MW01201348

Growth Modeling

Methodology in the Social Sciences
David A. Kenny, Founding Editor
Todd D. Little, Series Editor
www.guilford.com/MSS

This series provides applied researchers and students with analysis and research design books that emphasize the use of methods to answer research questions. Rather than emphasizing statistical theory, each volume in the series illustrates when a technique should (and should not) be used and how the output from available software programs should (and should not) be interpreted. Common pitfalls as well as areas of further development are clearly articulated.

RECENT VOLUMES

DOING STATISTICAL MEDIATION AND MODERATION
  Paul E. Jose

LONGITUDINAL STRUCTURAL EQUATION MODELING
  Todd D. Little

INTRODUCTION TO MEDIATION, MODERATION, AND CONDITIONAL
PROCESS ANALYSIS: A REGRESSION-BASED APPROACH
  Andrew F. Hayes

BAYESIAN STATISTICS FOR THE SOCIAL SCIENCES
  David Kaplan

CONFIRMATORY FACTOR ANALYSIS FOR APPLIED RESEARCH, SECOND EDITION
  Timothy A. Brown

PRINCIPLES AND PRACTICE OF STRUCTURAL EQUATION MODELING, FOURTH EDITION
  Rex B. Kline

HYPOTHESIS TESTING AND MODEL SELECTION IN THE SOCIAL SCIENCES
  David L. Weakliem

REGRESSION ANALYSIS AND LINEAR MODELS:
CONCEPTS, APPLICATIONS, AND IMPLEMENTATION
  Richard B. Darlington and Andrew F. Hayes

GROWTH MODELING: STRUCTURAL EQUATION
AND MULTILEVEL MODELING APPROACHES
  Kevin J. Grimm, Nilam Ram, and Ryne Estabrook

PSYCHOMETRIC METHODS: THEORY INTO PRACTICE
  Larry R. Price

Growth Modeling

Structural Equation and Multilevel Modeling Approaches

Kevin J. Grimm
Nilam Ram
Ryne Estabrook

Series Editor's Note by Todd D. Little

THE GUILFORD PRESS
New York   London

Library of Congress Cataloging-in-Publication Data

Names: Grimm, Kevin J., author. | Ram, Nilam, author. | Estabrook, Ryne, author.
Title: Growth modeling : structural equation and multilevel modeling approaches / Kevin J. Grimm,
    Nilam Ram, and Ryne Estabrook.
Description: New York, NY : Guilford Press, [2017] | Series: Methodology in the social sciences | Includes
    bibliographical references and index.
Identifiers: LCCN 2016021792 | ISBN 9781462526062 (hardcover : alk. paper)
Subjects: LCSH: Social sciences—Statistical methods. | Social sciences—Mathematical models. |
    Longitudinal method.
Classification: LCC HA29 .G7734 2016 | DDC 300.72/7—dc23
LC record available at *https://lccn.loc.gov/2016021792*

Series Editor's Note

When I look at the growth of the contributions in Guilford's Methodology in the Social Sciences series, I see some spectacular contributions spanning essential areas of advanced modeling and statistical analysis procedures. This work by Kevin J. Grimm, Nilam Ram, and Ryne Estabrook is yet another staple for social science researchers to read and digest. These authors are in the group of new innovators and leaders in the field of developmental methodology; they are to this academic generation what the likes of John Nesselroade, Jack McArdle, John Horn, Bill Meredith, and Keith Widaman are to my academic generation. This book also illustrates the new age of longitudinal growth modeling techniques that mature research areas need to be able to model the complex dynamic process of change and growth. These authors play the roles of innovator and educator with equal aplomb.

This book has a number of features that you will particularly enjoy. First, it contextualizes longitudinal research by outlining the fundamental goals of longitudinal research—the raisons d'être for collecting longitudinal data in the first place! Its focus is not on the panel model for longitudinal data, but rather on the varieties of growth models that are possible. The authors begin with the basics of growth modeling but then add some "miracle grow" to the soil and bring to fruition models for nonlinear growth, growth mixture models, models for non-normal data, models with categorical indicators and outcomes, and the whole complement of change score models that have caught the fancy of many researchers.

One of the features you will find particularly useful is the extensive code that the authors present. They provide the code for each model in one of two proprietary software platforms (SAS and Mplus) and in the world of R. For those not familiar with R, put the letter R into your favorite search engine and the first page that comes up will be *http://www.r-project.org/*. As you will see, R is the free and open-source software development platform created by a thriving community of scholars who are contributing to the development of statistical procedures and techniques. The two packages that Grimm, Ram, and Estabrook use are `nlme` and `OpenMx`; they have contributed to the development of the latter.

This book is a treasure and a very good complement and extension to my own contribution to this series, *Longitudinal Structural Equation Modeling*. You will find this book by Grimm, Ram, and Estabrook to be everything that you would like it to be: authoritative, accessible, and avant-garde. As with all of the books in the series, I entreat you to "enjoy!"

TODD D. LITTLE
Montecatini Terme, Italy

Preface

Growth Modeling: Structural Equation and Multilevel Modeling Approaches is the product of a collaboration that began when we arrived in graduate school. We sat next to each other (often in the same office), wrestling with concepts of change, data, and an array of stats programs. Our advisors, Jack McArdle (J. J. M.) and John Nesselroade (J. R. N.), encouraged us to engage with longitudinal data, and we became fascinated. When we would ask whether it was better to approach the data using Analysis A, Analysis B, or Analysis C, our advisors rarely gave direct answers. Instead, they usually suggested we try all three to see what happened—also implicitly suggesting that we question whether any of the options were actually appropriate for these data and the phenomena we were seeking to understand. We tried many things—some that worked, and many that did not. After a while we realized that each analysis led us somewhere, even if it was back to where we started. This book is our attempt to chronicle and share what we have learned on these journeys. Like J. J. M. and J. R. N., we do not attempt to provide definitive answers about which analysis to do when. Rather, our hope is that each chapter will facilitate discussion about longitudinal data, longitudinal analysis, and theories of change—and through those discussions readers might be inspired to explore their data in new ways, recognize the subtle signs of change, and present their findings with poise and precision.

Longitudinal data are exceptional. They provide opportunity to describe how and when people change and explain why. The richness of the resulting descriptions and range of possible explanations can challenge existing theoretical perspectives and push us toward new models of behavior. In pulling together the contents of this book, we have worked through the many thoughts that emerge from our practical experience applying growth models to longitudinal data collected from samples that range in size from 1 to 50,000 persons and at cadences that range from milliseconds to decades. Beyond the common set of expletives that often accompany data analysis, we find that when the data can support the inquiry (sufficient number of occasions and sufficiently sensitive measures), the change trajectories are *nonlinear* and the structure of between-person differences is *complex*.

Thus, the book is structured with the intent to lead readers from the basics of linear growth modeling toward models that provide for description of complex, nonlinear change. Complementing other excellent books on longitudinal growth modeling (*Applied Longitudinal Data Analysis* by Singer & Willett, 2003; *Latent Curve Modeling: A Structural Equation Perspective* by Bollen & Curran, 2006) and longitudinal analysis (*Longitudinal Data Analysis Using Structural Equation Models* by McArdle & Nesselroade, 2014; *Longitudinal Structural Equation Modeling* by Little, 2013), we purposely push consideration of *nonlinearity* and how its presence influences choice of study design. We also believe that the best way to learn growth modeling is to do it—"hands on" with real data. The disappointments and triumphs that one experiences during analysis of one's own data are memorable and rewarding. We encourage you to get your hands dirty and have fun with the real-data examples, the programming codes, and our annotation of output from multiple programs. Then, do it again with your data!

The 18 chapters are organized into five sections. Part I, Introduction and Organization, reviews the goals of longitudinal research and practical steps for preparing data prior to analysis of change (descriptive statistics and plotting of longitudinal trajectories). Part II, The Linear Growth Model and Its Extensions, introduces the linear growth model, with detailed discussion of different ways to handle the *time* variable, time-invariant predictors of change, multiple groups (e.g., boys, girls), growth mixtures, and multivariate outcomes. Early presentation of these "advanced" topics within the context of linear change is meant to facilitate cohesive understanding of how the models work and can be applied in many situations. With the basics in place, Part III, Nonlinearity in Growth Modeling, proceeds through an array of nonlinear models—growth models that are nonlinear with respect to time, growth models that are nonlinear with respect to parameters, and growth models that are nonlinear with respect to random coefficients (latent variables). The stepwise presentation is organized to facilitate adoption of increasingly complex forms of nonlinearity. Part IV, Modeling Change with Latent Entities, illustrates application of growth models to binary (dichotomous) and ordered polytomous variables, as well as to latent variables that are indicated by multiple continuous and categorical variables. Part V, Latent Change Scores as a Framework for Studying Change, introduces a process-oriented version of the growth model, first outlining univariate and bivariate versions of the model (with connection back to Part II), and then describing recent advancements in how these models can be used to study nonlinear change.

To facilitate practical application of growth models to readers' own longitudinal data, all of the models are introduced with detailed presentation of real-data examples, code, and interpretation of output. Remaining agnostic to modeling framework, each topic is introduced in both multilevel and structural equation modeling formats, and with code for use with both popular proprietary software (SAS and Mplus) and freely available R software (nlme and OpenMx). Thus, all readers will be able to work through the examples in at least two programs. Of note, our programming structures closely follow the mathematical presentations of the models so as to aid translation of one's own models into new code.

We have had the luck to work with many wonderful colleagues who willingly share ideas and data. The bits of their vast knowledge that we have gathered in this book are a tribute to the efforts of the many people who contributed over many decades to the advancement of behavioral science and how we think about and study behavioral change. In the same way that our mentors provoked exploration of ideas, we hope that this collection of models and examples can support inquisitive researchers looking for change and graduate students learning to study change. Discover more and let us know what you find!

We thank our families and our many colleagues for their patience and encouragement and for their fruitful and exciting engagement with us over more than a decade of working together. Specific thanks to Jonathan Helm (The Pennsylvania State University) for his assistance with `nlme` and answering R questions at all hours; Zhiyong Johnny Zhang and Lijuan Peggy Wang (University of Notre Dame) for their assistance with LyX and ability to answer all questions about its use; David Kaplan (University of Wisconsin), Jeffrey Harring (University of Maryland), Dan Powers (The University of Texas at Austin), Yasuo Miyazaki (Virginia Polytechnic Institute and State University), John (Jack) McArdle (University of Southern California), and Betsy McCoach (University of Connecticut, Storrs), who all provided extremely thoughtful and helpful comments when reviewing the book; the Health and Developmental Research Methods Labs at the University of California, Davis, and Arizona State University, the methods group at Penn State, and the Center for Advanced Study in the Behavioral Sciences at Stanford University. Big thanks to C. Deborah Laughton for her encouragement and ebullient optimism, and to Todd D. Little for his comments and support during the creative process. Finally, a dedication to our cherished mentors, Jack McArdle and John Nesselroade. Thank you for giving us the knowledge of and love for longitudinal data and analysis.

Contents

11 • Growth Models with Nonlinearity in Parameters 234

12 • Growth Models with Nonlinearity in Random Coefficients 275

PART IV.   MODELING CHANGE WITH LATENT ENTITIES

13 • Modeling Change with Ordinal Outcomes

14 • Modeling Change with Latent Variables Measured by Continuous Indicators

15 • Modeling Change with Latent Variables Measured by Ordinal Indicators

PART V.   LATENT CHANGE SCORES AS A FRAMEWORK FOR STUDYING CHANGE

16 • Introduction to Latent Change Score Modeling   403

17 • Multivariate Latent Change Score Models   422

18 • Rate-of-Change Estimates in Nonlinear Growth Models   445

The companion website *www.guilford.com/grimm-materials*
provides datasets and syntax for the book's examples,
along with additional code in SAS/R for linear
mixed-effects modeling.

Growth Modeling

Part I

Introduction
and Organization

1

Overview, Goals of Longitudinal Research, and Historical Developments

OVERVIEW

This book is written with the intent to lead readers from the basics of growth modeling to several advanced topics including growth mixture models, nonlinear change models, growth models for non-normal outcomes, growth models of latent variables, and the recent advances in latent change score modeling. In its entirety, the book is meant to support graduate courses on longitudinal data analysis and latent growth modeling in the social, educational, and behavioral sciences, or researchers interested in incorporating these methods into their research programs.

The 18 chapters are organized into five parts. In the first part, *Introduction and Organization*, we review the goals of longitudinal research and some practical preliminary steps that should be taken prior to examining change (descriptive statistics and plotting of longitudinal data). In the second part, *The Linear Growth Model and Its Extensions*, we introduce the linear growth model and several ways to expand the model to examine between-person differences in linear change and study multivariate change. Specifically, we cover different ways to handle time, the inclusion of time-invariant covariates as predictors of the growth factors (intercept and slope), multiple-group growth models, growth mixture models, and multivariate growth models. Several advanced topics are introduced in this part but are presented in the context of the linear growth model. The third part, *Nonlinearity in Growth Modeling*, proceeds through an array of nonlinear models—growth models that are nonlinear with respect to time, growth models that are nonlinear with respect to parameters, and growth models that are nonlinear with respect to random coefficients (latent variables). The stepwise presentation is organized to facilitate adoption of increasingly complex models. The fourth part, *Modeling Change with Latent Entities*, addresses the application of growth models that are fit directly to binary (dichotomous) and ordered polytomous outcomes, and latent variables that are indicated by multiple continuous and ordinal variables. The fifth and final part, *Latent Change Scores as a Framework for Studying Change*, introduces a process-oriented version of the growth model. We discuss univariate and bivariate models, and then describe recent advancements in how these models can be used to study individual rates of change in nonlinear growth models.

With intent to facilitate practical application of growth models to longitudinal data, all of the models are introduced with detailed presentation of real-data examples, code for fitting the models to the example data using multiple statistical packages, discussion of the output from those programs, and interpretation of the modeling results. Remaining agnostic to the modeling framework, we introduce each topic through the multilevel and structural equation modeling frameworks. Within the multilevel modeling framework we provide code for PROC NLMIXED in SAS (Littell, Milliken, Stroup, Wolfinger, & Schabenberger, 2006) and the nlme package (Pinheiro, Bates, DebRoy, Sarkar, & R Development Core Team, 2013) in R. Within the structural equation modeling framework we provide code for Mplus (Muthén & Muthén, 1998–2012) and the OpenMx package (Boker et al., 2011) in R. In each framework, we have purposively paired a popular proprietary program (SAS and Mplus) with a freely available R package (nlme and OpenMx) so that all readers will be able to work through the examples in at least two programs. Of practical note, we have utilized the nonlinear mixed-effects modeling programs (NLMIXED and nlme) instead of their associated linear mixed-effects modeling programs (MIXED and lme) because the nonlinear programs are more flexible and therefore can be used to fit more of the models we present. Additionally, the programming of these procedures closely follow the mathematical presentations of the models, which we feel aids understanding. Finally, we provide code for the linear mixed-effects modeling programs on our website.

FIVE RATIONALES FOR LONGITUDINAL RESEARCH

In working through the chapters, it may be useful to keep in mind specific research questions and how the longitudinal data being analyzed help to propel those questions. In the dialectic surrounding lifespan development in the 1970s, Baltes and Nesselroade (1979) outlined five main rationales for conducting longitudinal research. At the time, these rationales described opportunities that longitudinal research designs afforded and laid the groundwork and impetus for the development of new methods to analyze longitudinal data. Growth models can be viewed, in part, as an answer to the call—these methods provided a statistically rigorous framework that enabled researchers to take advantage of the opportunities brought about by the collection of longitudinal data (see McArdle & Nesselroade, 2014). In the chapters that follow we often refer back to Baltes and Nesselroade's five rationales, and thus present them here, at the outset, as an overarching framework within which to consider one's research goals.

• **Rationale 1.** The first rationale and primary reason for conducting longitudinal research is the *direct identification of intraindividual change (and stability)*. Measuring the same individual (entity) repeatedly allows researchers to identify if and how specific attributes of the individual changed (or remained the same) over time. Developmental (and other) theories of change often conceptualize and describe change as either an incremental or a transformational process (see Ram & Grimm, 2015). Incremental change is observed and identified as change in the magnitude (quantitative) of the same construct along a continuum over a specific time interval. Transformational change is observed and identified as a change or transition between discrete states during a specific time interval (e.g., Piaget's stage theory of development; Piaget, 1952). Analytically, the main goal is to obtain a parsimonious and accurate description of how and when attributes of the individual change over time. Importantly, Baltes and Nesselroade noted that stability and constancy over time are special cases of intraindividual change. As we shall see in the rest of the book, growth models are designed specifically to articulate a wide variety of possible (linear and nonlinear) patterns of intraindividual change.

• **Rationale 2.** Once the pattern of intraindividual (within-person) change is identified (in terms of magnitude or sequential steps), a logical next question to ask is whether different individuals change in different ways. Thus, the second rationale for longitudinal research is the *direct identification of interindividual differences (or similarity) in intraindividual change*. This rationale invokes research questions like Do different individuals change different amounts or in different directions?, or Do different individuals transition from one stage to another at different times? Baltes and Nesselroade (1979) suggested that heterogeneity in change is the norm given the "existence of diversity, multidirectionality, and large interindividual differences in developmental outcomes" (p. 24). As discussed in Chapters 3, 5, 6, and 7, growth models are structured specifically to describe interindividual differences in intraindividual change.

• **Rationale 3.** Acknowledging that change rarely occurs in isolation, the third rationale for longitudinal research is the *analysis of interrelationships in behavioral change*. As Baltes and Nesselroade (1979) note, "The examination of interrelationships in change among distinct behavioral classes is particularly important if a structural, holistic approach to development is taken" (p. 25). This holistic approach centers on the idea that changes in multiple constructs are expected to occur simultaneously and/or sequentially. Analytically, the task requires simultaneous analysis of multiple variables and the evaluation of how changes in one variable precede, covary, and/or follow changes in another variable. In Chapter 8 we discuss multivariate growth models and dynamic predictors, and in Chapter 17 we cover how latent change score models may be used to examine such interrelationships.

• **Rationale 4.** The fourth rationale, *analysis of causes (determinants) of intraindividual change*, centers on explaining or accounting for the observed within-person change process. Specifically, the objective is to identify the time-varying factors and/or mechanisms that impact and/or drive the within-person changes identified in Rationale 1. Key in our presentation is that changes are likely to proceed at different rates at different periods of time. For example, when learning a new skill, intraindividual changes may proceed quickly early on, but more slowly later as individuals reach asymptotic levels of performance. In Chapter 8 we cover how time-varying predictors can be introduced into the growth model, and later in Part III (Chapters 9 to 12), we address nonlinear models for intraindividual change.

   • **Rationale 5.** The fifth rationale for longitudinal research is the *analysis of causes (determinants) of interindividual differences in intraindividual change.* Given that individuals differ in how they change over time (Rationale 2), researchers are often interested in identifying the factors and/or mechanisms that can account for those between-person differences. The objective is to identify the time-invariant variables that are related to specific aspects of within-person change. For example, demographic/background characteristics, experimental manipulations (e.g., interventions), and characteristics of the individuals' proximal and distal contexts may all influence how and when change proceeds. Research questions proceeding from Rationale 5 are often examined through the inclusion of time-invariant covariates (Chapter 5), the use of multiple-group growth models (Chapter 6), and growth mixture models (Chapter 7).

   Together, these five rationales for longitudinal research provide the foundation for building precise research questions that can be examined using contemporary growth models and the extensions covered in this book. As you work through the chapters, we encourage you to articulate how your research paradigms map on to these rationales. What is your theory of intraindividual change? What is your theory of between-person differences? and so on. You can then select specific models that are appropriate for those questions, and you can thoughtfully consider if and how the data afford and/or limit your ability to obtain accurate answers.

HISTORICAL DEVELOPMENT OF GROWTH MODELS

Before proceeding to the specifics of contemporary growth models and their recent extensions, we discuss the historical context in which growth models were developed. The methods we use to analyze change emerged from almost a century's worth of innovations. This summary provides a brief and selective overview of the innovations that contributed to the models presented throughout this book.

   The beginning of growth modeling and the ideas underlying many of the methods used today can be traced back to Wishart's (1938) critique of a study examining the weight gain of three groups of bacon pigs that were on three different diets (Woodman, Evans, Callow, & Wishart, 1936). Woodman et al. (1936) had calculated each pig's overall weight gain as the difference between the pig's weight at baseline and at week 16, and used the resulting change scores as the dependent variable in an analysis of variance to examine differences in weight gain in relation to diet type. The results were lackluster, with no significant differences in total weight gain between the three diet groups. Discouraged, but persistent, the authors then conducted an analysis of covariance that included baseline weight as a covariate. This analysis supported the initial hypothesis and provided evidence of a significant difference in weight gain between two of the three diet groups. Wishart (1938) was concerned, not with the soundness of the statistical analysis, which were indeed proper, but with the extent of *unanalyzed data*. The weights of the pigs were recorded weekly. However, the analysis only used the measurements obtained at baseline (week 0) and week 16. The original analysis used only those data that would conform to a straightforward analysis of variance and covariance. That is, the researchers selected data that fit into a specific analytic technique, rather than utilizing all of the data that were collected. Wishart (1938) thought that analyzing all 17 repeated observations would yield a more reliable and valid answer to the research question Do pigs' diets impact their rates of growth? The predicament was that it was not yet clear how all the repeated measures could be used to track the within-pig changes and the between-pig differences in within-pig change.

In his critique, Wishart (1938) approximated the formal methods that would be developed 50 years later. Following good practices, he first plotted the data—pigs' weight and the log transform of the pigs' weight on the *y*-axis and time (weeks since the beginning of the study from 0 through 16) on the *x*-axis. Then, examining these plots, he sought to identify a mathematical function that would provide the best representation of each pig's growth trajectory. After considering a few options, Wishart decided on a quadratic polynomial of the form $y_t = b_1 + b_2 \cdot (t - 8) + b_3 \cdot \{(t - 8)^2 - 24\}$ and estimated the parameters of the quadratic curve (i.e., b_1, b_2, and b_3) that best described each pig's data. These included an intercept (centered at week 8), a linear change component interpreted as "average growth rate in pounds per week," and a quadratic change component interpreted as "half the rate of change in the growth rate in pounds per week" (i.e., a scaling of acceleration). Thus, Wishart reduced the dimensionality of the original data (17 repeated measures) down to three specific aspects of growth that he thought had substantive meaning and that, hopefully, sufficiently described the entirety of the growth process. Wishart then used an analysis of variance to determine whether differences in the pigs' "average growth rate" (linear component) were related to diet. Wishart found a significant difference between two of the three diets in the linear aspect of change. As with the original analysis, Wishart then conducted an analysis of covariance accounting for the pigs' initial weights (specifically, predicted initial weight from the individual quadratic models). Replicating the original results, he found significant differences in "average growth rate" between two of the three diet groups. He then conducted similar analyses for the 'rate of change in the growth rate' (quadratic component). Wishart found that the three diet groups differed significantly in how their rate of weight gain accelerated over time.

Overall, Wishart's results were more robust (results were stronger) when using all of the longitudinal data, and he attempted to capture multiple aspects of the change process. Wishart's point was that there was important information embedded in *all* of the repeated measures and that information could be used to provide more accurate descriptions of the within-pig change process and the between-pig differences in the within-pig change process. The density of the repeated measures provided a more complex representation of growth and a better understanding of the growth process.

The general approach that Wishart used provides the foundation for understanding the core aspects of contemporary growth models. Key aspects of Wishart's approach were that (1) an individual's observed change trajectory can be described by a mathematical function of time, plus noise (error), (2) the parameters of the function represent specific, meaningful aspects of the within-individual change process (Rationale 1), (3) variation in those parameters constitutes information about between-individual differences in the change process (Rationale 2), and (4) how the variation in the growth parameters can be associated with other predictor variables or covariates provides information about exogenous (diet) and endogenous (initial weight) determinants of the between-individual differences in the within-individual change process (Rationale 5). The utility of Wishart's approach prevails today. Initial steps in the study of individual change often include plotting individual trajectories and fitting individual regressions to estimate individual growth parameters (see Singer & Willett, 2003).

Twenty years after Wishart's analysis, Tucker (1958) and Rao (1958) presented work that is often cited as the foundation of growth models within the structural equation modeling framework. Rao and Tucker each proposed an approach wherein the sums of squares and cross-products matrix obtained from repeated measures data were subjected to a principal components analysis. The principal components model decomposed the repeated measures data into a set of *generalized learning curves*, component loadings representing distinct patterns of change, and *individual component weights* (component scores) indicating the degree to which an individual's observed trajectory was saturated by each of the *generalized learning curves* (components). The generalized learning curves were interpreted as the fundamental aspects of change that all individuals shared (Rationale 1), and the individual component weights indicated how individual trajectories were different from one another (Rationale 2). Tucker (1966) subsequently refined the techniques for determining the number of generalized learning curves (components) to retain and described rotation procedures that would aid interpretation of the learning curves. In the same way that Wishart used a specific mathematical function (quadratic polynomial) to reduce the 17 repeated measurements of a pig's weight down to three meaningful parameters (intercept, rate of change, rate of acceleration) and examined between-pig differences in those parameters, Tucker and Rao used principal components analysis to reduce the dimensionality of the repeated measures data obtained from multiple individuals down to a smaller number of learning curves and examined between-person differences in the weighting of those curves/components. Key links to the application of growth models fit in the structural equation modeling framework are the use of a multivariate approach (i.e., factor-analytic) to reduce dimensionality, the way component (factor) loadings represent the dominant change trajectories, and the use of component (factor/latent variable) scores to provide information about between-person differences in change (see Grimm, Steele, Ram, & Nesselroade, 2013).

Through the 1970s and into the early 1980s the individual growth modeling (from Wishart) and generalized learning curve (from Tucker) approaches were used to examine how individuals changed over time. Of course, estimation routines were updated along the way, with the facility afforded by least squares, nonlinear least squares, and Bayesian approaches to estimating growth parameters (see Berkey, 1982; Box, 1950; Potthoff & Roy, 1964; Rogosa, Brandt, & Zimowski, 1982). Then, Harville (1977) introduced a class of linear mixed-effects models, and Laird and Ware (1982) developed more efficient estimation techniques for those models (see also Rao, 1965), which provided the main foundations that would support the fitting of growth models in the multilevel modeling framework. Specifically, Laird and Ware (1982) proposed that two-stage models should be used to study change. Using repeated measures of pulmonary function, they demonstrated how the new, unified approach to estimation (simultaneous estimation of level-1 [within-person] and level-2 [between-person] model parameters) could be used to study between-person differences in within-person change (Rationale 2). Further, their demonstration showed how exposure to air pollution had an effect on the long-term development of pulmonary function and highlighted how this framework could handle incomplete and highly unbalanced data—a common feature of longitudinal data. In the years that followed, Rogosa and Willett (1985) and Bryk and Raudenbush (1987) refined how the mixed-effects framework could be used to study individual change. These works highlighted common misconceptions regarding the study of change, demystified how the models articulated theory about individuals' initial state and rates of change (and the assumptions therein), and outlined a variety of change trajectories, linear and nonlinear, that could be examined using the mixed-effects modeling framework. Their presentations of accessible examples prompted many psychologists and educational researchers to adopt these techniques and made them a central part of the statistical toolbox used by social scientists.

In parallel, Jöreskog and Sörbom (1979) developed the structural equation modeling framework and supplied the research community with accessible software that provided the facility for simultaneously modeling mean and covariance structures. Using this framework and giving a nod to the approach introduced by Tucker (1958) and Rao (1958), Meredith and Tisak (1984, 1990) provided a general framework for fitting latent curve models in the structural equation modeling framework. Specifically, they illustrated how the linear growth model can be specified as a restricted confirmatory factor model with a mean structure, and discussed extensions to multiple-group growth models, higher-order polynomial models, spline models, and a variety of models with nonlinear change patterns. The flexibility of the structural equation modeling framework immediately enabled researchers to extend Meredith and Tisak's (1984, 1990) work. In the 1980s, for example, McArdle (1986) combined additive genetic models and latent growth models in the analysis of longitudinal data from twins to assess the additive genetic (heritability), common environmental, and unique environmental components of initial test performance, change in performance over time, and unique (individual) variability. McArdle (1988) also extended the model into the multivariate space, proposing several ways in which growth models could be used to study the development of two or more processes as well as changes in latent variables. The first of these models was the bivariate (or parallel process) growth model where the changes in two variables are simultaneously examined and the associations between intercepts and slopes are evaluated to study whether individual changes in one process are associated with individual changes in the second process. The second model was the curve of factors model or second-order growth model (Hancock, Kuo, & Lawrence, 2001), where changes in a multiply indicated latent variable were modeled. The third model was the factor of curves model where the associations among growth factors (as in the bivariate growth model) were modeled with second-order factors instead of covariance paths. The introduction of these models spurred discussions of how to test whether the same construct was measured in the same scale over time (longitudinal measurement invariance) and how to study the interplay between multiple developmental processes.

As the advances in computational power and efficiency increased, the possibilities for estimating nonlinear mixed-effects models were greatly enhanced (see Davidian & Giltinan, 1995; Pinheiro & Bates, 1995; Vonesh & Chinchilli, 1996). This allowed for the examination of interindividual differences in a wider set of within-person change models in the multilevel modeling framework. Work on this topic was conducted by Lindstrom and Bates (1990), Burchinal and Appelbaum (1991), Beal and Sheiner (1992), Vonesh (1992a, 1992b), Wolfinger (1993), Lin (Wolfinger & Lin, 1997), and Davidian and Gallant (1993). In the structural equation modeling framework, work on this topic was conducted by Browne and du Toit (1991; see also Browne, 1993), who showed how complex nonlinear mixed-effects models could be approximated through Taylor series expansion following the work of Beal and Sheiner (1982). This opened new opportunities to merge the flexibility of the structural equation modeling framework (e.g., measurement models) with the study of inherently nonlinear trajectories (see Blozis, 2004; Grimm, Ram, & Estabrook, 2010).

In the midst of these innovations, the growth modelers working in the multilevel framework (also called mixed-effects or random coefficient models) and the growth modelers working in the structural equation modeling framework realized that the two frameworks could be used to fit the same model and obtain identical results (see Willett & Sayer, 1994). In this book we present the multilevel and structural equation approaches and note that the choice of modeling framework is mostly a matter of preference because nearly all of the models we present can be fit in both frameworks. However, certain models are easier to specify and estimate in one framework versus the other. For example, the mixed-effects modeling framework handles individually varying time scales and modeling of inherently nonlinear trajectories more easily than the structural equation modeling framework, whereas the structural equation modeling framework provides more flexibility into modeling residual structures, fitting multivariate change models, and incorporating multiply indicated latent variables (see Ghisletta & Lindenberger, 2003), although these differences have been minimized over time (Grimm & Widaman, 2010; Kwok, West, & Green, 2007; Sterba, 2014).

Around the turn of the century, there was an increased interest in considering qualitative differences in within-person change (e.g., Magnusson, 2003). Researchers needing facility to group individuals based on their change patterns (e.g., early learners, late learners) introduced semiparametric group-based models, that represented between-person differences in change as a collection of latent classes (Jones, Nagin, & Roeder, 2001; Nagin, 1999), and growth mixture models that represented between-person differences in change as a combination of latent classes *and* continuous between-person differences within each latent class. Despite some limitations and ambiguity in their use (Bauer & Curran, 2003; Grimm, Ram, Shiyko, & Lo, 2013; Ram, Grimm, Gatzke-Kopp, & Molenaar, 2011), the popularity of these models has produced a great deal of knowledge about how individuals differ in how they change and prompted a rich set of advanced modeling possibilities (see Grimm & Ram, 2009; Grimm, Ram, & Estabrook, 2010; Li, Duncan, Duncan, & Hops, 2001; Ram & Grimm, 2009).

In the 2000s there were also innovations in how growth models could be used to simultaneously model individual changes and examine time-dependent lead-lag associations with longitudinal panel data. McArdle and Hamagami (2001) showed how latent difference (change) variables could be specified through fixed structural paths in the structural equation modeling framework—an extension that allowed researchers to examine the interplay between changes in two or more variables. At the same time, Curran and Bollen (2001) highlighted how autoregressive and cross-lagged effects could be included directly in growth models specified in the structural equation modeling framework. These efforts subsequently led to second-order difference models (Hamagami & McArdle, 2007) to study acceleration and its determinants and latent differential models (Boker, Neale, & Rausch, 2004), which treat time continuously instead of discretely, multiple-group and growth mixture models to examine group differences in lead–lag associations (Ferrer et al., 2007; Grimm, 2006), and the examination of between-person differences in the rate of change in nonlinear models (Grimm, Castro-Schilo, & Davoudzadeh, 2013; Grimm, Zhang, Hamagami, & Mazzocco, 2013). The latent change score framework allows for the examination of all of Baltes and Nesselroade's rationales for longitudinal research (see McArdle, 2009; McArdle & Nesselroade, 2014).

MODELING FRAMEWORKS AND PROGRAMS

As mentioned, we discuss both the structural equation modeling and multilevel modeling frameworks for specifying and fitting growth models. The majority of growth models can be specified in both frameworks (see Curran, 2003; Ghisletta & Lindenberger, 2003; Willett & Sayer, 1994); however, certain models can only be specified in one framework or the other because of program limitations. For example, inherently (fully) nonlinear models can only be directly fit within the (nonlinear) multilevel modeling framework, and second-order growth models can only be fit within the structural equation modeling framework. Furthermore, some models are more easily fit within a certain framework, although these models can be fit in both frameworks. For example, fitting growth models to data where individuals vary in their timing metric (individually varying time metrics) are more easily fit in the multilevel modeling framework, even though such models can be fit in the structural equation modeling framework (not necessarily with all structural equation modeling programs). Similarly, growth models with mixture distribution and growth models with different residual structures are more easily specified in the structural equation modeling framework even though certain multilevel modeling programs allow mixture distributions (e.g., PROC NLMIXED) and different residual structures (e.g., PROC MIXED; see Kwok, West, & Green, 2007). Thus, when moving into more advanced models, experience working in *both* the multilevel and structural equation modeling frameworks is beneficial.

As we noted, we discuss the programming of growth models using Mplus and OpenMx in the structural equation modeling framework and using PROC NLMIXED and nlme in the multilevel modeling framework. Mplus is a comprehensive latent variable modeling program (it can handle multilevel data, mixture distributions, and a variety of non-normal data [e.g., binary, ordinal, categorical, count, zero-inflated]), has efficient estimation routines (e.g., maximum likelihood, weighted least squares, Bayesian), a straightforward programming language, and is continually being improved. At the time of writing, Mplus is probably the most utilized structural equation modeling program. The Mplus website (*www.statmodel.com*) contains a demonstration version of the program that is only limited by the number of variables included in the analysis, the user manual, a collection of examples, discussion forums, and a series of papers highlighting new features of the program.

OpenMx can be seen as a recent update to Mx (Neale, Boker, Xie, & Maes, 2003), a freely available stand-alone structural equation modeling program. However, OpenMx is more of a transformation than an update because of the magnitude of its capabilities and how it is embedded within R, a freely available comprehensive statistical package. Thus, OpenMx is a free comprehensive structural equation modeling program that can handle binary and ordinal outcomes and mixture distributions. There are a variety of ways to specify models using OpenMx (path specification using RAM notation and matrix specification), but we note that regardless of the approach, the programming of OpenMx is more intense than Mplus, and familiarity with the R statistical package is beneficial. The OpenMx website (*http://openmx.psyc.virginia.edu*) contains program documentation, programming examples, a wiki, and forums where questions can be posed to the developers. Finally, the OpenMx development team is continuing to expand and improve its capabilities.

PROC MIXED and NLMIXED in SAS are two of the most popular procedures for mixed-effects or multilevel models. Singer (1998) provides an excellent overview of PROC MIXED, which increased its use among educational and psychological researchers. NLMIXED is a general modeling program that can handle multilevel data structures. Because of its generality, NLMIXED is not as efficient as MIXED; however, NLMIXED can handle inherently (fully) nonlinear models, non-normal outcomes (e.g., binary, ordinal, count, zero-inflated), and mixture distributions—topics that are of interest here. Additionally, the programming of NLMIXED is straightforward, although some knowledge of the SAS statistical language is beneficial.

The nlme package has been the primary mixed-effects modeling package available through R and includes both a linear mixed-effects modeling procedure (lme) and a nonlinear mixed-effects modeling procedure (nlme)—similar to MIXED and NLMIXED in SAS. Throughout this book we discuss the nlme procedure (over the lme procedure) because of its ability to fit inherently (fully) nonlinear models. The lme4 package (Bates,

Mächler, & Bolker, 2015; Bates, Mächler, Bolker, & Walker, 2011) is a newer package for fitting linear and nonlinear mixed-effects models (procedures include `lmer` and `nlmer`) in R and is able to fit mixed-effects models to non-normal outcomes (an advantage over `nlme`); however, `nlme` is more flexible when it comes to fitting inherently nonlinear models and its programming is more straightforward. For these reasons we focus on `nlme` instead of `lme4`; however, `lme4` syntax is available on our website, and Long's (2012) recent book of longitudinal data analysis discusses the use of `lme4`.

2

Practical Preliminaries
Things to Do before Fitting Growth Models

In the educational, behavioral, and social sciences, growth models are typically applied to data obtained from longitudinal panel studies or accelerated longitudinal studies (Bell, 1953, 1954)—that is, studies where several repeated measures were obtained from multiple individuals. Traditionally, longitudinal panel studies were designed such that the number of repeated assessments was relatively few (i.e., < 8) and the number of individuals was relatively large (i.e., > 200). However, advances in both the theoretical considerations of change (e.g., nonlinearity) and the technology for data collection (e.g., web-based surveys, smart phones) have greatly expanded the possibilities for collection and analysis of longitudinal data. Our experiences applying growth models to longitudinal data obtained from between 1 and 50,000 persons on between 2 and 1,000 occasions suggest the wide variety of behavioral changes that can be captured using the methods covered in this book. However, there are a number of *practical preliminaries* that should be considered at the outset—before jumping in to the model fitting (see also discussions in Grimm, Davoudzadeh, & Ram, 2015; Grimm & Ram, 2011; Kim-Spoon & Grimm, 2016; Ram & Gerstorf, 2009; Ram & Grimm, 2015).

Effective growth modeling requires, on the front end, thoughtful consideration of and facility working with both the attributes of longitudinal data and how those data are connected to theoretical models of change. On the data side, growth modelers should become well versed in (1) the manipulation of longitudinal *data structures* (e.g., reshaping wide and long data), (2) the *plotting* of longitudinal data, and (3) the *screening* of longitudinal data. In considering the connections to theory, growth modelers should be able to discuss and defend the specifics of their *longitudinal measurement* (choice of y-axis) and *time metric* (choice of x-axis). Taking the time to properly prepare their data and explore these issues on the front end of an analysis will both save time and increase the potential impact of one's findings.

DATA STRUCTURES

Longitudinal data typically come in two forms: *wide* and *long*. The first few rows of a datafile in each format are shown in Table 2.1. Table 2.1a contains the data in the long format, where each individual's data are organized in multiple rows. Each row contains the variables measured at a single occasion for a given individual. Thus, the length of the datafile depends on the number of participants and the number of repeated assessments per participant. The variable names in this dataset are *id*, which identifies the rows of the dataset that belong to the same individual; *time*, which is the timing metric variable; and *y*, which is the outcome of interest. It's important to note that the values of the *time* variable do not have to be shared by all individuals. For example, in the dataset, *id* = 1 was measured at times 3, 4, 6, and 7, whereas *id* = 2 was measured at times 2, 3, 4, 5, and 6. Long-form data are typically used in plotting and fitting growth models in the multilevel modeling framework. Table 2.1b contains the same data in the wide format, where each individual's data are organized in a single row and the repeated measures are contained in multiple columns (e.g., *y2, y3, y4*). Thus, the length of the wide datafile depends only on the number of participants; however, the number of variables depends on the number of variables measured at each occasion and the number of measurement occasions. In our example dataset, there is a separate column for every possible value of the timing metric. Thus, we have separate *y* variables for *time* = 2, 3, 4, 5, 6, and 7 (i.e., *y2* through *y7*). In this format, it is easier to see that the two individuals were not measured at the same time points because there are missing values (represented by the .) at *y2* and *y5* for *id* = 1 and at *y7* for *id* = 2. Wide-form data are typically used in data screening and when fitting growth models in the structural equation modeling framework.

TABLE 2.1. Example Longitudinal Data Structures

(a) Long format

id	time	y
1	3	8
1	4	14
1	6	24
1	7	30
2	2	4
2	3	7
2	4	17
2	5	20
2	6	22

(b) Wide format

id	y2	y3	y4	y5	y6	y7
1	.	8	14	.	24	30
2	4	7	17	20	22	.

Given that plotting, data screening, and analysis often require different data structures, developing skill in restructuring wide-form data into long-form data and vice versa is necessary. Throughout the book our example datasets are typically available in both formats. However, we assume that those working through the examples have the facility to reshape or transform datasets between the wide and long formats as needed. When working with one's own data, fluid transfer between formats greatly facilitates analysis and enables the production of meaningful presentation of results.

To illustrate how to restructure data in SAS and R, we introduce an example dataset. The data come from the National Longitudinal Survey of Youth—Children and Young Adults (NLSY-CYA; Center for Human Resource Research, 2004). The initial organization of the data is in the long format, and the data are stored in an ASCII text file. We note that it is often easier to store data in the long format because there may be multiple timing metrics with which to organize the same data in the wide format (e.g., measurement occasion, age, grade) and to switch from one to the other would involve first restructuring the data to the long format. Script 2.1 contains SAS code for reading the ASCII text file into the program, restructuring the data to a *wide* format by age, and then restructuring the data back to the long format. First, the data are read in using a datastep. Here, we name the datafile wght_long, state where the file is located using INFILE, and provide variable names using INPUT. As with all SAS datasteps and procedures, we end the datastep with RUN;. We now want to restructure the data using the variable age; however, age is measured very precisely (using several decimal places). Thus, to begin restructuring, we first round age to the nearest whole year, and we do this in a datastep. We create a new dataset called wght_long1, which is first set equal to the wght_long dataset using the SET statement, and create a new variable named age_r, which is the rounded value of age (ROUND(age)). Lastly, we eliminate rows in the long dataset where the variable wght is missing (IF wght ne .;). Next, we use PROC FREQ to display a frequency table for our timing variable, age_r. We do this to check the values of age_r to make sure they are whole numbers and to obtain the minimum and maximum values because this information is helpful when restructuring. The values of age_r are indeed whole numbers and range from 5 to 19. Thus, when we restructure the data to the wide format, we will have weight variables from age 5 (wght5) to 19 (wght19). The last step prior to restructuring is to sort the data, and we sort the data by the participant identification variable (id) and the timing variable (age_r).

We're now ready to restructure the data, which is done in a datastep. The datastep begins by naming the new dataset wght_wide and creating a collection of variables using an ARRAY statement. In the ARRAY statement, we provide names of the elements in the array and the names of the variables created in the array. Here, the names of the array elements are wght_5 through wght_19, and the names of the variables are wght5 to wght19. Next, the variable names are listed in a RETAIN statement, which makes the listed variables retain their values from one iteration of the datastep to the next. We then SET the wght_long1 dataset, which is our originating long-format file. Next, we use a BY statement to indicate that the aspects of this datastep should be done separately for each participant (remember that in the originating dataset there are multiple records per

Script 2.1. SAS Code for Reading, Restructuring, and Writing Data

```
DATA wght_long;
    INFILE 'C:\Data\wght_data.dat';
    INPUT id occ occ_begin year time_in_study grade age gyn_age wght;
RUN;

*Restructuring the data by age;
DATA wght_longi;
    SET wght_long;
    age_r = ROUND(age);
    IF wght ne .;
RUN;

PROC FREQ DATA = wght_long1;
    TABLES age_r;
RUN;

PROC SORT DATA = wght_long1;
    BY id age_r;
RUN;

DATA wght_wide;
    ARRAY wght_[5:19] wght5-wght19;
    RETAIN wght5-wght19;
    SET wght_long1;
    BY id;
    IF FIRST.id THEN DO I = 5 TO 19;
        wght_[I] = .;
    END;
    wght_[age_r] = wght;
    IF LAST.id THEN OUTPUT;
    KEEP id wght5-wght19;
RUN;

DATA _NULL_;
    SET wght_wide;
    FILE 'C:\Data\wght_wide.dat';
    PUT id wght5-wght19;
RUN;

*Restructuring wght_wide back into long format;
DATA wght_long_new;
    SET wght_wide;
    ARRAY wght_[5:19] wght5-wght19;
    DO age_r = 5 to 19;
        wght = wght_[age_r];
        OUTPUT;
    END;
    KEEP id age_r wght;
RUN;

DATA wght_wide_new1;
    SET wght_wide_new;
    IF wght ne .;
RUN;
```

participant). We then use a series of statements to populate the variables created in the ARRAY statement. First, an IF-THEN statement is used to populate the variables with missing values. The statement begins with IF FIRST.id, which is true at the first record for each participant. So, when the first record of each participant is encountered, the elements wght_5 through wght_19 (and therefore the variables wght5 through wght19) are populated with missing values. Next, the elements wght_5 through wght_19 are populated with the appropriate wght value based on age_r (i.e., wght_[age_r] = wght;). An IF-THEN statement is then used to determine when the data should be recorded. In this statement, IF LAST.id is used to indicate when the final record for each person is reached, and only when this is true are the variables wght5 through wght19 complete and ready to be placed in the datafile. Finally, a KEEP statement is used only to keep the id variable and wght5 through wght19. The data restructuring from long to wide is now complete. As a last step, we output the wght_wide data into an ASCII text file using a datastep. The FILE and PUT statements are used to indicate the path and file name along with the variables (and their order) to be included in the datafile. Such a file could then be read by structural equation modeling programs for analyses.[1]

In the next two datasteps, we now restructure the wide-format dataset back to a long-format dataset. The datastep begins by giving the new datafile the name wght_long_new and setting the wide-format datafile (SET wght_wide). Next, the variables wide5 through wide19 are put into an ARRAY, so that we can call each one individually in the following DO loop. The DO loop then populates a new variable named wght with each value of wght5 through wght19 based on age_r, which is a new variable that begins at 5 and goes to 19. The wght variable is then OUTPUT after each iteration of the DO loop, which creates multiple records per person, and the DO loop is completed. The KEEP statement is then used to keep the id, age_r, and wght variables. In the next datastep, the rows in which the wght variable is missing are removed.

R code for reading, restructuring, and writing data is contained in Script 2.2. Data are read in from an ASCII datafile using read.table. In this statement, the path to the datafile along with the file name and extension are contained within quotes, and the missing data indicator is specified using na.strings=. The datafile is given the name wght_long. In the next statement, names() is used to provide variable names. To begin restructuring the data from the long to wide format, we round the age variable using round().[2] We then use the reshape() command to restructure the data. In this command, we list the originating datafile (wght_long) and name the variable that varies with time in v.names, the identification variable in idvar, the timing variable in timevar, and then the direction of the restructure (i.e., wide). This statement efficiently restructures the data, but the following two statements are used to reorganize the data. First, the

---

[1] If several variables are being read into SAS or output from SAS, then using a linesize statement may be needed depending on the number of columns in the datafile.

[2] To refer to the variable in R, we use the name of the datafile (wght_long), followed by $ and then the variable name (e.g., age).

Script 2.2. R **Code for Reading, Restructuring, and Writing Data**

```
# reading data
wght_long = read.table('C:/Data/wght_data.dat', na.strings='.')
names(wght_long) = c('id','occ','occ_begin','year','time_in_study',
                     'grade','age','gyn_age','wght')

# restructuring data from long to wide
wght_long$age_r = round(wght_long$age)

wght_wide = reshape(wght_long, v.names='wght', idvar='id', timevar=
                    'age_r', direction='wide')

wght_wide1 = wght_wide[,c('id','wght.5','wght.6','wght.7','wght.8',
                          'wght.9','wght.10','wght.11','wght.12',
                          'wght.13','wght.14','wght.15','wght.16',
                          'wght.17','wght.18','wght.19']

names(wght_wide 1) = c('id','wght5','wght6','wght7','wght8','wght9',
                       'wght10','wght11','wght12','wght13','wght14',
                       'wght15','wght16','wght17','wght18','wght19')

# writing out file
write.table(wght_wide1, 'C:/Data/wght_wide.dat', sep=" ",
            row.names=FALSE, col.names=FALSE, na='.')

# restructuring data from wide back to long
wght_long_new = reshape(wght_wide1, idvar='id',
      varying=c('wght5','wght6','wght7','wght8','wght9','wght10',
                'wght11','wght12','wght13','wght14','wght15',
                'wght16','wght17','wght18','wght19'),
      times=c(5,6,7,8,9,10,11,12,13,14,15,16,17,18,19),
      v.names='wght', direction='long')

wght_long_new = wght_long_new[order(wght_long_new$id,
                wght_long_new$time),]

wght_long_new1 = wght_long_new[which(!is.na(wght_long_new$wght)),]
```

dataset wght_wide1 is created, and in this dataset the variables are simply reordered. In the second statement, new names are provided for the variables. We then use write. table to write the data to a space delimited ASCII text file with . as the missing value code, and this datafile can be read by structural equation modeling programs.

To restructure this data back to the wide format, we can also use reshape(). In this command, we begin by listing the originating datafile (wght_wide1) and identification variable using idvar. Next, the variables that represent the same variable over time are listed in the varying statement. Here, we list the 15 weight variables. Next, the times statement is used to specify the time at which the measurements of the variables listed in varying took place. Thus, we list the age associated with each weight variable. Next, we provide a name for the variable that will contain the repeatedly measured weight variables. We then report the direction of the restructuring, which is long. The next two statements sort the data according to time, which is the new timing variable, and we remove rows in the dataset where the wght variable was incomplete.

Lastly, we note a third data format that may be encountered. This data format is similar to the wide format because there is one record or row for each participant. However, instead of the data being organized according to a chosen time metric (like *age* in our example), the data are organized into a minimum number of variables. For example, each participant's first assessment would be in variable *y1*, each participant's second assessment would be in variable *y2*, and so on. Additionally, there would be a series of timing variables, such that *time1* would have the timing information of the first assessment *y1*, *time2* would have the timing information of the first assessment *y2*, and so forth. Thus, *time1* may contain information about the participant's age when his or her first assessment took place. The main difference between this format and the wide format is that the timing information is contained in a series of variables as opposed to the variable names of the outcome. This format is very flexible and allows researchers to include multiple timing variables in a wide-type format dataset. However, this format has little need; typically, it is only needed when fitting growth models in the structural equation modeling framework when allowing different participants to have different time metrics (i.e., individually varying time metrics, covered in Chapter 4).

LONGITUDINAL PLOTS

As in any statistical analysis, it is important to take a close look at the data. This includes producing both quantitative summaries and visualizations. Typically, the summaries and plots are examined iteratively, each new piece of information leading into and informing the next. Here we present the visualizations first to highlight the importance of actually looking at one's data. Plots provide extremely useful information about potential models, measurement issues, possible time metrics, outliers, and miscodings. Many later problems can be avoided by carefully examining a robust selection of plots for unusual observations. Individual change trajectories can be plotted to evaluate whether one's hypotheses may actually map onto the data (e.g., is a linear change model appropriate?).

A useful longitudinal plot is shown in Figure 2.1 where the weights of a subset of participants are plotted against their age at the time of measurement. Syntax to produce such a plot in SAS and R is given in Scripts 2.3 and 2.4, respectively. For SAS, we present code for making plots using the SGPLOT and GPLOT procedures. Longitudinal plots made using the SGPLOT procedure are delivered through the Output Delivery System (ODS). The first two lines of code turn on the graphics system and provide a set of options, including file type, image resolution, image format, image size, and file name. Once the graphics environment is set up as desired, the PROC SGPLOT line specifies the dataset, which must be in the long format. In this script we subset the data to plot values from a smaller number of participants using the where command (i.e., (where = (id > 1300 AND id < 1600))). Here, we subset the data when plotting so that the plot is sparse enough (e.g., *n* < 50) to follow and examine individual trajectories. The procedure would be repeated looking at different subsets in order to obtain a full picture of the data.

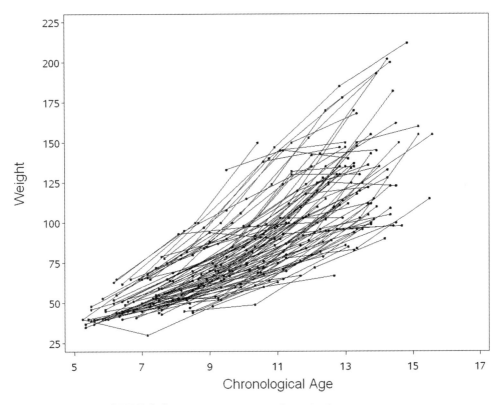

FIGURE 2.1. Longitudinal plot of weight data against age.

The SERIES command is used to specify the type of plot (time series) as well as the variables to be used on the *x*-axis, age, on the *y*-axis, wght, and to group the data, id. The GROUP=id statement indicates that the repeated measures should be linked using the individual identifier. Specific attributes of the plot are controlled using the LINEATTRS = ... (line attributes) and MARKERATTRS = ... (marker attributes) statements. Labels, range, and placement of tick marks for the axes are defined using the YAXIS and XAXIS statements. Finally, the ODS graphics system is turned off.

The GPLOT procedure, although a bit older and sometimes clunky, can also be used to obtain informative longitudinal plots. The PROC GPLOT line specifies the dataset, which must be in the long format. Again, we subset the data to plot a small number of cases using the where statement. The SYMBOL statement controls the line and marker attributes. In the symbol statement, we specify I=join to connect datapoints belonging to the same participant with a straight line, R=5000 to reuse the same symbol statement 5,000 times, V=dot to represent each datapoint by a closed circle, H=.5 to control the size of the closed circle, W=1 to control the thickness of the line connecting the datapoints, and C=black to specify the color of the datapoints and lines. Multiple SYMBOL statements can be used to differentiate groups provided that the data are sorted by the grouping variable and the REPEAT statement for each symbol/group is exactly equal to the number of cases in each group.

Script 2.3. SAS **Scripts for Plotting Longitudinal Data with SGPLOT and GPLOT**

```
ODS LISTING STYLE = journal image.dpi=300;
ODS GRAPHICS ON / RESET-ALL IMAGEFMT=png WIDTH=4in
IMAGENAME='Long_Plot';

PROC SGPLOT DATA = wght_long (where = (id > 1300 AND id < 1600));
   SERIES X=age Y=wght / GROUP=id
       LINEATTRS = (COLOR=black PATTERN=solid THICKNESS=1)
       MARKERATTRS = (COLOR=black SIZE=3 SYMBOL=circlefilled)
       MARKERS;
   YAXIS LABEL = "Height" VALUES = (25 to 225 BY 25);
   XAXIS LABEL = "Chronological Age" VALUES = (5 to 17 BY 2);
RUN;

ODS GRAPHICS OFF;

GOPTIONS
   HTEXT = 1.5
   CTEXT = black
   FTEXT = 'Albany AMT';

PROC GPLOT DATA = wght_long (where = (id > 1300 AND id < 1600));
   SYMBOL1
       I=join R=5000 V=dot H=.5 W=1 C=black;
   AXIS1
       LABEL = (A=90 F='Albany AMT' H=2 'Weight')
       ORDER = (25 to 225 BY 25)
       MINOR = none
       OFFSET = (2 pct, 2 pct);
   AXIS2
       LABEL = (F='Albany AMT' H=2 'Chronological Age')
       ORDER = (5 to 17  BY  2)
       MINOR = none
       OFFSET = (2 pct, 2 pct);
   PLOT wght*age=id /VAXIS = AXIS1 HAXIS = AXIS2 NOLEGEND;
RUN;
```

The AXIS statements control the axis labels, value range, tickmarks, and offset. For example, in defining AXIS1, the LABEL statement is used to describe the aspects of the label for the y-axis. In this statement the text is rotated by setting A=90, the font is set to Albany AMT (F='Albany AMT'), the font size is set by H=2, and the text of the label is Weight. The ORDER statement sets the range, 25 to 225, and location of the major tick marks—at every 25. MINOR=NONE indicates that minor tick marks should not be printed, and OFFSET indicates that the minimum and maximum values in the range should be set a small distance, 2% of total size, away from the edges of the plot space.

The PLOT statement then indicates the main content of the plot. In this case, wght*age=id creates a scatterplot with wght on the y-axis, and age on the x-axis; the repeated measures are linked using the individual identifier id. Because the datapoints for each individual will be connected in the order in which they appear in the dataset, it is important that the data are sorted by both the identifying variable and the time (x-axis) variable. The VAXIS (vertical axis) and HAXIS (horizontal axis) statements indicate how the previously defined AXIS1 and AXIS2 content should be placed in the plot space, and the NOLEGEND statement suppresses the automatic generation of a legend. All aspects of the plot can be changed to accommodate both aesthetic tastes and the specifics of the data being examined. We typically edit multiple aspects of the plots (colors, fonts, size, etc.) for presentation and publication.

In R, we use the functions provided in the ggplot2 package (Wickham, 2009) to plot the longitudinal trajectories; this code is contained in Script 2.4. The script begins by loading the ggplot2 package and putting a subset of the sample (in this case participants with ids between 1,300 and 1,600) into a new object, wght_long1. The plot_obs object is defined using the ggplot function, to which we pass the name of the dataset, data=wght_long1, and an aesthetics function, aes(), that identifies which variables are to be used on each axis and to group the repeated measures, (x=age, y=wght, group=id). Specific plot geometries and characteristics are then added (using a +). We include geom_line(), which connects observations in order of the x-variable for each group; geom_point(), which plots the individual data-points; theme_classic(), which provides a classic layout for the background and x- and y-axes (one may also try theme_bw()); and scale_x_continuous() and scale_y_continuous(), which control the range and breaks for the major tick marks, and the name for the text labels of the axes. Finally, print(plot_obs) displays the plot object.

The human visual system is extremely good at pattern recognition. Thus, plots are very useful for both data screening and obtaining initial ideas about one's data. Often we examine upwards of 50 plots *before* beginning an analysis. As noted earlier, these efforts provide us with a comprehensive view of the opportunities, potential, limitations, and problems we shall encounter in the modeling process. Given the plethora of good books and materials on data vizualization in both SAS and R, we have only provided very basic code here. Additional guidance and code can be found in *Longitudinal Data Analysis for the Behavioral Sciences Using R* (Long, 2012), *R Graphics Cookbook* (Chang, 2013), *Statistical Graphics Procedures by Example: Effective Graphs Using SAS* (Matange & Heath,

Script 2.4. R Script for Plotting Longitudinal Data

```
library(ggplot2)

wght_long1 <- wght_long[which(wght_long$id>1300 & wght_long$id<1600),]

plot_obs <- ggplot(data=wght_long1, aes(x=age, y=wght, group=id)) +
                geom_line() +
                geom_point() +
                theme_classic() +
                scale_x_continuous(breaks = c(5,7,9,11,13,15,17),
                                   name = "Chronological Age") +
                scale_y_continuous(breaks = c(25,50,75,100,125,150,175,
                                   200,225), name = "Weight")

print(plot_obs)
```

2011) and *A Handbook of Statistical Graphics Using SAS ODS* (Der & Everitt, 2014). Lastly, we note that we do not provide range restrictions on the plots at the outset to determine if there are participants with out-of-range values on the timing metric or outcome variable.

DATA SCREENING

Before fitting growth models, it is important to examine the data and obtain basic information about the variables to be used in the analysis. Preliminary screening should include examinations of the distribution of scores for each variable. As usual, key univariate descriptives include the mean, median, variance (standard deviation), skewness, kurtosis, minimum, maximum, range, and the number of observations for each variable based on the chosen time metric. Bivariate descriptives include correlations/covariances and bivariate frequency tables for nominal or ordinal variables. All these descriptives can be examined for patterns and nonlinear relations, as well as potential outliers and miscodes. Longitudinal data are special because they are ordered, which can be indexed along one or more time metrics (variables such as measurement occasion, age, calendar date, time since an event, number of exposures, etc.). For example, it is immediately informative to examine how the mean, variance, and number of available cases change across the repeated measures (e.g., wght5, wght6, wght7). As will be discussed in the next section, selection of the time metric greatly influences how results from any specific growth model can be interpreted. Thus, in the data screening stage it is important to consider how various properties of the longitudinal data differ when the data are organized in relation to different time metrics. Although we only illustrate a very basic set of evaluations, the main objective of the data screening process is to learn as much as possible about one's data. Any and all descriptives (and plots) that can be obtained/produced using both wide-form and long-form data should be examined.

Data for this example are the weight data from the NLSY-CYA briefly described above and plotted longitudinally against age in Figure 2.1. To describe the data by age, we first restructure the data into the wide format with age rounded to the nearest year, which was done in Scripts 2.1 and 2.2. Scripts 2.5 and 2.6 are then implemented to calculate a selection of univariate descriptive statistics for the age-specific weight variables in SAS and R, respectively. In SAS, PROC MEANS is used to obtain the sample size (N), mean (MEAN), standard deviation (STD), minimum (MIN), maximum (MAX), skewness (SKEW), and kurtosis (KURT) (with 2 decimal precision, MAXDEC=2) for the age-specific weight variables (VAR wght5-wght19). Bivariate relations among the repeated observations are obtained using PROC CORR, and corresponding plots are obtained using PROC SGSCATTER. In SGSCATTER, repeated measures of weight are listed on the MATRIX statement, and DIAGONAL=(HISTOGRAM) is specified to plot the univariate distributions along the diagonal of the matrix.

Similar statistical information is obtained in the R script. The script begins by creating a dataset that only contains the weight variables. Thus, the dataset wght_vars is created from the wght_wide1 dataset, and only the variables listed are retained. This

Script 2.5. SAS Script for Basic Data Screening

```
PROC MEANS DATA = wght_wide N MEAN STD MIN MAX SKEW KURT MAXDEC=2;
    VAR wght5-wght19;
RUN;

PROC CORR DATA = wght_wide;
    VAR wght5-wght19;
RUN;

ODS LISTING STYLE = journal image_dpi=300;
ODS GRAPHICS ON / RESET=ALL IMAGEFMT=png WIDTH=6in IMAGENAME='Matrix';

PROC SGSCATTER DATA = wght_wide;
    MATRIX wght5-wght19 / DIAGONAL=(HISTOGRAM);
RUN;

ODS GRAPHICS OFF;
```

Script 2.6. R Code for Basic Data Screening

```
wght_vars = wght_wide1[ ,c('wght5','wght6','wght7','wght8','wght9',
                           'wght10','wght11','wght12','wght13',
                           'wght14','wght15','wght16','wght17',
                           'wght18','wght19')]

#Descriptives
library(psych)
describe(wght_vars)

# Bivariate Descriptives
cor(wght_vars, use='pairwise.complete.obs')

panel.hist <- function(x, ...)
{
    usr <- par("usr"); on.exit(par(usr))
    par(usr = c(usr[1:2], 0, 1.5))
    h <- hist(x, plot = FALSE)
    breaks <- h$breaks; nB <- length(breaks)
    y <- h$counts; y <- y/max(y)
    rect(breaks[-nB], 0, breaks[-1], y, col="cyan", ...)
}

pairs(~wght5+wght6+wght7+wght8+wght9+
       wght10+wght11+wght12+wght13+wght14+
       wght15+wght16+wght17+wght18+wght19,
       data=wght_wide1, diag.panel=panel.hist)
```

step facilitates production of descriptives in subsequent steps. After loading the psych package, the describe() function is used to obtain univariate statistics for the previously defined selection of weight variables, wght_vars. This function provides, among other statistics, the sample size, mean, standard deviation, median, range, min, and max. The cor() function is then used to obtain bivariate correlations.

The next section of code defines a function, `panel.hist()`, that will be used to obtain a corresponding matrix of bivariate scatterplots and univariate histograms (on the diagonal). Details can be found at *http://astrostatistics.psu.edu/su07/R/html/graphics/html/pairs.html* or in the *R Graphics Cookbook* (Recipe 5.13, Chang, 2013). The actual plot is generated using the `pairs()` function, wherein the selection of weight variables is listed separated by + signs, `wght_wide1` is the dataset for the weight data in wide format, and `diag.panel=panel.hist` calls the `panel.hist` function to place univariate histograms on the diagonals.

Output

A selection of SAS and R output for the univariate descriptive statistics is shown in Outputs 2.1 and 2.2, respectively. For the most part, they are self-explanatory, but close examination highlights important aspects of these data. However, we first begin by noting a discrepancy between the numbers from SAS and R. The differences in the reported statistics between programs are due to how the programs round numbers. Specifically, SAS rounded all ages halfway between two whole numbers to the higher whole number (e.g., 12.5 rounds to 13). R, on the other hand, rounds ages halfway between two whole numbers to the nearest even number (e.g., 12.5 rounds to 12). Thus, when restructuring the data to the *wide* format, you should note some discrepancies between the datafiles.

Returning to the descriptive statistics, we see, first, that sample size changes dramatically across age, with approximately 1,200 participants assessed at ages 10, 11, and 12 and less than 10 participants assessed at age 19. Second, there appear to be some potential coding/reporting errors in the data. Minimum values for weight at ages 7, 8, and 12 were less than 10 pounds, and maximum values for weights at ages 8, 9, and 10 were in the 200s. Both extremes would be unusual in early and middle childhood and require further investigation and/or cleaning. Third, the age-specific means display an increasing

Output 2.1. SAS Output for Univariate Descriptive Statistics

Variable	N	Mean	Std Dev	Minimum	Maximum	Skewness	Kurtosis
wght5	171	43.47	9.26	30.00	90.00	1.64	4.55
wght6	772	47.68	9.97	27.00	110.00	1.53	4.68
wght7	921	53.90	12.25	8.00	127.00	1.38	3.39
wght8	1067	62.49	17.67	7.00	280.00	2.72	22.47
wght9	1092	72.22	19.50	30.00	220.00	1.40	3.82
wght10	1219	82.55	22.89	20.00	200.00	1.19	2.03
wght11	1246	96.13	27.11	44.00	265.00	1.16	2.26
wght12	1196	108.74	29.05	1.00	249.00	1.08	1.98
wght13	1106	121.84	32.68	42.00	313.00	1.27	2.52
wght14	995	130.59	34.56	62.00	324.00	1.51	2.98
wght15	202	129.57	26.52	87.00	235.00	0.88	0.90
wght16	70	135.46	33.09	90.00	240.00	1.10	0.85
wght17	50	136.62	32.97	96.00	255.00	1.71	3.14
wght18	14	137.64	51.47	101.00	280.00	2.22	4.44
wght19	8	148.63	31.38	115.00	200.00	0.75	-0.76

Output 2.2. R Output for Univariate Descriptive Statistics

	var	n	mean	sd	median	trimmed	mad	min	max	range	skew	kurtosis	se
wght5	1	171	43.47	9.26	41.0	42.45	5.93	30	90	60	1.61	4.29	0.71
wght6	2	837	47.85	9.84	46.0	46.86	8.90	27	110	83	1.48	4.46	0.34
wght7	3	856	54.21	12.46	51.0	52.69	8.90	8	127	119	1.35	3.20	0.43
wght8	4	1157	62.77	17.57	60.0	60.72	14.83	7	280	273	2.59	21.02	0.52
wght9	5	1002	72.77	19.70	68.5	70.49	15.57	37	220	183	1.40	3.81	0.62
wght10	6	1320	83.08	23.03	79.0	80.51	20.76	20	200	180	1.16	1.88	0.63
wght11	7	1145	96.72	27.31	91.0	93.90	23.72	44	265	221	1.16	2.27	0.81
wght12	8	1288	108.90	28.75	104.0	106.12	23.72	1	249	248	1.05	1.91	0.80
wght13	9	1014	122.82	33.15	116.0	119.06	25.20	42	313	271	1.26	2.41	1.04
wght14	10	1054	130.42	34.12	122.0	125.78	25.20	62	324	262	1.50	2.98	1.05
wght15	11	143	130.41	26.88	128.0	127.90	23.72	87	235	148	0.93	1.10	2.25
wght16	12	72	135.03	32.76	126.5	130.91	25.95	90	240	150	1.09	0.70	3.86
wght17	13	48	137.31	33.42	129.0	132.62	20.76	96	255	159	1.56	2.28	4.82
wght18	14	15	136.13	42.94	119.0	127.77	14.83	101	280	179	1.88	2.31	12.89
wght19	15	7	153.43	30.55	145.0	153.43	22.24	118	200	82	0.39	-1.67	11.55

trend over time, going from 43.47 pounds at age 5 up to 148.63 pounds at age 19 (from the SAS output). The increases, though, are not constant (i.e., linear) as age-to-age differences ranged from –1 (between ages 14 and 15) to +13 (between ages 12 and 13), highlighting the fact that gains in weight across this age range are nonlinear (i.e., a linear growth model will not fit these data when age is the time metric). Fourth, age-to-age differences in the standard deviations indicate that the amount of between-child differences in weight also increased through early and middle childhood and stabilized around age 11 (although some caution in interpretation is warranted given that the sample size also decreased rapidly after age 11). Many developmental processes are characterized by such increases (differential development), and increases in the standard deviation are typical of many developmental processes and often highlight positive associations between initial values and subsequent changes. Fifth, the skew and kurtosis values show that the distributions of weight, at most ages, are both positively skewed, which is typical of weight data since weight cannot go below zero, and platykurtic. The similarity of skew and kurtosis across ages (except for the age 8 data, where kurtosis was 22.47 and should be examined for errors and/or miscoding) suggests that non-normality may be a key feature of these data and that a model that accounts for non-normality may be warranted. Thus, we have already learned a good deal about how the weight data are organized with respect to chronological age.

The matrix scatterplots from SAS and R are shown in Figures 2.2a and 2.2b, respectively. For clarity, the plots shown are only 6 × 6, covering ages 5 to 10. They need to be supplemented with additional ages (with overlap) for a full evaluation. Again, close examination highlights some important aspects of these data, and note that the ranges of the x- and y-axes are age–pair specific. First, the positive skew of the distribution at each age is prominent along the diagonal. Second, the bivariate scatterplot showing the relation between age 5 weights and age 6 weights is empty, which means that no individuals were measured at both ages. Considering the data collection setup for the NLSY-CYA, this missingness is expected because assessments were obtained approximately every other year. The frequency of assessment has implications for how closely the observed changes can be mapped to an ongoing process. Third, a number of unusual observations are evident. For example, in the 8/9 year bivariate scatterplot there is an observation very far to the right that is all alone. Checking the axes, this individual appeared to have gained 100 pounds in one year, which is unlikely and suggests that additional cleaning of these data is required.

As we hope to have demonstrated, basic longitudinal plots and descriptive statistics produced here are useful for data screening. Our conclusion is that these weight data from the NLSY-CYA have some potential when organized with respect to age, but that they are not ready for analysis. With local datasets, potential problems can be further investigated through careful examination of the forms and/or files (paper or electronic) used in data collection. In large, publicly available databases like the NLSY-CYA, though, those forms cannot be accessed (or may no longer exist). Thus, recoding and/or deleting observations must be made post hoc using one's best judgment. Removing highly unusual observations may be relatively straightforward and follow highly defensible decision rules. But removal of borderline observations may not be so easy. There are always exceptions to even well-formulated procedures. In such cases, we suggest that the modeling enterprise proceed in parallel, both with and without outliers. Informed decisions can then be made regarding how robust the findings are with respect to those observations. In addition to the purely practical aspects of data screening, the plots and descriptives are extremely useful when considering the ways in which one's longitudinal data can be connected to specific theories of within-person change and between-person differences in within-person change.

LONGITUDINAL MEASUREMENT

Growth models are typically used to examine how individuals' attributes change over time. The data for analysis are *repeated measures*, wherein the attributes of one or more individual entities (e.g., persons) are obtained on multiple occasions that have known ordering or locations in *time*. For example, in the data used in the above examples, children's physical attributes (e.g., weight) were measured multiple times at 2-year intervals. These data (after some cleaning) provide the raw materials for examining how individuals' weight changes with age. Implicit in our presentation so far is the assumption that the weight scores have the same meaning across all measurement occasions and across all individuals. In this section, we hint at some of the measurement issues that must be considered when fitting growth models.

Before fitting any growth models, it is important to consider whether the repeatedly measured variables are suitable for examining individual change. How reliable are the scores at each measurement occasion? Can the scores from one measurement occasion be quantitatively compared to those obtained at a later occasion? Were the scores obtained in the same way? Are the scores scaled in the same metric? Did the passage of time in some way change the meaning of the measurement procedure? These questions should be asked every time an analysis is prepared, so that the measurement assumptions are explicit and/or tested. Our intent here is not to provide a comprehensive treatment of these often complex issues. Readers are referred to the many more comprehensive treatments of longitudinal measurement (Little, 1997; Meredith & Horn, 2001; Millsap, 2011; Widaman & Reise, 1997). However, we underscore the importance of measurement in the modeling of change by highlighting three basic considerations: reliability, scaling/sensitivity of measures to the analysis of change, and measurement invariance across time (see also Chapters 14 and 15).

Reliability

As in all analyses, researchers should examine the reliability of their measurement instruments. Typical evaluations include assessment/calculation of internal consistency (Cronbach's α) and test–retest reliability. The general concept of reliability is that the rank ordering of the scores is stable over repeated testings. Historically, this has meant

(a) Using SGSCATTER in SAS

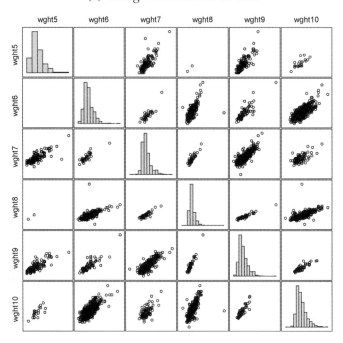

(b) Using pairs in R

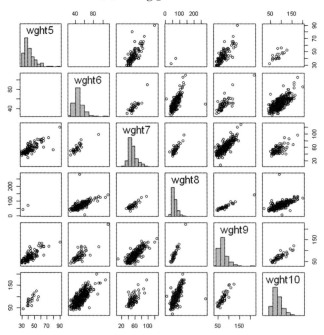

FIGURE 2.2. Matrix scatterplot.

consistency or stability of between-person differences. For example, test–retest reliability is operationalized as the rank-order stability (correlation) of scores obtained on two occasions. High stability (e.g., > 0.80) across time is interpreted as an indication of good reliability. However, when we are interested in and purposively examining change, judging reliability in terms of stability (i.e., the opposite of change) runs counter to our goals. Thus, we do not recommend using test–retest reliability in a longitudinal setting where change is expected. High internal consistency (e.g., Cronbach's α > 0.80) of multiple-item questionnaires is interpreted as an indication of good reliability and is a good starting point. Cronbach's α can be calculated separately at each measurement occasion to evaluate whether the test, scale, or survey is internally reliable over the course of the study. For example, had weight been measured using multiple items/methods, we could calculate Cronbach's α at each age and evaluate if and how the reliability of weight scores changed from age 5 to age 19. This possibility highlights that assessments of reliability are (sub)sample and occasion-specific. Good reliability across *all* occasions of measurement (ages) provides some evidence of longitudinal reliability. However, we must keep in mind that reliability of the observed scores does not translate to reliability of *change*. That is, just because between-person differences are reliably measured at a given point in time, does not mean the same scores are useful in measuring how an individual changes across time.

Scaling/Sensitivity

The study of change is facilitated by the use of measurement tools that are appropriately scaled and sensitive to change. Does the measurement tool capture the changes of interest? Many measurement instruments do not. For example, IQ scores are explicitly age normed, such that the average is 100 and the standard deviation is 15. Normed scores are not appropriate for growth modeling because the very information (i.e., changes in the mean and variance) upon which the growth model is built have already been removed. While there are some exceptions, growth modeling should be conducted with scores that can vary over time (e.g., raw/sum scores, IRT theta scores). Generally, these scores contain the most information and are most useful for modeling change. Transformations, whether linear or nonlinear, should be considered carefully and if applied, should be applied in the same manner at each measurement occasion so that the change information is retained.

Further, it is important to consider the sensitivity of the measurement tool to within-person changes over the chosen time period. Some tools, particularly those developed in research settings focused on the assessment of between-person differences, are not necessarily sensitive to within-person changes. For example, a scale that measures weight in units of stone (14-pound increments) is not nearly as sensitive as a scale that measures weight in ounces. Occasion-to-occasion changes in individuals' weight measured on the two scales will look quite different—potentially quite stable when using one instrument and quite variable using the other. Granular measurement tools (e.g., 5-point Likert-type scales on questionnaires) can lead to conclusions that the measured constructs are relatively stable, while fine-grained measures (e.g., 0- to 100-point slider-type interface) can lead to conclusions that the measured constructs are quite variable. Our recommendation is to use more fine-grained measures when they are available and known to be reliable. An additional consideration for measurement is whether the measurement instrument can represent the entire range of skills present at each measurement occasion, so that the full range of change can be adequately tracked. Violations of this consideration may be evident when ceiling or floor effects are observed. In such cases, the measurement instrument is unable to adequately measure individual change at the upper or lower end of the continuum. In sum, measurement properties of the scale being used have severe consequences for how much can be learned from investigations of individual change. Thus, the choice of measurement instrument and its qualities should be considered thoughtfully; this decision can impact substantive conclusions garnered from the analyses (see Grimm, Kuhl, & Zhang, 2013).

Measurement Invariance

When working with repeated measures data, comparability of scores across measurement occasions requires a certain level of measurement invariance. Does the measurement tool measure the same construct in the same metric at each occasion? Formally, measurement invariance ensures that scores are comparable across both persons and measurement occasions. For example, measurement invariance across the repeated measures of individuals' weight is facilitated by use of the same measurement device (scale) each year—provided that the scale is calibrated in the same way each year. If the scale is calibrated differently on different occasions or if different units of measurement are used, the resulting scores cannot be quantitatively compared—the measurement instrument is noninvariant. When working with physical devices, measurement invariance is tested and assured through calibration. When working with psychological scales, measurement invariance is either assumed (not ideal) or tested using formal measurement models—usually longitudinal factor or item response models (see Little, 1997; Meredith, 1993; Meredith & Horn, 2001; Millsap, 1995, 2011; Widaman & Reise, 1997). Covered in more detail in Chapters 14 and 15, the general idea is to use these models to test whether the items or tests are functioning in the same way at all measurement occasions. In brief, we test whether specific parameters (discrimination/factor loading and threshold/intercept) are reasonably the same across occasions, and if possible fix them to be invariant. If the measurement parameters are deemed invariant across measurement occasions, then the construct-level scores can be quantitatively compared. That is, measurement invariance ensures that the observed changes reflect changes in the persons and *not* changes in the measurement instrument.

Typical problems faced in studying measurement invariance in longitudinal research are related to sample size and age appropriateness. Longitudinal studies tend to rely on relatively small (select) samples, especially with large data collection protocols (i.e., large numbers of surveys/tests/scales with several items). When sample size is small, tests of measurement invariance are underpowered, and the combination of small samples and many items or tests make it difficult to estimate models to test for measurement invariance. In the absence of the formal tests, special care is needed to be both explicit and thoughtful about the measurement assumptions being made. Another approach to the study of measurement invariance is to have a parallel cross-sectional study, where measurement invariance models can be fit. One limitation of this approach is the inability to test for measurement invariance related to repeated testing. The second problem of studying measurement invariance in longitudinal studies is age appropriateness. Longitudinal researchers are often faced with the task of measuring the *same* construct at *different* ages. The rapidity of development means that different measurement tools are likely to be most appropriate at different measurement occasions. For example, accurately measuring mathematics skills in kindergarten and sixth grade require different items. That is, the items used to measure mathematics ability in kindergarten are inappropriate for measuring mathematics ability in sixth grade and vice versa. In these instances, it is very difficult or potentially impossible to examine measurement invariance (see Edwards & Wirth, 2009; Meredith & Horn, 2001), and there is little guarantee that the scores obtained at one age can be meaningfully compared to the scores obtained at other ages. Often, we make assumptions about measurement invariance because of our inability to test for it.

TIME METRICS

Following the rationales for longitudinal research presented in the previous chapter, growth models provide opportunities to examine within-person change and between-person differences in within-person change. Our brief discussion on longitudinal measurement highlighted some of the issues surrounding the selection and scaling of the *y*-axis; how the construct is measured. In this section we highlight some of the issues surrounding selection and scaling of the *x*-axis: *time*. Conceptually, the metric on which time is indexed can be considered a vehicle (variable) representing and condensing a particular set of processes (Wohlwill, 1973). Time is used as a proxy against which to track the within-person change process. For example, when indexed by chronological age (time since birth), time represents a set of age-related processes. When indexed by grade in school, time represents a set of school-related processes. When indexed by time-in-study, time represents a set of processes invoked upon meeting the research staff. Thus, depending on the set of processes one is interested in, different time metrics may be of use and multiple time metrics may be of interest.

Figure 2.3 is a series of longitudinal plots of the repeated measures of weight obtained from a subsample of females who participated in the NLSY-CYA plotted against different time metrics (*x*-axis). As a collection, these plots inform us about what time metrics may be of greatest use for describing the between-person differences in within-person change. In Figure 2.3a, the repeated measures of weight are plotted with respect to *individual measurement occasion*, a design variable that indicates how many times the participant had his or her weight measured by the research staff (count of the exposure to the measurement protocol). In this case, time represents the extent of exposure to the research staff.

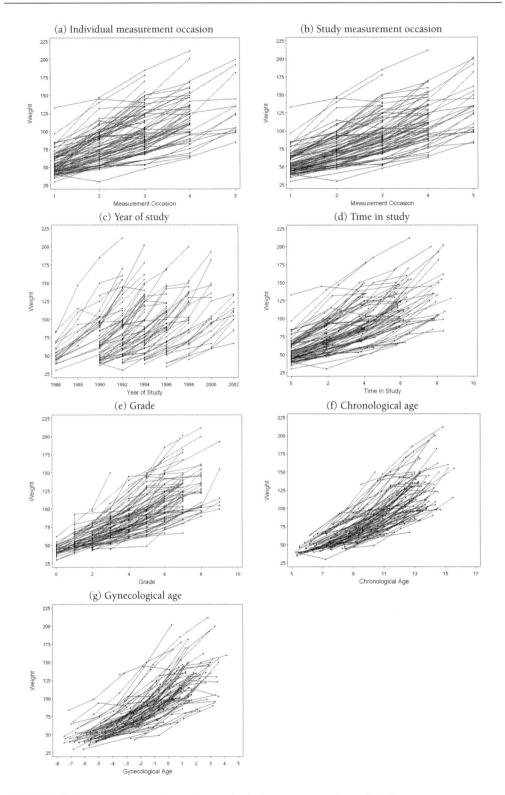

FIGURE 2.3. Longitudinal plots of individual changes in weight with different timing metrics.

In Figure 2.3b, the same data are plotted with respect to *study measurement occasion*, a design variable that indicates when a measurement was obtained with respect to the overall study design (ordinal ranking of repeated measures beginning with each participant's first measurement occasion). In this case, time represents a study design process—study measurement occasion since the participant's first. From Figures 2.3a and 2.3b, the individual trajectories of weight appear to increase over time, with a more or less constant rate of change (increasing about the same amount for each unit of time). This pattern of within-person change might be relatively well described by a linear growth model.

The individual and study measurement occasion time metrics are commonly used in growth modeling applications, in part because these time variables are easy to obtain. In fact, they are assigned by the research staff during data collection. Which wave of data collection are we in? Did the participant show up in this wave? With no information actually needed from the participant, these *time* variables are easy to produce, tend to have comparatively few missing values, and highlight the importance of the research staff's time in the data collection process. However, as we hope to have shown, they are researcher-assigned study design variables that may or may not map on to the *developmental/change process* of interest. The extent to which these variables can serve as proxies for the actual processes driving within-person change depends on the congruence between the actual change process and the study design. In some cases, the congruence is known and controlled experimentally (i.e., in the study of exposure or practice effects; e.g., McArdle & Woodcock, 1997), but often it is not (e.g., in study of development).

Although not always useful with respect to one's research question, individual and study measurement occasion time metrics are extremely useful for understanding the data structure and potential implications of study design for analysis and interpretation of results. For example, in both Figures 2.3a and 2.3b, the extent of longitudinal attrition can be seen in the differences in data density between the first and fifth measurement occasions. The extent of incomplete data will need to be reported and interpreted with respect to common threats to internal and external validity. Note also that when plotted with respect to measurement occasion, the repeated measures of weight are all aligned in five perfectly vertical columns. This alignment is facilitated by the fact that measurement occasion is a count or ordinal variable that has a limited number of values. This organizational scheme aids some types of analysis, but also makes strong and often inappropriate assumptions about how time proceeds. For example, traditional repeated measures analysis of variance is well suited to such time metrics because time is often treated as a categorical variable. However, in many growth models, time is treated as a continuous variable where it is assumed that the distance between *time* = 1 and *time* = 2 is equivalent to the distance between *time* = 4 and *time* = 5. These assumptions (interval scale of measurement) regarding time are convenient but may not match the reality of the study design or one's research goals.

Two more study design variables are shown in Figures 2.3c and 2.3d. In these panels, the repeated measures of weight are plotted with respect to *calendar year* (1986–2002) and *time in study* (0 to 10 years), respectively. Calendar year represents how weight changes with respect to historical processes. The lack of a distinct, homogeneous pattern across time suggests that historical processes operating in the late 20th century are not driving within-person changes in weight. However, the plot does highlight the cohort-sequential study design and the potential need to explicitly test for cohort effects either as a potential explanation of between-person differences in change (do later-born cohorts grow at faster rates than earlier-born cohorts?) or as an element of the study design (can the sequential cohorts be pooled together?). Calendar year may be an important proxy when studying how macro-level social processes (e.g., historical changes in nutrition) affect within-person change and the between-person differences therein. In contrast, time in study (years since the participant's first measurement) represents the influence on more proximal processes. Specifically, this time metric highlights how children's weight changed with respect to meeting the research staff for the first time—not a particularly viable hypothesis in this case. However, we can use this time metric to examine an important aspect of the study design. From Figure 2.3d, we can see the individual differences in the measurement schedules. Individuals' repeated measures were not always obtained at 2-year intervals. Some were measured a bit sooner and some a bit later. Furthermore, along this time metric, the individual changes appear to show some nonlinearity, with acceleration as individuals get further into the study. The presence of nonlinear trajectories may prompt consideration of a wider set of growth models.

Longitudinal plots utilizing two time metrics obtained during data collection are shown in Figures 2.3e and 2.3f. *Grade in school* is a measured variable that serves as a proxy for school-related change processes that include processes occurring within a child and within his or her environment. This time metric is often used for academic variables because changes in children's academic abilities should be, at least in part, influenced by what takes place during school. However, this time metric may not serve as an appropriate marker of the biological processes hypothesized to influence weight gain. The use of grade also highlights an important aspect of time. Time is special because it always marches forward. Time never sits still and never goes backwards (unfortunately). However, time metrics may or may not maintain these properties. For example, some children repeat a grade in school and thus may provide two repeated measures at exactly the same time even though they occurred in different years. Furthermore, the practical realities of data collection mean that differences in grade may not be coincident with differences in calendar time. That is, one-year differences in grade may reflect less than a year of calendar time (e.g., May 2000 → October 2000) or more than a year of calendar time (e.g., October 2000 → May 2002), even in situations where no children skip or repeat grades.

Age is another measured variable, usually calculated as the difference between the child's birthdate (obtained directly from study participants or their proxies) and the date of assessment. Generally, age serves as a proxy for the set of age-related biological, physical, psychological, and social processes. Use of this time metric presumes that at least some of these age-related processes are determinants of the observed changes in weight. Examining the trajectories in Figure 2.3f, we see the type of heterogeneity we expect when using a continuously measured *time* variable—no two individuals were measured at exactly the same age. We also see nonlinearity, again with acceleration as individuals get older. Generally, age is a popular and useful time metric for understanding many developmental processes. However, care should be taken when interpreting changes along an age time metric because age is a proxy for an unspecified set of age-related processes and because it cannot be manipulated, age has limited value for establishing causality.

In the final panel, Figure 2.3g, the repeated measures of weight are plotted with respect to *gynecological age*, here defined as the difference between chronological age at assessment and individuals' self-reported age at menarche (*time* = 0). As a time metric, gynecological age represents a set of age-related processes that proceed to and from a specific biological event. The spacing of individuals' repeated measures remains the same as when age was used as the *x*-axis, but the individuals have been aligned to a different *time* = 0 location (birth vs. menarche). That is, realignments of the individual trajectories with respect to birth or menarche provide different perspectives on the between-person differences in within-person change (within-person changes are the same). Viewed in relation to gynecological age, we see more evidence of nonlinearity, with changes in weight being somewhat more rapid in the years relatively close to menarche (e.g., −2 < *time* < +1) than in the years further away from menarche. Depending on one's research question, chronological age, gynecological age, or another alignment of age (relative to death, crawling, walking, etc.) may allow for a more precise articulation of the patterns embedded in the data. More generally, a plethora of time metrics are available in any longitudinal study. All possible alternatives should be considered and explored until the variable on the *x*-axis, the processes proxied by that variable, and one's research goals are well aligned.

After considering how seven different time metrics may be used as proxies for different sets of change processes, one might consider whether there are multiple processes involved. Are changes in weight influenced by both age-related processes (chronological age time metric) and macro-level social changes in nutrition (calendar-year time metric)? Probably yes. But the same reasons that make *time* special make the separation of multiple time-related processes difficult. For example, academic ability may be influenced by both school-related and age-related processes. But once children are in school, time spent in school (grade) is highly related with chronological age. When one increases, the other almost always does too (i.e., multicollinearity). Creative study designs can sometimes produce separation. In this situation, an administrative rule provides an opportunity to separate the time metrics. Typically, there is a cutoff date for school enrollment. Children who turn 5 before a specific date, say September 1, may enter school in the fall. Children who turn 5 after the date must wait until the following fall. Thus, two children who are only 1 week apart in age (e.g., born August 30 and September 7) will be 1 year apart in grade. Assuming that the two children are identical in all other respects, the similarity in age and the discrepancy in grade provide an opportunity to separate the influence of age-related and school-related processes (see Morrison, Smith, & Dow-Ehrensberger, 1995). Similarly, McArdle and Woodcock (1997) showed how age-related change can be untangled from practice effects by having an age-heterogeneous sample and varying the time lag between the repeated measures. In sum, the choice of time metric has important consequences for the modeling of change and the interpretation of growth modeling results. The possibilities should be considered thoughtfully and comprehensively (see Ram, Gerstorf, Fauth, Zarit, & Malberg, 2010; Wohlwill, 1973).

CHANGE HYPOTHESES

Once an appropriate, and theoretically derived, time metric is chosen, researchers need to consider hypotheses revolving around change. Specifically, researchers need to make hypotheses for how the observed scores are related to the time metric at the individual level (individual change function) and hypotheses regarding where, in the within-person change function, between-person differences manifest. With respect to the individual change function, the goal is to mathematically describe how the developmental process unfolds within each person. When examining individual change patterns, like those presented in Figure 2.1, it is important to think about mathematical functions that may be able to characterize the shape of individual changes. This leads to discussions regarding how the individual change patterns can be summarized. Of course, we note that many descriptions are possible. Researchers should consider mathematical representations that may adequately summarize the individual change patterns, are not unnecessarily complex, and provide meaningful information about the individual. Many times researchers emphasize one of these three desires for an appropriate mathematical representation. For example, many researchers fit a linear growth model (maximizing *not unnecessarily complex* and *provide meaningful information*) to describe each individual's trajectory by two parameters: an intercept, or predicted score at a specific point in time, and a slope representing the individual's rate of linear growth during the observation period. Although simple and a good starting point, the linear growth model can be an oversimplification of a complex developmental process and may lose many nuances of the individual trajectory. At times, researchers emphasize finding a mathematical function that strongly captures the individual change trajectory at the expense of the other objectives. For example, the study of individual changes in physical stature (i.e., height) have led to the development of many mathematical functions that are compared by examining the magnitude of residuals (see Karkach, 2006). Many of these models have parameters that do not provide meaningful information regarding important aspects of individual growth (see, however, Preece & Baines, 1978).

Additional considerations are whether the mathematical function is able to represent the entirety of the developmental process, not just the part of the developmental process that is observed, and whether the developmental process contains multiple phases that should be modeled separately (e.g., before and after the death of a spouse, birth of a child; see Cudeck & Klebe, 2002; Ram & Grimm, 2007). If there is not a strong theory regarding the individual change process, we recommend that researchers begin with simple models and move onto more complex models. Additionally, the fitting of unstructured or data-driven/exploratory growth models may be warranted (see McArdle & Epstein, 1987; Meredith & Tisak, 1990; Grimm et al., 2013).

In addition to thinking about a mathematical model for the relation between the time metric and observed scores, researchers need to consider time-varying covariates that may affect the individual change trajectory. For example, when studying change in cognitive abilities in a sample of older adults, it may be important to include measures of significant life events that occur during the observation period, such as the death of a close relative or a fall that leads to a physical disability. Such events may have a sizable and measurable effect on the individual's change trajectory. Another example is accounting for the timing of pubertal changes when studying individual changes in depression in a sample of children and adolescents.

Once the individual change model is considered, the next key issue is to determine which parameters of the individual change model are allowed to differ across individuals. For example, in most applications of the linear growth model, both the intercept and slope are allowed to vary over persons. Thus, between-person differences in these two particular aspects of change should account for the between-person differences in the change trajectories. Take, as a second example, the logistic curve, a more complex nonlinear function with four parameters: a lower asymptote related to the preexisting level of the attribute, an upper asymptote related to the potential level of the attribute, an inflection point capturing the timing of rapid change, and a rate of change capturing how quickly an individual moves from the lower to upper asymptote. It may be that all four parameters need to vary over individuals to capture the differences in the observed trajectories; however, in certain applications this may not be reasonable for theoretical or practical reasons. Marceau, Ram, Houts, Grimm, and Susman (2011) fit logistic models to describe individual changes in pubertal development and only allowed for between-person differences in the timing of the inflection point and the rate of change because, by definition of the observed scores (Tanner stages), all individuals began at Stage 1 and ended at Stage 5. Thus, the lower and upper asymptotes were not allowed to vary between individuals. Theoretical notions of key change aspects should drive the location of between-person differences in the model; however, data constraints (e.g., number of time points, observation period) may limit the number and location of between-person differences.

INCOMPLETE DATA

Incomplete data are present in all longitudinal studies. Take, as an example, the different time metrics discussed for the longitudinal weight data. Even if we assume that all participants were measured every 2 years, we still, in essence, have incomplete data if we structure the data by age. That is, each participant, although measured on the predetermined 2-year interval, was not measured at all potential ages. Moreover, if we use a fine-grained time metric, there is no way for all participants to be measured at all time points. Thus, when working with longitudinal data, it is important to be aware of the various approaches to handling incomplete data. Here, we describe how incomplete data are handled throughout the book. Readers interested in complete treatments of incomplete data approaches are referred to Enders (2010) and Molenberghs, Fitzmaurice, Kenward, Tsiatis, and Verbeke (2015).

Incomplete data in longitudinal studies are often handled by using *full information maximum likelihood* (FIML) estimation. Multiple imputation (MI) approaches, which are frequently used with cross-sectional data, are not often used with longitudinal data. One likely reason for this is that longitudinal data often have a high amount of data incompleteness and MI approaches are often recommended when the amount of incomplete data is comparatively small. Whether FIML or MI is used to handle the incomplete data, the incomplete data must be *missing at random* (MAR) or *missing completely at random* (MCAR; see Rubin, 1976). MAR means that the probability of observing an incomplete score is related to other *observed* variables in the analysis and unrelated to the potential value of the incomplete score or other unobserved data. With longitudinal data, this means that the likelihood of an incomplete value is related to previously (or subsequently) measured data, such as the previous scores on the outcome of interest and covariates (e.g., sex, age, education level). MCAR means that the incomplete data occur independently of observed and unobserved variables (e.g., purely at random).

FIML handles the incompleteness by integrating the incomplete values into the estimation routine. Unlike MI, FIML does not impute plausible values. Instead, the marginal probability of observing the measured variables for each individual is computed by integrating over the variables with incomplete data (Allison, 2012). One way to conceptualize FIML estimation is to consider the patterns of complete and incomplete data. If we group individuals together who have the same pattern of complete and incomplete data (the same set of observed and unobserved variables), we can then specify a model for the observed variables in each one of these *groups*. Across groups, we specify the same model (for the complete variables) and constrain the model parameters to be equivalent over groups (see McArdle, 1994). This multiple-group approach yields one set of parameters regardless of group membership, and each individual contributes to the estimation of the model parameters as much as he or she can, given his or her available data. One assumption inherent in this approach is that the same model (and parameters) holds across groups (defined by their pattern of complete and incomplete data). If this assumption does not hold (and MCAR and MAR are violated), then FIML (and MI) will produce biased results. There are approaches to handling non-ignorable data incompleteness (also referred to as missing not at random) in longitudinal studies. These methods include pattern mixture models (Little & Rubin, 2002), shared-parameter models (e.g., Beunckens, Molenberghs, Verbeke, & Mallinckrodt, 2008), and selection models (e.g., Diggle & Kenward, 1994). We recommend Muthén, Asparouhov, Hunter, and Leuchter (2011) for a discussion of these approaches and extensions.

FIML estimation has become the main approach to handle incomplete data in the structural equation modeling framework, and most structural equation modeling programs use FIML estimation by default. We note that some programs (e.g., Mplus) only handle incomplete data on the endogenous variables by default and additional model specifications are needed to accommodate incomplete data on exogenous variables. Multilevel modeling programs inherently use FIML approaches and handle incomplete data on endogenous variables. If one is using multilevel modeling programs and exogenous variables are incomplete, we recommend using MI to handle the incomplete data on the exogenous variables and then utilize FIML to handle incomplete data on the endogenous variables. Throughout the book, we use FIML estimation in our examples.

MOVING FORWARD

These practical preliminaries are extremely important and, as we noted, can save a lot of hassle later on. In the next section, we begin our discussion of linear growth models and their extensions. We limit ourselves to linear growth models in this section to concentrate on the complexities brought about by the *extensions* (covariates, multivariate outcomes, multiple groups, and mixture distributions). In Chapter 3, we begin our discussion of linear growth models, their specification in the multilevel and structural equation modeling frameworks, and the interpretation of model parameters. We utilize a longitudinal dataset, with repeated measures of mathematics for illustrative purposes.

Part II

The Linear Growth Model and Its Extensions

3

Linear Growth Models

In discussing growth models, we begin with linear models because of their simplicity and common use. Additionally, linear growth models are often a starting point when attempting to understand within-person change. Longitudinal data for this chapter come from the NLSY-CYA (Center for Human Resource Research, 2004), where children were repeatedly administered mathematics tests. The mathematics scores come from the Peabody Individual Achievement Test (PIAT; Dunn & Markwardt, 1970), which have been analyzed in Grimm, Stelle, Mashburn, Burchinal, and Pianta (2010). In this chapter, we use a reduced dataset for simplicity. A longitudinal plot of mathematics scores against grade at testing is contained in Figure 3.1a for the sample. From this plot, it is difficult to see individual trajectories; however, several features of the data are noticeable. Participants vary in the number of assessments, were assessed from second to eighth grade, but were not measured in each grade, partially due to the assessment protocol in the NLSY-CYA (assessments were spaced approximately 2 years apart) as well as random and nonrandom incompleteness. Overall, there appears to be positive growth over time as scores tend to increase with increases in grade. A similar plot is contained in Figure 3.1b; however, fewer trajectories are plotted. In this plot, it is easier to see the individual trajectories and the variability in individual trajectories in terms of scores at each grade, rates of growth, shapes of growth, and individual variability over time. Some individuals appear to follow more or less smooth trajectories, whereas others show greater fluctuations in performance around their trend.

Data from the sample will be subjected to two linear growth models; the *no-growth* or *intercept only* model and the *linear growth* model. We present the no-growth model because it is a common and logical starting point for any study of change as this model predicts that scores do not change with increases in time. Thus, the no-growth model is a model we often want to reject. The no-growth model has one latent variable, an intercept, which represents the overall level of performance over time. The linear growth model

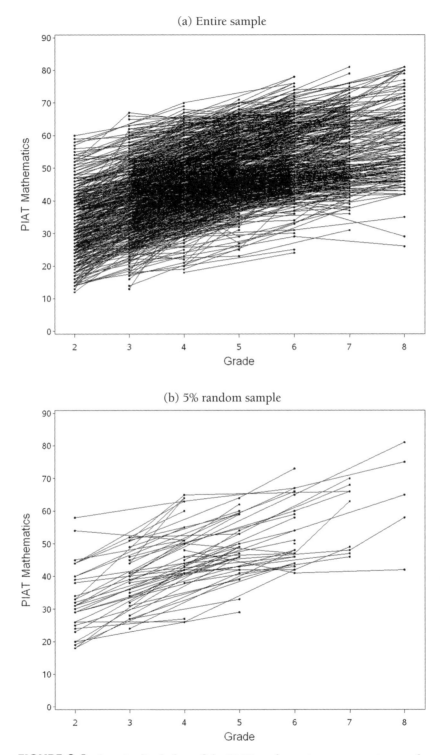

FIGURE 3.1. Longitudinal plots of the PIAT mathematics scores against grade.

allows for a specific type of within-person change trajectory, such that the rate of change is constant within an individual but is allowed to differ between individuals. The linear growth model has two latent variables, an intercept, usually centered at an initial point in time, and a linear slope, representing the rate of change over the observation period. The intercept and slope are allowed to vary over persons and to covary with one another. The linear growth model is similar to fitting a linear regression model to each individual's data and then summarizing the estimated intercepts and slopes by their means, variances, and covariance.

MULTILEVEL MODELING FRAMEWORK

As a multilevel model, the no-growth and linear growth models are two-level models as the repeated scores are nested within individuals. The level-1 (individual) equation for the no-growth model can be written as

$$y_{ti} = b_{1i} + u_{ti} \tag{3.1}$$

where y_{ti} is the repeatedly measured score (e.g., mathematics score) for individual i at time t, b_{1i} is the random intercept (intercept for individual i), and u_{ti} is the time-specific residual score. The time-specific residual score is assumed to follow a normal distribution with a mean of zero and constant variance (e.g., $u_{ti} \sim N(0, \sigma_u^2)$). The level-2 (sample) equation for the random intercept is specified as

$$b_{1i} = \beta_1 + d_{1i} \tag{3.2}$$

where β_1 is the sample mean for the intercept and d_{1i} is individual i's deviation from the sample mean. The individual deviations are assumed to follow a normal distribution with a mean of zero and an estimated variance (e.g., $d_{1i} \sim N(0, \sigma_1^2)$). Equations 3.1 and 3.2 are sometimes combined into a single equation, which yields

$$y_{ti} = (\beta_1 + d_{1i}) + u_{ti} \tag{3.3}$$

This combined level-1 and level-2 equation is common in economics, and this format of programming is required for certain programs. In the no-growth model, each individual has an intercept, but no change in scores is predicted by the model because there is no function of time (e.g., grade) in the level-1 equation (Equation 3.1). Estimated parameters from the no-growth model include the sample-level mean of the random intercept (β_1), the variance of the random intercept (σ_1^2), and the residual variance (σ_u^2). The variance of the random intercept provides information about the magnitude of between-person differences in scores at each measurement occasion, and the residual variance provides information about the magnitude of within-person fluctuations in scores over time.

The second model is the linear growth model, which allows individual scores to change linearly over time and permits individuals to differ in their rates of change. In this model, the rate of change is constant within a given individual, but different individuals are allowed to change at different rates. The level-1 equation for the linear growth model is specified as

$$y_{ti} = b_{1i} + b_{2i} \cdot \left(\frac{t - k_1}{k_2} \right) + u_{ti} \tag{3.4}$$

where y_{ti} is the repeatedly measured variable at time t for individual i, b_{1i} is the random intercept or predicted score for individual i when $t = k_1$, b_{2i} is the random slope or rate of change for individual i for a one-unit change in t/k_2, t represents time and could represent grade at assessment, age at assessment, time in study, time until death, and the like, and u_{ti} is the time-specific residual score. As in the no-growth model, $u_{ti} \sim N(0, \sigma_u^2)$. The constants k_1 and k_2 are chosen to center the intercept and scale the slope, respectively. Often, k_1 is set to 1 to center the intercept at the first occasion, assuming t begins with 1 (e.g., second grade), and k_2 is set to 1 to scale the linear slope in terms of the unit of time given in the timing variable t (e.g., grade or yearly change).

The level-2 equation for the random intercept and slope is written as

$$\begin{aligned} b_{1i} &= \beta_1 + d_{1i} \\ b_{2i} &= \beta_2 + d_{2i} \end{aligned} \tag{3.5}$$

where β_1 and β_2 are sample-level means for the intercept and slope, and d_{1i} and d_{2i} are individual deviations from their respective sample-level mean. Individual deviations are assumed to follow a multivariate normal distribution with zero means, estimated variances, and a covariance; for example,

$$d_{1i}, d_{2i} \sim MVN \left(\begin{bmatrix} 0 \\ 0 \end{bmatrix}, \begin{bmatrix} \sigma_1^2 & \\ \sigma_{21} & \sigma_2^2 \end{bmatrix} \right)$$

Combining Equations 3.4 and 3.5 leads to

$$y_{ti} = (\beta_1 + d_{1i}) + (\beta_2 + d_{2i}) \cdot \left(\frac{t - k_1}{k_2} \right) + u_{ti} \tag{3.6}$$

In the linear growth model, there are six estimated parameters. Estimated parameters include the mean intercept (β_1) and slope (β_2), representing the predicted average score for the sample when $t = k_1$ and the predicted average rate of change for the sample with respect to the chosen time metric (i.e., t/k_2); the variances of the intercept (σ_1^2) and slope (σ_2^2) indicating the magnitude of between-person differences in predicted scores when $t = k_1$ and in the rate of change; the covariance between the intercept and slope (σ_{21}) indicating the degree to which individual deviations in the intercept are associated with individual deviations in the rate of change; and the residual variance (σ_u^2). Practically, researchers are often interested in whether or not the estimate of β_2 is significantly different from zero as an indication of mean change over time. However, in many situations, researchers should pay closer attention to whether the estimate for the variance in change (σ_2^2) is significantly different from zero, indicating individuals vary in their amount of change. Variation in change is important because this variation may be due to experimental manipulations (e.g., treatment effects), individual background characteristics (e.g., gender), and so on. If there is no significant variance in change, then individuals are expected to change in highly similar ways.

MULTILEVEL MODELING IMPLEMENTATION

Data for this example are the longitudinal mathematics data contained in Figure 3.1a, and *grade at testing* is used as the timing variable. In order to fit growth models using multilevel modeling software, data must be in the long format with multiple records per person (one record per measurement occasion per person). The datafile is named `nlsy_math_long`, the mathematics variable is `math`, the timing variable is `grade`, and `id` is the child identification variable.

No-Growth Model

The `NLMIXED` script for the no-growth model fit to the mathematics data is presented in Script 3.1. The script begins by calling the `NLMIXED` procedure and the `nlsy_math_long` dataset. Next, the level-2 (Equation 3.2) is written where `b_1i` is the individual intercept, `beta_1` is the mean intercept, and `d_1i` is the individual deviation from the intercept mean. Next, the level-1 (Equation 3.1; individual trajectory) equation is written without the time-dependent residual term. For the no-growth model, this equation is simply `traject = b_1i`. Next, the `MODEL` statement in `NLMIXED` indicates the dependent variable and its distribution. In this model, `math` is the dependent variable, and it is assumed to follow a `NORMAL` distribution with a mean equal to `traject`, which was previously defined, and a residual variance equal to `v_u`—the residual (level-1) variance, which will be estimated. The `RANDOM` statement is used to identify the random coefficients (parameters that vary over persons) and their estimated parameters.

Script 3.1. NLMIXED Script for the No-Growth Model

```
PROC NLMIXED DATA = nlsy_math_long;
    b_1i = beta_1 + d_1i;
    traject = b_1i;
    MODEL math ~ NORMAL(traject, v_u);
    RANDOM d_1i ~ NORMAL([0], [v_1]) SUBJECT = id;
    PARMS beta_1 = 40 v_1 = 30 v_u = 50;
RUN;
```

In the no-growth model, the random coefficient is d_1i, the individual deviation from the mean intercept, and is assumed to follow a NORMAL distribution with a mean of 0 and a variance equal to v_1—a parameter to be estimated. Also on the RANDOM line is SUBJECT = id, which indicates that the random coefficients vary over children because id is the child's identification variable. The final part of the NLMIXED script contains the starting values for the estimated parameters. Here, we provide *reasonable* starting values for the three parameters to be estimated in the no-growth model. Good starting values can often be found by examining the longitudinal plots (Figure 3.1a) and fitting simpler models, such as linear regression models that do not account for the clustered nature of the repeated measures data. Providing good starting values becomes increasingly important as the models become more complex.

The nlme script for a no-growth model is contained in Script 3.2 and includes calling the nlme library, which must be installed into R.[1] The object ng.math.nlme is then created, and this is where the output from the nlme procedure is held. Naming objects with descriptive names is very useful, and ng.math.nlme stands for a <u>n</u>o-growth model fit to the <u>math</u>ematics variable with the <u>nlme</u> procedure. The statements to specify the model in nlme follow the <-. In this statement, the no-growth model for mathematics is specified. In nlme, the combined level-1 and level-2 equation (Equation 3.3) without the residual term is specified (math ~ beta_1 + d_1i) and is followed by specifying the dataset. The fixed and random statements come next. In the no-growth model, there is a fixed intercept (fixed=beta_1~1) and a random intercept (random=d_1i~1). The cluster, or in this case, subject identification, variable is specified using the group command (group=~id). Specifying the fixed effect for beta_1 estimates the mean of the intercept (β_1), and specifying the random effect for d_1i estimates its variance (σ_1^2). Next, a starting value is provided for the mean of the intercept (start=c(beta_1=40)). Finally, na.action="na.omit" is specified to omit observations where an incomplete value is present. Without this statement, nlme won't estimate the model when missing data are present. Requesting summary(ng.math.nlme) prints the output from the nlme procedure.

SAS and R output for the no-growth model is contained in Output 3.1 and Output 3.2, respectively. Output from NLMIXED and nlme begins with likelihood-based fit statistics. Fit statistics provided by NLMIXED include the −2 log likelihood (−2LL) and a series of information criteria (i.e., Akaike information criterion [AIC], Akaike information criterion corrected [AICc], and the Bayesian information criterion [BIC]). nlme provides the AIC, BIC, and log likelihood value. The AIC, AICc, and BIC are based on the −2LL and a penalty function for the number of estimated parameters. The AIC is equal to −2LL + 2p, where p is the number of estimated parameters. The AICc applies a correction to the AIC for finite samples. The correction, $(2p[p + 1])/(N − p − 1)$, is added to the AIC. The AICc has been recommended for small sample sizes and heavily parameterized

---

[1]This can be done using install.packages("nlme") and selecting a local mirror from which to download the package.

Script 3.2. `nlme` Script for the No-Growth Model

```
library (nlme)

ng.math.nlme <- nlme (math ~ beta_1 + d_1i,
                      data=nlsy_math_long,
                      fixed=beta_1~1,
                      random=d_1i~1,
                      group=~id,
                      start=c(beta_1=40),
                      na.action="na.omit")

summary (ng.math.nlme)
```

models (Burnham & Anderson, 2002). The BIC is equal to $-2LL + \ln(N) \cdot p$, where $\ln(N)$ is the natural log of the sample size and p is the number of estimated parameters. The $-2LL$ can be used to statistically compare *nested* models, such as the no-growth and linear growth models, whereas the information criteria can be used to compare models that are or are not nested. At this time, the fit statistics are noted and will be used later when discussing the linear growth model.

Parameter estimates from NLMIXED are labeled according to how they were labeled in the script, which makes descriptive labeling of parameters helpful. Parameter estimates from nlme are grouped by the type of parameter (random vs. fixed), with random-effects parameters followed by fixed-effects parameters. Parameter estimates for the no-growth model include the mean of the intercept (beta_1 in NLMIXED, Fixed effect of beta_1 in nlme), which equaled 45.91; the variance (or standard deviation) of the intercept (v_1, Random effect of d_1i), which equaled 46.92 (standard deviation was 6.85 and reported in nlme); and the residual variance (v_u, Random effect of Residual), which equaled 116.68 (standard deviation was 10.80). The parameter estimates for the no-growth model indicate the average participant had a score of 45.91 and was not predicted to change across time. There was significant variability in the intercept indicating that children differed in their level of mathematics ability, and the residual variance was significant and sizable indicating a large amount of unexplained variance in the observed mathematics trajectories (potentially because the no-growth model doesn't adequately represent the data).

NLMIXED provides appropriate standard errors for parameter estimates, degrees of freedom, *t*-values, and associated *p*-values for examining the statistical significance of the parameter estimates. Additionally, 95% confidence intervals are calculated. Finally, the gradient is reported. The gradient represents how quickly the parameter estimate was changing at convergence. For the no-growth model, the gradients for all estimated parameters were very small, indicating that parameter estimates were not changing rapidly when the model converged—a sign that the solution was stable. If the gradient for a parameter is large, then the solution is unstable and results should be interpreted cautiously. This may also indicate a local optimum as opposed to the global optimum in the

Output 3.1. NLMIXED Output for the No-Growth Model

```
                                Fit Statistics

                         -2 Log Likelihood           17492
                         AIC (Smaller Is Better)      17498
                         AICC (Smaller Is Better)     17498
                         BIC (Smaller Is Better)      17512


                              Parameter Estimates

                     Standard
Parameter  Estimate    Error    DF  t Value  Pr > |t|  Alpha   Lower     Upper    Gradient

beta_1     45.9147    0.3240    931  141.72   <.0001    0.05   45.2789   46.5505   0.00009
v_1        46.9175    4.8322    931    9.71   <.0001    0.05   37.4342   56.4008   0.000028
v_u        116.68     4.5479    931   25.66   <.0001    0.05   107.76   125.61    -6.28E-6
```

Output 3.2. `nlme` Output for the No-Growth Model

```
Nonlinear mixed-effects model fit by maximum likelihood
  Model: math ~ b_1i
  Data: nlsy_math_long
       AIC      BIC     logLik
   17497.9  17515.02  -8745.952

Random effects:
 Formula: b_1i ~ 1 | id
            b_1i  Residual
StdDev: 6.849582  10.80196

Fixed effects: b_1i ~ 1
         Value  Std.Error   DF   t-value   p-value
b_1i  45.91468   0.323796  1289  141.8013        0
```

likelihood function. In these situations, it is beneficial to rerun the model with new starting values to help determine whether or not the solution is optimal.

nlme provides appropriate standard errors for fixed-effects parameters, degrees of freedom, *t*-values and associated *p*-values. We note that nlme calculates degrees of freedom differently than NLMIXED. In nlme, degrees of freedom are calculated based on the amount of longitudinal information or the number of observed datapoints (2,221) minus the sample size (932). Thus, the reported *df* = 2,221 − 932 = 1,289. NLMIXED calculates degrees of freedom as the sample size minus the number of random effects, *df* = 932 − 1. Differences in reported degrees of freedom are based on differences in the amount of information from the data and the amount of information estimated from the data. nlme takes a regression-like approach where the degrees of freedom are based on the number of datapoints, and an intercept, in the case of the no-growth model, is estimated for each person. NLMIXED takes the view that the mean of the intercept is a single level-2 parameter and the amount of available information at level-2 is based on sample size.

We note that nlme does not output significance tests for the random-effects estimates. However, the significance of the random-effects parameters can be evaluated by using the intervals statement (intervals(ng.math.lme)) or by fitting a model where the random effect is not included in the model and calculating the change in −2*LL*. If the change in −2*LL* is significant given the change in the number of estimated parameters, then estimating the random effect improves model fit, indicating that the parameter is significantly different from zero. However, when there are more than one random-effect parameter (as in the linear growth model), this approach can yield a multiple parameter comparison, which does not provide a separate significance test of each random-effect estimate.

Linear Growth Model

The NLMIXED and nlme scripts for the linear growth model are contained in Scripts 3.3 and 3.4, respectively. We highlight the major changes from the no-growth scripts. In

Script 3.3. NLMIXED Script for the Linear Growth Model

```
PROC NLMIXED DATA = nlsy_math_long;
    b_1i = beta_1 + d_1i;
    b_2i = beta_2 + d_2i;
    traject = b_1i + b_2i * (grade-2);
    MODEL math ~ NORMAL (traject, v_u);
    RANDOM d_1i d_2i ~ NORMAL ([0,0], [v_1,
                                       c_21, v_2])
    SUBJECT = id OUT = estimates;
    PARMS beta_1 = 20 beta_2 = 6 v_1 = 60 v_2 = .8 c_21 = 0 v_u = 50;
RUN;
```

Script 3.4. nlme Script for the Linear Growth Model

```
lg.math.nlme <- nlme(math~(beta_1+d_1i)+(beta_2+d_2i)*(grade-2),
                data=nlsy_math_long,
                fixed=beta_1+beta_2~1,
                random=d_1i+d_2i~1,
                group=~id,
                start=c(beta_1=35,beta_2=4),
                na.action="na.omit")

summary (lg.math.nlme)
```

NLMIXED, the first part of the script now contains the level-2 equations for the random intercept and random slope (Equation 3.5). The level-1 equation (Equation 3.4) now specifies the linear growth model, with grade-2 as the timing variable. Two is subtracted from grade to center the intercept at the second-grade measurement occasion. Thus, parameters associated with the intercept will reflect predicted values in second grade. The intercept can be centered at any point in time and is often centered at the initial measurement occasion; however, it is ideal to center the intercept at a theoretically important point in time, if one exists. The RANDOM line of the linear growth script now has two random coefficients, d_1i and d_2i. These random variables are assumed to follow multivariate normal (NORMAL) distributions with zero means and a variance–covariance matrix as specified. In the variance–covariance matrix, v_1 is the intercept variance, c_21 is the intercept–slope covariance, and v_2 is the slope variance. Finally, starting values are provided for all estimated parameters.

The nlme script begins by creating an R object named lg.math.nlme to contain the output. The combined level-1 and level-2 equation for the linear growth model (Equation 3.6) without the residual term is then specified and followed by naming the dataset. In the linear growth model, there is a fixed intercept and slope (fixed=beta_1+beta_2~1), a random intercept and slope (random=d_1i+d_2i~1), and the cluster variable is id. Starting values are specified for the fixed effects (start=c(beta_1=35,beta_2=4)), and the na.action statement follows.

Select output from NLMIXED and nlme for the linear growth model is contained in Output 3.3 and 3.4, respectively. This time, we begin with the fit statistics because the first question is whether the linear growth model fit better than no-growth model. The –2LL for the linear growth model was 15,937, whereas the –2LL for the no-growth model was 17,492. The improvement or change in –2LL between the no-growth and linear growth models was 17,492 – 15,937 = 1,555. Under the null hypothesis that the models fit equally well, the change in –2LL is distributed as a chi-square statistic with degrees of freedom equal to the difference in the number of estimated parameters between the models. The difference in the number of estimated parameters was 3. Thus, the linear growth model fit significantly better than the no-growth model based on the change in –2LL relative to the difference in the number of estimated parameters ($\chi^2(3) = 1,555$, $p <$ .01). This is supported by examining the information criteria reported by NLMIXED and nlme, as the linear growth model had lower AIC, AICc, and BIC values compared to the no-growth model.

Next, we move onto the parameter estimates from the linear growth model. The mean intercept (beta_1; Fixed effect of beta_1) was 35.27, which is the mean predicted mathematics score in second grade for our sample. The mean slope (beta_2; Fixed effect of beta_2) was 4.34 and is the mean predicted annual change in mathematics scores from second through eighth grade. This is the average annual rate of change because a one-unit change in the variable grade is one year. Parameter estimates for the random effects indicate there was significant variation in *true* mathematics scores in second grade because the intercept variance (v_1, Random effect of d_1i) was estimated to be 64.56 (standard deviation was 8.04) and significantly different from zero. Additionally, there was significant variation in annual true changes in mathematics because the slope variance (v_2, Random effect of d_2i) was estimated to be 0.73 (standard deviation was 0.86) and significantly different from zero. There was a nonsignificant negative covariance between true mathematics scores in second grade and true annual changes in mathematics (c_21, Corr between d_1i and d_2i), which was estimated to be –0.18 (correlation was $r = -.03$). Thus, children's level of math performance in second grade was unrelated to how quickly they changed from second through eighth grade. The final parameter estimate is the residual variance (v_u, Random effect of Residual), which was estimated to be 36.23 (standard deviation is 6.02) and indicates individual variability not accounted for by the linear growth model.

Predicted Trajectories and Residuals

Individual estimates of the intercept and slope were output from NLMIXED and nlme. In NLMIXED, this was done by specifying OUT=estimates immediately following SUBJECT=id. This creates a dataset called estimates, which contains two lines per subject. The first line contains the estimate for d_1i, and the second contains the estimate for d_2i. Script 3.5 contains brief statements to reorganize this dataset and merge this new dataset with the original dataset to create predicted and residual values. In the

Output 3.3. NLMIXED Output for the Linear Growth Model

Fit statistics

-2 Log Likelihood	15937
AIC (smaller is better)	15949
AICC (smaller is better)	15949
BIC (smaller is better)	15978

Parameter Estimates

Parameter	Estimate	Standard Error	DF	t Value	Pr > |t|	Alpha	Lower	Upper	Gradient
beta_1	35.2673	0.3554	930	99.23	<.0001	0.05	34.5698	35.9648	-0.00024
beta_2	4.3393	0.08831	930	49.14	<.0001	0.05	4.1660	4.5126	-0.00008
v_1	64.5616	5.6594	930	11.41	<.0001	0.05	53.4549	75.6682	-0.00001
v_2	0.7325	0.3273	930	2.24	0.0254	0.05	0.09024	1.3749	-0.00016
c_21	-0.1815	1.1501	930	-0.16	0.8747	0.05	-2.4385	2.0756	-0.00007
v_u	36.2298	1.8666	930	19.41	<.0001	0.05	32.5667	39.8930	0.000022

Output 3.4. `nlme` Output for the Linear Growth Model

```
Nonlinear mixed-effects model fit by maximum likelihood
 Model: math ~ (beta_1 + d_1i) + (beta_2 + d_2i) * (grade - 2)
 Data: nlsy_math_long
       AIC      BIC     logLik
  15949.39 15983.62 -7968.693

Random effects:
 Formula: list(d_1i ~ 1, d_2i ~ 1)
 Level: id
 Structure: General positive-definite, Log-Cholesky parametrization
        StdDev    Corr
d_1i      8.0350382 d_1i
d_2i      0.8558994 -0.026
Residual 6.0191140

Fixed effects: beta_1 + beta_2 ~ 1
          Value Std.Error   DF  t-value  p-value
beta_1 35.26736 0.3551568 1288 99.30082        0
beta_2  4.33933 0.0873767 1288 49.66231        0
```

Script 3.5. `SAS` Script to Calculate Individual Predicted and Residual Values

```
PROC SORT DATA = estimates;
    BY id;
RUN;
DATA estimates1;
    SET estimates;
    RETAIN;
    BY id;
    IF first.id = 1 THEN d_1i = estimate;
    IF last.id = 1 THEN d_2i = estimate;
    IF last.id = 1 THEN OUTPUT;
    KEEP id d_1i d_2i;
RUN;
DATA nlsy_prediction;
    MERGE nlsy_math_long estimates1;
    BY id;
    pred = (35.2673 + d_1i) + (4.3393 + d_2i) * (grade - 2);
    resid = math - pred;
RUN;
```

first part of this script, the dataset `estimates1` is created, which is a restructured form of the `estimates` dataset with one row per individual. This dataset was then merged with the original dataset using a data step, and then the predicted and residual values are calculated using the fixed-effects parameter estimates along with the estimated individual intercept and slope scores.

Script 3.6. R Script to Calculate Individual Predicted and Residual Values

```
b_1i_hat = ranef(lg.math.nlme)[,1] + fixef(lg.math.nlme)[1]
b_2i_hat = ranef(lg.math.nlme)[,2] + fixef(lg.math.nlme)[2]
child_id = as.numeric(rownames(ranef(lg.math.nlme)))

estimates <- data.frame(child_id, b_1i_hat, b_2i_hat)
estimates1 = merge(x = nlsy_math_long, y = estimates,
             by.x = c('id'), by.y = c('child_id'),
             all = TRUE)

estimates1$pred = estimates1$b_1i_hat + estimates1$b_2i_hat *
                  (estimates1$grade - 2)
estimates1$resid = estimates1$math - estimates1$pred
```

Similarly, Script 3.6 contains R code to take information from `nlme` to calculate individual predicted and residual values. Fixed-effect estimates (`beta_1` and `beta_2`) and individual random-effect estimates (`d_1i` and `d_2i`) can be obtained from `nlme` using `fixef(lg.math.nlme)` and `ranef(lg.math.nlme)`, respectively. This information was then combined to create individual estimates of the intercept, `b_1i_hat`, and slope, `b_2i_hat`. These data were then merged with the original dataset to calculate predicted and residual values.

The predicted and residual values are plotted in Figure 3.2a and 3.2b, respectively. The predicted plot is useful for understanding what the linear growth model is expecting from the data, whereas the residual plot is useful for understanding model fit and misfit as well as checking model assumptions. The residual plot appears to highlight potential model misspecification as the residuals show a trend over time. Residuals for the second, seventh, and eighth grades have negative means, whereas residuals for third, fourth, fifth, and sixth grades have positive means. This indicates unmodeled nonlinearity in the development of mathematics. A second model assumption check is whether or not the residuals have equal variance over time. The residual plot indicates similar residual variability at each grade, and checking the standard deviation of the residuals at each grade agrees with this conclusion as they varied from 4.10 to 5.06.

STRUCTURAL EQUATION MODELING FRAMEWORK

As a structural equation model, growth models are fit as restricted common factor models with latent variables for the intercept and slope. The restricted common factor model for the growth model can be written as

$$y_i = \Lambda\eta_i + u_i \tag{3.7}$$

where y_i is a $T \times 1$ vector of the repeatedly measured observed scores for individual i, where T represents the number of repeated assessments based on the chosen time metric, Λ is a $T \times R$ matrix of factor loadings defining the growth factors (latent variables), where R is the number of growth factors ($R = 1$ for no-growth model, $R = 2$ for linear growth

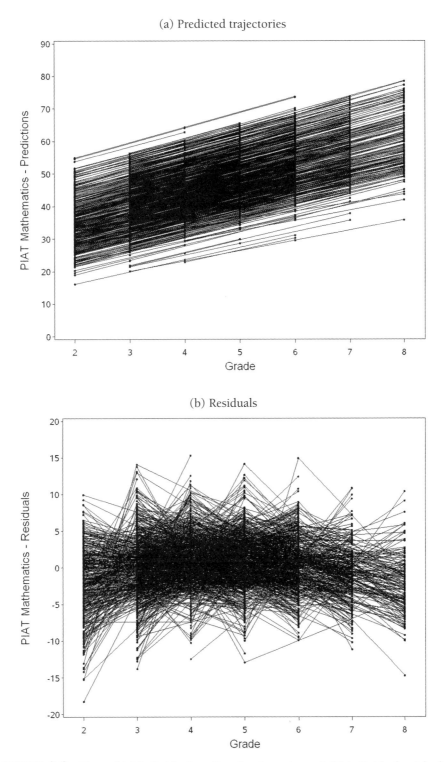

FIGURE 3.2. Plots of (a) individual predicted trajectories and (b) individual residuals.

model), η_i is an $R \times 1$ vector of factor scores for individual i, and $\mathbf{u}_i$ is a $T \times 1$ vector of residual or unique scores for individual i. The factor scores can be written as deviations from the sample-level means, such that

$$\eta_i = \alpha + \xi_i \tag{3.8}$$

where α is an $R \times 1$ vector of factor means and ξ_i is an $R \times 1$ vector of mean deviations for i.

The growth model of Equations 3.7 and 3.8 leads to a series of expectations for the mean and covariance structure of the observed data. Model expectations are utilized in the structural equation modeling framework to calculate parameter estimates and model fit indices. The expected mean (μ) and covariance (Σ) structure based on the growth model are

$$\mu = \Lambda\alpha$$
$$\Sigma = \Lambda\Psi\Lambda' + \Theta \tag{3.9}$$

where Ψ is an $R \times R$ latent variable covariance matrix and Θ is a $T \times T$ residual diagonal covariance matrix. The diagonal elements of Θ are often forced to be equal to map onto the homogeneity of variance assumption common in multilevel models; however, in the structural equation modeling framework this constraint is often not necessary and is testable (see Grimm & Widaman, 2010).

Different types of growth models are specified by changing the dimensions and values contained within the Λ matrix. For the no-growth model, Λ is a $T \times 1$ (column) matrix because there is only one latent variable in the no-growth model. The column matrix contains a series of 1s, which defines the latent variable as the intercept. Thus, the Λ matrix would be specified as

$$\Lambda = \begin{bmatrix} 1 \\ 1 \\ 1 \\ 1 \\ 1 \\ 1 \\ 1 \end{bmatrix} \tag{3.10}$$

for our illustrative data where there are seven occasions (second through eighth grade). In the linear growth model, $R = 2$ because we must define both the intercept and linear slope, which makes Λ a $T \times 2$ matrix. The first column of the matrix contains a series of 1s to define the intercept, and the second column contains values that change linearly with respect to the chosen timing metric. For our example data with seven equally spaced time points and a linear growth model, the Λ matrix is specified as

$$\boldsymbol{\Lambda} = \begin{bmatrix} 1 & \dfrac{1 - k_1}{k_2} \\[2mm] 1 & \dfrac{2 - k_1}{k_2} \\[2mm] 1 & \dfrac{3 - k_1}{k_2} \\[2mm] 1 & \dfrac{4 - k_1}{k_2} \\[2mm] 1 & \dfrac{5 - k_1}{k_2} \\[2mm] 1 & \dfrac{6 - k_1}{k_2} \\[2mm] 1 & \dfrac{7 - k_1}{k_2} \end{bmatrix} \qquad (3.11)$$

where the first column defines the intercept and the second defines the linear slope with constants k_1 and k_2 to center the intercept and scale the slope, respectively.

A path diagram of a linear growth model with seven occasions of measurement (math2 through math8 to map onto our illustrative data) is given in Figure 3.3. Path diagrams are a common way of communicating a specified model in the structural equation

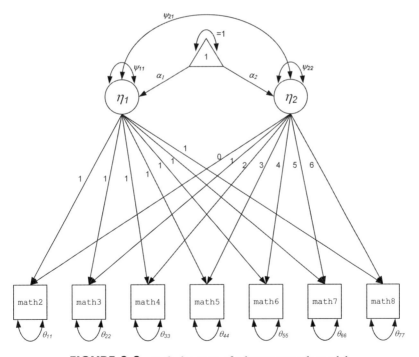

FIGURE 3.3. Path diagram of a linear growth model.

modeling framework. In these diagrams, squares represent observed variables, circles represent latent variables, and the triangle denotes a constant (a variable with a value of 1 for each participant). One-headed arrows represent directional relationships, such as regression coefficients and factor loadings, and two-headed arrows represent nondirectional or symmetric relations, such as variances and covariances. In this specification, k_1 is set to 2 and k_2 is set to 1 to center the intercept at the second-grade measurement occasion and scale the slope in terms of years. Following path diagram tracing rules (Wright, 1921; McArdle & McDonald, 1984), the covariance and mean structure of the observed scores can be derived from the path diagram, and this path diagram exactly replicates the necessary matrix algebra to specify the linear growth model given above.

The specification of growth models in the structural equation modeling framework can map directly onto the specification of growth models in the multilevel modeling framework. For example, Equation 3.7 maps onto the level-1 equations (Equations 3.1 and 3.4) of the no-growth and linear growth models specified above. In the mapping to the linear growth model, η_i is a vector that contains the intercept (η_1) and slope (η_2) latent variables, which map onto b_{1i} and b_{2i}. The factor loading matrix, Λ, in the structural equation modeling framework can be mapped onto the functional relationship between the random coefficients and the repeatedly measured scores in the level-1 equations from the multilevel modeling framework. For the linear growth model in the multilevel modeling framework, these functional relationships are 1 for b_{1i} and $(t - k_1)/k_2$ for b_{2i}. The vector $\mathbf{u}_i$ from the structural equation modeling framework would contain the various values of u_{ti} from the multilevel modeling approach. The α vector in the structural equation modeling framework, which contains the means of the latent factors, α_1 and α_2, map onto β_1 and β_2 from the multilevel modeling framework. The vector of individual mean deviations in the structural equation modeling framework, ξ_i, map onto d_{1i} and d_{2i} from the multilevel modeling framework, and Ψ, which contains the latent variable variances and covariances, would contain (σ_1^2) in the no-growth model and

$$\begin{pmatrix} \sigma_1^2 & \\ \sigma_{21} & \sigma_2^2 \end{pmatrix}$$

in the linear growth model. Lastly, the Θ matrix would contain the estimated residual variances along the diagonal,

$$\begin{pmatrix} \sigma_u^2 & 0 & 0 \\ 0 & \ddots & 0 \\ 0 & 0 & \sigma_u^2 \end{pmatrix}$$

STRUCTURAL EQUATION MODELING IMPLEMENTATION

The no-growth and linear growth models can be fit in many ways using Mplus and OpenMx. Here, and throughout the book, we use the standard structural equation modeling framework with few variations. We do so to be consistent because several models discussed in later chapters can only be fit using the standard framework and to provide an easier link to programs not discussed throughout this book. In the structural equation modeling framework, data are organized in the wide (person-level) format where there is a single record per person and the repeatedly measured variables are organized by the chosen time metric (e.g., grade). For our example data, variables are named math2, math3, ..., math8 to indicate the mathematics scores in second through eighth grades. Data for this example are the same longitudinal mathematics data, but organized in the wide format with observations grouped by grade—the chosen time metric. As with the multilevel modeling programs, we describe the fitting of the no-growth and linear growth models.

No-Growth Model

The Mplus script for fitting the no-growth model is contained in Script 3.7. The script begins with the standard elements. These include a title (TITLE:), the datafile (DATA: FILE=), and then information regarding the variables (VARIABLE:), including the names of the variables contained in the dataset (NAMES=), the missing data indicator (MISSING=.), and the variables to be used in the present analysis (USEVAR=). Next is the ANALYSIS: command where we specify TYPE=MEANSTRUCTURE to model means and covariances, which is now the default in Mplus, and we specify COVERAGE=0. The COVERAGE statement refers to the lower limit for the covariance coverage—the proportion of the sample with the combination of each variable pair. If the covariance coverage falls below 0.10 (at least 10% of the sample has each combination of variables), then global fit indices will not be reported. We put the lower bound for the covariance coverage to 0 in order for the global fit indices to be reported.

The most important part of the script is the MODEL: statement, where the structural model is specified. There are specific keywords (e.g., BY, ON, WITH) that appear

Script 3.7. Mplus Script for the No-Growth Model

```
TITLE: No Growth Model - PIAT Mathematics Data;
DATA: FILE = nlsy_math_wide_R.dat;
VARIABLE: NAMES = id female lb_wght anti_k1
         math2-math8 age2-age8 men2-men8 spring2-spring8
         anti2-anti8;
    MISSING = .;
    USEVAR = math2-math8;
ANALYSIS: TYPE= MEANSTRUCTURE;
         COVERAGE=0;
MODEL: eta_1 BY math2-math8@1;
       eta_1;
       [eta_1];
       math2-math8 (theta);
       [math2-math8@0];
OUTPUT: SAMPSTAT;
```

throughout the `Mplus` scripts, and we briefly mention them here. The keyword `BY` is used to define factor loadings for latent variables, such that latent variables are indicated `BY` the manifest variables. The keyword `WITH` is used to define covariances, such that variable X covaries `WITH` variable Y. The keyword `ON` is used to define regression coefficients, such that the outcome variable, Y, is regressed `ON` the input variable, X. Additionally, variable names are listed to refer to their variances, and variable names are listed within square brackets (i.e., `[]`) to refer to their means or intercepts (i.e., one-headed arrow from the constant).

In the `MODEL` statement for the no-growth model, we begin by defining a latent variable, `eta_1`, which is indicated by all of the repeated measures with factor loadings fixed to 1 using the `@` symbol to denote a fixed parameter. This latent variable represents the intercept for the no-growth model because all factor loadings are set equal to 1. Next, `eta_1` is listed to indicate its variance (ψ_{11}), and this is followed by `[eta_1]` to indicate its mean (α_1). Next, we list all of the repeatedly observed variables, `math2`-`math8`, followed by (`theta`). Listing the variable names refers to their residual or unique variances (because they are outcomes in the factor model) and `theta` is a label, which forces the unique variances for these variables to be equal over time. The final part of the `MODEL` statement is `[math2-math8@0]`, which refers to the intercepts of the observed variables. In growth models, the intercepts of observed scores are set equal to 0 because the mean structure is derived from the latent variables. The last part of the script is the `OUTPUT` statement, where we ask for estimated sample statistics to be reported (`SAMPSTAT`).

There are multiple ways to program structural equation models in `OpenMx`. In an attempt to mirror the programming of `Mplus`, where aspects of the model are separately specified (e.g., factor loadings, variances, intercepts), we specify each part of the model using separate `mxPath` statements and utilize reticular action model (RAM) notation (McArdle, 2005; McArdle & McDonald, 1984), which maps directly onto the path diagram presented in Figure 3.3.

The `OpenMx` script for the no-growth model is contained in Script 3.8. The specification begins with `mxModel`, providing a title, indicating that RAM notation (`type='RAM'`) will be used, specifying the dataset, indicating that it contains `raw` data, and providing names of the manifest and latent variables to be included in the model specification. For the no-growth model we specify three sets of paths using `mxPath`. The paths contain the (1) variances, (2) factor loadings, and (3) means and intercepts. First, variances are specified stating that these paths go `from` each of our manifest and latent variables, are two-headed arrows (`arrows=2`), and are estimated parameters (`free=TRUE`). We then provide starting values (`values=`) and give the parameter estimates labels (`labels=`). In this specification, the residual variances are constrained to be invariant over time; thus, the labels for the variances of manifest variables are the same—`th`. Next, the factor loadings are specified for the intercept, `eta_1`. These one-headed arrows go from `eta_1` to the repeated measures (`math2` through `math8`), with fixed (`free=FALSE`) weights equal to 1 (`values=1`). The final `mxPath` statement in the no-growth model is the mean

Script 3.8. OpenMx Script for the No-Growth Model

```
ng.math.omx <- mxModel('No Growth, Path Specification',
    type='RAM', mxData(observed=nlsy_math_wide, type='raw'),
    manifestVars=c('math2','math3','math4','math5','math6','math7',
                   'math8'),latentVars='eta_1',

# variance paths
mxPath(from=c('eta_1','math2','math3','math4','math5','math6',
              'math7','math8'),
    arrows=2, free=TRUE, values=c(80, 60, 60, 60, 60, 60, 60, 60),
    labels=c('psi_11', 'th', 'th', 'th', 'th', 'th', 'th', 'th')),

# factor loadings
mxPath(from='eta_1', to=c('math2','math3','math4','math5','math6',
                          'math7','math8'),
    arrows=1, free=FALSE, values=1),

# means and intercepts
mxPath(from='one', to='eta_1',
    arrows=1, free=TRUE, values=40, labels='alpha_1')

) # close model

ng.math.fit <- mxRun(ng.math.omx)

summary(ng.math.fit)
```

of the latent variable intercept and is a path from the constant to eta_1. In OpenMx, paths beginning at the constant go from='one' and in this case go to='eta_1', the intercept. This one-headed path is freely estimated, assigned a starting value of 40, and labeled alpha_1. The model is then closed and estimated using mxRUN. The output is placed in ng.math.fit, which is printed using summary(ng.math.fit).

Select Mplus and OpenMx output for the no-growth model is contained in Outputs 3.5 and 3.6, respectively. In Mplus, output begins with MODEL FIT INFORMATION, where the various measures of model fit are reported, followed by the MODEL RESULTS, where parameter estimates along with standard errors, t-values, and p-values are reported. The MODEL FIT INFORMATION begins with the number of estimated parameters (3) and two log likelihood values: the H0 Value and the H1 Value. The H0 Value is the log likelihood for the fitted model, and multiplying this value by -2 provides the $-2LL$ (17,491.904), which is identical to the $-2LL$ produced by the multilevel modeling programs. The H1 Value is the log likelihood for the saturated model where all means, variances, and covariances are estimated. Multiplying both log likelihood values by -2 and taking their difference yields the chi-square measure of model fit mentioned below. Next, a series of information criteria are reported including the AIC, BIC, and Sample Size Adjusted BIC. As mentioned earlier, these information criteria are based on the $-2LL$ plus a penalty function for the number of estimated parameters. The sample size adjusted BIC uses a modified value (i.e., $[N + 2]/24$) for sample size. In all cases, lower values indicate better model–data fit.

Output 3.5. `Mplus` Output for the No-Growth Model

```
MODEL FIT INFORMATION

Number of Free Parameters                          3
Loglikelihood
            H0 Value                        -8745.952
            H1 Value                        -7866.567
Information Criteria
            Akaike (AIC)                    17497.903
            Bayesian (BIC)                  17512.415
            Sample-Size Adjusted BIC        17502.888
               (n* = (n + 2)/24)
Chi-Square Test of Model Fit
            Value                            1758.769
            Degrees of Freedom                     32
            P-Value                           0.0000
RMSEA (Root Mean Square Error Of Approximation)
            Estimate                          0.241
            90 Percent C.I.                   0.231   0.250
            Probability RMSEA <= .05          0.000
CFI/TLI
            CFI                               0.000
            TLI                              -0.347

MODEL RESULTS
                                                      Two-Tailed
                    Estimate      S.E.    Est./S.E.    P-Value
ETA_1     BY
    MATH2            1.000       0.000     999.000     999.000
    ...
    MATH8            1.000       0.000     999.000     999.000
Means
    ETA_1           45.915       0.324     141.721       0.000
Intercepts
    MATH2            0.000       0.000     999.000     999.000
    ...
    MATH8            0.000       0.000     999.000     999.000
Variances
    ETA_1           46.917       4.832       9.709       0.000
Residual Variances
    MATH2          116.682       4.548      25.656       0.000
    ...
    MATH8          116.682       4.548      25.656       0.000
```

Next, the chi-square test of model fit, a test of perfect model–data fit, is reported. For the no-growth model, the χ^2 = 1,758.769 on 32 degrees of freedom (*df*) with a *p*-value less than .0001. The chi-square is not often used as the sole measure of fit because models are never expected to fit the data perfectly and the chi-square statistic is sensitive to sample size. Thus, nearly every model would be rejected based on the chi-square if a decent sample size is available. However, the chi-square, just like

Output 3.6. OpenMx Output for the No-Growth Model

```
free parameters:
        name      matrix        row         col     Estimate    Std.Error
1         th           S      math2       math2    116.68281     4.547869
2     psi_11           S      eta_1       eta_1     46.91614     4.832891
3    alpha_1           M          1       eta_1     45.91468     0.323980

observed statistics:   2221
estimated parameters:   3
degrees of freedom:   2218
-2 log likelihood:   17491.9
saturated -2 log likelihood:   NA
number of observations:   933
chi-square:   NA
p:   NA
Information Criteria:
          df  Penalty  Parameters     Penalty   Sample-Size    Adjusted
AIC:    13055.903                     17497.90                       NA
BIC:     2324.321                     17512.42                 17502.89
CFI:   NA
TLI:   NA
RMSEA:   NA
```

the −2LL, is useful when comparing *nested* models. It's important to note that the *df* reported by Mplus is based on the number of unique pieces of information in the covariance matrix and the mean vector. When data are incomplete, Mplus uses the same approach; however, other programs (e.g., OpenMx) report degrees of freedom based on the number of observations.

The next set of fit statistics provided in the MODEL FIT INFORMATION are the global fit indices, which can be used to evaluate how well the model represents the data. Mplus reports the root mean square error of approximation (RMSEA), the comparative fit index (CFI), and the Tucker–Lewis index (TLI). All of these fit indices tend to range between 0 and 1. For the RMSEA, lower values indicate better fit with values less than 0.10 and 0.05 indicating adequate and good model fit, respectively. For the CFI and TLI, higher values indicate better fit with values over 0.90 and 0.95 indicating adequate and good fit, respectively. However, we note that the CFI and TLI are not calculated appropriately when modeling longitudinal data (see Widaman & Thompson, 2003). Thus, these fit indices should be used cautiously with longitudinal data or calculated using the appropriate null model. The RMSEA for the no-growth model was 0.241, and the CFI and TLI were both poor, suggesting the no-growth model was inappropriate for these data.

Fit statistics from OpenMx are presented toward the end of the output and include the −2LL (17,491.90), degrees of freedom based on the number of observed scores (2,221) minus the number of estimated parameters (3), and information criteria (AIC and BIC). OpenMx reports information criteria based on multiple penalty functions. The first values are based on a penalty function based on degrees of freedom. These values are calculated by subtracting a penalty function from the $-2LL$. The penalty functions for the AIC and BIC are $2 \cdot df$ and $(\ln[N] \cdot df)/2$, respectively, where df are the reported degrees of freedom. Next, OpenMx reports the AIC and BIC with a penalty function based on the number of estimated parameters, which is how Mplus, SAS, and nlme calculate these information criteria. Lastly, OpenMx reports the Sample-Size Adjusted BIC in the third column. We note that the various calculations of the AIC and BIC can lead to the same conclusions when evaluating the fit of two competing models. That is, differences in the AIC when calculated using degrees of freedom or the number of estimated parameters are identical, and differences in the BIC when using degrees of freedom versus the number of estimated parameters are different by a factor of 1/2. OpenMx does not report global fit indices (e.g., RMSEA, CFI, TLI) by default when raw data are used; however, these indices can be calculated by fitting the saturated and null models and inputting their likelihood and associated degrees of freedom (using SaturatedLikelihood=, SaturatedDoF=, IndependenceLikelihood=, and IndependenceDoF=), or the appropriate R object.[2]

Parameter estimates are reported in the MODEL RESULTS section of Mplus and at the beginning of the OpenMx ouput. In Mplus, parameter estimates along with parameters that were fixed to specific values (fixed parameter estimates are reported with 0.000 for the standard error and 999.000 for the t- and p-values) are reported along with standard errors, t-values, and two-tailed p-values. OpenMx only reports *estimated* parameters, which are organized by the labels provided during specification, along with standard errors. Parameters for the no-growth model are the mean of the latent variable eta_1, the variance of the latent variable eta_1, and the residual variance. The estimated mean of eta_1 was 45.92 (Means of ETA_1 in Mplus, alpha_1 in OpenMx), indicating the predicted average score on the intercept. The variance of eta_1 was 46.92 (Variances of ETA_1; psi_11), indicating the magnitude of between-person differences in the intercept, and the residual variance was 116.68 (Residual Variances of MATH2 through MATH8; th)—variability in scores not accounted for by the no-growth model.

Linear Growth Model

The Mplus and OpenMx scripts for the linear growth model are presented in Scripts 3.9 and 3.10, respectively. For Mplus, we present the MODEL statement, and for OpenMx we present the mxModel statement. In Mplus, the additions to the no-growth script include the specification of a second latent variable, eta_2, the linear slope, which is indicated BY all of the observed scores with factor loadings that change linearly with respect to grade. Changes in the factor loadings are in one unit increments to scale the linear slope in terms of annual changes because the change in time between consecutive observed

---

[2] We note that mxRefModels (ng.math.fit, run=TRUE) can be used to fit the saturated model and typical independence model and that specifying summary (ng.math.fit, refModels=ref), where ref is the name of the object created by mxRefModels (), can also be used to obtain these fit indices.

Script 3.9. *Mplus* Script for the Linear Growth Model

```
MODEL:
    eta_1 BY math2-math8@1;
    eta_1;
    [eta_1];
    eta_2 BY math2@0
                math3@1
                math4@2
                math5@3
                math6@4
                math7@5
                math8@6;
    eta_2;
    [eta_2];
    eta_1 WITH eta_2;
    math2-math8 (theta);
    [math2-math8@0];
OUTPUT: SAMPSTAT;

PLOT:
    TYPE = PLOT3;
    SERIES = math2-math8(eta_2);
SAVEDATA:
    FILE = factor_scores.dat;
    SAVE = FSCORES;
```

scores is one year. Additionally, the first factor loading for eta_2 is fixed @0 to center the intercept at the second-grade assessment to mimic the centering done with the multilevel modeling programs. As with eta_1, the variance and mean of eta_2 are specified by listing the variable name and then putting the variable name within square brackets. The final addition to the script is eta_1 WITH eta_2, which allows for the estimation of the covariance between the intercept and linear slope. In the PLOT: statement, we have requested a series plot for the mathematics variables (PLOT: TYPE=PLOT3; SERIES=math2-math8(eta_2);), which allows for the generation of a series of plots that can be used to help diagnose model fit. Specifically, a plot of the observed and predicted individual trajectories (e.g., Figure 3.1a and 3.2a) as well as the estimated and predicted mean trajectories can be viewed after running the model using the Plot drop-down menu. Lastly, we have requested the estimation of factor scores, which can also be used to create predicted and residual plots using external software, such as SAS or R.

In OpenMx, we've made several changes to specify the linear growth model. First, in the mxModel we now include two latent variables, eta_1 and eta_2, for the intercept and slope. The variance paths now only contain the residual variances of observed variables. These two-headed paths go from the mathematics variables, are freely estimated, given starting values of 60, and labeled th. The next mxPath statement is new and contains the latent variable variances and covariance. In this statement, we have listed both latent variables in from= and have used connect='unique.pairs' to specify the variances of eta_1 and eta_2 along with their covariance. Starting values

Script 3.10. `OpenMx` Script for the Linear Growth Model

```
lg.math.omx <- mxModel('Linear Growth, Path Specification',
    type='RAM', mxData(observed=nlsy_math_wide, type='raw'),
    manifestVars=c('math2','math3','math4','math5','math6',
                    'math7','math8'),
    latentVars=c('eta_1','eta_2'),

# residual variance paths
mxPath(from=c('math2','math3','math4','math5','math6','math7',
            'math8'),
    arrows=2, free=TRUE, values=60, labels='th'),

# latent variable variances and covariance paths
mxPath(from=c('eta_1','eta_2'), arrows=2, connect='unique.pairs',
    free=TRUE, values=c(1,0,1), labels=c('psi_11','psi_21','psi_22')),

# factor loadings
mxPath(from='eta_1', to=c('math2','math3','math4','math5','math6',
                        'math7','math8'),
    arrows=1, free=FALSE, values=1),

mxPath(from='eta_2', to=c('math2','math3','math4','math5','math6',
                        'math7','math8'),
    arrows=1, free=FALSE, values=c(0, 1, 2, 3, 4, 5, 6)),

# means and intercepts
mxPath(from='one', to=c('eta_1','eta_2'),
    arrows=1, free=TRUE, values=c(40, 4), labels=c('alpha_1',
                                                    'alpha_2'))

) # close model

lg.math.fit <- mxRun(lg.math.omx)

summary(lg.math.fit)
```

are then provided (`values=c(1,0,1)`) as well as labels (`labels=c('psi_11',
'psi_21','psi_22')`). The `mxPath` for the intercept factor loadings is identical to
the no-growth model, but now an `mxPath` statement for the slope factor loadings has
been added. These one-headed arrows go from `eta_2` to the mathematics measures with
fixed values beginning with 0 and linearly increasing in steps of 1. The last `mxPath` command is for the means of the latent variables—one-headed arrows from the unit constant
(`one`) to the intercept, `eta_1`, and slope, `eta_2`. These parameters are freely estimated,
given starting values, and labeled `alpha_1` and `alpha_2`. The model is then closed,
estimated using `mxRun`, and output is printed using `summary(lg.math.fit)`.

Output from fitting the linear growth model to the mathematics data in `Mplus` and
`OpenMx` is contained in Output 3.7 and 3.8, respectively. In examining model fit, we first
compare the linear growth model to the no-growth model by examining the change in
the chi-square (or $-2LL$ in `OpenMx`). This comparison is carried out in the same way as
was done with the $-2LL$ when fitting models with the multilevel modeling programs. The
improvement in chi-square was $\chi^2_{\text{no growth}} - \chi^2_{\text{linear growth}} = 1,758.769 - 204.252 = 1,554.517$,
with a difference of 3 degrees of freedom, which indicates the linear growth model fit

Output 3.7. Mplus Output for the Linear Growth Model

```
MODEL FIT INFORMATION

Number of Free Parameters                        6
Loglikelihood
            H0 Value                    -7968.693
            H1 Value                    -7866.567
Information Criteria
            Akaike (AIC)                15949.386
            Bayesian (BIC)              15978.410
            Sample-Size Adjusted BIC    15959.354
                (n* = (n + 2)/24)
Chi-Square Test of Model Fit
            Value                        204.252
            Degrees of Freedom           29
            P-Value                      0.0000
RMSEA (Root Mean Square Error Of Approximation)
            Estimate                     0.081
            90 Percent C.I.              0.070 0.091
            Probability RMSEA <= .05     0.000
CFI/TLI
            CFI                          0.792
            TLI                          0.849
```

```
MODEL RESULTS

                                              Two-Tailed
                 Estimate    S.E.   Est./S.E.   P-Value
ETA_1    BY
    MATH2          1.000    0.000    999.000    999.000
    ...
    MATH8          1.000    0.000    999.000    999.000
ETA_2 BY
    MATH2          0.000    0.000    999.000    999.000
    MATH3          1.000    0.000    999.000    999.000
    MATH4          2.000    0.000    999.000    999.000
    MATH5          3.000    0.000    999.000    999.000
    MATH6          4.000    0.000    999.000    999.000
    MATH7          5.000    0.000    999.000    999.000
    MATH8          6.000    0.000    999.000    999.000
ETA_1    WITH
    ETA_2         -0.181    1.150     -0.158      0.875
Means
    ETA_1         35.268    0.355     99.230      0.000
    ETA_2          4.339    0.088     49.136      0.000
Variances
    ETA_1         64.562    5.659     11.408      0.000
    ETA_2          0.733    0.327      2.238      0.025
Residual Variances
    MATH2         36.229    1.867     19.410      0.000
    ...
    MATH8         36.229    1.867     19.410      0.000
```

Output 3.8. `OpenMx` **Output for the Linear Growth Model**

```
free parameters:
        name    matrix    row      col    Estimate      Std.Error
1         th       S    math2    math2   36.2295121    1.88201524
2      psi_11      S    eta_1    eta_1   64.5621973    5.72696169
3      psi_21      S    eta_1    eta_2   -0.1815431    1.17776670
4      psi_22      S    eta_2    eta_2    0.7325821    0.33346285
5     alpha_1      M      1      eta_1   35.2674178    0.35541335
6     alpha_2      M      1      eta_2    4.3393314    0.08833084

observed statistics:   2221
estimated parameters:   6
degrees of freedom:   2215
-2 log likelihood:   15937.39
saturated -2 log likelihood:   NA
number of observations:   933
chi-square:  NA
p:  NA
Information Criteria:
        df Penalty    Parameters    Penalty    Sample-Size    Adjusted
AIC:   11507.3857                   15949.39                        NA
BIC:     790.3181                   15978.42                  15959.36
CFI:  NA
TLI:  NA
RMSEA:  NA
```

significantly better than the no-growth model. Note that the change in chi-square was equivalent to the change in $-2LL$ reported above. In terms of global fit, the linear growth model showed adequate fit based on the RMSEA (0.081), but poor fit based on the reported CFI (0.792) and TLI (0.849). Thus, the linear growth model fit better than the no-growth model, but has a somewhat questionable fit to the observed changes in mathematics from second through eighth grade based on the global fit indices.

Moving to the parameter estimates, we find that the mean of the intercept and slope (Means of ETA_1 and ETA_2; alpha_1 and alpha_2) from the linear growth model indicate the average child had a score of 35.27 in second grade and increased his or her score 4.34 points per year. There was significant variation in both the intercept (Variances of ETA_1; psi_11) and slope (Variances of ETA_2; psi_22), indicating that students significantly differed in their predicted scores in second grade and in their linear rate of growth. Additionally, there was a nonsignificant covariance (ETA_1 WITH ETA_2; psi_21) between the intercept and slope, suggesting that children's mathematics scores in second grade did not relate to their annual changes in mathematics. Finally, the residual variance (Residual Variances of MATH2 through MATH8; th) was 36.23, indicating the magnitude of individual variation not accounted for by the linear growth model.

Predicted Trajectories and Residuals

As we noted, the PLOT command at the end of the Mplus script can be used to generate predicted individual trajectories; however, the residual plot is not available directly through `Mplus`. For this, factor scores were saved using the `SAVEDATA` command. The `SAVEDATA` command outputs a dataset containing the variables used in the model as well as the factor score estimates and their standard errors. This dataset can be read into `SAS`, `R`, or any statistical program, and the predicted and residual plots can be made within these computing environments. In `OpenMx`, there is no default estimation of factor scores; however, factor scores can be estimated in a variety of ways using the `OpenMx` output and the `R` statistical environment (see Estabrook & Neale, 2013). From these values, predicted trajectories and residual values can be calculated and examined.

IMPORTANT CONSIDERATIONS

Linear growth models are an appropriate starting place for any study of individual change. In many cases, these models are able to capture the observed change process well; however, there are numerous times when this is not the case. Thus, it's always useful to fit and compare additional models (described in later chapters) and consider group differences in change. As we noted, fitting growth models in the multilevel and structural equation modeling frameworks has benefits and limitations, and one of the benefits of the structural equation modeling framework was evident here as global fit indices were available to evaluate the fit of the model based on how well the model captured the observed data (e.g., using the RMSEA, CFI, and TLI) as opposed to basing model–data fit on comparative model fitting (e.g., AIC & BIC) and diagnostics (e.g., residual plot). We note that the global fit indices were not available by default in `OpenMx`, but these indices are easily obtained.

Regardless of the framework used to fit linear growth models, there are a few important considerations to keep in mind. First is the timing metric. In the current example, we used grade at testing as the time metric, but others are, of course, possible. Specifically, age at testing may be more relevant, as this timing metric can better capture the spacing between assessments. Additionally, there may be some limitations to using grade, such as students repeating or skipping a grade. Thus, years since second grade may be a more appropriate timing metric. A second consideration is the residual structure. In these examples, we specified a constant residual variance. The flexibility of the structural equation modeling framework allows us to easily change the residual structure, and this flexibility may have important effects on latent variable covariances (Grimm & Widaman, 2010). In the multilevel modeling framework, `PROC MIXED`, `NLMIXED`, and `nlme` have the capability of fitting more complex residual structures (see Harring & Blozis, 2014; Kwok, West, & Green, 2007); however, the implementation may be more challenging with certain programs.

A third consideration is the location of the intercept. In our illustrative example, the intercept was centered at the second-grade assessment because this was the earliest measurement occasion and researchers are often interested in individual differences at an initial point in time. The intercept could be located at any time point, but choosing a relevant time point, one with observed data and with meaning outside of the specific study, is ideal. For example, centering an intercept at the end of eighth grade may be important with the mathematics data if we were interested in high school preparedness. Additionally, it's possible to fit the linear growth model with two intercepts (see Willett, 1997) instead of an intercept and a slope. This type of model is useful if there are two important points in time where researchers want to study individual differences and still use the linear growth model. For example, researchers in an intervention study may be interested in scores at baseline (before the intervention) and the postintervention follow-up while modeling linear change between the two.

A fourth consideration is an appropriate scale for the linear slope. We chose to scale the slope in terms of years, which holds meaning relative to schooling. However, scaling the slope in terms of milliseconds, seconds, minutes, days, weeks, months, decades, or millennia may provide an appropriate scale to study change, depending on the nature of the outcome. The location of the intercept and scaling of the slope do not affect model fit, but parameter estimates vary accordingly. These choices are important for interpretation and insight into what the linear growth model is projecting from the data.

MOVING FORWARD

In the next chapter, we continue to work with the linear growth model and discuss how to fit models when individuals vary in their assessment schedules. That is, the timing variable varies on an individual basis. Longitudinal data with these characteristics are often said to have individually varying time metrics. As we mentioned above, a variety of time metrics may be useful to track change against. Some of these metrics will be fairly common to most participants (e.g., grade in our current example), but there are time metrics where no two individuals will be assessed at the exact same time. If you think about measuring time very precisely (e.g., seconds, milliseconds), then you will have such data. Having such data can lead to model fitting complications, especially considering how the data are organized in the structural equation modeling framework (i.e., wide format with a variable for each assessment). In Chapter 4, we discuss approaches to handling such data.

4

Continuous Time Metrics

Often a first decision when attempting to understand within-person change is deciding on an appropriate time scale to track change against. In the illustrative example discussed in the previous chapter, *grade in school* was the chosen time scale, and the observations were organized around this time metric. This is, of course, not the only time metric that may be reasonable for these data. Additional, potentially meaningful time metrics include *age* as well as *measurement occasion*. In discussing time metrics, there are time metrics that represent discrete time intervals, such as *measurement occasion* and our use of *grade* in the previous chapter, where the time metric takes on discrete values (e.g., 1, 2, 3) that are more or less common to participants. However, we note that not all participants need to be assessed at each of these measurement occasions. Alternatively, there are time metrics that represent more continuous time scales, such as age, where age is measured precisely with values that are not common to multiple participants (e.g., 12.34 years). It is possible, of course, for the same time metric to be used in a discrete or continuous fashion. For example, age could be rounded to the nearest year or half year, and grade could be measured more precisely as year in school plus the number of days since the beginning of the school year. In this chapter, we discuss various techniques for fitting growth models with a time metric that is more or less continuous, sometimes referred to as an *individually varying time metric*.

Data for this chapter are the same longitudinal data on mathematics achievement collected from the NLSY-CYA (Center for Human Resource Research, 2004) and analyzed in the previous chapter. However, in this chapter we use *age at testing* as the time metric. A longitudinal plot of the mathematics scores against age at testing is contained in Figure 4.1 for a 5% random sample. From this plot, it is easy to see that children were assessed at individually varying ages. These data are now subjected to a linear growth model in the multilevel and structural equation modeling frameworks. We note that the treatment of continuous time metrics is straightforward in the multilevel modeling framework but

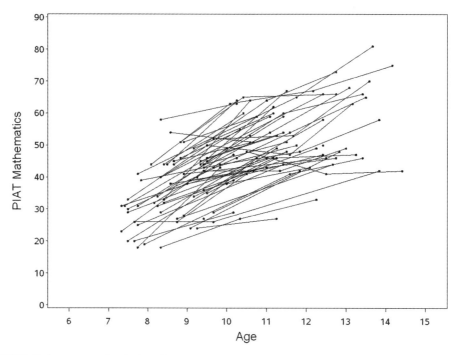

FIGURE 4.1. Longitudinal plot of the PIAT mathematics scores against age: 5% sample.

not in the structural equation modeling framework. Thus, this chapter focuses mainly on handling continuous time metrics in the structural equation modeling framework. In doing so, we discuss two alternatives, their benefits, and their limitations.

MULTILEVEL MODELING FRAMEWORK

The linear growth model with an individually varying time metric, age_{ti}, can be written as

$$y_{ti} = b_{1i} + b_{2i} \cdot \left(\frac{age_{ti} - k_1}{k_2} \right) + u_{ti} \tag{4.1}$$

where y_{ti} is the repeatedly measured variable at time t for participant i, b_{1i} is the random intercept or predicted score for individual i when $age_{ti} - k_1 = 0$, b_{2i} is the random slope or rate of change for individual i for a one-unit change in age_{ti}/k_2, age_{ti}/k_2 is the time metric that varies over individuals, and u_{ti} is the time-specific residual score ($u_{ti} \sim N(0, \sigma_u^2)$). The constants k_1 and k_2 are chosen to center the intercept and scale the slope. With individually varying time metrics, k_1 is often set equal to a value of the time metric where data is observed near the beginning of the observation period. For example, we will center the intercept at age 8, and the intercept will represent predicted mathematics scores at this age; however, we note that participants were assessed prior to age 8 and this choice is arbitrary in this example. k_2 scales the slope according to the chosen time metric. For example, age_{ti} could be scaled in terms of decades, years, months, days, and so on, and this scaling is needed to understand the scale of the slope, b_{2i} (e.g., changes per decade, year, month, day).

The level-2 equation for the random intercept and slope is written as

$$b_{1i} = \beta_1 + d_{1i}$$
$$b_{2i} = \beta_2 + d_{2i}$$

(4.2)

where β_1 and β_2 are expected sample-level means for the intercept and slope and d_{1i} and d_{2i} are individual deviations from their respective sample-level mean. Individual deviations are assumed to follow a multivariate normal distribution with zero means, estimated variances, and a covariance; for example,

$$d_{1i}, d_{2i} \sim MVN\left(\begin{bmatrix} 0 \\ 0 \end{bmatrix}, \begin{bmatrix} \sigma_1^2 & \\ \sigma_{21} & \sigma_2^2 \end{bmatrix}\right)$$

The combined expression of Equations 4.1 and 4.2 leads to

$$y_{ti} = (\beta_1 + d_{1i}) + (\beta_2 + d_{2i}) \cdot \left(\frac{age_{ti} - k_1}{k_2}\right) + u_{ti}$$

(4.3)

MULTILEVEL MODELING IMPLEMENTATION

The linear growth model with age at testing as the time metric was fit using `NLMIXED` and `nlme`. Programming scripts are contained in Scripts 4.1 and 4.2, respectively. The datafile is named `nlsy_math_long`, the mathematics variable is `math`, the timing variable is `age`, and `id` is the child identification variable. The original scaling of the variable `age` is *months* (i.e., age in months).

Script 4.1. NLMIXED Script for the Linear Age-Based Growth Model

```
PROC NLMIXED DATA = nlsy_math_long;
    b_1i = beta_1 + d_1i;
    b_2i = beta_2 + d_2i;
    traject = b_1i + b_2i*(age/12-8);
    MODEL math ~ NORMAL(traject, s_u*s_u);
    RANDOM d_1i d_2i ~ NORMAL([0,0], [s_1*s_1,
                                      s_2*r_21*s_1, s_2*s_2])
                                                   SUBJECT = id;
    PARMS beta_1 = 30 beta_2 = 5 s_1 = 10 r_21 = 0 s_2 = 2 s_u = 7;
RUN;
```

Script 4.2. nlme Script for the Linear Age-Based Growth Model

```
lg.math.age.nlme <- nlme(math~b_1i+b_2i*(age/12-8),
                         data=nlsy_math_long,
                         fixed=b_1i+b_2i~1,
                         random=b_1i+b_2i~1,
                         group=~id,
                         start=c(b_1i=35, b_2i=4),
                         na.action="na.omit")
summary(lg.math.age.nlme)
```

Script 4.1 begins by calling the NLMIXED procedure and the nlsy_math_long dataset. Next, the level-2 equation is written where b_1i and b_2i are a function of sample-level means, beta_1 and beta_2, plus the individual deviations, d_1i and d_2i. Next, the level-1 equation is written with (age/12 - 8) as the time metric. Age was divided by 12 to scale the slope in years, as opposed to months, and 8 was subtracted to center the intercept at 8 years. For the linear growth model, the level-1 equation is traject = b_1i + b_2i*(age/12-8). As with previous NLMIXED scripts, the level-1 residual term is not included in this trajectory equation. Next, the MODEL statement in NLMIXED indicates the dependent variable and its distribution. In this model, math is the dependent variable, which is assumed to follow a NOR-MAL distribution with a mean equal to traject, which was previously defined, and a variance equal to s_u*s_u—the level-1 residual variance in terms of a product of standard deviations. In this script, we illustrate that NLMIXED can be programmed to estimate standard deviations and correlations as opposed to variances and covariances. In this case, s_u is the standard deviation, which will be estimated, and s_u*s_u is the variance. The random coefficients are then listed on the RANDOM line and include d_1i and d_2i, which are assumed to follow NORMAL distributions with means equal to 0 and a variance–covariance matrix with the following elements: s_1*s_1, s_2*r_21*s_1, and s_2*s_2. In this specification, s_1 is the standard deviation of the intercept, r_21 is the correlation between the intercept and slope, and s_2 is the standard deviation of the linear slope. Also on the RANDOM line is SUBJECT = id, which indicates that the random effects vary over children because id is the child iden-tification variable. The final part of the NLMIXED script contains the starting values for the estimated parameters.

The nlme script for a linear age-based growth model is contained in Script 4.2. The object lg.math.age.nlme is created to hold output from the nlme procedure. The nlme statement follows, and the linear age-based growth model is specified following Equation 4.1, the level-1 individual growth trajectory, with (age/12-8) as the time metric. In this script, we wrote the level-1 model (as opposed to the combined equation—Equation 4.3) as an alternative way to program growth models in nlme. In this specification, the ran-dom coefficients, b_1i and b_2i, have both fixed- (fixed=b_1i+b_2i~1) and random-effects (random=b_1i+b_2i~1) parameters and the random-effects parameters are based on the child identification variable, `group=~id`. Starting values are then specified for the means of the intercept and age-based linear slope (`start=c(b_1i=35, b_2i=4)`). Requesting `summary(lg.math.age.nlme)` prints the output from the `nlme` procedure.

Results for the linear growth model with age as the time metric estimated using `NLMIXED` and `nlme` are contained in Outputs 4.1 and 4.2, respectively. An initial desire is to compare the fit of this model with the fit of the linear growth model, with grade as the time metric ($-2LL$ = 15,937; Chapter 3 example) to determine which time metric is more appropriate. Even though there is no formal statistical test to make this comparison (e.g., change in $-2LL$ is inappropriate because the models are not nested), this can be a worthwhile thought process as long as the limitations are understood. The major limitation is that the same growth model, in this case, the linear growth model, may not be the appropriate within-person change trajectory in both time metrics. For example, it is possible for an exponential growth model to be appropriate based on one time metric (e.g., age) and a linear growth model to be appropriate in the second time metric (e.g., measurement occasion). This is especially true of accelerated longitudinal (Bell, 1954) or cohort-sequential (Schaie, 1965) designs, where participants are age-heterogeneous at the first measurement occasion. Going back to our illustrative example, we find that it does appear that the linear age-based model fits the data better than the linear grade-based model, based on likelihood-based fit statistics (BIC, AIC, and AICC). This may be due to the finer measurement of the time metric (especially the differences in time between assessments) because age was measured more or less continuously, whereas grade was measured discretely; it may be due to age being a more appropriate time metric than grade; or it may be due to other factors. However, we note that the correlation between age and grade was .95 (intraclass correlation = .56).

Parameter estimates for the linear age-based growth model include the means of the random intercept (`beta_1`; `Fixed effect of b_1i`) and slope (`beta_2`; `Fixed effect of b_2i`), the standard deviations of the random intercept (`s_1`, `Random effect estimate for b_1i`) and slope (`s_2`, `Random effect estimate for b_2i`), the correlation between the random intercept and slope (`r_21`, `Corr between b_1i and b_2i`), and the standard deviation of the level-1 residual (`s_u`, `Random effect for Residual`). The mean of the random intercept was 35.17, and the standard deviation of the random intercept was 8.05. These estimates indicate the predicted average mathematics score for the sample at age 8 and the magnitude of between-child differences in the predicted scores at age 8. Moving on to the parameters associated with the random slope, the mean of the linear age-based slope was 4.26 and represents the predicted average annual rate of change in mathematics for the sample; the standard deviation of the slope was 0.82 and indicates the magnitude of between-child differences in the annual rate of change. Next, the intercept–slope correlation was .20 and not significant, suggesting that predicted mathematics performance at age 8 was unrelated to predicted changes in mathematics during the observation period. Finally, the residual standard deviation was 5.67, indicating the amount of individual variability not accounted for by the linear age-based growth model.

Output 4.1. NLMIXED Output for the Linear Age-Based Growth Model

Fit Statistics

-2 Log Likelihood	15843
AIC (smaller is better)	15855
AICC (smaller is better)	15855
BIC (smaller is better)	15884

Parameter Estimates

Parameter	Estimate	Standard Error	DF	t Value	Pr > |t|	Alpha	Lower	Upper	Gradient
beta_1	35.1731	0.3466	930	101.48	<.0001	0.05	34.4929	35.8533	-0.00012
beta_2	4.2566	0.08095	930	52.58	<.0001	0.05	4.0977	4.4154	-0.00037
s_1	8.0517	0.3426	930	23.50	<.0001	0.05	7.3793	8.7240	-0.00027
r_21	0.1997	0.1888	930	1.06	0.2903	0.05	-0.1707	0.5702	0.000437
s_2	0.8217	0.1706	930	4.82	<.0001	0.05	0.4869	1.1564	0.000141
s_u	5.6706	0.1499	930	37.83	<.0001	0.05	5.3764	5.9647	-0.00055

STRUCTURAL EQUATION MODELING FRAMEWORK

The handling of individually varying time metrics in the structural equation modeling framework is not straightforward, and there are multiple ways this idea can be conceptualized in this framework. We discuss two approaches to handle individually varying time metrics. The first approach is more precise than the second; however, the second approach has some benefits over the first. In this section we present both approaches and discuss how the models are implemented in `Mplus` and `OpenMx`.

The first approach utilizes what are often referred to as *definition* variables (see McArdle & Hamagami, 1996; Mehta & Neale, 2005). A definition variable simply contains information to be used in the definition of one or more model parameters. The growth model remains the restricted common factor model previously discussed and written as

$$\mathbf{y}_i = \boldsymbol{\Lambda} \boldsymbol{\eta}_i + \mathbf{u}_i \tag{4.4}$$

where $\mathbf{y}_i$ is a $T \times 1$ vector of the repeatedly measured scores for individual i, where T represents the number of measurement occasions (i.e., maximum number of measurement occasions across all participants), $\boldsymbol{\Lambda}$ is a $T \times R$ matrix of factor loadings defining the latent growth factors, where R is the number of growth factors, $\boldsymbol{\eta}_i$ is an $R \times 1$ vector of factor scores for individual i, and $\mathbf{u}_i$ is a $T \times 1$ vector of unique scores for individual i. In the

Output 4.2. `nlme` Output for the Linear Age-Based Growth Model

```
Nonlinear mixed-effects model fit by maximum likelihood
 Model: math ~ b_1i + b_2i * (age/12-8)
 Data: nlsy_math_long
       AIC        BIC      logLik
  15855.14   15889.37   -7921.568

Random effects:
 Formula: list(b_1i ~ 1, b_2i ~ 1)
 Level: id
 Structure: General positive-definite, Log-Cholesky parametrization
          StdDev    Corr
  b_1i    8.0516851 b_1i
  b_2i    0.8216873 0.2
  Residual 5.6705739

Fixed effects: b_1i + b_2i ~ 1
            Value  Std.Error   DF    t-value  p-value
  b_1i   35.17313  0.3463334  1288  101.55857       0
  b_2i    4.25656  0.0804631  1288   52.90071       0

Number of Observations: 2221
Number of Groups: 932
```

definition variable approach, the Λ matrix does not contain fixed values (e.g., 0, 1, 2) but values based on the definition variables. For example, if there are four measurement occasions and we wish to track changes against age at testing, then the Λ matrix is specified as

$$\Lambda = \begin{bmatrix} 1 & \dfrac{age_{1i} - k_1}{k_2} \\[2ex] 1 & \dfrac{age_{2i} - k_1}{k_2} \\[2ex] 1 & \dfrac{age_{3i} - k_1}{k_2} \\[2ex] 1 & \dfrac{age_{4i} - k_1}{k_2} \end{bmatrix} \tag{4.5}$$

where the first column defines the intercept and the second defines the linear age-based slope. The variables age_{1i}, age_{2i}, age_{3i}, and age_{4i} are the definition variables and represent the age of the participant at the measurement occasion. As previously described, k_1 and k_2 are constants to center the intercept and scale the slope, respectively. Thus, based on this specification, the factor loading matrix varies across individuals. This approach should provide identical results as those obtained with the multilevel modeling programs. Additionally, when using this approach only likelihood-based fit indices are available. Thus, indices of global fit, common within the structural equation modeling framework, are no longer available.

The second approach is to use a time metric that closely approximates the individually varying time metric, but does not become truly individually varying. For example, we can round age to the nearest half or quarter year and create a dataset where observations are grouped according to these refined metrics and then fit growth models as they were fit in the previous chapter. We refer to this approach as the *time-window* approach (see McArdle, Ferrer-Caja, Hamagami, & Woodcock, 2002) as there is a window of time where each observation is placed. This approach is feasible and can provide many of the benefits of the structural equation modeling framework; however, this approach to the measurement of time remains approximate. Smaller windows of time (e.g., one-eighth year) are, of course, possible; however, there are limits. If the data matrix becomes too sparse, then estimation becomes difficult and the global fit indices can become unreliable and under certain circumstances will not be reported. Additionally, some programs (e.g., Mplus) require that each variable have at least two observations that are different from one another. Thus, if the time window becomes too small, such that one of the variables contains a single datapoint, then the model will not be estimated. One approach to understanding how the refinement of the time metric affects parameter estimation and model fit is to utilize the multilevel modeling framework and fit growth models while varying the precision of the time metric. If parameter estimates and model fit do not change much when moving to the less precise time metric, then it may be reasonable to utilize the less precise time metric.

STRUCTURAL EQUATION MODELING IMPLEMENTATION

The linear age-based growth model is fit using the definition variable approach as well as the time-window approach with Mplus and OpenMx. For the definition variable approach, the dataset is organized by measurement occasion and there are up to four repeated measurements per person. In this dataset there are four math variables named math1, math2, math3, and math4, along with four definition variables named age1, age2, age3, and age4. The original metric of the age variables is *months*. For the time-window approach, the dataset is organized by age at testing rounded to the nearest half year. In this dataset there are 16 math variables named math70, math75, ..., math140, and math145 to indicate the mathematics scores from age 7 through 14.5 years in half-year increments.

Definition Variable Approach

In Mplus there are multiple ways to use the definition variable approach to fitting growth models. The first approach is by using the TSCORES command, where TSCORES stands for *time scores* and the four age variables (age1 to age4) are the time scores. The second approach utilizes the MODEL CONSTRAINT command and is a more general way to approach the estimation of such models. For example, the TSCORES approach is limited to polynomial (e.g., linear, quadratic) growth models where the MODEL CONSTRAINT approach can be used for linear and nonlinear models (Sterba, 2014). We note that the definition variables must be complete for this approach to estimate the model properly. Thus, before outputting the data for Mplus, the incomplete values of age1 to age4 were set equal to 150 (months), an arbitrary value that has no impact on estimation because they are connected with incomplete mathematics scores. We note, however, that choosing values that are drastically different from the ages in the dataset can harm model convergence.

The Mplus script for fitting the linear growth model using the definition variable approach is contained in Script 4.3. The script begins with the standard elements; however, there are a few new elements. First, the CONSTRAINT statement contains the names of the definition variables, age1-age4. This statement is used for variables that are not part of the model, but are used in the MODEL CONSTRAINT command. These variables will be used to constrain the factor loadings of the slope to vary according to the values of the definition variables. The MODEL command follows, and the basic linear growth model with an intercept, eta_1, and a slope, eta_2, is specified. The factor loadings for the intercept are fixed at 1 (@1), but the slope factor loadings are not fixed at specific values. Instead, they are given labels (L1 through L4). We note that there is an * after the first indicator of the linear slope, which is needed to override the default that the first factor loading is fixed at 1. The labels for the slope factor loadings will be used at the end of the script in the MODEL CONSTRAINT command. The remainder of the MODEL statement follows typical specification including the variances (eta_1 eta_2), covariance (eta_1 WITH eta_2), and means ([eta_1 eta_2]) of latent variables; residual variances of observed scores were set equal (math1-math4 (theta)), and the intercepts of observed scores were set to 0 ([math1-math4@0]). The MODEL CONSTRAINT command comes

Script 4.3. `Mplus` Script for the Linear Age-Based Growth Model Using the Definition Variable Approach

```
TITLE: Linear Growth Model - Definition Variable Approach;
DATA: FILE= nlsy_math_wide_occ_A.dat;
VARIABLE: NAMES = id female lw_brth anti_k1
                  math1-math4 age1-age4 grade1-grade4
                  men1-men4 spring1-spring4 anti1-anti4;
     MISSING = .;
     USEVAR = math1-math4;
     CONSTRAINT = age1-age4;
ANALYSIS: TYPE = MEANSTRUCTURE;

MODEL: eta_1 BY math1-math4@1;
       eta_2 BY math1* (L1)
               math2  (L2)
               math3  (L3)
               math4  (L4);
       eta_1 eta_2;
       eta_1 WITH eta_2;
       [eta_1 eta_2];

       math1-math4 (theta);
       [math1-math4@0];

MODEL CONSTRAINT:
       L1 = (age1/12 - 8);
       L2 = (age2/12 - 8);
       L3 = (age3/12 - 8);
       L4 = (age4/12 - 8);
OUTPUT: SAMPSTAT STANDARDIZED;
```

next, and the labels from the slope factor loadings (L1 through L4) are set equal to the appropriate definition variable (e.g., L1 = age1/12-8). As in the multilevel modeling specification, the ages were divided by 12, and then 8 was subtracted to scale the slope in years and center the intercept at 8 years.

The OpenMx script for a linear growth model using the definition variable approach is contained in Script 4.4. The specification begins with an initial step to center and scale the definition variables by dividing by 12 and subtracting 8. Now, the variables age1_c8 through age4_c8 are scaled in terms of years and centered at age 8. The OpenMx package is then loaded, and the model is specified using mxModel. This specification contains the typical elements from the linear grade-based growth model discussed in Chapter 3. Specifically, there are mxPath statements for the residual variances of the observed variables, the latent variable variances and covariance using connect='unique.pairs', the factor loadings for the intercept and slope, and the means of the latent variables. The major difference with this specification is the factor loadings for the slope. As expected, these paths go from eta_2 to the math variables, math1 through math4. These one-headed arrows are fixed (free=FALSE) because they will be set equal to the definition variables using the labels statement. The labels statement begin with data., which invokes

Script 4.4. `OpenMX` **Script for the Linear Age-Based Growth Model Using the Definition Variable Approach**

```
nlsy_math_occ$age1_c8 <- age1/12 - 8
nlsy_math_occ$age2_c8 <- age2/12 - 8
nlsy_math_occ$age3_c8 <- age3/12 - 8
nlsy_math_occ$age4_c8 <- age4/12 - 8

library(OpenMx)

lg.math.age.omx <- mxModel('Linear Growth, Path Specification',
  type='RAM', mxData(observed=nlsy_math_occ,type='raw'),
  manifestVars=c('math1','math2','math3','math4'),
  latentVars=c('eta_1','eta_2'),

# residual variance paths
mxPath(from=c('math1','math2','math3','math4'),
  arrows=2, free=TRUE, values=40, labels='th'),

# latent variable variances and covariance
mxPath(from=c('eta_1','eta_2'), arrows=2, connect='unique.pairs',
free=TRUE, values=c(1,0,1),
  labels=c('psi_11','psi_21','psi_22')),

# regression weights
mxPath(from='eta_1', to=c('math1','math2','math3','math4'),
  arrows=1, free=FALSE, values=1),

mxPath(from='eta_2', to=c('math1','math2','math3','math4'),
arrows=1, free=FALSE,
  labels=c('data.age1_c8','data.age2_c8','data.age3_c8','data.age4_c8')),

# means and intercepts
mxPath(from='one', to=c('eta_1','eta_2'),
  arrows=1, free=TRUE, values=c(40, 4), labels=c('alpha_1','alpha_2'))

) # close model

lg.math.age.fit <- mxRun(lg.math.age.omx)

summary(lg.math.age.fit)
```

the definition variable framework, and this is followed by the name for the definition variable. Thus, the first factor loading is labeled `data.age1_c8` because it is set equal to `age1_c8`. The remainder of the script is identical to what would be programmed for a linear growth model with four measurement occasions. The model is run using `mxRun`, and output is printed using `summary(lg.math.age.fit)`.

Fit statistics and parameter estimates from `Mplus` and `OpenMx` for the linear age-based growth model using the definition variable approach are contained in Outputs 4.3 and 4.4, respectively. Since the measurement occasions are individually varying, the programs only produce likelihood-based fit statistics (e.g., $-2LL$, AIC, BIC). The fit indices

Output 4.3. `Mplus` Output for Linear Age-Based Growth Model Using the Definition Variable Approach

```
MODEL FIT INFORMATION

Number of Free Parameters                              6
Loglikelihood
        H0 Value                                 -7921.568
Information Criteria
        Akaike (AIC)                             15855.137
        Bayesian (BIC)                           15884.161
        Sample-Size Adjusted BIC                 15865.105
        (n* = (n + 2) / 24)
MODEL RESULTS
```

	Estimate	S.E.	Est./S.E.	Two-Tailed P-Value
ETA_1 BY				
MATH1	1.000	0.000	999.000	999.000
MATH2	1.000	0.000	999.000	999.000
MATH3	1.000	0.000	999.000	999.000
MATH4	1.000	0.000	999.000	999.000
ETA_2 BY				
MATH1	999.000	0.000	999.000	999.000
MATH2	999.000	0.000	999.000	999.000
MATH3	999.000	0.000	999.000	999.000
MATH4	999.000	0.000	999.000	999.000
ETA_1 WITH				
ETA_2	1.321	1.016	1.300	0.194
Means				
ETA_1	35.173	0.347	101.479	0.000
ETA_2	4.257	0.081	52.580	0.000
Variances				
ETA_1	64.830	5.517	11.752	0.000
ETA_2	0.675	0.280	2.409	0.016
Residual Variances				
MATH1	32.155	1.700	18.916	0.000
MATH2	32.155	1.700	18.916	0.000
MATH3	32.155	1.700	18.916	0.000
MATH4	32.155	1.700	18.916	0.000

reported by `Mplus` and `OpenMx` are identical to those reported by the multilevel modeling programs. Parameter estimates reported by both programs are identical to each other and to those obtained from `NLMIXED` and `nlme`. Parameter estimates include the means of the intercept (Means of ETA_1; alpha_1; 35.17) and slope (Means of ETA_2; alpha_2; 4.26) representing the predicted average score at age 8 and the predicted average yearly rate of change. Variances of the intercept (Variances of ETA_1; psi_11; 64.83) and slope (Variances of ETA_2; psi_22; 0.68) indicate the magnitude of between-person differences in predicted scores at age 8 and between-person differences in predicted annual changes. The covariance between the intercept and slope (ETA_1

Output 4.4. `OpenMx` **Output for the Linear Age-Based Growth Model Using the Definition Variable Approach**

```
free parameters:
      name   matrix    row     col    Estimate    Std.Error
1       th       S    math1   math1   32.155103   1.68320829
2   psi_11       S    eta_1   eta_1   64.831504   5.43664706
3   psi_21       S    eta_1   eta_2    1.321083   0.97891480
4   psi_22       S    eta_2   eta_2    0.675238   0.27406093
5  alpha_1       M        1   eta_1   35.173137   0.34659212
6  alpha_2       M        1   eta_2    4.256553   0.08095491

observed statistics:  2221
estimated parameters:   6
degrees of freedom:  2215
-2 log likelihood:  15843.14
saturated -2 log likelihood:   NA
number of observations:   932
chi-square:  NA
p:  NA
Information Criteria:
       df Penalty  Parameters  Penalty  Sample - Size Adjusted
AIC:   11413.1366                15855.14                     NA
BIC:     698.4444                15884.16                15865.11
CFI:  NA
TLI:  NA
RMSEA:  NA
```

`WITH ETA_2; psi_21; 1.32)` suggests that predicted mathematics scores at age 8 were unrelated to predicted annual changes in mathematics during the observation period. Lastly, the residual variance (`Residual Variances` of MATH1 to MATH4; `th`; 32.16) indicates the amount of individual variability unaccounted for by the linear age-based growth model.

Time-Window Approach

The scripts for the linear age-based growth model fit with `Mplus` and `OpenMx` using the *time-window approach* are contained in Scripts 4.5 and 4.6, respectively. In both scripts, the specification follows the previous chapter, where factor loadings for the slope were fixed at specific values that change linearly with respect to age. The factor loading at age 8 years was fixed to 0 to center the intercept at 8 years, and factor loadings increased in increments of 0.50 because age was rounded to the nearest half year. Thus, the slope was scaled in terms of years. We note that the factor loadings for `math70` and `math75` are negative because these scores were collected prior to 8 years of age.

Fit statistics and parameter estimates from fitting the linear age-based growth model using the time-window approach in `Mplus` and `OpenMx` are contained in Output 4.5 and 4.6, respectively. The −2LL for this model was 15,856 compared with 15,843 when age was measured more precisely. Thus, there appears to be a slight loss

Script 4.5. `Mplus` Script for the Linear Age-Based Growth Model Using the Time-Window Approach

```
MODEL:
    eta_1 BY math70-math145@1;
    eta_2 BY math70@-1 math75@-.5  math80@0  math85@.5
            math90@1  math95@1.5  math100@2 math105@2.5
            math110@3 math115@3.5 math120@4 math125@4.5
            math130@5 math135@5.5 math140@6 math145@6.5;
    eta_1 eta_2;
    eta_1 WITH eta_2;
    [eta_1 eta_2];
    math70-math145 (theta);
    [math70-math145@0];
```

of information for the linear growth when age was rounded to the nearest half year. However, global fit indices are now available through `Mplus,` and based on these fit indices, the age-based linear growth model appears to fit well based on the RSMEA; however, the CFI and TLI still indicate poor fit. Parameter estimates were similar, but not identical, to those obtained when using the definition variable approach. The mean of the intercept (Means of `ETA_1`; `alpha_1`; 35.07) and the mean of the slope (Means of `ETA_2`; `alpha_2`; 4.23) were slightly off from the estimates obtained using the definition variable approach (35.17 and 4.27, respectively). Furthermore, the variances and covariances were also slightly different (65.12 vs. 64.83 for the variance of the intercept [Variances of `ETA_1`; `psi_11`] ; 0.72 vs. 0.68 for the variance of the slope [Variances of `ETA_2`; `psi_22`]; 1.17 vs. 1.32 for the intercept–slope covariance [`ETA_1 WITH ETA_2`; `psi_21`]; and 32.22 vs. 32.15 for the residual variance [Residual Variances of `MATH70` through `MATH145`; th]). However, the general conclusions regarding the growth process were highly similar.

IMPORTANT CONSIDERATIONS

The handling of individually varying time metrics is straightforward with multilevel modeling programs, and this is one of the big advantages to fitting growth models in this framework. Furthermore, a precisely measured time metric can aid model fit and interpretation. For example, even a measurement occasion based time metric could be measured more accurately and reflect days (hours, minutes) since the first measurement occasion. This type of time metric may be useful when studying responsiveness to an intervention. The two approaches to handling individually varying time metrics in the structural equation modeling framework have benefits and limitations besides those previously mentioned. For example, moving toward modeling changes in a latent variable, such as those presented in Chapter 14, the definition variable approach is more straightforward because there would be a latent variable at four occasions (based on our illustrative data) with the definition variable approach instead of 17 occasions with the

Script 4.6. OpenMx Script for the Linear Age-Based Growth Model Using the Time-Window Approach

```
lg.math.age.omx <- mxModel('Linear Growth, Path Specification', type='RAM',
  mxData(observed=nlsy_math_age, type='raw'),
  manifestVars=c('math70',   'math75',   'math80',   'math85',   'math90',   'math95',
                 'math100',  'math105',  'math110',  'math115',  'math120',  'math125',
                 'math130',  'math135',  'math140',  'math145'),

  latentVars=c('eta_1', 'eta_2'),

# residual variance paths
  mxPath(from=c('math70',   'math75',   'math80',   'math85',   'math90',   'math95',
                'math100',  'math105',  'math110',  'math115',  'math120',  'math125',
                'math130',  'math135',  'math140',  'math145'),
  arrows=2, free=TRUE, values=40, labels='th'),

# latent variable variances and covariances
  mxPath(from=c('eta_1','eta_2'), arrows=2, connect='unique.pairs',
  free=TRUE, values=c(1,0,1), labels=c('psi_11','psi_21','psi_22')),

# regression weights
  mxPath(from='eta_1',
  to=c('math70',   'math75',   'math80',   'math85',   'math90',   'math95',
       'math100',  'math105',  'math110',  'math115',  'math120',  'math125',
       'math130',  'math135',  'math140',  'math145'),
  arrows=1, free=FALSE, values=1),

  mxPath(from='eta_2',
  to=c('math70',   'math75',   'math80',   'math85',   'math90',   'math95',
       'math100',  'math105',  'math110',  'math115',  'math120',  'math125',
       'math130',  'math135',  'math140',  'math145'),
  arrows=1, free=FALSE,
  values=c(-1, -.5, 0, .5, 1, 1.5, 2, 2.5, 3, 3.5, 4, 4.5, 5, 5.5, 6, 6.5)),

# means and intercepts
  mxPath(from='one', to=c('eta_1','eta_2'),
  arrows=1, free=TRUE, values=c(40, 4), labels=c('alpha_1','alpha_2'))
) # close model

lg.math.age.fit <- mxRun(lg.math.age.omx)

summary(lg.math.age.fit)
```

Output 4.5. **Mplus** **Output for the Linear Age-Based Growth Model Using the Time-Window Approach**

```
MODEL FIT INFORMATION

Number of Free Parameters                              6
Loglikelihood
            H0 Value                          -7927.945
            H1 Value                          -7781.391
Information Criteria
            Akaike (AIC)                      15867.890
            Bayesian (BIC)                    15896.914
            Sample-Size Adjusted BIC          15877.859
              (n* = (n + 2) / 24)
Chi-Square Test of Model Fit
            Value                               293.108
            Degrees of Freedom                       95
            P-Value                              0.0000
RMSEA(Root Mean Square Error Of Approximation)
            Estimate                              0.047
            90 Percent C.I.                       0.041        0.054
            Probability RMSEA <= .05              0.756
CFI/TLI
            CFI                                   0.799
            TLI                                   0.854
SRMR(Standardized Root Mean Square Residual)
            Value                                 0.316
```

```
MODEL RESULTS
```

	Estimate	S.E.	Est./S.E.	Two-Tailed P-Value
ETA_1 BY				
MATH70	1.000	0.000	999.000	999.000
...				
MATH145	1.000	0.000	999.000	999.000
ETA_2 BY				
MATH70	-1.000	0.000	999.000	999.000
MATH75	-0.500	0.000	999.000	999.000
...				
MATH140	6.000	0.000	999.000	999.000
MATH145	6.500	0.000	999.000	999.000
ETA_1 WITH				
ETA_2	1.165	1.015	1.147	0.251
Means				
ETA_1	35.074	0.349	100.625	0.000
ETA_2	4.229	0.081	51.988	0.000
Variances				
ETA_1	65.120	5.562	11.708	0.000
ETA_2	0.728	0.275	2.646	0.008
Residual Variances				
MATH70	32.219	1.686	19.107	0.000
...				
MATH145	32.219	1.686	19.107	0.000

Output 4.6. `OpenMx` **Output for the Linear Age-Based Growth Model Using the Time-Window Approach**

```
free parameters:
         name  matrix      row        col     Estimate     Std.Error
1          th     S     math70      math70    32.2186746   1.69205224
2      psi_11     S      eta_1       eta_1    65.1221634   5.61061586
3      psi_21     S      eta_1       eta_2     1.1645448   1.03480061
4      psi_22     S      eta_2       eta_2     0.7283302   0.27732660
5     alpha_1     M          1       eta_1    35.0739983   0.34855852
6     alpha_2     M          1       eta_2     4.2290589   0.08134569

observed statistics:  2221
estimated parameters:  6
degrees of freedom:  2215
-2 log likelihood:  15855.89
saturated -2 log likelihood:  NA
number of observations:  932
chi-square:  NA
p:  NA
Information Criteria:
            df Penalty    Parameters Penalty        Sample-Size Adjusted
AIC:        11425.8900           15867.89                             NA
BIC:          711.1979           15896.91                       15877.86
CFI:  NA
TLI:  NA
RMSEA:  NA
```

time-window approach. Having this many time points would likely harm model convergence in most programs due to the high number of variables (e.g., three to four variables per latent variable would lead to 51 to 68 variables in the model) and the amount of data incompleteness. Moving toward linear dynamic models, such as those presented in Chapter 16, the time-window approach is better suited because linear dynamic models have not been fit using the definition variable approach (rather not say it is possible, but it hasn't been done as of yet). In conclusion, the handling of individually varying time metrics is addressable in both frameworks. It is more straightforward in the multilevel modeling framework, but knowing how these time metrics can be handled in the structural equation modeling framework is important as we move forward and deal with more complex models.

MOVING FORWARD

In the subsequent chapters we explore approaches to studying between-person differences in growth trajectories. Specifically, we examine three types of models that capture between-person differences in change. First, we discuss adding predictors that do not vary over time (i.e., time-invariant covariates) of the intercept and slope. Next, we describe how the multiple-group framework can aid our understanding of between-person differences in change when dealing with categorical or grouping variables. Finally, we describe the use of growth mixture models as an exploratory approach to search for group differences in change.

5

Linear Growth Models with Time-Invariant Covariates

Building on the linear growth models described in Chapter 3, we consider the question: Are the noted between-person differences in the trajectories of change related to other measured between-person difference variables? In particular, this chapter introduces models that examine whether or not the variability in the intercept and slope from the linear growth model can be explained by one or more *time-invariant covariates*. In this context time-invariant covariates are person-level variables—the values of which do not change over time. Common examples include gender, experimental conditions or manipulations (e.g., level of dosage in a drug intervention), and socioeconomic status. Such variables are essentially included as input or independent variables in a multiple regression-type model where the intercept and slope of the linear growth model are the outcomes or dependent variables. We note that, as in regression, the time-invariant covariates can be continuous, ordinal, and/or categorical and should be coded properly for inclusion into a regression framework (e.g., dummy or effect coding categorical input variables). By studying how the between-person differences in the intercept and slope are related to other person-level variables, we gain understanding of the potential reasons why individuals change in different ways. Although based on longitudinal outcomes, the results from these models do not provide for any additional inferences regarding causality than do typical regression models. Users should be cautious when discussing such effects, keeping in mind whether the time-invariant covariate has been assigned and/or manipulated within a proper experimental protocol (e.g., with random assignment).

Example data for this chapter are the same as those used in Chapter 3—longitudinal data on mathematics achievement collected as part of the NLSY-CYA. In Chapter 3, the within-person changes in mathematics from second through eighth grades and between-person differences therein were represented using a linear growth model, with grade as the time metric and the intercept centered at second grade. Here, we extend that model by introducing two time-invariant covariates: (1) whether or not the child had a low birthweight and (2) the child's antisocial behaviors in kindergarten as reported by the child's parent. The low-birthweight variable (lb_wght) is a dichotomous variable coded 0 if the child had a birthweight greater than 5.5 pounds and coded 1 if the child's birthweight was less than 5.5 pounds. The antisocial behavior rating (anti_k) variable is treated as a continuous variable and has values ranging from 0 to 8. The research questions examined are: Do low-birthweight children have different intercepts and slopes of mathematics achievement from normal-birthweight children? and Is antisocial behavior related to the intercept and slope of mathematics achievement?

MULTILEVEL MODEL FRAMEWORK

In the multilevel modeling framework, the linear growth model with time-invariant covariates is a straightforward extension of the model introduced in Chapter 3. The level-1 (within-person) model remains the same as in Chapter 3,

$$y_{ti} = b_{1i} + b_{2i} \cdot t + u_{ti} \tag{5.1}$$

where y_{ti} is the repeatedly measured variable (e.g., *mathematics achievement*) collected at time t for individual i, b_{1i} is the random intercept or predicted score for individual i when $t = 0$, b_{2i} is the random slope or rate of change for individual i for a one-unit change in t, t represents the chosen time metric (e.g., *grade*), and u_{ti} is the time-specific residual score at time t for individual i.

The level-2 (between-person) model follows the same form used in the previous chapters but is expanded to include the time-invariant covariates, X_{1i} through X_{Ci}, as predictors of the random intercept and slope. With these additions, the level-2 equations become

$$b_{1i} = \beta_{01} + \beta_{11} \cdot X_{1i} + \beta_{21} \cdot X_{2i} + \ldots + \beta_{C1} \cdot X_{Ci} + d_{1i}$$
$$b_{2i} = \beta_{02} + \beta_{12} \cdot X_{1i} + \beta_{22} \cdot X_{2i} + \ldots + \beta_{C2} \cdot X_{Ci} + d_{2i} \tag{5.2}$$

where β_{01} and β_{02} are sample-level parameters indicating the expected intercept and slope when X_{1i} through X_{Ci}, the time-invariant covariates, equal 0; and β_{11}, β_{21}, . . ., β_{C1} and β_{12}, β_{22}, . . ., β_{C2} are level-2 regression parameters indicating the relation between the time-invariant covariates and the individual-level intercepts and slopes, respectively. The final components of the level-2 equation are d_{1i} and d_{2i}, disturbance or residual scores, which capture between-person differences in the intercept and slope that are not explained by the time-invariant covariates. The level-2 parameters are interpreted in the same way as they would in a standard regression model. Typically kept in the unstandardized form, they indicate the expected difference in the intercept or slope (outcomes) for a one-unit difference in $X_{1i}, X_{2i}, \ldots, X_{Ci}$ (predictors). With much of the research utilizing growth models being focused on if and how the between-person differences in within-person change (e.g., in intercept and slope) are related to other between-person difference factors (e.g., birthweight, antisocial behavior), many hypotheses can be tested by examining whether the level-2 regression parameters ($\beta_{11}, \ldots, \beta_{C1}$ and $\beta_{12}, \ldots, \beta_{C2}$) are significant. If they are, then the time-invariant covariates are related to individuals' growth trajectories.

It is important to note that the substantive interpretation of the level-2 regression parameters is affected by the scaling and centering of the time-invariant covariates. As in standard regression models, when time-invariant covariates are centered at their sample-level means, the β_{01} and β_{02} parameters indicate the expected intercept and slope for a participant with average scores rather than for a hypothetical person with scores of zero on all the covariates. In some cases, individuals with zero scores are an important comparison group. For example, in cases where the time-invariant covariate, X_{1i}, is a dichotomous variable, such as gender or experimental condition, dummy coding (0, 1) often provides for easier interpretation than sample-mean centering. When used with dummy codes, β_{01} and β_{02} indicate the expected intercept and slope for the group coded 0 (e.g., the control group) and β_{11} and β_{12} indicate the expected difference between the intercept and slope for the group coded 0 and the group coded 1 (e.g., difference between control and experimental groups). Thus, with the 0/1 dummy coding, the expected intercept and slope for the group coded 1 is calculated as $\beta_{01} + \beta_{11}$ and $\beta_{02} + \beta_{12}$, respectively. Alternatively, if X_{1i} is a dichotomous variable that is effect coded (e.g., $-.5, +.5$), β_{01} and β_{02} represent the grand mean of the intercept and slope (assuming equal sample sizes in each group), and β_{11} and β_{12} are the expected difference between the two groups. In sum, scaling and centering should be used to obtain the interpretations needed for answering specific research questions.

In practice, it can be useful to combine Equations 5.1 and 5.2 as certain multilevel programs require models to be written out in this extended form. Placing the level-2 equations into the appropriate places in the level-1 equation yields

$$
\begin{aligned}
y_{ti} = & (\beta_{01} + \beta_{11} \cdot X_{1i} + \beta_{21} \cdot X_{2i} + \ldots + \beta_{C1} \cdot X_{Ci} + d_{1i}) + \\
& (\beta_{02} + \beta_{12} \cdot X_{1i} + \beta_{22} \cdot X_{2i} + \ldots + \beta_{C2} \cdot X_{Ci} + d_{2i}) \cdot t + u_{ti}
\end{aligned}
\tag{5.3}
$$

Further algebraic combination (distributing t) gives

$$
\begin{aligned}
y_{ti} = & (\beta_{01} + \beta_{11} \cdot X_{1i} + \beta_{21} \cdot X_{2i} + \ldots + \beta_{C1} \cdot X_{Ci} + d_{1i}) + \\
& (\beta_{02} \cdot t + \beta_{12} \cdot X_{1i} \cdot t + \beta_{22} \cdot X_{2i} \cdot t + \ldots + \beta_{C2} \cdot X_{Ci} \cdot t + d_{2i} \cdot t) + u_{ti}
\end{aligned}
\tag{5.4}
$$

The combined equation highlights that β_{11} through β_{C1} can be interpreted as *main effects* (in standard ANOVA language) and that β_{12} through β_{C2} can be interpreted as *covariate by time interactions* (often referred to as cross-level interactions). Although the multilevel equations (Equations 5.1 and 5.2) are often used when communicating about the model and its results, the combined equation (Equation 5.4) often eases the burden of programming the models.

MULTILEVEL MODELING IMPLEMENTATION

Growth models with time-invariant covariates are easily implemented using multilevel software. Here, we illustrate implementation in NLMIXED and nlme. As in previous chapters, the longitudinal data are organized in the long format with multiple records per person. In our example (following Chapter 3), the outcome is the repeatedly measured children's mathematics scores obtained from second through eighth grades, and the timing variable is grade. The time-invariant covariates evaluated here include lb_wght, a dummy-coded dichotomous variable indicating whether the child was of normal (coded 0) or low (coded 1) birthweight, and anti_k1, a continuous variable with values ranging from 0 to 8 indicating the extent to which the child displayed antisocial behaviors in kindergarten or first grade (higher scores indicate more antisocial behavior). Written out in the multilevel framework, the model is

$$math_{ti} = b_{1i} + b_{2i} \cdot (grade_{ti} - 2) + u_{ti} \qquad (5.5)$$

$$b_{1i} = \beta_{01} + \beta_{11} \cdot lb\_wght_i + \beta_{21} \cdot anti\_k1_i + d_{1i}$$
$$b_{2i} = \beta_{02} + \beta_{12} \cdot lb\_wght_i + \beta_{22} \cdot anti\_k1_i + d_{2i} \qquad (5.6)$$

with the main research questions being whether β_{11}, β_{12}, β_{21}, and β_{22} are significantly different than zero.

An NLMIXED script for fitting this model is shown in Script 5.1. As usual, the script begins by calling the NLMIXED procedure and nlsy_math_long dataset. Next, highlighting the explicit mathematical nature of NLMIXED code, we specify the level-2 model by coding Equation 5.6 in a very literal manner. The level-1 model is specified next, with

Script 5.1. NLMIXED Script for the Linear Growth Model with Time-Invariant Covariates

```
PROC NLMIXED DATA = nlsy_math_long;
    b_1i = beta_01 + beta_11*lb_wght + beta_21*anti_k1 + d_1i;
    b_2i = beta_02 + beta_12*lb_wght + beta_22*anti_k1 + d_2i;

    traject = b_1i + b_2i*(grade - 2);
    MODEL math ~ NORMAL(traject, v_u);
    RANDOM d_1i d_2i ~ NORMAL([0,0], [v_1, c_21, v_2])

    SUBJECT = id;
    PARMS
        beta_01 = 35   beta_02 = 4
        beta_11 = 0    beta_12 = 0    beta_21 = 0    beta_22 = 0
        v_1 = 70       v_2 = 1        c_21 = 0       v_u = 36;
RUN;
```

only slight adjustment of Equation 5.5. Specifically, the linear growth model is specified as `traject = b_1i + b_2i * (grade - 2)`, with `traject` as the predicted value of the outcome (i.e., no residual term, u_{ti}). The `MODEL` and `RANDOM` lines are identical to the linear growth model described in Chapter 3. As was previously specified, `math` is the repeatedly measured outcome variable that is assumed to follow a `NORMAL` distribution with a mean equal to the `traject` equation with residual variance `v_u`. The `RANDOM` line indicates that the level-2 disturbances, `d_1i` and `d_2i`, are assumed to follow multivariate normal distributions, with zero means specified in the first set of brackets (`[0,0]`) and the residual variance–covariance matrix specified in the second set of brackets (`[...]`). Specifically, in the variance–covariance matrix, `v_1` is the residual intercept variance, `c_21` is the residual intercept–slope covariance, and `v_2` is the residual slope variance. Unlike in previous chapters, these estimates now represent residual variance and covariance parameters because the intercept and slope, `b_1i` and `b_2i`, are being predicted by the time-invariant covariates. Thus, the total variance of the intercept and slope is a combination of explained variance (predictions from the time-invariant covariates) and unexplained variance (residual variability). Finally, starting values are provided for all estimated parameters on the `PARMS` line, and the model is closed with `RUN`.

Implementing the model in `nlme` is facilitated by first writing the combined model. Following from Equation 5.3, our example model becomes

$$math_{ti} = (\beta_{01} + \beta_{11} \cdot lb\_wght_i + \beta_{21} \cdot anti\_kl_i + d_{1i}) +$$
$$(\beta_{02} + \beta_{12} \cdot lb\_wght_i + \beta_{22} \cdot anti\_kl_i + d_{2i}) \cdot (grade_{ti} - 2) + u_{ti} \tag{5.7}$$

This form of the equation is translated into `nlme` as shown in Script 5.2. The script begins by creating an R object named `lg.math.nlme` to contain the output from the `nlme` function. Within the `nlme` function, we first specify the model of interest, Equation 5.7, replacing the equal sign with a ~ and leaving out the time-specific residual term, u_{ti}. The dataset to be analyzed is then indicated by `data=nlsy_math_long`, and we indicate which of the model parameters are the fixed effects, `fixed=beta_01+ beta_11+beta_21+beta_02+beta_12+beta_22~1`, and which are the random effects, `random=d_1i+d_2i~1`. The next line, `group=~id`, indicates the variable in the dataset that is the clustering variable. As elsewhere, the `start=` command is used to specify starting values for all fixed-effects parameters, and the `na.action=` command is used to indicate how missing data are to be handled. This command will drop observations where the time-invariant covariates are incomplete—the way incomplete data on exogenous variables are handled in the multilevel modeling framework. Thus, in some cases, it may be useful to use multiple imputation techniques to handle this type of incomplete data when fitting growth models in the multilevel modeling framework. Finally, output from the `nlme` procedure is obtained using the `summary` function.

Excerpts of the output from `NLMIXED` and `nlme` are shown in Outputs 5.1 and 5.2, respectively. The outputs contain likelihood-based fit statistics and parameter estimates. Of relevance here, we focus on interpretation of the parameter estimates and return to fit

Script 5.2. nlme Script for the Linear Growth Model with Time-Invariant Covariates

```
lg.math.nlme <- nlme(math ~ (beta_01 + beta_11*lb_wght + beta_21*anti_k1 + d_1i) +
                             (beta_02 + beta_12*lb_wght + beta_22*anti.k1 + d_2i)*(grade-2),
          data=nlsy_math_long,
          fixed=beta_01+beta_11+beta_21+beta_02+beta_12+beta_22~1,
          random=d_1i+d_2i~1,
          group=~id,
          start=c(beta_01=30, beta_11=0, beta_21=0, beta_02=4, beta_12=0, beta_22=0),
          na.action="na.omit")

summary(lg.math.nlme)
```

Output 5.1. NLMIXED Output for the Linear Growth Model with Time-Invariant Covariates

Fit Statistics

-2 Log Likelihood	15923
AIC (smaller is better)	15943
AICC (smaller is better)	15943
BIC (smaller is better)	15992

Parameter Estimates

Parameter	Estimate	Standard Error	DF	t Value	Pr > |t|	Alpha	Lower	Upper	Gradient
beta_01	36.2899	0.4968	930	73.05	<.0001	0.05	35.3150	37.2648	0.000086
beta_02	4.3152	0.1218	930	35.42	<.0001	0.05	4.0761	4.5543	0.000739
beta_11	-2.7160	1.2939	930	-2.10	0.0361	0.05	-5.2554	-0.1766	0.000129
beta_12	0.6246	0.3334	930	1.87	0.0613	0.05	-0.02972	1.2789	0.000045
beta_21	-0.5509	0.2325	930	-2.37	0.0180	0.05	-1.0072	-0.09463	-0.00054
beta_22	-0.01929	0.05892	930	-0.33	0.7435	0.05	-0.1349	0.09635	-0.00028
v_1	63.0664	5.6097	930	11.24	<.0001	0.05	52.0572	74.0756	7.866E-6
v_2	0.7133	0.3264	930	2.19	0.0291	0.05	0.07270	1.3539	0.00051
c_21	-0.07895	1.1447	930	-0.07	0.9450	0.05	-2.3254	2.1676	-0.00054
v_u	36.2569	1.8683	930	19.41	<.0001	0.05	32.5903	39.9235	0.000269

Output 5.2. nlme Output for the Linear Growth Model with Time-Invariant Covariates

```
Data: nlsy_math_long
       AIC        BIC      logLik
  15943.14    16000.2   -7961.57

Random effects:
 Formula: list(d_1i ~ 1, d_2i ~ 1)
 Level: id
 Structure: General positive-definite, Log-Cholesky parametrization
           StdDev      Corr
 d_1i      7.9413082   d_1i
 d_2i      0.8445044   -0.012
 Residual  6.0213584

Fixed effects: beta_01 + beta_11 + beta_21 + beta_02 + beta_12 + beta_22 ~ 1
             Value     Std.Error      DF     t-value    p-value
 beta_01    36.28987   0.4969765    1284    73.02130    0.0000
 beta_11    -2.71621   1.2953406    1284    -2.09691    0.0362
 beta_21    -0.55088   0.2327789    1284    -2.36655    0.0181
 beta_02     4.31516   0.1207520    1284    35.73573    0.0000
 beta_12     0.62464   0.3335738    1284     1.87256    0.0614
 beta_22    -0.01929   0.0589361    1284    -0.32731    0.7435

Number of Observations: 2221
Number of Groups: 932
```

statistics at the conclusion of the chapter. The parameter estimates indicate that a child who had a normal birthweight (lb_wght= 0) and for whom no antisocial behaviors were reported (anti_k1= 0) was predicted to have a math score of 36.29 (beta_01) in second grade (where grade - 2= 0) and grew by 4.32 (beta_02) points per grade. Low-birthweight children (lb_wght= 1) were predicted to have significantly lower mathematics scores in second grade by 2.72 (beta_11, $p = .03$) points but did not significantly differ with respect to the linear rate of growth (beta_12= 0.62, $p = .06$). Similarly, each unit of reported antisocial behaviors was associated with a –0.55 difference in true math scores in second grade (beta_21, $p = .02$); however, the level of antisocial behavior was unrelated to the rate of linear growth (beta_22= –0.02, $p = .77$) from second through eighth grades. Visual representation of these results is given in Figure 5.1. In Figure 5.1a, the bold black line is the predicted trajectory for a normal-birthweight child with an average antisocial behavior score, and the dashed line is the predicted trajectory for a low-birthweight child with an average antisocial behavior score. As seen in this figure, the predicted trajectory for the normal-birthweight child was higher at second grade reflecting the significant difference in the intercept. The two trajectories show increases over time at slightly different rates of growth, but we note that the differences in the growth rates were not significant. In Figure 5.1b we have plotted three predicted trajectories. The solid line is the predicted trajectory for a normal-birthweight child with

(a) Based on low-birthweight variable

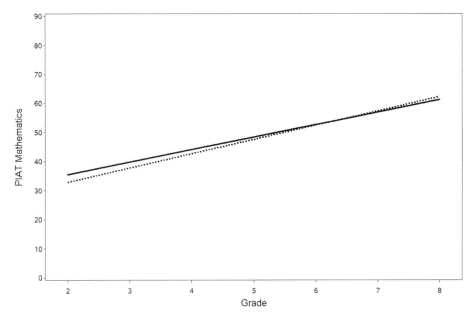

(b) Based on antisocial behavior variable

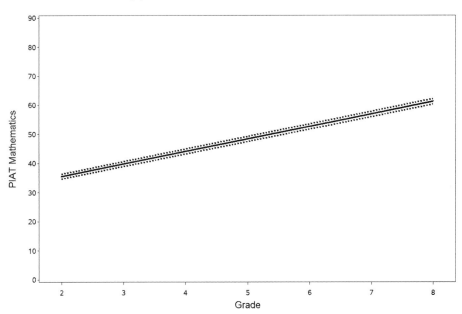

FIGURE 5.1. Example predicted trajectories based on the linear growth model with time-invariant covariates.

an average antisocial behavior score (`anti_k1`=1.42); the upper dashed line is the predicted trajectory for a normal-birthweight child with an antisocial behavior score equal to 0 (i.e., lowest possible value and closer to the mean than a score that was one standard deviation below the mean due to the skewed nature of the antisocial behavior variable); and the lower dashed line is the predicted trajectory for a normal-birthweight child with an antisocial behavior score that is one standard deviation above the mean (`anti_k1`=2.92). As seen in this figure, the main difference between these trajectories is in the intercept, with higher intercepts associated with lower antisocial behavior scores and lower intercepts associated with higher antisocial behavior scores.

In addition to the fixed effects, it is important to consider the random effects. `NLMIXED` provides estimates in terms of variances and covariances, and `nlme` provides estimates in terms of standard deviations and correlations. Parameter estimates include the residual variance of the intercept (`v_1`=63.07; `Random effect of d_1i`= 7.94), the residual variance of the slope (`v_2`= 0.71; `Random effect of d_2i`= 0.84), the residual covariance between the intercept and slope (`c_21`= –0.08; correlation between `d_1i` and `d_2i`= –0.01), and the level-1 residual variance (`v_u`= 36.27; `Random effect of Residual`= 6.02). The residual variance of the intercept and slope is individual variation in the random coefficients that was not accounted for by the low-birthweight and antisocial behavior variables, and the residual covariance represents the linear association between the residual deviations of the random intercept and slope. The level-1 residual variance represents individual occasion-specific variability in mathematics scores unexplained by the linear growth model with time-invariant covariates.

STRUCTURAL EQUATION MODELING FRAMEWORK

As a structural equation model, the linear growth model with time-invariant covariates is fit as a multiple-indicator multiple-cause (MIMIC) model (see Jöreskog & Goldberger, 1975; McArdle & Epstein, 1987). Conceptually, the intercept and slope are latent variables indicated by multiple observed measures, and the time-invariant covariates are considered multiple-causal predictors of those latent variables. The restricted common factor model for linear growth presented in prior chapters is the foundation. Specifically,

$$\mathbf{y}_i = \mathbf{\Lambda}\boldsymbol{\eta}_i + \mathbf{u}_i \tag{5.8}$$

where $\mathbf{y}_i$ is a $T \times 1$ vector of the repeatedly measured observed scores for individual i, where T represents the number of repeated assessments based on the chosen time metric, $\mathbf{\Lambda}$ is a $T \times 2$ matrix of factor loadings defining the latent growth factors, $\boldsymbol{\eta}_i$ is a 2×1 vector of factor scores (intercept and slope) for individual i, and $\mathbf{u}_i$ is a $T \times 1$ vector of residual or unique scores for individual i. The latent factor scores (intercept and slope) are then regressed on the time-invariant covariates. Specifically,

$$\boldsymbol{\eta}_i = \boldsymbol{\alpha} + \mathbf{B}\mathbf{X}_i + \boldsymbol{\xi}_i \tag{5.9}$$

where α is a 2×1 vector of latent variable intercepts (mapping on β_{01} and β_{02} in the multi-level framework), $\mathbf{B}$ is a $2 \times C$ matrix of regression coefficients (mapping onto $\beta_{11}, \ldots, \beta_{C1}$ and $\beta_{12}, \ldots, \beta_{C2}$), where C is the number of covariates, X_i is a $C \times 1$ matrix of time-invariant covariates for individual i, and ξ_i is a 2×1 vector of residual deviations for individual i. The model implied mean vector (μ) and covariance matrix (Σ) for $\mathbf{y}$ based on the linear growth model with time-invariant covariates is

$$\mu = \mathbf{\Lambda}\alpha + \mathbf{\Lambda}\mathbf{B}\omega \qquad (5.10)$$
$$\Sigma = \mathbf{\Lambda}\mathbf{\Psi}\mathbf{\Lambda}' + \mathbf{\Lambda}\mathbf{B}\mathbf{\Phi}\mathbf{B}'\mathbf{\Lambda}'\mathbf{\Theta}$$

where ω is a $C \times 1$ vector of means for the time-invariant covariates, $\mathbf{\Psi}$ is a 2×2 residual latent covariance matrix, $\mathbf{\Phi}$ is a $C \times C$ covariance matrix for the time-invariant covariates, and $\mathbf{\Theta}$ is a $T \times T$ diagonal residual covariance matrix. A path diagram of a linear growth model with two time-invariant covariates, X_1 and X_2, as predictors of the intercept and slope is given in Figure 5.2. In this path diagram, the variables X_1 and X_2 have means (ω_1 and ω_2), variances (ϕ_{11} and ϕ_{22}), and a covariance (ϕ_{21}). There are one-headed arrows from X_1 and X_2 to the latent intercept (labeled β_{11} and β_{21}) and slope (labeled β_{12} and β_{22}) representing the effects of these two time-invariant covariates on the intercept and slope from the growth model.

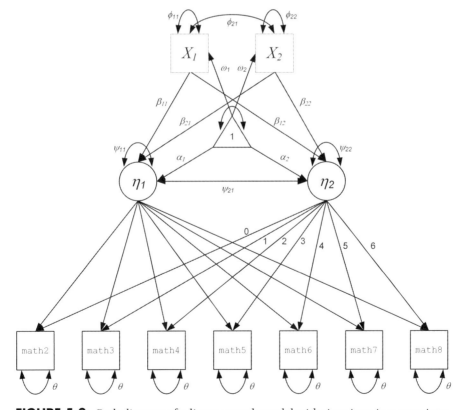

FIGURE 5.2. Path diagram of a linear growth model with time-invariant covariates.

STRUCTURAL EQUATION MODELING IMPLEMENTATION

Growth models with time-invariant covariates are also easily implemented with structural equation modeling software. As in previous chapters, the longitudinal data are in the wide format with one record per person. In our example (following from Chapter 3) the outcomes are the repeatedly measured children's mathematics scores obtained from second through eighth grades, math2 through math8. The time-invariant covariates of interest are lb_wght, a dummy-coded dichotomous variable indicating whether the child was of normal (coded 0) or low (coded 1) birthweight, and anti_k1, a continuous measure with values ranging from 0 to 8 indicating the extent to which the child displayed antisocial behaviors in kindergarten or first grade (higher scores indicate more antisocial behavior).

The MODEL statement from the Mplus script for fitting the linear growth model with low birthweight and antisocial behavior as time-invariant covariates is shown in Script 5.3. We note that prior to the MODEL statement, lb_wght and anti_k1 were added to the USEVARIABLE line. In the MODEL statement the linear growth model is specified just as in Chapter 3. The latent intercept and slope, eta_1 and eta_2, are defined using the BY keyword. Factor loadings for eta_1 are fixed at 1 to define the intercept and factor loadings for eta_2 are specified to follow a linear change pattern beginning at 0 (centering the intercept at second grade) and ending at 6. The latent variable intercepts, variances, and covariance are specified with the lines [eta_1 eta_2];, eta_1 eta_2;, and eta_1 WITH eta_2;. The observed variable intercepts are fixed to 0

Script 5.3. Mplus Script for the Linear Growth Model with Time-Invariant Covariates

```
MODEL: eta_1 BY math2-math8@1;
       eta_2 BY math2@0 math3@1
                math4@2 math5@3
                math6@4 math7@5
                math8@6;

       eta_1 eta_2;
       [eta_1 eta_2];
       eta_1 WITH eta_2;

       math2-math8 (theta);
       [math2-math8@0];

!Introducing Covariate
       eta_1 eta_2 ON lb_wght anti_k1;

       lb_wght anti_k1;
       [lb_wght anti_k1];
       lb_wght WITH anti_k1;

OUTPUT: SAMPSTAT STANDARDIZED;
```

with [math2-math8@0]; and a constant residual variance is specified with math2-math8 (theta);. As noted in the comments embedded in the script, the time-invariant covariates are then introduced into the model. There are two approaches by which time-invariant covariates can be included in *Mplus*. In the first approach, the line eta_1 eta_2 ON lb_wght anti_k1; (Equation 5.9 above) is added to indicate that the latent factors should be regressed on the time-invariant covariates. When only this line is added, incomplete data are handled in the same way as in the multilevel modeling programs. That is, when a participant has an incomplete value for *any* time-invariant covariate, the participant is dropped from the analysis. In the second approach, additional statements are included to indicate that the means ([lb_wght anti_k1];), variances (lb_wght anti_k1;), and covariances (lb_wght WITH anti_k1;) of the time-invariant covariates should also be modeled. These additions, which explicitly model the structure of the time-invariant covariates, override *Mplus* defaults so that participants with data for any of the observed variables being modeled (exogenous or endogenous) are included when estimating the model (i.e., use all of the data regardless of whether the data are complete or partially incomplete in any way). This is the approach we use here, which also maintains concordance between *Mplus* and OpenMx.

The OpenMx script for fitting the linear growth model with low birthweight and antisocial behavior as time-invariant covariates is contained in Script 5.4. The script begins with the linear growth model specification from Chapter 3 with a few minor changes. When the model is initiated, we include the variables lb_wght and anti_k1 to the list of manifest variables, manifestVars=c('math2',..., 'lb_wght','anti_k1'). Then, as highlighted toward the end of the model specification, four mxPath statements are added to indicate how the time-invariant covariates enter into the model. The first of these mxPath statements establishes the means of the time-invariant covariates by specifying one-headed arrows (arrows=1) from the constant, one, to the two time-invariant covariates, lb_wght and anti_k1, with the starting values given by values=c(.1,1), and labels given by labels=c('omega_1', 'omega_2'). The second mxPath statement specifies the variances and covariance among the time-invariant covariates. This statement uses connect='unique.pairs' and arrows=2 to specify the full variance–covariance matrix for the time-invariant covariates. Starting values (values=c(.1,0,1)) and labels (labels=c('phi_11', 'phi_21', 'phi_22') are then provided for these paths. Lastly, the regression coefficients are specified in the final two mxPath statements. The first of these statements is for the one-headed arrows from lb_wght to eta_1 and eta_2, and the second of these statements is for the one-headed arrows from anti_k1 to eta_1 and eta_2. These four paths are given starting values of 0 and labeled beta_11, beta_12, beta_21, and beta_22, respectively. The model is then closed and run using mxRUN. The output is put into lg.math.fit, the contents of which are printed using summary(lg.math.fit).

Excerpts from the output of the *Mplus* and OpenMx analyses are shown in Output 5.3 and 5.4, respectively. *Mplus* indicates that the model estimation terminated normally, but highlights a potential issue. The output states that the standard errors may not be trustworthy and that Parameter 15 may be a problem. Adding TECH1 on the OUTPUT line

Script 5.4. OpenMx Script for the Linear Growth Model with Time-Invariant Covariates

```
lg.math.omx <- mxModel('Linear Growth with Time Invariant Covariates',
type='RAM', mxData(observed=nlsy_math_wide, type='raw'),
manifestVars=c('math2','math3','math4','math5','math6','math7','math8','lb_wght','anti_k1'),
latentVars=c('eta_1','eta_2'),

# residual variance paths
mxPath(from=c('math2','math3','math4','math5','math6','math7','math8'),
arrows=2, free=TRUE, values=60, labels='th'),

# latent variable variances and covariance
mxPath(from=c('eta_1','eta_2'), connect='unique.pairs',
arrows=2, free=TRUE, values=c(1,0,1), labels=c('psi_11',  'psi_21',  'psi_22')),

# factor loadings
mxPath(from='eta_1', to=c('math2','math3','math4','math5','math6','math7','math8'),
arrows=1, free=FALSE, values=1),

mxPath(from='eta_2', to=c('math2','math3','math4','math5','math6','math7','math8'),
arrows=1, free=FALSE, values=c(0, 1, 2, 3, 4, 5, 6)),

# means and intercepts
mxPath(from='one', to=c('eta_1','eta_2'),
arrows=1, free=TRUE, values=c(40, 4), labels=c('alpha_1','alpha_2')),

###Including Time - Invariant Covariates
# means
mxPath(from='one', to=c('lb_wght','anti_k1'),
arrows=1, free=TRUE, values=c(.1, 1), labels=c('omega_1','omega_2')),

# variances and covariance paths
mxPath(from=c('lb_wght','anti_k1'), connect='unique.pairs',
arrows=2, free=TRUE, values=c(.1, 0, 1), labels=c('phi_11',  'phi_21',  'phi_22')),

# regression coefficients
mxPath(from='lb_wght', to=c('eta_1', 'eta_2'),
arrows=1, free=TRUE, values=0, labels=c('beta_11',  'beta_12')),

mxPath(from='anti_k1', to=c('eta_1', 'eta_2'),
arrows=1, free=TRUE, values=0, labels=c('beta_21',  'beta_22'))
) # close model

lg.math.fit <- mxRun(lg.math.omx)

summary(lg.math.fit)
```

Output 5.3. `Mplus` Output for the Linear Growth Model with Time-Invariant Covariates

```
THE MODEL ESTIMATION TERMINATED NORMALLY
    THE STANDARD ERRORS OF THE MODEL PARAMETER ESTIMATES MAY NOT BE
    TRUSTWORTHY FOR SOME PARAMETERS DUE TO A NON-POSITIVE DEFINITE
    FIRST-ORDER DERIVATIVE PRODUCT MATRIX. THIS MAY BE DUE TO THE
    STARTING VALUES BUT MAY ALSO BE AN INDICATION OF MODEL NONIDENTI-
    FICATION. THE CONDITION NUMBER IS -0.373D-16. PROBLEM INVOLVING
    PARAMETER 15.

MODEL FIT INFORMATION

Number of Free Parameters                        15
Loglikelihood
            H0 Value                       -9785.085
            H1 Value                       -9675.110
Information Criteria
            Akaike (AIC)                   19600.171
            Bayesian (BIC)                 19672.747
            Sample-Size Adjusted BIC       19625.108
            (n* = (n + 2) / 24)
Chi-Square Test of Model Fit
            Value                            219.951
            Degrees of Freedom                    39
            P-Value                           0.0000
RMSEA (Root Mean Square Error Of Approximation)
            Estimate                           0.071
            90 Percent C.I.                    0.062 0.080
            Probability RMSEA <=.05            0.000
CFI/TLI
            CFI                                0.789
            TLI                                0.811

MODEL RESULTS
                                           Two-Tailed
              Estimate    S.E.    Est./S.E.   P-Value
ETA_1    BY
    MATH2       1.000    0.000     999.000    999.000
    MATH3       1.000    0.000     999.000    999.000
    ...
    MATH7       1.000    0.000     999.000    999.000
    MATH8       1.000    0.000     999.000    999.000
ETA_2    BY
    MATH2       0.000    0.000     999.000    999.000
    MATH3       1.000    0.000     999.000    999.000
    ...
    MATH7       5.000    0.000     999.000    999.000
    MATH8       6.000    0.000     999.000    999.000
ETA_1    ON
    LB_WGHT    -2.716    1.294      -2.099      0.036
    ANTI_K1    -0.551    0.232      -2.369      0.018
```

(continued)

Output 5.3. (Continued)

ETA_2 ON				
LB_WGHT	0.625	0.333	1.873	0.061
ANTI_K1	-0.019	0.059	-0.327	0.743
ETA_1 WITH				
ETA_2	-0.078	1.145	-0.068	0.946
LB_WGHT WITH				
ANTI_K1	0.007	0.014	0.548	0.584
Means				
LB_WGHT	0.080	0.009	9.031	0.000
ANTI_K1	1.454	0.050	29.216	0.000
Intercepts				
ETA_1	36.290	0.497	73.052	0.000
ETA_2	4.315	0.122	35.420	0.000
Variances				
LB_WGHT	0.074	0.003	21.599	0.000
ANTI_K1	2.312	0.107	21.599	0.000
Residual Variances				
MATH2	36.257	1.868	19.407	0.000
MATH3	36.257	1.868	19.407	0.000
. . .				
MATH7	36.257	1.868	19.407	0.000
MATH8	36.257	1.868	19.407	0.000
ETA_1	63.064	5.609	11.242	0.000
ETA_2	0.713	0.326	2.185	0.029

produces an additional table of output that includes the parameter specification of the model and the starting values for each parameter. Looking through the TECH1 table, we find that Parameter 15 is the variance of anti_k1, one of the time-invariant covariates. Even though the error mesage indicates that the problem is with Parameter 15, the actual problem Mplus is having involves the variance of the low-birthweight variable (Parameter 13 in Mplus), a dichotomous variable. This is because the variance of a dichotomous variable (coded 0/1) is perfectly related to its mean, such that the variance is equal to its mean multiplied by one minus its mean. Knowing that this issue is at the root of the error message alleviates the concern with the estimation of this particular model. With experience and sustained attention to the mathematical details, diagnosis of such issues becomes easier.[1]

After the estimation note, the Mplus output contains a selection of model fit indices. The model appears to fit the data adequately when evaluating the RMSEA (e.g., < 0.08),

---

[1]A MODEL CONSTRAINT command can be added where the variance of the lb_wght is set equal to its mean multiplied by 1 minus its mean. The mean and variance of lb_wght would be given labels, and these labels would be used in the MODEL CONSTRAINT command, such that v_lb_wght = m_lb_wght * (1 - m_lb_wght). Additionally, m_lb_wght is given a nonzero starting value. Note that the inclusion of this constraint results in Mplus believing and reporting one additional degree of freedom, which is not actually the case. Thus, corrections to fit statistics are necessary.

Output 5.4. `OpenMx` **Output for the Linear Growth Model with Time-Invariant Covariates**

```
free parameters:
      name matrix      row       col      Estimate      Std.Error
1   beta_11      A    eta_1   lb_wght   -2.716253328    1.289265837
2   beta_12      A    eta_2   lb_wght    0.624639201    0.332623809
3   beta_21      A    eta_1   anti_k1   -0.550885010    0.232304379
4   beta_22      A    eta_2   anti_k1   -0.019290257    0.058916563
5        th      S    math2     math2   36.256735852    1.998888785
6    phi_11      S  lb_wght   lb_wght    0.073923930    0.003422626
7    phi_21      S  lb_wght   anti_k1    0.007412999    0.013537666
8    phi_22      S  anti_k1   anti_k1    2.312232833    0.107115158
9    psi_11      S    eta_1     eta_1   63.064391665    6.470825418
10   psi_21      S    eta_1     eta_2   -0.078331721    1.466959740
11   psi_22      S    eta_2     eta_2    0.713184940    0.383770639
12  omega_1      M        1   lb_wght    0.080385750    0.008901344
13  omega_2      M        1   anti_k1    1.454447628    0.049793179
14  alpha_1      M        1     eta_1   36.289875065    0.496602084
15  alpha_2      M        1     eta_2    4.315158538    0.121894609

observed statistics: 4087
estimated parameters: 15
degrees of freedom: 4072
-2 log likelihood: 19570.17
saturated -2 log likelihood: NA
number of observations: 933
chi-square: NA
p: NA
Information Criteria:
      df Penalty Parameters Penalty  Sample-Size Adjusted
AIC    11426.171            19600.17                    NA
BIC    -8275.815            19672.75              19625.11
CFI: NA
TLI: NA
RMSEA: NA
```

but the fit remains poor when evaluating the CFI and TLI (e.g., < 0.90); however, we note that the CFI and TLI are not calculated in the proper way for longitudinal data. We will come back to the evaluations of model fit later in the chapter. Next, the Mplus output contains parameter estimates and associated standard errors. The OpenMx output is similar, providing parameter estimates along with likelihood-based fit information.

As above, we focus on the interpretation of the effects relating the time-invariant covariates to the latent intercept and slope. The intercepts for ETA_1 and ETA_2 (Intercepts of ETA_1 and ETA_2 in Mplus output; alpha_1 and alpha_2 in OpenMx output) are the latent variable intercept parameters and equaled 36.29 and 4.32, respectively. These parameters represent the predicted math score in second grade and the annual rate of change in mathematics, respectively, for a normal-birthweight child with no reported antisocial behavior problems. The regression parameters representing the effects of low birthweight and antisocial behaviors on the intercept indicate that low birthweight and antisocial behaviors were significantly related to the intercept (ETA_1 ON LB_WGHT and ETA_1 ON ANTI_K1; beta_11 and beta_21), but not the slope (ETA_2 ON LB_WGHT and ETA_2 ON ANTI_K1; beta_12, beta_22). Specifically, low-birthweight children had lower intercept scores by 2.72 points controlling for antisocial behaviors; and children who had higher antisocial behavior scores had lower intercept scores—a decrease of 0.55 points for a one-unit change in the number of reported antisocial behaviors controlling for low-birthweight status. The results coincide with the patterns of predicted trajectories shown in Figure 5.1.

IMPORTANT CONSIDERATIONS

The majority of research in growth modeling seeks to understand how between-person characteristcs (i.e., time-invariant covariates) are associated with between-person differences in within-person change captured by longitudinal data. In our illustrative example, we limited ourselves to *two* time-invariant covariates for simplicity. However, several time-invariant covariates, and the interactions between them, can be included simultaneously in the model. As in all regression analyses, appropriate scaling and centering of time-invariant covariates are essential to obtaining substantively meaningful parameter estimates. All the common practices in regression, such as examining interactions (moderation) between time-invariant covariates, nonlinear relations, and tests of mediation are possible and implemented in typical ways. For example, product variables can be calculated, included in the dataset, and entered as additional predictors to examine interactive effects. Additionally, the effects of time-invariant covariates can be added to the model in a hierarchical fashion to isolate whether their addition significantly improved model fit (akin to examining whether there was a significant change in the R^2).

Model Fit

A common question asked about this approach to understanding associations between time-invariant covariates and individual trajectories is whether the addition of the time-invariant covariates was useful. In the multilevel modeling framework, the $-2LL$s obtained when fitting models with and without the time-invariant covariates can be directly compared (if no participants were dropped from the analysis because of incomplete data on the time-invariant covariates), which provides a way to evaluate relative model fit. Specifically, we can examine the difference between the $-2LL$s relative to the difference in the number of parameters being estimated (or difference in degrees of freedom). In our example, the $-2LL$ for the linear growth model was 15,937 (obtained in Chapter 3) and the $-2LL$ for the linear growth model with two time-invariant predictors (low birthweight and antisocial behaviors) of the intercept and slope was 15,923, a difference of 14. The difference in the number of estimated parameters was $(19 - 15) = 4$. Thus, the improvement in fit was significant ($\chi^2(4) = 14$, $p < .01$), indicating that low birthweight and antisocial behaviors were useful as predictors. This test of model improvement is similar to an omnibus test of significance in factorial analysis of variance (ANOVA). That is, it is not necessary to demonstrate significant change in model fit to examine variable-by-variable effects. In parallel to the differences in –2LL, the differences in AIC and BIC also indicated improvement in model fit (lower information criteria indicates better fit) when the time-invariant covariates were included in the model.

In the structural equation modeling framework, it is typical to evaluate global fit (e.g., RMSEA, CFI, TLI); however, rarely does the addition of time-invariant covariates significantly change these indices. The global fit of the models was approximately the same, whether or not the time-invariant covariates were included. The relative fit of the models may be quite informative as in the multilevel modeling framework. As above, differences in –2LL (or χ^2) can be calculated to test whether the inclusion of the time-invariant covariates significantly improved model fit. In the structural equation modeling framework, the comparison (baseline) model is not simply a model without the time-invariant covariates. Rather, it is a model that includes the time-invariant covariates but constrains their effects on the intercept and slope to 0. In Mplus the statement eta_1 eta_2 ON lb_wght@0 anti_k1@0; is used to force the effects of the time-invariant covariates to 0. In OpenMx, the two MxPath statements for the effects of the time-invariant covariates are changed, such that FREE=FALSE and VALUES=0. The difference in the –2LL between these two models was 14, with a difference of 4 degrees of freedom, $\chi^2(4) = 14$, $p < .01$. This difference is identical to the one obtained when comparing models in the multilevel modeling framework. We come to the same conclusion regarding the importance of low birthweight and antisocial behaviors when examining differences in children's mathematics trajectories.

Explained Variance

In addition to assessing the importance of the time-invariant covariates, researchers also want to know how much variance in the intercept and slope was explained by the time-invariant covariates. That is, what proportion of the between-person differences in the intercept and slopes was explained by the time-invariant covariates. In both the multilevel and structural equation modeling frameworks, variance estimates of the intercept and slope obtained in models with and without time-invariant covariates can be compared. In our example, for instance, the estimate of intercept variance was 64.562 for the linear growth model without time-invariant covariates and 63.064 when low birthweight and antisocial behaviors were included as time-invariant covariates. The difference between the estimated variances was 1.498. Converted to a proportion of the original variance, we find that the time-invariant covariates explained 0.023 (1.498/64.562) or 2.3% of the between-person differences in intercept. Similar calculations for the slope yielded an explained variance of 0.027 (2.7%).

Two limitations of this approach should be acknowledged. First, care should be taken in the comparison of these variances because the models may not have been fit to exactly the same data. Recall that within the multilevel modeling framework any person who is missing data on any time-invariant covariate is eliminated from the analysis; however, data from these participants would have been included in the estimation of the linear growth model without time-invariant covariates. Thus, estimation of the two models may be based on two different samples making the direct comparison of variance estimates inappropriate. Note that this is only problematic within the multilevel modeling implementations and some specifications in the structural equation modeling framework (e.g., using `Mplus` and only specifying the regression effects). In either case, parameters can be set to 0, so that the same data are analyzed with both models (e.g., put a 0 in the place of `beta_11`, `beta_12`, `beta_21`, and `beta_22` in the `NLMIXED` and `nlme` scripts). Second, it should be kept in mind that the intercept and slope are *unobserved* variables and therefore do not have calculated variances. That is, the variances of these variables are estimated parameters. In some cases, the estimated variance increases when time-invariant covariates are added. When calculated as described in the previous paragraph, the explained variance would be negative, which is obviously problematic. An appropriate calculation for explained variance, although quite labor intensive, can be done using information from the model that includes the time-invariant covariates. For the intercept, explained variance is calcuated as

$$R^2 = \frac{\left(\beta_{11} \cdot \sigma_{x1}^2 \cdot \beta_{11}\right) + \left(\beta_{21} \cdot \sigma_{x2}^2 \cdot \beta_{21}\right) + 2 \cdot (\beta_{11} \cdot \sigma_{x1,x2} \cdot \beta_{21})}{\sigma_I^2 + \left(\beta_{11} \cdot \sigma_{x1}^2 \cdot \beta_{11}\right) + \left(\beta_{21} \cdot \sigma_{x2}^2 \cdot \beta_{21}\right) + 2 \cdot (\beta_{11} \cdot \sigma_{x1,x2} \cdot \beta_{21})}$$

where σ_{x1}^2 and σ_{x2}^2 are the variances of the time-invariant covariates, $\sigma_{x1,x2}$ is the covariance between the time-invariant covariates, and σ_I^2 is the estimated residual intercept variance. Similar calculations can be made for the slope. Applying this approach, the R^2 for the example is calculated as .020 for the intercept and .040 for the slope. The formula generalizes for cases when there are more than two time-invariant covariates; however, the process requires taking into account the variances and covariances of all time-invariant covariates. Fortunately, in `Mplus`, when `STANDARDIZED` is requested on the `OUTPUT:` line, explained variance estimates are included at the bottom of the output. For our example, the output lists the explained variance of the intercept and slope as .020 and .040, respectively.

Standardized Coefficients

In addition to calculating explained variance, researchers may want to calculate standardized coefficients to help determine the importance of each predictor and to use as a measure of effect size. The level-2 regression coefficients (paths) from the time-invariant covariates to the intercept and slope are unstandardized. Standardized coefficients can be calculated by multiplying the unstandardized coefficient by the ratio of the standard deviation of the predictor (i.e., time-invariant covariate) to the outcome (i.e., intercept or slope). Thus, the standardized coefficient for the effect from antisocial behaviors to the intercept is

$$\beta_{21}^* = \beta_{21} \cdot \frac{\sqrt{\sigma_{x2}^2}}{\sqrt{\sigma_1^2 + (\beta_{11} \cdot \sigma_{x1}^2 \cdot \beta_{11}) + (\beta_{21} \cdot \sigma_{x2}^2 \cdot \beta_{21}) + 2 \cdot (\beta_{11} \cdot \sigma_{x1,x2} \cdot \beta_{21})}},$$

where β_{21}^* is the standardized coefficient, β_{21} is the unstandardized coefficient, σ_{x2}^2 is the variance of antisocial behaviors, and $\sigma_1^2 + (\beta_{11} \cdot \sigma_{x1}^2 \cdot \beta_{11}) + (\beta_{21} \cdot \sigma_{x2}^2 \cdot \beta_{21}) + 2 \cdot (\beta_{11} \cdot \sigma_{x1,x2} \cdot \beta_{21})$ is the total variance of the intercept, whose determination was discussed earlier. This yields

$$-0.551 \cdot \frac{\sqrt{2.312}}{\sqrt{63.065 + (0.080 \cdot 0.074 \cdot 0.080) + (-0.551 \cdot 2.312 \cdot -0.551) + 2 \cdot (0.080 \cdot 0.007 \cdot -0.551)}}$$

$$= -0.105$$

Thus, the effect of antisocial behaviors on second-grade mathematics scores was small. In `Mplus` and `OpenMx` (and the majority of, if not all, structural equation modeling programs), standardized coefficients can be requested, eliminating the need for hand calculations. In `Mplus`, requesting `STANDARDIZED` on the output line gives a variety of standardized coefficients (fully standardized, standardized endogenous variables, and standardized exogenous variables) and in `OpenMx`, `mxStandardizeRAMpaths()` can be specified with the name of the fitted model within the parentheses.

MOVING FORWARD

In this chapter we have considered the linear growth model with time-invariant covariates—a model often fit to examine individual differences in growth and change. When this model is used, a variety of assumptions are invoked. The model assumes invariance of the structure of change across all persons. That is, we assume that all children, regardless of their scores on the time-invariant covariates, follow a linear growth trajectory. Further, we assumed that the magnitude of residual variance in the intercept and slope, and the residual covariance between the intercept and slope are the same for children with different values on the time-invariant covariates. Additionally, we assume that the residual variance of the observed scores is equivalent across all children. That is, no matter the values of the time-invariant covariates, the misfit of the linear model is identical. In our example, we assume that the magnitude of year-to-year fluctuations in mathematics performance of children with lower and higher levels of antisocial behavior was equivalent. Given that these assumptions may or may not be true, they should be thoroughly considered before taking up such analyses. In the next chapter, we discuss multiple-group growth models that facilitate thorough examination of these assumptions for certain types of time-invariant covariates, namely, ones that are categorical, ordinal, or continuous variables that have been categorized (e.g., median split).

6

Multiple-Group Growth Modeling

Building on the growth models with time-invariant covariates described in the previous chapter, we now work through an alternative framework for examining between-person differences in change—the multiple-groups framework (McArdle, 1989; McArdle & Hamagami, 1996). Growth models with time-invariant covariates are useful for studying differences in *average* growth trajectories but have limited utility for examining differences in other aspects of the within-person change process and the between-person differences in that process. Without extension, such time-invariant covariate models tell us nothing about differences in the variances and covariance among growth factors, residual variability, and the structure of within-person changes. In this chapter we illustrate how the multiple-groups framework can be used to examine differences in any aspect of the growth model. This flexibility can provide additional insight into how and why individuals differ in their development. Further extensions to search for developmental differences in unmeasured groups follow in Chapter 7 (i.e., growth mixture models).

The additional flexibility in understanding group differences provided by the multiple-groups framework is extremely useful when examining group differences in the amount of variation at both level-1 (measurement) and level-2 (structural). For example, in studying group differences in externalizing behaviors from age 2 through 7, we observed that boys and girls had different amounts of variance at the within (level-1) and between-person (level-2) levels of the growth model. That is, boys showed greater residual variance indicating that their trajectories were more difficult to capture—greater variance remained after accounting for the growth model. In addition, boys also showed greater variability in the intercept and slope, indicating that boys' trajectories were more different from one another than girls' trajectories. Furthermore, the structure of within-person changes varied across groups. That is, boys showed slow linear decline in externalizing behaviors through elementary school, whereas girls showed exponential decline in externalizing behaviors during that same time period. These aspects of group differences are difficult to study using the time-invariant covariate models discussed in Chapter 5, but they can be studied with the multiple-groups growth model discussed here. It must be noted, however, that the multiple-group approach is not recommended for all situations. Typically, it is reserved for inquiry into differences between a relatively small number of groups that are designated by a single categorical variable. In some situations the approach is useful when considering several grouping variables. These situations are accommodated by combining the grouping variables together (e.g., two two-group variables would create a four-group model), but as the net number of groups gets larger, multiple-group models become more and more unwieldy. Continuous variables can always be degraded into ordinal categorical grouping variables, but the reductions in precision and the arbitrary nature of cutoff choices can be difficult to justify. When continuous variables are available, we encourage using them in their originally intended form, if possible.

Example data for this chapter are the same data used in the previous chapters—longitudinal data on mathematics achievement collected from the NLSY-CYA. In Chapter 3, the within-person changes in mathematics from second grade through eighth grade and the between-person differences therein were represented using a linear growth model, with grade as the time metric and the intercept centered at second grade. Here, we use the multiple-groups framework to examine differences between groups defined by birth-weight (0 = normal, 1 = low), a medical distinction assigned to children at birth based on whether or not their weight was less than 5.5 pounds.

MULTILEVEL MODELING FRAMEWORK

In the multilevel modeling framework, the multiple-group linear growth model is conceptualized as a collection of two-level models—one model for each group. Within each group, the level-1 model is similar to the linear growth model introduced in Chapter 3, but with an additional group-specific designation given by the superscript (g). Thus, for $i = 1$ to N individuals in $g = 1$ to G groups, the model is specified as

$$y_{ti}^{(g)} = b_{1i}^{(g)} + b_{2i}^{(g)} \cdot t + u_{ti}^{(g)} \tag{6.1}$$

where $y_{ti}^{(g)}$ is the repeatedly measured variable collected at time t for individual i in group g, $b_{1i}^{(g)}$ is the random intercept or predicted score for individual i in group g when $t = 0$, $b_{2i}^{(g)}$ is the random slope or rate of change for individual i in group g for a one-unit change in t, t represents the chosen time metric in an appropriate scale—that is, t could be replaced by $(t - k_1)/k_2$, and $u_{ti}^{(g)}$ is the time-specific residual score at time t for individual i in group g. The time-specific residual is assumed to be normally distributed with group-specific variance, $u_{ti}^{(g)} \sim N\left(0, \sigma_u^{2(g)}\right)$. Similarly, the group-specific level-2 equations are written as

$$b_{1i}^{(g)} = \beta_1^{(g)} + d_{1i}^{(g)}$$
$$b_{2i}^{(g)} = \beta_2^{(g)} + d_{2i}^{(g)} \tag{6.2}$$

where $\beta_1^{(g)}$ and $\beta_2^{(g)}$ are group-specific means of the intercept and slope, and $d_{1i}^{(g)}$ and $d_{2i}^{(g)}$ are individual deviations from the respective group-specific mean for individual i in group g. The individual deviations are assumed to follow a multivariate normal distribution in each group with zero means, estimated variances, and a covariance; for example,

$$d_{1i}^{(g)}, d_{2i}^{(g)} \sim MVN\left(\begin{bmatrix} 0 \\ 0 \end{bmatrix}, \begin{bmatrix} \sigma_1^{2(g)} & \\ \sigma_{21}^{(g)} & \sigma_2^{2(g)} \end{bmatrix}\right)$$

In essence, the data are split by the grouping variable, and separate growth models are fit to each group simultaneously.

The multilevel model of Equations 6.1 and 6.2 is specified with each parameter of the linear growth model as group specific (each parameter is superscripted by (g)). In practice, variants of this model are fit to articulate and test specific types of group differences. Typically, four models, ordered to allow for more and more group specificity, are estimated and compared. The first model (M1) is the *invariance* model where all estimated parameters are invariant (identical) across groups. This model has the fewest parameters (simplest model) and maps onto the linear growth model described in Chapter 3. One set of parameters is used to describe change, without any group specificity. Parameter estimates from this model should be identical to those obtained from the linear growth model that does not include the grouping variable. With a linear growth trajectory, this model has six estimated parameters: intercept and slope means, intercept and slope variances, intercept–slope covariance, and residual variance—one set for all groups.

The second model (M2) is the *means* model where the latent variable means, β_1 and β_2, are estimated separately for each group, while all other parameters remain invariant across groups. This model follows the logic of commonly utilized statistical models, such as in the *analysis of variance* and *independent samples t-test*, which are used to examine differences in group-level means. Notably, the means model also maps directly onto the growth model with a single dichotomous time-invariant predictor of the intercept and slope (the type of model described in the previous chapter).

The third model (M3) is the *means and covariances* model and allows for group-specific latent variable means, variances, and covariances, while the remaining parameters (i.e., residual variance and linear structure) are held invariant across groups. Finally, the fourth model (M4) is the *means, covariances, and residual variances* model where all estimated parameters are allowed to be group specific. By comparing the relative fit of these four models, we can identify if and how the groups differ from one another with respect to (1) average trajectory, (2) the magnitude of between-person variability and covariability of the growth trajectories, and (3) the magnitude of unexplained within-person variability over time.

MULTILEVEL MODELING IMPLEMENTATION

Although multiple-group models are not often fit in the multilevel modeling framework, the flexibility of NLMIXED and nlme allows for the direct estimation of these models.

The longitudinal mathematics data are organized in the long format with multiple records per person. The repeatedly measured outcome is the child-level mathematics variable (math), and the grouping variable is lb_wght, coded 0 for normal-birthweight children and 1 for low-birthweight children.

The NLMIXED script for Model M4 (means, covariances, and residual variances) is shown in Script 6.1. Although inverted from the ordering (M1 to M4) outlined above, we present the M4 script because it is the most general. Models M1, M2, and M3 are obtained by making minor changes to this script (often removing elements). As in the previous chapters, the script begins by calling the NLMIXED procedure and nlsy_math_long dataset. Next, several IF-THEN statements are used to subset the data by the grouping variable, lb_wght. The statements invoke the general form of Equation 6.2, where the individual intercept (b_1i) and slope (b_2i) are a function of group-level means (beta_1_N and beta_2_N, or beta_1_L and beta_2_L) and deviations (d_1i_N and d_2i_N, or d_1i_L and d_2i_L). The letters N for *Normal* (lb_wght = 0) and L for *Low* birthweight (lb_wght = 1) are used to distinguish the group-specific parameters. After outlining the level-2 equations, two more IF-THEN statements are used to indicate that the residual variance, v_u, is group specific. Specifically, the residual variance, v_u, is set equal to v_u_N for the normal-birthweight

Script 6.1. NLMIXED Script for the Means, Covariances, and Residual Variances Model

```
PROC NLMIXED DATA = nlsy_math_long;
    IF lb_wght = 0 THEN b_1i = beta_1_N + d_1i_N;
    IF lb_wght = 0 THEN b_2i = beta_2_N + d_2i_N;

    IF lb_wght = 1 THEN b_1i = beta_1_L + d_1i_L;
    IF lb_wght = 1 THEN b_2i = beta_2_L + d_2i_L;

    IF lb_wght = 0 THEN v_u = v_u_N;
    IF lb_wght = 1 THEN v_u = v_u_L;

    traject = b_1i + b_2i * (grade - 2);

    MODEL math ~ NORMAL (traject, v_u);
    RANDOM d_1i_N d_2i_N d_1i_L d_2i_L ~
            NORMAL ([0,0,0,0], [v_1_N,
                                c_21_N, v_2_N,
                                0,      0,  v_1_L,
                                0,      0, c_21_L, v_2_L])
    SUBJECT = id;
    PARMS
    beta_1_N = 40 beta_2_N = 5 beta_1_L = 4 beta_2_L = 5
    v_1_N = 70    v_2_N = 1    c_21_N = 0
    v_1_L = 70    v_2_L = 1    c_21_L = 0
    v_u_N = 40    v_u_L = 40;
RUN;
```

group and equal to `v_u_L` for the low-birthweight group. Next, the trajectory equation is written without the level-1 residual variance. The `MODEL` statement follows where the outcome, `math`, is assumed to follow a `NORMAL` distribution with mean `traject` and variance `v_u`. Both of these statements are identical to the statements needed for a single-group growth model.

The `RANDOM` line comes next, designating that the four level-2 individual deviations (`d_1i_N`, `d_2i_N` and `d_1i_L`, `d_2i_L`), two for each group, are assumed to follow `NORMAL` distributions with 0 means (`[0,0,0,0]`) and the specified variance–covariance matrix. The variance–covariance matrix contains parameters for the variance of the intercept for each group (`v_1_N` and `v_1_L`), variance of the slope for each group (`v_2_N` and `v_2_L`), and intercept–slope covariance for each group (`c_21_N` and `c_21_L`). Given that no child is in both groups (exclusive coding of `lb_wght`), between-group covariances are fixed at 0. That is, all the across-group random-effects parameters are fixed to 0 by placing zeroes in the appropriate locations (lower left block) of the variance–covariance matrix. Next, the statement `SUBJECT = id` is used to indicate that the random effects are random over individuals. Finally, the `PARMS` statement is used to provide starting values for the 12 (6 per group) estimated parameters.

To estimate Models M1, M2, and M3, this script is slightly modified. Working backwards, for Model M3, the residual variance, `v_u`, should be invariant across groups. Thus, the two `IF-THEN` statements that separate the residual variance are removed. In parallel, the `PARMS` statement is modified by removing the starting values for `v_u_N` and `v_u_L` and providing a starting value for `v_u` (for a total of 11 estimated parameters). Continuing to Model M2, we additionally modify the variance–covariance matrix in the `RANDOM` statement so that the variances and covariances of the individual deviations are invariant across groups. This is achieved by adjusting the parameter labels in the variance–covariance matrix so that they are no longer group-specific. The labels for the intercept variance (`v_1_N` and `v_1_L`), slope variance (`v_2_N` and `v_2_L`), and intercept–slope covariance (`c_21_N` and `c_21_L`) are changed to `v_1`, `v_2`, and `c_21`, respectively. Using the same labels for the normal- and low-birthweight groups forces the latent variable variances and covariance to be equal across groups. Again, the `PARMS` statement must be adjusted to provide starting values for `v_1`, `v_2`, and `c_21` and remove those for `v_1_N`, `v_2_N`, `c_21_N`, `v_1_L`, `v_2_L`, and `c_21_L` (now a total of eight estimated parameters). Finally, Model M1 is specified by modifying the first two sets of `IF-THEN` statements. These statements are modified by replacing the group-specific means, `beta_1_N`, `beta_2_N`, `beta_1_L`, and `beta_2_L`, with sample-level means, `beta_1` and `beta_2` (e.g., `IF lb_wght = 0 THEN b_1i = beta_1 + d_1i_N;` and `IF lb_wght = 1 THEN b_1i = beta_1 + d_1i_L;`). This forces the mean intercept and slope to be the same (invariant) across the two groups. As before, the `PARMS` statement is modified, now providing starting values for the six estimated parameters that remain.

The flexibility of `nlme` also allows for the direct estimation of multiple-group growth models; however, compared with `NLMIXED`, it does have some limitations. As before, the longitudinal data are organized in the long format with multiple records per person.

The outcome variable is the child-level mathematics score (math). The grouping variable is lb_wght, coded 0 for normal-birthweight children and coded 1 for low-birthweight children. Additionally, we introduce another grouping variable nb_wght that is coded in the opposite way of lb_wght. That is, nb_wght is coded 0 for the low-birthweight group and coded 1 for the normal-birthweight group. Thus, lb_wght identifies if the child is in the low-birthweight group, and nb_wght identifies if the child is from the normal-birthweight group and these variables are used to invoke multiple-groups within the nlme package.

The nlme script for Model M4 is shown in Script 6.2. First, we create the nb_wght variable in the nlsy_math_long dataset by reverse coding lb_wght. With the dummy variables now in place, we can proceed to specify the model. An object named mg4.math.nlme is created that will hold the output from the nlme function. The equation for the multiple-group model is written in two parts, each of which is invoked when one of the dummy variables equals 1. In the first part nb_wght is multiplied by a linear growth model with beta_1_N and beta_2_N as fixed effects and d_1i_N and d_2i_N as random coefficients. Since nb_wght is coded 1 for the normal-birthweight group, this part of the model is for the normal-birthweight children. Thus, beta_1_N and beta_2_N are the means of the intercept and slope, and d_1i_N and d_2i_N are the random coefficients for the normal-birthweight group. In the second part of the model, lb_wght is multiplied by a linear growth model, with beta_1_L and beta_2_L as fixed effects and d_1i_L and d_2i_L as random coefficients. Since lb_wght is coded 1 for the low-birthweight group, this part of the model is invoked for low-birthweight children. Thus, beta_1_L and beta_2_L are the means of the intercept and slope, and d_1i_L and d_2i_L are the random coefficients for the low-birthweight group.

The next lines of script specifies the datafile for analysis and lists the fixed and random effects. The fixed command specifies all four fixed effects (mean intercept and slope for each group), and the random command specifies a Blocked structure for

Script 6.2. nlme Script for the Means, Covariances, and Residual Variances Model

```
nlsy_math_long$nb_wght <- 1 - nlsy_math_long$lb_wght

mg4.math.nlme<-nlme(math~nb_wght*((beta_1_N+d_1i_N)+
                                  (beta_2_N+d_2i_N)*(grade-2))+
                    lb_wght*((beta_1_L+d_1i_L)+
                             (beta_2_L+d_2i_L)*(grade-2)),
                    data=nlsy_math_long,
                    fixed=beta_1_N+beta_2_N+beta_1_L+beta_2_L~1,
                    random=pdBlocked(list(d_1i_N+d_2i_N~1,
                                          d_1i_L+d_2i_L~1)),
                    group=~id,
                    start=c(35, 4, 35, 4),
                    weights=varIdent(form=~1|factor(lb_wght)),
                    control=(list(returnObject=TRUE)))
summary (mg4.math.nlme)
```

the latent variable covariance matrix. The `Blocked` structure estimates correlations (or covariances) for random effects within the same block and will fix the across-block correlations to zero. Using a comma-separated list, the first block contains `d_1i_N` and `d_2i_N`, the random effects for the normal-birthweight group, and the second block contains `d_1i_L` and `d_2i_L`, the random effects for the low-birthweight group. As was done in `NLMIXED`, the `Blocked` structure invokes estimation of the correlation between the intercept and slope within each group but does not estimate correlations among the random coefficients from different groups. The `group` command follows and indicates that the random effects apply over participants, and the `start` command provides the starting values for the four fixed effects. The `weights` command is then used to allow for group-specific level-1 residual variances. The `varIdent` option specifies that the residual variances should be organized as a matrix with no off-diagonal elements and `form` is used to specify a variance covariate, which allows for a heteroskedastic error structure that differs by `lb_wght`. Finally, the `control` command is used to obtain additional ouput that is useful when diagnosing problems with model convergence. Here the command indicates that the parameter estimates obtained at the last iteration should be output, even if convergence issues are encountered. The `summary` function is used to obtain the output from fitting the model.

Script 6.2 is easily modified to fit Models M1, M2, and M3. For Model M3, the `weights` command is removed, which forces the residual variance to be equal across the two groups. For Model M2, we make two additional changes. In the model equation, the group-specific deviations (`d_1i_N`, `d_2i_N` and `d_1i_L`, `d_2i_L`) are replaced by `d_1i` and `d_2i`, and the `random` statement is changed to `d_1i+d_2i~1`. These changes force the latent variable covariance matrix (i.e., intercept and slope variances and covariance) to be invariant over groups. Continuing to Model M1, two more changes are needed. The model equation is further adjusted so that the group-specific means (`beta_1_N`, `beta_2_N` and `beta_1_L`, `beta_2_L`) are replaced by `beta_1` and `beta_2`, and the `fixed` command is changed to `beta_1+beta_2~1`. Thus, the mean intercept and slope are invariant over groups. The estimated parameters should be the same as those obtained in the single-group model fit in Chapter 3.

Fit statistics and parameter estimates from Model M4 are shown in Output 6.1 and 6.2 for `NLMIXED` and `nlme`, respectively. The fit statistics will be used for model comparisons discussed at the end of the chapter. Here we walk through the parameter estimates from Model M4. In both the `NLMIXED` and `nlme` output, estimates labeled with an `_N` are for the normal-birthweight group, and estimates labeled with an `_L` are for the low-birthweight group. In a few instances, interpretation of the `nlme` output requires a bit of additional calculation. Overall, parameter estimates describing individual changes in mathematics growth are interpreted in the same manner as discussed in Chapter 3; however, these estimates are now group specific. Thus, the normal-birthweight group had a mean intercept of 35.48 (`beta_1_N`; `Fixed effect of beta_1_N`) and a mean linear slope of 4.29 (`beta_2_N`; `Fixed effect of beta_2_N`) points per year. The variance of the intercept was 62.13 (`v_1_N`; `Random effect of d_1i_N` is given as a standard devation and must be squared), the variance of the slope was 0.78

Output 6.1. NLMIXED Output for the Means, Covariances, and Residual Variances Model

Fit Statistics

-2 Log Likelihood	15926
AIC (smaller is better)	15950
AICC (smaller is better)	15950
BIC (smaller is better)	16008

Parameter Estimates

Parameter	Estimate	Standard Error	DF	t Value	Pr > |t|	Alpha	Lower	Upper	Gradient
beta_1_N	35.4818	0.3644	928	97.38	<.0001	0.05	34.7667	36.1968	0.007959
beta_2_N	4.2976	0.09111	928	47.17	<.0001	0.05	4.1188	4.4764	0.000736
beta_1_L	32.7313	1.3755	928	23.80	<.0001	0.05	30.0319	35.4307	-0.01019
beta_2_L	4.8971	0.3435	928	14.26	<.0001	0.05	4.2229	5.5713	0.019715
v_1_N	62.1335	5.7001	928	10.90	<.0001	0.05	50.9470	73.3201	-0.01076
v_2_N	0.7801	0.3338	928	2.34	0.0196	0.05	0.1250	1.4352	-0.02959
c_21_N	-0.06246	1.1564	928	-0.05	0.9569	0.05	-2.3319	2.2070	-0.01321
v_1_L	73.0535	23.0337	928	3.17	0.0016	0.05	27.8493	118.26	-0.01856
v_2_L	0.009963	0.9575	928	0.01	0.9917	0.05	-1.8691	1.8890	0.139719
c_21_L	0.8507	4.5391	928	0.19	0.8514	0.05	-8.0574	9.7589	-0.0216
v_u_N	35.0704	1.8944	928	18.51	<.0001	0.05	31.3527	38.7882	-0.03962
v_u_L	48.5132	7.5707	928	6.41	<.0001	0.05	33.6556	63.3708	-0.00261

Output 6.2. `nlme` Output for the Means, Covariances, and Residual Variances Model

```
Nonlinear mixed-effects model fit by maximum likelihood
  Model: math~nb_wght*((beta_1_N+d_1i_N)+(beta_2_N+d_2i_N)*
                      (grade-2))+lb_wght*((beta_1_L+d_1i_L)+
                      (beta_2_L+d_2i_L)*(grade-2))
  Data: nlsy_math_long
        AIC        BIC        logLik
   15950.12   16018.59   -7963.061

Random effects:
 Composite Structure: Blocked

 Block 1: d_1i_N, d_2i_N
 Formula: list(d_1i_N ~ 1, d_2i_N ~ 1)
 Level: id
 Structure: General positive-definite
          StdDev      Corr
 d_1i_N   7.8922007   d_1i_N
 d_2i_N   0.8795757   -0.009

Block 2: d_1i_L, d_2i_L
 Formula: list(d_1i_L ~ 1, d_2i_L ~ 1)
 Level: id
 Structure: General positive-definite
            StdDev       Corr
 d_1i_L     8.99408209   d_1i_L
 d_2i_L     0.02847274   0.988
 Residual   5.93062209

Variance function:
 Structure: Different standard deviations per stratum
 Formula: ~1 | factor (lb_wght)
  Parameter estimates:
          0           1
   1.000000   1.170216

Fixed effects: beta_1_N + beta_2_N + beta_1_L + beta_2_L ~ 1
              Value    Std.Error     DF     t-value     p-value
 beta_1_N   35.48131   0.3647427    930    97.27763          0
 beta_2_N    4.29731   0.0901739   1288    47.65582          0
 beta_1_L   32.79780   1.4062468    930    23.32293          0
 beta_2_L    4.87806   0.3382249   1288    14.42253          0

Number of Observations: 2221
Number of Groups: 932
```

(v_2_N; Random effect of d_2i_N), and the intercept–slope covariance was –0.06 (c_21_N; Corr between d_1i_N and d_2i_N given as a correlation). Finally, the level-1 residual variance was 35.07 (v_u_N; Random effect of Residual). In nlme, the residual standard deviation for the normal-birthweight group is calculated by multiplying the reported residual standard deviation (5.93) by the parameter estimate listed under Variance function for the group coded 0 on the lb_wght variable. This parameter was 1.00, which yields a residual standard deviation equal to 5.93 for the normal-birthweight group.

The low-birthweight group had a mean intercept of 32.73 (beta_1_L; Fixed effect of beta_1_L) and a mean linear slope of 4.90 (beta_2_L; Fixed effect of beta_2_L) points per year. In this group, the variance of the intercept was 73.05 (v_1_L; Random effect of d_1i_L), the variance of the slope was 0.01 (v_2_L; Random effect of d_2i_L), the intercept–slope covariance was 0.85 (c_21_L; Corr between d_1i_L and d_2i_L), and the level-1 residual variance was 48.51 (v_u_L; Random effect of Residual multiplied by 1.17). As before, the residual standard deviation for the low-birthweight group is calculated by multiplying the reported residual standard deviation (5.93) by the parameter estimate listed under Variance function for the group coded 1 on the lb_wght variable. This estimate was 1.17, and multiplying these values yields a residual standard deviation equal to 6.94 for the low-birthweight group.

STRUCTURAL EQUATION MODELING FRAMEWORK

There is a long history of modeling multiple-group data in the structural modeling framework (Jöreskog, 1971). In brief, a linear growth model is specified for each group (group-specific model specification), and parameter labels are used to constrain parameters to be equal across groups to test hypotheses regarding group differences in specific aspects of the linear growth model. The multiple-group linear growth model can be written as

$$\mathbf{y}_i^{(g)} = \mathbf{\Lambda}\eta_i^{(g)} + \mathbf{u}_i^{(g)} \tag{6.3}$$

where $\mathbf{y}_i^{(g)}$ is a $T \times 1$ vector of the repeatedly measured observed scores for individual i in group g, T represents the number of repeated assessments based on the chosen time metric, $\mathbf{\Lambda}$ is a $T \times 2$ matrix of factor loadings defining the latent growth factors, $\eta_i^{(g)}$ is a 2×1 vector of latent factor scores for individual i in group g, and $\mathbf{u}_i^{(g)}$ is a $T \times 1$ vector of residual or unique scores for individual i in group g. Note that the $\mathbf{\Lambda}$ matrix is *not* group specific (not superscript by g). Rather, both groups are assumed to follow a linear growth trajectory. In the structural equation modeling framework, it is possible to accommodate different shapes or structures of change by making the $\mathbf{\Lambda}$ matrix group specific (similarly, different functions of change can be specified in the multilevel modeling framework). Because of our focus on the linear growth model, we assume the change pattern is linear and invariant across groups.

As in the previous chapters, the latent factor scores are written as deviations from group-specific means, such that

$$\eta_i^{(g)} = \alpha^{(g)} + \xi_i^{(g)} \tag{6.4}$$

where $\alpha^{(g)}$ is a 2×1 vector of latent factor means for group g and $\xi_i^{(g)}$ is a 2×1 vector of residual deviations for individual i in group g. In this multiple-group setting, the implied population mean vector ($\mu^{(g)}$) and covariance matrix ($\Sigma^{(g)}$) are also group specific. These expectations are

$$\mu^{(g)} = \Lambda \alpha^{(g)}$$

$$\Sigma^{(g)} = \Lambda \Psi^{(g)} \Lambda' + \Theta^{(g)} \tag{6.5}$$

where $\Psi^{(g)}$ is a 2×2 latent variable covariance matrix for group g and $\Theta^{(g)}$ is a $T \times T$ residual diagonal covariance matrix for group g.

As in the specification presented for the multilevel modeling framework, all matrices containing estimated parameters of the multiple-group linear growth model are group specific (i.e., $\alpha^{(g)}$, $\Psi^{(g)}$, and $\Theta^{(g)}$). The four models discussed above, M1 to M4, are specified by imposing equality constraints on specific matrices. Model M1 is specified by placing equality constraints on all three matrices containing estimated parameters (i.e., $\alpha^{(g)} = \alpha$, $\Psi^{(g)} = \Psi$ and $\Theta^{(g)} = \Theta$). Model M2 is specified by placing equality constraints on the Ψ and Θ matrices (i.e., $\alpha^{(g)}$, $\Psi^{(g)} = \Psi$, and $\Theta^{(g)} = \Theta$). Model M3 is specified by only placing equality constraints on Θ (i.e., $\alpha^{(g)}$, $\Psi^{(g)}$, and $\Theta^{(g)} = \Theta$). Finally, Model M4 is specified with no equality constraints across groups—all of the estimated parameters of the multiple-group linear growth model are estimated separately for each group (i.e., $\alpha^{(g)}$, $\Psi^{(g)}$, and $\Theta^{(g)}$).

Figure 6.1 is a path diagram of a multiple-group linear growth model with four repeated measurements in y_i. As seen in this figure, there are separate path diagrams for each group (g = 1 and g = 2), each of which contains a linear growth model. Across the group-specific path diagrams, parameter labels that are identical indicate where an equality constraint has been imposed. In contrast, parameter labels that are superscripted by the group number indicate that those parameters are estimated separately for each group. Given the equality constraints presented in this path diagram, this figure represents Model M2 because only the labels for the means of the intercept and linear slope are superscripted by the group number.

STRUCTURAL EQUATION MODELING IMPLEMENTATION

For the structural equation modeling implementation, the longitudinal data are organized in the wide format, with one record per person. In our example, the repeated outcomes of interest are the child-level mathematics scores (math2 through math8) and

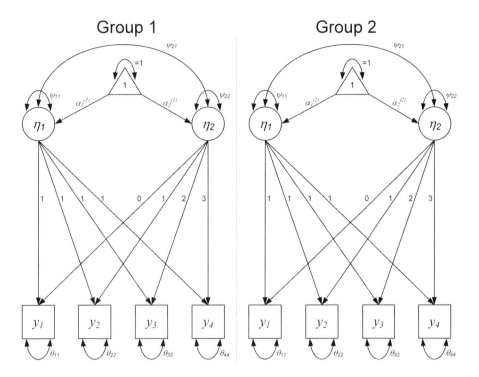

FIGURE 6.1. Path diagram of the multiple-group linear growth model.

the grouping variable is `lb_wght`, which is coded 0 for normal-birthweight children and 1 for low-birthweight children.

The `VARIABLE`, `ANALYSIS`, and `MODEL` statements from the `Mplus` script for fitting Model M4 are shown in Script 6.3. In the `VARIABLE` statement, the repeatedly measured variables are listed on the `USEVAR` line. Additionally, `lb_wght` is specified as the `GROUPING` variable, along with specific mapping between the values of the grouping variable and group-specific labels (0 = `normal`, 1 = `low`). These labels are used in the script to designate the group-specific model statements. As in previous chapters, in the `ANALYSIS` line we specify `TYPE=MEANSTRUCTURE` and the minimum covariance coverage.

The `MODEL` statement is used to specify the linear growth model. This is done in the usual manner, except that labels are included for all estimated parameters. This is done because `Mplus` has several defaults for multiple-group models, some of which are inappropriate for growth models. The labels override some of these defaults by initially imposing equality constraints on all estimated parameters, some of which are subsequently relaxed. The general model is followed by two group-specific model statements utilizing the labels defined in the `GROUPING` statement (`MODEL normal:` and `MODEL low:`). In `MODEL normal:`, the latent variable means (`[eta_1 eta_2];`), latent variable variances (`eta_1 eta_2;`) and covariance (`eta_1 WITH eta_2;`), and the residual variance of observed variables (`math2-math8 (theta1);`) are respecified

Script 6.3. `Mplus` Script for the Means, Covariances, and Residual Variances Model

```
VARIABLE: NAMES = id female lb_wght anti_k1
                  math2-math8 age2-age8 men2-men8
                  spring2-spring8 anti2-anti8;
    MISSING = .;
    USEVAR = math2-math8;
    GROUPING = lb_wght (0 = normal, 1 = low);

ANALYSIS: TYPE=MEANSTRUCTURE; COVERAGE=0;

MODEL:
    eta_1 BY math2-math8@1;
    eta_2 BY math2@0 math3@1 math4@2 math5@3 math6@4 math7@5 math8@6;
    [eta_1](alpha_1); [eta_2] (alpha_2);
    eta_1 (psi_11); eta_2 (psi_22);
    eta_1 WITH eta_2 (psi_21);
    [math2-math8@0];
    math2-math8 (theta);

MODEL normal:
    [eta_1 eta_2];
    eta_1 eta_2;
    eta_1 WITH eta_2;
    math2-math8 (theta1);

MODEL low:
    [eta_1 eta_2];
    eta_1 eta_2;
    eta_1 WITH eta_2;
    math2-math8 (theta2);
```

to make the estimation of these parameters specific to the normal-birthweight group. Similar statements are contained in MODEL low: to ensure that the model parameters are estimated separately for each group.[1] The parameters in the group-specific model statements will be estimated separately for each group, unless they are given common labels. Additionally, to constrain the residual variances to be equal across time, but to remain group specific, we give these parameters different labels (i.e., theta1 and theta2) in the group-specific model statements.

Models M1 through M3 are specified by making small adjustments to the M4 script, either by removing select statements from the group-specific models or by adding common labels to parameters in the group-specific models. For example, to obtain Model M3, we can remove the math2-math8 (theta1); and math2-math8 (theta2);

---

[1]In two-group models, respecifying the model specification for the second group is unnecessary. Moving to models with more than two groups, having a model specification for each group is important to be able to constrain or free parameters over groups.

statements or we can add a common label to both statements so that the final lines read `math2-math8 (theta);`. To specify Model M2, we remove the lines or add labels to the group-specific designations of the latent variable variances (`eta_1 eta_2;`) and covariance (`eta_1 WITH eta_2;`). Finally, for Model M1, common labels are applied to the means of the intercept and slope in the group-specific model statements. (Removing the statements for the latent variable means in the group-specific model will result in having the first group's mean intercept and slope to be fixed at 0 due to the `Mplus` default specification.)

The `OpenMx` code for specifying Model M4 is shown in Script 6.4. The script begins by creating two datasets with exclusive content, one for the normal-birthweight group and one for the low-birthweight group. These datasets are created using the `subset` command in R. The `mathdata_N` dataset contains the observations that belong to the normal-birthweight group (`lb_wght==0`) and `mathdata_L` contains the subset of observations that belong to the low-birthweight group (`lb_wght==1`). Separate datasets are needed to conduct multiple-group analyses in `OpenMx` (as opposed to having all data in one file that includes a group membership variable).

After the two datasets are created, the models are specified separately for each group. First, the linear growth model is specified for the normal-birthweight group using the `mathdata_N` dataset. The model specification follows the single-group specification of the linear growth model described in Chapter 3 using multiple `mxPath` statements to specify the model. `mxPath` statements for the residual variances of the observed scores, the intercept–slope variances and covariance, factor loadings for the intercept and slope, and means for the intercept and slope are given. Importantly, the labels given to each parameter are group specific. For the normal-birthweight group all parameter labels end with `_N` (e.g., `th_N` for the residual variance). After closing the first group-specific model, the same linear growth model is specified for the low-birthweight group using the `mathdata_L` dataset and group-specific labels that end with `_L`. The group specificity of the labels is important because it is this designation that allows parameter estimates to be separately estimated for each group. After closing the second group-specific model, `mxAlgebra` and `mxFitFunctionAlgebra` statements are used to specify the overall objective function as the sum of the group-specific objective functions, and then the full model is closed. Finally, `mxRun` and `summary` functions are used to fit the model and display the results.

As with the other implementations, Models M1 to M3 are specified by making small adjustments to this script. Here, these modifications are implemented by using common labels for specific parameters to constrain them to be invariant across groups. For example, to specify Model M3, the labels for the group-specific residual variances (`th_N` and `th_L`) are replaced by a common label (i.e., `th`). Similarly, Model M2 is specified by also replacing the group-specific labels for the latent variable variances and covariance by a set of common labels (i.e., `psi_11`, `psi_22`, and `psi_21`). Finally, Model M1 is specified by making the labels for the latent variable means the same across groups (i.e., `alpha_1` and `alpha_2`).

The `Mplus` and `OpenMx` results from Model M4 are shown in Output 6.3 and 6.4, respectively. Before discussing parameter estimates and model fit, we note that the `Mplus`

Script 6.4. OpenMx Script for the Means, Covariances, and Residual Variances Model

```r
mathdata_N <- subset(nlsy_math_wide,lb_wght==0)
mathdata_L <- subset(nlsy_math_wide,lb_wght==1)

mg4.math.omx <- mxModel('Multiple-group Growth Model, Means, Covariances, Residuals, Path Specification',
    mxModel('group1',type='RAM', mxData(observed=mathdata_N, type='raw'),
    manifestVars=c('math2','math3','math4','math5','math6','math7','math8'),
    latentVars=c('eta_1','eta_2'),

# residual variance paths
mxPath(from=c('math2','math3','math4','math5','math6','math7','math8'),
    arrows=2, free=TRUE, values=60, labels='th_N'),

# latent variable variances and covariance paths
mxPath(from=c('eta_1','eta_2'), connect='unique.pairs',
    arrows=2, free=TRUE, values=c(60,0,5), labels=c('psi_11_N','psi_21_N','psi_22_N')),

# Factor Loadings
mxPath(from='eta_1', to=c('math2','math3','math4','math5','math6','math7','math8'),
    arrows=1, free=FALSE, values=1),

mxPath(from='eta_2', to=c('math2','math3','math4','math5','math6','math7','math8'),
    arrows=1, free=FALSE, values=c(0, 1, 2, 3, 4, 5, 6)),

# means and intercepts
mxPath(from='one', to=c('eta_1','eta_2'),
    arrows=1, free=c(TRUE,TRUE), values=c(100, 15), labels=c('alpha_1_N','alpha_2_N'))
), # close Normal Birthweight Model
```

```r
mxModel('group2', type='RAM', mxData(observed=mathdata_L, type ='raw'),
    manifestVars=c('math2','math3','math4','math5','math6','math7','math8'),
    latentVars=c('eta_1','eta_2'),

# residual variance paths
mxPath(from=c('math2','math3','math4','math5','math6','math7','math8'),
    arrows=2, free=TRUE, values=60, labels='th_L'),

# latent variable variances and covariance paths
mxPath(from=c('eta_1','eta_2'), connect='unique.pairs',
    arrows=2, free=TRUE, values=c(60,0,5), labels=c('psi_11_L','psi_21_L','psi_22_L')),

# Factor Loadings
mxPath(from='eta_1', to=c('math2','math3','math4','math5','math6','math7','math8'),
    arrows=1, free=FALSE, values=1),

mxPath(from='eta_2', to=c('math2','math3','math4','math5','math6','math7','math8'),
    arrows=1, free=FALSE, values=c(0, 1, 2, 3, 4, 5, 6)),

# means and intercepts
mxPath(from='one', to=c('eta_1','eta_2'),
    arrows=1, free=c(TRUE,TRUE), values=c(100, 15), labels=c('alpha_1_L','alpha_2_L'))

), # Close Low Birthweight Model

mxAlgebra(group1.objective + group2.objective, name='mg_objective'), mxFitFunctionAlgebra('mg_objective')

) # Close Model

mg4.math.fit <- mxRun(mg4.math.omx)

summary(mg4.math.fit)
```

Output 6.3. Mplus Output for the Means, Covariances, and Residual Variances Model

THE MODEL ESTIMATION TERMINATED NORMALLY
       WARNING: THE LATENT VARIABLE COVARIANCE MATRIX (PSI) IN GROUP
       LOW IS NOT POSITIVE DEFINITE. THIS COULD INDICATE A NEGATIVE
       VARIANCE/RESIDUAL VARIANCE FOR A LATENT VARIABLE, A CORRELATION
       GREATER OR EQUAL TO ONE BETWEEN TWO LATENT VARIABLES, OR A LINEAR
       DEPENDENCY AMONG MORE THAN TWO LATENT VARIABLES. CHECK THE TECH4
       OUTPUT FOR MORE INFORMATION. PROBLEM INVOLVING VARIABLE ETA_2.

```
MODEL FIT INFORMATION
Number of Free Parameters                        12
Loglikelihood
           H0 Value                       -7963.056
           H1 Value                       -7840.549
Information Criteria
           Akaike (AIC)                   15950.111
           Bayesian (BIC)                 16008.159
           Sample-Size Adjusted BIC       15970.048
           (n* = (n + 2) / 24)
Chi-Square Test of Model Fit
           Value                            245.013
           Degrees of Freedom                    57
           P-Value                           0.0000
Chi-Square Contributions From Each Group
           NORMAL                           190.639
           LOW                               54.374
RMSEA (Root Mean Square Error Of Approximation)
           Estimate                           0.084
           90 Percent C.I.                    0.073        0.095
           Probability RMSEA <= .05           0.000
CFI/TLI
           CFI                                0.780
           TLI                                0.842


MODEL RESULTS

                                                  Two-Tailed
                 Estimate    S.E.    Est./S.E.     P-Value
Group NORMAL
ETA_1    BY
     MATH2        1.000     0.000     999.000       999.000
     ...
     MATH8        1.000     0.000     999.000       999.000
ETA_2    BY
     MATH2        0.000     0.000     999.000       999.000
     ...
     MATH8        6.000     0.000     999.000       999.000
```

```
ETA_1    WITH
    ETA_2     -0.063     1.161        -0.054        0.957
Means
    ETA_1     35.481     0.365        97.257        0.000
    ETA_2      4.297     0.091        47.145        0.000
Variances
    ETA_1     62.287     5.729        10.873        0.000
    ETA_2      0.774     0.334         2.314        0.021
Residual Variances
    MATH2     35.173     1.904        18.473        0.000
    ...
    MATH8     35.173     1.904        18.473        0.000


Group LOW
ETA_1    BY
    MATH2      1.000     0.000       999.000      999.000
    ...
    MATH8      1.000     0.000       999.000      999.000
ETA_2    BY
    MATH2      0.000     0.000       999.000      999.000
    ...
    MATH8      6.000     0.000       999.000      999.000
ETA_1    WITH
    ETA_2      0.746     5.522         0.135        0.892
Means
    ETA_1     32.800     1.407        23.314        0.000
    ETA_2      4.873     0.341        14.298        0.000
Variances
    ETA_1     79.626    25.630         3.107        0.002
    ETA_2     -0.158     1.477        -0.107        0.915
Residual Variances
    MATH2     48.689     8.445         5.766        0.000
    ...
    MATH8     48.689     8.445         5.766        0.000
```

output begins with a warning about the estimation of the latent variable covariance matrix (PSI) for the low-birthweight group and highlights variable ETA_2 as the problem. As we will see when parsing through the output, the estimated variance of the linear slope for the low-birthweight group was small and negative (–0.16). Given that variances cannot be less than zero, the error message and this parameter estimate indicate that the model was not viable. Thus, in practice, the parameter estimates should not be interpreted. We do describe the output here for pedagogical reasons, given that readers may encounter either similar error messages or viable output.

Parameter estimates from Mplus and OpenMx are organized according to group. Mplus reports all fixed and estimated parameters, first for Group NORMAL and then for Group LOW. Output from OpenMx includes only the estimated parameters with designations starting with group1. or group2. in the matrix column to indicate their group association. We note that parameter estimates constrained to be equal across

Output 6.4. OpenMx Output for the Means, Covariances, and Residual Variances Model

```
free parameters:
         name     matrix     row      col      Estimate      Std.Error
1        th_N     group1.S   math2    math2    35.17197839   1.87799257
2     psi_11_N    group1.S   eta_1    eta_1    62.28975865   5.58685757
3     psi_21_N    group1.S   eta_1    eta_2    -0.06320182   1.09799941
4     psi_22_N    group1.S   eta_2    eta_2     0.77373272   0.32227432
5     alpha_1_N   group1.M       1    eta_1    35.48131985   0.36482093
6     alpha_2_N   group1.M       1    eta_2     4.29730928   0.09112965
7        th_L     group2.S   math2    math2    48.68704569   8.39569515
8     psi_11_L    group2.S   eta_1    eta_1    79.62008119  25.35468150
9     psi_21_L    group2.S   eta_1    eta_2     0.74648044   5.41729561
10    psi_22_L    group2.S   eta_2    eta_2    -0.15728435   1.45729012
11    alpha_1_L   group2.M       1    eta_1    32.79999194   1.40680570
12    alpha_2_L   group2.M       1    eta_2     4.87300524   0.34077354

observed statistics: 2221
estimated parameters: 12
degrees of freedom: 2209
-2 log likelihood: 15926.11
saturated -2 log likelihood: NA
number of observations: 933
chi-square: NA
p: NA
Information Criteria:
         df Penalty Parameters Penalty    Sample-Size Adjusted
AIC:    11508.1112              15950.11                     NA
BIC:      820.0741              16008.17                15970.06
```

groups will only appear once, with a group1. designation. Parameter estimates describing the growth process in mathematics from second through eighth grade for the normal-birthweight group (Group NORMAL; group1.) include the mean intercept (35.48; Means of ETA_1; alpha_1_N) and slope (4.30; Means of ETA_2; alpha_2_N), variance of the intercept (62.29; Variances of ETA_1; psi_11_N) and slope (0.77; Variances of ETA_2; psi_22_N), intercept–slope covariance (–0.06; ETA_1 WITH ETA_2; psi_21_N), and residual variance (35.17; Residual Variances of MATH2 through MATH8; th_N). That is, on average, normal-birthweight children had a mathematics score of 35.48 in second grade and increased 4.30 points per year from second through eighth grades. Although there were significant between-child differences in both the intercept and slope, these individual differences were not significantly associated with one another.

In parallel, parameter estimates describing the growth process in mathematics from second through eighth grades for the low-birthweight group (Group_LOW; group2.) include the mean intercept (32.80; Means of ETA_1; alpha_1_L) and slope (4.87; Means of ETA_2; alpha_2_L), variance of the intercept (79.63; Variances of ETA_1; psi_11_L) and slope (–0.16; Variances of ETA_2; psi_22_L), intercept–slope covariance (0.75; ETA_1 WITH ETA_2; psi_21_L), and residual variance (48.69; Residual Variances of MATH2 through MATH8; th_L). On average, low-birthweight children had a mathematics score of 32.80 in second grade, and their scores increased 4.87 points per year from second through eighth grade. Keeping in mind the problem with model convergence noted earlier, one can see significant between-child differences in mathematics scores in second grade but not in the annual rate of change.

IMPORTANT CONSIDERATIONS

Model Comparisons

Contrasted with the inclusion of time-invariant predictors covered in the previous chapter, the multiple-groups framework provides some additional opportunities for examining between-person differences in change. By comparing the relative fit of the four fitted models, M1 to M4, we can identify if and how the groups differed from one another with respect to their means (M2), means and covariances (M3), and means, covariances, and residuals (M4). Because the models are *nested* (e.g., M1 is a constrained version of M4), model comparisons can be done using likelihood ratio tests (LRTs). To aid our comparisons, likelihood-based fit indices, along with the −2LL, are organized in Table 6.1. First, we compare the fit of Model M2 to that of Model M1. This comparison examines whether the groups differ in their average trajectories. Changes in the −2LL (or χ^2) are χ^2 distributed, with degrees of freedom equal to the difference in the number of estimated parameters. Thus, examining the M1 and M2 columns of Table 6.1, we find that the two additional parameters (group-specific vs. group-invariant means) in Model M2 led to a reduction in the −2LL of 5(16,937 − 16,932), a nonsignificant ($\chi^2(2) = 5$, $p = .08$) improvement in model fit. The increase in the BIC and the minor change in the AIC confirm the conclusion that Model M2 did not fit significantly better than Model M1. That is, the groups did not significantly differ in their average trajectories. Second, we compared the fit of Model M3 to that of Model M2. Again, the LRT was nonsignificant ($\chi^2(3) = 3$, $p = .39$) indicating that the latent variable covariance matrix was invariant over groups. Finally, Model M4 was compared with Model M3 to determine whether the groups differed in their residual variability. Again, the LRT was nonsignificant ($\chi^2(1) = 3$, $p = .08$) indicating that the residual variance was not significantly different over groups. In summary, the sequential model fitting and comparison indicated that the four models fit similarly, which suggests that the invariance model (Model M1) was the most parsimonious model that represents the observed data with nearly the same precision as the three multiple-group models that allowed for differences in the means, variances, and covariances, and residual variance.[2] Thus, we conclude that the normal- and low-birthweight

---

[2]In a similar way, Model M3 and Model M4 can also be compared directly to Model M1. Comparing Model M3 to Model M1, we conclude that, together, the differences in means and covariances are nonsignificant ($\chi^2(5) = 8$, $p = .16$), and comparing Model M4 to Model M1 we conclude that all the differences in means, covariances, and residual variance are nonsignificant ($\chi^2(6) = 11$, $p = .09$).

TABLE 6.1. Fit Statistics for the Multiple-Group Linear Growth Models

	Model M1	Model M2	Model M3	Model M4
Parameters	6	8	11	12
−2LL	15937	15932	15929	15926
BIC	15978	15987	16005	16008
AIC	15949	15948	15951	15950
Δ parameters	−	2	3	1
Δ−2LL	−	5	3	3

children did not differ in their average growth trajectories of mathematics, the extent of between-person differences in those trajectories, or the extent of fluctuation around their individual trajectories.

It may be noted that the conclusions about birthweight-related differences in the growth trajectories for mathematics reached here, in the multiple-groups framework, were not congruent with the conclusions reached in the previous chapter when birthweight group was used as a time-invariant covariate. In the time-invariant covariate analysis, low-birthweight children were found to have lower mathematics scores in second grade, while in the multiple-group analysis no differences were noted. This is because of two reasons. First, in the multiple-group models we did not control for antisocial behaviors. Second, the statistical tests were conducted in different ways. Here, in the multiple-groups framework, we tested for differences in the average trajectory, operationalized as a two degrees of freedom test of differences in the mean of both the intercept and the slope. In the time-invariant covariate models, we conducted separate one degree of freedom tests of the difference in the mean of the intercept and difference in the mean of the slope. The discrepancy between a global test of all latent factor means versus a series of one-parameter-at-a-time tests might be considered a limitation of the multiple-group approach. Single-parameter tests can be implemented in the multiple-groups framework (e.g., Model M1.5 can be specified where only the mean of the intercept differs between groups), with the additional flexibility that a wide variety of intermediate models can be used to test group differences. The key issue is more a philosophical one—Do the intercept and slope components of change hold specific interpretive value in isolation, or are they only meaningful in bulk as multiple components of a trajectory?

Ordering of Model Comparisons

There are two possible ways to structure the comparisons among the four multiple-group models, M1 to M4. One approach is to fit and compare the models in *ascending* order. That is, begin with Model M1, the most constrained model, and proceed to Models M2, M3, and finally M4, the model with the fewest constraints. In this approach, the first model in the sequence has the smallest number of parameters and the greatest misfit, in terms of the size of the −2LL and χ^2, and the last model in the sequence has the greatest number of parameters and the smallest misfit. Advantages of this sequencing include the following: (1) the simplest models (in terms of the number of estimated parameters) are fit first, (2) the second model in the sequence has direct parallels with the time-invariant covariate model and thus provides a common starting point for describing between-person differences in within-person change, and (3) the sequence generally follows the expansion of ANOVA (assuming equal variances followed by unequal variances). The alternative approach is to fit and compare models in *descending* order, beginning with the most relaxed model, the means, covariances, and residual variances model, and then gradually imposing constraints in sequence through the models—to M3, M2, and then M1. This approach follows the sequencing most often used when studying factorial invariance (Meredith, 1993) over groups or time. No matter the sequence, the same conclusions should be drawn.

MOVING FORWARD

The multiple-group approach to studying between-person differences in within-person change is powerful, even more so than we have covered. Thus far, we have limited our presentation to linear growth models for describing within-person change and between-person differences in change. In later chapters, we move to more complex nonlinear models and highlight the potential for studying group differences in the shape of change over time—an examination that is not available when working with models that include a time-invariant covariate as a predictor of the intercept and slope. For example, in some situations we may expect one group to follow a linear growth trajectory (e.g., control group), whereas another group would follow exponential growth (e.g., intervention group). As soon as we push beyond hypotheses about differences in the magnitude of within-person change trajectories, and consider the possibility that groups of individuals may follow different within-person change trajectories, the usefulness of the multiple-groups framework is magnified.

We have presented the multiple-groups framework as an alternative to the time-invariant covariates approach; however, the two frameworks can be integrated. As outlined in the previous chapter, time-invariant covariates are used to explain between-person differences in the intercept and slope. Adding time-invariant covariates into the multiple-groups framework allows us to explain variability in the intercept and slope within each group. We can then test whether the relations between the time-invariant covariates and the intercept and slope (regression parameters) differ across groups. Models where the regression parameters are invariant across groups allow for main effects of time-invariant covariates. Models where the regression parameters differ across groups examine how the time-invariant covariate and the grouping variable interact to affect individuals' change trajectories.

The multiple-groups framework is the foundation for understanding latent class growth models (Nagin, 1999) and growth mixture models (Muthén & Shedden, 1999). These models have received considerable attention in the last decade as an additional way of examining between-person differences in within-person change. Yet, they are not so different from the models just covered. The key distinction between these models and the multiple-group model is whether or not the grouping variable is known *a priori* (Ram & Grimm, 2009). In the multiple-groups framework, the grouping variable is known ahead of time. It is in the datafile, and it can be used to identify the cases that belong to each group. Group-specific models are used to understand how the groups differ in their growth trajectories. In contrast, for both the latent class growth model and the growth mixture model, the grouping variable is not known *a priori*. Rather, the grouping variable is inferred from differences manifested in the growth trajectories. In brief, these models attempt to recover the grouping variable by pulling apart the sample in ways that maximize between-group or between-class differences and minimize within-group or within-class differences. In the next chapter, we follow the approach taken here and illustrate how unknown or latent classes can differ in various aspects of the change trajectory—latent variable means, latent variable covariances, and residual variances (e.g., Ram & Grimm, 2009).

7

Growth Mixture Modeling

Growth models are used to describe how individuals change over time and examine the between-person differences in those changes. As with all models, certain assumptions are inherent to growth models. One such assumption is about the structure of between-person differences in the intercept and slope. For example, the models covered in Chapters 3 and 4 assume that the between-person differences in the intercept and linear slope exist along a continuum (low to high) and are normally (Gaussian) distributed. Thus, it is assumed that the sample is drawn from a single population. Substantively, though, we are often interested in and deal with samples from multiple populations (e.g., we collect data from males and females, adolescents with few behavior problems and adolescents with behavior problems, adults with signs of preclinical dementia and adults with no sign of dementia). The growth modeling extensions discussed thus far allow for slight alterations to the single population assumption in ways that accommodate such interests. For example, the distributions of the intercept and slope are assumed to be normally distributed *conditional* on the time-invariant covariates in the growth model with time-invariant covariates and the intercept and slope are assumed to be normally distributed within each group in multiple-group growth models. Extending the logic of multiple-group growth models where groups are defined *a priori*, the growth mixture model (GMM) allows for groups (often referred to as classes) of individuals to be identified post hoc. That is, GMMs search for groups of individuals in the dataset, such that individuals thought to be in the same group have similar trajectories and individuals thought to be in different groups have sufficiently different trajectories. As with the multiple-group growth model, the distributions of intercepts and slopes in each class are assumed to be multivariate normal and the distributions of intercepts and slopes over classes can be complex and highly non-normal.

We present the GMM as an extension of the multiple-group growth model where the grouping variable is latent or unobserved (Ram & Grimm, 2009). Just as the multiple-group model can be used to describe differences in how change proceeds in subsamples in the data, the GMM can also be used to describe differences in how change proceeds in subsamples in the data. The difference is that the multiple-group model is used when we know how to split the data and the GMM is used when we must *discover* how to split the data. The general idea is depicted in Figure 7.1, where distributions (e.g., of an intercept or a slope from a growth model) for two groups are shown with dotted lines and the distribution from the total sample is shown with a solid line. In the multiple-groups framework we know, *a priori*, that there are two groups and the group that each individual belongs to. Thus, the dashed lines of Figure 7.1 are observed in a multiple-group growth model; however, only the solid line is observed if we don't know how to split the sample into groups. Through an iterative estimation process, the GMM attempts to uncover the two underlying normal distributions, their parameters, and obtain a probabilistic determination of which individuals are part of which group. Following the logic underlying finite mixture models (Lazarsfeld & Henry, 1968), this is done by introducing a categorical latent variable into the growth model and iteratively obtain parameters of each group and the size of each group (Muthén & Shedden, 1999). Once model parameters are estimated, we can obtain a posterior estimate of the probability that each individual belongs to each group. Thus, a goal of researchers using GMMs is to obtain *probable* representations of the unobserved groups, how those groups differ, and who is a member of which group.

While in practice the GMM is used to describe unobserved group differences in change, one must be cautious when interpreting such results. GMMs are an exploratory analysis. Thus, the interpretation of the parameters as descriptions of unobserved

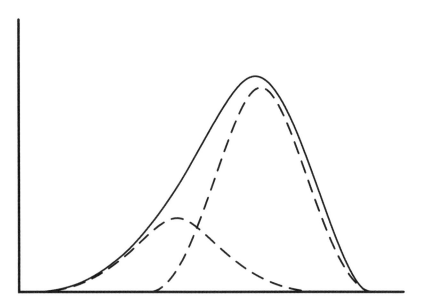

FIGURE 7.1. Non-normal distribution approximated by mixture distribution.

groups only provides circumstantial evidence of unseen groups. Other interpretations are equally viable. For example, the distribution depicted by the solid line in Figure 7.1 may truly represent how a particular aspect of change is distributed in a single population. Demonstrating this possibility, Bauer and Curran (2003) simulated longitudinal growth data for a single group that was normally distributed. These data were transformed to be slightly skewed and kurtotic. The degree of non-normality was relatively minor and considered typical of social science data. The data were then subjected to a series of growth and growth mixture models. Using typically employed and recommended fit indices, Bauer and Curran found that GMMs were almost universally favored, suggesting the presence of multiple subpopulations, even though the data came from a single population. This paper highlighted how the GMM, and the finite mixture model more generally, are simply trying to account for the non-normality in the data and that any non-normality in the observed distribution, whether driven by sampling multiple populations, incomplete sampling of a single population, measurement distortion, or nonlinear associations (Bauer, 2005) can manifest as a mixture of normal distributions. Thus, it is important to consider alternative explanations before jumping to the conclusion that the data were drawn from multiple populations (see also Ram & Grimm, 2009), and the replication of findings is key. Keeping this caution in mind, we walk through the specification, fitting, and interpretation of model results from GMMs.

The example data used in this chapter were drawn from the Early Childhood Longitudinal Study—Kindergarten Cohort (ECLS-K; National Center for Education Statistics, 2001), a longitudinal study of more than 21,000 children followed from kindergarten through eighth grade. From the full sample, we selected a 10% random sample of children assessed during kindergarten and first grade. The outcome variable, child weight measured in pounds, was collected on four occasions—fall and spring of kindergarten and first grade. The time metric, grade at testing, was coded with 0 representing the fall of kindergarten and 1.5 representing the spring of first grade. The trajectories of child weight across grade are shown in Figure 7.2. Generally, the trajectories appear to be relatively linear, with large between-child differences in the fall of kindergarten and larger between-child differences in the spring of first grade. Of note, the distribution of children's weights at each occasion were non-normal—positively skewed with a heavy tail on the upper end of the distribution. The research objective is to study individual changes in weight and between-person differences in weight change. We examine whether there is any evidence for multiple subpopulations based on the observed trajectories. That is, we wish to examine whether there is evidence that between-person differences in weight change are better represented by considering there to be more than one typology—potentially a group of individuals who show more or less typical change and a group of individuals who have a riskier change pattern. If this is the result, we want to identify the individuals who are likely to be in this group and the characteristics of this group to highlight potential mechanisms.

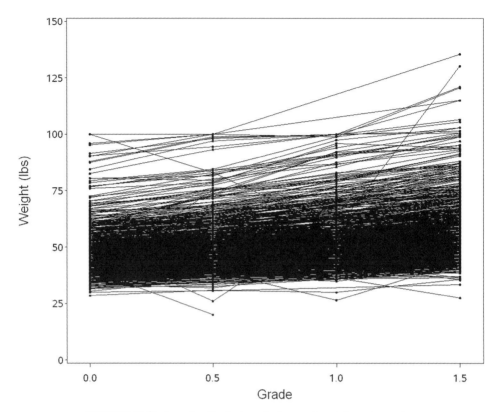

FIGURE 7.2. Longitudinal plot of observed weight trajectories.

MULTILEVEL MODELING FRAMEWORK

In the multilevel modeling framework, the GMM is conceptualized similarly to the multiple-group growth model covered in the previous chapter, as a collection of two-level models, one for each class. Within each class, the level-1 model is identical to the linear growth model initially described in Chapter 3, but with an additional class-specific designation given by the superscript (k). Thus, for $i = 1$ to N individuals and $k = 1$ to K classes, the model is specified as

$$y_{ti}^{(k)} = b_{1i}^{(k)} + b_{2i}^{(k)} \cdot t + u_{ti}^{(k)} \tag{7.1}$$

where $y_{ti}^{(k)}$ are the repeated scores (e.g., *weight*) collected at time t for individual i in class k, $b_{1i}^{(k)}$ is the random intercept or predicted score when $t = 0$ for individual i in class k, $b_{2i}^{(k)}$ is the random slope or rate of change for a one-unit change in t for individual i in class k, t represents the chosen time metric, and $u_{ti}^{(k)}$ is the time-specific residual score at time t for individual i in class k. As usual, the time-specific residuals are assumed to be normally distributed in each class with a class-specific variance, $u_{ti}^{(k)} \sim N(0, \sigma_u^{2(k)})$.

The class-specific level-2 equations are specified as

$$b_{1i}^{(k)} = \beta_1^{(k)} + d_{1i}^{(k)}$$
$$b_{2i}^{(k)} = \beta_2^{(k)} + d_{2i}^{(k)}$$

(7.2)

where $\beta_1^{(k)}$ and $\beta_2^{(k)}$ are class-specific means for the intercept and slope, and $d_{1i}^{(k)}$ and $d_{2i}^{(k)}$ are individual deviations for individual i in class k from the respective class-specifc mean. Individual deviations are assumed to follow a multivariate normal distribution in each class with means equal to zero, estimated variances, and covariance; for example,

$$d_{1i}^{(k)}, d_{2i}^{(k)} \sim MVN\left(\begin{bmatrix} 0 \\ 0 \end{bmatrix}, \begin{bmatrix} \sigma_1^{2(k)} & \\ \sigma_{21}^{(k)} & \sigma_2^{2(k)} \end{bmatrix}\right)$$

We note that the superscript (k) on each of the model parameters indicates that each parameter can be class specific in the same sense as how all model parameters can be group specific in multiple-group growth models.

We have specified the GMM of Equations 7.1 and 7.2 in a very general way, allowing each parameter to be class specific (each parameter is superscripted by (k)). However, in practice, researchers fit more specific models to examine class differences in certain parameters of the linear growth model. Paralleling the approach presented in the previous chapter, four models are used to examine different types of class differences. The first model (M1) is the *baseline* (*invariance*) model where all estimated parameters are invariant across classes. This model treats the data as though there is only one class and maps on to the linear growth model discussed in Chapter 3. The second model (M2) is the *means* model, where the means of the intercept and slope are class specific. In principle, individuals are probabilistically placed in classes that differ in their baseline levels (expected scores when $t = 0$) and rates of change. This specification, where only the mean trajectories differ across classes, is very common and is often the only model examined. However, as we saw in the previous chapter, classes may also differ with respect to other model parameters. The third model (M3) is the *means* and *covariances* model, where the latent variable (intercept and slope) distributions are class specific. That is, the average trajectories, the magnitude of between-person differences in the intercept and slope, and the association between intercepts and slopes within each class are class specific. Finally, in the fourth model (M4), classes may differ in all estimated parameters of the linear growth model: *means*, *covariances*, and *residual variances*.

Due to not knowing either the number of classes or the model parameters that differ over classes, we recommend fitting each type of model (M2, M3, and M4) while gradually increasing the number of classes (e.g., two classes, three classes). For each type of model, the number of classes can be increased until the model encounters convergence issues or model fit (discussed later) indicates that additional classes are unlikely to produce viable results. Once all models are fit, they are compared, based on fit criteria and the substantive interpretation of model parameters, in an attempt to determine whether there are multiple classes and, if so, how many classes and how their growth trajectories are different.

MULTILEVEL MODELING IMPLEMENTATION

GMMs are not often, or cannot be fit, in the widely available multilevel modeling programs. For example, GMMs can be fit using `NLMIXED` but not `nlme`. In `NLMIXED` we have often experienced convergence issues and/or obtained parameter estimates that were not the same as those obtained from commonly used structural equation modeling programs. Given these difficulties and discrepancies, the `NLMIXED` code is not described here but is included on our website.

STRUCTURAL EQUATION MODELING FRAMEWORK

The GMM is commonly conceptualized and fit in the structural equation modeling framework. As a structural equation model, the linear growth mixture model can be written as

$$\mathbf{y}_i^{(k)} = \mathbf{\Lambda}\eta_i^{(k)} + \mathbf{u}_i^{(k)} \tag{7.3}$$

where $\mathbf{y}_i^{(k)}$ is a $T \times 1$ vector of the repeatedly measured observed scores for individual i in class k, $\mathbf{\Lambda}$ is a $T \times 2$ matrix of factor loadings defining the latent variable intercept and slope, $\eta_i^{(k)}$ is a 2×1 vector of latent factor (intercept and slope) scores for individual i in class k, and $\mathbf{u}_i^{(k)}$ is a $T \times 1$ vector of unique scores for individual i in class k. Although it can be, the Λ matrix is not class specific here (however, see Ram & Grimm, 2009). Rather, we assume that all classes follow a linear growth trajectory. The latent factor scores are then written as deviations from class-specific means, such that

$$\eta_i^{(k)} = \alpha^{(k)} + \xi_i^{(k)} \tag{7.4}$$

where $\alpha^{(k)}$ is a 2×1 vector of latent factor means for class k and $\xi_i^{(k)}$ is a 2×1 vector of residual deviations for individual i in class k. The within-class model implied mean ($\mu^{(k)}$) and covariance ($\Sigma^{(k)}$) structure is

$$\mu^{(k)} = \mathbf{\Lambda}\alpha^{(k)}$$
$$\Sigma^{(k)} = \mathbf{\Lambda}\Psi^{(k)}\mathbf{\Lambda}' + \Theta^{(k)} \tag{7.5}$$

where $\Psi^{(k)}$ is a 2×2 latent covariance matrix for class k, and $\Theta^{(k)}$ is a $T \times T$ diagonal residual covariance matrix for class k. In the mixture model setting, the implied mean (μ)

and covariance ($\mathbf{\Sigma}$) structure of the full model cannot be expressed directly because we do not know, *a priori*, how to weight the class-specific models. Instead, we can represent the full density function of $\mathbf{y}$, $f(\mathbf{y})$, which is conceived as the weighted sum of class-specific densities and $f(\mathbf{y}^{(k)}, \mu^{(k)}, \mathbf{\Sigma}^{(k)})$. Specifically,

$$f(\mathbf{y}) = \sum_{k=1}^{K} \pi^{(k)} f\left(\mathbf{y}^{(k)} \mid \mu^{(k)}, \mathbf{\Sigma}^{(k)}\right) \tag{7.6}$$

where the proportion of the sample in latent class k, $\pi^{(k)}$, is estimated in the model fitting process. These class-specific proportions take on a value between 0 and 1 and sum to 1 (i.e., $\sum_{k=1}^{K} \pi^{(k)} = 1$).

The GMM specified above is general in that each matrix (except for Λ) is class specific. In practice, restricted versions of the model are used to determine the number of classes in combination with the parameters that vary over classes. As in the previous model chapter, four types of models (M1 to M4) are specified. In Model M1, the *invariance* model, there are no class-specific differences, and the data are modeled as though they were sampled from a single nonmixture population. Class-specific differences are then added in sequence. In the *means* model (M2) the latent variable means are allowed to be class specific ($\alpha^{(k)}$). In the literature, this is often the only model examined. However, classes may also differ in other meaningful ways. In the *means and covariances* model (M3) the latent variable means, variances, and covariance are class specific ($\alpha^{(k)}$ and $\mathbf{\Psi}^{(k)}$). Finally, in the *means*, *covariances*, and *residual variances* model (M4), all estimated parameters of the linear growth model are class specific ($\alpha^{(k)}$, $\mathbf{\Psi}^{(k)}$, and $\Theta^{(k)}$). As noted above, all three types of GMMs (M2 to M4) should be studied in order to determine the number of classes and the type of class differences that best represent the data.

In previous chapters we have also represented models in the structural equation modeling framework using path diagrams. Although GMMs, with the probabilistic class membership, include elements that do not conform to the mathematical logic behind path diagrams, researchers have developed a few heuristic path diagram-like representations to convey useful information about the setup of the models. One popular representation of the GMM is shown in Figure 7.3. Here, the latent class variable is depicted as a predictor of the intercept and slope latent variables. This conveys the idea that the latent class variable has an effect on the means of the intercept and slope—depicting a model similar to the means model (M2). Unfortunately, this representation of the GMM does not accommodate potential class differences in the latent variable variances, covariance, or residual variances. These might be incorporated by including superscripted (k)s on the specific parameters that are allowed to vary across classes. Although useful and a general depiction of the GMM, we have concern that the regression-type associations between

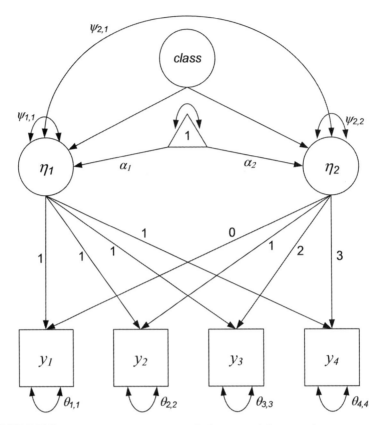

FIGURE 7.3. Commonly presented path diagram of the growth mixture model.

the latent class variable and the other latent variables do not accurately represent the mathematics of the GMM or the way results obtained from the models are organized.

An alternative path diagram-like representation of the GMM is shown in Figure 7.4. This representation follows the logic of the path diagrams used to depict multiple-group models, where separate path diagrams are drawn for each group and common parameter labels are used to indicate the parameters that are held invariant over groups. Thus, this figure represents a two-class means model (M2). Two path diagrams depict linear growth models, one for each class, and only the means of the intercept and slope are class specific (superscripted by their respective class numbers: 1 and 2). In addition, the arrows between the latent class variable and the two class-specific diagrams indicate that the latent class variable is related to the class-specific models in their entirety, probabilistically clustering individuals into each class. This multidiagram graphical representation more closely matches the mathematical underpinnings of the GMM. However, unlike the other approach, this representation lacks generality as one moves from a specific number of classes (e.g., two class-specific models) to an unknown number of classes (e.g., K class-specific models). Nonetheless, such diagrams are extremely useful when developing and conveying the research intentions and use of GMMs.

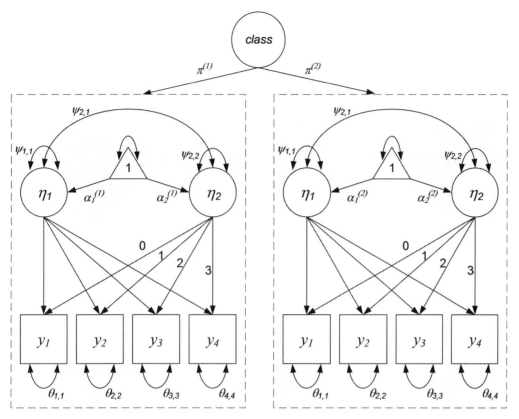

FIGURE 7.4. Uncommonly presented path diagram of the growth mixture model.

STRUCTURAL EQUATION MODELING IMPLEMENTATION

To fit the GMMs described above with structural equation modeling programs, the longitudinal data are organized in the wide format with one record per person. In our example, the repeatedly measured outcome is children's weight (wght1 through wght4) measured in the fall and spring of kindergarten and first grade, which are shown in Figure 7.2. Script 7.1 contains the VARIABLE, ANALYSIS, and MODEL statements from Mplus to estimate a two-class linear growth mixture model with the latent variable means (M2: means) allowed to vary over classes. In the VARIABLE statement, the weight variables (wght1 through wght4) are listed on the USEVAR line and CLASSES=c(2) is specified to indicate the name of the latent class variable (c) and the number of classes (2) for this model. This number is changed to obtain estimates for models with more latent classes. The finite mixture model is then invoked in the ANALYSIS statement with TYPE=MIXTURE.

The model is then specified in multiple parts within the MODEL section. The %OVERALL% statement designates the portion of the script where all model parameters are specified.

Script 7.1. `Mplus` Script for the Two-Class Means Model

```
VARIABLE: NAMES =    id            female
                     math1-math4   read1-read4    gk1-gk4
                     hght1-hght4   wght1-wght4;
     MISSING = .;
     USEVAR = wght1-wght4;
     CLASSES = c(2);

ANALYSIS: TYPE=MIXTURE;

MODEL:
%OVERALL%
     eta_1 BY wght1-wght4@1;
     eta_2 BY wght1@0 wght2@.5 wght3@1 wght4@1.5;

     eta_1 (psi_11); eta_2 (psi_22);
     eta_1 WITH eta_2 (psi_21);
     [eta_1 eta_2];

     wght1-wght4 (theta);
     [wght1-wght4@0];

%c#1%
     [eta_1*30 eta_2*3];
%c#2%
     [eta_1*60 eta_2*8];

OUTPUT: TECH11 TECH14;
```

This is done in the usual manner with, as in the multiple-group growth models, labels given for all estimated parameters. In this example, the latent variable intercept and slope, `eta_1` and `eta_2`, are indicated by the weight variables (`wght1` through `wght4`) with factor loadings that are fixed at 1 for the intercept and increase in a linear manner (e.g., `@0`, `@.5`, `@1`, and `@1.5`) for the slope. Latent variable variances, covariances, and means are then specified for `eta_1` and `eta_2`. Next, residual variances of `wght1` through `wght4` are specified and constrained to be equal across time. Lastly, measurement intercepts are specified and fixed to 0. In this `%OVERALL%` model, we have provided labels for all parameters that are invariant over latent classes. The labels place an equality constraint on these parameters and force them to be invariant across classes. This `%OVERALL%` model is followed by two class-specific model statements, `%c#1%` and `%c#2%`, utilizing the class name from the `CLASSES` statement and the respective class number. In the class-specific model statements, we respecify the model parameters that are separately estimated for each class. In this example, the class-specific statements for the means of `eta_1` and `eta_2` indicate that the classes may differ in the means of the latent variable intercept and slope (e.g., `[eta_1*30 eta_2*3];`). These class-specific parameters are given *reasonable* starting values (after the `*`) to aid estimation. In practice, we often choose values near the lower and upper ends of the distribution of intercepts and slopes, which can be obtained from fitting a linear growth model (i.e., one-class model). It is important that the starting values for each class are different from one another, which helps the estimation algorithm. Finally, in the `OUTPUT` section, the `TECH11` and `TECH14` outputs are requested. The `TECH11` output includes the Lo–Mendell–Rubin adjusted likelihood ratio test (LMRa LRT) and the Vuong–Lo–Mendell–Rubin likelihood ratio test (VLMR LRT), and `TECH14` output includes the bootstrap likelihood ratio test.[1] These approximate likelihood ratio tests are useful when comparing models with a different number of classes (Nylund, Asparouhov, & Muthén, 2007).

Models M3 and M4 are specified by adding additional statements to the class-specific models. For example, a two-class means and covariances model (M3) is specified by adding statements to indicate that the latent variable variances and covariance are also class specific. That is, the section labeled `%c#1%` becomes `[eta_1*30 eta_2*3]; eta_1 eta_2; eta_1 WITH eta_2;` and in the section labeled `%c#2%` becomes `[eta_1*60 eta_2*8]; eta_1 eta_2; eta_1 WITH eta_2;`. Providing starting values for the variances and covariances is not necessary. In Model M4 (means, covariances, and residual variances), statements for the residual variances are also contained in the class-specific models. Section `%c#1%` becomes `[eta_1*30 eta_2*3]; eta_1 eta_2; eta_1 WITH eta_2; wght1-wght4 (theta1);` and section `%c#2%` becomes `[eta_1*60 eta_2*8]; eta_1 eta_2; eta_1 WITH eta_2; wght1-wght4 (theta2);`. These statements allow the residual variance to be estimated separately for each class, but the labels `theta1` and `theta2` constrain the residual variance to be equal across time within each class.

Given that the number of classes is not known *a priori*, it must be determined by comparing models that differ in the number of classes. To do this, each type of model (M2 to M4) is run, and the number of classes is varied. The `Mplus` script is modified by changing the number of classes in the `VARIABLE` command (e.g., `CLASSES=c(3)` for a three-class model) and including additional class-specific model statements (e.g., `%c#3%`) to indicate the parameters that are allowed to differ in that class. Once beyond two classes, a full array of *hybrid* models are also possible. For example, a parameter may be invariant in two classes (designated by using the same label), but different in the third class (designated by using a different label). These possibilities continue down the path of exploratory analyses and models that are highly tailored to the empirical data, which highlight the need for replication.

An `OpenMx` Script for a two-class means model (M2) is shown in Script 7.2. The script begins by defining an object called `class1` that houses the first class-specific growth model. After specifying the manifest (`wght1-wght4`) and latent variables (`eta_1` and `eta_2`) included in the model, `mxPath` statements are used to specify the model. Paths for the residual variances, latent variable variances and covariance, factor loadings for the intercept and slope, and the means for the intercept and slope are all specified with `mxPath` statements and follow the specifications from previous chapters. We note that class-specific labels ending in `_c1` are used to allow specific parameters to vary over classes. In the two-class means model, the labels for the means of the latent variable intercept and slope include this notation. The `class1` object finishes with `mxFitFunctionML(vector=TRUE)`. Typically, we don't have to specify a fit

---

[1]Increasing the number of bootstrap draws using `LRTBOOTSTRAP` in the `ANALYSIS` command increases the precision of the bootstrap likelihood ratio test.

Script 7.2. OpenMx Script for the Two-Class Means Model

```
class1 <- mxModel('Class1', type='RAM',
    manifestVars=c('wght1', 'wght2', 'wght3', 'wght4'),
    latentVars=c('eta_1', 'eta_2'),

# residual variances
mxPath(from=c('wght1', 'wght2', 'wght3', 'wght4'), arrows=2,
    free=TRUE, values=6, labels='theta'),

# latent variances and covariance
mxPath(from=c('eta_1', 'eta_2'), arrows=2, connect='unique.pairs',
    free=TRUE, values=c(40, 7, 3), labels=c('psi_11', 'psi_12', 'psi_22')),

# intercept loadings
mxPath(from='eta_1', to=c('wght1', 'wght2', 'wght3', 'wght4'), arrows=1,
    free=FALSE, values=1),

# slope loadings
mxPath(from='eta_2', to=c('wght1', 'wght2', 'wght3', 'wght4'), arrows=1,
    free=FALSE, values=c(0, .5, 1, 1.5)),

# latent variable means
mxPath(from='one', to=c('eta_1', 'eta_2'), arrows=1,
    free=TRUE, values=c(44, 6), labels=c('alpha_1_c1', 'alpha_2_c1')),
```

```r
# ML Fit Function to run for each individual
mxFitFunctionML(vector=TRUE)
) # close model for class 1

class2 <- mxModel(class1,
# latent means
mxPath(from='one', to=c('eta_1', 'eta_2'), arrows=1,
free=TRUE, values=c(65, 15), labels=c('alpha_1_c2', 'alpha_2_c2')),

name='Class2') # close model

classRP <- mxMatrix('Full', 2, 1, free=c(TRUE, FALSE),
values=1, lbound=0.001, labels=c('p1', 'p2'), name='RProps')

classP <- mxAlgebra(RProps %x% (1 / sum(RProps)), name='Props')

algObj <- mxAlgebra(-2* sum(log(Props[1,1] %x% Class1.objective + Props[2,1] %x% Class2.objective)),
name='mixtureObj')

obj <- mxFitFunctionAlgebra('mixtureObj')

gmm.2.means <- mxModel('2Class Means Growth Mixture Model',
mxData(observed=ecls_wide, type='raw'),
class1, class2, classRP, classP, algObj, obj)

gmm.2.means.fit <- mxRun(gmm.2.means)

summary(gmm.2.means.fit)
```

function when using type='RAM' because it is automatically generated. However, finite mixture models require that every row of our data have its own likelihood, so we have to request this from the fit function. The vector=TRUE argument to mxFitFunctionML specifies that class1 return not a single likelihood value for the dataset, but a vector of likelihoods that will subsequently be combined.

The script continues by defining an object called class2 that houses the second class-specific growth model. The model specification begins by calling the class1 object, thereby defining the class2 model to be identical to the class1 model. Now, we only need to specify mxPath statements for the parameters that differ for the second class. In the means model (M2), this requires one mxPath statement to re-label the means of the latent variable intercept and slope, so that they end in _c2. In this statement, we provide starting values that are different from those in the class1 model. This completes the two class-specific model statements.

The next section of the script specifies the finite mixture part of the model. We begin by creating the object classRP that contains the relative class proportions. Using the mxMatrix function, we define the object as a full matrix with two rows and one column, a 2 × 1 matrix. The first element is labeled p1 and is freely estimated (free=TRUE), and the second element is labeled p2 and is not freely estimated (free=FALSE). The element p1 is given a starting value of 1 and a lower bound of 0.0001. The p2 element is fixed at 1. The parameter p1 represents the number of individuals classified into the first latent class for every one person classified into the second class. Thus, if p1 is estimated to be 2, then 66.6% of the sample is in the first class and 33.3% is in the second class. Starting p1 at 1 begins the iterative estimation routine with an equal proportion of individuals in each class. The matrix is named RProps. The mxAlgebra function is then used to convert the matrix of relative class proportions, RProps, to a matrix of absolute proportions, Props, by dividing the elements of RProps by its sum.

Now that all the necessary matrices are in place, we use them to specify the objective function for the two-class means (M2) GMM. For this, two objects are created. The mxAlgebra function is used to create an object, algObj, that specifies the −2 log likelihood (−2LL; objective function) for the mixture model. Specifically, the −2LL is calculated as −2 multiplied by the sum of the log of the class proportions multiplied by their respective class-specific objective functions (e.g., Props[1,1] %x% Class1.objective). This mxAlgebra is named mixtureObj, which is then used with mxFitFunctionAlgebra to formally define the algebraic function used for model estimation. Finally, all the pieces are put together using mxModel, such that gmm.2.means is an object that links together the name of the model, raw data, class-specific models, class proportions, and the objective function. The full model is run using the mxRun function, and the output is displayed using the summary function.

As in the previous chapter, small modifications are needed to specify Models M3 and M4 and models with more than two classes. The means and covariances model (M3) is specified by including an additional class-specific statement in the class2 object: mxPath(from=c('eta_1','eta_2'), arrows=2, connect='unique.pairs', free=TRUE, values=c(40,7,3), labels=c('psi_11_c2','psi_12_c2', 'psi_22_c2')), which allows the latent variable variances and covariance to vary over classes. For the means, covariances, and residual variances model (M4), an mxPath statement for the residual variances is added to the class2 object: mxPath(from= c('wght1','wght2','wght3','wght4'), arrows=2, free=TRUE, values=6, labels='theta_c2'). Additional latent classes can be included by adding more class-specific models (e.g., class3), where parameters allowed to differ for that class are specified and designated with class-specific labels (e.g., alpha_1_c3); modifying the classRP object to be a $K \times 1$ matrix, where K is the number of latent classes; expanding the objective function (algObj) to include the additional classes in the likelihood function; and adding class-specific objects to the mxModel statement (e.g., class3). The flexibility of OpenMx allows for the specification of the full array of models.

The output from Mplus and OpenMx for the two-class linear growth mixture model with latent variable means allowed to differ across latent classes (M2) is shown in Outputs 7.1 and 7.2. The extensive output from Mplus begins with model fit information, including the number of free parameters, log likelihood value, and a listing of information criteria. The information criteria (e.g., AIC, BIC, and sample size adjusted BIC) are commonly used to evaluate the relative fit of mixture models. We return to our recommendations to evaluate model fit later in the chapter. Next, Mplus provides estimates of the number of individuals in each latent class. Classification information is provided in three different ways. First, classification information is provided based on the ESTIMATED MODEL. Here, the estimated class proportions are based directly on the estimated model parameters—specifically the mean of the latent class variable (reported later in the output as the mean of C#1). Second, classification information is based on the ESTIMATED POSTERIOR PROBABILITIES. Each individual has an *estimated* posterior probability of class membership, and these estimated probabilities are summed together to estimate the total number of individuals in each class. Often, the estimates of class size based on the model and the posterior probabilities are very similar. Third, the estimated posterior probabilities are used to assign each individual to a single class based on their MOST LIKELY LATENT CLASS MEMBERSHIP. This ensures that any given individual is not *split* across classes, making the total number of individuals in each class a whole number (as would be the case in a multiple-group model with known group membership).

Information regarding the proportion of individuals in each class can be used to determine the substantive viability of a GMM. First, it is important to examine whether each latent class is a small set of *outliers* or a *viable* latent class. Some researchers have suggested that each latent class should contain at least 1% of the total sample for the latent class to be meaningful (Jung & Wickrama, 2008). Second, the three estimates of class size discussed should, ideally, produce very similar estimates. If the estimates diverge sharply, then confidence of class assignment is low and the results should be interpreted cautiously. In our example, the three estimates were all quite close, with class 1 containing approximately 91% of the sample and class 2 containing the remaining 9%. Provided the rest of the output looks good, this model appears to be viable because each class was well populated.

Output 7.1. `Mplus` Output for the Two-Class Means Model

```
MODEL FIT INFORMATION
Number of Free Parameters                          9
Loglikelihood
        H0 Value                          -11800.529
        H0 Scaling Correction Factor          8.727
           for MLR
Information Criteria
        Akaike (AIC)                        23619.058
        Bayesian (BIC)                      23663.945
        Sample - Size Adjusted BIC          23635.359
           (n* = (n + 2) / 24)
```

```
FINAL CLASS COUNTS AND PROPORTIONS FOR THE LATENT CLASSES BASED ON THE
ESTIMATED MODEL
    Latent
    Classes
        1         990.61361         0.91469
        2          92.38639         0.08531
```

```
FINAL CLASS COUNTS AND PROPORTIONS FOR THE LATENT CLASS PATTERNS BASED
ON ESTIMATED POSTERIOR PROBABILITIES
    Latent
    Classes
        1         990.61370         0.91469
        2          92.38630         0.08531
```

```
CLASSIFICATION OF INDIVIDUALS BASED ON THEIR MOST LIKELY LATENT CLASS
MEMBERSHIP
Class Counts and Proportions
    Latent
    Classes
        1              994         0.91782
        2               89         0.08218
```

```
CLASSIFICATION QUALITY
Entropy                               0.944
```

```
Average Latent Class Probabilities for Most Likely Latent Class Member-
ship (Row) by Latent Class (Column)
           1        2
    1   0.990    0.010
    2   0.077    0.923
```

```
MODEL RESULTS
```

	Estimate	S.E.	Est./S.E.	Two-Tailed P-Value
Latent Class 1				
ETA_1 WITH				
ETA_2	6.694	1.210	5.531	0.000
Means				
ETA_1	44.060	0.230	191.526	0.000
ETA_2	5.818	0.130	44.662	0.000

```
Variances
    ETA_1        40.082     2.737      14.644       0.000
    ETA_2         3.117     1.351       2.308       0.021
Residual Variances
    WGHT1         5.574     1.344       4.147       0.000
    ...
    WGHT4         5.574     1.344       4.147       0.000

Latent Class 2
ETA_1    WITH
    ETA_2         6.694     1.210       5.531       0.000
Means
    ETA_1        64.305     2.518      25.537       0.000
    ETA_2        15.301     0.704      21.744       0.000
Variances
    ETA_1        40.082     2.737      14.644       0.000
    ETA_2         3.117     1.351       2.308       0.021
Residual Variances
    WGHT1         5.574     1.344       4.147       0.000
    ...
    WGHT4         5.574     1.344       4.147       0.000

Categorical Latent Variables
Means
    C#1           2.372     0.187      12.694       0.000

TECHNICAL 11 OUTPUT
    Random Starts Specifications for the k-1 Class Analysis Model
            Number of initial stage random starts            10
            Number of final stage optimizations               2
    VUONG-LO-MENDELL-RUBIN LIKELIHOOD RATIO TEST FOR 1 (H0) VERSUS
    2 CLASSES
            H0 Loglikelihood Value                     -11994.423
            2 Times the Loglikelihood Difference          387.789
            Difference in the Number of Parameters              3
            Mean                                          -24.775
            Standard Deviation                            146.841
            P-Value                                        0.0043
    LO-MENDELL-RUBIN ADJUSTED LRT TEST
            Value                                         370.132
            P-Value                                        0.0052

TECHNICAL 14 OUTPUT
    PARAMETRIC BOOTSTRAPPED LIKELIHOOD RATIO TEST FOR 1 (H0) VERSUS 2
    CLASSES
            H0 Loglikelihood Value                     -11994.423
            2 Times the Loglikelihood Difference          387.789
            Difference in the Number of Parameters              3
            Approximate P-Value                            0.0000
            Successful Bootstrap Draws                          5
```

Output 7.2. `OpenMx` Output for the Two-Class Means Model

```
free parameters:
         name      matrix    row      col    Estimate  Std.Error lbound ubound
1          p1      RProps      1        1  10.722685  1.4383818  0.001
2       theta   Class1.S  wght1    wght1   5.574039  0.1757217
3      psi_11   Class1.S  eta_1    eta_1  40.082067  2.1323574
4      psi_12   Class1.S  eta_1    eta_2   6.694213  0.6425100
5      psi_22   Class1.S  eta_2    eta_2   3.117379  0.4613173
6  alpha_1_c1   Class1.M      1    eta_1  44.060436  0.2233393
7  alpha_2_c1   Class1.M      1    eta_2   5.818469  0.1006631
8  alpha_1_c2   Class2.M      1    eta_1  64.305698  1.0543901
9  alpha_2_c2   Class2.M      1    eta_2  15.300968  0.3768798

observed statistics: 4141
estimated parameters: 9
degrees of freedom: 4132
-2 log likelihood: 23601.06
number of observations: 1083

Information Criteria:
      df Penalty Parameters Penalty   Sample-Size Adjusted
AIC   15337.058              23619.06                    NA
BIC   -5271.252              23663.95               23635.36
```

Next, a measure of CLASSIFICATION QUALITY called *entropy* is reported. In this context, the entropy statistic ranges from 0 and 1, with higher values indicating the classes are more easily distinguished. Higher values are better, with some researchers suggesting that models with entropy values less than 0.80 should not be considered further. In our example, entropy was 0.94, supporting the notion that the classes identified in this model were easy to distinguish. Finally, `Mplus` provides the average latent class probabilities for each class. These values are based on the estimated posterior probabilities and are calculated by first assigning individuals to a class and then calculating the average probability of membership for each class. Here, the average probability of membership in class 1 for individuals who would be assigned to class 1 based on their posterior probabilities was 0.99. In complement, the average probability of membership in class 2 for individuals who would be assigned to class 2 was 0.92. These values, also above 0.80, confirm that classification was relatively easy. In sum, all the fit information discussed thus far suggests that the two classes in this model were relatively easy to distinguish and that individuals were classified into their respective classes with a high level of confidence.

In the next section of output, the parameter estimates for each class are provided in the MODEL RESULTS. As with the output from multiple-group models, parameter estimates are displayed separately for each class. An important first check is whether there are any out-of-bound parameter estimates (e.g., negative variances). Given the complexity of GMMs and the exploratory nature of the search procedure, out-of-bound parameter estimates are common.

When they appear, the model should be discarded.[2] In our illustrative example, model parameters are all in-bounds. Parameter estimates for class 1 describe a growth trajectory with a mean intercept of 44.06 and a mean slope equal to 5.82 pounds per year. Parameter estimates for class 2 describe a growth trajectory with a mean intercept of 64.31 and a mean slope of 15.30 pounds per year. Substantively, the first class might be considered a *normative* group because it contained 91% of the sample. In complement, the second class might be considered an *at-risk* group because this class had a higher mean weight in the fall of kindergarten and had a mean rate of change that was more than twice the rate of the *normative* group. The remaining parameters were specified as invariant across classes and thus describe characteristics of both groups. The covariance parameters describe the magnitude of between-child differences in the growth trajectory for members of the same class. The variances of the intercept (40.08) and slope (3.12) were both significant, indicating there were individual differences in the growth trajectories within each class. The intercept–slope covariance (6.69) was positive and significant, indicating that children who weighed more in the fall of kindergarten tended to gain more weight over time than children (in the same class) who weighed less in the fall of kindergarten. The residual variance (5.57) was also significant, indicating the magnitude of individual fluctuations around the predicted linear trajectories. Finally, the output provides the estimated mean of the latent class variable. Labeled as C#1, this parameter is in the logit (log-odds) metric and describes the proportion of individuals in each class. Here, the mean of the latent class variable for class 1 (#1) was 2.37, representing a point on the logit scale that can be transformed into a probability or proportion. A logit of 2.37 equals .915, the proportion of the sample that was classified in class 1; that is, $1/[1 + exp(-2.37)] = .915$. This point estimate has a standard error (0.187), which can be used to calculate a confidence interval around the proportion of individuals classified into each class.

The final sections of the `Mplus` output include the likelihood ratio tests produced by the `TECH11` and `TECH14` outputs. These likelihood ratio tests, with their associated *p*-values, compare the fitted model with K classes ($K = 2$ in our example) to a model with $K - 1$ classes. P-values that are less than .05 indicate that the model with K classes fit significantly better than the model with $K - 1$ classes. In our example, the *p*-values for both the Vuong–Lo–Mendell–Rubin and parametric bootstrapped likelihood ratio tests were less than .05, indicating that the two-class linear GMM with latent variable means (M2) allowed to differ across latent classes fit better than a one-class model. Note that these tests are used to compare models of the same type (i.e., different number of classes within means, M2; means and covariances, M3; or means, covariances, and residual variances, M4), but are not used to compare models of different types (e.g., a three-class M2 to a two-class M3 model). As will be covered below, comparison across different types of models is done with information criteria, classification quality, and the substantive interpretation of model parameters.

The output from `OpenMx` begins with parameter estimates. The first parameter, `p1`, is the *relative* proportion of children classified into class 1 compared to class 2. Following

---

[2]Although these models should be discarded, the results of such models may suggest the estimation of additional models.

the specification for the Rprops matrix given above, the estimate indicates that for every child in class 2, there were 10.72 children in class 1. As per the specification of the Props matrix, the relative proportion is converted to the proportion of children in each class and yields 91.5% of the sample in class 1—matching the proportion reported in Mplus. Next, the parameter estimates for each class are reported. The matrix associated with each parameter designates whether the parameter is for the first (e.g., class1.M) or second class (e.g., class2.M). Parameters that are not class specific are reported as coming from the lower numbered class. Based on our specification, the latent variable variances and covariances, as well as the residual variances were invariant over classes. Thus, the estimates of these parameters are reported as coming from class 1 (i.e., class1.).

We begin our discussion of model parameters with the means of the intercept and slope. The OpenMx output lists these estimates as coming from the Class1.M and Class2.M vectors. The mean intercept (alpha_1_c1) and slope (alpha_2_c1) for class 1 were 44.06 and 5.82, respectively. Thus, class one contained approximately 91.5% of the sample and had a mean weight of 44.06 pounds in the fall of kindergarten and gained 5.82 pounds per year, on average. The mean intercept (alpha_1_c2) and slope (alpha_2_c2) for class 2 were 64.31 and 15.30, respectively. Thus, the second class, which contained 8.5% of the sample, had a mean weight of 64.31 pounds in the fall of kindergarten and gained 15.30 pounds per year, on average. The class-invariant parameters included the residual variance (theta), which equaled 5.57; the intercept variance (psi_11), which equaled 40.08; the variance of the slope (psi_22), which equaled 3.11; and the covariance between the intercept and slope (psi_12), which equaled 6.69. These values are designated as coming from the Class1.S matrix; however, following the model specification, these parameters apply to both classes. The final section of the OpenMx output summarizes model fit by reporting the –2LL and information criteria (AIC, BIC, and sample-size adjusted BIC). Classification summaries and the entropy statistic can be calculated but are not provided automatically.

MODEL FIT, MODEL COMPARISON, AND CLASS ENUMERATION

Our objective in using GMMs is to identify groups with different change trajectories. The grouping variable is unmeasured and extracted in an exploratory way. Many models are fit, and the best (i.e., most likely) model for the data is selected. In our ECLS-K child weight example, we fit three different types of GMMs: means, M2; means and covariances, M3; and means, covariances, and residuals, M4. Within each model type, we fit models with a different number of classes, starting with two-class models, and increased the number of latent classes incrementally (three-class, four-class, etc.) until the BIC plateaued or convergence issues were encountered. Fit statistics from all models fit are organized into a table, which is then used to select the model that provides the best representation of the data. For our example, we report all fit information obtained from Mplus in Table 7.1.

Model selection is probably the most controversial and debated issue in mixture modeling. The straightforward comparisons that we did in the multiple-groups framework,

TABLE 7.1. Model Fit Information for the Linear Growth Mixture Models Applied to ECLS-K Weight Data

Fit statistic	Linear growth (M1 model)	Means (M2 models)			Means and covariances (M3 models)		Means, covariances, and residual variances (M4 models)	
		Two-class	Three-class	Four-class*	Two-class*	Three-class*	Two-class	Three-class*
Class proportions	1.00	.91/.09	.89/.09/.02	.89/.09/.02/.00	.76/.24	.66/.30/.03	.76/.24	.62/.34/.04
AIC	24,001	23,619	23,425	23,400	23,166	23,090	21,986	21,658
BIC	24,031	23,664	23,485	23,475	23,226	23,180	22,052	21,758
ABIC	24,012	23,635	23,447	23,427	23,188	23,122	22,010	21,695
Entropy	–	.94	.95	.96	.69	.71	.81	.76
VLMR p-value	–	<.01	.08	.53	.02	.04	<.01	<.01
LMR p-value	–	<.01	.09	.53	.02	.04	<.01	<.01
Bootstrap p-value	–	<.01	<.01	<.01	<.01	<.01	<.01	<.01

Note. Asterisks indicate convergence issues were encountered.

when the grouping variable was measured, are not appropriate. Although models with a different number of latent classes are nested, differences in –2LL cannot be used for comparison and model selection. Thus, debates have ensued. Different researchers, using a variety of different simulation conditions to study the problem of model selection in finite mixture models, have favored the use of (and highlighted the limitations of) different fit statistics, including the LMR LRT (noted in Muthén, 2003), the Bayesian information criterion (BIC; Nylund, Asparouhov, & Muthén, 2007), the sample size adjusted BIC (Enders & Tofighi, 2008; Henson, Reise, & Kim, 2007; Tofighi & Enders, 2007), and the bootstrap likelihood ratio test (BLRT; Nylund, Asparouhov, & Muthén, 2007). Our recommendation is to consider all available fit information when selecting a model and to supplement this information with substantive knowledge of the phenomena being studied (see also Muthén, 2003). In our experience, the different indices (e.g., BIC, BLRT) rarely point to a single model. The information must be considered as a whole, and the process of model selection should be described clearly, especially when defending the choice of the *best model* in a manuscript. Our model selection process follows the steps described by Ram and Grimm (2009).

First, we examine model convergence. As noted by asterisks in Table 7.1, several models did not properly converge. The four-class means model, the two- and three-class means and covariances models, and the three-class means, covariances, and residual variances model all had parameters that were out of bounds. In most cases, the variance of the intercept or slope was negative in one or more of the classes. Thus, these models are set aside. Second, we examine the information criteria: BIC, AIC, and sample size adjusted BIC. Generally, the BIC, because it imposes a harsher penalty for model complexity, is preferred to the AIC for model comparison. One approach to examining the BIC (or other information criteria) is to plot its value against the number of classes for the different types of models (similar to a scree plot). BICs for the models fit are graphically presented in Figure 7.5. Following the lines, it is evident that the relative change in the BIC was large when moving from one to two classes for all models fit. The amount of change gets smaller when moving from the two- to three-class models. This suggests that the complexity of the three-class and four-class models may not be necessary. The information criteria suggest that the two-class models should be further evaluated.

Third, we examine the likelihood ratio tests. These tests provide additional information for model selection within model type (e.g., M2 models). For example, the likelihood ratio tests for the means (M2) models indicate that the two-class model is preferred to the one-class model (all $ps < .01$). Looking at whether the three-class model is preferred to the two-class model, we see that the p-values for the VLMR LRT and the LMRa LRT indicate that the three-class means (M2) model did not fit significantly better than the two-class model (p-values greater than .05); however, the bootstrap likelihood ratio test favored the three-class over the two-class model. Similarly, the likelihood ratio tests for the two-class means, covariances, and residual variances (M4) model indicated that the two-class model was favored over the single class model (all $ps < .01$). Although the likelihood ratio tests also suggest that the three-class model was favored over the two-class model (all $ps < .01$), the

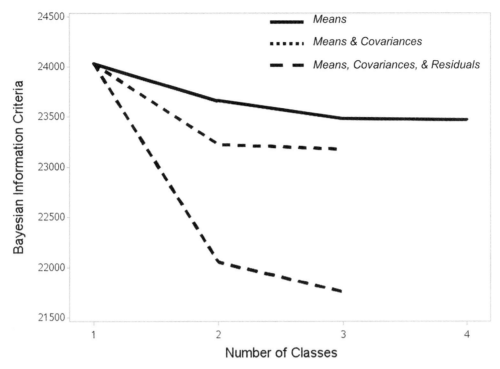

FIGURE 7.5. BIC plotted against the number of classes.

three-class model was already set aside because of convergence issues. Due to the various likelihood ratio tests, two models remain under consideration: the two-class means (M2) model and the two-class means, covariances, and residual variances (M4) model. Fourth, we examine the entropy statistic. Generally, models with greater confidence of classification are preferred. The two-class means (M2) model had an entropy of .94 and the two-class means, covariances, and residual variances (M4) model had an entropy of .81. Both are acceptable (e.g., entropy > .80) and therefore both models remain viable, but the entropy statistic was stronger for two-class means (M2) model.

Finally, we look back at all the statistical fit information and weigh the pros and cons along with substantive considerations. The two-class means (M2) model had higher entropy (0.94 vs. 0.81). The two-class means, covariances, and residual variances (M4) model had lower information criteria (e.g., BIC of 22,052 vs. 23,664). There is no right answer. Arguments for selecting either model are easily made, and each model is defensible. Examination of parameter estimates from a substantive perspective highlight differences between the two classes uncovered from the models. The two-class means model separates a homogeneous small class of individuals (9% of the sample) with higher weights at kindergarten entrance and more rapid weight gain over time. The variances of the intercept and slope, intercept–slope covariance, and residual variance were invariant over classes for the two-class means model. Thus, the classes are the same in terms of magnitude of between-person differences in the intercept and slope and the average amount of weight fluctuation over time around the predicted trajectory. In the two-class means, covariances, and residual variances model, the minority group was larger, containing 24% of the sample. Children likely to be in this class were heavier in kindergarten and gained more weight over time, on average. Additionally, the variances of the intercept and slope were much larger for this class. Thus, children in this class varied greatly in their weights at kindergarten entrance and their rate of weight change. Furthermore, a defining feature of this class was their larger residual variance, indicating that children likely to be in this class had a lot of weight fluctuation over time. Highlighting the importance of entropy and the easier to consume substantive interpretation, we selected the two-class means (M2) model as the most appropriate representation of the between-person differences in weight changes from the beginning of kindergarten through the end of first grade.

Parameter estimates from this model are shown in Table 7.2. Class 1 contained the majority, 91%, of the sample (n_1 = 990.61) and is referred to as the *normative* group. The mean weight for children in this class at the beginning of kindergarten was 44.06 pounds, and the mean rate of change was 5.82 pounds per year. Class 2 contained 9% of the sample and is referred to as the *minority* group. Children in this class had a mean weight at the beginning of kindergarten of 64.31 pounds and a mean rate of growth equal to 15.30 pounds per year. In both classes, there were significant between-person differences in the intercept (40.08) and slope (3.12) and a positive covariance (6.69; $r = 0.58$) between the two, indicating that children who weighed more at the beginning of kindergarten tended to gain more weight between the beginning of kindergarten and the end of first grade compared to other children in the same class. The residual variance was 5.57 indicating a small amount of individual fluctuation around the linear growth trajectories.

To visualize the trajectories for the two classes, we plotted the mean trajectories for each class as well as the 95% confidence bounds on the magnitude of between-person differences for each class in Figure 7.6. Here we can see that the two classes show slight overlap—a positive sign that the classes are sufficiently different from one another. Not only were their mean trajectories different from one another, but the percent overlap in their distribution at any measurement occasion was small. Researchers often plot mean trajectories to examine the size of the differences between classes; however, researchers

TABLE 7.2. Parameter Estimates for the Two-Class Means Model

Parameter	Class 1	Class 2
nc	990.61	92.39
α_1	44.06	64.31
α_2	5.82	15.30
ψ_{11}	40.08	40.08
ψ_{22}	3.12	3.12
ψ_{21}	6.69	6.69
θ_{tt}	5.57	5.57

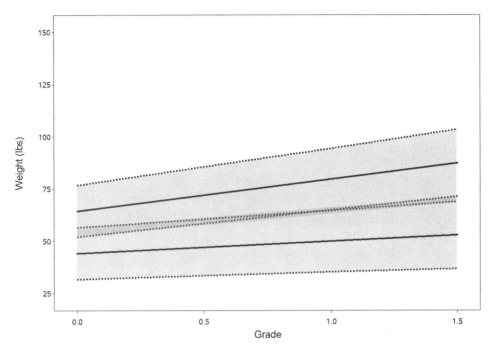

FIGURE 7.6. Predicted class trajectories from the chosen two-class growth mixture model.

should consider the magnitude of between-person differences in the growth trajectories within each class as was done here. This approach ensures that the amount of overlap between classes is shown and not hidden.

IMPORTANT CONSIDERATIONS

Approaching Growth Mixture Models

GMMs are extremely useful for exploring and describing longitudinal data; however, they must be approached carefully and with a high degree of thought and precaution. In preparation, it is important to examine univariate and bivariate descriptive statistics and plots—and to develop preliminary ideas about what may emerge from this exploration. These ideas can be developed based on the literature, previous examinations of the same data, and/or newly obtained descriptive statistics and plots. The general principle is to know as much as possible about the phenomena and the data before engaging in model fitting. Not only will one avoid garbage-in, garbage-out pitfalls, but interpretation of results will be easier. When the preliminaries are done and it is time to fit the GMMs, we recommend fitting multiple types of models (means, M2; means and covariances, M3; means, covariances, and residuals, M4) and increasing the number of classes (within each type of model) until the information criteria plateau or convergence problems are encountered. This approach provides a systematic and defensible strategy for obtaining a robust understanding of how many latent classes there may be and how those latent classes may differ with respect to each aspect of the growth model, while avoiding the potential overabundance of useless models. In our experience, this search often provokes consideration of additional alternative models, tailored to the specifics of the phenomenon and data. For example, if the parameters of a two-class means and covariances model describe one class having a linear slope mean near 0 *and* a linear slope variance near 0, we would be provoked to formulate and explore the viability of a two-class model where one class follows a linear growth trajectory and the second class follows an intercept-only model. Although rarely formulated at the outset (unless following previous findings), GMMs where the class-specific models differ in form (e.g., with and without linear slope factor) provide extremely useful, tailored descriptions of many phenomena. Through thoughtful and careful consideration of the exploratory process, one may find some real gems.

Pitfalls in Growth Mixture Modeling

When fitting mixture models, it is important to look out for and avoid common stumbling blocks. Four pitfalls, in particular, can induce high levels of frustration and eat lots of time. First, the uncertainty embedded in the mixture and the enormity of possible class assignments mean that GMM solutions are notoriously unstable. Often, the estimation routines working toward the optimal solution get stuck at local maxima in the likelihood function. Thus, parameter estimates can be very sensitive to starting values, making it important to fit each model several times with different sets of starting values in order to determine whether the optimal solution has been found. By default, Mplus uses 10 sets of random starting values when fitting mixture models, reports the log likelihoods obtained from each of those runs, and provides a warning when the best log likelihood was not replicated—an indication that the results are dependent on the starting values. When such problems arise, the number of random sets of starting values should be increased using the STARTS command, and the viability of the solution checked carefully. Multiple runs with different starting values can be implemented in OpenMx with some additional code (details on the website).

Second, as represented in Figure 7.1, mixture models seek to describe the shape of an overall distribution as a collection of normal distributions. In essence, skewness and kurtosis are re-represented as a collection of discrete classes (see Grimm et al., 2013). Different classes will be identified depending on the shape of distribution. Often, GMMs are specified with the (implicit) assumption that the residuals are normally distributed within each class. This assumption may not be realistic, particularly when working with binary, ordinal, or count variables (e.g., smoking behavior). Misspecifying the distribution of the repeatedly measured outcomes when fitting GMMs is especially problematic because it may lead to the identification of spurious classes (see Bauer & Curran, 2003). Luckily, as will be discussed in a later chapter, outcome variables with many types of non-normal distributions (e.g., Bernoulli, Poisson) can be accommodated using the appropriately selected link function (see Muthén & Asparouhov, 2009). Much time can be saved through careful examination of the raw data and thoughtful consideration of the underlying assumptions.

Third, care should be taken to accommodate or at least consider multiple types of change. Thus far, we have only discussed linear growth models and used GMMs to describe groups that follow different linear trajectories. In reality, though, individuals follow nonlinear trajectories. As we shall promote through the remainder of this book, this nonlinearity should be modeled. In the fitting of GMMs, this means that researchers should consider and examine whether groups differ in the *shape* or *pattern* of change. As mentioned briefly above, class-specific models may differ qualitatively in their pattern of change. For example, one class may exhibit exponential growth, whereas another class may exhibit quadratic change. Thus, the structure of change, the Λ matrix in the structural equation modeling specification, can be class specific. This flexibility allows for a wide variety of qualitative differences in the ways in which change unfolds over time. Accommodating those differences may lead to quite different conclusions than those reached if only considering linear models. Some examples of nonlinear growth mixture modeling can be found in McArdle and Nesselroade (2003), Kaplan and Sweetman (2006), Ram and Grimm (2009), Grimm, Ram, and Estabrook (2010), and Li et al. (2001).

Fourth, care should be taken when deciding how and when to include covariates as predictors or outcomes of class membership. Generally, once an unmeasured latent class variable has been identified, we would like to examine if and how class membership is related to other constructs. For example, a next step in our examination of the changes in children's weight is whether the normative versus the at-risk classification is related to birthweight, gender, or later behavior (e.g., substance use). The issue is that the addition of covariates into the model can significantly affect the type of classes found as well as class membership. That is, classification in a model with covariates may look substantially different than classification based only on the longitudinal trajectories. Knowing this problem, researchers have proposed a number of potential solutions. Some researchers (e.g., Li & Hser, 2011; Lubke & Muthén, 2007; Muthén, 2004) have recommended using the model with covariates when determining the appropriate number of latent classes, whereas others (e.g., Tofighi & Enders, 2007) have argued that class enumeration should be done without covariates. Generally, we advocate using the latter approach because we are assured that the latent classes are based on the longitudinal trajectories and not the covariates. The covariates can then be added and examined in a separate, postclassification analysis while tracking and evaluating the consistency of classification at each step. Recently, this has become easier as several multistep procedures have been proposed for evaluating the effects of covariates without having them affect class membership (Vermunt, 2010). A recent simulation study (Asparouhov & Muthén, 2013) has demonstrated the viability and utility of these approaches.

The recommended approach has three steps, though in some programs these happen behind the scenes. First, the latent class or mixture model is estimated without covariates. Second, individual probabilities of class membership estimated from the latent class posterior probabilities are used to classify individuals into one or another class, while retaining knowledge of the uncertainty of that classification (in principle, the standard error of that classification). Third, a new latent class model is formulated that examines the relations among the covariates and the latent class variable. In this model, the latent class variable is indicated with uncertainty by the assigned class variable (obtained in Step 2). Thus, the effects of covariates can be studied while both assuring that the latent class variable is only derived from the repeated measures and the uncertainty inherent in the classification is taken into consideration. Implementation of this procedure is available in Mplus using the AUXILIARY command.

MOVING FORWARD

GMMs are extremely useful for understanding and describing between-person differences in within-person change. In the subsequent chapters, we discuss various types of multivariate change models, nonlinear change models, modeling of non-normal outcomes, modeling change in latent entities, and latent difference score models. GMMs can be combined with all of these models to understand between-person differences in various aspects of change as well as leading and lagging indicators in the study of multivariate change. We encourage you to consider the possibilities of GMMs in combination with the various models discussed in the remainder of the book.

8

Multivariate Growth Models and Dynamic Predictors

Developmental processes rarely unfold in isolation. Thus, researchers often wish to study two or more constructs over time attempting to understand their joint development and the way the constructs and their changes are related over time. A variety of statistical models have been proposed to simultaneously study change in multiple entities, and we cover two models in this chapter. The first, termed the *multivariate growth model* (MGM; also referred to as a parallel process and correlated growth model; McArdle, 1988), examines the interrelations of two distinct growth processes. The second, called the *growth model with time-varying covariate* (TVC), estimates the effect a time-varying variable has on the scores while simultaneously modeling change in those scores with a growth model. The time-varying variable is often referred to as a *dynamic* predictor because its value changes over time. These models are commonplace in developmental research and answer specific questions regarding the associations between two or more simultaneously changing entities (see Grimm, 2007) as well as associations among changes for related individuals (e.g., husbands and wives).

Choosing between the MGM and the TVC (or any statistical model) depends on the research question and the ability to properly estimate model parameters given the available data. With bivariate panel data, either model can be fit, but each model provides information for specific research questions and the models should be applied thoughtfully to ensure model assumptions are tenable and meaningful information can be obtained. To demonstrate the use of each, we extend the prior example that examined longitudinal changes in mathematics achievement with data collected from the NLSY-CYA (Center for Human Resource Research, 2004). Here, we expand the example with two separate illustrations to *simultaneously* investigate mathematics achievement and two other repeatedly measured variables. The first is the child's level of *hyperactivity*, which was measured concurrently with mathematics achievement. The second is the *season* of the assessment, a dichotomous variable indicating whether the assessment occurred in the fall or spring of the school year. Note that these two additional variables differ in important ways and were specifically chosen to illustrate differences between the models discussed in the chapter. Greater details about these differences are discussed at the conclusion of the chapter after the two models are presented.

MULTILEVEL MODELING FRAMEWORK

Multivariate Growth Model

The MGM examines individual changes in each repeatedly measured variable and allows the growth factors (i.e., intercepts and slopes) and unique factors to covary between constructs. With two repeatedly measured variables, the level-1 equation for the MGM can be written as

$$y_{ti} = b_{1i} + b_{2i} \cdot \left(\frac{t - k_1}{k_2} \right) + u_{ti}$$

$$x_{ti} = h_{1i} + h_{2i} \cdot \left(\frac{t - k_3}{k_4} \right) + s_{ti}$$

(8.1)

where y_{ti} and x_{ti} are the observed scores at time t for individual i, b_{1i} and h_{1i} are the random intercepts, or predicted scores of y_{ti} and x_{ti} for individual i when $t - k_1 = t - k_3 = 0$, b_{2i} and h_{2i} are the random slopes for individual i representing the predicted linear rate of change in y_{ti} and x_{ti} (scaled in terms of t/k_2 and t/k_4), respectively, t is the original metric of time, and u_{ti} and s_{ti} are time-specific residual scores for y_{ti} and x_{ti}, respectively. The level-1 residual scores are assumed to follow multivariate normal distributions, often with constant variance across time and a constant within-time covariance,

$$u_{ti},\ s_{ti} \sim MVN \left(\begin{bmatrix} 0 \\ 0 \end{bmatrix}, \begin{bmatrix} \sigma_u^2 & \\ \sigma_{s,u} & \sigma_s^2 \end{bmatrix} \right)$$

The constants, k_1 and k_3, center the intercepts, and k_2 and k_4 scale the slopes. Often, $k_1 = k_3$ to center the random intercepts at a common point in time (e.g., second grade) and $k_2 = k_4$ to scale the slopes in the same metric (e.g., years).

The level-2 equation for the random intercepts and slopes is written as

$$\begin{aligned} b_{1i} &= \beta_1 + d_{1i} \\ b_{2i} &= \beta_2 + d_{2i} \\ h_{1i} &= \alpha_1 + f_{1i} \\ h_{2i} &= \alpha_2 + f_{2i} \end{aligned}$$

(8.2)

where β_1 and α_1 are the means of the random intercepts, β_2 and α_2 are the means for the random slopes, d_{1i} and f_{1i} are individual deviations from their respective mean intercepts, and d_{2i} and f_{2i} are individual deviations from their respective mean slopes. Individual deviations are assumed to follow a multivariate normal distribution with zero means, estimated variances, and covariances,

$$
d_{1i}, d_{2i}, f_{1i}, f_{2i} \sim MVN \left(\begin{bmatrix} 0 \\ 0 \\ 0 \\ 0 \end{bmatrix}, \begin{bmatrix} \sigma_{d1}^2 & & & \\ \sigma_{d2,d1} & \sigma_{d2}^2 & & \\ \sigma_{f1,d1} & \sigma_{f1,d2} & \sigma_{f1}^2 & \\ \sigma_{f2,d1} & \sigma_{f2,d2} & \sigma_{f2,f1} & \sigma_{f2}^2 \end{bmatrix} \right)
$$

The additional pieces of information provided by the MGM, beyond when univariate growth models are fit to each process separately, are the covariances between the intercepts and slopes across constructs and the covariance among the residuals within time. Of particular interest is the covariance between the random slopes ($\sigma_{f2,d2}$) because this parameter indicates whether changes in the first construct are associated with changes in the second. Additionally, this covariance is the only covariance that remains invariant when the intercepts are centered at different points in time. That is, different values for k_1 and k_3 will lead to different estimates for all covariances in the matrix above *except* $\sigma_{f2,d2}$ (Rogosa & Willett, 1985). Nevertheless, the remaining covariances provide additional information regarding the joint development of the two constructs. The covariance between the intercepts indicates the sign and strength of association between the predicted scores of the constructs at a specific point in time depending on the location of the intercepts. If the intercepts are centered at second grade, the covariance between the intercepts indicates the degree to which predicted scores covary in second grade. The two remaining cross construct latent variable covariances are intercept–slope covariances and indicate the degree to which the predicted values in the first construct at the location of the intercept are associated with linear changes in the second construct over the observation period, and vice versa.

The last piece of additional information from the MGM is the covariance among the residual scores ($\sigma_{s,u}$), which represents the degree to which perturbations from the smooth predicted trajectories are associated with one another at any given point in time. This covariance is needed to capture covariability that is unique or specific to the measurement occasion. For example, if a participant recently failed a test in school, he or she may not show his or her typical performance on a variety of tests/surveys at that measurement occasion. This would lead to a higher degree of covariance between scores collected during that measurement occasion than would be expected. Additionally, this extra degree of covariance would only affect scores at this measurement occasion and would not be carried by the associations among the intercepts and slopes.

Time-Varying Covariate Model

The TVC model examines change in one construct while accounting for a secondary variable that also changes with time—the time-varying covariate. The TVC model can be written as

$$y_{ti} = b_{1i} + b_{2i} \cdot \left(\frac{t - k_1}{k_2} \right) + b_3 \cdot x_{ti} + u_{ti} \tag{8.3}$$

where y_{ti} is the outcome of interest measured at time t for individual i, b_{1i} is the random intercept for individual i conditional on x_{ti}, the time-varying covariate, b_{2i} is the random slope for individual i conditional on x_{ti}, t is the original metric of time, k_1 and k_2 are constants chosen to center the intercept and scale the slope, b_3 is the effect of the time-varying covariate, and u_{ti} is the time-dependent residual. The interpretation of the intercept and slope is complicated by the addition of the time-varying covariate. Now the intercept and slope are conditional upon the time-varying covariate (i.e., holding the time-varying covariate constant), as would be the case in a multiple regression model. In the multilevel specification of the TVC model, b_{1i} and b_{2i} are also forced to be uncorrelated with the time-varying covariate, x_{ti}, which can affect estimates obtained from the model if this assumption does not hold (Curran & Peterman, 2005).

Two additional specifications of the time-varying covariate model are worth mentioning. The first involves a lagged effect of the time-varying covariate. Specifically, x_{t-1i} can be included as the time-varying covariate instead of x_{ti}. Thus, instead of controlling for the current level of the time-varying covariate, one can control for the prior level of the time-varying covariate. One issue with this specification in the multilevel modeling framework is data incompleteness. Within the multilevel modeling framework, observations are dropped if an exogenous variable is incomplete. Thus, if an individual was assessed at time t, but not assessed at time $t - 1$, then the observation for this individual at time t will not be included when the model is estimated because the lagged time-varying covariate is incomplete. The second specification allows the effect of the time-varying covariate to vary with time. Thus, b_3 is replaced with b_{3t}. Estimation of this model is possible in the multilevel modeling framework as long as the data are balanced with respect to time—similar to how the data are set up for the growth model in the structural equation modeling framework (see Skibbe, Grimm, Bowles, & Morrison, 2012). To estimate this model, a series of dummy-coded variables are created to differentiate the measurement occasions from one another. For example, this model can be written as

$$y_{ti} = b_{1i} + b_{2i} \cdot \left(\frac{t - k_1}{k_2} \right) + b_{31} \cdot d_1 \cdot x_{ti} + \ldots + b_{3T} \cdot d_T \cdot x_{ti} + u_{ti} \tag{8.4}$$

where b_{31} is the effect of the time-varying covariate at the first occasion, d_1 is a dummy coded variable that takes on a value of 1 at the first occasion and 0 elsewhere, b_{3T} is the effect of the time-varying covariate at the last occasion (occasion T), d_T is a dummy-coded variable that takes on a value of 1 at the last occasion and 0 elsewhere, and x_{ti} is the time-varying covariate at the last occasion (see Skibbe et al., 2012).

MULTILEVEL MODELING IMPLEMENTATION

Multivariate Growth Model

Longitudinal changes in hyperactivity were jointly examined with longitudinal changes in mathematics to determine whether changes in hyperactivity were associated with changes in mathematics performance. Hyperactivity was measured through parental ratings on the Behavior Problems Index (Zill & Peterson, 1986). As a first step, individual changes in hyperactivity are plotted in Figure 8.1. Changes in hyperactivity are sharply different from changes observed for mathematics. Mathematics scores increased over time for most, if not all, children, whereas hyperactivity scores increased for some children, decreased for others, or remained relatively stable. At the sample level, there does not appear to be much mean change in hyperactivity from second through eighth grade.

To fit multivariate growth models in the multilevel modeling framework, the data need to be reorganized in such a way that there is a *single* variable that contains the outcome data for the two (or more) variables. This new dataset will have two rows for each

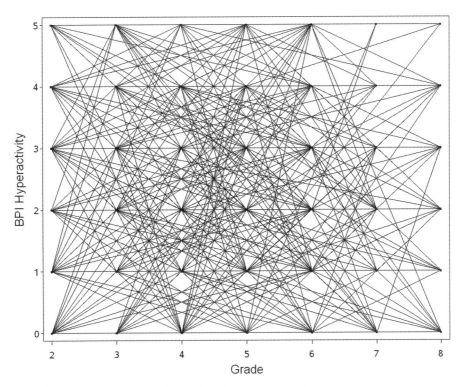

FIGURE 8.1. Longitudinal plot of the hyperactivity scores against grade.

person–occasion, such that the first outcome variable is on the first row and the second outcome variable is on the second row for a given person at a given occasion. Thus, the datafile for a bivariate growth model will be twice as long (i.e., twice as many rows) as the datafile used for a univariate growth model. Additionally, two dummy-coded variables are required to indicate whether the new variable is taking on the value of the first or second outcome. This design is similar to how multiple-group models were estimated in the previous chapter, where a dummy-coded variable indicated the low- and normal-birthweight groups. In fact, the data arrangement and model specification are highly similar for the multiple-group and bivariate growth models.

The SAS script to fit a bivariate linear growth model in NLMIXED is contained in Script 8.1. The script begins by restructuring the datafile to accommodate two outcome variables. A datastep creates the dataset multivariate. This datastep replaces each row with two rows. The first row contains the mathematics variable (var = math;), and the second contains the hyperactivity variable (var = hyp;). Both rows have dummy-coded variables, d_math and d_hyp, which indicate whether the variable, var, takes on the value of the mathematics or hyperactivity score. Lastly, var_num has a value of 1 for the mathematics measure and 2 for hyperactivity measure.[1] Variables that are carried over from the nlsy_math_long dataset and appear on both lines of the new dataset include id, grade, and age.

Within SAS, fitting the bivariate linear growth model begins by calling the NLMIXED procedure and multivariate datafile. Next, a combined level-1 and level-2 equation is specified without the level-1 residual. This equation has two parts—one for each outcome variable. The first part has d_math as a multiplier. Since d_math takes on a value of 1 for the *mathematics* variable, this part of the model is specific to the mathematics outcome. The model for mathematics is a linear growth model with beta_1 and beta_2 as fixed effects and d_1i and d_2i as random coefficients. The second part of the trajectory equation has d_hyp as a multiplier to indicate that this part of the model is specific to the *hyperactivity* variable. The model for hyperactivity is a linear growth model with alpha_1 and alpha_2 as fixed effects and f_1i and f_2i as random coefficients. The next part of the script contains two conditional statements to allow for two level-1 variances—one for each outcome. The level-1 residual, v_e, equals v_u for the mathematics variable (d_math = 1), and equals v_s for the hyperactivity variable (d_math = 0).

The MODEL and RANDOM statements follow. In the MODEL statement, the variable var is the outcome, which is assumed to be normally distributed with mean traject, from the combined level-1 and level-2 equation specified above, and residual variance v_e. The RANDOM statement contains the random coefficients of the linear growth model for mathematics followed by the random coefficients of the linear growth model for hyperactivity. These random coefficients have 0 means and a variance–covariance matrix as specified. In the variance–covariance matrix, we allow for variances of all random coefficients, intercept–slope covariances within each variable, and covariances of random coefficients across

---

[1] The var_num variable is only necessary in the PROC MIXED script available online.

Script 8.1. NLMIXED Script for the Bivariate Linear Growth Model

```
* Stacking data to fit a multivariate growth model;
DATA multivariate;
    SET nlsy_math_long;
    var = math;          d_math = 1;      d_hyp = 0;      var_num = 1;      OUTPUT;
    var = hyp;           d_math = 0;      d_hyp = 1;      var_num = 2;      OUTPUT;
    KEEP id grade age var d_math d_hyp;
RUN;

* Multivariate Growth Model;
PROC NLMIXED DATA = multivariate;
    traject = d_math * ((beta_1 + d_1i) + (beta_2 + d_2i) * (grade - 2)) +
              d_hyp * ((alpha_1 + f_1i) + (alpha_2 + f_2i) * (grade - 2));

    IF d_math = 1 THEN v_e = v_u;
    IF d_math = 0 THEN v_e = v_s;

    MODEL var ~ NORMAL(traject, v_e);

    RANDOM d_1i d_2i f_1i f_2i
              ~ NORMAL([0,0,0,0], [ v_d1,
                                    c_d2d1,   v_d2,
                                    c_f1d1,   c_f1d2,   v_f1,
                                    c_f2d1,   c_f2d2,   c_f2f1,   v_f2] )      SUBJECT = id;

    PARMS
    beta_1 = 35      beta_2 = 4           v_d1 = 65      v_d2 = .76      c_d2d1 = 0      v_u = 36.2
    alpha_1 = 2      alpha_2 = -.06       v_f1 = 1.6     v_f2 = .005     c_f2f1 = 0      v_s = 1.1
/* Bivariate Information */
    c_f1d1 = -3      c_f2d1 = 0           c_f1d2 = 0     c_f2d2 = 0;
RUN;
```

171

variables. As described above, this last set of covariances is the main added benefit of fitting the bivariate growth model over two univariate growth models—specifically, the covariance between the intercepts (c_f1d1), the covariance between the intercept for hyperactivity and slope for mathematics (c_f1d2), the covariance between the slope for hyperactivity and the intercept for mathematics (c_f2d1), and the covariance between the slopes (c_f2d2). Next, the subject identification variable is indicated (subject = id). Lastly, starting values are provided for all estimated parameters in the PARMS statement. We note that NLMIXED is unable to estimate the covariance between the level-1 residuals ($\sigma_{s,u}$). Thus, NLMIXED is able to produce unbiased estimates of model parameters when the residual covariance is zero (or near zero). If the residual covariance is sizable and different from zero, then NLMIXED will yield biased results or may fail to converge. PROC MIXED, the linear mixed-effects modeling procedure available through SAS, is able to estimate this parameter, and scripts for its use are available on our website.

The R script for fitting the bivariate linear growth model using nlme is contained in Script 8.2. The script begins by separating the dataset into two parts. The first dataset, called math, contains the mathematics data. This dataset contains the following variables: id, the child identification variable; var, which contains the mathematics scores;

Script 8.2. nlme Script for the Bivariate Linear Growth Model

```
# creating a multivariate form of the data
math <- data.frame(id      = nlsy_math_long$id,
                   var     = nlsy_math_long$math,
                   grade   = nlsy_math_long$grade,
                   d_math  = 1,
                   d_hyp   = 0,
                   grp     = 'math')

hyp <- data.frame(id      = nlsy_math_long$id,
                  var     = nlsy_math_long$hyp,
                  grade   = nlsy_math_long$grade,
                  d_math  = 0,
                  d_hyp   = 1,
                  grp     = 'hyp')

multivariate <- rbind(math, hyp)

# bivariate linear growth model
math.hyp.nlme<-nlme(var~d_math*(b_1i+b_2i*(grade-2))+
                 d_hyp*(h_1i+h_2i*(grade-2)),
            data = multivariate,
            fixed = b_1i+b_2i+h_1i+h_2i~1,
            random = b_1i+b_2i+h_1i+h_2i~1,
            group = ~id,
            start = c(35, 4, 1, -1),
            weights = varIdent(c(hyp =.3),
            form = ~1|grp),
            na.action = na.omit)

summary(math.hyp.nlme)
```

grade, the timing variable; d_math, which is set equal to 1; d_hyp, which is set equal to 0; and grp, a character variable that is set equal to math. The second dataset, called hyp, contains the hyperactivity data and is organized in a similar manner with the same set of variables. In this dataset, var now contains the hyperactivity scores, d_math is set equal to 0, d_hyp is set equal to 1, and grp equals hyp. Finally, the dataset multivariate is created by stacking these two datasets using the rbind command.

The bivariate linear growth model is then specified using nlme. In this script, the outcome variable, var, is set equal to d_math multiplied by a linear growth model with b_1i and b_2i as the intercept and slope plus d_hyp multiplied by a linear growth model with h_1i and h_2i as the intercept and slope. Since d_math equals 1 for the mathematics scores and 0 for the hyperactivity scores, b_1i and b_2i are the intercept and slope for mathematics. Similarly, h_1i and h_2i are the intercept and slope for hyperactivity. The dataset is then specified as the multivariate dataset that was recently created. Next are the fixed- and random-effects parameters. In this specification, the fixed effects were not separated from the random effects as was done in many of the previous specifications. Thus, b_1i, b_2i, h_1i, and h_2i have fixed-effects (i.e., means) and random-effects (variances and covariances) parameters. The grouping (or cluster) variable, id, indicates the nesting or cluster variable. Starting values are then provided for the fixed effects and arranged according to the order of elements in the fixed statement. The weights statement is used to specify separate level-1 variances for mathematics and hyperactivity. This statement is used in a similar way to when multiple-group models were constructed. The level-1 variances vary according to the grp variable. A new addition to this statement is c(hyp=.3), which provides a starting value for the size of the level-1 variance for hyperactivity as a proportion of size of the level-1 variance for mathematics. This starting value aids estimation because the level-1 variances for mathematics and hyperactivity are very different given their respective scales.

Parameter estimates for the bivariate linear growth model estimated by NLMIXED and nlme are contained in Output 8.1 and 8.2, respectively. For mathematics, the mean intercept was 35.25 (beta_1, Fixed effect of b_1i), and the mean slope was 4.34 points per year (beta_2, Fixed effect of b_2i). The intercept variance was 64.98 (v_d1, Random effect of b_1i), the slope variance was 0.70 (v_d2, Random effect of b_2i), the intercept–slope covariance was –0.17 (c_d2d1, Corr between b_1i and b_2i), and the level-1 residual variance was 36.82 (v_u, Random effect of Residual). For hyperactivity, the mean intercept was 1.90 (alpha_1, Fixed effect of h_1i) and the mean slope was –0.06 points per year (alpha_2, Fixed effect of h_2i). The intercept variance was 1.54 (v_f1, Random effect of h_1i), the slope variance was 0.005 (v_f2, Random effect of h_2i), the intercept–slope covariance was –0.02 (c_f2f1, Corr between h_1i and h_2i), and the level-1 residual variance was 1.10 (v_s, Random effect of Residual variance multiplied by 0.17—reported in Variance function for hyp).

The added value of the bivariate model are the covariances among the growth factors. For mathematics and hyperactivity, the covariance between the intercepts was –3.03 (c_f1d1, Corr between h_1i and b_1i), the covariance between the slope for

Output 8.1. NLMIXED Output for the Bivariate Linear Growth Model

Parameter Estimates

Parameter	Estimate	Standard Error	DF	t Value	Pr > |t|	Alpha	Lower	Upper	Gradient
beta_1	35.2457	0.3558	928	99.05	<.0001	0.05	34.5474	35.9441	-0.09656
beta_2	4.3435	0.08792	928	49.40	<.0001	0.05	4.1709	4.5160	0.14042
v_d1	64.9902	5.6863	928	11.43	<.0001	0.05	53.8307	76.1497	0.041092
v_d2	0.6943	0.3221	928	2.16	0.0314	0.05	0.06205	1.3265	-0.57753
c_d2d1	-0.06631	1.1417	928	-0.06	0.9537	0.05	-2.3069	2.1743	0.143932
v_u	36.1982	1.8626	928	19.43	<.0001	0.05	32.5429	39.8536	-0.03121
alpha_1	1.9043	0.05825	928	32.69	<.0001	0.05	1.7900	2.0187	0.053651
alpha_2	-0.05681	0.01431	928	-3.97	<.0001	0.05	-0.08490	-0.02872	-0.44446
v_f1	1.5471	0.1560	928	9.92	<.0001	0.05	1.2408	1.8533	0.216526
v_f2	0.004728	0.008598	928	0.55	0.5825	0.05	-0.01215	0.02160	-0.79665
c_f2f1	-0.02066	0.03096	928	-0.67	0.5047	0.05	-0.08142	0.04009	-0.23259
v_s	1.1036	0.05685	928	19.41	<.0001	0.05	0.9920	1.2151	0.04637
c_f1d1	-2.9902	0.6225	928	-4.80	<.0001	0.05	-4.2118	-1.7686	0.083706
c_f2d1	0.1103	0.1511	928	0.73	0.4656	0.05	-0.1862	0.4067	0.24928
c_f1d2	0.09491	0.1469	928	0.65	0.5185	0.05	-0.1935	0.3833	-0.16386
c_f2d2	-0.04047	0.03008	928	-1.35	0.1788	0.05	-0.09951	0.01857	0.10773

Output 8.2. `nlme` Output for the Bivariate Linear Growth Model

```
Random effects:
 Formula: list(b_1i ~ 1, b_2i ~ 1, h_1i ~ 1, h_2i ~ 1)
 Level: id
 Structure: General positive-definite, Log-Cholesky parametrization
         StdDev       Corr
b_1i     8.04436620 b_1i     b_2i    h_1i
b_2i     0.86704196 -0.029
h_1i     1.24184756 -0.299    0.093
h_2i     0.06810481  0.201   -0.698 -0.235
Residual 6.01038401

Variance function:
 Structure: Different standard deviations per stratum
 Formula: ~1 | grp
 Parameter estimates:
      math         hyp
  1.0000000 0.1748218

Fixed effects: b_1i + b_2i + h_1i + h_2i ~ 1
        Value Std.Error   DF  t-value p-value
b_1i 35.25849 0.3551053 3456 99.29024    0e+00
b_2i  4.34307 0.0873764 3456 49.70531    0e+00
h_1i  1.90349 0.0581508 3456 32.73367    0e+00
h_2i -0.05663 0.0142229 3456 -3.98155    1e-04
```

hyperactivity and intercept for mathematics was 0.11 (`c_f2d1`, Corr between `h_2i` and `b_1i`), the covariance between the intercept for hyperactivity and the slope for mathematics was 0.11 (`c_f1d2`, Corr between `h_1i` and `b_2i`), and the covariance between the slopes was –0.04 (`c_f2d2`, Corr between `h_2i` and `b_2i`). The results from the bivariate linear growth model indicate that only the intercepts of the growth models for mathematics and hyperactivity were significantly related. The covariance was negative, indicating that children's predicted mathematics scores in second grade were negatively associated with their predicted hyperactivity scores in second grade. Thus, children of parents who reported greater levels of hyperactivity tended to show worse mathematics performance in second grade.

Time-Varying Covariate Model

The data for the time-varying covariate model are the longitudinal mathematics data previously analyzed using linear growth models augmented by a time-varying covariate, which is the *season* in which the measurement took place. Observations from the NLSY-CYA were selected, in part, according to when testing occurred. Specifically, observations were selected if they were collected during the fall (i.e., September–December) or spring (i.e., March–June). This information is summarized with the variable `spring`, which was coded 0 if the testing took place in the fall and coded 1 if the testing took place in the spring. This variable represents a time-varying covariate because it varies within individuals over time. Additionally, this variable is expected to be associated with the outcome and is unlikely to correlate with an individual's intercept and slope (necessary to obtain unbiased parameter estimates when using the multilevel modeling framework). Thus, the assumption of the lack of correlation between the time-varying covariate and the intercept and slope inherent in the multilevel specification should hold.

The SAS script for the time-varying covariate model fit to the longitudinal mathematics data with spring as the time-varying covariate is provided in Script 8.3. The script follows the linear growth model specification from Chapter 3 with two minor changes. First, the time-varying covariate, spring, is included on the trajectory (level-1) equation with regression coefficient b3. Second, a starting value for b3 is provided in the PARMS statement. The remainder of the script follows typical specification for a linear growth model because there were no changes made to the MODEL or RANDOM statements.

The nlme script for the TVC model fit to the longitudinal mathematics data with spring as the time-varying covariate is provided in Script 8.4. The only modifications to the script from the linear growth model in Chapter 3 are in the combined level-1 and level-2 equation, an additional parameter on the fixed statement, and a starting value for that additional parameter. The first change is the inclusion of spring with regression coefficient b3 to the trajectory equation. Next, the fixed statement now includes b3 to

Script 8.3. NLMIXED Script for the Linear Growth Model with Time-Varying Covariate

```
PROC NLMIXED DATA = nlsy_math_long;
      b_1i = beta_1 + d_1i;
      b_2i = beta_2 + d_2i;

      traject = b_1i + b_2i * (grade - 2) + b3 * spring;

      MODEL math ~ NORMAL(traject, v_u);
      RANDOM d_1i d_2i ~ NORMAL ([0,0], [v_1,
                                         c_21, v_2])
      SUBJECT = id;
      PARMS
      beta_1 = 40 beta_2 = 5 b3 = 0
      v_1 = 70    v_2 = 1    c_21 = 0
      v_u = 40;
RUN;
```

Script 8.4. nlme Script for the Linear Growth Model with Time-Varying Covariate

```
math.tvc.nlme<-nlme(math~(beta_1+d_1i)+(beta_2+d_2i)*(grade-2)+b3*spring,
                    data = nlsy_math_long,
                    fixed = beta_1+beta_2+b3~1,
                    random = d_1i+d_2i~1,
                    group = ~id,
                    start = c(35, 4, 0),
                    na.action = na.omit)

summary(math.tvc.nlme)
```

Output 8.3. NLMIXED Output for the Linear Growth Model with Time-Varying Covariate

Parameter Estimates

Parameter	Estimate	Standard Error	DF	t Value	Pr > |t|	Alpha	Lower	Upper	Gradient
beta_1	32.6479	0.4036	930	80.89	<.0001	0.05	31.8558	33.4400	0.000052
beta_2	4.1587	0.08762	930	47.46	<.0001	0.05	3.9867	4.3306	0.000079
b3	4.6940	0.3957	930	11.86	<.0001	0.05	3.9175	5.4705	0.000053
v_1	55.7575	5.1325	930	10.86	<.0001	0.05	45.6849	65.8301	0.00003
v_2	0.6892	0.3195	930	2.16	0.0312	0.05	0.06225	1.3161	-0.00022
c_21	0.4679	1.0745	930	0.44	0.6633	0.05	-1.6408	2.5767	0.000105
v_u	34.7210	1.8007	930	19.28	<.0001	0.05	31.1872	38.2549	-0.00001

estimate the effect of the time-varying covariate. Lastly, a starting value of 0 is given to b3 in the start statement. The remaining model specification is unchanged.

Parameter estimates from PROC NLMIXED and nlme for the TVC model are contained in Output 8.3 and 8.4, respectively. Parameter estimates describing the growth of mathematics were similar to those obtained from the linear growth model without the time-varying covariate; however, their interpretation is different because they are conditioned on the time-varying covariate. We first describe the effect of the time-varying covariate (b3). Here the variable spring had a significant positive effect on mathematics scores, indicating that children measured in the spring scored, on average, 4.69 points greater than children measured in the fall of the same school year (controlling for the random intercept and slope). This could be interpreted as the effect that schooling has on mathematics achievement because children measured in the spring spent more time in school compared to children who were measured in the same grade, but in the fall. Alternatively, the effect could also be related to age because children measured in the spring tend to be older than children in the same grade, but measured in the fall.

As noted, the growth parameters have different interpretations when compared to the linear growth model without the time-varying covariate. For example, the mean intercept (32.65, beta_1) now represents the expected mathematics performance in the fall of second grade rather than the expected mathematics performance in second grade. The intercept variance (55.76, v_1; Random effect of d_1i) is also conditional upon the time-varying covariate and therefore represents the magnitude of between-person differences in expected mathematics scores in the fall or spring of second grade. The mean slope (4.16, beta_2) still represents annual change, but annual change for measurements that took place during the same season—fall or spring. This is best seen in Figure 8.2, which is a plot of the expected mean trajectory for mathematics based on the TVC model. In this plot, predictions for the whole numbered grades (e.g., 2.0, 3.0) are for measurements that took place in the fall, whereas predictions for the half-numbered grades (e.g., 2.5, 3.5) are for measurements taken in the spring. Thus, the predicted

Output 8.4. nlme Output for the Linear Growth Model with Time-Varying Covariate

```
Random effects:
 Formula: list(d_1i ~ 1, d_2i ~ 1)
 Level: id
 Structure: General positive-definite, Log-Cholesky parametrization
          StdDev      Corr
d_1i      7.4670738   d_1i
d_2i      0.8301924   0.075
Residual 5.8924545

Fixed effects: beta_1 + beta_2 + b3 ~ 1
          Value Std.Error    DF  t-value  p-value
beta_1 32.64789 0.4021616  1287 81.18102        0
beta_2  4.15866 0.0868214  1287 47.89896        0
b3      4.69404 0.3931912  1287 11.93830        0
```

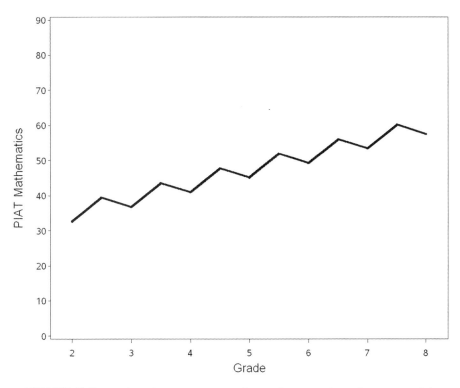

FIGURE 8.2. Predicted mean trajectory for mathematics from the TVC model.

change from grade 2.0 to 3.0 or from grade 2.5 to 3.5 (or any other one-year increment) is 4.16—the mean slope; however, this is not the case for a one-unit change in grade when the season of the assessment changed (e.g., fall of second grade to spring of third grade). This plot is also helpful for understanding the effect of the time-varying covariate, such that there appears to be an overall positive effect during school (i.e., fall to spring), but an overall negative effect during the summer (i.e., spring to fall), which may highlight a summer effect (Skibbe et al., 2012) where academic skills decline over the summer.

STRUCTURAL EQUATION MODELING FRAMEWORK

Multivariate Growth Model

The structural equation modeling framework easily accommodates multiple developmental processes. The bivariate growth model can be expressed using the restricted common factor model described in Chapter 3. Thus, the common factor model for a bivariate growth model can be written as

$$\mathbf{y}_i = \mathbf{\Lambda}\boldsymbol{\eta}_i + \mathbf{u}_i \tag{8.5}$$

where $\mathbf{y}_i$ is a $2T \times 1$ vector of the repeatedly measured observed scores for individual i (one series of scores for each variable), where T represents the number of repeated assessments based on the chosen time metric, Λ is a $2T \times R$ matrix of factor loadings defining the latent growth factors, where R is the number of growth factors for the two processes (e.g., four for a bivariate linear growth model), η_i is an $R \times 1$ vector of latent factor scores for individual i, and $\mathbf{u}_i$ is a $2T \times 1$ vector of residual or unique scores for individual i. In this specification, the vector $\mathbf{y}_i$ contains the repeatedly measured variables for the outcome variables (referred to as y_{ti} and x_{ti} in the multilevel specification). Similarly, the factor scores, η_i, are the intercept and slope factors for both outcome variables, and the residual factors, $\mathbf{u}_i$, include residuals from both sets of observed scores.

The latent factor scores are written as deviations from the mean, such that

$$\eta_i = \alpha + \xi_i \tag{8.6}$$

where α is an $R \times 1$ vector of latent factor means and ξ_i is an $R \times 1$ vector of mean deviations for individual i. The population mean (μ) and covariance (Σ) structure based on the bivariate latent growth model are

$$\mu = \Lambda \alpha$$
$$\Sigma = \Lambda \Psi \Lambda' + \Theta \tag{8.7}$$

where Ψ is a $R \times R$ latent variable covariance matrix containing covariances among growth factors (intercepts and slopes) and Θ is a $2T \times 2T$ residual covariance matrix. In the bivariate growth model, the diagonal elements of Θ are often forced to be equal for each variable. Thus, the first T diagonal elements of Θ are set equal, and the second T diagonal elements of Θ are set equal. Additionally, in the bivariate growth model, off-diagonal elements of Θ corresponding to the same measurement occasions are estimated and often set to be equal. For example, a common specification of Θ with three measurement occasions is

$$\begin{pmatrix} \theta_y & & & & & \\ 0 & \theta_y & & & & \\ 0 & 0 & \theta_y & & & \\ \theta_{x,y} & 0 & 0 & \theta_x & & \\ 0 & \theta_{x,y} & 0 & 0 & \theta_x & \\ 0 & 0 & \theta_{x,y} & 0 & 0 & \theta_x \end{pmatrix} \tag{8.8}$$

where θ_y are the unique variances for the first process, θ_x are the unique variances for the second process, and $\theta_{x,y}$ are the unique time-specific covariances across variables. Thus, the Ψ and Θ matrices contain the across variable associations from the bivariate growth model (i.e., covariances among growth factors and unique covariances).

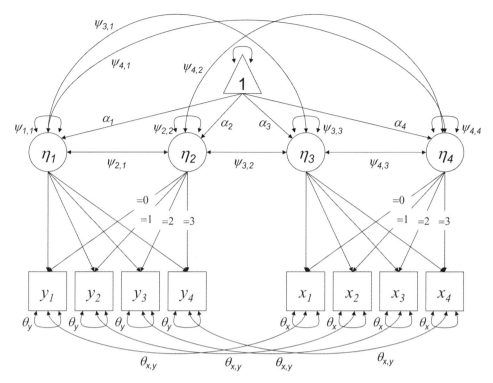

FIGURE 8.3. Path diagram of a bivariate linear growth model.

Figure 8.3 is a path diagram of a bivariate linear growth model with four measurement occasions. Parameter labels map onto the specification presented above with few exceptions. The observed variables are labeled y_1 through y_4 and x_1 through x_4 to highlight the two sets of repeatedly measured variables, and the intercepts and slopes are labeled η_1, η_2, η_3, and η_4. For each set of variables, we have defined a linear growth model where the factor loadings for the intercepts (η_1 and η_3) are set to 1 and the factor loadings for the slopes (η_2 and η_4) change linearly with respect to time. These latent growth factors have means (α_1, α_2, α_3, and α_4), variances ($\psi_{1,1}$, $\psi_{2,2}$, $\psi_{3,3}$, and $\psi_{4,4}$), and covariances ($\psi_{2,1}$, $\psi_{3,1}$, $\psi_{4,1}$, $\psi_{4,2}$, $\psi_{3,2}$, and $\psi_{4,3}$) with one another. The unique or residual variances are set equal across time for each set of repeated variables (θ_y and θ_x), and the uniquenesses of the two variables are allowed to covary within time ($\theta_{x,y}$). The bivariate or cross-variable information comes from certain latent variable covariances ($\psi_{3,1}$, $\psi_{3,2}$, $\psi_{4,1}$, and $\psi_{4,2}$) and the residual covariance ($\theta_{x,y}$).

The flexibility of the structural equation modeling framework allows for directional associations (regressions) between latent variables as opposed to the nondirectional associations (covariances) presented thus far.[2] Specifically, associations between intercepts and slopes can be made directional, such that intercepts predict slopes. The rationale

---

[2]The flexibility of NLMIXED also allows for these directional associations.

behind this adjustment is often based on the location of the intercept relative to the slope. Often, intercepts are centered at the first measurement occasion where the factor loadings from the slopes are set equal to 0. In this specification, slopes are assumed to be unaffected by the first measurement occasion because of its zero factor loading (following traditional factor analytic logic), and intercepts are thought to come *before* the slopes because the slopes only have nonzero factor loadings after the first measurement occasion. Hence, the intercept is measured at an earlier point in time and may affect the slope, which represents changes that occurred after the initial point in time. However, this perspective is not as simple as this logic alludes. Scores measured at the first occasion do, in fact, contribute to the slope because of the restricted mean structure in growth models. This can be seen by centering the intercept at different time points and how model fit is unaltered even though the slope has nonzero values at different time points. The intercept and slope actually occur simultaneously at all time points, and in most situations it is inappropriate to treat them as independent and occurring sequentially.

A second consideration is the study at hand. In several developmental studies there is an ongoing developmental process under observation. The developmental process was taking place before the study began and will continue after the study is complete. Such is the case with the mathematics data from the NLSY. Children's mathematics skills were developing prior to the project's commencement, and the process was simply observed at specific points in time. Consequently, the first measurement occasion for the study did not coincide with initial mathematics achievement, nor was it a *special* day in the lives of the participants. In such situations, it is unreasonable to treat the intercept as anything more than a piece of information about the change trajectory of the developmental process. However, in situations where the first measurement occasion occurred at an important point in time for the participants, then it can be reasonable to treat the intercept as having greater meaning and the intercept could be used as a predictor of the slope. Examples of such experiences include an operation, birth of a child, and divorce. In these cases, it might be appropriate to exclude the first assessment from the growth model and treat it as a time-invariant covariate.

Time-Varying Covariate Model

The structural equation modeling framework offers greater flexibility than the multilevel modeling framework when fitting the TVC model; however, this flexibility can come at a cost of convergence. The TVC model can be written as

$$\mathbf{y}_i = \boldsymbol{\Lambda}\boldsymbol{\eta}_i + \mathbf{B}\mathbf{x}_i + \mathbf{u}_i \tag{8.9}$$

where $\mathbf{y}_i$ is a $T \times 1$ vector of repeatedly measured scores for individual i, where T represents the number of repeated assessments based on the chosen time metric, $\boldsymbol{\Lambda}$ is a $T \times R$ matrix of factor loadings defining the latent growth factors, where R is the number of growth factors, $\boldsymbol{\eta}_i$ is an $R \times 1$ vector of latent factor scores for individual i, $\mathbf{B}$ is a $T \times T$ matrix of regression coefficients for the time-varying covariate, $\mathbf{x}_i$ is a $T \times 1$ vector of repeatedly measured scores that vary with time (i.e., the time-varying covariate), and $\mathbf{u}_i$ is a $T \times 1$ vector of residual or unique scores for individual i.

As in the basic growth modeling framework, the latent factor scores are written as deviations from the mean, such that

$$\eta_i = \alpha + \xi_i \tag{8.10}$$

where α is an $R \times 1$ vector of latent factor means and ξ_i is an $R \times 1$ vector of mean deviations for individual i. Additionally, the vector of time-varying covariates can be expressed as

$$\mathbf{x}_i = \tau + \zeta_i \tag{8.11}$$

where τ is a $T \times 1$ vector of means and ζ_i is a $T \times 1$ vector of individual deviations around the means. The population mean (μ) and covariance (Σ) structure for $\mathbf{y}_i$ based on the TVC model are

$$\mu = \Lambda\alpha + \mathbf{B}\tau$$
$$\Sigma = \Lambda\Psi\Lambda' + \mathbf{B}\Phi\mathbf{B}' + \Theta \tag{8.12}$$

where Ψ is the latent variable covariance matrix, Φ is the covariance matrix for the time-varying covariate, and Θ is the residual covariance matrix. This specification mirrors the common specification of the TVC model described for the multilevel modeling framework when the matrix $\mathbf{B}$ is diagonal with elements set equal to force the effect of the time-varying covariate to be invariant with respect to time. In this specification, the time-varying covariates are unrelated to the latent growth factors. However, the flexibility of the structural equation modeling framework allows for the estimation of these covariances (see Grimm, 2007).

A path diagram of the TVC model is contained in Figure 8.4. On the left-hand side of the figure is the growth model for the repeated measurements of y with a latent variable intercept, η_1, and slope, η_2. On the right-hand side of the diagram is the time-varying covariate, x_1 through x_4. In the structural equation modeling framework, the time-varying covariate actually represents multiple variables. At each measurement occasion, the time-varying covariate has a mean (τ_1 to τ_4), variance ($\phi_{1,1}$ to $\phi_{4,4}$), and covariances across time ($\phi_{2,1}$ to $\phi_{4,3}$). The time-varying covariate has a direct effect on y with regression coefficients $\beta_{1,1}$ through $\beta_{4,4}$.

In the structural modeling framework it is easy to see how the effect of the time-varying covariate could vary with time, how lagged time-varying covariate effects could be modeled, and how the time-varying covariate could be allowed to covary with the intercept and slope. However, this flexibility comes at the cost of estimation difficulty. That is, the TVC model is computationally more difficult to estimate in the structural equation modeling framework because the model for the time-varying covariate variables is saturated and can therefore have many parameters to estimate. These difficulties are accentuated when incomplete data are present because all of the covariances among the

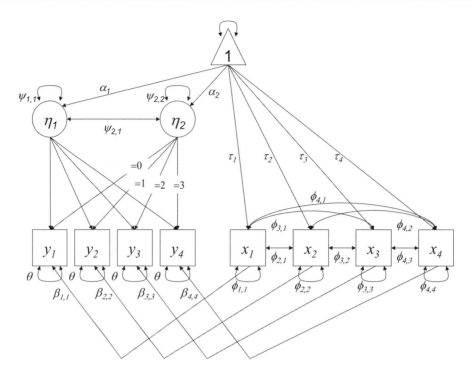

FIGURE 8.4. Path diagram of a TVC model.

time-varying covariate are estimated. Thus, the time-varying covariates should be jointly observed. If they are not jointly observed (as may be the case with our illustrative data), then the covariances among the time-varying covariates are impossible to estimate. In these situations, the covariances can be fixed to 0, but this constraint may not be valid if the time-varying covariate is expected to have a degree of stability (e.g., hyperactivity).

STRUCTURAL EQUATION MODELING IMPLEMENTATION

Multivariate Growth Model

The example data for the bivariate linear growth model are the same as above. However, the data are structured in the wide format with a single record per person. Each record contains the variables math2 through math8 and hyp2 through hyp8 for the mathematics and hyperactivity data from second through eighth grade, respectively. The growth model for mathematics and hyperactivity assumes the trajectories are linear with respect to grade.

The MODEL statement for fitting the bivariate linear growth model in Mplus is contained in Script 8.5. The MODEL statement begins by defining eta_1 and eta_2 using the keyword BY to define the intercept and linear slope for mathematics. Factor loadings for eta_1 are fixed at 1, and factor loadings for eta_2 are fixed and change linearly

Script 8.5. *Mplus* Script for the Bivariate Linear Growth Model

```
MODEL:
! Growth Model for Mathematics
    eta_1 BY math2-math8@1;
    eta_2 BY math2@0 math3@1 math4@2 math5@3 math6@4 math7@5 math8@6;
    eta_1 eta_2;
    eta_1 WITH eta_2;
    [eta_1 eta_2];
    math2-math8 (theta_M);
    [math2-math8@0];

! Growth Model for Hyperactivity
    eta_3 BY hyp2-hyp8@1;
    eta_4 BY hyp2@0 hyp3@1 hyp4@2 hyp5@3 hyp6@4 hyp7@5 hyp8@6;
    eta_3 eta_4;
    eta_3 WITH eta_4;
    [eta_3 eta_4];
    hyp2-hyp8 (theta_H);
    [hyp2-hyp8@0];

! Bivariate Information
    eta_1 WITH eta_3;
    eta_1 WITH eta_4;
    eta_2 WITH eta_3;
    eta_2 WITH eta_4;

    math2 WITH hyp2 (theta_MH);
    math3 WITH hyp3 (theta_MH);
    math4 WITH hyp4 (theta_MH);
    math5 WITH hyp5 (theta_MH);
    math6 WITH hyp6 (theta_MH);
    math7 WITH hyp7 (theta_MH);
    math8 WITH hyp8 (theta_MH);
```

with respect to grade beginning with 0 to center the intercept at second grade. Next, latent variable variances (eta_1 eta_2;), the covariance between the intercept and slope (eta_1 WITH eta_2;), and the intercept and slope means ([eta_1 eta_2];) are specified. Residual variances for the mathematics variables are specified and labeled theta_M (math2-math8 (theta_M);) to constrain the residual variances to be equal across time. The last part of the linear growth model for mathematics is to fix to observed variable intercepts to 0 ([math2-math8@0];).

In the second part of the script, a linear growth model for hyperactivity is specified with eta_3 and eta_4 as the intercept and slope. The specification of the growth model for hyperactivity mimics the specification for mathematics. First, the intercept and slope latent variables are defined using the keyword BY, and then latent variable variances, covariance, and means are specified. Residual variances of observed variables are then specified and forced to be equal over time using the label theta_H. Lastly, observed variable intercepts are set equal to 0.

In the last part of the script, the parameters describing the associations between the mathematics and hyperactivity variables are specified. Here, covariances of intercepts and slopes across variables are specified as well as covariances among uniquenesses. The latent variable covariances include the covariance between the intercepts (eta_1 WITH eta_3;), the covariance between the intercept for mathematics and the slope for hyperactivity (eta_1 WITH eta_4;), the covariance between the slope for mathematics and the intercept for hyperactivity (eta_2 WITH eta_3;), and the covariance between the slopes (eta_2 WITH eta_4;). Lastly, the covariances between the residuals are specified. In these statements, the observed variables measured in the same grade are specified to covary (e.g., math2 WITH hyp2). Since these variables are endogenous variables, the estimated parameter is the *unique* or *residual* covariance as opposed to the covariance between the variables. These covariances are specified with a common label (theta_MH), which forces them to be equal over time. This constraint is common when the unique variances are equal over time; however, this constraint is inappropriate when unique variances are allowed to be time-dependent.

The code to fit the bivariate linear growth model in OpenMx is provided in Script 8.6. In this script, we specify growth models for mathematics and hyperactivity together as opposed to specifying them separately. The script begins by indicating the datafile and stating the manifest and latent variables included in the model. The manifest variables include the seven mathematics variables and the seven hyperactivity variables. Latent variables comprise the intercepts and slopes for mathematics (eta_1 and eta_2) and hyperactivity (eta_3 and eta_4). Next, the model is specified using several mxPath statements. The first two mxPath statements specify the residual variances of the observed variables. The paths for mathematics originate at each of the mathematics variables, are two-headed arrows (arrows=2), given starting values of 60, and all labeled th_M to constrain them to be equal across time. The residual variances for the hyperactivity variables are specified in a similar manner, but given starting values of 1 and labeled th_H. Next, the residual covariances are specified. These two-headed arrows originate from the mathematics variables and go to the hyperactivity variables, are freely estimated, given a starting value of 0, and are all labeled th_MH. Again, we note that a single parameter for the residual covariance is estimated because a common label is utilized for these paths. The latent variable variances and covariances are specified in the next mxPath statement. These two-headed arrows (arrows=2) originate from each latent variable, and connect='unique.pairs' is used to specify all variances, and covariances among the specified variables. All of these paths are freely estimated (free=TRUE), given starting values, and labeled accordingly.

The next four mxPath statements define the intercepts and slopes for mathematics and hyperactivity. First, the intercept for mathematics (eta_1) is defined with factor loadings to the seven mathematics variables that are fixed at 1. Next, the linear slope for mathematics (eta_2) is defined with factor loadings to the seven mathematics variables that change linearly with respect to time and begin with 0. In a similar fashion, the intercept (eta_3) and slope (eta_4) for hyperactivity are defined. Next, the means of the latent variables are specified as one-headed arrows from the constant (one) to each latent variable. These paths are freely estimated, given starting values, and appropriate labels.

Script 8.6. OpenMx Script for the Bivariate Linear Growth Model

```
blgm.math.hyp.omx <- mxModel('Bivariate Linear Growth Model, Path
Specification',
 type='RAM',mxData(observed=nlsy_math_wide, type='raw'),
 manifestVars=c('math2','math3','math4','math5','math6','math7','math8',
                'hyp2','hyp3','hyp4','hyp5','hyp6','hyp7','hyp8'),
 latentVars=c('eta_1','eta_2','eta_3','eta_4'),

# residual variances
mxPath(from=c('math2','math3','math4','math5','math6','math7','math8'),
 arrows=2, free=TRUE, values=60, labels='th_M'),

mxPath(from=c('hyp2','hyp3','hyp4','hyp5','hyp6','hyp7','hyp8'),
 arrows=2, free=TRUE, values=1, labels='th_H'),

# residual covariances
mxPath(from=c('math2','math3','math4','math5','math6','math7','math8'),
 to=c ('hyp2','hyp3','hyp4','hyp5','hyp6','hyp7','hyp8'),
 arrows=2, free=TRUE, values=0,
 labels=c('th_MH','th_MH','th_MH','th_MH','th_MH','th_MH','th_MH'))

# latent variable variances and covariances
mxPath(from=c('eta_1','eta_2','eta_3','eta_4'), connect='unique.pairs',
 arrows=2, free=TRUE, values=c(50,0,0,0,1,0,0,1),
 labels=c('psi_11','psi_21','psi_31','psi_41',
                   'psi_22','psi_32','psi_42',
                            'psi_33','psi_43',
                                     'psi_44'

# factor loadings
mxPath(from='eta_1',
 to=c('math2','math3','math4','math5','math6','math7','math8'),
 arrows=1, free=FALSE, values=1),

mxPath(from='eta_2',
 to=c('math2','math3','math4','math5','math6','math7','math8'),
 arrows=1, free=FALSE, values=c(0, 1, 2, 3, 4, 5, 6)),

mxPath(from='eta_3',
 to=c('hyp2','hyp3','hyp4','hyp5','hyp6','hyp7','hyp8'),
 arrows=1, free=FALSE, values=1),

mxPath(from='eta_4',
 to=c ('hyp2','hyp3','hyp4','hyp5','hyp6','hyp7','hyp8'),
 arrows=1, free=FALSE, values=c(0, 1, 2, 3, 4, 5, 6)),

# means and intercepts
mxPath(from='one', to=c('eta_1','eta_2','eta_3','eta_4'),
 arrows=1, free=TRUE, values=c(100, 15, 1, 0),
 labels=c('alpha_1','alpha_2','alpha_3','alpha_4')),

) # Close Model

blgm.math.hyp.fit <- mxRun(blgm.math.hyp.omx)

summary(blgm.math.hyp.fit)
```

The model is then closed and run using mxRun. Fit indices and parameter estimates are viewed using summary.

Parameter estimates from the bivariate linear growth model fit using Mplus and OpenMx are contained in Output 8.5 and 8.6, respectively. The linear growth model for mathematics had a mean intercept of 35.26 (Mean of ETA_1; alpha_1) and a mean annual rate of change of 4.34 (Mean of ETA_2; alpha_2) points. There was significant variability in the intercept (64.71; Variance of ETA_1; psi_11) and slope (0.75; Variance of ETA_2; psi_22), and a nonsignificant covariance between the intercept and slope (–0.20; ETA_1 WITH ETA_2; psi_21). The linear growth model for hyperactivity had a mean intercept of 1.90 (Mean of ETA_3; alpha_3) and a significant mean annual rate of change equal to –0.06 (Mean of ETA_4; alpha_4) points. There was significant variability in the intercept (1.54; Variance of ETA_3; psi_33), but not the slope (0.01; Variance of ETA_4;

Output 8.5. Mplus Parameter Estimates for the Bivariate Linear Growth Model

MODEL RESULTS

		Estimate	S.E.	Est./S.E.	Two-Tailed P-Value
ETA_1	WITH				
ETA_2		-0.204	1.154	-0.176	0.860
ETA_3		-2.979	0.673	-4.426	0.000
ETA_4		0.107	0.164	0.654	0.513
ETA_3	WITH				
ETA_4		-0.020	0.031	-0.644	0.520
ETA_2	WITH				
ETA_3		0.098	0.161	0.608	0.543
ETA_4		-0.040	0.038	-1.061	0.289
MATH2	WITH				
HYP2		-0.011	0.233	-0.046	0.963
...					
MATH8	WITH				
HYP8		-0.011	0.233	-0.046	0.963
Means					
ETA_1		35.259	0.356	99.178	0.000
ETA_2		4.343	0.088	49.139	0.000
ETA_3		1.903	0.058	32.702	0.000
ETA_4		-0.057	0.014	-3.950	0.000
Variances					
ETA_1		64.711	5.664	11.424	0.000
ETA_2		0.752	0.329	2.282	0.023
ETA_3		1.542	0.156	9.908	0.000
ETA_4		0.005	0.009	0.539	0.590
Residual Variances					
MATH2		36.126	1.863	19.390	0.000
...					
MATH8		36.126	1.863	19.390	0.000
HYP2		1.104	0.057	19.404	0.000
...					
HYP8		1.104	0.057	19.404	0.000

Output 8.6. `OpenMx` **Parameter Estimates for the Bivariate Linear Growth Model**

	name	matrix	row	col	Estimate	Std.Error
1	th_M	S	math2	math2	36.126276844	1.839264080
2	th_MH	S	math2	hyp2	-0.010736501	0.233577456
3	th_H	S	hyp2	hyp2	1.104125879	0.056896723
4	psi_11	S	eta_1	eta_1	64.711077297	5.414988264
5	psi_21	S	eta_1	eta_2	-0.203518436	1.065187297
6	psi_22	S	eta_2	eta_2	0.751586255	0.317819734
7	psi_31	S	eta_1	eta_3	-2.979502771	0.677650648
8	psi_32	S	eta_2	eta_3	0.097702665	0.160619040
9	psi_33	S	eta_3	eta_3	1.542132569	0.155562786
10	psi_41	S	eta_1	eta_4	0.107216732	0.164822192
11	psi_42	S	eta_2	eta_4	-0.040159313	0.037905973
12	psi_43	S	eta_3	eta_4	-0.019894808	0.030878829
13	psi_44	S	eta_4	eta_4	0.004628299	0.008589374
14	alpha_1	M	1	eta_1	35.258686586	0.355496873
15	alpha_2	M	1	eta_2	4.342993508	0.088357340
16	alpha_3	M	1	eta_3	1.903468154	0.058198520
17	alpha_4	M	1	eta_4	-0.056592836	0.014327333

psi_44). Additionally, there was a nonsignificant covariance between the intercept and slope for hyperactivity (–0.02; ETA_3 WITH ETA_4; psi_43).

We now turn to the additional information provided by the bivariate linear growth model. The covariance between the intercepts (–2.98; ETA_1 WITH ETA_3; psi_31) was significant and negative. Thus, children with lower expected mathematics scores in second grade tended to have higher expected levels of hyperactivity in second grade. The covariance between the intercept for mathematics and the slope for hyperactivity was not significant (0.11; ETA_1 WITH ETA_4; psi_41), indicating that children's expected mathematics scores in second grade were not associated with their expected rate of change in hyperactivity between second and eighth grade. The covariance between the intercept for hyperactivity and the slope for mathematics was also not significant (0.10; ETA_2 WITH ETA_3; psi_32), indicating that children's expected level of hyperactivity in second grade was unrelated to their expected rate of change in mathematics between second and eighth grade. The covariance between the slope for mathematics and the slope for hyperactivity was not significant (–0.04; ETA_2 WITH ETA_4; psi_42) indicating that children's expected rate of change in mathematics scores was unrelated to their expected rate of change in their hyperactivity scores over the observation period. Lastly, the covariance between the residuals for mathematics and the residuals for hyperactivity was not significant (–0.01; MATH2 WITH HYP2; th_MH), indicating that there was no detectable association between mathematics and hyperactivity beyond the associations between their growth processes.

Time-Varying Covariate Model

The MODEL statement for the TVC model fit in Mplus is contained in Script 8.7. The script begins with the specification of a linear growth model for the mathematics variables,

Script 8.7. `Mplus` Script for the TVC Model

```
MODEL:
    eta_1 BY math2-math8@1;
    eta_2 BY math2@0 math3@1 math4@2 math5@3 math6@4 math7@5 math8@6;
    eta_1*60 eta_2*1;
    eta_1 WITH eta_2;
    [eta_1*35 eta_2*4];
    math2-math8*35 (theta);
    [math2-math8@0];

! Adding the Time-Varying Covariate
    math2 ON spring2*4 (beta);
    math3 ON spring3*4 (beta);
    math4 ON spring4*4 (beta);
    math5 ON spring5*4 (beta);
    math6 ON spring6*4 (beta);
    math7 ON spring7*4 (beta);
    math8 ON spring8*4 (beta);

    spring2-spring8;
    spring2-spring8 WITH spring2-spring8@0;
    [spring2-spring8];

! Covariances with intercept and slope
    eta_1 eta_2 WITH spring2-spring8@0;
```

which follows previous specifications. The factor loadings for the intercept, `eta_1`, and slope, `eta_2`, are defined using the keyword BY. Latent variables variances (`eta_1*60 eta_2*1;`) and covariance (`eta_1 WITH eta_2;`) are then specified and followed by the latent variable means (`[eta_1*35 eta_2*4];`). Next, residual variances are specified (`math2-math8 (theta);`) and constrained to be equal across time. Lastly, the intercepts for the mathematics variables are set equal to 0 (`[math2-math8@0];`).

The model components for the time-varying covariate are then specified. First, the effect of the time-varying covariate is specified. In the structural equation modeling framework, this is a series of statements because the data are organized in the wide format. The first of these statements is `math2 ON spring2*4 (beta);`. In these statements, the mathematics variable at each measurement occasion (e.g., `math2`) is regressed on the time-varying covariate measured at the same occasion (e.g., `spring2`). A label (i.e., `beta`) is used to constrain the effect of the time-varying covariate to be equal across time, which mimics the specification of this model in the multilevel modeling framework. Next, the mean and covariance stucture of the time-varying covariate are specified. First, the variances of the time-varying covariate are specified (`spring2-spring8;`), which are then followed by their covariances (`spring2-spring8 WITH spring2-spring8;`). In this model, these covariances are set equal to 0 (i.e., `@0`) to aid estimation because of data incompleteness. In this case, fixing these covariances to 0 should not be problematic because the time-varying covariate was not expected to show a high degree of covariation across time. The means of the time-varying covariate are then specified and freely estimated (`[spring2-spring8];`). Lastly, the covariances between the intercept and slope from the growth model for mathematics and the time-varying covariate are specified and set equal to 0 (eta_1 eta2 WITH spring2-spring8@0). As noted, these constraints mimic the specification in the multilevel modeling framework and are logical for these data (e.g., the season in which the child was assessed was likely to be unrelated to his or her intercept and slope). However, in certain cases it is reasonable to estimate these covariances.

The OpenMx script for the TVC model fit to the mathematics data with season as the time-varying covariate is contained in Script 8.8. The script begins by listing the data-file as well as the manifest and latent variables contained in the model. The model is then specified with a series of mxPath statements. The path specification begins with the typical matrices necessary to fit a linear growth model. Specifying this part of the model follows our previous specification from Chapter 3. Here, we briefly mention each of the mxPath statements. First, residual variances of the mathematics variables are specified and constrained to be equal across time. Next, we specify the intercept and slope variances and covariance and use connect='unique.pairs' to specify both the variances and covariance in a single statement. The factor loadings that define the intercept and slope are then specified and followed by an mxPath statement for the means of the intercept and slope. As we noted, the specification of these mxPath statements follows the specification of the linear growth model for mathematics without the time-varying covariate.

The additions to the script for the TVC model are the final three mxPath statements. First, the means of the repeatedly measured time-varying covariate are specified. These are one-headed arrows from the constant (one) to each measurement of the time-varying covariate (spring2 through spring8). These parameters are freely estimated, given starting values of .5, and labeled tau_1 through tau_7. Next, the variances of the repeatedly measured time-varying covariate are specified. These parameters are given starting values of .25 and labeled phi_11 through phi_77. Lastly, the effect of the time-varying covariate on the outcome variable is specified. These paths go from the time-varying covariates (spring2 through spring8) to the mathematics scores (math2 through math8). These parameters are given starting values of 0 and a common label (beta) to constrain them to be equal over time mimicking the specification in the multi-level modeling framework. If different labels are provided for these parameters, then the effect of the time-varying covariate would be allowed to vary with time. Additionally, covariance paths between the time-varying covariate and the intercept and slope as well as covariance paths among the time-varying covariates could be specified. Because they were not specified here, they are fixed to 0.

Parameter estimates obtained from the TVC model fit in Mplus and OpenMx are contained in Output 8.7 and 8.8, respectively. The effect of the time-varying covariate was 4.69 (math2 ON spring2; beta), indicating that the timing of the assessment had a positive effect on mathematics scores, such that children assessed during the spring scored, on average, 4.69 points greater than children assessed during the fall. The means of the intercept and slope were 32.65 and 4.16 (Means of ETA_1 and ETA_2; alpha_1 and alpha_2), respectively. These values represent the predicted average mathematics score in the *fall* of second grade and the predicted average annual change in mathematics conditional on the time-varying covariate. The variances of the intercept and slope

Script 8.8. OpenMx Script for the TVC Model

```
tvc.math.spr.omx <- mxModel('Time Varying Covariate Model, Path Specification',
type='RAM', mxData(observed=nlsy_math_wide, type='raw'),
manifestVars=c('math2', 'math3', 'math4', 'math5', 'math6', 'math7', 'math8',
               'spring2', 'spring3', 'spring4', 'spring5', 'spring6', 'spring7', 'spring8'),

latentVars=c('eta_1', 'eta_2'),

# Residual variances of mathematics scores
mxPath(from=c('math2', 'math3', 'math4', 'math5', 'math6', 'math7', 'math8'),
arrows=2, free=TRUE, values=60, labels='theta'),

# Latent variable variances and covariances
mxPath(from=c('eta_1', 'eta_2'),
arrows=2, connect='unique_pairs', free=TRUE,
values=c(80, 0, 1), labels=c('psi_11', 'psi_21', 'psi_22')),

# Factor Loadings
mxPath(from='eta_1',
to=c('math2', 'math3', 'math4', 'math5', 'math6', 'math7', 'math8'),
arrows=1, free=FALSE, values=1),

mxPath(from='eta_2',
to=c('math2', 'math3', 'math4', 'math5', 'math6', 'math7', 'math8'),
arrows=1, free=FALSE, values=c(0, 1, 2, 3, 4, 5, 6)),
```

```
# Latent Variable Means
mxPath(from='one', to=c('eta_1','eta_2'),
    arrows=1, free=TRUE, values=c(40, 5), labels=c('alpha_1','alpha_2')),

### TVC
# means
mxPath(from='one',
    to=c('spring2','spring3','spring4','spring5','spring6','spring7','spring8'),
    arrows=1, free=TRUE,
    values=.5, labels=c('tau_1','tau_2','tau_3','tau_4','tau_5','tau_6','tau_7')),

# variances
mxPath(from=c('spring2','spring3','spring4','spring5','spring6','spring7','spring8'),
    arrows=2, free=TRUE,
    values=-.25, labels=c('phi_11','phi_22','phi_33','phi_44','phi_55','phi_66','phi_77')),

# Effect of TVC
mxPath(from=c('spring2','spring3','spring4','spring5','spring6','spring7','spring8'),
    to=c('math2','math3','math4','math5','math6','math7','math8'),
    arrows=1, free=TRUE, values=0, labels='beta')

) # Close Model

tvc.math.spr.fit <- mxRun(tvc.math.spr.omx)

summary(tvc.math.spr.fit)
```

Output 8.7. *Mplus* **Output from the TVC Model**

MODEL RESULTS

	Estimate	S.E.	Est./S.E.	Two-Tailed P-Value
MATH2 ON				
SPRING2	4.694	0.396	11.863	0.000
MATH3 ON				
SPRING3	4.694	0.396	11.863	0.000
MATH4 ON				
SPRING4	4.694	0.396	11.863	0.000
MATH5 ON				
SPRING5	4.694	0.396	11.863	0.000
MATH6 ON				
SPRING6	4.694	0.396	11.863	0.000
MATH7 ON				
SPRING7	4.694	0.396	11.863	0.000
MATH8 ON				
SPRING8	4.694	0.396	11.863	0.000
ETA_1 WITH				
ETA_2	0.468	1.074	0.436	0.663
Means				
SPRING2	0.609	0.027	22.840	0.000
SPRING3	0.545	0.024	22.732	0.000
SPRING4	0.646	0.025	26.235	0.000
SPRING5	0.661	0.025	26.950	0.000
SPRING6	0.708	0.023	30.728	0.000
SPRING7	0.786	0.031	25.217	0.000
SPRING8	0.718	0.038	19.029	0.000
ETA_1	32.648	0.404	80.890	0.000
ETA_2	4.159	0.088	47.462	0.000
Variances				
SPRING2	0.238	0.018	12.942	0.000
SPRING3	0.248	0.017	14.680	0.000
SPRING4	0.229	0.017	13.748	0.000
SPRING5	0.224	0.016	13.638	0.000
SPRING6	0.207	0.015	13.964	0.000
SPRING7	0.168	0.018	9.301	0.000
SPRING8	0.202	0.024	8.426	0.000
ETA_1	55.756	5.132	10.864	0.000
ETA_2	0.689	0.319	2.158	0.031
Residual Variances				
MATH2	34.719	1.801	19.283	0.000
...				
MATH8	34.719	1.801	19.283	0.000

were estimated to be 55.76 and 0.69 (Variances of ETA_1 and ETA_2; psi_11 and psi_22), respectively, and represent between-person differences in mathematics performance in the *fall* or *spring* of second grade and annual changes in mathematics conditional on the time-varying covariate. Thus, the intercept variance represents variability in mathematics performance in the *fall* or *spring* of second grade, and the slope variance represents

Output 8.8. `OpenMx` Output from the TVC Model

```
free parameters:
     name   matrix      row       col      Estimate     Std.Error
1    beta      A     math2    spring2    4.6940050    0.39551825
2    theta     S     math2     math2    34.7209703    1.79945847
3    phi_11    S   spring2    spring2    0.2381279    0.01839924
4    phi_22    S   spring3    spring3    0.2479524    0.01689051
5    phi_33    S   spring4    spring4    0.2288282    0.01664462
6    phi_44    S   spring5    spring5    0.2239847    0.01642365
7    phi_55    S   spring6    spring6    0.2068631    0.01481369
8    phi_66    S   spring7    spring7    0.1681304    0.01807744
9    phi_77    S   spring8    spring8    0.2023398    0.02401290
10   psi_11    S     eta_1     eta_1   55.7573364    5.16141907
11   psi_21    S     eta_1     eta_2    0.4678683    1.08187956
12   psi_22    S     eta_2     eta_2    0.6892236    0.31867306
13   tau_1     M         1    spring2    0.6089548    0.02666175
14   tau_2     M         1    spring3    0.5452431    0.02398552
15   tau_3     M         1    spring4    0.6455022    0.02460377
16   tau_4     M         1    spring5    0.6612898    0.02453806
17   tau_5     M         1    spring6    0.7076918    0.02303079
18   tau_6     M         1    spring7    0.7861262    0.03117449
19   tau_7     M         1    spring8    0.7183089    0.03774743
20   alpha_1   M         1     eta_1   32.6479030    0.40360401
21   alpha_2   M         1     eta_2    4.1586564    0.08761774
```

variability in the annual changes in mathematics if the season (i.e., fall and spring) of the assessments does not change. Thus, these estimates are slightly smaller than estimates from the linear growth model without the time-varying covariate. The conditional covariance between the intercept and slope was 0.47 (ETA_1 WITH ETA_2; psi_21) and was not significantly different from zero. Lastly, the residual variance for mathematics was 34.72 (Residual Variance of MATH2; theta) and represents variability in mathematics scores not accounted for by the TVC model.

When using the structural equation modeling framework for the TVC model, the means and variances of the time-varying covariates are estimated across time. These estimates are noteworthy and informative about how the time-varying covariate varies with time, but this information often goes uninterpreted. The means of the time-varying covariate (Means of SPRING2-SPRING8; tau_1 to tau_7) ranged from 0.55 to 0.79, indicating that most assessments took place during the spring compared to the fall. Additionally, the means do not appear to fluctuate much over time—at least in any systematic way. The variances of the time-varying covariates (Variances of SPRING2-SPRING8; phi_11 through phi_88) provide information on between-person differences in these scores. However, since the time-varying covariate was dichotomous, these variances are not informative (variance of a dichotomous variable is perfectly related to its mean).

Lastly, we note that if the covariances between the intercept and slope with the time-varying covariate were estimated, the effect of the time-varying covariate dropped from

4.69 to 3.60 even though only 3 of the 14 covariances were significantly different from zero. The remaining parameter estimates were highly similar across models. Finally, we note that attempting to estimate all covariances among the seven measurements of the time-varying covariate led to convergence issues.

IMPORTANT CONSIDERATIONS

The bivariate growth model and TVC model are two of the most commonly fit bivariate longitudinal models in the social sciences. Their common use is likely due to two factors—the models can answer specific questions regarding developmental processes, and these models are not difficult to specify with different statistical programs—especially the TVC model in the multilevel modeling framework. The models do answer different questions and should not be used interchangeably (Grimm, 2007). Not only do the two models conceive the question of the association between two or more constructs in drastically different ways, but different types of variables may not be appropriate for each approach (see also Singer & Willett, 2003).

The bivariate growth model conceives the two constructs as ongoing developmental processes. In our example, hyperactivity, like mathematics, was conceptualized as having an underlying individual change process. In this sense, hyperactivity and mathematics were both endogenous variables. Furthermore, the between-construct associations are *between-person* associations. For example, the slope–slope covariance examines whether individuals who changed more positively in one construct tended to change more positively in the other construct *relative* to the individuals in the sample. In constrast, the time-varying covariate in the TVC model does not necessarily have an underlying change process. Furthermore, it may be inappropriate if the time-varying covariate does have an underlying systematic change process. Ideally, the time-varying covariate is exogenous to the developmental process being modeled. Additionally, the effect of the time-varying covariate is a *within-person* effect, such that its effect alters an individual's change trajectory. Lastly, we note that the effect of the time-varying covariate has an instantaneous effect on the trajectory—the effect does not persist or affect scores at subsequent occasions.[3]

We note that an endogenous variable, like hyperactivity, can be modeled as a time-varying covariate. However, there are several limitations to this approach (Grimm, 2007). First, the researcher must determine the primary variable of interest (e.g., mathematics) and the time-varying covariate (e.g., hyperactivity). This decision is not always obvious or easy to justify. Two separate models can be estimated to let each variable serve as the primary variable, but the results from the two models can contradict one another, which is difficult to explain. Second, in the multilevel modeling framework, the time-varying covariate is assumed to be uncorrelated with the intercept and slope (Curran &

---

[3]A model like this could be specified but is not typically done.

Peterman, 2005), and this is unreasonable if both variables are endogenous (hyperactivity is likely to be associated with the developmental process of mathematics achievement). Lastly, there are questions as to whether the time-varying covariate should be centered, and if so, the best way to center (i.e., person-centered or time-centered). These limitations have led researchers to propose new approaches to handling time-varying covariates. These recommendations typically involve fitting a growth-type model (e.g., intercept-only model) to the TVC, regressing the intercept and slope from the growth model on the growth factors from the TVC, and regressing the outcome scores on the TVC (see Curran & Bauer, 2011; Hoffman, 2015). These proposed approaches get closer to the multivariate growth model discussed above with regressions between the uniqueness (see also Grimm, 2007).

Proper Interpretation

Moving back to the bivariate growth model, we need to discuss the interpretation of the correlation or covariance among the slopes. This correlation can be tricky to interpret because change has both *direction* and *magnitude*. If change is positive in both constructs for all individuals, then a positive correlation among slopes indicates that people who show more growth in one construct tend to show more growth in the second construct. However, if change is positive for all individuals for the first construct, but negative for all individuals for the second, then a positive correlation indicates that people who show more growth in the first construct tend to show less decline (less change as opposed to more change) in the second construct. The interpretation becomes more clouded when direction of change varies between individuals (i.e., some show positive change whereas others show negative change) as we had with the hyperactivity scores. Within this scenario, a positive correlation between slopes can suggest that people who showed more positive change in one construct tended to show more positive change in the second construct. In this statement we refer to both the magnitude (i.e., more) and direction (i.e., positive) of the changes.

MOVING FORWARD

The bivariate growth model and TVC model answer key developmental questions when used and interpreted properly. Additional bivariate models that involve latent change or difference scores (McArdle, 2001) will be discussed later in the book. These models allow for an additional type of association between constructs—one that is time-sequential. In the next section of the book, we begin to examine additional types of individual trajectories—trajectories where the individual rate of change varies with time. In this section we describe several types of nonlinear models that vary in complexity in an attempt to understand more complex forms of individual change. We note that MGM and TVC models can be fit and results interpreted in similar ways when more complex change patterns are evident (see Grimm & Marcoulides, 2016).

Part III

Nonlinearity in Growth Modeling

9

Introduction to Nonlinearity

Thus far we have discussed the linear growth model and several of its extensions. The linear growth model is the most commonly fit growth model in the social sciences and is often an adequate model for understanding change within limited time spans. However, if the process under study is measured more often and/or measured over a long span of time, then the process is likely to show some degree of nonlinearity, such that the individual rate of change is not constant. For example, cortisol levels are plotted against measurement occasion during an experimental intervention (Seeman, Berkman, et al., 1995; Seeman, Singer, & Charpentier, 1995) in Figure 9.1a, and verbal ability estimates are plotted against age for participants of the Berkeley Growth Study (Jones & Bayley, 1941) and Guidance Study (Macfarlane, 1919) in Figure 9.1b. The individual trajectories for cortisol and verbal ability are obviously not linear—a linear growth model would be unable to capture the complexity present in the individual trajectories. Thus, it is appropriate to be aware of the various ways to model nonlinear change.

The next three chapters cover models able to capture nonlinear change. In this chapter, we describe a general framework for nonlinear change models. We categorize non-linear change models into three types according to their complexity and the programs necessary to fit such models: Type I models are nonlinear with respect to *time*; Type II models are nonlinear with respect to *parameters*; and Type III models are nonlinear with respect to *random coefficients* or *latent variables*. Throughout the next three chapters, we use the terms *random coefficient* and *latent variable* interchangeably. Random coefficient is the common term in multilevel, mixed-effect, or random coefficient models, whereas latent variable is the common term in structural equation models, but both represent an unobserved or latent entity that varies over persons.

This organization for nonlinear change models is important because of the type of programs needed to estimate each model. For example, Type I models can be estimated with linear multilevel or mixed-effects programs (e.g., PROC MIXED and lme) and all

(a) Cortisol trajectories over the course of an experimental manipulation

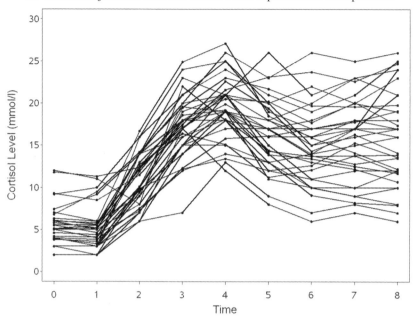

(b) Verbal ability trajectories from the Berkeley Growth and Guidance Studies

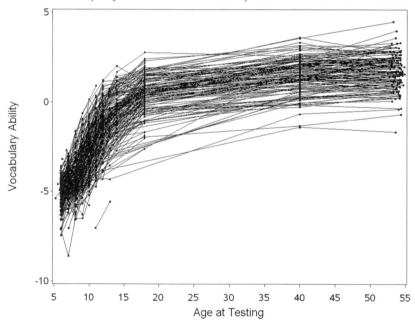

FIGURE 9.1. Longitudinal data showing various forms of nonlinearity.

structural equation modeling programs. To estimate such models in the multilevel framework, a nonlinear function of time (e.g., t^2 and $\log(t)$) is calculated and then input as a predictor of the repeatedly measured outcome. In a similar vein, these models can be estimated in the structural equation modeling framework by setting the factor loadings for the slope(s) to equal the values calculated from the nonlinear function of time. Type II models can only be fit with nonlinear multilevel modeling programs and structural equation models that allow for nonlinear constraints. In these models, one or more parameters of the nonlinear function are estimated, but the random coefficients enter the model in an additive (linear) fashion. Type III models can only be fit with nonlinear multilevel modeling programs because one or more random coefficients are part of the nonlinear function and therefore enter the model in a multiplicative (nonlinear) fashion. These models cannot be fit directly in the structural equation modeling framework; however, they can be *approximated* in the structural equation modeling framework using Taylor series expansion (Beal & Sheiner, 1982; Browne & du Toit, 1991). This approach to estimate model parameters is also useful in the multilevel modeling framework due to estimation difficulties often encountered with Type III nonlinear models.

ORGANIZATION FOR NONLINEAR CHANGE MODELS

In this section we provide context for our organizational framework for nonlinear change models and specifically state the mathematical differences between the three types of nonlinear change models. This organizational framework revolves around the calculation of partial derivatives of the level-1 equation with respect to each random coefficient. Calculating these partial derivatives is a necessary step to obtain parameter estimates for each model, which highlights the estimation complexities inherent in each model.

Type I models have partial derivatives that only depend on *time* or a known function of time (no unknowns). One example of a Type I model is the quadratic growth model, which can be written as

$$y_{ti} = b_{1i} + b_{2i} \cdot t + b_{3i} \cdot t^2 + u_{ti} \tag{9.1}$$

where b_{1i} is the intercept or predicted value when $t = 0$, b_{2i} is the linear component of change and represents the rate of change when $t = 0$, b_{3i} is the quadratic component of change representing acceleration (how quickly the rate of change is changing), t represents the chosen time metric, and u_{ti} is the time-dependent residual. As a first step, we calculate the derivative of Equation 9.1 with respect to t to highlight that the rate of change (first derivative) is not constant, indicating that the function is indeed nonlinear with respect to time. The derivative of Equation 9.1 with respect to t is

$$dy_{ti}/dt = b_{2i} + 2 \cdot b_{3i} \cdot t \tag{9.2}$$

and it can be seen that the derivative or the instantaneous rate of change is dependent on t. Thus, the rate of change depends on time, indicating that the quadratic model is (at least) nonlinear with respect to time. As a second step, the partial derivatives of Equation 9.1 are calculated with respect to each random coefficient (b_{1i}, b_{2i}, and b_{3i}). These partial derivatives are

$$\partial y_{ti}/\partial b_{1i} = 1$$
$$\partial y_{ti}/\partial b_{2i} = t$$
$$\partial y_{ti}/\partial b_{3i} = t^2 \tag{9.3}$$

and it can be seen that these partial derivatives are dependent on a constant, *time* (t) or a function of *time* (t^2), but none of the partial derivatives are dependent on an unknown parameter or random coefficient. If one or more of these partial derivatives is a function of an estimated parameter, then the model is nonlinear with respect to parameters (Type II), and if one or more of these partial derivatives is dependent on a random coefficient, then the model is nonlinear with respect to random coefficients (Type III).

Here, we note that the partial derivatives in Equation 9.3 can simply be calculated because they are only dependent on time, t, an observed variable. In the multilevel modeling framework, these functions of time are calculated and entered as predictors of the outcome according to Equation 9.1. In the structural equation modeling framework, these partial derivatives are the factor loadings for the latent variables of the quadratic growth model, and again, the factor loadings are set equal to these values because t is known.

As a second example, we present an exponential trajectory following the form

$$y_{ti} = b_{1i} + b_{2i} \cdot (1 - \exp(-\gamma \cdot t)) + u_{ti} \tag{9.4}$$

where b_{1i} is the intercept or predicted value when $t = 0$ for individual i, b_{2i} is the amount of change from the intercept to the asymptotic level for individual i, γ is an estimated parameter and represents the rate of approach to the asymptotic level, t is the chosen time metric, and u_{ti} is the time-dependent residual. The derivative of Equation 9.4 with respect to t is

$$dy_{ti}/dt = \gamma \cdot b_{2i} \cdot \exp(-\gamma \cdot t) \tag{9.5}$$

and indicates the model is nonlinear with respect to time because its first derivative with respect to t depends on t. The partial derivatives of Equation 9.4 with respect to the random coefficients are

$$\partial y_{ti}/\partial b_{1i} = 1$$
$$\partial y_{ti}/\partial b_{2i} = 1 - \exp(-\gamma \cdot t) \tag{9.6}$$

and indicate that this exponential model is nonlinear with respect to parameters (Type II) because $\partial y_{ti}/\partial b_{2i}$ is dependent on γ, an unknown parameter. Fitting this model in the multilevel modeling framework requires the nonlinear modeling framework because the partial derivative of Equation 9.4 with respect to b_{2i} cannot be calculated directly due to γ being an unknown parameter that needs to be estimated. In the structural equation modeling framework, the factor loadings for the b_{2i} are set equal to $1 - \exp(-\gamma \cdot t)$, as opposed to fixed values of time, and γ needs to be estimated. To do this, the structural equation modeling program must allow for nonlinear constraints on model parameters (e.g., factor loading parameters for b_{2i} are set equal to a nonlinear function that includes an unknown parameter; see Grimm & Ram, 2009). Most structural equation modeling programs allow for this type of parameter constraint.

As a third example, we present a slightly different variation of the exponential growth model, which can be written as

$$y_{ti} = b_{1i} + b_{2i} \cdot (1 - \exp(-b_{3i} \cdot t)) + u_{ti} \qquad (9.7)$$

where b_{1i} is the intercept or predicted value when $t = 0$ for individual i, b_{2i} is the amount of change to the upper asymptote for individual i, b_{3i} is the rate of approach to the upper asymptote for individual i, t is the chosen time metric, and u_{ti} is the time-dependent residual. The key difference between Equations 9.4 and 9.7 is that the rate of approach in Equation 9.7 is a random coefficient and therefore varies over individuals. Allowing for variation in the rate of approach leads to more diversity in the predicted trajectories because the individual rate of change depends on two random coefficients (b_{2i} and b_{3i}) instead of one (b_{2i} in Equation 9.4). The derivative of Equation 9.7 with respect to t is

$$dy_{ti}/dt = b_{3i} \cdot b_{2i} \cdot \exp(-b_{3i} \cdot t) \qquad (9.8)$$

and indicates the model is nonlinear with respect to time because its first derivative with respect to t depends on t. The partial derivatives of Equation 9.7 with respect to the random coefficients are

$$\partial y_{ti}/\partial b_{1i} = 1$$
$$\partial y_{ti}/\partial b_{2i} = 1 - \exp(-b_{3i} \cdot t)$$
$$\partial y_{ti}/\partial b_{3i} = b_{2i} \cdot t \cdot \exp(-b_{3i} \cdot t) \qquad (9.9)$$

and indicate that the model is nonlinear with respect to random coefficients because $\partial y_{ti}/\partial b_{2i}$ and $\partial y_{ti}/\partial b_{3i}$ are dependent on one or more random coefficients (i.e., b_{2i} and b_{3i}). To estimate the parameters of this type of model, a nonlinear multilevel modeling program is needed. The structural equation modeling framework cannot directly estimate the model parameters of Equation 9.7 because the structural equation modeling framework is a *linear* modeling framework (latent variables must be additive). However, the model of Equation 9.7 can be approximated using a first-order Taylor series expansion. The first-order Taylor series expansion is a linear approximation of the inherently nonlinear function around a target function, which approximates the mean trajectory. Since it is a linear approximation, the model can be estimated in the structural equation modeling framework.

MOVING FORWARD

In the next chapter, we describe and fit three commonly specified models that are nonlinear with respect to time. These models are fit to longitudinal height data collected as part of the Berkeley Growth Study (Jones & Bayley, 1941). In the two subsequent chapters, we describe a few Type II and Type III nonlinear change models and fit them to the same longitudinal data. In these chapters we discuss the specification of these models, the challenges, and the opportunites these models afford.

10

Growth Models with Nonlinearity in Time

In this chapter we describe and fit two types of models that are nonlinear with respect to time. The two models are the *quadratic* and *spline growth* models. These two models are commonly used to account for nonlinear trajectories and are often a first step to studying nonlinear trends. Additionally, these models can and have been combined in various ways to explain complex nonlinear trends and individual differences therein (Cudeck & Klebe, 2002; Ram & Grimm, 2007). The quadratic model accounts for nonlinearity by adding a second-order power of time (e.g., t^2), and the spline model accounts for nonlinearity by allowing for separate growth models for distinct spans of time. The spline model has also been referred to as the piecewise growth model (see Li, Duncan, Duncan, & Hops, 2001) or the multiphase model (see Cudeck & Klebe, 2002) because the change process under study is viewed as having multiple phases or pieces (e.g., two distinct linear phases, a quadratic phase and a linear phase).

To illustrate their use, these models are fit to longitudinal height data collected as part of the Berkeley Growth Study (Jones & Bayley, 1941). The Berkeley Growth Study initially tracked the development of $N = 61$ children from birth through adulthood. Several children were added to the study to replace children who were lost due to attrition. The illustrative data come from $N = 83$ children measured from 1 through 36 months. Assessments took place at 1, 3, 6, 9, 12, 15, 18, 24, and 36 months of age. A longitudinal plot of these data is contained in Figure 10.1. As seen in this figure, height changes are rapid initially, before growth begins to slow, and the rate of change is more or less constant from 12 to 36 months.

MULTILEVEL MODELING FRAMEWORK

Quadratic Growth Model

The quadratic growth model accounts for nonlinearity by adding a second-order power of time to the linear growth model. The quadratic growth model can be written as

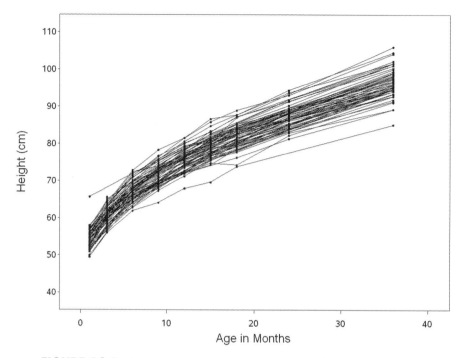

FIGURE 10.1. Longitudinal height data from the Berkeley Growth Study.

$$y_{ti} = b_{1i} + b_{2i} \cdot \left(\frac{t - k_1}{k_2} \right) + b_{3i} \cdot \left(\frac{t - k_1}{k_2} \right)^2 + u_{ti} \qquad (10.1)$$

where y_{ti} is the dependent variable measured at time t for individual i, b_{1i} is the random intercept, or predicted score of y_{ti} for individual i when $t - k_1 = 0$, b_{2i} is the linear component and predicted rate of change for individual i when $t - k_1 = 0$, b_{3i} is the quadratic component representing acceleration of the trajectory for individual i, t represents the chosen time metric, and u_{ti} is the time-specific residual at time t for individual i. The time-specific residuals are assumed to follow normal distributions with constant variance, $u_{ti} \sim N\left(0, \sigma_u^2\right)$. The constants, k_1 and k_2, center the intercept and scale the linear and quadratic components.

The level-2 equation for the random intercept, linear, and quadratic components is written as

$$\begin{aligned} b_{1i} &= \beta_1 + d_{1i} \\ b_{2i} &= \beta_2 + d_{2i} \\ b_{3i} &= \beta_3 + d_{3i} \end{aligned} \qquad (10.2)$$

where β_1, β_2, and β_3 are fixed effects for the intercept, linear, and quadratic components describing the mean predicted trajectory, and d_{1i}, d_{2i}, and d_{3i} are individual deviations from their respective fixed effect. Individual deviations are assumed to follow a multivariate normal distribution with zero means, estimated variances, and covariances,

$$d_{1i}, d_{2i}, d_{3i} \sim MVN \left(\begin{bmatrix} 0 \\ 0 \\ 0 \end{bmatrix}, \begin{bmatrix} \sigma_1^2 & & \\ \sigma_{21} & \sigma_{22}^2 & \\ \sigma_{31} & \sigma_{32} & \sigma_3^2 \end{bmatrix} \right)$$

Higher-order polynomial (e.g., cubic, quartic) models can be estimated by the addition of random coefficients multiplied by the time metric, $((t - k_1)/k_2)$ raised to the associated power. However, in practice researchers rarely test models beyond the cubic model.

The quadratic growth model, and polynomial models more generally, are often fit when the linear model shows poor fit and/or the observed data show some degree of nonlinearity. Polynomial models are often fit before other nonlinear models because they can capture a variety of developmental trajectories and are relatively easy to fit. However, these models are not without their limitations. The biggest limitation is the interpretation of model parameters. That is, the interpretation of the linear (rate of change when $t - k_i = 0$) and quadratic (acceleration) components is often difficult to map onto theoretical notions of the change process under study. The problem of interpretation gets worse with higher-order polynomial models. Cudeck and du Toit (2002) presented a reparameterized version of the quadratic model to highlight aspects of the curve that may be of interest to researchers. The parameters included the intercept, the time at which the maximum (or minimum) was reached, and the maximum (or minimum) value. This reparametrization is useful when the maximum (or minimum) value is observed in the data and less useful when the maximum (or minimum) occurs outside the range of the data. Additionally, the estimation of this model is more complex and requires a nonlinear mixed-effects modeling program.

A second limitation of polynomial models deals with model convergence and estimation. Polynomial models can be difficult to estimate due to the collinearity between the power terms. For this reason, it is important to center the intercept toward the middle of the observation period. For example, the correlation between t and t^2 is 0.96 with seven measurement occasions when t is coded from 0 to 6. The correlation drops to 0 when t is coded from −3 to 3. However, when moving to higher-order polynomials (e.g., cubic), odd-ordered (e.g., 1, 3, 5) powers tend to have a high degree of collinearity regardless of centering, as do even-ordered (e.g., 2, 4, 6) powers.

Spline Growth Models

Spline growth models separate time into discrete phases and attempt to account for the observed changes within each phase with simple (often polynomial) growth models. The segments of the growth model connect at *knot* points, sometimes referred to as *transition* points, where one phase is ending and another phase is beginning. Spline models are especially useful when there are theoretical reasons to separate time into discrete phases. For example, age can be separated based on age at crawling when modeling changes in infant sleep behavior. That is, it is expected that learning to crawl has an effect on the infant's sleep behavior, and the spline model would be able to model changes in sleep behavior before and after the infant learns to crawl. The age when the infant learns to crawl would be the *knot* point—the point where the precrawling change model ends and the postcrawling change model begins. This situation is visualized in Figure 10.2, where sleep behavior improves until the infant begins to crawl and then sleep behavior subsequently declines. As seen in this figure, the overall trajectory is nonlinear with respect to time because the rate of change is not constant over the time. A second example comes from modeling changes in depressive symptoms for mothers relative to the birth of their first child. In this example, there would be a rate of change in depression before the birth of the child and a distinct rate of change after the child was born.

Spline growth models can contain any type of linear or nonlinear change function within each phase of development and any number of phases (there are, of course, data limitations). However, for simplicity, we describe the bilinear spline growth model where there are two phases and a linear change model within each. The bilinear spline growth model can be written as

$$y_{ti} = b_{1i} + b_{2i} \cdot \min(t - k_1, 0) + b_{3i} \cdot \max(t - k_1, 0) + u_{ti} \qquad (10.3)$$

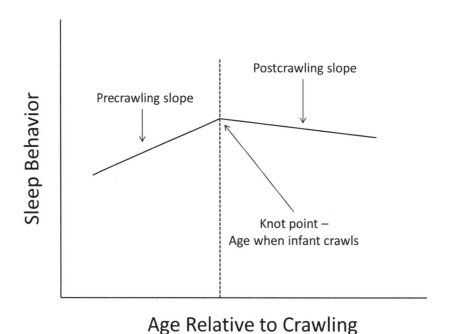

FIGURE 10.2. Visualization of a bilinear spline growth model.

where y_{ti} is the dependent variable measured for individual i at time t, b_{1i} is the random intercept centered at the knot point, k_1, or predicted score of y_{ti} for individual i when $t = k_1$, b_{2i} is the preknot random linear slope or the linear rate of change prior to the knot point for individual i, b_{3i} is the postknot random linear slope or the linear rate of change after the knot point for individual i, t represents the time metric, and u_{ti} is the time-specific residual score at time t for individual i. The residuals are assumed to follow normal distributions with constant variance, $u_{ti} \sim N(0, \sigma_u^2)$. As with the quadratic growth model, the level-2 equation for the bilinear spline growth model is

$$b_{1i} = \beta_1 + d_{1i}$$
$$b_{2i} = \beta_2 + d_{2i} \qquad (10.4)$$
$$b_{3i} = \beta_3 + d_{3i}$$

where β_1, β_2, and β_3 are the fixed-effects parameters for the intercept, preknot linear slope, and postknot linear slope describing the predicted mean trajectory, and d_{1i}, d_{2i}, and d_{3i} are individual deviations from their respective fixed effect. Individual deviations are assumed to follow a multivariate normal distribution with zero means, estimated variances, and covariances,

$$d_{1i}, d_{2i}, d_{3i} \sim MVN\left(\begin{bmatrix} 0 \\ 0 \\ 0 \end{bmatrix}, \begin{bmatrix} \sigma_1^2 & & \\ \sigma_{21} & \sigma_{22}^2 & \\ \sigma_{31} & \sigma_{32} & \sigma_3^2 \end{bmatrix} \right)$$

Spline growth models are very flexible and can account for a wide variety of change trajectories, even with linear change models in each phase. And when simple change models are fit within each phase, the interpretation of model parameters is straightforward. Furthermore, spline models can be fit with *jump* points where the two segments do not meet at the knot point. This type of model may be appropriate when the event dividing time has a substantial and instantaneous effect on the outcome (e.g., unexpected death of a spouse and depression). One limitation of spline models is that the overall change pattern is not smooth. Thus, fitting spline models to developmental processes where development is expected to be more or less continuous is difficult to justify theoretically, especially when the location of the knot point does not have a strong theoretical justification. Lastly, the spline models discussed in this chapter have *fixed* knot points, such that the number and location of the knot points are chosen *a priori* and all participants share the same set of knot points. Spline models can be fit with estimated knot points and with knot points that vary in location over participants; however, these models are Type II and Type III nonlinear models, respectively. Thus, these models will be discussed in subsequent chapters.

MULTILEVEL MODELING IMPLEMENTATION

The longitudinal height data are in the long format with variables id, age, and hght for the participant identifier, age in months, and height at each assessment, respectively.

Quadratic Growth Model

The quadratic growth model of Equation 10.1 was fit to the longitudinal height data using PROC NLMIXED and nlme. The NLMIXED script for this model is contained in Script 10.1. The script begins with the level-2 equation (Equation 10.2) and is followed by the level-1 equation (Equation 10.1), with age centered at 18 months and scaled in years (divided by 12). We note that ** in SAS means *to the power of.* Thus, ((age - 18)/12)**2 is the square of ((age - 18)/12). Next, the MODEL statement is used to indicate that hght is the outcome variable, which is assumed to follow a NORMAL distribution with a mean equal to traject and residual variance v_u. The RANDOM statement comes next and indicates that d_1i, d_2i, and d_3i are the random coefficients, which are assumed to follow a multivariate normal distribution with 0 means and a variance–covariance matrix as specified. Lastly, the PARMS statement contains starting values for all estimated parameters.

The nlme script for fitting the quadratic growth model is contained in Script 10.2. In this script, the outcome variable, hght, is set equal to the quadratic growth model of

Script 10.1. NLMIXED Script for the Quadratic Growth Model

```
PROC NLMIXED DATA = hght_long;
    b_1i = beta_1 + d_1i;
    b_2i = beta_2 + d_2i;
    b_3i = beta_3 + d_3i;

    traject = b_1i + b_2i * (age - 18)/12 + b_3i * ((age - 18)/12)**2;

    MODEL hght ~ NORMAL(traject, v_u);
    RANDOM d_1i d_2i d_3i ~ NORMAL ([0,0,0], [v_1,
                                              c_21,  v_2,
                                              c_31, c_32, v_3])
    SUBJECT = id;
    PARMS
        beta_1 = 80    beta_2 = 15    beta_3 = -3
        v_1 = 10       v_2 = 1        v_3 = .1
        c_21 = 0       c_31 = 0       c_32 = 0
        v_u = 10;
RUN;
```

Script 10.2. nlme Script for the Quadratic Growth Model

```
hght.quad.nlme <- nlme(hght~b_1i+b_2i*((age-18)/12)+b_3i*((age-18)/12)^2,
                   data=hght_long,
                   fixed=b_1i+b_2i+b_3i~1,
                   random=b_1i+b_2i+b_3i~1,
                   groups=~id,
                   start=c(30, 10, -3),
                   na.action=na.omit)
summary(hght.quad.nlme)
```

Equation 10.1, with age centered at 18 months (18 subtracted from age) and scaled in years (divided by 12). The random coefficients (b_1i, b_2i, and b_3i) have estimated fixed-effects (fixed=b_1i+b_2i+b_3i~1) parameters describing the mean trajectory and random-effects (random=b_1i+b_2i+b_3i~1) parameters to describe the extent of between-person differences in each change component as well as their covariability. The random coefficients are random over participants (groups=~id). Starting values are then provided for the fixed effects and na.action is set to na.omit, which will omit observations with incomplete values for hght or age.

The quadratic growth model, as specified, failed to converge. We note that this is not uncommon with this model, and convergence issues with this model can often be attributed to two reasons. First, the quadratic growth model may be inappropriate for the observed developmental trajectories. Second, the variability in the quadratic component (b_{3i}) may be very small. A common approach to the second problem is to fix the variance of b_{3i} to 0. This can be done in NLMIXED by changing b_3i = beta_3 + d_3i; to b_3i = beta_3; and removing d_3i from the RANDOM line and deleting its associated parameters (c_31, c_32, and v_3) from the specified covariance matrix. In nlme, b_3i is deleted from the random line to remove its associated random-effects parameters.

This adjusted quadratic growth model was fit in NLMIXED and nlme, and parameter estimates from this model are contained in Output 10.1 and 10.2, respectively. The mean intercept was 83.02 cm (beta_1, Fixed effect of b_1i) indicating the predicted mean height at 18 months. The mean of the linear component was 13.78 cm per year (beta_2, Fixed effect of b_2i), indicating the annual rate of growth at 18 months, and the quadratic component (beta_3, Fixed effect of b_3i) was −3.43 cm per year and is one-half the acceleration of the individual curves. We note that the quadratic growth model is sometimes specified as $y_{ti} = b_{1i} + b_{2i} \cdot t + (b_{3i}/2) \cdot t^2 + u_{ti}$, which makes b_{3i} the individual acceleration. The intercept variance was 7.31 (v_1, Random effect of b_1i), indicating the magnitude of true between-person variability in height at 18 months; the linear component variance was 0.79 (v_2, Random effect of b_2i), indicating between-person differences in the rate of growth at 18 months; and the intercept–slope covariance was 1.49 (c_21, Corr between b_1i and b_2i), indicating that children who were taller at 18 months tended to be growing at a faster rate at 18 months. Lastly, the level-1 residual variance was 2.66 (v_u, Random effect of Residual). Since the quadratic component had no variability between children, the curvature of the quadratic model was identical for all participants.

Individual predictions from the adjusted quadratic growth model are contained in Figure 10.3. From this figure, several features of the parameter estimates are evident. First, the curvature of the individual predictions does not vary greatly because the variance of the quadratic component was fixed at 0. Second, the positive correlation ($r = .62$) between the intercept, which was centered at 18 months, and the linear component is evident. That is, at 18 months (and elsewhere) the taller children appeared to grow at the fastest rate and the shorter children tended to grow at a slower rate. It

Output 10.1. NLMIXED Output for the Adjusted Quadratic Growth Model

Parameter Estimates

Parameter	Estimate	Standard Error	DF	t Value	Pr > |t|	Alpha	Lower	Upper	Gradient
beta_1	83.0164	0.3243	81	256.02	<.0001	0.05	82.3712	83.6616	0.00051
beta_2	13.7843	0.1345	81	102.45	<.0001	0.05	13.5166	14.0520	-0.0016
beta_3	-3.4294	0.08692	81	-39.45	<.0001	0.05	-3.6024	-3.2565	0.00006
v_1	7.3119	1.2621	81	5.79	<.0001	0.05	4.8007	9.8230	0.000079
v_2	0.7895	0.2269	81	3.48	0.0008	0.05	0.3381	1.2408	0.000898
c_21	1.4896	0.4289	81	3.47	0.0008	0.05	0.6362	2.3431	-0.00041
v_u	2.6582	0.1838	81	14.46	<.0001	0.05	2.2925	3.0239	0.000374

Output 10.2. nlme Output for the Adjusted Quadratic Growth Model

```
Random effects:
 Formula: list(b_1i ~ 1, b_2i ~ 1)
 Level: id
 Structure: General positive-definite, Log-Cholesky parameterization
          StdDev      Corr
 b_1i     2.7040353   b_1i
 b_2i     0.8885105   0.62
 Residual 1.6303875

Fixed effects: b_1i + b_2i + b_3i ~ 1
          Value     Std.Error   DF    t-value     p-value
 b_1i     83.01636  0.3248686   496   255.5383          0
 b_2i     13.78432  0.1344658   496   102.5117          0
 b_3i     -3.42943  0.0870154   496   -39.4118          0
```

is also evident that the quadratic growth model is inappropriate for these data given the visual discrepancies between the data in Figure 10.1 and the predictions in Figure 10.3. That is, the observed trajectories show greater curvature during infancy and more linearity during the toddler years compared to the predictions from the adjusted quadratic growth model.

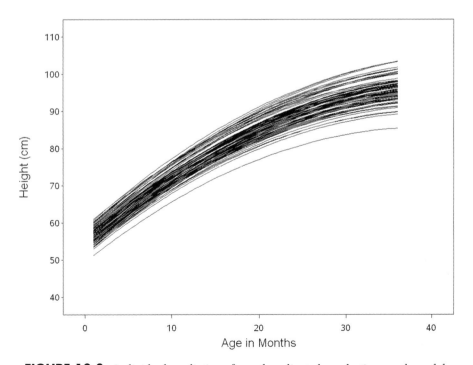

FIGURE 10.3. Individual predictions from the adjusted quadratic growth model.

Spline Growth Models

The NLMIXED script for the bilinear spline growth model is provided in Script 10.3. The script for the bilinear spline growth model is written very similarly to the quadratic growth model above with one major change—the trajectory equation now follows the level-1 equation for the bilinear spline growth model. The script begins with specifying the level-1 equation (Equation 10.3) with a knot point at 9 months and random coefficients b_1i, b_2i, and b_3i. The MIN and MAX functions are used in NLMIXED to return the minimum and maximum value of 0 and age-9 for each record in the dataset. Thus, the chosen knot point is 9 months of age—the point at which the early rapid growth appears to slow based on Figure 10.1. The MODEL statement follows and is typically specified with hght as the outcome, which is assumed to be normally distributed with a mean equal to traject and v_u as the level-1 variance. The RANDOM statement comes next. The random coefficients in this specification are b_1i, b_2i, and b_3i, which have estimated means (beta_1, beta_2, and beta_3) and a covariance matrix as specified. The SUBJECT=id indicates the random effects are random over participants (id), and the PARMS statement is used to provide starting values for all estimated parameters to begin the iterative estimation routine.

The nlme script for the bilinear spline growth model fit to the longitudinal height data is provided in Script 10.4. The script for the bilinear spline growth model is very similar to the script for the quadratic growth model. There are only two changes. The first is the level-1 equation, which now follows Equation 10.3 utilizing the pmin and pmax commands and setting the knot point to nine months. The pmin and pmax commands return a vector of minimum and maximum values, taking vectors as arguments. We note that this is needed because we want the minimum and maximum values for each record in our dataset and note that the min and max commands do not work because they are used to compare two values. The second change is the start command, where

Script 10.3. NLMIXED Script for the Bilinear Spline Growth Model

```
PROC NLMIXED DATA = hght_long;
        traject = b_1i + b_2i * MIN (0,age-9) + b_3i * MAX (0,age-9);

        MODEL hght ~ NORMAL(traject, v_u);
        RANDOM b_1i b_2i b_3i ~ NORMAL([beta_1,beta_2,beta_3],
                                               [v_1,
                                                c_21, v_2,
                                                c_30, c_32, v_3])
        SUBJECT=id;
        PARMS
        beta_1 = 60    beta_2 = 2    beta_3 = 1
        v_1 = 5        v_2 = .05     v_3 = .2
        c_21 = 0       c_31 = 0      c_32 = 0
        v_u = 2;
RUN;
```

Script 10.4. nlme Script for the Bilinear Spline Growth Model

```
hght.spline.nlme <- nlme(hght~b_1i+b_2i*(pmin(0,age-9))+
                                b_3i*(pmax(0,age-9)),
                data=hght_long,
                fixed=b_1i+b_2i+b_3i~1,
                random=b_1i+b_2i+b_3i~1,
                groups=~id,
                start=c(60, 10, 6),
                na.action=na.omit)

summary(hght.spline.nlme)
```

appropriate starting values are provided for the fixed-effects parameters of the bilinear spline growth model. The remainder of the script follows Script 10.2.

Parameter estimates from PROC NLMIXED and nlme for the bilinear spline growth model are contained in Output 10.3 and 10.4, respectively. The mean of the random intercept was 73.35 cm (beta_1, Fixed effect of b_1i), indicating the predicted average height for a 9-month-old child. The mean of the preknot slope was 2.23 cm per month (beta_2, Fixed effect of b_2i), indicating the monthly rate of growth prior to 9 months (from 1 to 9 months). The mean postknot slope was 0.89 cm per month (beta_3, Fixed effect of b_3i), indicating the rate of growth after 9 months (from 9 to 36 months). The variances of the random coefficients were all significant, indicating that children varied in each aspect of the growth model. The variance of the random intercept was 6.12 (v_1, Random effect of b_1i), indicating the magnitude of between-person differences in height at 9 months; the preknot slope variance was 0.04 (v_2, Random effect of b_2i), indicating between-person differences in the rate of growth prior to 9 months; and the postknot slope variance was 0.002 (v_3, Random effect of b_3i), indicating between-person differences in the monthly rate of growth after 9 months. The covariances among the random coefficients were also significant, indicating that the various individual parameters of the change process based on the bilinear spline growth model were related to one another. Specifically, the intercept–preknot slope covariance was 0.23 (c_21, Corr between b_1i and b_2i), indicating that children who were taller at 9 months tended to grow more rapidly before 9 months; the intercept–postknot slope covariance was 0.08 (c_31, Corr between b_1i and b_3i) indicating that children who were taller at 9 months tended to grow more rapidly after 9 months; and the pre-postknot slope covariance was 0.01 (c_32, Corr between b_2i and b_3i), indicating that children who grew faster before 9 months tended to grow faster after 9 months of age. Lastly, the level-1 residual variance was 1.81 (v_u, Random effect of Residual) and relates to the magnitude of individual fluctuations around the individual trajectories that was not captured by the model.

Figure 10.4 is a plot of the individual predicted growth trajectories from the bilinear spline growth model. As seen in this figure, the rate of growth prior to the knot point

Output 10.3. NLMIXED Output for the Bilinear Spline Growth Model

Parameter Estimates

Parameter	Estimate	Standard Error	DF	t Value	Pr > |t|	Alpha	Lower	Upper	Gradient
beta_1	73.3507	0.2939	80	249.55	<.0001	0.05	72.7657	73.9356	0.00079
beta_2	2.2267	0.03335	80	66.77	<.0001	0.05	2.1603	2.2931	-0.00011
beta_3	0.8874	0.009502	80	93.40	<.0001	0.05	0.8685	0.9063	-0.00732
v_1	6.1244	1.0991	80	5.57	<.0001	0.05	3.9370	8.3117	-0.00006
v_2	0.04363	0.01404	80	3.11	0.0026	0.05	0.01568	0.07157	0.007665
v_3	0.002174	0.001085	80	2.00	0.0486	0.05	0.000014	0.004334	0.18495
c_21	0.2333	0.09581	80	2.44	0.0171	0.05	0.04263	0.4240	-0.00225
c_31	0.08389	0.02522	80	3.33	0.0013	0.05	0.03371	0.1341	-0.00222
c_32	0.008394	0.002764	80	3.04	0.0032	0.05	0.002894	0.01389	0.026482
v_u	1.8120	0.1355	80	13.37	<.0001	0.05	1.5423	2.0818	0.000582

Output 10.4. `nlme` Output for the Bilinear Spline Growth Model

```
Random effects:
 Formula: list(b_1i ~ 1, b_2i ~ 1, b_3i ~ 1)
 Level: id
 Structure: General positive-definite, Log-Cholesky parameterization
         StdDev       Corr
b_1i     2.47477711   b_1i     b_2i
b_2i     0.20887672   0.451
b_3i     0.04662073   0.727    0.862
Residual 1.34611421

Fixed effects: b_1i + b_2i + b_3i ~ 1
         Value    Std.Error   DF    t-value     p-value
b_1i  73.35059   0.29455032  496   249.02568         0
b_2i   2.22669   0.03329296  496    66.88174         0
b_3i   0.88742   0.00949461  496    93.46612         0
```

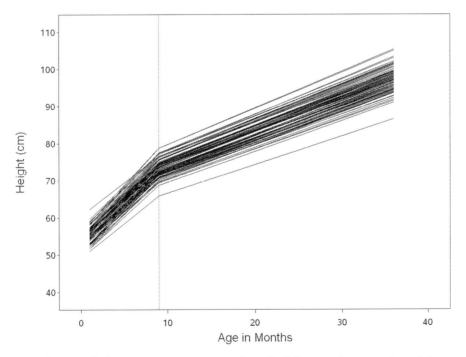

FIGURE 10.4. Individual predictions from the bilinear spline growth model.

(in infancy) was more rapid than the rate of growth after the knot point (toddler years), which is mirrored in the observed trajectories. It is also apparent that all children were predicted to experience this change in their individual rate of growth at the same point in time (i.e., 9 months), the chosen knot point for this example. This figure also highlights a key feature of many spline models—the rate of growth can change sharply at the knot point. We note that this is a common feature of the bilinear spline growth model; however, the sharp changes at the knot point can be smoothed by incorporating additional functions of time. For example, Cudeck and Klebe (2002) fit a quadratic-linear spline growth model, which allowed for a smooth transition between the two phases. In any case, having sharp changes before and after the knot point is a common feature of spline models, and its theoretical rationale must be considered. In the current situation, a sharp change does not seem reasonable; however, in other situations this type of model is quite reasonable.

STRUCTURAL EQUATION MODELING FRAMEWORK

The structural equation modeling framework easily accommodates models that are non-linear with respect to time. The growth model is expressed in the same way, and modifications are made to the Λ matrix. The common-factor model for the growth model can be written as

$$\mathbf{y}_i = \mathbf{\Lambda}\eta_i + \mathbf{u}_i \tag{10.5}$$

where $\mathbf{y}_i$ is a $T \times 1$ vector of the repeatedly measured observed scores for individual i, where T represents the number of repeated assessments based on the chosen time metric, $\mathbf{\Lambda}$ is a $T \times R$ matrix of factor loadings defining the latent growth factors, where R is the number of latent variables (i.e., growth factors), η_i is an $R \times 1$ vector of latent factor scores for individual i, and $\mathbf{u}_i$ is a $T \times 1$ vector of residual or unique scores for individual i. The latent factor scores are written as deviations from the mean, such that

$$\eta_i = \alpha + \xi_i \tag{10.6}$$

where α is an $R \times 1$ vector of latent factor means and ξ_i is an $R \times 1$ vector of mean deviations for individual i. The population mean (μ) and covariance (Σ) structure based on the latent growth model are

$$\mu = \mathbf{\Lambda}\alpha$$
$$\Sigma = \mathbf{\Lambda}\mathbf{\Psi}\mathbf{\Lambda}' + \mathbf{\Theta} \tag{10.7}$$

where $\mathbf{\Psi}$ is an $R \times R$ latent covariance matrix containing covariances among growth factors and $\mathbf{\Theta}$ is a $T \times T$ residual covariance matrix.

Quadratic Growth Model

The quadratic growth model is fit by adjusting the Λ matrix to accommodate the additional growth factor (compared with the linear model) with the elements of the columns of the Λ matrix set equal to different powers of time. For example, the Λ matrix for a quadratic growth model with five equally spaced occasions of measurement is

$$\Lambda = \begin{pmatrix} 1 & \dfrac{1-k_1}{k_2} & \left(\dfrac{1-k_1}{k_2}\right)^2 \\[2ex] 1 & \dfrac{2-k_1}{k_2} & \left(\dfrac{2-k_1}{k_2}\right)^2 \\[2ex] 1 & \dfrac{3-k_1}{k_2} & \left(\dfrac{3-k_1}{k_2}\right)^2 \\[2ex] 1 & \dfrac{4-k_1}{k_2} & \left(\dfrac{4-k_1}{k_2}\right)^2 \\[2ex] 1 & \dfrac{5-k_1}{k_2} & \left(\dfrac{5-k_1}{k_2}\right)^2 \end{pmatrix} \tag{10.8}$$

where the first column defines the intercept, the second column defines the linear component with values that change linearly with time (t), and the third column defines the quadratic component and contains squares of the elements from the second column. As in the linear model, the intercept can be centered at any measurement occasion (or point in time) by altering the value of k_1, and the linear and quadratic components can be scaled in various ways by changing the value of k_2. For example, the Λ matrix for a quadratic growth model with the intercept centered at the third occasion, $k_1 = 3$, with $k_2 = 1$ yields

$$\Lambda = \begin{pmatrix} 1 & -2 & 4 \\ 1 & -1 & 1 \\ 1 & 0 & 0 \\ 1 & 1 & 1 \\ 1 & 2 & 4 \end{pmatrix} \tag{10.9}$$

and Figure 10.5 is a path diagram of this specification of the quadratic growth model. Parameter and variable labels map onto the specification presented above. There are three latent variables ($\eta_1, \eta_2,$ and η_3) defined by factor loadings specified in Equation 10.9 with estimated means ($\alpha_1, \alpha_2,$ and α_3), variances ($\psi_{1,1}, \psi_{2,2},$ and $\psi_{3,3}$), and covariances ($\psi_{2,1}, \psi_{3,1},$ and $\psi_{3,2}$).

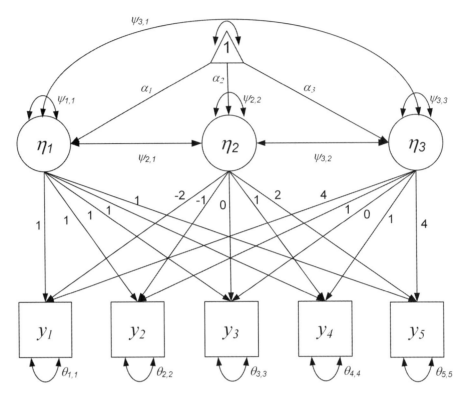

FIGURE 10.5. Path diagram of a quadratic growth model.

Spline Growth Models

Spline growth models with fixed knot points are fit by adjusting the dimensions and elements of the Λ matrix to follow the function of time in Equation 10.3. For example, the Λ matrix for a bilinear spline growth model with five equally spaced measurement occasions is

$$\Lambda = \begin{pmatrix} 1 & \min\left(\dfrac{1-k_1}{k_2}, 0\right) & \max\left(\dfrac{1-k_1}{k_2}, 0\right) \\ 1 & \min\left(\dfrac{2-k_1}{k_2}, 0\right) & \max\left(\dfrac{2-k_1}{k_2}, 0\right) \\ 1 & \min\left(\dfrac{3-k_1}{k_2}, 0\right) & \max\left(\dfrac{3-k_1}{k_2}, 0\right) \\ 1 & \min\left(\dfrac{4-k_1}{k_2}, 0\right) & \max\left(\dfrac{4-k_1}{k_2}, 0\right) \\ 1 & \min\left(\dfrac{5-k_1}{k_2}, 0\right) & \max\left(\dfrac{5-k_1}{k_2}, 0\right) \end{pmatrix} \quad (10.10)$$

where the first column defines the intercept, the second column defines the preknot slope, and the third column defines the postknot slope. The knot point is located at k_1 in the original time metric (i.e., when $k_2 = 1$) or k_1/k_2 in the rescaled time metric. If the knot point was specified at the third measurement occasion, the Λ matrix for the bilinear spline growth model would be

$$\Lambda = \begin{pmatrix} 1 & -2 & 0 \\ 1 & -1 & 0 \\ 1 & 0 & 0 \\ 1 & 0 & 1 \\ 1 & 0 & 2 \end{pmatrix} \tag{10.11}$$

As can be seen in these factor loadings, both the preknot and postknot slopes have 0 factor loadings at the third measurement occasion, which indicates the location of the intercept. The preknot slope has values that change linearly with time before the knot point, after which the factor loadings for the preknot slope do not change, indicating that this factor does not produce changes in the observed scores after the knot point. The postknot slope has factor loadings that do not change prior to the knot point, indicating that this factor does not impact changes in the observed scores prior to the knot point, and factor loadings that change linearly with time after the knot point.

A path diagram of this bilinear spline growth model is contained in Figure 10.6, with the observed variables labeled y_1 through y_5, and the intercept, preknot slope, and post-knot slope labeled η_1, η_2, and η_3, respectively. The factor loadings in this diagram follow Equation 10.11, with η_2 having 0 factor loadings to the last three observed variables and η_3 having 0 factor loadings to the first three observed variables. The three latent variables have estimated means (α_1, α_2, and α_3), variances ($\psi_{1,1}$, $\psi_{2,2}$, and $\psi_{3,3}$) and covariances ($\psi_{2,1}$, $\psi_{3,1}$, and $\psi_{3,2}$).

STRUCTURAL EQUATION MODELING IMPLEMENTATION

The longitudinal height data are now in the wide format, with separate variables for height measured at 1, 3, 6, 9, 12, 15, 18, 24, and 36 months (hght01-hght36).

Quadratic Growth Model

The Mplus MODEL statement for fitting the quadratic growth model is contained in Script 10.5. The statement begins by defining eta_1, eta_2, and eta_3 using the keyword BY to define the intercept, linear component, and quadratic component. Factor loadings for eta_1 are fixed at 1 (@1), factor loadings for eta_2 change linearly with respect to age centered at 18 months and scaled in terms of years, and factor loadings for eta_3

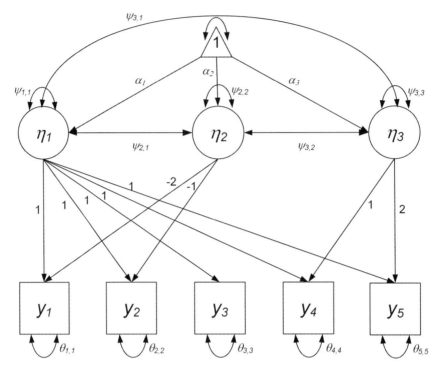

FIGURE 10.6. Path diagram of the bilinear spline growth model.

are squares of the factor loadings for eta_2. Next, latent variable variances (eta_1*60 eta_2*4 eta_3*.3;), covariances among the latent variables (eta_1 WITH eta_2 eta_3; eta_2 WITH eta_3;), and means ([eta_1*65 eta_2*2 eta_3*-.1];) are specified. Starting values are provided for the means and variances of the latent variables to aid model estimation. Residual variances for the height variables are

Script 10.5. *Mplus* Script for the Quadratic Growth Model

```
MODEL:
    eta_1 BY hght01-hght36@1;
    eta_2 BY hght01@-1.4167 hght03@-1.25 hght06@-1   hght09@-.75 hght12@-.5
            hght15@-.25    hght18@0     hght24@.5   hght36@1.5;
    eta_3 BY hght01@2.1169  hght03@1.5625 hght06@1    hght09@.5625 hght12@.25
            hght15@.0625   hght18@0      hght24@.25  hght36@2.25;

    eta_1*60 eta_2*4 eta_3*.3;
    eta_1 WITH eta_2 eta_3;
    eta_2 WITH eta_3;

    [eta_1*65 eta_2*2 eta_3*-.1];

    hght01-hght36*10 (theta);
    [hght01-hght36@0];
```

then specified and forced to be equal over time (hght01-hght36 (theta);). The last statement for the quadratic growth model fixes the observed variable intercepts to 0 ([hght01-hght36@0];).

The code to fit the quadratic growth model in OpenMx is provided in Script 10.6. The script begins by indicating the datafile and listing the manifest and latent variables. The manifest variables include the nine height variables, and the latent variables include the intercept (eta_1), linear component (eta_2), and quadratic component (eta_3). Next, the model is specified with multiple mxPath statements. The first specifies the residual variances of the observed variables—two-headed arrows (arrows=2) that are freely estimated (free=TRUE) and originate from each height variable. A starting value of 10 and a common label (theta) are applied to all residual variances to constrain them to be equal over time. Latent variable variances and covariances are then specified. The latent variables are listed as the originating variables (from=c('eta_1', 'eta_2','eta_3')), and connect='unique.pairs' is used to request variances and covariances among all specified variables. Starting values are then provided along with appropriate labels. We note that the order for these elements follows the order of the variables listed and organized according to an upper triangular matrix. Factor loadings are then specified to define eta_1, eta_2, and eta_3. These one-headed arrows orginate from the latent variable, go to the observed height variables, and are fixed (free=FALSE). The factor loadings for eta_1 are set equal to 1; the factor loadings for eta_2 change linearly with age, centered at 18 months, and scaled in terms of years; and the factor loadings for eta_3 are squares of the factor loadings for eta_2. Lastly, the means of eta_1, eta_2, and eta_3 are specified as one-headed arrows originating from the constant (one) and going to each of the three latent variables. These paths are given starting values and labels. The mxModel statement is then closed.

The structural equation modeling programs also encountered estimation issues when fitting the quadratic growth model to the height data. Mplus reported a warning stating that the latent variable covariance matrix was not positive definite, and we find that the estimated correlation between the linear and quadratic components was out of bounds ($r =$ −1.27). OpenMx reports no issues, but requesting mxStandardizeRAMpaths (quad. hght.fit) yields the standardized output where the out-of-bounds correlation between eta_2 and eta_3 is reported. The adjusted quadratic model was then fit in both programs. In Mplus, the variance of eta_3 was fixed at 0 along with the covariances involving the quadratic component (i.e., eta_3@0; eta_1 WITH eta_3@0; eta_2 WITH eta_3@0;). In OpenMx, eta_3 was removed from the mxPath statement for latent variable variances and covariances. Starting values and labels of the associated parameters were also removed.

Parameter estimates from the adjusted quadratic growth model from Mplus and OpenMx are contained in Output 10.5 and 10.6, respectively. The adjusted quadratic growth model for height had a mean intercept (predicted average height at 18 months) of 83.01 cm (Mean of ETA_1; alpha_1), a linear rate of 13.73 cm per year at 18 months (Mean of ETA_2; alpha_2), and one-half the acceleration was −3.40 cm per year

Script 10.6. OpenMx Script for the Quadratic Growth Model

```
quad.hght.omx <- mxModel('Quadratic Growth Model, Path Specification',
    type='RAM', mxData(observed=hght_wide, type='raw'),
    manifestVars=c('hght01','hght03','hght06','hght09','hght12','hght15','hght18','hght24','hght36'),
    latentVars=c('eta_1','eta_2','eta_3'),

# residual variances
mxPath(from=c('hght01','hght03','hght06','hght09','hght12','hght15','hght18','hght24','hght36'),
    arrows=2, free=TRUE, values=10, labels='theta'),

# latent variable variances & covariances
mxPath(from=c('eta_1','eta_2','eta_3'), connect='unique.pairs',
    arrows=2, free=TRUE,
    values=c(60,0,0,4,0,.3),
    labels=c('psi_11','psi_21','psi_31','psi_22','psi_32','psi_33')),

# factor loadings
mxPath(from='eta_1', to=c('hght01','hght03','hght06','hght09','hght12','hght15','hght18','hght24','hght36'),
    arrows=1, free=FALSE, values=1),

mxPath(from='eta_2', to=c('hght01','hght03','hght06','hght09','hght12','hght15','hght18','hght24','hght36'),
    arrows=1, free=FALSE,
    values=c(-1.4167, -1.25, -1, -.75, -.5, -.25, 0, .5, 1.5)),

mxPath(from='eta_3', to=c('hght01','hght03','hght06','hght09','hght12','hght15','hght18','hght24','hght36'),
    arrows=1, free=FALSE,
    values=c(2.1169, 1.5625, 1, .5625, .25, .0625, 0, .25, 2.25)),

# latent variable means
mxPath(from='one', to=c('eta_1','eta_2','eta_3'),
    arrows=1, free=TRUE, values=c(65, 2, -.1),
    labels=c('alpha_1','alpha_2','alpha_3'))

) # Close Model
```

Output 10.5. `Mplus` **Estimates for the Adjusted Quadratic Growth Model**

		Estimate	S.E.	Est./S.E.	Two-Tailed P-Value
ETA_1	WITH				
ETA_2		1.519	0.431	3.527	0.000
ETA_3		0.000	0.000	999.000	999.000
ETA_2	WITH				
ETA_3		0.000	0.000	999.000	999.000
Means					
ETA_1		83.008	0.323	256.810	0.000
ETA_2		13.730	0.135	102.059	0.000
ETA_3		-3.395	0.082	-41.497	0.000
Variances					
ETA_1		7.356	1.263	5.825	0.000
ETA_2		0.825	0.227	3.627	0.000
ETA_3		0.000	0.000	999.000	999.000
Residual Variances					
HGHT01		2.447	0.169	14.453	0.000
...					
HGHT36		2.447	0.169	14.453	0.000

Output 10.6. `OpenMx` **Estimates for the Adjusted Quadratic Growth Model**

free parameters:

	name	matrix	row	col	Estimate	Std.Error
1	theta	S	hght01	hght01	2.4473267	0.16933185
2	psi_11	S	eta_1	eta_1	7.3557571	1.26277758
3	psi_21	S	eta_1	eta_2	1.5186301	0.43052339
4	psi_22	S	eta_2	eta_2	0.8249223	0.22745399
5	alpha_1	M	1	eta_1	83.0084342	0.32322858
6	alpha_2	M	1	eta_2	13.7301429	0.13453193
7	alpha_3	M	1	eta_3	-3.3945093	0.08180253

(Mean of ETA_3; alpha_3). There was significant variability in the intercept (7.36; Variance of ETA_1; psi_11) and linear component (0.83; Variance of ETA_2; psi_22) and a significant positive covariance between the intercept and linear change component (1.52; ETA_1 WITH ETA_2; psi_21). Lastly, the residual variance was 2.45 (Residual Variances of HGHT01, theta). Overall, the parameter estimates obtained from the structural equation modeling programs were highly similar to the estimates from the multilevel modeling programs.

Spline Growth Model

The MODEL statement for the bilinear spline growth model from `Mplus` is contained in Script 10.7. The organization of the script follows the specification for the quadratic growth model with the same elements. The only changes are in the factor loadings for eta_2 and

Script 10.7. `Mplus` Script for the Bilinear Spline Growth Model

```
MODEL:
    eta_1 BY hght01-hght36@1;
    eta_2 BY hght01@-8 hght03@-6 hght06@-3 hght09@0  hght12@0
             hght15@0  hght18@0  hght24@0  hght36@0;
    eta_3 BY hght01@0  hght03@0  hght06@0  hght09@0  hght12@3
             hght15@6  hght18@9  hght24@15 hght36@27;

    eta_1*60 eta_2*4 eta_3*3;
    eta_1 WITH eta_2 eta_3;
    eta_2 WITH eta_3;
    [eta_1*65 eta_2*3 eta_3*1];
    hght01-hght36*10 (theta);
    [hght01-hght36@0];
```

eta_3. The factor loadings for eta_2 increase linearly from the 1-month assessment to the 9-month assessment (from –8 to 0). The factor loadings for the subsequent measurement occasions are maintained at 0 because eta_2 does not impact the changes in height after 9 months. The factor loadings for eta_3 are set equal to 0 for the 1-, 3-, 6-, and 9-month assessments because eta_3 does not impact the changes in height at these occasions (noting that the lack of impact is reflected by having the same factor loading across time). After the 9-month assessment, eta_3 has linearly changing factor loadings. Given the factor loadings for eta_2 and eta_3, the intercept, eta_1, is centered at the 9-month assessment (both eta_2 and eta_3 have 0 factor loadings at the 9-month assessment) and eta_2 and eta_3 reflect changes before and after the knot point, respectively, and both slopes are scaled in months. The remainder of the script specifies variances for the latent variables, covariances among the latent variables, means of the latent variables, and residual variances of the observed variables; all of which are specified in the same manner as in the quadratic growth model with some minor differences in the starting values.

The OpenMx script for the bilinear spline growth model fit to the height data is contained in Script 10.8. As in Mplus, the only changes from the script for the quadratic growth model involve the specification of the factor loadings. The factor loadings for eta_2 change linearly with age in months up to the 9-month assessment, after which a constant factor loading is maintained. Factor loadings for eta_3 are set to 0 up through the 9-month assessment and then begin to change linearly with age in months. The remainder of the script from the quadratic growth model is maintained with minor adjustments to starting values.

Parameter estimates obtained from fitting the bilinear spline growth model in Mplus and OpenMx are contained in Output 10.7 and 10.8, respectively. The mean intercept was 73.35 cm (Mean of ETA_1, alpha_1), which was the predicted average height for a 9-month-old child. The mean preknot slope was 2.23 cm per month (Mean of ETA_2, alpha_2) and is the average rate of growth prior to 9 months of age. The mean postknot slope (Mean of ETA_3, alpha_3) was 0.89 cm per month and is the average rate of growth after 9 months. The intercept variance was 6.13 (Variance of ETA_1, psi_11), indicating the magnitude of between-person differences in height

Script 10.8. OpenMx Script for the Bilinear Spline Growth Model

```
spl.hght.omx <- mxModel('Spline Growth Model, Path Specification',
type='RAM', mxData(observed=hght_wide, type='raw'),
manifestVars=c('hght01','hght03','hght06','hght09','hght12','hght15','hght18','hght24','hght36'),
latentVars=c('eta_1','eta_2','eta_3')),

# Residual Variances
mxPath(from=c('hght01','hght03','hght06','hght09','hght12','hght15','hght18','hght24','hght36'),
arrows=2, free=TRUE,
values=10, labels='theta'),

# Latent Variable Covariances
mxPath(from=c('eta_1','eta_2','eta_3'), connect='unique.pairs',
arrows=2, free=TRUE,
values=c(1,0,1,0,1),
labels=c('psi_11','psi_21','psi_31','psi_22','psi_32','psi_33')),

# Factor Loadings
mxPath(from='eta_1', to=c('hght01','hght03','hght06','hght09','hght12','hght15','hght18','hght24','hght36'),
arrows=1, free=FALSE, values=1),

mxPath(from='eta_2', to=c('hght01','hght03','hght06','hght09','hght12','hght15','hght18','hght24','hght36'),
arrows=1, free=FALSE,
values=c(-8, -6, -3, 0, 0, 0, 0, 0, 0)),

mxPath(from='eta_3', to=c('hght01','hght03','hght06','hght09','hght12','hght15','hght18','hght24','hght36'),
arrows=1, free=FALSE,
values=c(0, 0, 0, 3, 6, 9, 15, 27)),

# Latent Variable Means
mxPath(from='one', to=c('eta_1','eta_2','eta_3'),
arrows=1, free=TRUE, values=c(80, 15, 10),
labels=c('alpha_1','alpha_2','alpha_3'))
) # Close Model
```

229

Output 10.7. `Mplus` **Parameter Estimates for the Bilinear Spline Growth Model**

MODEL RESULTS

		Estimate	S.E.	Est./S.E.	Two-Tailed P-Value
ETA_1	WITH				
ETA_2		0.233	0.096	2.435	0.015
ETA_3		0.084	0.025	3.327	0.001
ETA_2	WITH				
ETA_3		0.008	0.003	3.037	0.002
Means					
ETA_1		73.351	0.294	249.543	0.000
ETA_2		2.227	0.033	66.773	0.000
ETA_3		0.887	0.010	93.397	0.000
Variances					
ETA_1		6.125	1.099	5.572	0.000
ETA_2		0.044	0.014	3.107	0.002
ETA_3		0.002	0.001	2.003	0.045
Residual Variances					
HGHT01		1.812	0.136	13.369	0.000
...					
HGHT36		1.812	0.136	13.369	0.000

Output 10.8. `OpenMx` **Parameter Estimates for the Bilinear Spline Growth Model**

free parameters:

	name	matrix	row	col	Estimate	Std.Error
1	theta	S	hght01	hght01	1.812019110	0.135542633
2	psi_11	S	eta_1	eta_1	6.124533831	1.099204500
3	psi_21	S	eta_1	eta_2	0.233322362	0.095817144
4	psi_22	S	eta_2	eta_2	0.043629803	0.014042436
5	psi_31	S	eta_1	eta_3	0.083885673	0.025215431
6	psi_32	S	eta_2	eta_3	0.008394337	0.002763891
7	psi_33	S	eta_3	eta_3	0.002173550	0.001085268
8	alpha_1	M	1	eta_1	73.350594556	0.293940341
9	alpha_2	M	1	eta_2	2.226691165	0.033347415
10	alpha_3	M	1	eta_3	0.887424499	0.009501600

at 9 months; the preknot slope variance was 0.04 (Variance of ETA_2, psi_22), indicating between-person differences in the rate of growth prior to 9 months; and the postknot slope variance was 0.00 (Variance of ETA_3, psi_33), indicating between-person differences in the monthly rate of growth after 9 months. Although the postknot slope variance was quite small, it was significantly different from zero. Here, we may want to reestimate the model and change the scale of the pre- and postknot slopes from monthly rates of change to yearly rates of change by dividing the factor loadings by 12.

This will not alter model fit in any way, but the variance of the pre- and postknot slopes will be larger because of its new scale. We note that the level of significance will remain the same.

The growth factors were also significantly associated with one another. The intercept–preknot slope covariance was 0.23 (ETA_1 WITH ETA_2, psi_21), indicating that children who were taller at 9 months tended to grow more rapidly before 9 months; the intercept–postknot slope covariance was 0.08 (ETA_1 WITH ETA_3, psi_31), indicating that children who were taller at 9 months tended to grow more rapidly after 9 months; and the pre-postknot slope covariance was 0.01 (ETA_2 WITH ETA_3, psi_32), indicating that children who grew faster before 9 months tended to grow faster after 9 months. Lastly, the level-1 residual variance was 1.81 (Residual Variance of HGHT01-HGHT36, theta), indicating the magnitude of variability left unexplained by the bilinear spline growth model.

IMPORTANT CONSIDERATIONS

Several types of models fall under the Type I designation—nonlinear models with respect to time. Such models that may be appropriate for the height data include the logarithmic ($\log(age_{ti})$) and the square root ($\sqrt{age_{ti}}$) models. In all models that are nonlinear with respect to time, the transformations of time and/or the additional functions of time can be calculated directly and are not dependent on any unknown parameter. Thus, the factor loading pattern for specifying these models in the structural equation modeling framework is composed of fixed (prespecified) values.

Variations of Models Presented

The spline models presented in this chapter had fixed knot points, and we only fit models with *one* knot point. A single *a priori* chosen knot point is unlikely to be the *best* knot point for these data. Often, an ideal knot point is determined by *estimating* the knot point; however, this is a Type II nonlinear model. An alternative approach that falls under Type I nonlinear models is to fit a series of models with different knot points. The likelihoods of the different models (i.e., $-2LL$ or χ^2) can be plotted against the location of the knot point, and the knot point with the minimum $-2LL$ (or χ^2) is the ideal knot point. This approach is referred to as the profile likelihood approach (see McArdle & Wang, 2008). We note two limitations of this approach. First, the standard error of the knot point is unknown. Second, the ideal knot point may not be located at a specific measurement occasion. In this approach, multiple models are specified, and the knot point is often located at each measurement occasion. For example, the optimal knot point for the height data may be 8.5 months, and a model with the knot point located at 8.5 months is unlikely to be fit because there was not a measurement occasion at 8.5 months.

In the specification of the bilinear spline growth model, we centered the intercept at the knot point. This is a common approach with spline models because the knot point is often viewed as an important point in time (e.g., age at crawling, birth). However, as with other growth models, the intercept can be centered at any point in time. For example, with five equally spaced measurement occasions and a bilinear spline growth model with the knot point at the third measurement occasion,

$$\Lambda = \begin{pmatrix} 1 & 0 & 0 \\ 1 & 1 & 0 \\ 1 & 2 & 0 \\ 1 & 2 & 1 \\ 1 & 2 & 2 \end{pmatrix}$$

to center the intercept at the first measurement occasion. A key aspect of the Λ matrix is where each latent variable has factor loadings that are changing versus constant. Time points where factor loadings are changing indicate that the latent variable is affecting change at those measurement occasions.

A second alternative specification of the bilinear spline growth model is to have the first slope affect the scores at all time points and the second slope to only affect the scores after the knot point. For example,

$$\Lambda = \begin{pmatrix} 1 & 0 & 0 \\ 1 & 1 & 0 \\ 1 & 2 & 0 \\ 1 & 3 & 1 \\ 1 & 4 & 2 \end{pmatrix}$$

In this specification, the first slope remains the rate of change prior to the knot point, but the second slope is the change in the rate of change after the knot point. Some researchers may prefer this approach because it is easy to see how the linear growth model is nested under the bilinear spline growth model and the parameters of the second slope are associated with the change in the rate of change after the knot point. Thus, if the mean of the second slope was significantly different from 0, then the rate of change was significantly different after the knot point.

Spline models with jump points can also be specified. For example, with five equally spaced measurement occasions and a bilinear spline growth model with the jump point between the second and third measurement occasions,

$$\Lambda = \begin{pmatrix} 1 & 0 & 0 & 0 \\ 1 & 1 & 0 & 0 \\ 1 & 2 & 1 & 0 \\ 1 & 2 & 1 & 1 \\ 1 & 2 & 1 & 2 \end{pmatrix}$$

In this specification, the first column defines the intercept or predicted value at the first measurement occasion; the second column defines the pre-jump point linear rate of change; the third column defines the change in the intercept beginning at the third measurement occasion (the magnitude of the jump); and the fourth column defines the post-jump point linear rate of change. These types of models can be fit, but may be difficult to justify theoretically.

Extensions

In the same way that individually varying measurement schedules can be accounted for in the linear growth model, such measurement schedules can be accounted for with these nonlinear models. In the multilevel modeling approach, no changes are needed. In the structural equation modeling framework, the functions of time can be calculated and the definition variable approach can be used. Additionally, these models can, of course, be combined with the multiple-group and growth mixture modeling frameworks to allow for group differences in any parameter of the model (Li et al., 2001). With spline models, it is possible for different observed or unobserved groups to have different knot points, which allows for the study of differences in the *timing* of the transition between phases.

MOVING FORWARD

In the next chapter, we discuss more complex nonlinear models in which the structure of change is dependent on one or more unknown parameters. Most of these models require a nonlinear mixed-effects modeling program or structural equation modeling software that allows for nonlinear constraints.

## 11

Growth Models with Nonlinearity in Parameters

In this chapter we expand our discussion of nonlinearity in growth models and describe models in which the relationship between the random coefficients (latent variables) and the outcome of interest depends on one or more unknown parameters. In all previous models discussed, the functional form of change (linear, quadratic, spline) was fixed and only dependent on the timing of assessment, which was known. Moving to models where the structure of change is dependent on unknown entities requires us to use nonlinear multilevel modeling programs. That is, the linear mixed-effects or multilevel modeling programs, such as PROC MIXED and lme, are unable to fit these models. In the structural equation modeling framework, the majority of these nonlinear models require nonlinear constraints, and several programs now allow for such constraints (e.g., Mplus, OpenMx, lavaan, Lisrel). Several types of models fall into this category of nonlinear change models. Here, we present a few models and attempt to generalize to the class of models.

The first type of model that falls into this category is inherently nonlinear but conditionally linear (Blozis & Cudeck, 1999). Inherently nonlinear models are models that have unknown parameters appearing in the mathematical function of time (e.g., an unknown parameter contained within an exponent and/or an unknown parameter raised to an exponent; Burchinal & Appelbaum, 1991). Inherently nonlinear models are smooth functions that are able to represent a variety of developmental processes in their entirety. Thus, these models are more likely to represent true developmental functions compared to the linear and nonlinear time models previously discussed. Additionally, the parameters of these nonlinear models can describe interesting features of change, which may easily map onto developmental theory (e.g., rates of change, asymptotic levels, timing of accelerated change). The versions of the inherently nonlinear models discussed here are not *fully nonlinear* (Davidian & Giltinan, 1995) but are conditionally linear. Thus, their random coefficients (latent variables) enter the model in a linear fashion; only estimated parameters (and not random coefficients) appear in the mathematical function of time. Conditional linear forms of inherently nonlinear models that are commonly considered by developmentalists include the exponential ($y_{ti} = b_{1i} + b_{2i} \cdot (1 - \exp(-\gamma \cdot t))$), logistic ($y_{ti} = b_{1i} + \dfrac{b_{2i}}{1 + \exp(-\gamma(t - \delta))}$), Gompertz ($y_{ti} = b_{1i} + b_{2i} \cdot (\exp(-\exp(-\gamma(t - \delta))))$), and power models ($y_{ti} = b_{1i} + b_{2i} \cdot t^{\gamma}$), where γ and δ are unknown parameters. To illustrate the fitting of these types of inherently nonlinear models, we fit a variation of the *Jenss–Bayley growth model* (Jenss & Bayley, 1937), which was specifically developed to track changes in height during infancy and therefore should be appropriate for the illustrative height data.

The second model discussed is the latent basis (shape-factor, unstructured) growth model (McArdle & Epstein, 1987; Meredith & Tisak, 1990).[1] The latent basis model is a more or less exploratory growth model in which the pattern of change (e.g., linear, quadratic) is not specified *a priori*, but an optimal shape of change is derived from the data. One can think of this model as an optimal rescaling of time in the sense that the log time and square root time models are simple rescalings of time. The latent basis model is often considered when growth models are fit in the structural equation modeling framework because of the ease with which the model is fit; however, this model can be fit with nonlinear multilevel modeling programs as well.

The third model is an extension of the spline models discussed in the previous chapter. The spline models discussed here have an *estimated* knot point as opposed to a *fixed* knot point. These models optimize the location of the knot point and provide a standard error for the estimated knot point, which allows for the calculation of its confidence interval. All of these models are fit to the longitudinal height data collected as part of the Berkeley Growth Study (Jones & Bayley, 1941) and analyzed in the previous chapter.

MULTILEVEL MODELING FRAMEWORK

Jenss–Bayley Growth Model

The Jenss–Bayley growth model (Jenss & Bayley, 1937) was developed to model changes in the physical stature of infants and toddlers. The model combines an exponential and a linear growth model and proposes that early changes in height mimic an exponential trajectory, where growth acts to limit further growth, and that these early exponential changes gradually slow and the rate of change stabilizes, becoming more or less constant during the toddler years. The Jenss–Bayley growth model is typically written as

$$y_{ti} = b_{1i} + b_{2i} \cdot t - \exp(b_{3i} + b_{4i} \cdot t) + u_{ti} \tag{11.1}$$

---

[1]The latent basis model does not fit nicely into our organization of nonlinear models. It was placed in this chapter because there are unknown parameters in the function of time and because nonlinear mixed-effects modeling programs are needed to fit this model; however, all structural equation modeling programs can fit this model (i.e., nonlinear constraints are not required).

where y_{ti} is the dependent variable measured for individual i at time t, b_{1i} is the individual intercept for the linear asymptote, b_{2i} is the individual slope of the linear asymptote, $\exp(b_{3i})$ is the vertical distance between the actual intercept and the intercept of the linear asymptote for individual i, $\exp(b_{4i})$ is the individual ratio of acceleration of growth at time t to that at time $t - 1$, and u_{ti} is the time-specific residual score for individual i at time t, which are assumed to follow normal distributions with constant variance, $u_{ti} \sim N(0, \sigma_u^2)$. The Jenss–Bayley growth model can be reparameterized (rewritten) to define b_{1i} as the intercept, which is typical in growth models, and to define b_{3i} as the vertical distance between the actual intercept and the intercept of the linear asymptote for individual i. This specification is

$$y_{ti} = b_{1i} + b_{2i} \cdot t + b_{3i} \cdot (\exp(b_{4i} \cdot t) - 1) + u_{ti} \qquad (11.2)$$

where b_{1i} is now the individual intercept (predicted height when $t = 0$) and b_{3i} is the vertical distance between the actual intercept and the intercept of the linear asymptote for individual i. These versions of the Jenss–Bayley growth model are Type III nonlinear models because b_{4i}, a random coefficient, is contained within the nonlinear function of time (i.e., $\exp(b_{4i} \cdot t)$). This model can be modified into a Type II nonlinear model by replacing b_{4i}, a random coefficient, with γ, an estimated parameter, which does not vary over participants. This limits the types of trajectories that can be observed because all participants have the same exponential curvature. Thus,

$$y_{ti} = b_{1i} + b_{2i} \cdot t + b_{3i} \cdot (\exp(\gamma \cdot t) - 1) + u_{ti} \qquad (11.3)$$

will be the form of the Jenss–Bayley growth model fit and described in this chapter. The random coefficients in Equation 11.3 enter the model in a linear (additive) fashion as each random coefficient is a multiplier of a function of time that does not depend on a random coefficient.

The level-2 equation for the random coefficients is written as

$$\begin{aligned}
b_{1i} &= \beta_1 + d_{1i} \\
b_{2i} &= \beta_2 + d_{2i} \\
b_{3i} &= \beta_3 + d_{3i}
\end{aligned} \qquad (11.4)$$

where β_1, β_2, and β_3 are fixed-effects parameters and d_{1i}, d_{2i}, and d_{3i} are individual deviations from their respective fixed-effect parameter, which are assumed to follow a multivariate normal distribution with zero means, estimated variances, and covariances,

$$d_{1i}, d_{2i}, d_{3i} \sim MVN\left(\begin{bmatrix} 0 \\ 0 \\ 0 \end{bmatrix}, \begin{bmatrix} \sigma_1^2 & & \\ \sigma_{21} & \sigma_2^2 & \\ \sigma_{31} & \sigma_{32} & \sigma_3^2 \end{bmatrix}\right)$$

Latent Basis Growth Model

The *latent basis growth* model is a flexible model that can approximate a variety of non-linear trajectories. The latent basis model can be written as

$$y_{ti} = b_{1i} + b_{2i} \cdot A_t + u_{ti} \tag{11.5}$$

where y_{ti} is the outcome of interest for individual i measured at time t, b_{1i} is the intercept for individual i, b_{2i} is the *shape* factor for individual i (often referred to as a slope), A_t is the basis coefficient at time t, and u_{ti} is the time-dependent residual. The basis coefficients, contained within A, describe the pattern of change with respect to time. For identification and to give a scale to b_{2i}, two basis coefficients need to be fixed to different values. Often, A_1, the first basis coefficient, is fixed to 0, and A_T, the last basis coefficient, is fixed to 1. The remaining basis coefficients are estimated from the data. These identification constraints scale b_{2i} in terms of the total predicted amount of change for individual i from the first to the last measurement occasion. In the latent basis model, the rate of change is not necessarily constant across time and is allowed to differ between subjects. However, there is only one random coefficient, b_{2i}, influencing change over the course of the observation period. Thus, the general shape of change is constant across participants, but subjects are allowed to vary in the magnitude of that general shape.

The level-2 equation for the latent basis growth model is

$$\begin{aligned} b_{1i} &= \beta_1 + d_{1i} \\ b_{2i} &= \beta_2 + d_{2i} \end{aligned} \tag{11.6}$$

where β_1 and β_2 are fixed-effect parameters for the intercept and shape factor, and d_{1i} and d_{2i} are individual deviations from their respective fixed effect. The individual deviations are assumed to follow a multivariate normal distribution with zero means, estimated variances, and covariances; that is,

$$d_{1i}, \; d_{2i} \sim MVN\left(\begin{bmatrix} 0 \\ 0 \end{bmatrix}, \begin{bmatrix} \sigma_1^2 & \\ \sigma_{21} & \sigma_2^2 \end{bmatrix} \right)$$

The latent basis model is not as flexible as the previously discussed models in terms of the timing of assessments. In the latent basis model, discrete intervals of time are required. That is, the latent basis model cannot be fit in continuous time where participants have individually varying times of measurement without some level of accommodation. For example, the latent basis model can be fit when observations are placed in a discrete number of bins representing different measurement times (see time-window approach in Chapter 4; see also Sterba, 2014).

Spline Growth Models with Estimated Knot Points

Spline growth models are extended in this chapter. Specifically, we discuss spline models where the knot point is estimated from the data, as opposed to a fixed value chosen by the researcher. The *bilinear spline growth model with an estimated knot point* can be written as

$$y_{ti} = b_{1i} + b_{2i} \cdot \min(t - \gamma, 0) + b_{3i} \cdot \max(t - \gamma, 0) + u_{ti} \qquad (11.7)$$

where y_{ti} is the dependent variable measured for individual i at time t, b_{1i} is the random intercept located at the knot point, $t = \gamma$, b_{2i} is the preknot random linear slope or the linear rate of change prior to the knot point, b_{3i} is the postknot random linear slope or the linear rate of change after the knot point, γ is the estimated knot point, t represents the time metric, and u_{ti} is the time-specific residual at time t for individual i. The level-2 equation for this growth model is

$$\begin{aligned}
b_{1i} &= \beta_1 + d_{1i} \\
b_{2i} &= \beta_2 + d_{2i} \\
b_{3i} &= \beta_3 + d_{3i}
\end{aligned} \qquad (11.8)$$

where β_1, β_2, and β_3 are fixed-effects parameters for the intercept, preknot linear slope, and postknot linear slope and d_{1i}, d_{2i}, and d_{3i} are individual deviations from their respective fixed effect. These individual deviations are assumed to follow a multivariate normal distribution with zero means, estimated variances, and covariances; for example,

$$d_{1i},\, d_{2i},\, d_{3i} \sim \text{MVN}\left(\begin{bmatrix} 0 \\ 0 \\ 0 \end{bmatrix}, \begin{bmatrix} \sigma_1^2 & & \\ \sigma_{21} & \sigma_2^2 & \\ \sigma_{31} & \sigma_{32} & \sigma_3^2 \end{bmatrix}\right)$$

MULTILEVEL MODELING IMPLEMENTATION

The longitudinal height data (hght_long) are in the long format, with variables id, age, and hght for the identification variable, age in months, and height in centimeters.

Jenss–Bayley Growth Model

The Jenss–Bayley growth model of Equation 11.3 was fit to the longitudinal height data using PROC NLMIXED and nlme. The SAS script is contained in Script 11.1. The script begins with the level-1 equation following Equation 11.3 with age scaled in years (age/12). This is followed by the MODEL statement where the outcome (hght) is assumed to follow a NORMAL distribution with mean traject and level-1 variance v_u. The RANDOM statement comes next, where the random coefficients (b_1i, b_2i, and b_3i) are assumed to follow a multivariate normal distribution with estimated

Script 11.1. `NLMIXED` Script for the Jenss–Bayley Growth Model

```
PROC NLMIXED DATA = hght_long;
    traject = b_1i + b_2i * (age/12) + b_3i * (exp(gamma*(age/12))-1);
    MODEL hght ~ NORMAL(traject, v_u);
    RANDOM b_1i b_2i b_3i ~ NORMAL([beta_1,beta_2,beta_3],
                                            [v_1,
                                             c_21, v_2,
                                             c_31,  c_32, v_3])

    SUBJECT = id;
    PARMS
        beta_1 = 50    beta_2 = 10    beta_3 = -18    gamma = -2
        v_1 = 8        v_2 = 1        v_3 = 9
        c_21 = 0       c_31 = 0       c_32 = 0
        v_u = 2;
RUN;
```

means (`beta_1`, `beta_2`, `beta_3`) and a variance–covariance matrix as specified. The `PARMS` statement contains starting values for all estimated parameters.

The `nlme` script for fitting the Jenss–Bayley growth model is contained in Script 11.2. In this script, the outcome variable, `hght`, is set equal to Equation 11.3 with age scaled in years (`age` divided by 12). The random coefficients (`b_1i`, `b_2i`, and `b_3i`) have estimated fixed-effects parameters, which describe their mean values, and the unknown parameter, `gamma`, is also considered a fixed-effect parameter (fixed=b_1i+b_2i+b_3i+gamma~1). The random coefficients have random-effects parameters (random=b_1i+b_2i+b_3i~1), which describe their variability and covariability. These random coefficients are random over participants (groups=~id). The script finishes with starting values for the fixed-effects parameters, and `na.action` is set to `na.omit`.

The Jenss–Bayley growth model converged rather quickly in both `NLMIXED` and `nlme`. Parameter estimates from both programs are contained in Output 11.1 and 11.2, respectively. The mean of the intercept was 51.09 cm (`beta_1`, `Fixed effect` of `b_1i`), which is the predicted mean height of children at birth. The mean of the vertical distance between the intercept of the linear asymptote and the actual intercept was –17.88 cm (`beta_3`, `Fixed effect` of `b_3i`). The rate of linear growth during the toddler years was 9.27 cm per year (`beta_2`, `Fixed effect` of `b_2i`). The last fixed-effects parameter was the `gamma` parameter, which was estimated to be –2.06.

Script 11.2. `nlme` Script for the Jenss–Bayley Growth Model

```
hght.jb.nlme <- nlme(hght~b_1i+b_2i*(age/12)+b_3i*(exp(gamma*(age/12))-1),
                data=hght_long,
                fixed=b_1i+b_2i+b_3i+gamma~1,
                random=b_1i+b_2i+b_3i~1,
                groups=~id,
                start=c(50, 10, -18, -2),
                na.action=na.omit)

summary(hght.jb.nlme)
```

Output 11.1. NLMIXED Output for The Jenss–Bayley Growth Model

Parameter Estimates

Parameter	Estimate	Standard Error	DF	t Value	Pr > |t|	Alpha	Lower	Upper	Gradient
beta_1	51.0915	0.3524	80	144.98	<.0001	0.05	50.3902	51.7928	0.000025
beta_2	9.2749	0.1723	80	53.84	<.0001	0.05	8.9320	9.6177	-0.00002
beta_3	-17.8812	0.4635	80	-38.58	<.0001	0.05	-18.8036	-16.9588	2.419E-7
gamma	-2.0634	0.07804	80	-26.44	<.0001	0.05	-2.2187	-1.9081	-0.00029
v_1	7.3895	1.3519	80	5.47	<.0001	0.05	4.6991	10.0799	2.7E-6
v_2	0.7395	0.1812	80	4.08	0.0001	0.05	0.3790	1.1001	-5.63E-6
v_3	9.4221	2.1462	80	4.39	<.0001	0.05	5.1510	13.6931	-1.59E-7
c_21	0.6151	0.3748	80	1.64	0.1047	0.05	-0.1308	1.3610	1.563E-6
c_31	4.8592	1.4200	80	3.42	0.0010	0.05	2.0333	7.6851	-0.00001
c_32	0.6703	0.4894	80	1.37	0.1747	0.05	-0.3037	1.6442	0.00002
v_u	0.6710	0.05003	80	13.41	<.0001	0.05	0.5714	0.7705	-0.00005

Output 11.2. `nlme` Output for the Jenss–Bayley Growth Model

```
Random effects:
 Formula: list(b_1i ~ 1, b_2i ~ 1, b_3i ~ 1)
 Level: id
         StdDev        Corr
b_1i     2.7199531     b_1i    b_2i
b_2i     0.8590517     0.260
b_3i     3.0567734     0.583   0.248
Residual 0.8193595

Fixed effects: b_1i + b_2i + b_3i + gamma ~ 1
             Value     Std.Error   DF    t-value     p-value
b_1i        51.04753   0.3501220   495   145.79927         0
b_2i         9.31413   0.1649161   495    56.47799         0
b_3i       -17.81609   0.4537913   495   -39.26054         0
gamma       -2.08950   0.0731174   495   -28.57738         0
```

Exponentiating this parameter yields 0.13 (exp (–2.06)), which is the ratio of acceleration of growth at time t to that at time $t – 1$ (in years). Thus, this parameter indicates how quickly the rapid changes in height taking place during early infancy decelerate.

The variance of the intercept was 7.39 (v_1, Random effect of b_1i), which reflects individual differences in height at birth. The variance of the linear slope was 0.74 (v_2, Random effect of b_2i), indicating between-person differences in the linear rate of growth during the toddler years. The variance of the difference in the intercept and the intercept for the linear asymptote was 9.42 (v_3, Random effect of b_3i), indicating individual differences in this aspect of the model, which is related to differences in the amount of growth that occurred prior to when the changes became constant. The covariance between the intercept and the linear slope was 0.62 (c_21, Corr between b_1i and b_2i) and not statistically significant, indicating that birth height was unrelated to the linear rate of growth during the toddler years. The covariance between intercept and the difference between the intercept and the intercept of the linear asymptote was 4.86 (c_31, Corr between b_1i and b_3i), indicating that children who were taller at birth tended to have smaller (more positive) differences between the two intercepts (i.e., these children grew less before transitioning to their linear asymptote). The covariance between the difference in the intercepts and the linear rate of change was 0.67 (c_32, Corr between b_2i and b_3i), indicating that children who grew less before transitioning to their linear asymptote tended to grow at a faster rate during the toddler years. Lastly, the residual variance was 0.67 (v_u, Random effect of Residual).

Figure 11.1 is a plot of the predicted trajectories from the Jenss–Bayley growth model. The predicted trajectories are smooth and display the early rapid growth, which begins to slow during late infancy, and is followed by more or less constant growth from 15 through 36 months. The between-child variability in growth is also evident from this figure because several of the predicted trajectories cross. That is, it is not simply that the tallest children grow at the fastest rate at all times; there are sizable between-child

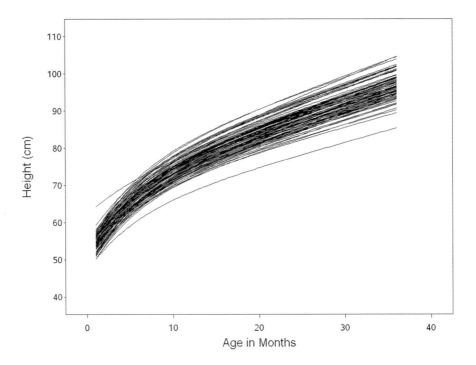

FIGURE 11.1. Individual predictions of the Jenss–Bayley growth model.

differences in the rate of growth during infancy that are not consistent with between-child differences in the rate of growth during the toddler years.

Latent Basis Growth Model

The NLMIXED script for the latent basis growth model is contained in Script 11.3. The script begins with a series of conditional statements. These conditional statements are used to define the basis coefficients (A_t). The basis coefficient at the first measurement occasion (age = 1) is set equal to 0, and the basis coefficient at the last measurement occasion (age = 36) is set equal to 1. The remaining basis coefficients are set equal to a series of unknown parameters (A_2 through A_8), which will be estimated. Next, the level-1 equation for the latent basis growth model (Equation 11.5) is specified with traject, the expected mean trajectory, as the outcome, b_1i as the intercept, and b_2i as the shape factor. The shape factor is scaled in terms of *total* change in height from 1 to 36 months. The MODEL statement follows and defines the outcome variable and its distribution with mean traject and residual variance v_u. The RANDOM statement is then used to define the random coefficients, b_1i and b_2i, which have estimated means (beta_1 and beta_2) and a variance–covariance matrix as specified. Lastly, starting values for parameter estimates are provided in the PARMS statement.

The nlme script for the latent basis growth model is contained in Script 11.4. Prior to the nlme command, the datafile is augmented to include a series of dummy-coded

Script 11.3. NLMIXED Script for the Latent Basis Growth Model

```
PROC NLMIXED DATA = hght_long;
    IF age = 1   THEN A_t = 0;
    IF age = 3   THEN A_t = A_2;
    IF age = 6   THEN A_t = A_3;
    IF age = 9   THEN A_t = A_4;
    IF age = 12 THEN A_t = A_5;
    IF age = 15 THEN A_t = A_6;
    IF age = 18 THEN A_t = A_7;
    IF age = 24 THEN A_t = A_8;
    IF age = 36 THEN A_t = 1;

    traject = b_1i + b_2i * A_t;

    MODEL hght ~ NORMAL(traject, v_u);
    RANDOM b_1i b_2i ~ NORMAL([beta_1, beta_2], [v_1,
                                                  c_21, v_2])

    SUBJECT = id;
    PARMS
        beta_1 = 40 beta_2 = 15
        A_2 = .2 A_3 = .3 A_4 = .4 A_5 = .6 A_6 = .7 A_7 = .8 A_8 = .9
        v_1 = 40 v_2 = 1   c_21 = 0
        v_u = 10;
RUN;
```

variables.[2] These variables, named age1 through age36, indicate each measurement occasion. For example, age1 is coded 1 when age equals 1 and age1 is coded 0 otherwise.

The nlme command begins with a modified version of the latent basis growth model. The model is written on an occasion-by-occasion basis using an indicator variable to turn on and off each part of the growth model depending on the measurement occasion. The programming of this model draws on our presentation of multiple-group models where an indicator variable was used to identify each group. For the first occasion, the measurement occasion indicator variable, age1, is multiplied by the growth model, with 0 as the basis coefficient (b_1i+b_2i*0). For the second through eighth measurement occasion, indicator variables (e.g., age3) are multiplied by the growth model with estimated basis coefficients, A_2 through A_8 (e.g., b_1i+b_2i*A_2). At the last measurement occasion, the indicator variable, age36, is multiplied by the growth model with 1 as the basis coefficient (b_1i+b_2i*1). The random coefficients, b_1i and b_2i, have fixed- and random-effects parameters, and the basis coefficients are considered fixed-effects parameters. Thus, the unknown basis coefficients appear in the fixed statement. The identification variable is indicated in the groups statement, and starting values are provided for all fixed-effects parameters.

Parameter estimates from NLMIXED and nlme are contained in Output 11.3 and 11.4, respectively. The mean of the intercept (beta_1, Fixed effect of b_1i) was

---

[2]The for loop goes to 747 because that is the number of observations in the datafile.

Script 11.4. `nlme` Script for the Latent Basis Growth Model

```
for(n in 1:747) {
        if (hght_long$age[n] == 1) {hght_long$age1[n]=1}
        if (hght_long$age[n] != 1) {hght_long$age1[n]=0}
        if (hght_long$age[n] == 3) {hght_long$age3[n]=1}
        if (hght_long$age[n] != 3) {hght_long$age3[n]=0}
        if (hght_long$age[n] == 6) {hght_long$age6[n]=1}
        if (hght_long$age[n] != 6) {hght_long$age6[n]=0}
        if (hght_long$age[n] == 9) {hght_long$age9[n]=1}
        if (hght_long$age[n] != 9) {hght_long$age9[n]=0}
        if (hght_long$age[n] == 12) {hght_long$age12[n]=1}
        if (hght_long$age[n] != 12) {hght_long$age12[n]=0}
        if (hght_long$age[n] == 15) {hght_long$age15[n]=1}
        if (hght_long$age[n] != 15) {hght_long$age15[n]=0}
        if (hght_long$age[n] == 18) {hght_long$age18[n]=1}
        if (hght_long$age[n] != 18) {hght_long$age18[n]=0}
        if (hght_long$age[n] == 24) {hght_long$age24[n]=1}
        if (hght_long$age[n] != 24) {hght_long$age24[n]=0}
        if (hght_long$age[n] == 36) {hght_long$age36[n]=1}
        if (hght_long$age[n] != 36) {hght_long$age36[n]=0}
        }

hght.latent.nlme  <- nlme(hght~age1*(b_1i+b_2i*0)+
                            age3*(b_1i+b_2i*A_2)+
                            age6*(b_1i+b_2i*A_3)+
                            age9*(b_1i+b_2i*A_4)+
                            age12*(b_1i+b_2i*A_5)+
                            age15*(b_1i+b_2i*A_6)+
                            age18*(b_1i+b_2i*A_7)+
                            age24*(b_1i+b_2i*A_8)+
                            age36*(b_1i+b_2i*1),
                        data=hght_long ,
                        fixed=b_1i+b_2i+A_2+A_3+A_4+A_5+A_6+A_7+A_8~1,
                        random=b_1i+b_2i~1,
                        groups=~id,
                        start=c(60, 20, .3, .4, .5, .6, .7, .8, .9),
                        na.action=na.omit)

summary(hght.latent.nlme)
```

54.54 cm and indicates the predicted mean height of 1-month-old infants because the basis coefficient at the 1-month measurement occasion was 0. The mean of the shape factor (beta_2, Fixed effect of b_2i) was 42.10 cm and is the total predicted mean change in height from 1 to 36 months. The basis coefficients describe the shape of change from 1 to 36 months. The basis coefficients, A_2 through A_8, were 0.15, 0.31, 0.41, 0.50, 0.59, 0.66, and 0.78. These basis coefficients represent the proportion of the total amount of change that has occurred up to that point in time. Thus, 15% of the total change from 1 to 36 months occurred by the 3-month measurement occasion. Similarly,

Output 11.3. NLMIXED Output for the Latent Basis Growth Model

Parameter Estimates

Parameter	Estimate	Standard Error	DF	t Value	Pr > |t|	Alpha	Lower	Upper	Gradient
beta_1	54.5425	0.2778	81	196.36	<.0001	0.05	53.9899	55.0952	-0.0007
beta_2	42.1001	0.4087	81	103.00	<.0001	0.05	41.2868	42.9133	0.000175
A_2	0.1471	0.003538	81	41.57	<.0001	0.05	0.1400	0.1541	-0.01821
A_3	0.3088	0.003426	81	90.15	<.0001	0.05	0.3020	0.3156	-0.0098
A_4	0.4096	0.003392	81	120.75	<.0001	0.05	0.4028	0.4163	0.005591
A_5	0.5030	0.003350	81	150.12	<.0001	0.05	0.4963	0.5096	-0.01422
A_6	0.5871	0.003551	81	165.35	<.0001	0.05	0.5800	0.5942	0.005325
A_7	0.6568	0.003552	81	184.92	<.0001	0.05	0.6498	0.6639	0.006554
A_8	0.7833	0.003641	81	215.12	<.0001	0.05	0.7760	0.7905	-0.00657
v_1	5.1383	0.8886	81	5.78	<.0001	0.05	3.3704	6.9063	-0.00031
v_2	10.2310	1.9807	81	5.17	<.0001	0.05	6.2900	14.1720	-0.00006
c_21	-0.9285	0.9730	81	-0.95	0.3428	0.05	-2.8644	1.0074	-0.00017
v_u	0.8158	0.05636	81	14.48	<.0001	0.05	0.7037	0.9279	0.000667

Output 11.4. nlme Output for the Latent Basis Growth Model

```
Random effects:
 Formula: list(b_1i ~ 1, b_2i ~ 1)
 Level: id
 Structure: General positive-definite, Log-Cholesky parametrization
         StdDev      Corr
b_1i     2.2669367   b_1i
b_2i     3.1982959   -0.128
Residual 0.9031948

Fixed effects: b_1i + b_2i + A_2 + A_3 + A_4 + A_5 + A_6 + A_7 + A_8 ~ 1
          Value    Std.Error   DF    t-value     p-value
b_1i    54.54834   0.2797289   490   195.00427        0
b_2i    42.08689   0.4113588   490   102.31187        0
A_2      0.14678   0.0035631   490    41.19609        0
A_3      0.30874   0.0034520   490    89.43782        0
A_4      0.40956   0.0034124   490   120.02170        0
A_5      0.50299   0.0033746   490   149.05122        0
A_6      0.58723   0.0035781   490   164.11636        0
A_7      0.65704   0.0035792   490   183.57248        0
A_8      0.78358   0.0036713   490   213.43595        0
```

50% of the total change occurred by 12 months of age. Therefore, infants were predicted to grow a similar amount from 12 to 36 months as they did from 1 to 12 months.

The variance of the intercept (v_1, Random effect of b_1i) was 5.14 and represents between-child variation in height at 1 month. The variability in the shape factor (v_2, Random effect of b_2i) was 10.23, indicating between-child variation in the total amount of change from 1 to 36 months. The intercept–shape covariance (c_21, Corr between b_1i and b_2i) was –0.93 and not significant. Thus, height at 1 month was unrelated to the predicted total amount of change in height from 1 to 36 months. The last estimated parameter was the residual variance (v_u, Random effect of Residual), which was 0.82, and represents within-child variability in height that was unexplained by the latent basis growth model.

Figure 11.2 is a plot of the individual trajectories from the latent basis growth model. The predicted trajectories closely match the mean growth trajectory and these trajectories are not as varied as the predicted trajectories from the Jenss–Bayley growth model. This can be seen in the growth trajectories from 12 through 36 months where the trajectories are almost parallel in the latent basis growth model and intersect more in the Jenss–Bayley growth model. This is because the latent basis growth model has a single individual differences factor controlling individual change (b_{2i}), whereas the Jenss–Bayley growth model has two (b_{2i} and b_{3i}). That is, predicted changes in height based on the latent basis growth model are always proportional to one another (e.g., participants who were predicted to show more growth during infancy showed more growth during the toddler years), whereas in the Jenss–Bayley growth model the individual rate of change is more dynamic and constantly evolving. Additionally, the between-person differences in the rate of change vary at each measurement occasion in the Jenss–Bayley growth model.

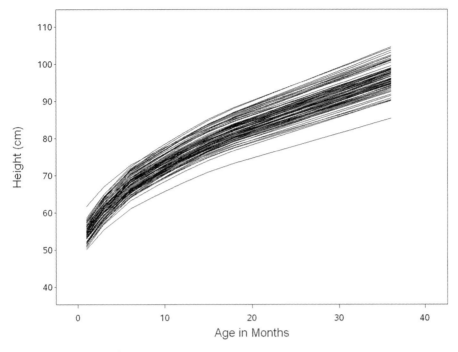

FIGURE 11.2. Individual predictions of the latent basis growth model.

Spline Growth Model with Estimated Knot Point

The NLMIXED script for the bilinear spline growth model with an estimated knot point is provided in Script 11.5. The script begins with the level-1 equation following Equation 11.7, with b_1i, b_2i, and b_3i as random coefficients and utilizing the MIN and MAX functions in SAS. In this script, age-gamma is contained in the MIN and MAX functions, and gamma is the *unknown* knot point. The remainder of the script follows the bilinear spline growth model presented in the previous chapter. The MODEL statement is specified with hght as the outcome, which is assumed to be normally distributed with a mean equal to traject and v_u as the level-1 variance. The RANDOM statement contains the random coefficients, b_1i, b_2i, and b_3i, which have estimated means (beta_1, beta_2, and beta_3) and a covariance matrix as specified. The remaining two statements are typically specified to indicate that the random effects are random over participant (id) and to provide starting values for estimated parameters to begin the iterative estimation routine.

The nlme script for the spline growth model with an estimated knot point fit to the longitudinal height data is provided in Script 11.6. The level-1 equation for the model is specified with b_1i, b_2i, and b_3i as random coefficients. The pmin and pmax functions are used to take the minimum and maximum of age-gamma and 0. The fixed command includes b_1i, b_2i, b_3i and gamma, the estimated knot point, and the random-effects parameters are estimated for b_1i, b_2i, b_3i. The random effects are random over participants (based on the subject identification variable, id). Lastly, starting values are provided for the fixed-effects parameters.

Script 11.5. `NLMIXED` Script for the Bilinear Spline Growth Model with an Estimated Knot Point

```
PROC NLMIXED DATA = hght_long;
    traject = b_1i + b_2i*(MIN(age-gamma,0)) + b_3i*(MAX(age-gamma,0));

    MODEL hght ~ NORMAL(traject, v_u);
    RANDOM b_1i b_2i b_3i ~ NORMAL([beta_1,beta_2,beta_3],
                                                [v_1,
                                                 c_21, v_2,
                                                 c_31, c_32, v_3])
    SUBJECT = id;
    PARMS
        beta_1 = 70   beta_2 = 7   beta_3 = .5   gamma = 9
        v_1 = 8       v_2 = 1      v_3 = 1
        c_21 = 0      c_31 = 0     c_32 = 0
        v_u = 2;
RUN;
```

Script 11.6. `nlme` Script for the Bilinear Spline Growth Model with an Estimated Knot Point

```
hght.spline.nlme <- nlme(hght~b_1i+b_2i*(pmin(0,age-gamma))+
                                b_3i*(pmax(0,age-gamma)),
                        data=hght_long,
                        fixed=b_1i+b_2i+b_3i+gamma~1,
                        random=b_1i+b_2i+b_3i~1,
                        groups=~id,
                        start=c(60, 5, 2, 8),
                        na.action=na.omit)

summary(hght.spline.nlme)
```

Parameter estimates from `PROC NLMIXED` and `nlme` for this bilinear spline growth model are contained in Output 11.5 and 11.6, respectively. The estimates obtained from `nlme` were slightly different from those obtained from `NLMIXED`. In this description, we report the estimates from `NLMIXED`. The mean intercept was 71.69 cm (`beta_1, Fixed effect of b_1i`), which is the predicted average height at the knot point, 7.52 months. The preknot slope mean was 2.57 cm per month (`beta_2, Fixed effect of b_2i`), indicating the average rate of change before 7.52 months, and the postknot slope mean (`beta_3, Fixed effect of b_3i`) was 0.90 cm per month, indicating the average rate of change after 7.52 months. The intercept variance was 5.91 (`v_1, Random effect of b_1i`), indicating between-person variability in height at 7.52 months; the preknot slope variance was 0.07 (`v_2, Random effect of b_2i`), indicating between-person differences in the rate of growth prior to the knot point; and the postknot slope variance was 0.003 (`v_3, Random effect of b_3i`), indicating between-person differences in the monthly rate of growth after the knot point. As we mentioned in the previous chapter, it is reasonable to rescale the slopes in terms of years to obtain a more accurate picture of the amount of variability in the rate of change after the knot point. The intercept–preknot slope covariance was 0.27 (`c_21, Corr between b_1i and b_2i`), indicating that children who were taller at 7.52 months tended

Output 11.5. NLMIXED Output for the Bilinear Spline Growth Model with an Estimated Knot Point

Parameter Estimates

Parameter	Estimate	Standard Error	DF	t Value	Pr > |t|	Alpha	Lower	Upper	Gradient
beta_1	71.6880	0.3330	80	215.27	<.0001	0.05	71.0253	72.3508	-0.00065
beta_2	2.5653	0.05274	80	48.64	<.0001	0.05	2.4603	2.6702	0.00005
beta_3	0.9031	0.009926	80	90.98	<.0001	0.05	0.8833	0.9228	0.000156
gamma	7.5167	0.1330	80	56.50	<.0001	0.05	7.2519	7.7815	0.000871
v_1	5.9071	1.0457	80	5.65	<.0001	0.05	3.8261	7.9880	-0.00024
v_2	0.06967	0.02047	80	3.40	0.0010	0.05	0.02892	0.1104	0.002703
v_3	0.003272	0.001122	80	2.91	0.0046	0.05	0.001038	0.005505	-0.00998
c_21	0.2656	0.1123	80	2.36	0.0205	0.05	0.04205	0.4891	0.002041
c_31	0.07563	0.02490	80	3.04	0.0032	0.05	0.02607	0.1252	0.004618
c_32	0.008192	0.003366	80	2.43	0.0172	0.05	0.001493	0.01489	-0.00572
v_u	1.4758	0.1103	80	13.38	<.0001	0.05	1.2563	1.6954	0.00014

Output 11.6. nlme Output for the Bilinear Spline Growth Model with an Estimated Knot Point

```
Random effects:
 Formula: list(b_1i ~ 1, b_2i ~ 1, b_3i ~ 1)
 Level: id
 Structure: General positive-definite, Log-Cholesky parametrization
           StdDev            Corr
b_1i       2.43555766        b_1i       b_2i
b_2i       0.26036626        0.418
b_3i       0.05674639        0.548      0.550
Residual   1.21623023

Fixed effects: b_1i + b_2i + b_3i + gamma ~ 1
           Value     Std.Error    DF      t-value      p-value
b_1i    71.82716    0.3353841     495    214.16390           0
b_2i     2.53762    0.0525520     495     48.28783           0
b_3i     0.90117    0.0098949     495     91.07447           0
gamma    7.62649    0.1372391     495     55.57085           0
```

to grow more rapidly before 7.52 months; the intercept–postknot slope covariance was 0.08 (c_31, Corr between b_1i and b_3i), indicating that children who were taller at 7.52 months tended to grow more rapidly after 7.52 months; and the preknot–postknot slope covariance was 0.01 (c_32, Corr between b_2i and b_3i), indicating that children who grew faster before 7.52 months tended to grow faster after 7.52 months. Lastly, the level-1 residual variance was 1.48 (v_u, Random effect of Residual).

At this point, it is relevant to compare the bilinear spline growth model fit in the previous chapter and the bilinear spline growth model with an estimated knot point fit here. These two models are *nested* and differ by a single parameter. Thus, we can statistically compare the models using a likelihood ratio test. The $-2LL$ from the bilinear spline growth model was 2339.2, and the $-2LL$ from the bilinear spline growth model with an estimated knot point was 2264.7. Subtracting these values yields 74.5 and indicates that estimating the knot point significantly improved model fit compared to having the knot point fixed at 9 months ($\chi^2(1) = 74.5$, $p < .001$). This result highlights the importance of estimating the knot point and allowing for the knot point to be located at a time point between measurement occasions (instead of being locked into a measurement occasion). Furthermore, this approach allows us to calculate the 95% confidence interval for the knot point, which was [7.25, 7.78]. This is especially relevant if we have hypotheses regarding the location of the knot point (e.g., how long after the death of a close relative do changes in depression change course?).

Figure 11.3 contains a plot of the individual predicted trajectories from the bilinear spline growth model with an estimated knot point, along with a reference line at the location of the knot point. As seen in this figure, the rate of change abruptly changes at the knot point. Interestingly, the knot point, 7.52 months, is between two measurement occasions. Thus, there is no measurement occasion that contributes to the estimation of both slopes. That is, when the knot point was fixed at 9 months, data from 9-month measurement occasion were at the junction of the pre- and postknot slopes and therefore part of both slopes. Here, each measurement occasion only contributes to the estimation of one slope because the knot point is located between two measurement occasions.

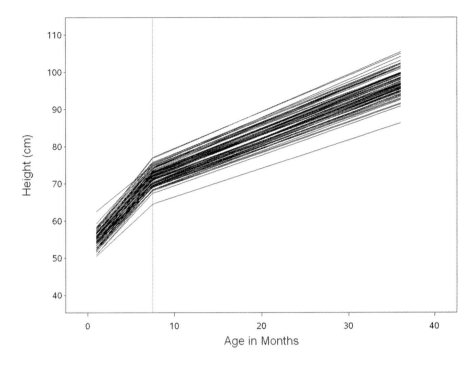

FIGURE 11.3. Individual predictions of the bilinear spline growth model with an estimated knot point.

STRUCTURAL EQUATION MODELING FRAMEWORK

The structural equation modeling framework can accommodate models that are nonlinear with respect to *parameters*; however, the structural equation modeling programs must allow for nonlinear constraints to fit the majority of these models (i.e., the latent basis model does not require nonlinear constraints). Many programs allow for nonlinear constraints (Mplus, OpenMx, Lisrel, PROC CALIS, lavaan), but certain programs may not allow for all needed functions (e.g., Mplus does not currently have MIN and MAX functions). The growth model is expressed in the same way, and modifications are made to the Λ matrix—the Λ matrix will now contain estimated elements and mathematical functions. Previously, all elements of the Λ matrix were fixed values (no unknowns).

The common factor model for the latent growth model can be written as

$$\mathbf{y}_i = \Lambda \eta_i + \mathbf{u}_i \qquad (11.9)$$

where $\mathbf{y}_i$ is a $T \times 1$ vector of the repeatedly measured observed scores for individual i, where T represents the number of repeated assessments based on the chosen time metric, Λ is a $T \times R$ matrix of factor loadings defining the latent growth factors, where R is the number of growth factors, η_i is an $R \times 1$ vector of latent factor scores for individual i, and $\mathbf{u}_i$ is a $T \times 1$ vector of residual or unique scores for individual i.

The latent factor scores are written as deviations from the sample mean and written as

$$\eta_i = \alpha + \xi_i \qquad (11.10)$$

where α is an $R \times 1$ vector of latent factor means and ξ_i is an $R \times 1$ vector of mean deviations for individual i. The population mean (μ) and covariance (Σ) structure based on the latent growth model are

$$\mu = \Lambda \alpha$$
$$\Sigma = \Lambda \Psi \Lambda' + \Theta \qquad (11.11)$$

where Ψ is a $R \times R$ latent covariance matrix containing covariances among the growth factors and Θ is a $T \times T$ residual covariance matrix.

Jenss–Bayley Growth Model

The Jenss–Bayley growth model of Equation 11.3 can be fit directly in the structural equation modeling framework because the latent variables (random coefficients) enter the model in a linear fashion—latent variables are additive. Within the structural equation modeling framework, the Λ matrix is augmented to include unknown parameters that require estimation. The Λ matrix for the Jenss–Bayley growth model with five equally spaced occasions of measurement is

$$\Lambda = \begin{pmatrix} 1 & \dfrac{1-k_1}{k_2} & \exp\left(\gamma\left(\dfrac{1-k_1}{k_2}\right)\right) - 1 \\[2mm] 1 & \dfrac{2-k_1}{k_2} & \exp\left(\gamma\left(\dfrac{2-k_1}{k_2}\right)\right) - 1 \\[2mm] 1 & \dfrac{3-k_1}{k_2} & \exp\left(\gamma\left(\dfrac{3-k_1}{k_2}\right)\right) - 1 \\[2mm] 1 & \dfrac{4-k_1}{k_2} & \exp\left(\gamma\left(\dfrac{4-k_1}{k_2}\right)\right) - 1 \\[2mm] 1 & \dfrac{5-k_1}{k_2} & \exp\left(\gamma\left(\dfrac{5-k_1}{k_2}\right)\right) - 1 \end{pmatrix} \qquad (11.12)$$

where the first column defines the intercept, the second column defines the slope of the linear asymptote with values that change linearly with time (t), and the third column defines the vertical distance between the actual intercept and the intercept of the linear asymptote. The constants, k_1 and k_2, are chosen to center the intercept and scale time in an appropriate metric. γ is an unknown parameter requiring estimation that is contained in the Λ matrix, and $\exp(\gamma)$ is the ratio of acceleration of growth at time t to that at time $t - 1$. Thus, the first and second columns of the Λ matrix contain fixed values (k_1 and k_2 are known), whereas the last column contains unknown values, which conform to a specific nonlinear function.

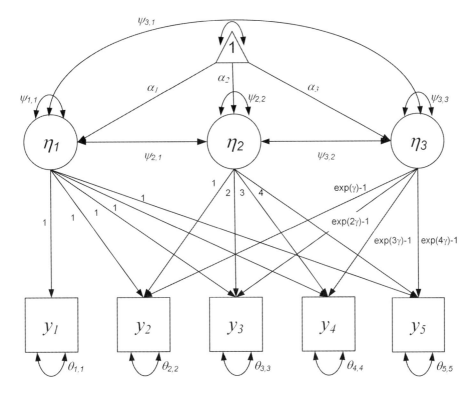

FIGURE 11.4. Path diagram of the Jenss–Bayley growth model.

Figure 11.4 is a path diagram of the Jenss–Bayley growth model with five measurement occasions and $k_1 = k_2 = 1$. Parameter labels map onto the specification presented above. The observed variables are labeled y_1 through y_5 and the latent variables representing the intercept, the slope of the linear asymptote, and the vertical difference between the actual intercept and intercept of the linear asymptote are labeled η_1, η_2, and η_3; γ is an unknown parameter contained in the factor loadings for η_3.

Latent Basis Growth Model

The latent basis growth model is specified by allowing certain elements of the Λ matrix to be freely estimated, whereas other elements are fixed for identification purposes. Allowing specific elements to be freely estimated allows the pattern of change to be determined by the data. For example, the Λ matrix for the latent basis growth model with five occasions of measurement can be specified as

$$\Lambda = \begin{pmatrix} 1 & 0 \\ 1 & \lambda_{22} \\ 1 & \lambda_{32} \\ 1 & \lambda_{42} \\ 1 & 1 \end{pmatrix} \tag{11.13}$$

where the first column defines the intercept and the second column defines the shape factor with two fixed loadings and three unknown loadings (λ_{22}, λ_{32}, λ_{42}) to be estimated. Fixing the first and last factor loading to 0 and 1, respectively, scales the shape factor in terms of total change. In this specification, the unknown factor loadings represent the proportion of the predicted total change from the first to the last occasion that occurred up to that point in time. Thus, the factor loadings for the latent basis model are not fixed, nor are they forced to follow a specific function of time, which is why this model is sometimes referred to as the unstructured growth model. Alternative specifications of the Λ matrix of the latent basis growth model, which scale the shape factor in different ways, are common. For example, in studying the initial increases and subsequent decreases in cortisol response, Ram and Grimm (2009) set the first factor loading to 0 and the factor loading for the time point when cortisol peaked to 1. This scaled the shape factor in terms of change from baseline to peak response.

A path diagram of the latent basis growth model is contained in Figure 11.5, with the observed variables labeled y_1 through y_5 and the intercept and the shape factor labeled η_1 and η_2, respectively. The factor loadings for η_1 are fixed at 1, the first factor loading for η_2 is fixed at 0 (it doesn't appear in path diagram), the last factor loading for η_2 is fixed at 1, and the loadings at occasions 2, 3, and 4 are estimated parameters.

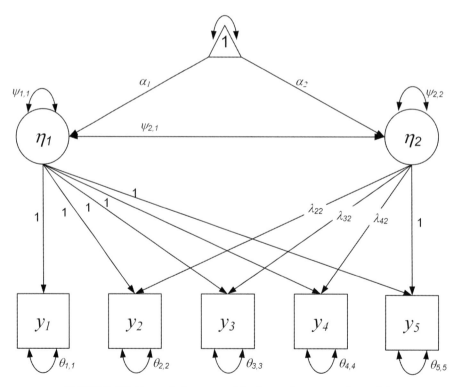

FIGURE 11.5. Path diagram of the latent basis growth model.

Spline Growth Model with Estimated Knot Point

Spline models with estimated knot points are also fit by adjusting the specification of the Λ matrix. For example, the Λ matrix for a bilinear spline growth model with an estimated knot point with five equally spaced measurement occasions is

$$\Lambda = \begin{pmatrix} 1 & \min\left(\dfrac{1-\gamma}{k_2}, 0\right) & \max\left(\dfrac{1-\gamma}{k_2}, 0\right) \\[2ex] 1 & \min\left(\dfrac{2-\gamma}{k_2}, 0\right) & \max\left(\dfrac{2-\gamma}{k_2}, 0\right) \\[2ex] 1 & \min\left(\dfrac{3-\gamma}{k_2}, 0\right) & \max\left(\dfrac{3-\gamma}{k_2}, 0\right) \\[2ex] 1 & \min\left(\dfrac{4-\gamma}{k_2}, 0\right) & \max\left(\dfrac{4-\gamma}{k_2}, 0\right) \\[2ex] 1 & \min\left(\dfrac{5-\gamma}{k_2}, 0\right) & \max\left(\dfrac{5-\gamma}{k_2}, 0\right) \end{pmatrix} \tag{11.14}$$

where the first column defines the intercept, the second column defines the preknot slope, and the third column defines the postknot slope. The knot point is located at γ, which is an estimated parameter in the original time metric or γ/k_2 in the rescaled time metric. As we noted above, some structural equation modeling programs do not allow for minimum and maximum functions, which prevents the specification of this Λ matrix. Fortunately, Harring, Cudeck, and du Toit (2006) showed how the bilinear spline growth model can be reparameterized and specified without using minimum and maximum functions. Following Harring and colleagues (2006), the Λ matrix is specified as

$$\Lambda = \begin{pmatrix} 1 & \dfrac{1-k_1}{k_2} & \sqrt{\left(\left(\dfrac{1-k_1}{k_2}\right)-\gamma\right)^2} \\[3ex] 1 & \dfrac{2-k_1}{k_2} & \sqrt{\left(\left(\dfrac{2-k_1}{k_2}\right)-\gamma\right)^2} \\[3ex] 1 & \dfrac{3-k_1}{k_2} & \sqrt{\left(\left(\dfrac{3-k_1}{k_2}\right)-\gamma\right)^2} \\[3ex] 1 & \dfrac{4-k_1}{k_2} & \sqrt{\left(\left(\dfrac{4-k_1}{k_2}\right)-\gamma\right)^2} \\[3ex] 1 & \dfrac{5-k_1}{k_2} & \sqrt{\left(\left(\dfrac{5-k_1}{k_2}\right)-\gamma\right)^2} \end{pmatrix} \tag{11.15}$$

In this parameterization, the interpretation of the latent variables (we refer to these latent variables as η_1^*, η_2^*, and η_3^*) changes due to the reparameterization. For example, the first column defines the average intercept of the two linear splines, the second column defines the average slope of the two linear splines, and the third column defines half the difference between the slopes of the two linear splines. Fortunately, the estimates of this model can be back-transformed to provide estimates for the parameters from the typical specification of the bilinear spline growth model. The mean of the preknot slope is the difference between the means of η_2^* and η_3^* (i.e., $\alpha_2^* - \alpha_3^*$); the mean of the post-knot slope is the sum of the means of η_2^* and η_3^* (i.e., $\alpha_2^* + \alpha_3^*$); and the mean intercept located at the knot point is the mean of η_1^* plus the knot point multiplied by the mean of η_2^* (i.e., $\alpha_1^* + \gamma \cdot \alpha_2^*$). A path diagram of this model is not presented but generally follows the presentation of the path diagram for the Jenss–Bayley growth model with factor loadings set equal to the factor loading matrix in either Equation 11.14 or 11.15.

STRUCTURAL EQUATION MODELING IMPLEMENTATION

The longitudinal height data are now in the wide format with separate variables for the height measured at 1, 3, 6, 9, 12, 15, 18, 24, and 36 months (hght01-hght36).

Jenss–Bayley Growth Model

The MODEL statement for fitting the Jenss–Bayley growth model in Mplus is contained in Script 11.7. The MODEL statement begins by defining eta_1, eta_2, and eta_3 using the keyword BY. The factor loadings for eta_1 and eta_2 are fixed values. The factor loadings of eta_1 are set equal to 1, and the factor loadings for eta_2 change linearly in terms of years. The factor loadings for eta_3 are not fixed values because the third column of the factor loading matrix in Equation 11.12 contains an estimated parameter, γ. In Mplus, these factor loadings are given labels (L13 through L93), and an asterisk is placed after the first variable to override the Mplus default that latent variables are identified by the first observed variable with a factor loading set equal to 1. The labels are needed to force the factor loadings to change according to a nonlinear function. The remainder of the MODEL statement follows the typical specification. Latent variable variances and covariances are specified next and followed by latent variable means. Reasonable starting values are given for the latent variable variances and means. Typically, good starting values for latent variable means and variances are needed for a model of this complexity. The last two statements of the MODEL command are for the residual variances, which are constrained to be equal across time, and the observed variable intercepts, which are set equal to 0.

The MODEL CONSTRAINT statement follows the MODEL statement. In the MODEL CONSTRAINT statement, the factor loadings for eta_3 are set equal to a nonlinear function of time with an estimated parameter. The first part of the statement, new(gamma*-2), creates a new unknown parameter to be estimated, which is named gamma and given a

Script 11.7. `Mplus` Script for the Jenss–Bayley Growth Model

```
MODEL:
    eta_1 BY hght01-hght36@1;
    eta_2 BY hght01@.0833 hght03@.25 hght06@.5 hght09@.75 hght12@1
             hght15@1.25  hght18@1.5 hght24@2  hght36@3;
    eta_3 BY hght01* (L13)
             hght03   (L23)
             hght06   (L33)
             hght09   (L43)
             hght12   (L53)
             hght15   (L63)
             hght18   (L73)
             hght24   (L83)
             hght36   (L93);

    eta_1*60 eta_2*4 eta_3*.1;
    eta_1 WITH eta_2 eta_3;
    eta_2 WITH eta_3;

    [eta_1*50 eta_2*.5 eta_3*-8];

    hght01-hght36*2 (theta);

    [hght01-hght36@0];
MODEL CONSTRAINT:
    new(gamma*-2);

    L13 = exp(gamma * 0.0833)-1;
    L23 = exp(gamma * 0.2500)-1;
    L33 = exp(gamma * 0.5000)-1;
    L43 = exp(gamma * 0.7500)-1;
    L53 = exp(gamma * 1.0000)-1;
    L63 = exp(gamma * 1.2500)-1;
    L73 = exp(gamma * 1.5000)-1;
    L83 = exp(gamma * 2.0000)-1;
    L93 = exp(gamma * 3.0000)-1;
```

starting value of –2. The next nine statements are the nonlinear constraints for the factor loadings of `eta_3`. On the left side of the equations are the labels of the factor loadings for `eta_3` (`L13` through `L93`), and on the right side of the equation is the nonlinear function (e.g., `exp(gamma * 0.0833)-1`). The nonlinear function is the exponent of `gamma`, the estimated parameter, multiplied by the timing of the assessment, scaled in years, and then 1 is subtracted. The only difference in this series of equations is the timing of the assessment, which ranges from `0.0833` to `3.0000`, which is 1 to 36 months scaled in years.

The code to fit the Jenss–Bayley growth model in `OpenMx` is provided in Script 11.8. The script begins by indicating the datafile and defining both manifest and latent variables. The manifest variables include the nine height variables, and the latent variables comprise the intercept, slope of the linear asymptote, and the difference between the actual intercept and intercept of the linear asymptote (`eta_1`, `eta_2`, `eta_3`). Next, the model is specified with `mxPath` commands. The first specifies the residual variances

Script 11.8. OpenMx Script for the Jenss–Bayley Growth Model

```
jb.hght.omx <- mxModel('Jenss Bayley Growth Model, Path Specification',
type='RAM', mxData(observed=hght_wide, type='raw'),
manifestVars=c('hght01','hght03','hght06','hght09','hght12','hght15','hght18','hght24','hght36'),
latentVars=c('eta_1','eta_2','eta_3'),

# Residual Variances
mxPath(from=c('hght01','hght03','hght06','hght09','hght12','hght15','hght18','hght24','hght36'),
arrows=2, free=TRUE, values=10, labels='theta'),

# Latent Variable Covariances
mxPath(from=c('eta_1','eta_2','eta_3'), connect='unique.pairs',
arrows=2, free=TRUE, values=c(1,0,0,1,0,1),
labels=c('psi_11','psi_21','psi_31','psi_22','psi_32','psi_33')),

# Factor Loadings
mxPath(from='eta_1', to=c('hght01','hght03','hght06','hght09','hght12','hght15','hght18','hght24','hght36'),
arrows=1, free=FALSE, values=1),

mxPath(from='eta_2', to=c('hght01','hght03','hght06','hght09','hght12','hght15','hght18','hght24','hght36'),
arrows=1, free=FALSE, values=c(.0833, .25, .5, .75, 1, 1.25, 1.5, 2, 3)),

mxPath(from ='eta_3', to=c('hght01','hght03','hght06','hght09','hght12','hght15','hght18','hght24','hght36'),
arrows=1, free=FALSE,
labels=c('Load[1,1]', 'Load[2,1]', 'Load[3,1]', 'Load[4,1]', 'Load[5,1]',
'Load[6,1]', 'Load[7,1]', 'Load[8,1]', 'Load[9,1]')),

# Latent Variable Means
mxPath(from ='one', to=c('eta_1','eta_2','eta_3'),
arrows=1, free=TRUE, values=c(80, 15, -1), labels=c('alpha_1','alpha_2','alpha_3')),

mxMatrix('Full', 9, 1, free = TRUE, values = -2, labels = 'g', name = 'gamma'),
mxMatrix('Full', 9, 1, free = FALSE, values = 1, name = 'one'),
mxMatrix('Full', 9, 1, free = FALSE, values = c(.0833,.25,.5,.75,1,1.25,1.5,2,3), name='time'),

mxAlgebra(exp(gamma * time)-one, name='Load')

) # Close Model

jb.hght.fit <- mxRun(jb.hght.omx)

summary(jb.hght.fit)
```

of the observed variables—two-headed arrows (`arrows=2`) that are freely estimated (`free=TRUE`), but constrained to be equal because of their common label (`theta`). Latent variable variances and covariances are then specified. The latent variables are listed as the originating variable (`from=c('eta_1','eta_2','eta_3')`), and `connect='unique.pairs'` is stated to indicate a full symmetric covariance matrix for these variables. Starting values are then provided along with labels.

Factor loadings are then specified to define the latent variables. Factor loadings for the intercept are fixed (`free=FALSE`) and set equal to 1; factor loadings for the linear asymptote change linearly with age scaled in years since birth, and factor loadings for the difference between the actual intercept and intercept of the linear asymptote are not freely estimated (`free=FALSE`) but will be specified to change according to the nonlinear function. For now, these factor loadings are given labels (`Load[1,1]` through `Load[9,1]`), which are elements of a named `mxAlgebra` statement that will follow, where the nonlinear function is specified. Next, the means of the latent variables are specified as one-headed arrows originating from the constant (`one`) and going to `eta_1`, `eta_2`, and `eta_3`.

The next series of commands are needed to force the factor loadings of `eta_3` to change according to a specific nonlinear function. The first matrix, created with `mxMatrix`, is for the new parameter to be estimated. This matrix has nine rows and one column (9×1) because there are nine measurement occasions. The values of this matrix are freely estimated (`free=TRUE`), given starting values of -2, and the label g. Lastly, the matrix is named `gamma`. We note that all the elements of this matrix are the same because the label g is given to all elements. Therefore, even though this matrix has nine elements, it represents a single parameter. The second `mxMatrix` is a 9×1 matrix that contains fixed values that are set equal to 1. This matrix is named `one` and is needed because 1 is subtracted from the exponent of gamma multiplied by age in the Jenss–Bayley growth model (Equation 11.12). The third `mxMatrix` contains information regarding the timing of the assessments. This 9×1 matrix contains fixed values corresponding to the timing of assessments scaled in years since birth and is named `time`. Lastly, the `mxAlgebra` command is used to specify the nonlinear function for the factor loadings of `eta_3`, which is based on the Jenss–Bayley growth model and is the difference between the exponent of `gamma` multiplied by `time` and `one`. The name given to the `mxAlgebra` is `Load`, which has nine elements, `Load[1,1]` through `Load[9,1]`, which were the labels given to the factor loadings of `eta_3`. The use of matrices when specifying these constraints is very useful, simplifies code, and reduces careless mistakes.

Parameter estimates from the Jenss–Bayley growth model fit in *Mplus* and OpenMx are contained in Output 11.7 and 11.8, respectively. The mean of the intercept was 51.09 cm (Mean of `eta_1`, `alpha_1`) and represents the predicted mean height of infants at birth. The mean of the linear asymptote was 9.27 cm per year (Mean of `eta_2`, `alpha_2`), indicating the average rate of growth during the toddler years. The mean of the vertical distance between the intercept of the linear asymptote and the actual asymptote was –17.88 cm (Mean of `eta_3`, `alpha_3`). Finally, the `gamma` parameter was –2.06, and exponentiating this parameter yields 0.13 (exp (–2.06)), which is the ratio of acceleration of growth at time t to that at time $t-1$ (in years) during the infant years.

Output 11.7. Mplus Output for the Jenss–Bayley Growth Model

		Estimate	S.E.	Est./S.E.	Two-Tailed P-Value
ETA_1	BY				
	HGHT01	1.000	0.000	999.000	999.000
	. . .				
	HGHT36	1.000	0.000	999.000	999.000
ETA_2	BY				
	HGHT01	0.083	0.000	999.000	999.000
	. . .				
	HGHT36	3.000	0.000	999.000	999.000
ETA_3	BY				
	HGHT01	-0.158	0.005	-28.849	0.000
	HGHT03	-0.403	0.012	-34.600	0.000
	HGHT06	-0.644	0.014	-46.275	0.000
	HGHT09	-0.787	0.012	-63.203	0.000
	HGHT12	-0.873	0.010	-88.043	0.000
	HGHT15	-0.924	0.007	-124.890	0.000
	HGHT18	-0.955	0.005	-180.080	0.000
	HGHT24	-0.984	0.003	-390.443	0.000
	HGHT36	-0.998	0.000	-2077.696	0.000
ETA_1	WITH				
	ETA_2	0.615	0.375	1.641	0.101
	ETA_3	4.859	1.420	3.422	0.001
ETA_2	WITH				
	ETA_3	0.671	0.489	1.370	0.171
Means					
	ETA_1	51.093	0.352	145.007	0.000
	ETA_2	9.274	0.172	53.830	0.000
	ETA_3	-17.881	0.464	-38.573	0.000
Variances					
	ETA_1	7.389	1.352	5.466	0.000
	ETA_2	0.740	0.181	4.082	0.000
	ETA_3	9.422	2.146	4.390	0.000
Residual Variances					
	HGHT01	0.671	0.050	13.411	0.000
	. . .				
	HGHT36	0.671	0.050	13.411	0.000
New/Additional Parameters					
	GAMMA	-2.063	0.078	-26.441	0.000

The variance of the intercept was 7.39 (Variance of eta_1, psi_11), indicating between-child differences in height at birth. The variance of the linear slope was 0.74 (Variance of eta_2, psi_22), which represents the magnitude of between-person differences in the linear rate of growth during the toddler years. The variance of the difference between the intercept of the linear asymptote and the actual intercept was 9.42 (Variance of eta_3, psi_33) and represents between-child differences in the relative amount of growth during the infant years before transitioning to the linear asymptote. The covariance between the intercept and the linear slope was 0.62 (eta_1

Output 11.8. OpenMx Output for the Jenns–Bayley Growth Model

```
free parameters:
      name    matrix     row      col      Estimate    Std.Error
1     theta        S   hght01   hght01    0.6709178   0.05002789
2    psi_11        S    eta_1    eta_1    7.3887284   1.35182881
3    psi_21        S    eta_1    eta_2    0.6152247   0.37484150
4    psi_22        S    eta_2    eta_2    0.7396280   0.18118753
5    psi_31        S    eta_1    eta_3    4.8584951   1.42004215
6    psi_32        S    eta_2    eta_3    0.6706145   0.48946779
7    psi_33        S    eta_3    eta_3    9.4221637   2.14634918
8   alpha_1        M        1    eta_1   51.0932819   0.35235184
9   alpha_2        M        1    eta_2    9.2744207   0.17229178
10  alpha_3        M        1    eta_3  -17.8807054   0.46354927
11        g    gamma        1        1   -2.0629730   0.07802278
```

WITH eta_2, psi_21) and nonsignificant, indicating that birth height was unrelated to the rate of growth during the toddler years. The covariance between intercept and the difference between the intercept of the linear asymptote and actual intercept was 4.86 (eta_1 WITH eta_3, psi_31), indicating that children who were taller at birth tended to transition to a steadier growth rate after less overall growth. The covariance between the difference in the intercepts and the linear rate of change was 0.67 (eta_2 WITH eta_3, psi_32) and not statistically significant. Lastly, the residual variance was 0.67 (Residual Variance, theta).

Latent Basis Growth Model

The MODEL statement for the latent basis growth model fit in Mplus is contained in Script 11.9. The script is a straightforward extension of the linear growth model, with changes only appearing in the specification of the factor loadings for eta_2. The script begins by defining the intercept, eta_1, and shape factor, eta_2. The factor loadings for the intercept are all fixed at 1, and the factor loadings for the shape factor are a combination of fixed and free values. In this specification, the factor loading to the first assessment is fixed at 0 (hght01@0), the factor loading to the last assessment is fixed at 1 (hght36@1),

Script 11.9. Mplus Script for the Latent Basis Growth Model

```
MODEL:
    eta_1 BY hght01-hght36@1;
    eta_2 BY hght01@0 hght03* hght06* hght09*  hght12*
            hght15*  hght18* hght24* hght36@1;

    eta_1*60 eta_2*4;
    eta_1 WITH eta_2;
    [eta_1*65 eta_2*20];

    hght01-hght36*10 (theta);
    [hght01-hght36@0];
```

and the factor loadings to the remaining observed variables (hght03 through hght24) are unknown and will be estimated. Next, the latent variable variances and covariance are specified, and starting values are provided for the variance of the intercept and shape factors. The latent variables means are then specified in square brackets, and appropriate starting values are provided. This is followed by specifying the residual variances of the observed variables, providing starting values, and applying a common label to place an equality constraint on them. Lastly, the observed variable intercepts are fixed to 0.

The mxModel statement for the latent basis growth model from OpenMx is contained in Script 11.10. The script begins with the specification of the residual variances, which are given a starting value of 10 and a common label, theta, to constrain them to be equal. Next, latent variable variances and covariance are specified for eta_1 and eta_2 using connect='unique.pairs' to specify a full covariance matrix among the elements. Starting values of 1 are given to the variances and a starting value of 0 is given to the covariance between eta_1 and eta_2. Appropriate labels are then provided. Next, factor loadings are specified for eta_1 and eta_2. Factor loadings for eta_1 are set equal to 1, and the factor loadings for eta_2 are a combination of fixed values and freely estimated parameters. The first and last factor loadings are fixed to 0 and 1, respectively, using a combination of the free and values commands. NAs appear in the labels statement for the fixed elements. The remaining factor loadings are freely estimated, and reasonable starting values are provided. Lastly, factor means for eta_1 and eta_2 are specified, and given starting values and labels.

Parameter estimates from Mplus and OpenMx are contained in Output 11.9 and 11.10, respectively. The factor loadings for eta_2 provide information about the shape and relative amounts of growth between measurement occasions. Thus, a careful examination of these parameters is worthwhile. The factor loading at 3 months was 0.15 and represents the proportion of predicted total change (from 1 to 36 months) that occurred by 3 months. Thus, 15% of the total growth occurred in the first two months of the observation period. The factor loading for 6 months was 0.31. Thus, 31% of the total change occurred between 1 and 6 months. Alternatively, we can state that 16% (16 = (0.31 − 0.15) · 100) of the total change occurred between 3 and 6 months. Extending this logic we can calculate the relative rate of change between measurement occasions. For example, between 3 and 6 months, the relative rate of change was 5.33% per month ([0.16/3] · 100). Calculating the relative rate of change suggests that the relative rate of growth declined with increasing age. The most rapid relative rate of change occurred between 1 and 3 months, where the relative rate of change was 7.35%, and the smallest relative rate of change was 1.81% between 24 and 36 months. Furthermore, we can include information from the mean of the shape factor, eta_2, to calculate the average rate of change between measurement occasions. The mean of eta_2 was 42.10, and represents the predicted total average growth from 1 to 36 months. Thus, the average rate of change between 1 and 3 months was 3.09 cm per month (7.35% · 42.10), and the average rate of change between 24 and 36 months was 0.76 cm per month.

Now that the general shape of change is understood, we turn to the remaining parameter estimates. The mean of the intercept (Mean of ETA_1, alpha_1) was 54.54 and represents

Script 11.10. OpenMx Script for the Latent Basis Growth Model

```
latent.hght.omx <- mxModel('Latent Basis Growth Model, Path Specification',
    type='RAM', mxData(observed=hght_wide, type='raw'),
    manifestVars=c('hght01','hght03','hght06','hght09','hght12','hght15','hght18','hght24','hght36'),
    latentVars=c('eta_1','eta_2')),

# Residual Variances
mxPath(from=c('hght01','hght03','hght06','hght09','hght12','hght15','hght18','hght24','hght36'),
    arrows=2, free=TRUE, values=10, labels='theta'),

# Latent Variable Covariances
mxPath(from=c('eta_1','eta_2'), connect='unique.pairs',
    arrows=2, free=TRUE, values=c(1,0,1), labels=c('psi_11','psi_21','psi_22')),

# Factor Loadings
mxPath(from='eta_1', to=c('hght01','hght03','hght06','hght09','hght12','hght15','hght18','hght24','hght36'),
    arrows=1, free=FALSE, values=1),

mxPath(from='eta_2', to=c('hght01','hght03','hght06','hght09','hght12','hght15','hght18','hght24','hght36'),
    arrows=1, free=c(FALSE,TRUE,TRUE,TRUE,TRUE,TRUE,TRUE,TRUE,FALSE), values=c(0,.2,.3,.4,.5,.6,.7,.8,1),
    labels=c(NA,'L22','L32','L42','L52','L62','L72','L82',NA)),

# Latent Variable Means
mxPath(from='one', to=c('eta_1','eta_2'),
    arrows=1, free=TRUE, values=c(50, 45), labels=c('alpha_1','alpha_2'))

) # Close Model
```

Output 11.9. `Mplus` Output from the Latent Basis Growth Model

		Estimate	S.E.	Est./S.E.	Two-Tailed P-Value
ETA_1	BY				
HGHT01		1.000	0.000	999.000	999.000
...					
HGHT36		1.000	0.000	999.000	999.000
ETA_2	BY				
HGHT01		0.000	0.000	999.000	999.000
HGHT03		0.147	0.004	41.572	0.000
HGHT06		0.309	0.003	90.148	0.000
HGHT09		0.410	0.003	120.745	0.000
HGHT12		0.503	0.003	150.125	0.000
HGHT15		0.587	0.004	165.354	0.000
HGHT18		0.657	0.004	184.921	0.000
HGHT24		0.783	0.004	215.121	0.000
HGHT36		1.000	0.000	999.000	999.000
ETA_1	WITH				
ETA_2		-0.928	0.973	-0.954	0.340
Means					
ETA_1		54.543	0.278	196.354	0.000
ETA_2		42.100	0.409	102.997	0.000
Variances					
ETA_1		5.139	0.889	5.783	0.000
ETA_2		10.231	1.981	5.165	0.000
Residual Variances					
HGHT01		0.816	0.056	14.476	0.000
...					
HGHT36		0.816	0.056	14.476	0.000

Output 11.10. `OpenMx` Output for the Latent Basis Growth Model

free parameters:

	name	matrix	row	col	Estimate	Std.Error
1	L22	A	hght03	eta_2	0.1470679	0.003537661
2	L32	A	hght06	eta_2	0.3088312	0.003425829
3	L42	A	hght09	eta_2	0.4095698	0.003392017
4	L52	A	hght12	eta_2	0.5029530	0.003350232
5	L62	A	hght15	eta_2	0.5870969	0.003550546
6	L72	A	hght18	eta_2	0.6568479	0.003552045
7	L82	A	hght24	eta_2	0.7832835	0.003641127
8	theta	S	hght01	hght01	0.8157824	0.056355942
9	psi_11	S	eta_1	eta_1	5.1385245	0.888690260
10	psi_21	S	eta_1	eta_2	-0.9284781	0.973303182
11	psi_22	S	eta_2	eta_2	10.2311654	1.980925851
12	alpha_1	M	1	eta_1	54.5425903	0.277776702
13	alpha_2	M	1	eta_2	42.1000298	0.408748261

the predicted average height, in centimeters, of 1-month old children (the timing of the first measurement occasion). The mean of the slope or shape latent variable (Mean of ETA_2, alpha_2) was 42.10 and is, as we have previously noted, the predicted average amount of growth from 1 to 36 months, in centimeters. The variances of the intercept (Variance of ETA_1, psi_11) and shape latent variables (Variance of ETA_2, psi_22) were 5.14 and 10.23, respectively, representing the amount of between-child differences in height at 1 month and between-child differences in the amount of total change in height from 1 to 36 months. The intercept–shape covariance (ETA_1 WITH ETA_2, psi_21) was –0.93 and nonsignificant, indicating that individual differences in height at 1 month were unrelated to individual differences in the changes in height from 1 to 36 months. Lastly, the residual variance (Residual Variances of HGHT01 to HGHT36, theta) was 0.82, indicating within-child variation around the individual predicted growth trajectories.

Spline Growth Model with Estimated Knot Point

The MODEL statement for the bilinear spline growth model with an estimated knot point from Mplus is contained in Script 11.11. The approach we take in Mplus follows the specification by Harring, Cudeck, and du Toit (2006) and Equation 11.15 because Mplus does not currently allow for minimum and maximum functions.[3] The organization of the script follows the Jenss–Bayley growth model as some of the factor loadings used to define the latent variables are fixed and others depend on an estimated parameter. The MODEL statement begins by defining the three latent variables: eta_1s, eta_2s, and eta_3s. We put an s at the end of the latent variables to remind us that this form of the bilinear spline growth model follows Harring, Cudeck, and du Toit's (2006) approach. Following Equation 11.15, the factor loadings for eta_1s are set equal to 1, the factor loadings for eta_2s change linearly with time, and factor loadings for eta_3s are specified to follow a nonlinear function that is specified in the MODEL CONSTRAINT command. For now, these factor loadings are given the labels L13 through L93. In the remainder of the MODEL statement, we specify the variances, covariances, and means of the latent variables, and constrain the residual variances to be equal across time. We provide labels for the parameters associated with the latent variables in order to use Mplus to calculate the parameters of the traditional specification of the bilinear spline growth model (Equation 11.14), which will also be done using the MODEL CONSTRAINT command.

The MODEL CONSTRAINT command follows the MODEL command in Mplus and is utilized for two purposes. First, the command is used to constrain the factor loadings of eta_3s to follow a specific nonlinear function with an estimated parameter, named gamma. To do this, gamma is listed in the new() statement, and the labels for the factor loadings of eta_3s are constrained to equal the square root of the square of the month of the assessment minus gamma (e.g., L13 = SQRT((1 - gamma)^2) for the

---

[3]This is likely to change in the near future; however, this approach is useful when allowing for between-person variation in the knot point (Preacher & Hancock, 2015) and shows additional useful features of the Mplus program.

Script 11.11. Mplus Script for the Bilinear Spline Growth Model with an Estimated Knot Point

```
MODEL:
    eta_1s BY hght01-hght36@1;
    eta_2s BY hght01@1  hght03@3  hght06@6  hght09@9  hght12@12
             hght15@15 hght18@18 hght24@24 hght36@36;
    eta_3s BY hght01* (L13)
              hght03* (L23)
              hght06* (L33)
              hght09* (L43)
              hght12* (L53)
              hght15* (L63)
              hght18* (L73)
              hght24* (L83)
              hght36* (L93);

    eta_1s*40 (psi_11s)
    eta_2s*1  (psi_22s)
    eta_3s*1  (psi_33s);
    eta_1s WITH eta_2s (psi_21s);
    eta_1s WITH eta_3s (psi_31s);
    eta_2s WITH eta_3s (psi_32s);

    [eta_1s*45]  (alpha_1s);
    [eta_2s*3]   (alpha_2s);
    [eta_3s*-1]  (alpha_3s);

    hght01-hght36*10 (theta);
    [hght01-hght36@0];
MODEL CONSTRAINT:
    new(gamma*8
        alpha_1 alpha_2 alpha_3
        psi_11 psi_22 psi_33
        psi_21 psi_31 psi_32);

    L13 = SQRT((1  - gamma)^2);
    L23 = SQRT((3  - gamma)^2);
    L33 = SQRT((6  - gamma)^2);
    L43 = SQRT((9  - gamma)^2);
    L53 = SQRT((12 - gamma)^2);
    L63 = SQRT((15 - gamma)^2);
    L73 = SQRT((18 - gamma)^2);
    L83 = SQRT((24 - gamma)^2);
    L93 = SQRT((36 - gamma)^2);

    alpha_1 = alpha_1s+gamma*alpha_2s;
    alpha_2 = alpha_2s-alpha_3s;
    alpha_3 = alpha_2s+alpha_3s;

    psi_11 = (psi_11s + gamma*gamma*psi_22s)+2*psi_21s*gamma;
    psi_22 = (psi_22s + psi_33s)-2*psi_32s;
    psi_33 = (psi_22s + psi_33s)+2*psi_32s;

    psi_21 = psi_21s - psi_31s + gamma*(psi_22s-psi_32s);
    psi_31 = psi_21s + psi_31s + gamma*(psi_22s+psi_32s);
    psi_32 = psi_22s - psi_33s;
```

assessment at the first month). In the nine constraints for the factor loadings, only the month associated with the measurement occasion changes.

Second, the MODEL CONSTRAINT command is used to specify a series of equations to calculate estimates of parameters from the traditional bilinear spline growth model. The specified model contains latent variables that are not necessarily of interest, and it would be beneficial to transform the parameters of the estimated model into parameters related to the preknot slope, the postknot slope, the intercept centered at the knot point, and the estimated knot point. The transformation equations are presented in the script, and these equations are utilized to calculate parameter estimates of the latent variables of interest (even though we do not model these latent variables). In the MODEL CONSTRAINT command, alpha_1, alpha_2, alpha_3, psi_11, psi_22, psi_33, psi_21, psi_31, and psi_32 are contained in the new() statement, and these parameters represent the means, variances, and covariances of the intercept (centered at the knot point), preknot slope, and postknot slope. A series of equations are then specified where these new estimated parameters appear on the left-hand side of the constraint and on the right-hand side are several equations with parameters from the estimated model. These equations are specified based on the means, variances, and covariances of linear combinations (e.g., sums and differences of variables). The benefit of doing this in conjunction with the model is that appropriate standard errors of these transformed parameters are calculated.

The OpenMx script for the bilinear spline growth model with an estimated knot point fit to the height data is contained in Script 11.12. The structure of the script is similar to the structure of the spline model with a fixed knot point; however, there are a few additions to allow for the estimation of the knot point. The first two mxPath statements specify the residual variances of the observed variables, which are constrained to be equal over time, and the latent variable variances and covariances, which are freely estimated. Three mxPath statements are then used to specify the factor loadings for the three latent variables: eta_1, eta_2, and eta_3. Factor loadings for eta_1 are fixed and set equal to 1. Factor loadings for eta_2 and eta_3 vary as a function of the knot point, which will be estimated. In the script, these one-headed arrows are not freely estimated nor set to fixed values. However, since these parameters vary according to a specified function with an estimated parameter, we specify free=FALSE. The labels for the factor loadings of eta_2 are L11[1,1] through L91[1,1] and the labels for the factor loadings of eta_3 are L12[1,1] through L92[1,1]. These labels are unique in that they are elements of a series of 1×1 matrices, which are subsequently defined with a series of mxAlgebra commands. Next, latent variable means are specified—one-headed arrows from the constant to eta_1, eta_2, and eta_3.

The next series of commands are needed to define the additional estimated parameter and set the factor loadings of eta_2 and eta_3 to vary according to the estimated knot point. The mxMatrix statement defines the additional parameter to be estimated. This matrix contains a single element (dimensions of the matrix are 1×1), which is given a starting value of 7 and labeled g. The matrix is named gamma, and the matrix name is needed when defining the constraints in OpenMx. Next, a collection of mxAlgebra statements are specified where the constraints for the factor loadings of eta_2 and eta_3 are specified. Thus, there are nine mxAlgebra statements for eta_2 and nine for eta_3. The

Script 11.12. OpenMx Script for the Bilinear Spline Growth Model with an Estimated Knot Point

```
spl.hght.omx <- mxModel('Spline Growth Model, Path Specification', type='RAM',
    mxData(observed=hght_wide, type='raw'),
    manifestVars=c('hght01', 'hght03', 'hght06', 'hght09', 'hght12', 'hght15', 'hght18', 'hght24', 'hght36'),
    latentVars=c('eta_1', 'eta_2', 'eta_3'),

# Residual Variances
    mxPath(from=c('hght01', 'hght03', 'hght06', 'hght09', 'hght12', 'hght15', 'hght18', 'hght24', 'hght36'),
        arrows=2, free=TRUE, values=10, labels='theta'),

# Latent Variable Covariances
    mxPath(from=c('eta_1', 'eta_2', 'eta_3'), connect='unique.pairs', arrows=2,
        free=TRUE, values=c(1,0,0,1,0,1), labels=c('psi_11','psi_21','psi_31','psi_22','psi_32','psi_33')),

# Factor Loadings
    mxPath(from='eta_1', to=c('hght01', 'hght03', 'hght06', 'hght09', 'hght12', 'hght15', 'hght18', 'hght24', 'hght36'),
        arrows=1, free=FALSE, values=1),

    mxPath(from='eta_2', to=c('hght01', 'hght03', 'hght06', 'hght09', 'hght12', 'hght15', 'hght18', 'hght24', 'hght36'),
        arrows=1, free=FALSE, values=0,
        labels=c('L11[1,1]', 'L21[1,1]', 'L31[1,1]', 'L41[1,1]', 'L51[1,1]',
                 'L61[1,1]', 'L71[1,1]', 'L81[1,1]', 'L91[1,1]')),

    mxPath(from='eta_3', to=c('hght01', 'hght03', 'hght06', 'hght09', 'hght12', 'hght15', 'hght18', 'hght24', 'hght36'),
        arrows=1, free=FALSE, values=0,
        labels=c('L12[1,1]', 'L22[1,1]', 'L32[1,1]', 'L42[1,1]', 'L52[1,1]',
                 'L62[1,1]', 'L72[1,1]', 'L82[1,1]', 'L92[1,1]')),
```

```
# Latent Variable Means
mxPath(from='one', to=c('eta_1','eta_2','eta_3'), arrows=1, free=TRUE, values=c(70, 3, 1),
       labels=c('alpha_1','alpha_2','alpha_3')),

# Additional Parameter and Constraints
mxMatrix ('Full', 1, 1, free=TRUE, values=7, labels='g', name='gamma'),

mxAlgebra(min(0,    1-gamma),  name='L11'),
mxAlgebra(min(0,    3-gamma),  name='L21'),
mxAlgebra(min(0,    6-gamma),  name='L31'),
mxAlgebra(min(0,    9-gamma),  name='L41'),
mxAlgebra(min(0,   12-gamma),  name='L51'),
mxAlgebra(min(0,   15-gamma),  name='L61'),
mxAlgebra(min(0,   18-gamma),  name='L71'),
mxAlgebra(min(0,   24-gamma),  name='L81'),
mxAlgebra(min(0,   36-gamma),  name='L91'),

mxAlgebra(max(0,    1-gamma),  name='L12'),
mxAlgebra(max(0,    3-gamma),  name='L22'),
mxAlgebra(max(0,    6-gamma),  name='L32'),
mxAlgebra(max(0,    9-gamma),  name='L42'),
mxAlgebra(max(0,   12-gamma),  name='L52'),
mxAlgebra(max(0,   15-gamma),  name='L62'),
mxAlgebra(max(0,   18-gamma),  name='L72'),
mxAlgebra(max(0,   24-gamma),  name='L82'),
mxAlgebra(max(0,   36-gamma),  name='L92')

) # Close Model
```

first mxAlgebra command contains the constraint for the first factor loading of eta_2. The functional constraint for this factor loading is the minimum of 0 and the timing of the measurement, 1 month, minus gamma (i.e., min(0, 1-gamma)), the estimated knot point. This mxAlgebra command is named L11; recall that the label of the first factor loading of eta_2 was L11[1,1], which is the connection between these two statements. The remaining mxAlgebra commands for eta_2 follow this form, with the only change being the timing of the assessment (e.g., min(0, 3-gamma)). The nine mxAlgebra commands for eta_3 are similar. The main difference is the functional constraint—max versus min—to take the maximum of 0 and the timing of the assessment minus gamma. The mxAlgebra statements for the factor loadings of eta_3 are given names L12 through L92 to map onto the labels for the factor loadings for eta_3. The model is then closed.

Parameter estimates obtained from the bilinear spline growth model with an estimated knot point fit in Mplus and OpenMx are contained in Output 11.11 and 11.12, respectively. The first parameter to interpret is the estimated knot point (gamma under New/Additional Parameters, g from the gamma matrix). The estimate was 7.52 and represents the age, in months, at which the change in the rate of growth is located. Next, we turn to the means to understand the predicted average growth trajectory. The mean intercept was 71.69 (alpha_1), indicating the predicted average height (in centimeters) for a 7.52-month-old child. The mean preknot slope was 2.57 (alpha_2), indicating the monthly rate of growth in centimeters before 7.52 months of age, and the postknot slope mean was 0.90 (alpha_3), indicating the average monthly rate of growth in centimeters after 7.52 months of age. The intercept variance was 5.91 (psi_11) and represents the magnitude of between-person differences in height at 7.52 months. The preknot slope variance was 0.07 (psi_22) indicating between-person differences in the rate of growth prior to 7.52 months and the postknot slope variance was 0.003 (psi_33) indicating between-person differences in the monthly rate of growth after 7.52 months. Next, the intercept–preknot slope covariance was 0.27 (psi_21) indicating that children who were taller at 7.52 months tended to grow more rapidly before 7.52 months. The intercept–postknot slope covariance was 0.08 (psi_31), indicating that children who were taller at 7.52 months tended to grow more rapidly after 7.52 months, and the pre–postknot slope covariance was 0.01 (psi_32), indicating that children who grew faster before 7.52 months of age tended to grow faster after 7.52 months of age. Lastly, the level-1 residual variance was 1.48 (Residual Variance of HGHT01-HGHT36, theta).

IMPORTANT CONSIDERATIONS

The move from Type I to Type II nonlinear models comes with infinite possibilities for modeling nonlinear change patterns because of the infinite number of mathematical functions to test as a basis for modeling within-person change and between-person differences in change. Allowing the structure of change to be, at least, partially based on the data (by having estimated parameters in the functions of time) enables the models to better account for the observed trajectories (e.g., the bilinear spline growth model with an

Output 11.11. Mplus Output from the Bilinear Spline Growth Model with an Estimated Knot Point

MODEL RESULTS

	Estimate	S.E.	Est./S.E.	Two-Tailed P-Value
ETA_1S BY				
HGHT01	1.000	0.000	999.000	999.000
...				
HGHT36	1.000	0.000	999.000	999.000
ETA_2S BY				
HGHT01	1.000	0.000	999.000	999.000
...				
HGHT36	36.000	0.000	999.000	999.000
ETA_3S BY				
HGHT01	6.517	0.133	48.980	0.000
HGHT03	4.517	0.133	33.948	0.000
HGHT06	1.517	0.133	11.400	0.000
HGHT09	1.483	0.133	11.149	0.000
HGHT12	4.483	0.133	33.697	0.000
HGHT15	7.483	0.133	56.245	0.000
HGHT18	10.483	0.133	78.793	0.000
HGHT24	16.483	0.133	123.890	0.000
HGHT36	28.483	0.133	214.082	0.000
ETA_1S WITH				
ETA_2S	0.003	0.048	0.057	0.954
ETA_3S	0.030	0.046	0.642	0.521
ETA_2S WITH				
ETA_3S	-0.017	0.005	-3.244	0.001
Means				
ETA_1S	58.653	0.264	222.307	0.000
ETA_2S	1.734	0.028	62.401	0.000
ETA_3S	-0.831	0.026	-32.163	0.000
Variances				
ETA_1S	4.604	0.820	5.615	0.000
ETA_2S	0.022	0.006	4.056	0.000
ETA_3S	0.014	0.005	2.667	0.008
Residual Variances				
HGHT01	1.476	0.110	13.379	0.000
...				
HGHT36	1.476	0.110	13.379	0.000
New/Additional Parameters				
GAMMA	7.517	0.133	56.496	0.000
ALPHA_1	71.688	0.333	215.270	0.000
ALPHA_2	2.565	0.053	48.640	0.000
ALPHA_3	0.903	0.010	90.984	0.000
PSI_11	5.907	1.046	5.649	0.000
PSI_22	0.070	0.020	3.403	0.001
PSI_33	0.003	0.001	2.915	0.004
PSI_21	0.266	0.112	2.364	0.018
PSI_31	0.076	0.025	3.037	0.002
PSI_32	0.008	0.003	2.434	0.015

Output 11.12. OpenMx Output for the Bilinear Spline Growth Model with an Estimated Knot Point

```
free parameters:
          name    matrix     row       col      Estimate      Std.Error
1        theta        S   hght01    hght01   1.475858661    0.110315026
2       psi_11        S    eta_1     eta_1   5.907146657    1.045698141
3       psi_21        S    eta_1     eta_2   0.265585607    0.112325672
4       psi_22        S    eta_2     eta_2   0.069665792    0.020472517
5       psi_31        S    eta_1     eta_3   0.075625276    0.024902494
6       psi_32        S    eta_2     eta_3   0.008191522    0.003366130
7       psi_33        S    eta_3     eta_3   0.003271379    0.001122327
8      alpha_1        M        1     eta_1  71.688102934    0.333014682
9      alpha_2        M        1     eta_2   2.565283804    0.052740943
10     alpha_3        M        1     eta_3   0.903088429    0.009925738
11           g    gamma        1         1   7.516692798    0.133048909
```

estimated knot point fit significantly better than the bilinear spline growth model with a fixed knot point). This additional flexibility, with respect to change patterns, comes with the cost of higher rates of nonconvergence and greater computational demand. We note that selecting good starting values becomes very important as poor, and even okay, starting values can lead to nonconvergence or convergence to local solutions, as opposed to the global solution, of the likelihood function. Thus, trying a variety of starting values is important as well as trying various programs to estimate model parameters. Good starting values for the fixed-effects (latent variable means) parameters can come from fitting nonlinear regression models to all of the data, which ignore the clustering of observations within individuals. Good starting values for the random-effects parameters (latent variable variances and covariances) can be found by fitting nonlinear regression models to each individual's data separately and calculating the variances and covariances of the model parameters across individuals.

The latent basis growth model is often specified in the way described above; however, slightly modified specifications warrant discussion. First, the location of the fixed factor loadings can be varied. Some researchers advocate for the first two factor loadings to be fixed at 0 and 1, respectively. This scales the shape factor in terms of change between the first two measurement occasions. This approach tends to have better convergence rates when oscillation patterns are present or when the first and last measurement occasions have similar means. Second, the latent basis model can be specified as a linear growth model with deviations from linearity. Specifically, the factor loading matrix with five measurement occasions can be specified as

$$\Lambda = \begin{pmatrix} 1 & 0 \\ 1 & 1+\delta_2 \\ 1 & 2+\delta_3 \\ 1 & 3+\delta_4 \\ 1 & 4 \end{pmatrix} \tag{11.16}$$

where δ_2 through δ_4 are estimated parameters representing deviations from the linear growth model. This model enables researchers to easily determine whether or not the basis coefficients significantly diverge from the linear growth trajectory. This idea can be expanded where an additional growth factor is included in the model, such that

$$\Lambda = \begin{pmatrix} 1 & 0 & 0 \\ 1 & 1 & \lambda_{23} \\ 1 & 2 & \lambda_{33} \\ 1 & 3 & \lambda_{43} \\ 1 & 4 & 1 \end{pmatrix} \tag{11.17}$$

where the first two columns define the intercept and linear component and the third column defines an additional latent basis component to determine how much the growth trajectory deviates from linearity (McArdle, 1988).

Individually Varying Measurement Schedules

Much like individually varying measurement schedules can be accounted for in the linear growth modeling framework, the same can be done with most of these nonlinear models. Specifically, the inherently nonlinear models and the spline models can accommodate individually varying measurement schedules in a straightforward manner. Additionally, having individually varying measurement schedules can aid model estimation. However, the latent basis growth model does not easily accommodate individually varying measurement schedules without some adjustment. As noted, the latent basis growth model can be fit using the time-window approach. However, see Sterba (2014) for an alternative approach that utilizes time deviations around measurement occasions.

Covariates, Multiple Groups, and Mixtures

The inclusion of covariates, multiple groups, and unobserved groups (latent classes) can now be expanded to include the *structure* of change. Previously, multiple groups and unobserved groups were allowed to affect the mean of the latent variables, latent variable variances and covariances, and residual variances. Since there are now estimated parameters in the function(s) of time, the structure of change or how change is expected to unfold over time within each person can be allowed to vary over observed groups, unobserved groups, and even modified by time-invariant covariates (i.e., regression-type equation can be set up for unknown parameters). For example, in the latent basis growth model, the basis coefficients can be allowed to vary over groups or be dependent on time-invariant covariates. Allowing the basis coefficients to vary indicates that the within-person change pattern varies as a function of the grouping variable or time-invariant covariate. In the multiple-group and latent class frameworks, the latent variable mean and covariance structure is often allowed to vary when allowing the structure of change to vary over groups or classes (see Ram & Grimm, 2009). Thus, this model often falls between the means and covariances model and the means, covariances, and residual variances model. In the time-invariant covariate framework, regression-like equations can be set up to allow the parameters of the function to depend on the time-invariant covariates. In NLMIXED and nlme, this can be set up in a similar manner to how the time-invariant covariate can predict the intercept and slope. In Mplus and OpenMx, these regression-like equations can be specified in a similar fashion to how individually varying measurement schedules are set up using the definition variable approach.

MOVING FORWARD

In the next chapter, we conclude our discussion of modeling nonlinear change patterns by allowing random coefficients to appear in the nonlinear function of time. Such random coefficients or latent variables enter the model in a nonlinear fashion. These models can be directly estimated in the nonlinear multilevel modeling framework and can be approximated in the structural equation modeling framework using Taylor series expansion. We discuss both approaches.

## 12

Growth Models with Nonlinearity in Random Coefficients

In this chapter we complete our discussion of nonlinearity in growth models and discuss models where random coefficients or latent variables enter the model in a nonlinear fashion. These types of models have been termed nonlinear random coefficient models and fully nonlinear models. Due to the way in which the random coefficients or latent variables enter into the model, these models cannot be directly estimated within the structural equation modeling framework because it is a linear modeling framework (LiSRel, the first commercial structural equation modeling program, stands for Linear Structural Relations). However, these models can be *approximated* following the procedures outlined by Beal and Sheiner (1982) and Browne and du Toit (1991) using Taylor series expansion. This procedure produces a model that approximates the fully nonlinear model and should therefore be utilized cautiously. A first-order Taylor series expansion is typically utilized because the first-order expansion is a linear approximation where random coefficients enter the model in a linear fashion. The first-order expansion is also a common approach to estimating these models in the multilevel modeling framework.

As in the previous chapter, many types of nonlinear models fall into this category (Type III nonlinear models), but we only discuss two models that build on the models discussed in the previous chapters. The first of these models is the Jenss–Bayley growth model with four random coefficients (in the previous chapter, the model had three random coefficients) and a bilinear spline growth model with variability in the knot point. The Jenss–Bayley growth model is a smooth, continuous function that is inherently nonlinear. As discussed in the previous chapter, these models are more likely to represent true developmental phenomena and often have parameters that describe interesting features of change, which may easily map onto developmental theory (e.g., rates of change, asymptotic levels, timing of accelerated change). Fully nonlinear models that are commonly considered by developmentalists include the exponential ($y_{ti} = b_{1i} + b_{2i} \cdot (1 -$ exp $(-b_{3i} \cdot t)))$, logistic ($y_{ti} = b_{1i} + \dfrac{b_{2i}}{1 + \exp(-b_{3i} (t - b_{4i}))}$), Gompertz ($y_{ti} = b_{1i} + b_{2i} \cdot (\exp$

$(-\exp(-b_{3i}(t - b_{4i}))))$, and power models $(y_{ti} = b_{1i} + b_{2i} \cdot t^{b_{3i}})$. We note that the versions of these inherently nonlinear models are fully nonlinear because b_{3i} and/or b_{4i} are part of the nonlinear function and are random coefficients (subscripted by i). The second model is the bilinear spline growth model with variability in the knot point, which is a combination of two growth segments that connect at a knot point that differs for different individuals. This model expands our discussion of spline models by allowing the knot point to be a random coefficient, which allows for between-person differences in the timing of the transition between phases. As in the previous chapter, these models are fit to the longitudinal height data collected as part of the Berkeley Growth Study (Jones & Bayley, 1941).

MULTILEVEL MODELING FRAMEWORK

Jenss–Bayley Growth Model

We extend the Jenss–Bayley growth model (Jenss & Bayley, 1937) that was fit in the previous chapter to allow for a greater degree of between-child differences in the predicted growth trajectories. The Jenss–Bayley growth model that we fit here can be written as

$$y_{ti} = b_{1i} + b_{2i} \cdot t + b_{3i} \cdot (\exp(b_{4i} \cdot t) - 1) + u_{ti} \qquad (12.1)$$

where y_{ti} is the dependent variable measured for individual i at time t, b_{1i} is the individual intercept, b_{2i} is the individual slope of the linear asymptote, b_{3i} is the individual vertical distance between the actual intercept and the intercept of the linear asymptote, $\exp(b_{4i})$ is the individual ratio of acceleration of growth at time t to that at time $t - 1$, and u_{ti} is a time-specific residual score, which is assumed to follow a normal distribution with 0 mean and constant variance, $u_{ti} \sim N(0, \sigma_u^2)$. As previously noted, this version of the Jenss–Bayley growth model is a Type III nonlinear model because b_{4i}, a random coefficient, is contained in the nonlinear function (i.e., $\exp(b_{4i} \cdot t) - 1$) and therefore enters the model in a nonlinear fashion. This allows for individual differences in the ratio of acceleration of growth during the exponential phase of development.

The level-2 equation for the random coefficients is written as

$$
\begin{aligned}
b_{1i} &= \beta_1 + d_{1i} \\
b_{2i} &= \beta_2 + d_{2i} \\
b_{3i} &= \beta_3 + d_{3i} \\
b_{4i} &= \beta_4 + d_{4i}
\end{aligned}
\qquad (12.2)
$$

where β_1, β_2, β_3, and β_4 are means of the random coefficients and d_{1i}, d_{2i}, d_{3i}, and d_{4i} are individual deviations from their respective mean. The individual deviations are assumed to follow a multivariate normal distribution with zero means, estimated variances, and covariances; for example,

$$
d_{1i}, d_{2i}, d_{3i}, d_{4i} \sim MVN \left(\begin{bmatrix} 0 \\ 0 \\ 0 \\ 0 \end{bmatrix}, \begin{bmatrix} \sigma_1^2 & & & \\ \sigma_{21} & \sigma_2^2 & & \\ \sigma_{31} & \sigma_{32} & \sigma_3^2 & \\ \sigma_{41} & \sigma_{42} & \sigma_{33} & \sigma_4^2 \end{bmatrix} \right)
$$

The Jenss–Bayley growth model of Equations 12.1 and 12.2, and fully nonlinear models more generally, can be difficult to estimate because of the multiplicative nature of their random coefficients. To ease the computational difficulty of estimation, the model can be approximated using a first-order Taylor series expansion (Beal & Sheiner, 1982). This process begins by writing the *target* function, which for our purposes is the individual trajectory with the fixed-effects parameters replacing the random coefficients. Thus, the *target* function is

$$
\mu_t = \beta_1 + \beta_2 \cdot t + \beta_3 \cdot (\exp(\beta_4 \cdot t) - 1) \tag{12.3}
$$

where the means of the random coefficients, β_1, β_2, β_3, and β_4, are in place of the random coefficients, b_{1i}, b_{2i}, b_{3i}, and b_{4i}. Next, the partial derivatives of the target function are calculated with respect to each unknown. The partial derivatives of Equation 12.3 are

$$
\partial \mu_t / \partial \beta_1 = 1
$$
$$
\partial \mu_t / \partial \beta_2 = t
$$
$$
\partial \mu_t / \partial \beta_3 = \exp(\beta_4 \cdot t) - 1 \tag{12.4}
$$
$$
\partial \mu_t / \partial \beta_4 = \beta_3 \cdot t \cdot \exp(\beta_4 \cdot t)
$$

Next, an individual-level model is specified with the partial derivatives as multipliers of new random coefficients. Thus,

$$
y_{ti} = x_{1i} + x_{2i} \cdot t + x_{3i} \cdot (\exp(\beta_4 \cdot t) - 1) + x_{4i} \cdot (\beta_3 \cdot t \cdot \exp(\beta_4 \cdot t)) + u_{ti} \tag{12.5}
$$

is the new level-1 model and this expression is a Type II nonlinear model because the new random coefficients, x_{1i}, x_{2i}, x_{3i}, and x_{4i}, are additive and therefore enter the model in a linear fashion. The random coefficients of Equation 12.5 are not exactly the same as the random coefficients of Equation 12.1 and are therefore written as xs instead of bs. However, these random coefficients have much in common with the random coefficients of Equation 12.1. The level-2 model for the random coefficients of Equation 12.5 is

$$
\begin{aligned}
x_{1i} &= \beta_1 + d_{1i} \\
x_{2i} &= \beta_2 + d_{2i} \\
x_{3i} &= \beta_3 + d_{3i} \\
x_{4i} &= d_{4i}
\end{aligned}
\tag{12.6}
$$

This level-2 equation is nearly identical to the level-2 equation for the fully nonlinear model, with one exception. We first concentrate on the similarities. The means of x_{1i}, x_{2i}, and x_{3i} are the same as the means of b_{1i}, b_{2i}, and b_{3i} (i.e., β_1, β_2, and β_3), and the individual-level deviations (d_{1i}, d_{2i}, d_{3i}, and d_{4i}) are also the same. The only difference is the mean of x_{4i}, which is 0 instead of β_4. The reason why x_{4i} has a mean of 0 is because the mean trajectory of Equation 12.5 is equal to the target function as long as the mean of x_{4i} is 0. That is, the mean trajectory of Equation 12.5 is

$$
\mu_t = \beta_1 + \beta_2 \cdot t + \beta_3 \cdot (\exp(\beta_4 \cdot t) - 1)
\tag{12.7}
$$

when the mean of x_{4i} is 0 and Equation 12.7 is the target function.

This process can be carried out in the same way for other Type III nonlinear models. As a general rule, random coefficients in the expanded version associated with former random coefficients that were contained in the nonlinear function of time (e.g., x_{4i} with b_{4i}) will have their means fixed to 0. This constraint also affects the way in which time-invariant covariates are scaled when entered as predictors of the random coefficients when using Taylor series expansion. Specifically, time-invariant covariates *must* be mean-centered when entered as predictors of the random coefficients. If time-invariant covariates are not mean-centered, then the random coefficients that need to have expected means of 0, will have intercepts of 0 but nonzero expected means causing issues with parameter estimation (i.e., direction and magnitude of effects can be incorrect).

Bilinear Spline Growth Model with Variability in the Knot Point

Spline models are extended in this chapter to allow for variability in the knot or transition point. As in the model discussed above, allowing for variability in the knot point means that a random coefficient is part of the function of time. In these models a random coefficient appears in the *min* and *max* functions. Thus, the bilinear spline growth model with variability in the knot point can be written as

$$
y_{ti} = b_{1i} + b_{2i} \cdot \min(t - b_{4i}, 0) + b_{3i} \cdot \max(t - b_{4i}, 0) + u_{ti}
\tag{12.8}
$$

where y_{ti} is the dependent variable measured for individual i at time t, b_{1i} is the individual random intercept located at the individual knot point ($t = b_{4i}$), b_{2i} is the individual preknot linear slope or the linear rate of change prior to the knot point for individual i, b_{3i} is the individual postknot linear slope or the linear rate of change after the knot point for individual i, b_{4i} is the knot point for individual i, t represents the time metric, and u_{ti} is the time-specific residual score.

The level-2 equation for the bilinear spline growth model is

$$
\begin{aligned}
b_{1i} &= \beta_1 + d_{1i} \\
b_{2i} &= \beta_2 + d_{2i} \\
b_{3i} &= \beta_3 + d_{3i} \\
b_{4i} &= \beta_4 + d_{4i}
\end{aligned}
\tag{12.9}
$$

where β_1, β_2, β_3, and β_4 are the means for the intercept, preknot linear slope, postknot linear slope, and knot point, respectively, and d_{1i}, d_{2i}, d_{3i}, and d_{4i} are individual deviations from their respective sample-level mean. Individual deviations are assumed to follow a multivariate normal distribution with zero means, estimated variances, and covariances; for example,

$$
d_{1i},\, d_{2i},\, d_{3i},\, d_{4i} \sim MVN\left(\begin{bmatrix} 0 \\ 0 \\ 0 \\ 0 \end{bmatrix}, \begin{bmatrix} \sigma_1^2 & & & \\ \sigma_{21} & \sigma_2^2 & & \\ \sigma_{31} & \sigma_{32} & \sigma_3^2 & \\ \sigma_{41} & \sigma_{42} & \sigma_{43} & \sigma_4^2 \end{bmatrix} \right)
$$

Of primary interest in this model is the variability in the knot point, σ_4^2, which provides information on the degree to which individuals vary in the timing of their transition from the first phase of development to the second.

MULTILEVEL MODELING IMPLEMENTATION

Jenss–Bayley Growth Model

Direct Optimization

The Jenss–Bayley growth model of Equation 12.1 was fit to the longitudinal height data using `PROC NLMIXED` and `nlme` in multiple ways to highlight the direct and approximation approaches to fitting the model. The `SAS` script for the direct estimation of the model is contained in Script 12.1. The script begins with calling the `NLMIXED` procedure and datafile. Additionally, on the first line is `QPOINTS` = 5, which refers to the number of quadrature points per random effect when approximating the likelihood function integrated over the random effects. Fully nonlinear models can be difficult to estimate, and reducing the number of quadrature points eases computational demand. However, reducing the number of quadrature points also reduces precision.

Script 12.1. NLMIXED Script for the Jenss–Bayley Growth Model

```
PROC NLMIXED DATA = height_long QPOINTS = 5;
  traject = b_1i + b_2i * age/12 + b_3i * (exp(b_4i*(age/12))-1);

MODEL hght ~ NORMAL(traject, v_u);
RANDOM b_1i b_2i b_3i b_4i ~ NORMAL([beta_1,beta_2,beta_3,beta_4], [v_1,
                                                                    c_21,  v_2,
                                                                    c_31,  c_32,  v_3,
                                                                    c_41,  c_42,  c_43,  v_4])

SUBJECT = id;

PARMS
    beta_1 = 51     beta_2 = 9      beta_3 = -18    beta_4 = -2
    v_1 = 10        v_2 = .8        v_3 = 12        v_4 = .01
    c_21 = 0        c_31 = -4       c_32 = 0        c_41 = 0       c_42 = 0       c_43 = 0
    v_u = .7;

RUN;
```

The level-1 equation (Equation 12.1) with age scaled in years (age/12) comes next, with `traject` as the name of the predicted individual function. This is followed by the MODEL statement where the outcome (hght) is assumed to follow a NORMAL distribution with mean, `traject`, and level-1 variance, v_u. The RANDOM statement follows, and the random coefficients (b_1i, b_2i, b_3i, b_4i) are assumed to follow a multivariate normal distribution with estimated means (beta_1, beta_2, beta_3, beta_4) and a variance–covariance matrix as specified. The PARMS statement contains starting values for all estimated parameters.

The nlme script for fitting the Jenss–Bayley growth model is contained in Script 12.2. In this script, the outcome variable, hght, is set equal to Equation 12.1 with age scaled in years (age divided by 12). The random coefficients (b_1i, b_2i, b_3i, b_4i) have estimated fixed-effects (fixed=b_1i+b_2i+b_3i+b_4i~1) and random-effects (random=b_1i+b_2i+b_3i+b_4i~1) parameters. The script ends by indicating that the random coefficients vary over participants (groups=~id), providing starting values for the fixed-effects parameters, and setting the na.action to na.omit.

The Jenss–Bayley growth model converged in both NLMIXED and nlme; however, we note that NLMIXED did not converge using the default quadrature setting (i.e., NLMIXED using adaptive quadrature to automatically select an appropriate number of quadrature points not to exceed 31), indicating that changing the number of quadrature points aided convergence (Smith & Blozis, 2014). Additionally, in NLMIXED the starting values were iteratively updated from prior runs where the model did not converge. Parameter estimates from the two programs are contained in Output 12.1 and 12.2, respectively. Parameter estimates from the two programs are similar but not exactly the same. The differences in the estimates are likely due to the additional complexity of fitting fully nonlinear models and the different ways of approximating the integral of the likelihood function. However, the differences in the parameter estimates are not so large that conclusions regarding the growth process would differ. Here, we discuss estimates from NLMIXED.

The mean of the intercept was 51.04 cm (beta_1, Fixed effect of b_1i), indicating the predicted average height at birth. The mean of the linear asymptote was 9.24 cm per year (beta_2, Fixed effect of b_2i) and represents the average rate of linear growth during the toddler years. The mean of the vertical distance between the intercept of the linear asymptote and the actual asymptote was –18.05 cm (beta_3, Fixed effect of b_3i) and provides a sense of the amount of growth during the infant years.

Script 12.2. nlme Script for the Jenss–Bayley Growth Model

```
hght.jb.nlme <- nlme(hght~b_1i+b_2i*(age/12)+b_3i*(exp(b_4i*(age/12))-1),
                data=hght_long,
                fixed=b_1i+b_2i+b_3i+b_4i~1,
                random=b_1i+b_2i+b_3i+b_4i~1,
                groups=~id,
                start=c(50, 10, -18, -2),
                na.action=na.omit)

summary(hght.jb.nlme)
```

Output 12.1. NLMIXED Output for the Jenss–Bayley Growth Model

Parameter Estimates

Parameter	Estimate	Standard Error	DF	t Value	Pr > |t|	Alpha	Lower	Upper	Gradient
beta_1	51.0437	0.3509	79	145.46	<.0001	0.05	50.3452	51.7421	0.000086
beta_2	9.2391	0.1760	79	52.48	<.0001	0.05	8.8887	9.5894	0.000224
beta_3	-18.0513	0.5043	79	-35.79	<.0001	0.05	-19.0551	-17.0475	-0.00052
beta_4	-2.1048	0.09031	79	-23.30	<.0001	0.05	-2.2845	-1.9250	-0.00274
v_1	7.3250	1.4821	79	4.94	<.0001	0.05	4.3749	10.2751	0.00009
v_2	0.8111	0.3007	79	2.70	0.0085	0.05	0.2125	1.4096	-0.00035
v_3	11.6634	2.9227	79	3.99	0.0001	0.05	5.8459	17.4808	-4.5E-6
v_4	0.08974	0.05363	79	1.67	0.0982	0.05	-0.01700	0.1965	-0.00468
c_21	0.6796	0.4735	79	1.44	0.1551	0.05	-0.2628	1.6220	-5.12E-6
c_31	4.5668	1.5268	79	2.99	0.0037	0.05	1.5278	7.6057	-0.00018
c_32	1.3368	0.7735	79	1.73	0.0878	0.05	-0.2028	2.8764	0.00041
c_41	-0.01599	0.2562	79	-0.06	0.9504	0.05	-0.5259	0.4939	-0.00085
c_42	-0.09637	0.1182	79	-0.82	0.4174	0.05	-0.3317	0.1389	-0.00067
c_43	-0.5482	0.3902	79	-1.41	0.1639	0.05	-1.3248	0.2284	0.000916
v_u	0.6397	0.05027	79	12.73	<.0001	0.05	0.5397	0.7398	-0.00212

Output 12.2. nlme Output for the Jenss–Bayley Growth Model

```
Random effects:
 Formula: list (b_1i ~ 1, b_2i ~ 1, b_3i ~ 1, b_4i ~ 1)
 Level: id
 Structure: General positive-definite, Log-Cholesky parametrization
          StdDev       Corr
b_1i     2.6774379     b_1i     b_2i     b_3i
b_2i     0.8718004     0.319
b_3i     3.4101698     0.491    0.449
b_4i     0.2746959     -0.120   -0.275   -0.642
Residual 0.8041708

Fixed effects: b_1i + b_2i + b_3i + b_4i ~ 1
          Value      Std.Error    DF      t-value      p-value
b_1i     50.99058    0.3422308    495    148.99470         0
b_2i      9.31951    0.1607690    495     57.96834         0
b_3i    -17.84859    0.4814531    495    -37.07234         0
b_4i     -2.13260    0.0769088    495    -27.72897         0
```

The mean of the log of the ratio of acceleration was –2.10 (beta_4, Fixed effect of b_4i), and exponentiating this value yields an average ratio of acceleration of growth at time t compared to $t - 1$ of 0.12 (exp (–2.10)), which indicates how quickly the early changes in height decelerated during the exponential phase of development.

The variance of the intercept was 7.33 (v_1, Random effect of b_1i), and reflects the magnitude of individual differences in height at birth. The variance of the linear slope was 0.81 (v_2, Random effect of b_2i), indicating between-child differences in the linear rate of growth during the toddler years. The variance of the difference between the actual intercept and intercept of the linear asymptote was 11.66 (v_3, Random effect of b_3i) and relates to individual differences in the amount of growth during the infant years, and the variance of b_4i, which relates to variability in the ratio of acceleration (exp (b_4i)), was 0.09 and not significantly different from 0, indicating that the ratio of acceleration did not vary much over individuals. The covariance between the intercept and the linear slope was 0.68 (c_21, Corr between b_1i and b_2i) and nonsignificant. The covariance between intercept and the difference between the intercept of the linear asymptote and actual intercept was 4.57 (c_31, Corr between b_1i and b_3i), indicating that children who were taller at birth tended to have smaller (more positive) differences between the two intercepts. Thus, children who were taller at birth tended to transition to their linear asymptote more quickly. The covariance between the intercept and the ratio of acceleration was –0.02 (c_41, Corr between b_1i and b_4i) and nonsignificant. The covariance between the difference in the intercepts and the linear rate of change was 1.34 (c_32, Corr between b_2i and b_3i) and nonsignificant. The covariance between the difference in the intercepts and the ratio of acceleration was –0.10 (c_42, Corr between b_2i and b_4i) and nonsignificant. Finally, the covariance between the linear rate of change and the ratio of acceleration was –0.55 (c_43,

`Corr` between `b_3i` and `b_4i`) and nonsignificant. Lastly, the residual variance was 0.64 (`v_u`, Random `effect` of `Residual`), which was slightly smaller than when the ratio of acceleration was not allowed to vary over participants.

Figure 12.1 is a plot of the individual predicted trajectories from the Jenss–Bayley growth model. The individual growth trajectories are smooth and show the sharp increases in height during infancy, which begin to slow and are followed by relative stability in the growth rate during the toddler years. Overall, the individual predictions do not appear to be drastically different from the individual predictions when the ratio of acceleration was a parameter, as opposed to a random coefficient. Furthermore, the difference in fit between the two models (with and without variation in the ratio of acceleration) based on the −2LL was not significant ($\Delta\chi^2(4) = 4.1$, $p = .39$), indicating that allowing for individual variation in the ratio of acceleration did not significantly improve model fit. We note that the change in the number of estimated parameters was four and include the variance of the ratio of acceleration (σ_4^2) as well as its covariances (σ_{41}, σ_{42}, and σ_{43}).

First–Order Approximation

The `NLMIXED` script for the Jenss–Bayley growth model using the first-order approximation approach is contained in Script 12.3. The level-1 equation (Equation 12.5) for the

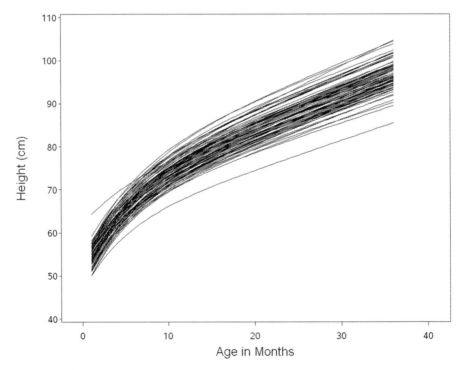

FIGURE 12.1. Individual predicted trajectories from the Jenss–Bayley growth model.

Script 12.3. NLMIXED Script for the First–Order Approximation of the Jenss–Bayley Growth Model

```
PROC NLMIXED DATA = height_long;
    traject = x_1i + x_2i*(age/12) + x_3i*(exp(beta_4*(age/12))-1) + x_4i*(beta_3*(age/12)*exp(beta_4*(age/12)));

    MODEL hght ~ NORMAL(traject, v_u);
    RANDOM x_1i x_2i x_3i x_4i ~ NORMAL([beta_1, beta_2, beta_3,0], [v_1,
                                                                      c_21, v_2,
                                                                      c_31, c_32, v_3,
                                                                      c_41, c_42, c_43, v_4])

    SUBJECT = id;
    PARMS
        beta_1 = 51      beta_2 = 9       beta_3 = -18     beta_4 = -2
        v_1 = 8          v_2 = .8         v_3 = 12         v_4 = .2
        c_21 = .6        c_31 = 4         c_32 = 1         c_41 = 0         c_42 = 0        c_43 = 0
        v_u = .7;
RUN;
```

285

approximation is now specified with `traject` as the predicted individual trajectory and age scaled in years (`age/12`). The `MODEL` statement is identical to the prior script, but the `RANDOM` statement has been modified. In the `RANDOM` statement, the random coefficients (`x_1i`, `x_2i`, `x_3i`, `x_4i`) are assumed to follow a multivariate normal distribution with estimated means for `x_1i`, `x_2i`, and `x_3i` (i.e., `beta_1`, `beta_2`, `beta_3`); however, the mean of `x_4i` is set equal to zero by placing a 0 in the mean vector. We note that `beta_4` (the mean of b_{4i} from Equation 12.1) is estimated as part of the trajectory equation. The specified covariance matrix is identical to the matrix specified in the prior script as the expectations for the variances and covariances for the new random coefficients are identical to the prior expectations. Lastly, the `PARMS` statement contains starting values for all estimated parameters. In `NLMIXED`, the same approximation approach can be utilized by specifying the fully nonlinear model (Equations 12.1 and 12.2) and stating `METHOD=FIRO` on the `PROC` line (instead of `QPOINTS=5`) because the first-order approximation is one of the options for approximating the integral of the likelihood function in `SAS`.

The `nlme` script for fitting the Jenss–Bayley growth model using the first-order approximation approach is contained in Script 12.4. In this script, the combined level-1 and level-2 equation (e.g., combining Equations 12.5 and 12.6) is specified with age scaled in years. The combined equation was needed for the first-order approximation approach because the mean of `x_3i` (`beta_3`) is part of the trajectory equation. That is, writing out `beta_3+d_3i` instead of `x_3i` allows the mean of `x_3i` to be given a label (`beta_3`), which is used in the nonlinear function (e.g., `beta_3*(age/12) *exp(beta_4*(age/12))`). The datafile is then specified and is followed by the fixed and random effects. The fixed effects are `beta_1`, `beta_2`, `beta_3`, and `beta_4` and the random coefficients are `d_1i`, `d_2i`, `d_3i`, and `d_4i`. The random coefficients are random over participants (`groups=~id`), and the model closes after providing starting values for the fixed effects and setting `na.action` to `na.omit`.

The Jenss–Bayley growth model estimated using the first–order approach converged rapidly in both `NLMIXED` and `nlme`. Parameter estimates from the two programs are contained in Output 12.3 and 12.4, respectively, and appear more similar to one another when compared against the similarity of estimates reported above. Also, note that the estimates here are not identical to those above but are not drastically different; however, significance levels are somewhat different—especially for the random-effects parameters. We don't discuss parameter estimates here because of our discussion above and because the parameter estimates from the structural equation modeling programs should be highly similar.

Bilinear Spline Growth Model with Variation in the Knot Point

The `NLMIXED` script for the bilinear spline growth model with variation in the knot point is contained in Script 12.5. Estimating model parameters for this model was challenging in `SAS`, and the presented script is the result of many iterations. We note that the full model converged when the number of quadrature points was set to 1 (`QPOINTS = 1`);

Script 12.4. `nlme` **Script for the First–Order Approximation of the Jenss–Bayley Growth Model**

```
hght.jb.nlme.fo <- nlme(hght~(beta_1+d_1i)+(beta_2+d_2i)*(age/12)+
                         (beta_3+d_3i)*(exp(beta_4*(age/12))-1)+
                         d_4i*(beta_3*(age/12)*exp(beta_4*(age/12))),
                    data=hght_long,
                    fixed=beta_1+beta_2+beta_3+beta_4~1,
                    random=d_1i+d_2i+d_3i+d_4i~1,
                    groups=~id,
                    start=c(50, 10, -18, -2),
                    na.action=na.omit)

summary(hght.jb.nlme.fo)
```

Output 12.3. NLMIXED Output for the First-Order Approximation of the Jenss–Bayley Growth Model

Parameter Estimates

Parameter	Estimate	Standard Error	DF	t Value	Pr > |t|	Alpha	Lower	Upper	Gradient
beta_1	51.0742	0.3529	79	144.74	<.0001	0.05	50.3719	51.7766	-0.01413
beta_2	9.2963	0.1739	79	53.47	<.0001	0.05	8.9503	9.6424	0.004992
beta_3	-17.8343	0.4923	79	-36.22	<.0001	0.05	-18.8142	-16.8543	0.011694
beta_4	-2.0770	0.08449	79	-24.58	<.0001	0.05	-2.2451	-1.9088	0.025261
v_1	7.4611	1.5321	79	4.87	<.0001	0.05	4.4114	10.5107	0.00498
v_2	0.8125	0.3409	79	2.38	0.0196	0.05	0.1340	1.4910	0.009715
v_3	11.7443	3.0483	79	3.85	0.0002	0.05	5.6767	17.8118	0.004387
v_4	0.07635	0.07931	79	0.96	0.3387	0.05	-0.08152	0.2342	0.065215
c_21	0.6530	0.5310	79	1.23	0.2225	0.05	-0.4040	1.7100	-0.00455
c_31	4.5326	1.5953	79	2.84	0.0057	0.05	1.3572	7.7080	0.029762
c_32	1.3652	0.8563	79	1.59	0.1149	0.05	-0.3393	3.0696	0.00341
c_41	0.02678	0.2636	79	0.10	0.9194	0.05	-0.4980	0.5515	0.029458
c_42	-0.07853	0.1437	79	-0.55	0.5862	0.05	-0.3645	0.2074	0.084053
c_43	-0.4925	0.3857	79	-1.28	0.2054	0.05	-1.2601	0.2752	-0.02275
v_u	0.6432	0.05280	79	12.18	<.0001	0.05	0.5381	0.7483	-0.04578

Output 12.4. nlme Output for the First-Order Approximation of the Jenss–Bayley Growth Model

```
Random effects:
 Formula: list (d_1i ~ 1, d_2i ~ 1, d_3i ~ 1, d_4i ~ 1)
 Level: id
 Structure: General positive-definite, Log-Cholesky parametrization
           StdDev      Corr
d_1i       2.7167245   d_1i     d_2i       d_3i
d_2i       0.8928475   0.267
d_3i       3.3840012   0.482    0.433
d_4i       0.2775613   0.027    -0.299     -0.525
Residual   0.8027912

Fixed effects: beta_1 + beta_2 + beta_3 + beta_4 ~ 1
           Value     Std.Error    DF     t-value     p-value
beta_1     50.96847  0.3478277    495    146.53366         0
beta_2      9.33387  0.1602771    495     58.23580         0
beta_3    -17.83233  0.4667396    495    -38.20616         0
beta_4     -2.11293  0.0752802    495    -28.06752         0
```

however, parameter estimates were unstable. In the specification in Script 12.5, we estimate standard deviations and correlations because some of the estimated variances were small, which can result in estimation difficulties. Also, as you'll see, a full covariance matrix for the random coefficients was not specified.

The specification of the model begins with the level-1 equation for the bilinear spline growth model with variation in the knot point (Equation 12.8), with b_1i, b_2i, b_3i, and b_4i as random coefficients and utilizing the MIN and MAX functions in SAS. In this script, as in Equation 12.8, age-b_4i is contained in the MIN and MAX functions and b_4i is a random coefficient. Thus, the knot point will be described by a mean and variance. The MODEL statement is specified with hght as the outcome with a mean equal to traject and s_u as the level-1 standard deviation. The RANDOM statement contains the random coefficients, b_1i, b_2i, b_3i, and b_4i, which have estimated means (beta_1, beta_2, beta_3, and beta_4) and a covariance matrix as specified. The covariances (or correlations) involving individual differences in the knot point were fixed to 0. This was done to aid model convergence and because, as you'll see, the variance in the knot point was quite small. The remaining two statements are typically specified to indicate the random effects are random with respect to participant (id) and to provide starting values for estimated parameters to begin the iterative estimation routine.

The nlme script for the bilinear spline growth model with variation in the knot point fit to the longitudinal height data is provided in Script 12.6. The level-1 equation for the model is specified with b_1i, b_2i, b_3i, and b_4i as random coefficients using the pmin and pmax functions. All of the random coefficients have fixed- (fixed=b_1i+b_2i+b_3i+b_4i~1) and random-effects (random=b_1i+ b_2i+b_3i+b_4i~1) parameters. The random effects are random with respect to participant (id), and starting values are provided for the fixed-effects parameters.

Script 12.5. NLMIXED Script for Bilinear Spline Growth Model with Variation in the Knot Point

```
PROC NLMIXED DATA = height_long QPOINTS = 1;
    traject = b_1i + b_2i*(MIN(age-b_4i,0)) + b_3i*(MAX(age-b_4i,0));

MODEL hght ~ NORMAL(traject, s_u*s_u);
RANDOM b_1i b_2i b_3i b_4i ~ NORMAL([beta_1, beta_2, beta_3, beta_4],
                                    [s_1*s_1,
                                     s_2*r_21*s_1,  s_2*s_2,
                                     s_3*r_31*s_1,  s_3*r_32*s_2,  s_3*s_3,
                                            0,             0,          0,    s_4*s_4])

SUBJECT = id;
PARMS
    beta_1 = 71.9    beta_2 = 2.51    beta_3 = .9     beta_4 = 7.9
    s_1 = 2.7        s_2 = .29        s_3 = .06       s_4 = .30
    r_21 = .1        r_31 = .5        r_32 = .4
    s_u = 1.21;

RUN;
```

Script 12.6. nlme Script for the Bilinear Spline Growth Model with Variation in the Knot Point

```
hght.spline.nlme <- nlme(hght~b_1i+b_2i*(pmin(0,age-b_4i))+
                               b_3i*(pmax(0,age-b_4i)),
                    data=hght_long,
                    fixed=b_1i+b_2i+b_3i+b_4i~1,
                    random=b_1i+b_2i+b_3i+b_4i~1,
                    groups=~id,
                    start=c(60, 5, 2, 8),
                    na.action=na.omit)

summary(hght.spline.nlme)
```

Parameter estimates from PROC NLMIXED and nlme for the bilinear spline growth model with variation in the knot point are contained in Output 12.5 and 12.6, respectively. As expected, estimates from nlme are somewhat different from those obtained through NLMIXED because of the different estimation routines and the different specifications (certain correlations were not estimated in NLMIXED). Here, we interpret the nlme parameter estimates. The mean intercept was 71.93 cm (beta_1, Fixed effect of b_1i), indicating the predicted average height at the knot point, which varied over children. The mean of the preknot slope was 2.51 cm per month (beta_2, Fixed effect of b_2i), indicating the monthly rate of growth before the individual knot point. The mean of the postknot slope was 0.90 cm (beta_3, Fixed effect of b_3i) per month, indicating the rate of growth after the individual knot point and the mean transition, or knot point, was 7.72 months (beta_4, Fixed effect of b_4i). The intercept standard deviation was 2.71 (s_1, Random effect of b_1i), indicating between-person differences in height at the knot point. The preknot slope standard deviation was 0.29 (s_2, Random effect of b_2i), indicating between-person differences in the rate of growth prior to the knot point. The postknot slope standard deviation was 0.06 (s_3, Random effect of b_3i), indicating between-person differences in the monthly rate of growth after the knot point, and the standard deviation of the knot point was 0.29, indicating the magnitude of between-child differences in the timing of their transition from the first phase of rapid growth to the second phase of slower growth.

Next, we focus on the correlations among the random coefficients. The intercept–preknot slope correlation was 0.11 (r_21, Corr between b_1i and b_2i) and is the degree of association between the rate of growth prior to the knot point and height at the knot point. The intercept–postknot slope correlation was 0.48 (r_31, Corr between b_1i and b_3i), indicating a relatively strong association between height at the knot point and the rate of growth after the knot point. The correlation between the intercept and the location of the knot point was 0.79 (not specified in NLMIXED, Corr between b_1i and b_4i) and suggests a very strong association between the child's height at the knot point and the child's timing of the transition between the two phases of development. This association should be expected as children who transitioned at an older age

Output 12.5. NLMIXED Output for the Bilinear Spline Growth Model with Variation in the Knot Point

Parameter Estimates

Parameter	Estimate	Standard Error	DF	t Value	Pr > |t|	Alpha	Lower	Upper	Gradient
beta_1	71.6883	0.3331	79	215.21	<.0001	0.05	71.0252	72.3513	0.004454
beta_2	2.5653	0.05273	79	48.65	<.0001	0.05	2.4603	2.6702	-0.03143
beta_3	0.9031	0.009922	79	91.02	<.0001	0.05	0.8833	0.9228	-0.08793
beta_4	7.5167	0.1330	79	56.50	<.0001	0.05	7.2519	7.7815	-0.02099
s_1	2.4315	0.2153	79	11.29	<.0001	0.05	2.0030	2.8601	0.015766
s_2	0.2638	0.03880	79	6.80	<.0001	0.05	0.1866	0.3410	-0.0216
s_3	0.05715	0.009817	79	5.82	<.0001	0.05	0.03761	0.07669	-0.09636
s_4	0.001486	0.1368	79	0.01	0.9914	0.05	-0.2708	0.2738	0.079414
r_21	0.4147	0.1308	79	3.17	0.0022	0.05	0.1544	0.6750	0.02536
r_31	0.5451	0.1711	79	3.19	0.0021	0.05	0.2046	0.8856	-0.00105
r_32	0.5463	0.2437	79	2.24	0.0278	0.05	0.06119	1.0313	0.060836
s_u	1.2149	0.04542	79	26.75	<.0001	0.05	1.1245	1.3053	-0.05472

Output 12.6. nlme Output for the Bilinear Spline Growth Model with Variation in the Knot Point

```
Random effects:
 Formula: list(b_1i ~ 1, b_2in ~ 1, b_3i ~ 1, b_4i ~ 1)
 Level: id
 Structure: General positive-definite, Log-Cholesky parametrization
          StdDev          Corr
b_1i      2.70806946      b_1i      b_2i      b_3i
b_2i      0.28601240      0.107
b_3i      0.05565713      0.476     0.443
b_4i      0.29339376      0.793     -0.506    0.238
Residual  1.21258824

Fixed effects: b_1i + b_2i + b_3i + b_4i ~ 1
          Value     Std.Error    DF      t-value     p-value
b_1i      71.92534  0.3602892    495     199.63224         0
b_2i      2.51075   0.0540702    495     46.43494          0
b_3i      0.90033   0.0098053    495     91.82080          0
b_4i      7.72076   0.1427390    495     54.09005          0
```

tended to be taller when they transitioned. The correlation between the preknot slope and postknot slope was 0.44 (r_32, Corr between b_2i and b_3i), indicating that the child's rate of growth prior to the knot point was positively related to the child's rate of growth after the knot point. The correlation between the preknot slope and the location of the knot point was –0.51 (not specified in NLMIXED, Corr between b_2i and b_4i), indicating that the child's rate of growth prior to the knot point was inversely related to the timing of the transition between developmental phases. Finally, the correlation between the postknot slope and the location of the knot point was 0.24 (not specified in NLMIXED, Corr between b_3i and b_4i), suggesting that the child's rate of growth in the second phase of development was positively related to the age at the transition between phases. Thus, children who transitioned between phases later tended to have a postknot rate of change that was more rapid than their peers. Lastly, the level-1 residual standard deviation was 1.21 (s_u, Random effect of Residual) and represents individual variability not captured by the model.

Figure 12.2 contains a plot of the individual predicted trajectories from the bilinear spline growth model with variation in the knot point, along with a vertical reference line at the mean age of the knot point. Although, children were allowed to transition at different ages, the variance of the knot point was relatively small, making it difficult to visually see which individuals transitioned before the mean transition time and which individuals transitioned after. Using the parameter estimates from nlme, we can calculate a 95% interval on the between-person differences in the timing of the transition between the two phases. The interval goes from 7.15 years to 8.29 years. This gives us a better sense of the degree to which individuals varied in the timing of this transition.

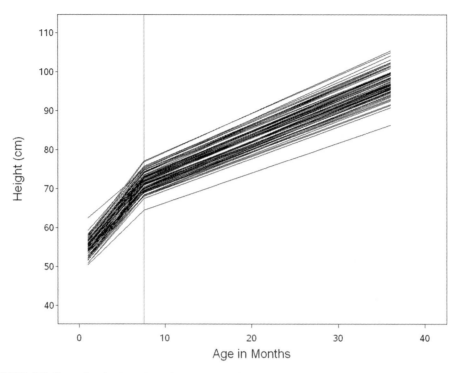

FIGURE 12.2. Individual predicted trajectories for the bilinear spline growth model with variation in the knot point.

Next, the question turns to whether or not allowing for variability in the knot point improved model fit. Thus, we compare the fit of the bilinear spline growth model with variation in the knot point to the bilinear spline growth model with an estimated knot point. The change in $-2LL$ was 2.30 (from nlme; change was 0 in NLMIXED) for the additional four parameters (σ_4^2, σ_{41}, σ_{42}, and σ_{43}), and this improvement in fit ($\Delta\chi^2(4) =$ 2.30, $p = .68$) was not statistically significant, indicating that allowing for variability in transition between the two phases of development did not significantly improve the match between the model and the observed data.

STRUCTURAL EQUATION MODELING FRAMEWORK

The structural equation modeling framework can accommodate *certain* models that are nonlinear in *coefficients*. Models that can be estimated in the structural equation modeling framework are those that can be specified using a first-order Taylor series expansion (e.g., Jenss–Bayley growth model in Equations 12.5 and 12.6). Generally, this eliminates spline models with variability in the knot point(s); however, as we noted in the prior chapter, Harring, Cudeck, and du Toit (2006) showed how the bilinear spline growth model can be reparameterized, which eliminated the need for *min* and *max* functions. If the spline model can be reparameterized in this fashion, then it is possible to fit this type of model and allow for variability in the knot point (see Preacher & Hancock, 2015). We take this approach here.

The structural equation modeling framework is a linear modeling framework; thus, the fully nonlinear model must be specified in a linear form where latent variables enter into the model in an additive fashion. Once the fully nonlinear model is specified as a linear model with unknown parameters, the model can be estimated in the structural equation modeling framework as long as the necessary nonlinear constraints are available. The growth model is expressed in the same way, and modifications are made to the Λ and α matrices. The Λ matrix contains the partial derivatives of the target function, and the α vector is not fully estimated as it has been specified thus far.

The basic setup of the model is identical to what has been presented previously with the common factor model written as

$$\mathbf{y}_i = \Lambda \eta_i + \mathbf{u}_i \tag{12.10}$$

and

$$\eta_i = \alpha + \xi_i \tag{12.11}$$

where $\mathbf{y}_i$ is a $T \times 1$ vector of the repeatedly measured observed scores for individual i, where T represents the number of repeated assessments based on the chosen time metric, Λ is a $T \times R$ matrix of factor loadings defining the latent growth factors, where R is the number of growth factors, η_i is an $R \times 1$ vector of latent factor scores for individual i, $\mathbf{u}_i$ is a $T \times 1$ vector of residual or unique scores for individual i, α is an $R \times 1$ vector of latent factor means, and ξ_i is an $R \times 1$ vector of mean deviations for individual i. The population mean (μ) and covariance (Σ) structure are

$$\mu = \Lambda \alpha$$
$$\Sigma = \Lambda \Psi \Lambda' + \Theta \tag{12.12}$$

where Ψ is a $R \times R$ latent covariance matrix containing covariances among growth factors and Θ is a $T \times T$ residual covariance matrix.

Jenss–Bayley Growth Model

The Jenss–Bayley growth model of Equation 12.5 can be estimated in the structural equation modeling framework because the latent variables (random coefficients) enter the model in a linear fashion. As mentioned above, the partial derivatives of Equation 12.5

compose the Λ matrix. Thus, with five equally spaced measurement occasions, the Λ matrix is specified as

$$
\Lambda = \begin{pmatrix}
1 & \dfrac{1-k_1}{k_2} & \exp\left(\alpha_4\left(\dfrac{1-k_1}{k_2}\right)\right)-1 & \alpha_3 \cdot \left(\dfrac{1-k_1}{k_2}\right) \cdot \exp\left(\alpha_4 \cdot \left(\dfrac{1-k_1}{k_2}\right)\right) \\[2ex]
1 & \dfrac{2-k_1}{k_2} & \exp\left(\alpha_4\left(\dfrac{2-k_1}{k_2}\right)\right)-1 & \alpha_3 \cdot \left(\dfrac{2-k_1}{k_2}\right) \cdot \exp\left(\alpha_4 \cdot \left(\dfrac{2-k_1}{k_2}\right)\right) \\[2ex]
1 & \dfrac{3-k_1}{k_2} & \exp\left(\alpha_4\left(\dfrac{3-k_1}{k_2}\right)\right)-1 & \alpha_3 \cdot \left(\dfrac{3-k_1}{k_2}\right) \cdot \exp\left(\alpha_4 \cdot \left(\dfrac{3-k_1}{k_2}\right)\right) \\[2ex]
1 & \dfrac{4-k_1}{k_2} & \exp\left(\alpha_4\left(\dfrac{4-k_1}{k_2}\right)\right)-1 & \alpha_3 \cdot \left(\dfrac{4-k_1}{k_2}\right) \cdot \exp\left(\alpha_4 \cdot \left(\dfrac{4-k_1}{k_2}\right)\right) \\[2ex]
1 & \dfrac{5-k_1}{k_2} & \exp\left(\alpha_4\left(\dfrac{5-k_1}{k_2}\right)\right)-1 & \alpha_3 \cdot \left(\dfrac{5-k_1}{k_2}\right) \cdot \exp\left(\alpha_4 \cdot \left(\dfrac{5-k_1}{k_2}\right)\right)
\end{pmatrix} \tag{12.13}
$$

where the first column defines the intercept, the second column defines the slope of the linear asymptote with values changing linearly with time, the third column defines the vertical distance between the actual intercept and the intercept of the linear asymptote, and the fourth column defines the ratio of acceleration. The values k_1 and k_2 are chosen to center the intercept and scale time, and α_3 and α_4 are estimated parameters. The α vector (means of latent variables) is specified as $\alpha = \begin{bmatrix} \alpha_1 & \alpha_2 & \alpha_3 & 0 \end{bmatrix}'$. The means of the first three latent variables (η_1, η_2, and η_3) are freely estimated; however, the mean of the fourth latent variable (η_4) is fixed equal to 0 because of the reasons described earlier; this latent variable only affects the covariance structure of the model and not the mean structure.

Figure 12.3 is a path diagram of this Jenss–Baley growth model with five measurement occasions. Parameter labels and variable names map onto the specification presented above. The latent variables include the intercept (η_1) with factor loadings equal to 1, the slope of the linear asymptote (η_2) with factor loadings that change linearly with time, vertical difference between the actual intercept and intercept of the linear asymptote (η_3) with factor loadings set equal to $\exp(t \cdot \alpha_4) - 1$, and the ratio of acceleration (η_4) with factor loadings set equal to $\alpha_3 \cdot t \cdot \exp(t \cdot \alpha_4)$. Importantly, η_4 does not have an estimated mean (no one–headed arrow from the constant).

Spline Growth Model with Variation in the Knot Point

Generally, spline growth models with variation in the knot point cannot be estimated in the structural equation modeling framework. However, a bilinear spline model can be approximated in the structural equation modeling framework (Preacher & Hancock, 2015) because the model can be reparameterized. The reparameterized version can then be specified using a first-order Taylor series expansion to allow the knot point to be its own latent variable.

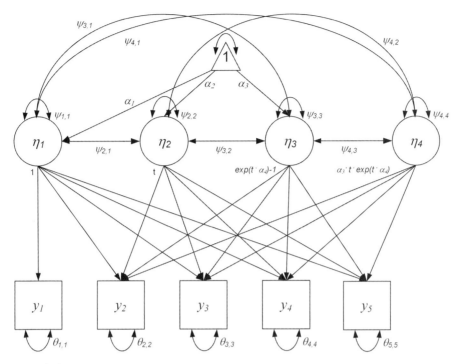

FIGURE 12.3. Path diagram of a Jenss–Bayley growth model using a first-order Taylor series expansion.

Following Harring, Cudeck, and du Toit (2006), the bilinear spline growth model with an estimated knot point can be written as

$$y_{ti} = b_{1i} + b_{2i} \cdot t + b_{3i} \cdot \sqrt{(t-\gamma)^2} + u_{ti} \tag{12.14}$$

where y_{ti} are the repeated measures, b_{1i} is the average intercept, b_{2i} is the average rate of change, b_{3i} is half the difference between the two slopes, and γ is the estimated knot point. Alternatively, this model can be written as

$$y_{ti} = b_{1i} + b_{2i} \cdot (t-\gamma) + b_{3i} \cdot \sqrt{(t-\gamma)^2} + u_{ti} \tag{12.15}$$

where b_{1i} is now the individual intercept at the knot point ($t = \gamma$). Here, we want the knot point to vary over individuals. Thus, we allow the knot point to be a random coefficient yielding

$$y_{ti} = b_{1i} + b_{2i} \cdot (t-b_{4i}) + b_{3i} \cdot \sqrt{(t-b_{4i})^2} + u_{ti} \tag{12.16}$$

which is a fully nonlinear model because b_{4i} is a random coefficient contained in the non-linear mathematical expression. To make the model estimable in the structural equation modeling framework, we utilize Taylor series expansion (Beal & Sheiner, 1982). Expanding Equation 12.16 yields

$$y_{ti} = x_{1i} + x_{2i} \cdot (t - \alpha_4) + x_{3i} \cdot \sqrt{(t - \alpha_4)^2} + x_{4i} \cdot \left(\frac{-\alpha_2 \cdot \sqrt{(t - \alpha_4)^2} + \alpha_3 \cdot t - \alpha_3 \cdot \alpha_4}{\sqrt{(t - \alpha_4)^2}} \right) + u_{ti}$$

(12.17)

which is estimable in the structural equation modeling framework. The random coefficients x_{1i}, x_{2i}, x_{3i}, and x_{4i} become the latent variables η_1, η_2, η_3, and η_4 with factor loadings set equal to 1, $(t - \alpha_4)$, $\sqrt{(t - \alpha_4)^2}$, and $\left(\dfrac{-\alpha_2 \cdot \sqrt{(t - \alpha_4)^2} + \alpha_3 \cdot t - \alpha_3 \cdot \alpha_4}{\sqrt{(t - \alpha_4)^2}} \right)$. The latent variable mean vector is $\alpha = \begin{bmatrix} \alpha_1 & \alpha_2 & \alpha_3 & 0 \end{bmatrix}'$, and the latent variable covariance matrix is fully specified.

STRUCTURAL EQUATION MODELING IMPLEMENTATION

The longitudinal height data in the wide format with separate variables for the height measured at 1, 3, 6, 9, 12, 15, 18, 24, and 36 months (hght01–hght36) will be used to illustrate the programming of the Jenss–Bayley growth model in Mplus and OpenMx. We do not present code for the bilinear spline growth model with variation in the knot point because this code is highly similar (only differences are in the constraints on the factor loading matrix) and fitting the model resulted in estimation issues (variance of the knot point was estimated to be negative). Mplus and OpenMx code for the bilinear spline growth model with variation in the knot point can be found on our website.

Jenss–Bayley Growth Model

The MODEL statement for fitting the Jenss–Bayley growth model in Mplus is contained in Script 12.7. The MODEL statement begins by defining eta_1, eta_2, eta_3, and eta_4 using the keyword BY and specifying their factor loading pattern. The factor loadings for eta_1 and eta_2 are fixed values and factor loadings for eta_3 and eta_4 are constrained to follow specific nonlinear functions with unknown parameters. Factor loadings for eta_1 are all 1s and factor loadings for eta_2 change linearly with time scaled in terms of years since birth. Factor loadings for eta_3 and eta_4 are then specified and given labels, L13 to L93 for eta_3 and L14 to L94 for eta_4. As mentioned earlier, an asterisk is placed after the first variable listed in the BY commands to override the default that latent variables are identified by the first listed variable with a factor loading set equal to 1. The labels will be used subsequently in the MODEL CONSTRAINT command to specify the functional form of the nonlinear constraints.

Latent variable variances and covariances are specified next. All of the latent variables have estimated variances and are allowed to covary with each other. Latent variable means are then specified in the next three statements. In the first, means for eta_1 and

Script 12.7. `Mplus` Script for Jenss–Bayley Growth Model

```
MODEL:
    eta_1 BY hght01-hght36@1;
    eta_2 BY hght01@.0833 hght03@.25 hght06@.5 hght09@.75 hght12@1
             hght15@1.25  hght18@1.5 hght24@2  hght36@3;
    eta_3 BY hght01* (L13)
             hght03  (L23)
             hght06  (L33)
             hght09  (L43)
             hght12  (L53)
             hght15  (L63)
             hght18  (L73)
             hght24  (L83)
             hght36  (L93);
    eta_4 BY hght01* (L14)
             hght03  (L24)
             hght06  (L34)
             hght09  (L44)
             hght12  (L54)
             hght15  (L64)
             hght18  (L74)
             hght24  (L84)
             hght36  (L94);

    eta_1*60 eta_2*4 eta_3 eta_4;

    eta_1 WITH eta_2 eta_3 eta_4;
    eta_2 WITH eta_3 eta_4;
    eta_3 WITH eta_4;

    [eta_1*60 eta_2*.5]; [eta_3*-8] (alpha_3); [eta_4@0];

    hght01-hght36*2 (theta);
    [hght01-hght36@0];

MODEL CONSTRAINT:
    new(alpha_4*.2);

    L13 = exp (alpha_4 * .0833) -1;
    L23 = exp (alpha_4 * .25  ) -1;
    L33 = exp (alpha_4 * .5   ) -1;
    L43 = exp (alpha_4 * .75  ) -1;
    L53 = exp (alpha_4 * 1    ) -1;
    L63 = exp (alpha_4 * 1.25 ) -1;
    L73 = exp (alpha_4 * 1.5  ) -1;
    L83 = exp (alpha_4 * 2    ) -1;
    L93 = exp (alpha_4 * 3    ) -1;

    L14 = alpha_3*.0833*(exp(alpha_4*.0833));
    L24 = alpha_3*  .25*(exp(alpha_4*.25));
    L34 = alpha_3*   .5*(exp(alpha_4*.5));
    L44 = alpha_3*  .75*(exp(alpha_4*.75));
    L54 = alpha_3*    1*(exp(alpha_4*1));
    L64 = alpha_3* 1.25*(exp(alpha_4*1.25));
    L74 = alpha_3*  1.5*(exp(alpha_4*1.5));
    L84 = alpha_3*    2*(exp(alpha_4*2));
    L94 = alpha_3*    3*(exp(alpha_4*3));
```

eta_2 are specified. In the second statement, the mean for eta_3 is specified and given the label alpha_3. The label is needed because it appears within the factor loadings for eta_4 (Equation 12.13). In the third statement, the mean of eta_4 is set equal to 0 following the specification of the Jenss–Bayley growth model using a first-order Taylor series expansion (Equations 12.5 and 12.6). The next two statements are for the residual variances, which are constrained to be equal over time, and for the observed variable intercepts, which are set to 0.

The MODEL CONSTRAINT statement follows, and the functional constraints for the factor loadings of eta_3 and eta_4 are specified. First, a new parameter, alpha_4, the mean of the log of the ratio of acceleration, is created using the new() statement. The next nine statements are for the functional constraints of the factor loadings for eta_3. On the left side of the equations are the labels for the factor loadings of eta_3, L13 to L93, and on the right side are the nonlinear functions of time (e.g., exp(alpha_4*age)). In the nine statements, only age varies. In a similar fashion, the functional constraints are then specified for the factor loadings of eta_4. On the left side of the equations are the labels of the factor loadings of eta_4, and on the right side are the functional constraints (e.g., alpha_2*age*(exp(alpha_3*age))) with estimated parameters alpha_3 and alpha_4.

The code to fit the Jenss–Bayley growth model in OpenMx is provided in Script 12.8. The script begins by indicating the datafile and defining both manifest and latent variables. The latent variables are named eta_1 through eta_4, and the manifest variables include the nine height variables, hght01 through hght36. The model is then specified with mxPath statements. The first mxPath command specifies the residual variances of the observed variables—two-headed arrows (arrows=2) that are freely estimated (free=TRUE). Starting values and common labels (theta) are applied to all residual variances to force them to be equal over time. Latent variable variances and covariances are then specified. The latent variables are listed as the originating variable (from=c ('eta_1','eta_2','eta_3','eta_4')), and connect='unique.pairs' is used to specify a full symmetric covariance matrix for these variables. Starting values are then provided along with labels.

Factor loadings for the four latent variables are specified next. Factor loadings for the intercept (eta_1) are fixed (free=FALSE) and set equal to 1, and the factor loadings for the linear asymptote (eta_2) are fixed and change linearly with age scaled in years since birth. The factor loadings for the difference between the actual intercept and intercept of the linear asymptote (eta_3) and the ratio of acceleration (eta_4) are not freely estimated (free=FALSE), but constrained to change according to nonlinear functions. For now, these factor loadings are given labels (L3[1,1] through L3[9,1] for eta_3 and L4[1,1] through L4[9,1] for eta_4). Next, the means of the latent variables are specified as one–headed arrows originating from the constant (one) and going to the first three latent variables (eta_1, eta_2, and eta_3). Again, we note that eta_4 does not have an estimated mean.

The next series of commands are needed for the functional constraints for the factor loadings of eta_3 and eta_4. The first matrix, created with mxMatrix, is

Script 12.8. OpenMx Script for the Jenss–Bayley Growth Model

```
jb.hght.omx <- mxModel('Jenss Bayley Growth Model, Path Specification',
  type='RAM', mxData(observed=hght_wide, type='raw'),
  manifestVars=c('hght01','hght03','hght06','hght09','hght12','hght15','hght18','hght24','hght36'),
  latentVars=c('eta_1','eta_2','eta_3','eta_4'),

# Residual Variances
mxPath(from=c('hght01','hght03','hght06','hght09','hght12','hght15','hght18','hght24','hght36'),
  arrows=2, free=TRUE, values=10, labels='theta'),

# Latent Variable Covariances
mxPath(from=c('eta_1','eta_2','eta_3','eta_4'),connect='unique.pairs',
  arrows=2, free=TRUE, values=c(1,0,0,0,1,0,0,1,0,1),
  labels=c('psi_11','psi_21','psi_31','psi_41','psi_22','psi_32','psi_42','psi_33','psi_43','psi_44')),

# Factor Loadings
mxPath(from='eta_1',to=c('hght01','hght03','hght06','hght09','hght12','hght15','hght18','hght24','hght36'),
  arrows=1, free=FALSE, values=1),

mxPath(from='eta_2',to=c('hght01','hght03','hght06','hght09','hght12','hght15','hght18','hght24','hght36'),
  arrows=1, free=FALSE, values=c(.0833, .25, .5, .75, 1, 1.25, 1.5, 2, 3)),

mxPath(from='eta_3', to=c('hght01','hght03','hght06','hght09','hght12','hght15','hght18','hght24','hght36'),
  arrows=1, free=FALSE,
  labels=c('L3[1,1]','L3[2,1]','L3[3,1]','L3[4,1]','L3[5,1]','L3[6,1]','L3[7,1]','L3[8,1]','L3[9,1]')),

mxPath(from='eta_4',to=c('hght01','hght03','hght06','hght09','hght12','hght15','hght18','hght24','hght36'),
  arrows=1, free=FALSE,
  labels=c('L4[1,1]','L4[2,1]','L4[3,1]','L4[4,1]','L4[5,1]','L4[6,1]','L4[7,1]','L4[8,1]','L4[9,1]')),

# Latent Variable Means
mxPath(from='one', to=c('eta_1','eta_2','eta_3'),
  arrows=1, free=TRUE, values=c(50,10,-15),
  labels=c('alpha_1','alpha_2','alpha_3')),

# Functional Constraints
mxMatrix('Full', 9, 1, free = FALSE, values = 1,       labels = 'number1', name = 'one'),
mxMatrix('Full', 9, 1, free = TRUE,  values = -15,      labels = 'alpha_3', name = 'a_3'),
mxMatrix('Full', 9, 1, free = TRUE,  values = -2,       labels = 'alpha_4', name = 'a_4'),
mxMatrix('Full', 9, 1, free = FALSE, values = c(.0833,.25,.5,.75,1.25,1.5,2,3), name = 'time'),

mxAlgebra((exp(a_4 * time)-one), name='L3'),
mxAlgebra(a_3*time*exp(a_4*time), name='L4')
) # Close Model
```

301

a 9 × 1 matrix of 1s and is needed because 1 is subtracted in the functional constraint for eta_3 (e.g., $\exp(\alpha_4 \cdot t) - 1$). The second is a 9 × 1 matrix of estimated elements (free=TRUE) labeled alpha_3. This label is identical to the label of the mean for eta_3 and simply allows us to use this parameter in the functional constraints. This matrix is named a_3, which will be used in the functional constraint. The third is a 9 × 1 matrix with freely estimated elements (free=TRUE) labeled alpha_4. This matrix contains a new parameter, which is the mean of the log of the ratio of acceleration. This matrix is named a_4, which is the name that will be used in the mxAlgebra statement. The fourth mxMatrix contains information regarding the timing of assessments scaled in years since birth and is named time. Finally, mxAlgebra commands are used to specify the functional constraints for the factor loadings of eta_3 and eta_4. The constraint for eta_3 is one less than the exponent of a_4, the new estimated parameter, multiplied by the timing of the assessment, time. The name given to the mxAlgebra is L3, which has nine elements L3[1,1] through L3[9,1], which were the labels given to the factor loadings of eta_3. In a similar vein, the constraint for eta_4 is the mean of eta_3, a_3, multiplied by the timing of the assessment, time, multiplied by the exponent of a_4 multiplied by the timing of the assessment. This mxAlgebra is named L4 with elements L4[1,1] through L4[9,1], which are the labels of the factor loadings for eta_4. The model is then closed.

Parameter estimates from the Jenss–Bayley growth model fit in Mplus and OpenMx are contained in Output 12.7 and 12.8, respectively. Estimates from Mplus and OpenMx are identical and close to estimates obtained from NLMIXED and nlme when the first-order approach was utilized. The mean of the intercept was 51.08 cm (Mean of ETA_1, alpha_1) and represents the predicted average height of infants at birth. The mean of the linear asymptote was 9.30 cm (Mean of ETA_2, alpha_2) and is the predicted rate of annual growth during the toddler years. The mean of the vertical difference between the intercept of the linear asymptote and the actual asymptote was –17.84 cm (Mean of ETA_3, alpha_3) and provides some information relevant to growth during the infant years. Finally, the average ratio of acceleration during infancy was 0.13 (i.e., $\exp(-2.08)$; alpha_4 under New/Additional Parameters, alpha_4) and represents how quickly, on average, growth was decelerating during infancy. The variance of the intercept was 7.41 (Variance of ETA_1, psi_11) and reflects individual differences in height at birth. The variance of the linear asymptote was 0.81 (Variance of ETA_2, psi_22), indicating between–person differences in the linear rate of growth during the toddler years. The variance of the difference between the intercept of the linear asymptote and the actual intercept was 11.63 (Variance of ETA_3, psi_33) and is related to the amount of between-child differences in growth during infancy. Lastly, the variance of the log of the ratio of acceleration was 0.08 (Variance of ETA_4, psi_44) and was not significantly different from 0, indicating that children did not show much systematic difference in how quickly their rate of growth decelerated during infancy.

Output 12.7. *Mplus* Output for Jenss–Bayley Growth Model

	Estimate	S.E.	Est./S.E.	Two-Tailed P-Value
ETA_1 BY				
HGHT01	1.000	0.000	999.000	999.000
...				
HGHT36	1.000	0.000	999.000	999.000
ETA_2 BY				
HGHT01	0.083	0.000	999.000	999.000
...				
HGHT36	3.000	0.000	999.000	999.000
ETA_3 BY				
HGHT01	−0.159	0.006	−26.838	0.000
HGHT03	−0.405	0.013	−32.228	0.000
HGHT06	−0.646	0.015	−43.194	0.000
HGHT09	−0.789	0.013	−59.136	0.000
HGHT12	−0.875	0.011	−82.592	0.000
HGHT15	−0.925	0.008	−117.484	0.000
HGHT18	−0.956	0.006	−169.901	0.000
HGHT24	−0.984	0.003	−370.674	0.000
HGHT36	−0.998	0.000	−1998.543	0.000
ETA_4 BY				
HGHT01	−1.250	0.040	−31.464	0.000
HGHT03	−2.653	0.113	−23.486	0.000
HGHT06	−3.158	0.194	−16.308	0.000
HGHT09	−2.818	0.229	−12.310	0.000
HGHT12	−2.236	0.227	−9.839	0.000
HGHT15	−1.663	0.203	−8.178	0.000
HGHT18	−1.188	0.170	−6.990	0.000
HGHT24	−0.561	0.104	−5.410	0.000
HGHT36	−0.105	0.028	−3.720	0.000
ETA_1 WITH				
ETA_2	0.639	0.528	1.211	0.226
ETA_3	4.448	1.572	2.829	0.005
ETA_4	0.030	0.262	0.113	0.910
ETA_2 WITH				
ETA_3	1.345	0.849	1.585	0.113
ETA_4	−0.078	0.143	−0.542	0.588
ETA_3 WITH				
ETA_4	−0.488	0.383	−1.273	0.203
Means				
ETA_1	51.076	0.352	145.136	0.000
ETA_2	9.296	0.174	53.480	0.000
ETA_3	−17.836	0.491	−36.333	0.000
ETA_4	0.000	0.000	999.000	999.000
Variances				
ETA_1	7.410	1.516	4.889	0.000
ETA_2	0.809	0.340	2.380	0.017
ETA_3	11.625	3.009	3.863	0.000
ETA_4	0.076	0.079	0.958	0.338
Residual Variances				
HGHT01	0.644	0.053	12.175	0.000
...				
HGHT36	0.644	0.053	12.175	0.000
New/Additional Parameters				
ALPHA_4	−2.076	0.084	−24.584	0.000

Output 12.8. `OpenMx` **Output for Jenss–Bayley Growth Model**

```
free parameters:
        name     matrix    row      col       Estimate    Std.Error
 1     theta        S    hght01   hght01     0.64361068   0.05285846
 2    psi_11        S    eta_1    eta_1      7.40983185   1.51601209
 3    psi_21        S    eta_1    eta_2      0.63918570   0.52741813
 4    psi_22        S    eta_2    eta_2      0.80917244   0.33976726
 5    psi_31        S    eta_1    eta_3      4.44830601   1.57227660
 6    psi_32        S    eta_2    eta_3      1.34529809   0.84805468
 7    psi_33        S    eta_3    eta_3     11.62504227   3.00640157
 8    psi_41        S    eta_1    eta_4      0.02957294   0.26218739
 9    psi_42        S    eta_2    eta_4     -0.07774225   0.14327950
10    psi_43        S    eta_3    eta_4     -0.48781365   0.38261606
11    psi_44        S    eta_4    eta_4      0.07590980   0.07914543
12   alpha_1        M      1      eta_1     51.07597943   0.35192099
13   alpha_2        M      1      eta_2      9.29555541   0.17381207
14   alpha_3        M      1      eta_3    -17.83600004   0.49089353
15   alpha_4       a_4     1        1       -2.07644521   0.08446366
```

All covariances, except one, were not significantly different from 0, indicating that most of the different aspects of growth from the Jenss–Bayley growth model were somewhat independent from one another. The significant covariance was between the intercept and the difference between the intercept of the linear asymptote and actual intercept, which was 4.45 (`ETA_1 WITH ETA_3, psi_31`), indicating that children who were taller at birth tended to have smaller (more positive) differences between the two intercepts. The final estimated parameter was the residual variance, which was 0.67 (`Residual Variance, theta`) and represents individual variation not accounted for by the model.

IMPORTANT CONSIDERATIONS

Fully nonlinear models have several benefits for modeling and understanding within-person change and between-person differences in change. These models allow for between-person differences in any parameter of the individual curve; however, these models often have convergence issues as seen in this chapter. For example, the bilinear spline growth model with variability in the knot point had convergence issues in `PROC NLMIXED`, which may indicate that the model was inappropriate for the data. However, programs have encountered convergence issues even in simulations where the population model was being fit to simulated data. To aid convergence, we reduced the number of quadrature points and tried multiple sets of starting values. Using Taylor series expansion is useful for generating starting values; however, relying solely on Taylor series expansion can be problematic (see Davidian & Giltinan, 2003).

MOVING FORWARD

This chapter concludes our presentation of the various types of models that are used to understand individual change patterns and between-person differences in individual change patterns. The next section focuses on ordinal outcomes and multivariate outcomes. Thus far, we have modeled changes for a single outcome that was assumed to have a normal distribution. In the next chapter, we consider models for ordinal outcomes, which is followed by chapters on multivariate normal and multivariate ordinal outcomes intended to measure a common construct that has been collected across time. Thus, we discuss measurement invariance and modeling change in latent variables.

# Part IV

Modeling Change with Latent Entities

13

Modeling Change
with Ordinal Outcomes

In this chapter we discuss how to model change with ordinal outcomes. So far, our outcome of interest has been continuous and assumed to follow a normal distribution; however, many variables are not normally distributed in the social, educational, and behavioral sciences. Treating non-normal and noncontinuous variables as such can lead to inaccurate parameter estimates and conclusions. Thus, it is important to use an appropriate distribution for the outcome variable. In this chapter we discuss models for dichotomous and the extension to polytomous outcomes as these types of outcomes are most common. Programs that can model non-normal outcomes and allow for between-person differences in the change process include `NLMIXED` in `SAS` (Sheu, 2002; Sheu, Chen, Su, & Wang, 2005), `Mplus`, and `OpenMx`. Although the `nlme` package cannot model non-normal outcomes, the `lme4` (Bates et al., 2011) package can model various types of non-normal distributions, and we include code on our webpage for `lme4`.

DICHOTOMOUS OUTCOMES

Dichotomous outcomes are common in the social, educational, and behavioral sciences. Examples include clinical diagnoses, such as depression and dementia, as well as the correctness of test questions (0 = wrong, 1 = correct). Treating such outcomes as continuous is riddled with problems (e.g., high degree of nonlinearity, out-of-bounds predictions) when distributions are uneven (80–20); however, there are fewer issues when more evenly distributed proportions (50–50) are observed. The logit and probit link functions are commonly used with dichotomous and polytomous outcomes and are described here.

The probit model can be thought of as having two parts. The first relates the dichotomous response to an underlying latent variable that is continuous and normally distributed, which is often referred to as the *latent response propensity*. The second relates the latent response propensity to the predictor variables (e.g., time). In the first part of the model, individual i's dichotomous response at time t, denoted y_{ti}, is the manifestation of individual i's latent response propensity at time t, denoted y_{ti}^*. Often, y_{ti}^*, the latent response propensity, is assumed to have a standard normal distribution or its residual is assumed to have a standard normal distribution. This relationship between y_{ti} and y_{ti}^* is conveyed through a threshold parameter, τ, which is the location on the latent response propensity separating respondents who have zeroes versus ones (e.g., incorrect vs. correct).

Mathematically, this is represented by

$$y_{ti} = \begin{cases} 0 & if \ y_{ti}^* \leq \tau \\ 1 & if \ y_{ti}^* > \tau \end{cases} \tag{13.1}$$

such that the observed response equals 0 or 1 depending on whether the score on the latent response propensity is less than or equal to τ or greater than τ, respectively. Figure 13.1 displays this relationship graphically where $\tau = 0.6$, which suggests that 27.43% of individuals scored 1 and 72.57% scored 0. The threshold, therefore, provides information regarding the proportion of individuals responding in each category. Longitudinally, the threshold, τ, is often assumed to be invariant with respect to time because the threshold is related to how the dichotomously scored variable is defined. That is, if the proportion of individuals who score a 1 increases over time, it is thought to be related to individuals changing positively (i.e., distribution of y_{ti}^* moving to the right in Figure 13.1) and not changes in how the variable was defined.

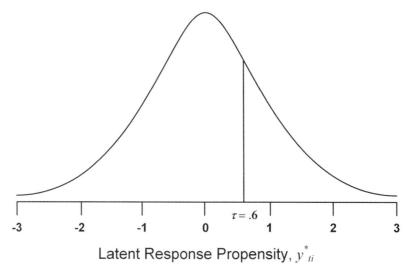

FIGURE 13.1. Graphical representation of the latent response propensity for dichotomous data.

In the second part of the model, changes in the latent response propensity are modeled by a linear or nonlinear growth model. For example, in a linear growth model, we can write

$$y_{ti}^* = b_{1i} + b_{2i} \cdot t + u_{ti} \tag{13.2}$$

where b_{1i} is the individual intercept, b_{2i} is the individual linear rate of change, and u_{ti} is the time-dependent residual. The intercept and slope are assumed to follow a multivariate normal distribution with means (β_1 and β_2), variances (σ_1^2 and σ_2^2), and a covariance (σ_{21}). The variance of the time-dependent residual, u_{ti}, is not estimated because y_{ti}^* is a latent variable and does not have an inherent scale. Typically, the variance of u_{ti} is fixed at 1.

In the structural equation modeling framework, we can write

$$\mathbf{y}_i^* = \mathbf{\Lambda}\eta_i + \mathbf{u}_i \tag{13.3}$$

and

$$\eta_i = \alpha + \xi_i \tag{13.4}$$

where $\mathbf{y}_i^*$ is a $T \times 1$ vector of the latent response propensities for individual i, where T represents the number of repeated assessments based on the chosen time metric, $\mathbf{\Lambda}$ is a $T \times R$ matrix of factor loadings defining the latent growth factors, where R is the number of growth factors, η_i is an $R \times 1$ vector of latent factor scores for individual i, and $\mathbf{u}_i$ is a $T \times 1$ vector of residual or unique scores for individual i. Lastly, α is an $R \times 1$ vector of latent factor means, and ξ_i is an $R \times 1$ vector of mean deviations for individual i.

There are two ways to identify growth models with dichotomous outcomes. The most common way is to estimate a single threshold parameter across time and fix the mean of the intercept to 0 ($\beta_1 = 0$, $\alpha_1 = 0$). This approach generalizes more easily to polytomous outcomes, and the threshold provides information regarding the distribution of zeroes and ones when time equals 0. The second approach is to fix the threshold at a specific value (often $\tau = 0$) and estimate the mean of the intercept. In this case, the mean of the intercept provides information regarding the location of the distribution of the response propensity when time equals 0. In either case, the slope provides information regarding the average rate of change in the response propensity and individual differences therein.

The logit link, the most common link function for regression with a dichotomous outcome, can also be used when modeling changes in a repeatedly measured dichotomous outcome. In the logit model, and following item response modeling notation, the log-odds of the probability is set equal to a linear function, which can be written as

$$\ln\left(\frac{\Pr(y_{ti} = 1)}{1 - \Pr(y_{ti} = 1)}\right) = \theta_{ti} - \omega \tag{13.5}$$

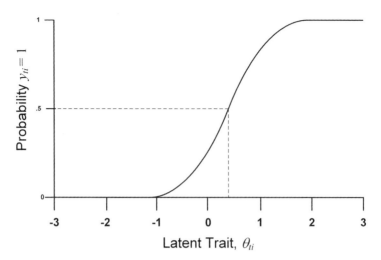

FIGURE 13.2. Example association between the probability of a positive response and the underlying latent trait based on the logit model.

where $\Pr(y_{ti} = 1)$ is the probability of obtaining a positive score (i.e., a score equal to 1), θ_{ti} is individual i's ability at time t (sometimes referred to as the *latent trait*, akin to response propensity in the probit model) and ω is the location parameter.[1] Solving Equation 13.5 for $\Pr(y_{ti} = 1)$ yields the logistic formula,

$$\Pr(y_{ti} = 1) = \frac{\exp(\theta_{ti} - \omega)}{1 + \exp(\theta_{ti} - \omega)} \tag{13.6}$$

The relation between the probability of a positive score and ability is plotted in Figure 13.2, where on the y-axis is the probability of a positive score, $\Pr(y_{ti} = 1)$, and on the x-axis is person ability, θ_{ti}. In this figure, the location parameter is $\omega = 0.40$, which indicates that a person with $\theta_{ti} = 0.40$ has a 0.50 probability of obtaining a positive score. Note that the curve is bounded by 0 and 1 as probability ranges between these values and that persons with lower ability have less than a 0.50 probability of obtaining a positive score and persons with higher ability have greater than a 0.50 probability of obtaining a positive score. In item response theory, this type of curve is referred to as the *item characteristic curve* or *trace line*. This figure also highlights the importance of having a single location parameter over time. That is, if the location parameter changed over time, then a person with the same ability at two points in time (or two people at two points in time) would have different probabilities of obtaining a positive score. If this were the case, then we would be unable to distinguish between changes in ability

---

[1]Typically, β is used for the location or difficulty parameter in item response models. We use ω to easily distinguish this parameter from the fixed-effects parameters β_1 and β_2 that have been used throughout the book.

and changes in the definition of scores (i.e., changes in the test). We also note that we do not have a discrimination (slope) parameter in Equations 13.5 and 13.6 because we have a single item that is repeatedly measured and an estimated discrimination parameter is not identified. It would only serve to change the scale of the model parameters, and we would have to fix another parameter to identify the discrimination parameter (i.e., if we fixed the variance of the intercept to be 1, then we would be able to estimate the discrimination parameter).

Now, we can write a model for how person ability, θ_{ti}, changes over time. If a linear model is warranted, we can write

$$\theta_{ti} = b_{1i} + b_{2i} \cdot t + u_{ti} \tag{13.7}$$

where b_{1i} is the individual intercept, b_{2i} is the individual linear rate of change, and u_{ti} is the time-dependent residual. As above, the intercept and slope are assumed to follow a multivariate normal distribution with means (β_1 and β_2), variances (σ_1^2 and σ_2^2), and a covariance (σ_{21}). Additionally, the variance of the time-dependent residual, σ_u^2, is not estimated because θ_{ti} is a latent variable and therefore does not have an inherent scale. In the logit model, the variance of u_{ti} is equal to the variance of the standard logistic distribution, which is $\pi^2/3$ where π is the mathematical constant (i.e., 3.14 . . .). As with the probit model, the growth model with a logit link can be identified in two ways. First, we can estimate a single location parameter, ω, for all measurement occasions and fix the mean of the intercept to zero ($\beta_1 = 0$). The alternative approach is to fix the location parameter to zero ($\omega = 0$) and estimate the mean of the intercept. In this approach ($\omega = 0$), it can be seen that the log of the odds is expected to follow the growth model, such that

$$\ln\left(\frac{\Pr(y_{ti} = 1)}{1 - \Pr(y_{ti} = 1)}\right) = b_{1i} + b_{2i} \cdot t + u_{ti} \tag{13.8}$$

In the structural equation modeling framework, we would write

$$\theta_i = \Lambda \eta_i + \mathbf{u}_i \tag{13.9}$$

and

$$\eta_i = \alpha + \xi_i \tag{13.10}$$

where θ_i is a $T \times 1$ vector of the latent traits for individual i, where T represents the number of repeated assessments based on the chosen time metric, Λ is a $T \times R$ matrix of factor loadings defining the latent growth factors, where R is the number of growth factors, η_i is an $R \times 1$ vector of latent factor scores for individual i, $\mathbf{u}_i$ is a $T \times 1$ vector of residual or unique scores for individual i, α is an $R \times 1$ vector of latent factor means, and ξ_i is an $R \times 1$ vector of mean deviations for individual i.

POLYTOMOUS OUTCOMES

Growth models for dichotomous outcomes can be extended to multicategory ordinal variables in a straightforward manner. Examples of multicategory variables include certain diagnoses (e.g., for dementia: normal, mild cognitive impairment, dementia) and Likert-type rating scales (e.g., strongly disagree, disagree, agree, strongly agree). In the probit model, additional thresholds are specified to divide the latent response propensity into multiple categories. For example, a four-category variable would have three thresholds (always one less than the number of categories), such that

$$
y_{ti} = \begin{cases}
0 & \text{if} \quad y_{ti}^* \leq \tau_1 \\
1 & \text{if} \quad \tau_1 < y_{ti}^* \leq \tau_2 \\
2 & \text{if} \quad \tau_2 < y_{ti}^* \leq \tau_3 \\
3 & \text{if} \quad y_{ti}^* > \tau_3
\end{cases}
\tag{13.11}
$$

where y_{ti} is the observed four-category response for individual i at time t, y_{ti}^* is the associated latent response propensity, and τ_1, τ_2, and τ_3 are the thresholds. Thus, τ_1 separates the first category (i.e., 0) from the second (i.e., 1), third (i.e., 2), and fourth categories (i.e., 3), τ_2 separates the first and second categories from the third and fourth categories, and τ_3 separates the first, second, and third categories from the fourth category. The thresholds are ordered, such that $\tau_1 < \tau_2 < \tau_3$. This relationship between the latent response propensity and a four-category item is depicted in Figure 13.3. Note that this relationship is considered a *cumulative* response process whereby each threshold distinguishes between

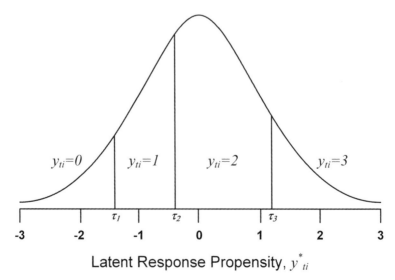

FIGURE 13.3. Graphical representation of the latent response propensity for a multicategory variable.

responding *in or above* a specific category versus responding below that specific category as opposed to an adjacent response process whereby the comparison is between two adjacent categories and is conditional on responding in one of those two response categories. In the cumulative model, all responses aid in the estimation of the threshold parameters. Changes in the latent response propensity can then be modeled with growth models as in Equations 13.2, 13.3, and 13.4.

The logit model of Equation 13.5 can also be expanded to include multiple categories. The cumulative logit model is more common than the adjacent logit model and is presented here. The cumulative logit model can be written as

$$\ln\left(\frac{\Pr(y_{ti} \geq c)}{1 - \Pr(y_{ti} \geq c)}\right) = \theta_{ti} - \omega_c \qquad (13.12)$$

where $\Pr(y_{ti} \geq c)$ is the probability of responding in or above category c, θ_{ti} is individual i's ability at time t, and ω_c is the location parameter separating categories $c - 1$ and c. Additionally, we note that $\omega_c < \omega_{c+1}$, which keeps order of the location parameters (e.g., scoring in the second category is more difficult than scoring in the first category). This constraint is sometimes imposed where $\omega_{c+1} = \omega_c + \delta_c$ (e.g., $\omega_2 = \omega_1 + \delta_1$) and δ_c is a positive number.

The relationship between the probability of responding in or above each category against ability is plotted in Figure 13.4 for a four-category item with $\omega_1 = -2.00$, $\omega_2 = 0.70$, and $\omega_3 = 1.50$. On the y-axis is the probability of responding in or above category c and ability is on the x-axis. As in Figure 13.2, each curve is bounded by 0 and 1, and

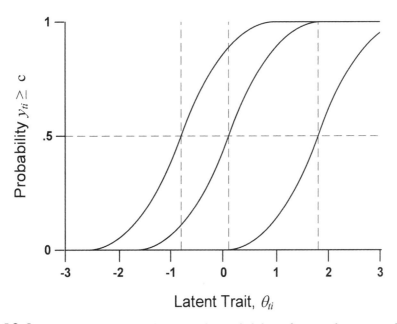

FIGURE 13.4. Example association between the probability of responding in or above each category and underlying latent trait.

the probability of responding in or above each category increases with ability. This figure also highlights how the distances between categories of a polytomous variable may not be equidistant. That is, a smaller increase in ability is needed to move from the second to the third category compared to the distance to move from the third to fourth category. In item response theory, this type of curve is referred to as the *operating characteristic curve*.

The probability of responding in a given category can be calculated by subtracting the probability of responding in or above category $c + 1$ from the probability of responding in or above category c. This leads to

$$\Pr(y_{ti} = c) = \frac{\exp(\theta_{ti} - \omega_c)}{1 + \exp(\theta_{ti} - \omega_c)} - \frac{\exp(\theta_{ti} - \omega_{c+1})}{1 + \exp(\theta_{ti} - \omega_{c+1})} \qquad (13.13)$$

Additionally, the probability of responding in the first category needs to be specified, which can be written as

$$\Pr(y_{ti} = 0) = 1 - \frac{\exp(\theta_{ti} - \omega_1)}{1 + \exp(\theta_{ti} - \omega_1)} \qquad (13.14)$$

where $c = 0$ is the first category. In essence, this equation states that a person has a 100% chance of responding in a category given that he or she responded to the variable.

Figure 13.5 is a plot of the relationship between the probability of scoring in each category against ability with probability on the y-axis and ability on the x-axis. This

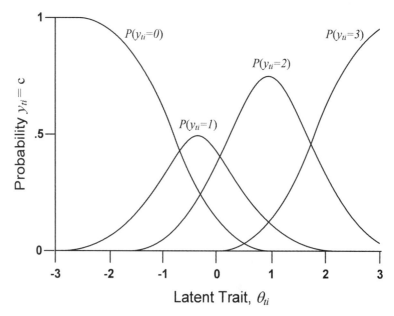

FIGURE 13.5. Example association between the probability of responding in each response category and underlying latent trait.

figure is useful to understand that each person with ability θ_{ti} has a probability of responding in each of the categories even though some of those probabilities are quite small. It is also useful for understanding how changes in ability relate to changes in the probability of responding in each category. In item response theory, this set of curves is referred to as the *category response curve*. Now that the link between the category response and ability is specified, changes in ability can be modeled as in Equations 13.7, 13.9, and 13.10.

ILLUSTRATION

We illustrate these approaches to modeling change in dichotomous and polytomously scored variables with data on smoking behavior collected as part of the NLSY-CYA. Young adults were asked about their recent smoking experiences. Specifically, participants were first asked if they had ever smoked cigarettes in their life. If they had smoked, they were then asked how recently and given multiple response options. Responses to these two questions were recoded into two variables. The first variable was created to make a dichotomy between participants who had smoked within the past 30 days and participants who had not. This variable aims to measure whether or not the participant is a *current* smoker. The second variable also measures smoking behavior, but to a finer degree. Specifically, the second variable created had four response categories: 0, participant never smoked; 1, participant had smoked but not within the past year; 2, participant smoked within the past year, but not within the past 30 days; and 3, participant smoked within the past 30 days.

MULTILEVEL MODELING IMPLEMENTATION

The smoking data (`smoke`) was set up in the long format for the multilevel programs with a variable named `c_smk` for the *current* smoking variable, `g_smk` for the *graded* smoking variable with four response categories, and `age` is used as the timing metric. Age ranged from 15 to 20 and is scaled in years.

Growth Model with a Dichotomous Outcome

SAS

The `NLMIXED` code for fitting the *linear growth* model with a dichotomous outcome using a logit link is contained in Script 13.1. The script begins by calling `NLMIXED` and specifying the dataset. Next, the linear growth model is written with `theta_ti` as the outcome, `b_1i` as the random intercept, and `b_2i` as the random slope multiplied by age centered at 15 years (`age-15`). This follows Equation 13.7 directly as changes

Script 13.1. NLMIXED Script for the Linear Growth Model with a Dichotomous Outcome Using the Logit Link

```
PROC NLMIXED DATA=smoke;
    theta_ti = b_1i + b_2i * (age-15);

    p = EXP(theta_ti-omega)/(1+EXP(theta_ti-omega));

    MODEL c_smk ~ BINARY(p);
    RANDOM b_1i b_2i ~ NORMAL([0, beta_2],[v_1, c_21, v_2]) SUBJECT=id;

    PARMS
        omega=4    beta_2=.5    v_1=6    c_21=0    v_2=.5;
RUN;
```

in the underlying latent ability, θ_{ti}, are modeled with a linear growth model. Next, we map the probability of being a current smoker, p, to person ability using the logistic function following Equation 13.6 with theta_ti as person ability and omega as the location parameter. The MODEL statement follows, and the outcome variable, c_smk, is a BINARY variable with probability, p. The RANDOM statement comes next and follows typical notation with b_1i and b_2i as random coefficients, which are assumed to follow a NORMAL distribution with means and a variance-covariance matrix as specified. We estimate the location parameter (omega), and therefore the mean of b_1i is fixed to 0 for identification. Lastly, starting values are provided in the PARMS statement.

The NLMIXED code for fitting the linear growth model with a dichotomous outcome using a probit link is contained in Script 13.2. The script is quite similar to the above script with a few minor changes. The growth model for ys_ti (ys for y star, y_{ti}^*), the latent response propensity, is specified with random coefficients b_1i and b_2i and age centered at 15 years (age-15). Next, the probability of being a current smoker, p, is equal to the probnorm function of ys_ti-tau. The probnorm function returns the probability of observing a value that is less than or equal to the specified function using a standard normal distribution. In essence, the probit link ys_ti-tau is contained in

Script 13.2. NLMIXED Script for the Linear Growth Model with a Dichotomous Outcome Using the Probit Link

```
PROC NLMIXED DATA = smoke;
    ys_ti = b_1i + b_2i*(age-15);

    p = probnorm(ys_ti-tau);

    MODEL c_smk ~ BINARY(p);
    RANDOM b_1i b_2i ~ normal([0,beta_2],[v_1, c_21, v_2]) SUBJECT = id;

    PARMS
        tau=-2   beta_2=.3   v_1=3   c_21=0   v_2=.2;
RUN;
```

the `probnorm` function to allow for the estimation of the threshold parameter, `tau`. The remainder of the script follows Script 13.1 with the `MODEL`, `RANDOM`, and `PARMS` statements. We note that slightly different starting values are provided that are more in line with the probit link.

Output

Select `NLMIXED` output from the linear growth model fit to the longitudinal smoking data using the logit and probit links is contained in Outputs 13.1 and 13.2, respectively. First, we note that the fits of the two models were highly similar (i.e., –2 log likelihoods were 13,637 and 13,641, respectively). Second, we note that the general conclusions from the parameter estimates and their levels of significance were highly similar. Thus, it makes little difference whether the logit or probit link is utilized; however, the interpretation of parameter estimates depends on the chosen link function.

Before discussing the interpretation of model parameters from the growth models, we note that the interpretation of these model parameters is complex and direct translation to probabilities and how probabilities are expected to change over time is troublesome. First, we begin with the interpretation of the model using the logit link and discuss the growth parameters, which are in the logit metric. The location parameter (`omega`) was 4.71 and represents the log-odds of *not* being a current smoker at age 15 (since $\theta_{ti} - \omega$). The variance of the intercept (`v_1`) was 9.43 and represents between-person differences in the log-odds of being a current smoker at 15 years of age. That is, at age 15, some individuals were less likely than others to be a current smoker. The mean of the linear slope (`beta_2`) was 0.43 and significantly different from zero, indicating that the log-odds of being a current smoker increased 0.43 units per year from 15 to 20 years of age. The variance of the linear slope (`v_2`) was 0.39 and also significantly different from zero, suggesting that individuals differed in how their log-odds of being a current smoker changed from 15 to 20 years of age. Lastly, the intercept–slope covariance was 0.12 and not significant. Thus, an individual's log-odds of being a current smoker at age 15 was unrelated to how their log-odds changed from 15 to 20 years of age.

Now, we turn to translating the parameters into understanding how the average probability of being a current smoker changed over time. We note that numerical integration is needed to calculate model-based probabilities. No simple formula is available to track changes in probability and tracking changes in the mean of θ_{ti} over time and translating it to probabilities using $\Pr(y_{ti} = 1) = \exp(\theta_{ti} - \omega)/(1 + \exp(\theta_{ti} - \omega))$ does not always provide accurate estimates of how the mean probability changed over time because θ_{ti} is assumed to be normally distributed and $\Pr(y_{ti} = 1)$ is not.[2] Here, we present an approach to *approximate* the model-based probabilities at each age. This approach is based on

---

[2]Doing these calculations can provide accurate estimates of how the *median* probability is expected to change over time.

Output 13.1. NLMIXED Output for the Linear Growth Model with a Dichotomous Outcome Using the Logit Link

Fit Statistics

-2 Log Likelihood	13637
AIC (smaller is better)	13647
AICC (smaller is better)	13647
BIC (smaller is better)	13682

Parameter Estimates

Parameter	Estimate	Standard Error	DF	t Value	Pr > |t|	Alpha	Lower	Upper	Gradient
Omega	4.7115	0.2591	7190	18.19	<.0001	0.05	4.2036	5.2193	0.003914
beta_2	0.4261	0.06116	7190	6.97	<.0001	0.05	0.3063	0.5460	-0.0229
v_1	9.4332	1.5833	7190	5.96	<.0001	0.05	6.3294	12.5369	-0.00017
c_21	0.1232	0.2135	7190	0.58	0.5640	0.05	-0.2954	0.5418	-0.00586
v_2	0.3880	0.09112	7190	4.26	<.0001	0.05	0.2094	0.5666	-0.00323

Output 13.2. NLMIXED Output for the Linear Growth Model with a Dichotomous Outcome Using the Probit Link

Fit Statistics

-2 Log Likelihood	13641
AIC (smaller is better)	13651
AICC (smaller is better)	13651
BIC (smaller is better)	13686

Parameter Estimates

Parameter	Estimate	Standard Error	DF	t Value	Pr > |t|	Alpha	Lower	Upper	Gradient
tau	2.5677	0.1296	7190	19.81	<.0001	0.05	2.3136	2.8218	-0.00068
beta_2	0.2313	0.03219	7190	7.18	<.0001	0.05	0.1682	0.2944	0.006401
v_1	2.6992	0.4250	7190	6.35	<.0001	0.05	1.8661	3.5323	-0.00003
c_21	0.04953	0.05994	7190	0.83	0.4087	0.05	-0.06798	0.1670	0.002201
v_2	0.1142	0.02563	7190	4.46	<.0001	0.05	0.06399	0.1645	0.001564

examining the model-based distribution of predicted scores at each age—that is, the estimated distribution of θ_{ti} at each age (i.e., $\hat{\theta}_{ti}$) and examining what proportion of this distribution is greater than the location parameter. For example, the variance of the random intercept was 9.43; therefore $\hat{\theta}_{15i}$ was expected to be normally distributed with a mean of 0 and a variance of 12.72, which is the sum of the variance of the random intercept and the variance of the standard logistic distribution. Thus, the standard deviation of $\hat{\theta}_{15i}$ is 3.57. From this distribution, we can calculate the percent of the distribution predicted to have an estimated latent trait greater than 4.71 ($\hat{\omega}$), which would suggest that this proportion of the sample had greater than a 0.50 probability of being a current smoker. At age 15, this percentage was approximately 9.33% of the sample. Thus, 9.33% of the sample was predicted to be a current smoker at age 15. These calculations were carried out at the remaining ages (i.e., $\hat{\theta}_{16i} \sim N$ (0.43, 3.65), $\hat{\theta}_{17i} \sim N$ (0.85, 3.84), $\hat{\theta}_{18i} \sim N$ (1.28, 4.12), $\hat{\theta}_{19i} \sim N$ (1.70, 4.46), and $\hat{\theta}_{20i} \sim N$ (2.13, 4.86)), which yielded 12.05%, 15.76%, 20.22%, 25.02%, and 29.78% of participants at ages 16, 17, 18, 19, and 20 years were expected to be smokers. Thus, we can see how the predicted probability of being a current smoker increased from 15 to 20 years and how this increase was not constant even though a linear growth model was fit (linear in the log-odds, but nonlinear in probability).

Similar information can be obtained from the results from fitting the linear growth model using the probit link. This model conveys much of the same information (i.e., logit and probit model carry highly similar predictions), but in a different metric (probability units instead of logits). The mean of the linear slope (beta_2) was 0.23 and significantly different from 0, indicating that there was an increase in the propensity of being a current smoker from 15 to 20 years of age. The variance of intercept (v_1) was 2.70 and significantly different from zero, suggesting that individuals varied in their propensity to smoke at 15 years. The variance of the linear slope (v_2) was 0.11 and significant, suggesting that individuals varied in how quickly their propensity to be a current smoker changed from 15 to 20 years of age. Lastly, the intercept–slope covariance (c_21) was 0.05 and not significantly different from 0, indicating that an individual's propensity to smoke at 15 years was unrelated to how his or her propensity changed over time.

As above, the parameters from this model can be used to determine predicted changes in the probability of being a current smoker over time. Again, this is based on the model-implied distribution of y_{ti}^* at each age and the proportion of the distribution above the threshold, τ. The model implied distribution of y_{15i}^*, the latent response propensity at 15 years, had a mean of 0 and a variance of 3.70. The model implied variance of y_{15i}^* is the variance of the random intercept plus 1, the residual variance in the probit model. This leads to a standard deviation of 1.98, and the percent of this distribution greater than 2.57 was 9.09%. Thus, the model predicts that 9.09% of participants were current smokers at 15 years. Expanding this rationale and making calculations for each age, we find that the model predicts the percentage of current smokers to increase to 11.88%, 15.65%, 20.16%, 24.99%, and 29.75% from 16 through 20 years. These percentages are highly similar to those obtained when the logit link was used, which, again, highlights the similarity in the predictions when using these two link functions.

Growth Model with a Polytomous Outcome

SAS

NLMIXED has the ability to fit linear and nonlinear growth models with polytomously scored ordinal outcomes using both the logit and probit link functions; however, NLMIXED does not have a built-in distribution that is appropriate. Thus, statements for the likelihood function must be included. The NLMIXED script for fitting a linear growth model with the polytomously scored smoking variable is given in Script 13.3. The script begins with a linear growth model specified for theta_ti following Equation 13.7, with random intercept, b_1i, random linear slope, b_2i, and age centered at 15 years (age-15). The next three statements are an intermediate step to specify the cumulative logit link. In these statements, the difference between ability, theta_ti, and the location parameters are specified, omega is the location parameter between the first and second categories (0 and 1), omega+delta_1 is the location parameter between the second and third categories (1 and 2), and omega+delta_1+delta_2 is the location parameter between the third and fourth categories (2 and 3). The differences between the latent ability and the location parameters are named e1, e2, and e3, which are included in the next four statements where the cumulative logit link is specified. Following Equations 13.13 and 13.14, the probability of responding in each of the four categories is specified. For example, the probability of responding in the first category (g_smk=0) is 1-EXP(e1)/(1+EXP(e1)).

The next two statements are for the likelihood function. These two statements are needed because NLMIXED does not have a built-in likelihood function for polytomous data. The log likelihood (ll) function is simply the log of the probability (LOG(p)). That is, for each response (e.g., g_smk=0), we want to maximize the probability of that response given the parameters to be estimated. However, if the probability, p, of a given response is very low ($1 \cdot 10^{-8}$), the value of the log likelihood function is replaced by a very large negative value (e.g., -1E100) to avoid a floating point problem (i.e., if the probability is very low, SAS reports 0 instead of the actual probability, and the log of 0 is undefined). The MODEL statement follows where g_smk is specified as the outcome, which is assumed to follow the GENERAL log likelihood function that was just defined. The RANDOM statement comes next and is typically specified with b_1i and b_2i as the random coefficients with means and variance-covariance matrix specified. Again, we highlight that the mean of the intercept is fixed at 0 for identification purposes. The PARMS statement provides starting values for all estimated parameters and the BOUNDS statement forces delta_1 and delta_2 to be positive, which ensures that the location parameters are ordered (e.g., the location parameter between category 2 and 3 is more positive than the threshold between category 1 and 2).

The script to estimate the linear growth model for a polytomous outcome using the probit link using NLMIXED is contained in Script 13.4. The script begins with a linear growth model for the latent response propensity, ys_ti, with random intercept, b_1i, random linear slope, b_2i, and age centered at 15 years (age-15). Next, the probit link is specified using four statements—one for each of the four categories of the outcome

Script 13.3. NLMIXED Script for the Linear Growth Model with a Polytomous Outcome Using the Logit Link

```
PROC NLMIXED DATA = smoke;
  theta_ti = b_1i+b_2i*(age-15);

  e1=(theta_ti-omega);
  e2=(theta_ti-(omega+delta_1));
  e3=(theta_ti-(omega+delta_1+delta_2));

  IF     g_smk=0 THEN p=1-EXP(e1)/(1+EXP(e1));
  ELSE IF g_smk=1 THEN p=EXP(e1)/(1+EXP(e1))-EXP(e2)/(1+EXP(e2));
  ELSE IF g_smk=2 THEN p=EXP(e2)/(1+EXP(e2))-EXP(e3)/(1+EXP(e3));
  ELSE IF g_smk=3 THEN p=EXP(e3)/(1+EXP(e3));

  IF (p > 1E-8) THEN ll = LOG(p);
  ELSE ll = -1E100;

  MODEL g_smk ~ GENERAL(ll);
  RANDOM b_1i b_2i ~ NORMAL([0,beta_2], [v_1,  c_21,  v_2]) SUBJECT = id;

  PARMS
    omega = 2    delta_1 = 1    delta_2 = 1    beta_2 = .4
    v_1 = 8      c_21 = 0       v_2 = .5;
  BOUNDS
    delta_1-delta_2 > 0;

RUN;
```

Script 13.4. NLMIXED Script for the Linear Growth Model with a Polytomous Outcome Using the Probit Link

```
PROC NLMIXED DATA = smoke;
  ys_ti = b_1i + b_2i*(age-15);

  IF       g_smk=0 THEN p = 1 - probnorm(ys_ti-tau1);
  ELSE IF g_smk=1 THEN p = probnorm(ys_ti-tau1) - probnorm(ys_ti-(tau1+tau2));
  ELSE IF g_smk=2 THEN p = probnorm(ys_ti-(tau1+tau2)) - probnorm(ys_ti-(tau1+tau2+tau3));
  ELSE IF g_smk=3 THEN p = probnorm(ys_ti-(tau1+tau2+tau3));

  IF (p > 1E-8) THEN ll = log(p);
  ELSE ll = -1E100;

  MODEL g_smk ~ general(ll);
  RANDOM b_1i b_2i ~ NORMAL([0,beta_2], [v_1, c_21, v_2]) SUBJECT = id;

  PARMS   tau1=1 tau2=1 tau3=1 beta_2=.5 v_1=2 c_21=0 v_2=.2;
  BOUNDS tau2-tau3 > 0;

RUN;
```

325

variable. The probability of responding in each category is given using the `probnorm` function. As with the logit model, the probability of responding in the first category is 1 minus the probability that the latent response propensity, `ys_ti`, is greater than the first threshold, `tau1`. For `gsmk=1`, the probability is the difference between responding in category 1 or above and the probability of responding in category 2 or above. Similarly, for category 2, the probability is the difference between responding in category 2 or above and the probability of responding in category 3, and for category 3, the probability is simply the probability that the latent response propensity is greater than the third threshold (`tau1+tau2+tau3`).

The log likelihood function is then specified on the next two lines in the same way as with the logit link. The log likelihood is the log of the probability, and the value of the log likelihood function is set to a very large negative value when the probability is very small (less than $1 \cdot 10^{-8}$). The MODEL and RANDOM statements follow and are typically specified. `g_smk` has a GENERAL log likelihood function that was just defined, and the random coefficients are `b_1i` and `b_2i` with means and variance–covariance matrix specified. As in the previous examples, the mean of the intercept is fixed at 0 for identification. In the PARMS statements starting values are provided, and the BOUNDS statements force the thresholds to be ordered by restricting `tau2` and `tau3` to positive values.

Output

Fit statistics and parameter estimates from NLMIXED for the linear growth model fit to the graded smoking variable using the logit and probit links are contained in Output 13.3 and 13.4, respectively. As before, the fit of the two models was highly similar, and the general conclusions from the parameter estimates were the same. Regardless of the link function utilized, we see that the variance of the intercept (`v_1`) was significant, indicating that, at 15 years of age, participants varied in their likelihood of engaging in smoking behaviors. The mean of the slope (`beta_2`) was positive and significant, indicating that the likelihood of engaging in smoking behaviors increased from 15 to 20 years, and the variance of the slope (`v_2`) was significant, indicating that participants varied in how their likelihood of engaging in smoking behavior changed across time. Lastly, we note that the intercept–slope covariance (`c_21`) was nonsignificant, indicating that an individual's likelihood of engaging in smoking behavior at age 15 was unrelated to how his or her likelihood changed across time.

We now turn to understanding and interpreting the location/threshold parameters in terms of the predicted probabilities of each response against age based on the linear growth model. Beginning with the logit link, we first calculate the distribution of $\hat{\theta}_{ti}$ at each measurement occasion. Based on the parameter estimates of the growth model, the distributions of the latent trait were $\hat{\theta}_{15i} \sim N(0, 3.53)$, $\hat{\theta}_{16i} \sim N(0.40, 3.56)$, $\hat{\theta}_{17i} \sim N(0.79, 3.69)$, $\hat{\theta}_{18i} \sim N(1.19, 3.93)$, $\hat{\theta}_{19i} \sim N(1.58, 4.25)$, and $\hat{\theta}_{20i} \sim N(1.98, 4.63)$. Combining this information with the location parameters, we calculated the percent of the distribution falling into each of the four categories at each age. This resulted in the

Output 13.3. NLMIXED Output for the Linear Growth Model with a Polytomous Outcome Using the Logit Link

Fit Statistics

-2 Log Likelihood	30308
AIC (smaller is better)	30322
AICC (smaller is better)	30322
BIC (smaller is better)	30370

Parameter Estimates

Parameter	Estimate	Standard Error	DF	t Value	Pr > |t|	Alpha	Lower	Upper	Gradient
omega	2.4046	0.09663	7190	24.88	<.0001	0.05	2.2151	2.5940	0.000024
delta_1	1.0045	0.03111	7190	32.29	<.0001	0.05	0.9435	1.0654	0.000687
delta_2	1.0909	0.03472	7190	31.41	<.0001	0.05	1.0228	1.1589	0.000281
beta_2	0.3961	0.02619	7190	15.12	<.0001	0.05	0.3448	0.4475	0.000726
v_1	9.1870	0.8163	7190	11.25	<.0001	0.05	7.5868	10.7872	-0.00005
c_21	-0.1087	0.1226	7190	-0.89	0.3749	0.05	-0.3490	0.1315	0.00011
v_2	0.4025	0.05044	7190	7.98	<.0001	0.05	0.3037	0.5014	-0.00026

Output 13.4. NLMIXED Output for the Linear Growth Model with a Polytomous Outcome Using the Probit Link

Fit Statistics

-2 Log Likelihood	30304
AIC (smaller is better)	30318
AICC (smaller is better)	30318
BIC (smaller is better)	30367

Parameter Estimates

Parameter	Estimate	Standard Error	DF	t Value	Pr > |t|	Alpha	Lower	Upper	Gradient
tau1	1.3553	0.05271	7190	25.71	<.0001	0.05	1.2519	1.4586	-0.00039
tau2	0.5665	0.01715	7190	33.03	<.0001	0.05	0.5329	0.6001	-0.00689
tau3	0.6129	0.01914	7190	32.03	<.0001	0.05	0.5754	0.6504	-0.00242
beta_2	0.2233	0.01450	7190	15.40	<.0001	0.05	0.1949	0.2518	0.005752
v_1	2.8614	0.2533	7190	11.30	<.0001	0.05	2.3648	3.3579	0.000175
c_21	-0.02151	0.03868	7190	-0.56	0.5782	0.05	-0.09732	0.05431	0.001533
v_2	0.1263	0.01600	7190	7.89	<.0001	0.05	0.09493	0.1577	0.006611

following: Age 15: 75% (never smoked), 8% (smoked in lifetime), 7% (smoked within past year), and 10% (smoked within past 30 days); Age 16: 71% (never smoked), 9% (smoked in lifetime), 7% (smoked within past year), and 12% (smoked within past 30 days); Age 17: 67% (never smoked), 9% (smoked in lifetime), 8% (smoked within past year), and 16% (smoked within past 30 days); Age 18: 62% (never smoked), 9% (smoked in lifetime), 9% (smoked within past year), and 20% (smoked within past 30 days); Age 19: 58% (never smoked), 9% (smoked in lifetime), 9% (smoked within past year), and 25% (smoked within past 30 days); and Age 20: 54% (never smoked), 8% (smoked in lifetime), 9% (smoked within past year), and 29% (smoked within past 30 days). As seen in these percentages, the major changes were in the first and last categories, whereas the percentages of the middle two categories showed little change over time. Thus, the percent of individuals who never smoked decreased over time, and the percentage of recent smokers increased over time.

Moving onto the probit link, the distributions of the latent response propensity were $\hat{y}^*_{15i} \sim N(0, 1.96)$, $\hat{y}^*_{16i} \sim N(0.22, 1.99)$, $\hat{y}^*_{17i} \sim N(0.45, 2.07)$, $\hat{y}^*_{18i} \sim N(0.67, 2.21)$, $\hat{y}^*_{19i} \sim N(0.89, 2.39)$, and $\hat{y}^*_{20i} \sim N(1.12, 2.61)$. Combining this information with the threshold parameters yields the following percentages in each category: Age 15: 75% (never smoked), 8% (smoked in lifetime), 7% (smoked within past year), and 10% (smoked within past 30 days); Age 16: 72% (never smoked), 9% (smoked in lifetime), 7% (smoked within past year), and 12% (smoked within past 30 days); Age 17: 67% (never smoked), 9% (smoked in lifetime), 8% (smoked within past year), and 16% (smoked within past 30 days); Age 18: 62% (never smoked), 9% (smoked in lifetime), 9% (smoked within past year), and 20% (smoked within past 30 days); Age 19: 58% (never smoked), 9% (smoked in lifetime), 9% (smoked within past year), and 24% (smoked within past 30 days); and Age 20: 54% (never smoked), 8% (smoked in lifetime), 9% (smoked within past year), and 29% (smoked within past 30 days). Thus, highly similar predictions for the changes in the percentages were obtained from the logit and probit links.

STRUCTURAL EQUATION MODELING IMPLEMENTATION

Mplus and OpenMx are able to fit growth models with dichotomous and multicategory variables. Mplus has been at the forefront of modeling dichotomous and ordinal variables in the structural equation modeling framework following the work of Muthén (1979, 1983, 1984). Mplus allows for both logit and probit links and offers several estimation techniques, including maximum likelihood and weighted least squares with several variants of each. The default estimator for categorical outcomes is weighted least squares mean and variance-adjusted (WLSMV). This approach has the advantage of reporting a scaled chi-square statistic and associated fit indices, such as the RMSEA, CFI, and TLI. However, this estimation technique has difficulty estimating the full polychoric correlation matrix with sparse data, which is needed for estimation. Alternatively, maximum likelihood estimation can be carried out but is often a more time-consuming estimation technique.

OpenMx utilizes a probit link, assuming that a latent continuous distribution underlies the ordinal variable with thresholds dividing the distribution into categories. In OpenMx, the mean and variance of the latent continuous distribution must be specified. Often the residual variance is fixed at 1, which follows the common specification of the probit link and is the scaling used by NLMIXED. An alternative approach is to fix the variance of the response propensity (as opposed to the residual variance) to 1 (e.g., Delta parameterization in Mplus). This choice of how to scale the response propensity does not have an effect on model fit (only affects parameter estimates and their interpretation), *unless* data are longitudinal. Thus, one has to consider whether the variance of the response propensity or the residual variance of the response propensity stays the same across time (see Grimm & Liu, 2016). Here, we fix the residual variance of the response propensity to 1. OpenMx utilizes maximum likelihood estimation for ordinal variables by generating expected covariance and mean matrices for the underlying continuous variables and then integrating the multivariate normal distribution defined by those covariances and means.

The smoking data (smoke) was set up in the wide form for the structural equation modeling programs, with separate variables for current smoking from 15 to 20 years (c_smk15 through c_smk20) and graded smoking (g_smk15 through g_smk20). In all analyses, the linear growth model is fit with the intercept centered at 15 years and the slope scaled in years.

Growth Model with a Dichotomous Outcome

Mplus

The Mplus script for a linear growth model fit to the current smoking variable using a logit link is contained in Script 13.5. The script begins with the typical elements of a title, data, and a list of variables in the datafile. In the VARIABLE command, the CATEGORI-CAL option is specified to indicate the ordinal variables that are included in the model. Thus, c_smk15-c_smk20, the current smoking dichotomous variables measured from age 15 to 20 years, are listed as being categorical. Next, in the ANALYSIS command, the estimation technique is set to maximum likelihood (ESTIMATOR=ML) and the link function is set to the logit link (LINK=LOGIT). The logit link is the default link when maximum likelihood estimation is utilized. Thus, the LINK=LOGIT statement is not needed; however, the probit link can be selected by stating LINK=PROBIT, and this is the only change needed to switch between the logit and probit links in Mplus. When using maximum likelihood estimation and a probit link, the *residuals* are assumed to follow a standard normal distribution.

The linear growth model is then specified in the MODEL command. First, the intercept, eta_1, and linear slope, eta_2, are defined using the keyword BY and are typically specified. The linear slope is scaled in years and the intercept is centered at 15 years to map onto the specification in the multilevel modeling programs. The variances of the intercept and slope are then requested and followed by the intercept–slope covariance using the keyword WITH. Next, the means of the intercept and slope are specified

Script 13.5. *Mplus* Script for the Linear Growth Model with a Dichotomous Outcome Using the Logit Link

```
TITLE: Linear Growth Model - Dichotomous Smoking Data;

DATA: FILE = nlsy_smoke_wide.dat;

VARIABLE:

  NAMES = id smk15-smk20 c_smk15-c_smk20 g_smk15-g_smk20;
  MISSING = .;
  USEVAR = c_smk15-c_smk20;
  CATEGORICAL = c_smk15-c_smk20;

ANALYSIS:

  TYPE=MEANSTRUCTURE;
  COVERAGE=0;
  ESTIMATOR=ML; LINK=LOGIT; !LINK=PROBIT; for a probit link function

MODEL:
  eta_1 BY c_smk15-c_smk20@1;
  eta_2 BY c_smk15@0 c_smk16@1 c_smk17@2 c_smk18@3 c_smk19@4 c_smk20@5;

  eta_1 eta_2;
  eta_1 WITH eta_2;

  [eta_1@0 eta_2*0];
  [c_smk15$1 c_smk16$1 c_smk17$1 c_smk18$1 c_smk19$1 c_smk20$1](omega);

OUTPUT: RESIDUAL STANDARDIZED;
```

using square brackets. The mean of the intercept is fixed at 0 (@0), and the mean of the slope is freely estimated and given a starting value of 0. The location (or threshold) parameters are then specified. The variables are listed in square brackets with $1 at the end. The $ sign indicates a location parameter, and the number designates the location parameter number. Thus, c_smk15$1 is the first location parameter for the c_smk15 variable. Since c_smk15 is a dichotomous variable, there is only one location parameter. Thus, this statement is to estimate the first location parameter for c_smk15 through c_smk20. Additionally, the label omega is included at the end of the statement, which constrains the location parameters for variables c_smk15 through c_smk20 to be equal over time. In the OUTPUT: statement, we've asked for the RESIDUAL output, which will print out the expected proportion of individuals with each response.

OpenMx

The OpenMx script to fit a linear growth model with a dichotomous outcome using the probit link is contained in Script 13.6. Before the growth model is specified, a preliminary step in OpenMx is needed. In this step, the ordinal variables are entered into mxFactor, and the levels of the factor are defined. The growth model is then specified using mxModel. The data and the manifest and latent variables included in the model are specified first. Next, the linear growth model is specified using multiple mxPath

Script 13.6. OpenMx Script for the Linear Growth Model with a Dichotomous Outcome Using the Probit Link

```
# Converting Items of Interest to Categorical Variables
smoke$c_smk15 <- mxFactor(smoke$c_smk15, levels=c(0,1))
smoke$c_smk16 <- mxFactor(smoke$c_smk16, levels=c(0,1))
smoke$c_smk17 <- mxFactor(smoke$c_smk17, levels=c(0,1))
smoke$c_smk18 <- mxFactor(smoke$c_smk18, levels=c(0,1))
smoke$c_smk19 <- mxFactor(smoke$c_smk19, levels=c(0,1))
smoke$c_smk20 <- mxFactor(smoke$c_smk20, levels=c(0,1))

################# Linear Growth Model ##################
lgm.smk.omx <- mxModel('Dichotomous Linear Growth Model, Path Specification',
    type='RAM', mxData(observed=smoke, type='raw'),
    manifestVars=c('c_smk15','c_smk16','c_smk17','c_smk18','c_smk19','c_smk20'),
    latentVars=c('eta_1','eta_2'),

# Residual variances
mxPath(from=c('c_smk15','c_smk16','c_smk17','c_smk18','c_smk19','c_smk20'),
    arrows=2, free=FALSE, values=1),

# Latent variable covariances
mxPath(from=c('eta_1','eta_2'), connect='unique.pairs',
    arrows=2, free=TRUE, values=c(1,0,1), labels=c('psi_11','psi_21','psi_22')),

# Factor loadings
mxPath(from='eta_1', to=c('c_smk15','c_smk16','c_smk17','c_smk18','c_smk19','c_smk20'),
    arrows=1, free=FALSE, values=1),
mxPath(from='eta_2', to=c('c_smk15','c_smk16','c_smk17','c_smk18','c_smk19','c_smk20'),
    arrows=1, free=FALSE, values=c(0,1,2,3,4,5)),

# Latent variable means
mxPath(from='one', to='eta_2',
    arrows=1, free=TRUE, values=.2, labels='alpha_2'),

# Thresholds
mxThreshold(vars=c('c_smk15','c_smk16','c_smk17','c_smk18','c_smk19','c_smk20'),
    nThresh=1, free=TRUE, values=2, labels='tau')
) # Close Model
```

332

statements. First, the residual variances of the dichotomous variables are set to 1 to define the scale of the underlying response propensities. The latent variable variances and covariances are then specified as two-headed arrows from eta_1 and eta_2 using connect='unique.pairs'. Starting values and labels are provided. Factor loadings for the intercept, eta_1, and slope, eta_2, come next. Factor loadings for the intercept are fixed values originating from eta_1 and going to the six dichotomous variables with values equal to 1. Factor loadings for the linear slope are fixed values orginating from eta_2 and going to the six dichotomous variables with values that change linearly with age and begin at 0 to scale the slope in terms of age and center the intercept at the first occasion, 15 years. The mean of the linear slope is then specified as one-headed arrows from one to eta_2 with a starting value of .2 and labeled alpha_2. The mean of the intercept is not specified and is therefore set to 0.

The thresholds for the dichotomous variables are then specified using mxThreshold. In this statement, the ordinal variables are listed in vars=, and the number of thresholds per variable is stated in nThresh. As in mxPath statements, we then indicate whether the thresholds are free to be estimated, provide starting values, and then labels. Here, our six current smoking variables each have one threshold because they are all dichotomous. The thresholds are freely estimated, given a starting value of 2, and labeled tau. The common label constrains them to be equal over time. The model is then closed and run using mxRun.

Output

Mplus output from the linear growth model with a dichotomous outcome using the logit link is contained in Output 13.5. When maximum likelihood estimation is used in Mplus with categorical outcomes, the log likelihood and its associated information criteria are the only fit information reported (the same information provided by the multilevel modeling programs). The log likelihood value was –6821.29 and multiplying this value by –2 yields 13642.59, which is approximately the value of the –2LL obtained by SAS when the logit link was utilized. Parameter estimates indicate that participants significantly varied in their likelihood of smoking at 15 years because the variance of the intercept (Variance of ETA_1) was significant. The mean of the slope (Mean of ETA_2) was 0.41 and significantly different from 0, suggesting that the likelihood of being a current smoker increased from 15 to 20 years, on average. The variance of the slope (Variance of ETA_2) was 0.34 and significantly different from 0, indicating that the rate of change in the likelihood of being a current smoker varied over individuals. Lastly, the likelihood of smoking at 15 years was unrelated to how this likelihood changed over time as the intercept–slope covariance (ETA_1 WITH ETA_2) was 0.19 and not significant. The location parameter for the logit link is listed under Thresholds and was estimated to be 4.54. As discussed above, this value along with approximate distributions of the underlying latent trait (i.e., $\hat{\theta}_{ti}$), based on the estimates from the growth model, can be used to determine predicted proportions of individuals who responded in each category. As we noted, this information is also available in the RESIDUAL output.

Output 13.5. Mplus Output for the Linear Growth Model with a Dichotomous Outcome Using the Logit Link

```
MODEL FIT INFORMATION

Number of Free Parameters                          5
Loglikelihood
          H0 Value                           -6821.294
Information Criteria
          Akaike (AIC)                       13652.588
          Bayesian (BIC)                     13686.992
          Sample-Size Adjusted BIC           13671.103
             (n* = (n + 2) / 24)
```

```
MODEL RESULTS
                                              Two-Tailed
                Estimate    S.E.   Est./S.E.   P-Value

ETA_1    BY
    C_SMK15      1.000     0.000    999.000    999.000
    C_SMK16      1.000     0.000    999.000    999.000
    C_SMK17      1.000     0.000    999.000    999.000
    C_SMK18      1.000     0.000    999.000    999.000
    C_SMK19      1.000     0.000    999.000    999.000
    C_SMK20      1.000     0.000    999.000    999.000

ETA_2    BY
    C_SMK15      0.000     0.000    999.000    999.000
    C_SMK16      1.000     0.000    999.000    999.000
    C_SMK17      2.000     0.000    999.000    999.000
    C_SMK18      3.000     0.000    999.000    999.000
    C_SMK19      4.000     0.000    999.000    999.000
    C_SMK20      5.000     0.000    999.000    999.000

ETA_1    WITH
    ETA_2        0.192     0.177      1.084      0.279

Means
    ETA_1        0.000     0.000    999.000    999.000
    ETA_2        0.408     0.054      7.504      0.000
Thresholds
    C_SMK15$1    4.540     0.217     20.891      0.000
    C_SMK16$1    4.540     0.217     20.891      0.000
    C_SMK17$1    4.540     0.217     20.891      0.000
    C_SMK18$1    4.540     0.217     20.891      0.000
    C_SMK19$1    4.540     0.217     20.891      0.000
    C_SMK20$1    4.540     0.217     20.891      0.000

Variances
    ETA_1        8.359     1.234      6.775      0.000
    ETA_2        0.344     0.082      4.214      0.000
```

Output 13.6. OpenMx **Output for the Linear Growth Model with a Dichotomous Outcome Using the Probit Link**

```
free parameters:
      name   matrix      row         col      Estimate      Std.Error
1  psi_11        S     eta_1       eta_1     2.5648821     0.38500230
2  psi_21        S     eta_1       eta_2     0.0656392     0.05538110
3  psi_22        S     eta_2       eta_2     0.1140258     0.02550067
4 alpha_2        M         1       eta_2     0.2218951     0.03065311
5     tau   thresh         1     c_smk15     2.5279868     0.12039924

observed statistics: 17112
estimated parameters: 5
degrees of freedom: 17107
-2 log likelihood: 13643.59
number of observations: 7192

Information Criteria:
        df Penalty  Parameters  Penalty  Sample-Size  Adjusted
AIC       -20570.41             13653.59                     NA
BIC      -138278.96             13688.00               13672.11
```

Output from OpenMx is contained in Output 13.6. Beginning with the fit information, the reported $-2LL$ was 13643.59 and very close to the value obtained from NLMIXED when the probit link was used (and very close to the $-2LL$ reported by Mplus when the probit link was used). Growth estimates were similar to those obtained by SAS and reported in Output 13.2. Overall, individuals' propensity to smoke increased from age 15 to 20 years as the mean of the linear slope (alpha_2) was 0.22 and significantly different from 0. Individuals varied in their propensity to smoke at age 15 (psi_11 was 2.56) and in how quickly their propensity to smoke changed with time (psi_22 was 0.11). Lastly, the intercept–slope covariance (psi_21) was nonsignificant, indicating that an individual's propensity to smoke at age 15 was unrelated to how quickly their propensity to smoke changed with age. The threshold parameter was 2.53 and can be used in conjunction with the growth estimates to determine the predicted proportion of individuals who responded in each category at each age.

Growth Model with a Polytomous Outcome

Mplus

Script 13.7 contains the Mplus input script for fitting the linear growth model using the logit link to the graded smoking behavior variable, which has four response categories. The graded smoking behavior variables, g_smk15-g_smk20, are listed on the CATEGORICAL line of the VARIABLE command to indicate that these variables are ordinal. Maximum likelihood estimation (ESTIMATOR=ML) and the logit link (LINK=LOGIT) are requested in the ANALYSIS command. A linear growth model is then specified in the MODEL command. The intercept, eta_1, is defined with factor loadings to the six ordinal

Script 13.7. `Mplus` Script for the Linear Growth Model with a Polytomous Outcome Using the Logit Link

```
TITLE: Linear Growth Model - Dichotomous Smoking Data;

DATA: FILE = nlsy_smoke_wide.dat;

VARIABLE:
  NAMES = id smk15-smk20 c_smk15-c_smk20 g_smk15-g_smk20;
  MISSING = .;
  USEVAR = g_smk15-g_smk20;
  CATEGORICAL = g_smk15-g_smk20;

ANALYSIS:
  TYPE=MEANSTRUCTURE;
  COVERAGE=0;
  ESTIMATOR=ML; LINK=LOGIT; !LINK=PROBIT; for probit link function

MODEL:
    eta_1 BY g_smk15-g_smk20@1;
    eta_2 BY g_smk15@0 g_smk16@1 g_smk17@2 g_smk18@3 g_smk19@4 g_smk20@5;

    eta_1 eta_2;
    eta_1 WITH eta_2;

    [eta_1@0 eta_2*0];
    [g_smk15$1-g_smk20$1] (omega1);
    [g_smk15$2-g_smk20$2] (omega2);
    [g_smk15$3-g_smk20$3] (omega3);

OUTPUT: RESIDUAL STANDARDIZED;
```

variables with weights equal to 1, and the slope, `eta_2`, is defined with factor loadings that change linearly with respect to age (slope is scaled in years and the intercept is centered at age 15). Latent variable variances (`eta_1 eta_2;`) and the intercept–slope covariance (`eta_1 WITH eta_2`) are then specified and followed by the latent variable means (`[eta_1@0 eta_2*0];`). The mean of the intercept is fixed at 0 for identification, and the mean of the slope is estimated and given a starting value of 0. Lastly, the location parameters are then specified. The first location parameter for the six ordinal variables is specified using the variable name followed by $1 (`[g_smk15$1-g_smk20$1]`). The label `omega1` is contained at the end of the statement in parentheses to force an equality constraint on the first location parameter for each variable. The remaining location parameters are specified similarly with $2 and $3 at the end of the variable name to refer to the second and third location parameters, respectively. The second location parameters are given the label `omega2`, and the third location parameters are given the label `omega3`, which forces them to be equal across time.

OpenMx

The `OpenMx` script for a linear growth model with a polytomous outcome and a probit link is contained in Script 13.8. Multiple `mxFactor` statements are used prior to model

Script 13.8. OpenMx Script for the Linear Growth Model with a Polytomous Outcome Using the Probit Link

```
#Converting Variables of Interest to Categorical Variables
smoke$g_smk15 <- mxFactor (smoke$g_smk15, levels=c(0,1,2,3))
smoke$g_smk16 <- mxFactor (smoke$g_smk16, levels=c(0,1,2,3))
smoke$g_smk17 <- mxFactor (smoke$g_smk17, levels=c(0,1,2,3))
smoke$g_smk18 <- mxFactor (smoke$g_smk18, levels=c(0,1,2,3))
smoke$g_smk19 <- mxFactor (smoke$g_smk19, levels=c(0,1,2,3))
smoke$g_smk20 <- mxFactor (smoke$g_smk20, levels=c(0,1,2,3))

############### Linear Growth Model ###############
lgm.g_smk.omx <- mxModel('Polytomous Linear Growth Model, Path Specification',
type='RAM', mxData(observed=smoke, type='raw'),
manifestVars=c('g_smk15','g_smk16','g_smk17','g_smk18','g_smk19','g_smk20'),
latentVars=c('eta_1','eta_2'),

# Residual Variances
mxPath(from=c('g_smk15','g_smk16','g_smk17','g_smk18','g_smk19','g_smk20'),
arrows=2, free=FALSE, values=1),

# Latent Variable Covariances
mxPath(from=c('eta_1','eta_2'), connect='unique.pairs',
arrows=2, free=TRUE, values=c(1,0,1), labels=c('psi_11','psi_21','psi_22')),

# Factor Loadings
mxPath(from='eta_1', to=c('g_smk15','g_smk16','g_smk17','g_smk18','g_smk19','g_smk20'),
arrows=1, free=FALSE, values=1),

mxPath(from='eta_2', to=c('g_smk15','g_smk16','g_smk17','g_smk18','g_smk19','g_smk20'),
arrows=1, free=FALSE, values=c(0,1,2,3,4,5)),

# Latent Variable Mean
mxPath(from='one', to='eta_2',
arrows=1, free=TRUE, values=.2, labels='alpha_2'),

# Thresholds
mxThreshold(vars=c('g_smk15','g_smk16','g_smk17','g_smk18','g_smk19','g_smk20'),
nThresh=3, free=TRUE, values=c(1,2,3), labels=c('tau1','tau2','tau3'))
) # Close Model
```

specification to allow OpenMx to recognize the variables as being ordinal and invoke the probit link. mxModel is then used to specify the model. First, the data, selected manifest variables, and latent variables included in the model are stated. The aspects of the linear growth model are then specified using a series of mxPath statements. The residual variances of the latent response propensities are fixed at 1. Next, the variances of the intercept and slope and their covariance are specified as two-headed arrows originating from eta_1 and eta_2 using connect='unique.pairs' for the intercept variance, intercept–slope covariance, and slope variance. These parameters are given starting values and labeled accordingly.

Factor loadings for the intercept and slope are then specified. Factor loadings for the intercept are one-headed arrows originating from eta_1 and going to the six polytomously scored smoking variables with weights equal to 1. Factor loadings for the slope are one-headed arrows originating from eta_2 and going to the six outcome variables with weights that change linearly with age and begin at 0. Thus, the slope is scaled in years and the intercept is centered at 15 years. The mean of the slope is then specified as a one-headed arrow from one to eta_2. The mean is given a starting value of .2 and labeled alpha_2. The thresholds for the six polytomous outcomes are then specified using mxThreshold. There are three thresholds for each of the graded smoking variables that are freely estimated, given starting values of 1, 2, and 3 and then labeled tau1, tau2, and tau3. The common labels force the three thresholds to be invariant over time. The model is then closed and run using mxRun.

Output

Mplus output from the linear growth model fit to the graded smoking variable using the logit link is contained in Output 13.7. As discussed above, Mplus reports the log likelihood and likelihood-based information criteria for model fit. The fit of the model was identical to that reported by NLMIXED. The estimates of growth describe overall increases in the latent trait over time as the mean of the slope (Mean of ETA_2) was 0.39 and significantly different from zero. There was significant variability in both the intercept (Variance of ETA_1; 9.12) and linear slope (Variance of ETA_2; 0.40) indicating that individuals varied in their likelihood of engaging in smoking behaviors at age 15 and how their likelihood of engaging in such behaviors changed over time. The intercept–slope covariance (ETA_1 WITH ETA_2) was negative but not significantly different from zero. Thus, participants' likelihood of engaging in smoking behaviors at age 15 was unrelated to how their likelihood changed from age 15 to 20.

Estimates for the location parameters of the logit link are contained under the header THRESHOLDS. The first location parameter was 2.40, the second was 3.40, and the third was 4.49. These values map on to the estimates obtained through NLMIXED, where the first location parameter was 2.40, the second was 3.40 (2.40 + 1.00), and the third was 4.49 (2.40 + 1.00 + 1.09). From these estimates and the estimates of the growth parameters, the predicted proportion of individuals responding in each category at each age can be calculated as was shown above.

Output 13.7. Mplus Output for the Linear Growth Model with a Polytomous Outcome Using the Logit Link

```
MODEL FIT INFORMATION

Number of Free Parameters                        7
Loglikelihood
        H0 Value                          -15154.210
Information Criteria
        Akaike (AIC)                       30322.419
        Bayesian (BIC)                     30370.584
        Sample-Size Adjusted BIC           30348.340
          (n* = (n + 2) / 24)

MODEL RESULTS
                                                Two-Tailed
                Estimate     S.E.    Est./S.E.    P-Value

ETA_1     BY
  G_SMK15       1.000      0.000    999.000      999.000
  . . .
  G_SMK20       1.000      0.000    999.000      999.000
ETA_2     BY
  G_SMK15       0.000      0.000    999.000      999.000
  . . .
  G_SMK20       5.000      0.000    999.000      999.000
ETA_1    WITH
  ETA_2        -0.099      0.121     -0.820        0.412
Means
  ETA_1         0.000      0.000    999.000      999.000
  ETA_2         0.394      0.026     15.138        0.000
Thresholds
  G_SMK15$1     2.396      0.096     25.031        0.000
  G_SMK15$2     3.400      0.110     30.935        0.000
  G_SMK15$3     4.491      0.127     35.439        0.000
  G_SMK16$1     2.396      0.096     25.031        0.000
  G_SMK16$2     3.400      0.110     30.935        0.000
  G_SMK16$3     4.491      0.127     35.439        0.000
  G_SMK17$1     2.396      0.096     25.031        0.000
  G_SMK17$2     3.400      0.110     30.935        0.000
  G_SMK17$3     4.491      0.127     35.439        0.000
  G_SMK18$1     2.396      0.096     25.031        0.000
  G_SMK18$2     3.400      0.110     30.935        0.000
  G_SMK18$3     4.491      0.127     35.439        0.000
  G_SMK19$1     2.396      0.096     25.031        0.000
  G_SMK19$2     3.400      0.110     30.935        0.000
  G_SMK19$3     4.491      0.127     35.439        0.000
  G_SMK20$1     2.369      0.096     25.031        0.000
  G_SMK20$2     3.400      0.110     30.935        0.000
  G_SMK20$3     4.491      0.127     35.439        0.000
Variances
  ETA_1         9.119      0.808     11.286        0.000
  ETA_2         0.403      0.051      7.893        0.000
```

Output 13.8. `OpenMx` Output for the Linear Growth Model with a Polytomous Outcome Using the Probit Link

```
free parameters:
     name         matrix      row        col     Estimate      Std.Error
1  psi_11              S     eta_1      eta_1    2.85859353     0.25061142
2  psi_21              S     eta_1      eta_2   -0.02188046     0.03732851
3  psi_22              S     eta_2      eta_2    0.12619314     0.01606315
4  alpha_2             M         1      eta_2    0.22325594     0.01391316
5     tau1     Thresholds      1     g_smk15    1.35424698     0.05155838
6     tau2     Thresholds      2     g_smk15    1.92062841     0.05899488
7     tau3     Thresholds      3     g_smk15    2.53337005     0.06792426

observed statistics: 17112
estimated parameters: 7
degrees of freedom: 17105
-2 log likelihood: 30304.58
number of observations: 7192
Information Criteria:
          |  df Penalty   |  Parameters Penalty   |  Sample-Size Adjusted
AIC:         -3905.417             30318.58                            NA
BIC:       -121600.211             30366.75                       30344.5
```

OpenMx output from the linear growth model with a polytomous outcome using the probit link is contained in Output 13.8. The fit of the model ($-2LL$ = 30,304.58) was very close to the fit of the model obtained through `NLMIXED`, highlighting the equivalence of the modeling frameworks for multicategory outcomes. As discussed earlier, the growth estimates describe overall increases in the latent response propensity with increasing age, as the mean of the linear slope (`alpha_2`) was 0.22 and significantly different from zero. Significant variability in the intercept (`psi_11`; 2.84) and linear slope (`psi_22`; 0.13) was observed, suggesting that individuals varied in the latent response propensity at age 15 and their changes in the response propensity from 15 to 20 years of age. Lastly, the latent response propensity at age 15 was unrelated to changes in the latent response propensity as the intercept–slope covariance (`psi_21`; –0.02) was nonsignificant. The three threshold parameters were estimated to be 1.35, 1.92, and 2.53, and these values map on to estimates obtained through `NLMIXED`, where the threshold parameters were estimated to be 1.36, 1.93 (1.36 + 0.57), and 2.54 (1.36 + 0.57 + 0.61). The threshold parameters in conjunction with the growth estimates can produce estimates of the predicted proportion of individuals responding in each category at each age.

IMPORTANT CONSIDERATIONS

In this chapter we discussed the fitting of linear growth models when the outcome variable is dichotomous or polytomous. Modeling change in these variables requires specialized programs able to appropriately handle such outcomes. Fortunately, `Mplus`, `OpenMx`, and NLMIXED are able to handle these distributions. When dealing with ordinal data, the following question often arises: When is it okay to treat an ordinal variable as having a continuous (normal) distribution? Specifically, how many response categories (e.g., 5, 7, 10) does a variable need to have for the variable to be continuous? The answer to this question depends on the distribution of responses as opposed to the number of response categories. With limited dependent variables, such as those with few response categories, there is a dependency between its mean and variance. In the most extreme case of dichotomous variables (coded 0/1), the variance is perfectly related to the mean by $\sigma^2 = \mu \cdot (1 - \mu)$, where σ^2 is the variance and μ is the mean. When there are more response categories, this dependency weakens; however, a strong dependency can remain depending on the distribution of responses. For example, if there are four response categories (0–3) and the mean is 0.10, then the variance must also be small. If the mean of the variable is 1.50, the variance can be small or large. Thus, there is less dependency between the mean and variance of an ordinal variable when the mean is near the center of the distribution. Therefore, it is important to examine the distributions of ordinal variables before making recommendations regarding whether the variable can be treated as continuous. In all cases, treating the variables as ordinal leads to fewer assumptions (e.g., interval scale).

Linear growth models were fit throughout this chapter; however, various types of nonlinear models can be fit. In NLMIXED, a nonlinear model of age (quadratic, exponential, etc.) can be written instead of the linear change trajectories specified in this chapter. In Mplus and OpenMx, a more complex factor loading matrix can be specified to allow for nonlinear trajectories of the latent trait or latent response propensity. Note that the linear growth models fit here result in logistic or probit (elongated s-shapes; Figure 13.2) changes in the probabilities, and nonlinear models of the underlying trait (latent response propensity) would lead to more complex change patterns for the probabilities.

Comparing the multilevel modeling and structural equation modeling approaches to modeling ordinal data, we find that the structural equation modeling programs tended to converge more quickly. Models fit using Mplus tended to converge within a few seconds, and models fit using OpenMx tended to converge within 40 seconds. NLMIXED generally took longer to converge, but this was greatly affected by the starting values provided in the PARMS statements. Models with poor starting values could take 20 to 40 minutes, whereas models with good starting values tended to take between 1 and 3 minutes. In the structural equation modeling framework, it is important to check whether each response category is observed at each measurement occasion because the data are in the wide format. For example, imagine a situation where all three of a three-response category variable were observed for the first two occasions and only the second and third response categories were observed at the third occasion. In this situation, the invariance of thresholds should be as follows: the first threshold for the third measurement occasion should be set equal to the second threshold for the first two measurement occasions because these thresholds distinguish between the second and third categories of the three response category variable.

Lastly, we note that other types of non-normality can be handled by the programs discussed. NLMIXED and Mplus can model outcomes that represent counts of events (e.g., number of times marijuana was smoked) using the Poisson or negative binomial distributions. `Mplus` also has built-in features to model count data that have a high density of 0 responses using the zero-inflated Poisson or zero-inflated negative binomial distributions. `NLMIXED` does not have these distributions built in; however, these types of models can be programmed using the general likelihood function. Lastly, `Mplus` can also model distributions with artificial ceiling or floor effects (see Wang, Zhang, McArdle, & Salthouse, 2008).

MOVING FORWARD

In this chapter, the latent entity modeled across time was a latent trait (logit) or underlying response propensity (probit) indicated by a single variable. In the next two chapters, we model changes of latent entities that are multivariately measured by either continuous or categorical indicators. In these chapters we discuss the importance of studying factorial invariance prior to modeling changes. Tests of factorial invariance are used to examine whether the latent entity is measuring the same construct in the same metric at each measurement occasion—something that is often taken for granted when modeling change in manifest variables.

## 14

Modeling Change with Latent Variables Measured by Continuous Indicators

In this chapter we discuss the common factor model as it is utilized in longitudinal data analysis and describe how changes in the common factors can be examined with growth models. This discussion focuses on common factors that are measured by continuously scored observed variables. We have reserved the discussion of common factors measured by ordinal variables for the next chapter. Modeling change in common factors is a logical extension of our previous discussions in the structural equation modeling framework where the data are arranged in a multivariate (wide) form, but not in the multilevel modeling framework where a single outcome variable is modeled (data are in the long form with a single outcome variable). There is nothing about the multilevel modeling framework that prohibits this type of model from being formulated and estimated, but limits in multilevel modeling software. NLMIXED and nlme require the outcomes to be organized into a single variable, and so these programs won't be discussed in this chapter (however, see Codd & Cudeck, 2014). WinBUGS, on the other hand, can fit these models and is programmed and written as a flexible multilevel modeling program. Thus, we present the mathematical specification based on both the multilevel and structural equation modeling frameworks, but only present programming scripts for the structural equation modeling programs.

A key concept when studying change in latent variables is establishing a common metric for the latent variables across time. (Unlike the observed variables analyzed in previous chapters, latent variables do not have an inherent scale, and longitudinally, it is necessary for that scale to be the same across time.) This is typically done by testing for factorial invariance (Meredith, 1964a, 1964b; Meredith & Horn, 2001; Widaman & Reise, 1997). Factorial invariance, or measurement equivalence, is the idea that the latent variable is measuring the same construct over time and measuring that construct in the same metric over time, such that a one-unit difference in the factor score at one time point means the same thing at all time points. If a single manifest variable is utilized, as was done throughout the book, measurement equivalence is assumed because we treat observed changes in the variable as changes in the construct giving rise to the scores. Only with a measurement model can we examine factorial invariance, and we begin our discussion here.

COMMON FACTOR MODEL

The common factor model (Spearman, 1904) relates a series of observed variables to a series of unmeasured factors thought to underlie the scores on the observed variables. The common factor model can be written as

$$y_{pi} = \tau_p + \lambda_{p1}\eta_{1i} + \lambda_{p2}\eta_{2i} + \ldots + \lambda_{pQ}\eta_{Qi} + u_{pi} \tag{14.1}$$

where y_{pi} is the pth variable measured for individual i, τ_p is the intercept for variable p, λ_{p1} is the factor loading for variable p on the first common factor, η_{1i} is the factor score for individual i on the first latent variable (factor), and so on for Q common factors, and u_{pi} is the unique factor score for p^{th} variable for individual i. This presentation of the common factor model mirrors the specification of a multilevel model where the observed data are thought of as distinct variables. In the structural equation modeling framework, factor models are more often thought about in terms of vectors and matrices. The same common factor model can be written as

$$\mathbf{y}_i = \tau + \mathbf{\Lambda}\eta_i + \mathbf{u}_i \tag{14.2}$$

where $\mathbf{y}_i$ is a $P \times 1$ vector of observed scores for individual i, τ is a $P \times 1$ vector of observed variable intercepts, $\mathbf{\Lambda}$ is a $P \times Q$ matrix of factor loadings, where Q is the number of common factors, η_i is a $Q \times 1$ vector of common factors for individual i, and $\mathbf{u}_i$ is a $P \times 1$ vector of unique factors. The models presented equivalently in Equations 14.1 and 14.2 lead to the same expected mean and covariance structures for the data, which are

$$\mu = \tau + \mathbf{\Lambda}\alpha \tag{14.3}$$

$$\Sigma = \mathbf{\Lambda}\mathbf{\Psi}\mathbf{\Lambda}' + \mathbf{\Theta} \tag{14.4}$$

where μ is a $P \times 1$ vector of expected means, Σ is a $P \times P$ matrix of expected variances and covariances, α is a $Q \times 1$ vector of factor means, $\mathbf{\Psi}$ is a $Q \times Q$ covariance matrix for the common factors η_i, and $\mathbf{\Theta}$ is a $P \times P$ covariance matrix for the unique factors.

Regardless of how the model is written, the parameters of a factor model have the same meaning. Factor loadings ($\mathbf{\Lambda}$ or λ) denote regressions of observed measurements on common factors, indicating the strength of the association between observed and latent variables. Like any other regression, a factor loading can be interpreted as the expected change in an observed variable per unit change in the factor. Intercepts (τ) are the means

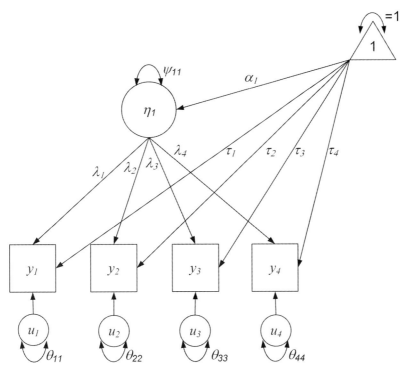

FIGURE 14.1. Path diagram of a common factor model.

of observed variables conditional on the common factors, just as intercepts in a regression reflect the mean of the dependent variable conditional on the independent variables. Finally, unique factors represent the part of the observed variables that is not accounted for by the factors, taking on the same function as residual terms in regression. Figure 14.1 is a path diagram of a common factor model with four observed variables (y_1 through y_4), one common factor (η_1) and four unique factors (u_1 through u_4). Factor loadings (λ_1 through λ_4) originate at the common factor and go to each of the observed variables. The common factor has a mean (α_1) and variance (ψ_{11}), the unique factors have variances (θ_{11} through θ_{44}), and the observed variables have intercepts (τ_1 through τ_4).

Identification

Latent variables (common factors) do not have an inherent scale, which creates both flexibility and causes problems for researchers. The same factor model will fit equally well if the latent variable has a variance of one or 100, provided all other model parameters are free to change along with the latent variable variance, meaning that there are an infinite number of solutions to any factor analytic model (i.e., the value of λ_1 in Figure 14.1 will vary depending on ψ_{11}). Researchers must place constraints on model parameters in such a way that only one of those solutions is possible—a process known as *model identification*. The most common method of identification is to constrain the factor means and variances directly, most often to zero and one, respectively. This method is straightforward, as it requires no manipulation of factor loadings, observed variable intercepts, or residual variances, and a one-unit change in the latent variable is a one standard deviation change, which aids interpretation. Alternative sets of identification criteria involve constraints on a reference indicator, typically constraining the intercept and factor loading for one observed variable to values of zero and one, respectively, and allowing the factor mean and variance to be freely estimated.

It is important to note that identification criteria may either be implicit in or interact with other constraints (e.g., equality constraints) placed on the model. Factorial invariance constraints (discussed in the next section of this chapter) typically constrain the scale of a latent variable to be the same for all time points, so only one time point will require identification constraints. Measuring change in latent variables is not as simple as using the same identification criteria at each time point—constraining the factor mean and variance to be equal at every measurement occasion is not an appropriate way to create an invariant scale. Creating an invariant common factor requires the structure of the common factor model to remain the same at each time point, which involves constraining some model parameters to be equal across time points. Specific tests and constraints are detailed next.

FACTORIAL INVARIANCE OVER TIME

To begin our discussion of factorial invariance over time, we must discuss the longitudinal common factor model. Extending the common factor model of Equation 14.2 to repeatedly measured variables, we can write

$$\mathbf{y}_{ti} = \boldsymbol{\tau}_t + \boldsymbol{\Lambda}_t \boldsymbol{\eta}_{ti} + \mathbf{u}_{ti} \tag{14.5}$$

where $\mathbf{y}_{ti}$ is a $P \times 1$ vector of observed variables at time t for individual i, $\boldsymbol{\tau}_t$ is a $P \times 1$ vector of intercepts at time t, $\boldsymbol{\Lambda}_t$ is a $P \times Q$ matrix of factor loadings at time t, $\boldsymbol{\eta}_{ti}$ is a $Q \times 1$ vector of common factor scores at time t for individual i, and $\mathbf{u}_{ti}$ is a $P \times 1$ vector of unique factor scores at time t for individual i.

Longitudinal factorial invariance refers to the equivalence of some parameters of the factor model across time. Having an invariant factor structure is an important aspect of using factor analysis as a scientific tool. Factors have no inherent scale or meaning; their interpretation is derived from their relationships with the set of observed variables. If a factor is to be treated as *the same* across different measurement occasions, that factor's association with other variables must remain constant over some set of variables. Because all of the parameters involved in factor analysis have their own inherent meaning, which parameters are held constant across time affects how we interpret change in common factors.

Methods for testing factorial invariance have a rich history in psychology. Early work on factorial invariance related exclusively to exploratory factor analysis and relied on the comparison and rotation of factor models fit separately to multiple groups. Cattell's (1944) parallel proportional profiles approach and Ahmavaara's (1954) work on the effects of group-based selection on simple structure are examples of early work on this topic. More modern treatments of factorial invariance come from Meredith (1964a, 1964b), who showed that the invariance of factor loadings across subgroups could be achieved when neither factors nor their loadings were standardized. Meredith's work persisted through the use of confirmatory factor analysis, where invariance is commonly tested by comparing multiple models with different parameter constraints. Subsequent work by Meredith (1993) established several nested *levels* of factorial invariance, where each level includes additional constraints on the model meant to attribute additional meaning to the factors. In the least constrained models, differences across time can be due either to changes in the factors or differences in the structure or characteristics of the observed variables. In the most constrained models, all of the changes in observed variable distributions over time can be attributed to the common factors, allowing researchers to study change at the factor level. Testing for factorial invariance is a multistep procedure that often involves fitting four models with an increasing number of constraints across time. The four models are the (1) *configural* invariance model, (2) *weak* invariance model, (3) *strong* invariance model, and (4) *strict* invariance model. Each of these models and their interpretations are discussed in turn.

The *configural* invariance model (Thurstone, 1947; Horn, McArdle, & Mason, 1983) constrains the number of factors and pattern of zero and nonzero loadings to be identical across measurement occasions. Factor variances, factor means, observed variable intercepts, and unique factor variances are free to vary across occasions, as are the magnitude and sign of any factor loadings not explicitly constrained to zero. While the factors extracted at each occasion may be interpreted similarly, these factors cannot be assumed to measure identical constructs at each occasion, nor can they be assumed to lie on the same scale. Longitudinal differences in observed means, variances, and covariances aren't necessarily due to changes in the factors and instead could be due to changes in the observed variables independent of the factors.

Configural invariance models are most commonly used as the initial model fit to serve as a comparison for the more constrained models. Longitudinal configural invariance models assume that the same number of factors are present at each measurement occasion, but this assumption may not be true. Factors may merge or split into different arrangements (e.g., the differentiation–dedifferentiation hypothesis in cognitive aging) or show a significant drop in variance such that certain factors aren't detectable at certain measurement occasions. While configural invariance is typically a starting point for subsequent invariance testing, researchers should pay close attention to both model fit and parameter values from this model to check that these assumptions (e.g., number of factors, same location of zero factor loadings) are met.

Weak (metric) factorial invariance is the least constrained of the three metric invariance models described by Meredith (1993). This model requires the full factor loading matrix (Λ) to be equal across all occasions but places no other restrictions on the model. As the factor loading matrix defines the covariances between the observed variables, weak factorial invariance creates proportional covariance structures across time. The magnitude of the covariances may increase or decrease with the variance of the common factors, but this increase or decrease affects all observed variable covariances equally. Observed variable intercepts remain free to vary across occasions, so the longitudinal changes in the observed variable means are not explained by the common factor(s). While the common factor(s) are sufficiently invariant to test regressions or covariances between the factors and additional variables, tests of longitudinal change in the factors demand a stronger form of invariance.

Strong invariance provides a higher level of measurement invariance by additionally constraining observed variable intercepts (τ) to be equal across measurement occasions and, at the same time, allows elements of the latent variable mean vector (α; minus any identification constraints) to vary over occasions. In doing so, strong factorial invariance restricts all longitudinal changes in the observed variable means and covariances to depend on the means, variances, and covariances among the common factors. Thus, changes in the observed variables are caused by changes in the common factors, which allows for the analysis of change in the common factor (i.e., second-order growth models described subsequently). As all mean-level change in the observed variables is attributable to the factors, strong invariance is sufficient to assume that the scale of the latent variable does not differ across measurement occasions.

Lastly, the *strict* factorial invariance places the strongest constraints on the longitudinal factor model. In addition to the constraints on factor loadings (Λ) and observed variable intercepts (τ), strict invariance models constrain unique variances (diagonal elements of Θ) to be equal across measurement occasions. In the strict factorial invariance model, all longitudinal changes in the observed means, variances, and covariances are attributed to the changes in the common factors over time.

Examining factorial invariance for a particular dataset and proposed measurement model requires the fitting of all four levels of factorial invariance. These four models are sequentially nested, such that any model may be compared with any other model using a likelihood ratio test. While weak factorial invariance establishes some degree of common measurement across occasions, either strong or strict invariance is required to attribute changes in the observed variables to changes in the common factors. Thus, these levels of factorial invariance are required to make the move to fitting growth models of common factors. A thorough discussion of measurement invariance and the appropriate tests of measurement invariance can be found in Millsap (2011).

Testing Factorial Invariance with Longitudinal Data

Testing factorial invariance with longitudinal data comes with additional modeling choices. While testing factorial invariance across groups with cross-sectional data is done in the multiple-group modeling framework, *longitudinal* factorial invariance is conducted in a single-group model with the data in wide form. The repeatedly measured variables are represented as separate variables, and the across-time factors are specified in the same model—like a multidimensional factor model along the time dimension. Figure 14.2 is a path diagram of a longitudinal factor model with a repeatedly measured factor (η_{11} through η_{T1}) and strict factorial invariance imposed because there is one set of factor loadings (λ_1 through λ_4), intercepts (τ_1 through τ_4), and unique variances (θ_{11} through θ_{44}). The mean and variance of the common factor at time 1 (η_{11}) is fixed at 0 and 1, which identifies the model and scales the latent variables. The latent variables at times 2 through T have estimated variances and means. As seen in Figure 14.2, the common factors are allowed to covary over time. These covariances provide information regarding the level of relative stability of the factors across time (e.g., high correlations indicate that the between-person differences in the factor are relatively stable across time).

Additionally, and not specified in Figure 14.2, we often allow for unique covariances across time. For example, the unique factors at time 1 are allowed to covary with the unique factors from time 2. That is, the unique factors for y_{11} and y_{12}, y_{21} and y_{22}, y_{31} and y_{32}, and y_{41} and y_{42} are allowed to covary. Similar covariances are typically specified for all observed variables that are the same across time (e.g., y_{11}, y_{12}, and y_{1T}). We do not often impose any equality constraints on these unique covariances; however, it may be reasonable to impose such constraints. For example, assuming a constant time lag between measurement occasions, the lag-1 unique covariances can be constrained to be equal, the lag-2 unique covariances can be constrained to be equal, and so on and so forth. These

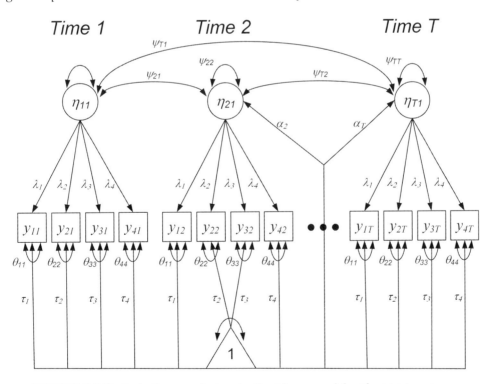

FIGURE 14.2. Path diagram of a longitudinal factor model with strict invariance.

unique covariances are often appropriate because the same observed variable correlates more strongly with itself over time than it does with the other observed variables over time. Failure to account for these autocorrelations can bias other parameters in a factor model and negatively affect model fit.

Strong invariance is needed to examine change at the factor level over time. If strong invariance does not hold across time, it indicates that the meaning of the factor changed over time (if *weak* invariance is not supported) or that the scale of the factor changed over time (if *strong* invariance is not supported). If weak invariance doesn't hold, then the interpretation of at least one (and possibly more) observed variable changed. This can happen when studying change because certain variables may no longer be appropriate. For example, a variable about biting behavior has a different meaning when asked about infants compared to school-age children. That is, biting is fairly common among infants and does not necessarily indicate a problem behavior, whereas biting is rare among school-age children and is indicative of externalizing behavior. Similar assessments can be made for questions related to crying in infants and school-age children (Flora, Curran, Hussong, & Edwards, 2008).

Another example comes from Widaman, Ferrer, and Conger (2010), who detailed a situation in which *numerical facility* had a noninvariant factor loading from second grade through college. Widaman et al. (2010) noted that while performance on the set of items exhibited a structure consistent with a common factor, elementary students relied on counting strategies whereas college students relied on memorization. Thus, the items were not measuring the same underlying skill at different ages. If *strong* invariance doesn't hold, then the factor is unable to account for all of the mean changes. This can happen in longitudinal research when the observed variables show different change patterns across time. For example, crystallized and fluid intelligence are two constructs that are often highly related to one another at any point in time; however, their change patterns are expected to differ, with crystallized intelligence peaking in late adulthood and showing minimal decline and fluid intelligence peaking in the early twenties and showing a strong subsequent decline (see McArdle et al., 2002). Similar discrepancies are apparent when examining changes in academic abilities measured by standardized tests (e.g., Woodcock–Johnson Tests of Achievement) and teacher rating scales (e.g., Academic Rating Scale) because the teacher ratings and standardized tests do not show the same change patterns (i.e., teacher ratings tend to show small changes, whereas standardized tests show large changes).

If strong invariance is not supported, then change models of the factors should not be fit because aspects of the measurement of the construct have changed and it is therefore difficult to distinguish between changes taking place in the individual and changes taking place in the measurement of the construct. At times, it is reasonable to investigate the cause of noninvariance. For example, if there are five observed variables at each measurement occasion and one of these variables has noninvariant parameters, it may be reasonable to simply remove this variable from the measurement model or allow this variable to have noninvariant measurement parameters. In the latter case, changes at the factor level reflect changes taking place in the observed variables that have invariant measurement parameters. If the lack of measurement invariance is due to multiple observed variables, it may not be reasonable to isolate a set of observed variables with invariant measurement parameters.

SECOND-ORDER GROWTH MODEL

Once the factors have been established at each occasion of measurement and *strong* or *strict* invariance is supported, we can begin to model changes at the factor level. The *second-order growth model* (Hancock et al., 2001; McArdle, 1988) is simply the merger of the longitudinal common factor model with the growth model. In this model, the factors for the measurement model (i.e., longitudinal common factor models) are considered *first-order* factors because they are immediately above the measured variables, and the growth factors (i.e., intercept and slope) are considered *second-order* factors because they are two levels above the measured variables. In this model, the second-order growth factors attempt to account for the changes in the mean, variance, and covariances of the first-order factors.

Working from the longitudinal factor model of Equation 14.5, Figure 14.2, and assuming a single common factor at each measurement occasion, the second-order growth model can be written as

$$\eta_i = \Gamma \xi_i + \upsilon_i \tag{14.6}$$

where η_i is a $T \times 1$ vector of common factor variables for individual i, Γ is a $T \times R$ factor loading matrix defining the latent growth factors (e.g., intercept and linear slope in the linear growth model), ξ_i is an $R \times 1$ vector of second-order latent growth factors, and υ_i is a $T \times 1$ vector of latent variable disturbance terms. The second-order factors are assumed to follow a multivariate normal distribution, such that $\xi_i \sim MVN(\kappa, \Phi)$, where κ is an $R \times 1$ vector of latent variable means and Φ is an $R \times R$ covariance matrix. The first-order factor disturbances (υ_i) are assumed to follow a normal distribution, such that $\upsilon_i \sim N(0, \psi)$ where ψ is a $T \times T$ diagonal covariance matrix of disturbances (e.g., latent variable residuals).

Identification, which was discussed for the factor model and the longitudinal factor model, is also an important consideration with second-order growth models. Typically, one factor loading for each first-order factor is fixed to 1, and the mean of the second-order latent variable intercept is fixed at 0. Alternatively, the disturbance variance can be set to a fixed value instead of fixing a factor loading, and an observed variable intercept can be fixed to 0 instead of fixing the second-order latent variable intercept mean to 0. The choice of identifying constraints does not affect model fit but does affect parameter estimates and their interpretation. Ideally, identification constraints are employed that provide the simplest interpretation of model parameters. One approach is to fix one factor loading per latent variable to a value, such that the total variance of the first first-order latent variable is expected to be 1, and fix the mean of the second-order latent variable intercept to 0 (K. Widaman, personal communication, October 12, 2014). With these identification constraints, the first first-order latent variable is essentially in a standardized metric, which makes the change parameters more interpretable. We adopt this approach here.

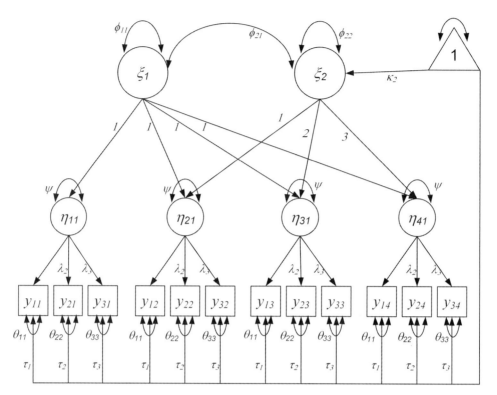

FIGURE 14.3. Path diagram of a second-order growth model.

Figure 14.3 is a path diagram of a second-order growth model following Equations 14.5 and 14.6. In this path diagram, there are three observed variables measured at each occasion (y_{11} through y_{34}), which indicate a single first-order factor at each time point (η_{11} through η_{41}). The changes in the first-order factors are modeled with second-order growth factors ξ_1 and ξ_2, which are the latent variable intercept and slope. The first factor loading for each latent variable is fixed at 1, and the mean of ξ_1 is fixed at 0 for identification; *strict* factorial invariance is imposed.

ILLUSTRATION

To illustrate the use of the longitudinal common factor model and the second-order growth model, we use a random sample of observations from the Early Childhood Longitudinal Study—Kindergarten Cohort (ECLS-K). Reading, mathematics, and science tests were administered in third, fifth, and eighth grades, and these three tests are considered indicators of an academic achievement common factor. The achievement tests in the ECLS-K were adaptive, and the scores used in this analysis are the estimated number of correct responses if the entire test was administered.

TABLE 14.1. Estimated Sample Statistics from the ECLS-K

	1.	2.	3.	4.	5.	6.	7.	8.	9.
Mean	51.01	127.27	99.75	64.81	150.30	123.78	83.35	169.20	140.57
Standard deviation	15.61	29.52	25.54	16.40	27.57	25.40	16.99	28.46	22.92
1. Science grade 3	1.00								
2. Reading grade 3	0.76	1.00							
3. Math grade 3	0.71	0.76	1.00						
4. Science grade 5	0.85	0.74	0.71	1.00					
5. Reading grade 5	0.74	0.86	0.73	0.78	1.00				
6. Math grade 5	0.69	0.72	0.88	0.75	0.76	1.00			
7. Science grade 8	0.76	0.72	0.71	0.82	0.75	0.75	1.00		
8. Reading grade 8	0.69	0.77	0.68	0.74	0.81	0.70	0.79	1.00	
9. Math grade 8	0.67	0.70	0.82	0.71	0.73	0.86	0.79	0.76	1.00

Estimated sample statistics for these scores from the three measurement occasions are presented in Table 14.1. The sample means increase over grade for all three tests, and the sample correlations are all strong—one indication that the reading, science, and math scores may be represented by a common underlying construct. The correlations within time tend to be stronger than the correlations across time, except for the correlations involving the same test over time (e.g., science in grade 3 and science in grade 5, $r = .85$).

STRUCTURAL EQUATION MODELING IMPLEMENTATION

Longitudinal Common Factor Model

Mplus

The Mplus script for fitting a longitudinal common factor model with *strict* factorial invariance to the ECLS-K data is presented in Script 14.1. We begin by defining the first-order factors (η_i) named eta_1, eta_2, and eta_3 for the academic achievement latent variable measured in third, fifth, and eighth grade. These latent variables are defined using the keyword BY, and labels are used to constrain the factor loadings to be equal over time. That is, the factor loadings to the science, reading, and mathematics variables are labeled lambda_S, lambda_R, and lambda_M, respectively. We note that an asterisk is placed after the first observed variable when defining each latent variable, which is needed to override the default that the first factor loading is fixed at 1. Constraining the loadings to be equal across time is in line with the specification of the strict invariance model. Next, latent variable variances and covariances are specified by listing the names of the latent variables to specify their variances and then using the WITH statement to specify each covariance. The variance of eta_1 is set to 1 as part of the model identification process. Latent variable means are then specified by listing the names of the latent variables in square brackets. The mean of eta_1 is fixed at 0 as the

Script 14.1. *Mplus* Script for the Longitudinal Factor Model with Strict Factorial Invariance

```
MODEL:
! Common Factors
     eta_1 BY s_g3 * (lambda_S)
               r_g3   (lambda_R)
               m_g3   (lambda_M);
     eta_2 BY s_g5 * (lambda_S)
               r_g5   (lambda_R)
               m_g5   (lambda_M);
     eta_3 BY s_g8 * (lambda_S)
               r_g8   (lambda_R)
               m_g8   (lambda_M);
! Latent Variable Variances & Covariances
     eta_1@1 eta_2 eta_3;
     eta_1 WITH eta_2 eta_3;
     eta_2 WITH eta_3;
! Latent Variable Means
     [eta_1@0 eta_2 *0 eta_3 *0];
! Unique Variances
     s_g3 s_g5 s_g8 (theta_S);
     r_g3 r_g5 r_g8 (theta_R);
     m_g3 m_g5 m_g8 (theta_M);
! Observed Variable Intercepts
     [s_g3 s_g5 s_g8] (tau_S);
     [r_g3 r_g5 r_g8] (tau_R);
     [m_g3 m_g5 m_g8] (tau_M);
! Unique Factor Covariances
     s_g3 WITH s_g5 s_g8;
     s_g5 WITH s_g8;
     r_g3 WITH r_g5 r_g8;
     r_g5 WITH r_g8;
     m_g3 WITH m_g5 m_g8;
     m_g5 WITH m_g8;
```

second part of the model identification process, and the means of eta_2 and eta_3 are freely estimated and given starting values of 0 (*0).

Next, unique variances are specified. These variances are specified for the observed variables and represent variability that is unique to the observed variable and not common with the other indicators of the common factor. These unique variances are given labels to constrain them to be equal across time. For example, the unique variances of the science variables are labeled theta_S. Again, this constraint is in line with the *strict* factorial invariance model. The observed variable intercepts are specified next. The intercepts are specified by listing the names of the observed variables in square brackets, and these parameters are constrained to be equal over time. For example, the intercepts for the science variables are specified together and labeled tau_S. Again, these constraints are in line with the strict invariance model. Lastly, the unique covariances are specified.

These covariances are specified between the same variable measured at different occasions. These covariances are specified using the WITH statement. For example, the science variable at third grade is allowed to covary with the science variables measured in fifth and eighth grades (s_g3 WITH s_g5 s_g8).

From the strict factorial invariance model specified in Script 14.1, we can remove equality constraints to specify the three other measurement invariance models. Working backwards, the strong invariance model is specified by removing the labels for the unique variances (theta_S, theta_R, and theta_M). The weak invariance model is specified by additionally removing the labels for the observed variable intercepts (tau_S, tau_R, and tau_M) and then fixing the means of eta_2 and eta_3 to 0 (for identification). Alternatively, two of the labels for the observed variable intercepts can be removed, and the means of eta_2 and eta_3 can remain freely estimated. The configural invariance model is specified by additionally removing the constraints on the factor loadings (lambda_S, lambda_R, and lambda_M) and fixing the variances of eta_2 and eta_3 to 1 (for identification). Alternatively, two of the labels for the factor loadings can be removed, and the variances of eta_2 and eta_3 can remain freely estimated.

OpenMx

The OpenMx script for the longitudinal factor model with *strict* factorial invariance is contained in Script 14.2. The script begins by stating the dataset and listing the manifest and latent variables included in the model. The model is then specified with a series of mxPath statements and begins with the unique variances. These are for the observed variables and are specified as two-headed arrows that originate from each observed variable. These paths are freely estimated, given a starting value of 100, and labeled appropriately. The labels for the unique variances of the science, reading, and math variables are constrained to be equal across time using a series of common labels. Thus, the labels for the science variables are th_s, the labels for the reading variables are th_r, and the labels for the mathematics variables are th_m. Next, the unique covariances are specified. In this mxPath statement, two-headed paths are specified for every pair of science variables, reading variables, and mathematics variables. These paths are freely estimated, given starting values of 50, and labeled appropriately. The latent variable variances and covariances are then specified. These paths originate from eta_1, eta_2, and eta_3, and we use connect='unique.pairs' to specify all the variances and covariances in a single mxPath statement. The factor variance for eta_1 is fixed at 1 (for identification purposes), but the remaining paths contained in this statement are freely estimated. Starting values of 1 are given to the variances of eta_2 and eta_3, and starting values of 0 are given to all covariances.

The factor loadings for the three latent variables are then specified in three mxPath statements. All factor loadings originate from a latent variable and go to the appropriate observed variable. All factor loadings are freely estimated, given starting values of 20 and common labels to constrain the factor loadings to be equal across time. That

Script 14.2. OpenMx Script for the Longitudinal Factor Model with Strict Factorial Invariance

```
strict.acad.omx <- mxModel('Strict Model, Path Specification',
  type='RAM', mxData(observed=eclsk, type='raw'),
  manifestVars=c('s_g3','r_g3','m_g3','s_g5','r_g5','m_g5','s_g8','r_g8','m_g8'),
  latentVars=c('eta_1','eta_2','eta_3'),

# Unique Variances
  mxPath(from=c('s_g3','r_g3','m_g3','s_g5','r_g5','m_g5','s_g8','r_g8','m_g8'),
    arrows=2, free=TRUE, values=100,
    labels=c('th_s','th_r','th_m','th_s','th_r','th_m','th_s','th_r','th_m')),

# Unique Covariances
  mxPath(from=c('s_g3','s_g3','s_g5','r_g3','r_g5','m_g3','m_g5'),
    to=c('s_g5','s_g8','s_g8','r_g5','r_g8','m_g5','m_g8'),
    arrows=2, free=TRUE, values=50,
    labels=c('th_s53','th_s83','th_s85','th_r53','th_r83','th_r85','th_m53','th_m83','th_m85')),

# Latent Variable Covariances
  mxPath(from=c('eta_1','eta_2','eta_3'), connect='unique.pairs',
    arrows=2, free=c(FALSE,TRUE,TRUE,TRUE,TRUE,TRUE), values=c(1,0,0,1,0,1),
    labels=c(NA,'psi_21','psi_31','psi_22','psi_32','psi_33')),

# Factor Loadings
  mxPath(from='eta_1', to=c('s_g3','r_g3','m_g3'),
    arrows=1, free=TRUE, values=20, labels=c('lambda_s','lambda_r','lambda_m')),

  mxPath(from='eta_2', to=c('s_g5','r_g5','m_g5'),
    arrows=1, free =TRUE, values=20, labels=c('lambda_s','lambda_r','lambda_m')),

  mxPath(from='eta_3', to=c('s_g8','r_g8','m_g8'),
    arrows=1, free=TRUE, values=20, labels=c('lambda_s','lambda_r','lambda_m')),

# Latent Variable Means
  mxPath(from='one', to=c('eta_2','eta_3'),
    arrows=1, free=TRUE, values=0, labels=c('alpha_2','alpha_3')),

# Observed Variable Intercepts
  mxPath(from='one', to=c('s_g3','r_g3','m_g3','s_g5','r_g5','m_g5','s_g8','r_g8','m_g8'),
    arrows=1, free=TRUE, values=70,
    labels=c('tau_s','tau_r','tau_m','tau_s','tau_r','tau_m','tau_s','tau_r','tau_m'))

) # Close Model
```

is, the factor loadings for the science variables are all labeled `lambda_s`, the factor loadings for the reading variables are labeled `lambda_r`, and the factor loadings for the mathematics variables are labeled `lambda_m`. Next, the latent variable means are specified for `eta_2` and `eta_3`—one-headed arrows originating at the constant and going to the two latent variables. These paths are given starting values of 0 and labeled `alpha_2` and `alpha_3`. Lastly, we specify the intercepts of the observed variables as one-headed arrows originating from the constant and going to each observed variable. These paths are given starting values of 70, and common labels are given to the science (`tau_s`), reading (`tau_r`), and mathematics (`tau_m`) variables to place an equality constraint on these parameters.

The `OpenMx` code in Script 14.2 is easily altered to specify the configural, weak, and strong invariance models. For the strong invariance model, different labels are given to the unique variances in the first `mxPath` statement. The weak invariance model can be specified by additionally providing different labels to the observed variable intercepts and removing the `mxPath` statement for the latent variable means. Alternatively, distinct labels can be provided for the intercepts of the reading and mathematics (or reading and science or mathematics and science) variables. The configural invariance model can be specified by providing different labels either to the factor loadings to the reading and mathematics (or reading and science or mathematics and science) variables, or to all factor loadings and constraining the latent variable variances to one.

Output

Before examining and interpreting parameter estimates from the longitudinal factor model with strict invariance, we report on the fit of the four invariance models. Fit statistics for the four models are contained in Table 14.2. Beginning with the configural invariance model, we see that the model fits the data well with an RMSEA of 0.030, a CFI of 0.998, and a TLI of 0.996. The fit of this model supports the notion of having a single common factor representing academic ability in third, fifth, and eighth grades. Moving to the weak invariance model, we see a significant increase in the χ^2 statistic ($\Delta\chi^2(4) = 81.31$, $p < .001$), a noticeable jump in the RMSEA, and smaller decreases in the CFI and TLI. Thus, there is a question of whether we are measuring the same construct in all

TABLE 14.2. Fit Statistics for the Measurement Invariance Model

Fit statistic	Configural invariance	Weak invariance	Strong invariance	Strict invariance
$\chi^2(df)$	35.52 (15)	116.83 (19)	540.75 (23)	600.61 (29)
AIC	83,914	83,987	84,403	84,451
BIC	84,120	84,173	84,567	84,584
RMSEA	0.030	0.059	0.123	0.115
CFI	0.998	0.992	0.955	0.951
TLI	0.996	0.984	0.930	0.939

grades; however, the overall fit of the model remains viable with a CFI of 0.992 and a TLI of 0.984. We therefore move onto the strong invariance model. Model fit was further degraded by the constraints imposed on the mean structure ($\Delta\chi^2(4) = 423.92$, $p < .001$) suggesting that the common factors may be unable to adequately capture the changes taking place in the observed variables. At the same time, the overall model fit is justifiable with a CFI of 0.955 and a TLI of 0.930, suggesting that the model adequately captures the observed data. We therefore move to the strict invariance model and find that the strict invariance model fit significantly worse than the strong invariance model ($\Delta\chi^2(6) = 59.86$, $p < .001$). However, again the strict invariance model shows adequate model fit with a CFI of 0.951 and a TLI of 0.939. Thus, we feel it is appropriate to interpret the parameters of the strict invariance model. We note that the power of likelihood ratio tests, as all statistical tests, is affected by sample size. Thus, having a large sample gives us a lot of power to detect noninvariance—even small effects. Researchers have advocated the examination of changes in global fit indices because of the power of likelihood ratio tests; at the same time, researchers should also consider absolute model fit as we did here.

Parameter estimates from Mplus and OpenMx are contained in Output 14.1 and 14.2, respectively. The factor loadings (BY statements in Mplus; lambda_s, lambda_r, and lambda_m in OpenMx) were significantly different from zero; however, in the current metric it is difficult to determine their strength. Thus, we look at the standardized output for this information. In Mplus, standardized output can be obtained by requesting STANDARDIZED in the OUTPUT: command, and mxStandardizeRAMpaths() can be used in OpenMx to obtain the standardized parameter estimates. We note that the standardized factor loadings can vary with time even when equality constraints are imposed on the raw (unstandardized) factor loadings. Examining the standardized factor loadings, we find that they were strong (> 0.84), indicating that the common factors were strongly indicated by their respective observed variables.

Focusing on the estimates associated with the common factors, we find that the mean of the latent variable (Means of eta_2 and eta_3; alpha_2 and alpha_3) was 1.02 in fifth grade and 1.95 in eighth grade. To give background to these estimates, we can use the distribution of the latent variable at third grade, which had a mean of 0 and a standard deviation of 1. Thus, from third to fifth grade the mean changed by a little more than a standard deviation of the third-grade distribution. Similarly, from fifth to eighth grade, the mean changes by a little less than a standard deviation based on the third-grade distribution. The variance (Variances of eta_2 and eta_3; psi_22 and psi_33) of the common factor in fifth and eighth grade was 1.01 and 0.97, respectively, indicating that the magnitude of between-person differences in academic achievement did not change much from third through eighth grade. Next, we examine the correlations among the common factors across time and find that the common factors were strongly correlated over time (WITH statements involving eta_1, eta_2, and eta_3; psi_21, psi_31, and psi_32). The latent variable covariances were reported in the outputs, but again, we can review the standardized output and see that the common factor correlations were all greater than 0.91, indicating that the between-person differences in the academic factor were very stable from third through eighth grades.

Output 14.1. `Mplus` Output for the Longitudinal Factor Model with Strict Factorial Invariance

MODEL RESULTS

		Estimate	S.E.	Est./S.E.	Two-Tailed P-Value
ETA_1	BY				
S_G3		15.176	0.319	47.527	0.000
R_G3		22.982	0.520	44.171	0.000
M_G3		21.236	0.473	44.917	0.000
ETA_2	BY				
S_G5		15.176	0.319	47.527	0.000
R_G5		22.982	0.520	44.171	0.000
M_G5		21.236	0.473	44.917	0.000
ETA_3	BY				
S_G8		15.176	0.319	47.527	0.000
R_G8		22.982	0.520	44.171	0.000
M_G8		21.236	0.473	44.917	0.000
ETA_1	WITH				
ETA_2		0.968	0.013	72.280	0.000
ETA_3		0.904	0.019	48.240	0.000
ETA_2	WITH				
ETA_3		0.949	0.027	35.095	0.000
S_G3	WITH				
S_G5		28.853	3.118	9.254	0.000
S_G8		6.616	3.301	2.004	0.045
S_G5	WITH				
S_G8		5.353	3.311	1.617	0.106
R_G3	WITH				
R_G5		112.069	8.673	12.921	0.000
R_G8		69.528	9.345	7.440	0.000
R_G5	WITH				
R_G8		79.187	9.640	8.214	0.000
M_G3	WITH				
M_G5		112.591	7.308	15.407	0.000
M_G8		93.469	7.990	11.698	0.000
M_G5	WITH				
M_G8		102.540	8.014	12.795	0.000
Means					
ETA_1		0.000	0.000	999.000	999.000
ETA_2		1.020	0.025	41.016	0.000
ETA_3		1.947	0.045	43.248	0.000
Intercepts					
S_G3		51.433	0.448	114.744	0.000
R_G3		126.363	0.702	179.898	0.000
M_G3		100.193	0.651	153.912	0.000
S_G5		51.433	0.448	114.744	0.000
R_G5		126.363	0.702	179.898	0.000
M_G5		100.193	0.651	153.912	0.000
S_G8		51.433	0.448	114.744	0.000
R_G8		126.363	0.702	179.898	0.000
M_G8		100.193	0.651	153.912	0.000

(continued)

Output 14.1. (Continued)

Variances				
ETA_1	1.000	0.000	999.000	999.000
ETA_2	1.011	0.026	38.332	0.000
ETA_3	0.971	0.036	27.168	0.000
Residual Variances				
S_G3	60.274	2.939	20.506	0.000
R_G3	208.700	8.172	25.537	0.000
M_G3	173.322	7.236	23.952	0.000
S_G5	60.274	2.939	20.506	0.000
R_G5	208.700	8.172	25.537	0.000
M_G5	173.322	7.236	23.952	0.000
S_G8	60.274	2.939	20.506	0.000
R_G8	208.700	8.172	25.537	0.000
M_G8	173.322	7.236	23.952	0.000

Output 14.2. OpenMx Output for the Longitudinal Factor Model with Strict Factorial Invariance

	name	matrix	row	col	Estimate	Std.Error
	free parameters:					
1	lambda_s	A	s_g3	eta_1	15.1749088	0.31829496
2	lambda_r	A	r_g3	eta_1	22.9806572	0.51768575
3	lambda_m	A	m_g3	eta_1	21.2362864	0.47104498
4	th_s	S	s_g3	s_g3	60.2698421	2.75251768
5	th_r	S	r_g3	r_g3	208.7606975	7.91909668
6	th_m	S	m_g3	m_g3	173.2977095	7.00338013
7	th_s53	S	s_g3	s_g5	28.8421738	2.94524110
8	th_r53	S	r_g3	r_g5	112.1324486	8.44106632
9	th_m53	S	m_g3	m_g5	112.5824844	7.07780122
10	th_s83	S	s_g3	s_g8	6.5929310	2.98503902
11	th_s85	S	s_g5	s_g8	5.3481884	2.63275428
12	th_r83	S	r_g3	r_g8	69.4982349	9.03710638
13	th_r85	S	r_g5	r_g8	79.1903571	9.34634205
14	th_m83	S	m_g3	m_g8	93.4654618	7.74374739
15	th_m85	S	m_g5	m_g8	102.4878349	7.76500982
16	psi_21	S	eta_1	eta_2	0.9679592	0.01338906
17	psi_22	S	eta_2	eta_2	1.0105512	0.02635231
18	psi_31	S	eta_1	eta_3	0.9038030	0.01875611
19	psi_32	S	eta_2	eta_3	0.9492382	0.02705506
20	psi_33	S	eta_3	eta_3	0.9707644	0.03580693
21	tau_s	M	1	s_g3	51.4331658	0.44774023
22	tau_r	M	1	r_g3	126.3627211	0.70221039
23	tau_m	M	1	m_g3	100.1927482	0.65088353
24	alpha_2	M	1	eta_2	1.0202422	0.02477327
25	alpha_3	M	1	eta_3	1.9470769	0.04487849

Next, we briefly review the estimates associated with the observed variables. The observed variable intercepts (Intercepts of s_g3, r_g3, m_g3; tau_s, tau_r, and tau_m) provide some information about the scale of the observed variables. These estimates can be used to help describe the expected means of the observed variables at the first occasion (when the mean of the common factor was 0). Since these variables are in their own unique metric, it is difficult to attribute much meaning to them outside the context of being part of the estimated model. The unique variances (Residual Variances of s_g3, r_g3, m_g3; th_s, th_r, and th_m) represent the amount of variability in the observed variable that was not accounted for by the common factor. Individually, these parameters are difficult to interpret, but turning to the standardized output, we can determine how much of the variance in the observed variables was accounted for by the common factors and we see that the common factor accounted for between 71 and 79% of the variability in the observed scores. This information is reflective of the magnitude of the standardized factor loadings. The unique covariances (WITH statement involving observed variables; th_s53, th_s83, and th_s85 for the science variables) were mostly significantly different from zero, suggesting that the unique aspects of these variables were associated over time. This highlights the importance of accounting for these unique aspects of covariation over time. We now build upon this strict invariance model and examine the changes in the first-order factors with a second-order growth model.

Second-Order Growth Model

Mplus

The Mplus script for a second-order latent basis growth model is contained in Script 14.3. The first part of the script follows the specification of the strict factorial invariance model with a few important changes that we highlight here. Beginning with the factor loadings for the first-order factors, we have fixed the factor loadings to the science variables to 15.176, which may seem like an arbitrary value. First, we note that this is an identification constraint. Second, this value was the estimate of the factor loading from the strict invariance model. In the strict invariance model, the variance of the eta_1 was fixed at 1. Thus, fixing this factor loading to the estimate from the strict invariance model would suggest that the expected variance of eta_1 will be approximately 1, and this can provide greater interpretation of the remaining estimated parameters from the second-order growth model. The first-order latent variable *disturbance* variances are now constrained to be equal across time and labeled psi. We note that they are disturbance variances because they represent variability in the common factors that is not accounted for by the second-order growth model. The first-order covariances are all fixed at 0 because the second-order growth model is expected to account for the covariances among the first-order factors. Similarly, the means of the first-order factors are fixed at 0 because the second-order growth model will attempt to account for the changes in the first-order means across time. The remainder of the common factor part of the script is unchanged.

Script 14.3. Mplus Script for the Second-Order Latent Basis Growth Model

```
MODEL:
! Common Factors
    eta_1 BY s_g3@15.176
            r_g3 (lambda_R)
            m_g3 (lambda_M);
    eta_2 BY s_g5@15.176
            r_g5 (lambda_R)
            m_g5 (lambda_M);
    eta_3 BY s_g8@15.176
            r_g8 (lambda_R)
            m_g8 (lambda_M);

! Latent Variable Variances & Covariances
    eta_1 eta_2 eta_3 (psi);
    eta_1 WITH eta_2@0 eta_3@0;
    eta_2 WITH eta_3@0;

! Latent Variable Means
    [eta_1@0 eta_2@0 eta_3@0];

! Unique Variances
    s_g3 s_g5 s_g8 (theta_S);
    r_g3 r_g5 r_g8 (theta_R);
    m_g3 m_g5 m_g8 (theta_M);

! Observed Variable Intercepts
    [s_g3 s_g5 s_g8] (tau_S);
    [r_g3 r_g5 r_g8] (tau_R);
    [m_g3 m_g5 m_g8] (tau_M);

! Unique Factor Covariances
    s_g3 WITH s_g5 s_g8;
    s_g5 WITH s_g8;
    r_g3 WITH r_g5 r_g8;
    r_g5 WITH r_g8;
    m_g3 WITH m_g5 m_g8;
    m_g5 WITH m_g8;

! Latent Basis Growth Model
    xi_1 BY eta_1@1 eta_2@1 eta_3@1;
    xi_2 BY eta_1@0 eta_2*.5 eta_3@1;
    xi_1 xi_2;
    xi_1 WITH xi_2;
    [xi_1@0 xi_2*2];
```

The second-order growth model is specified at the end of Script 14.3. First, we define xi_1, and xi_2. xi_1 is the latent variable intercept and has factor loadings that are fixed at 1, and xi_2 is the shape factor with two fixed and one estimated factor loading. The first and last factor loadings are fixed at 0 and 1, respectively, and the second factor loading will be estimated from the data following the unstructured or latent basis growth model specification. Next, latent variable variances and covariance are specified by listing xi_1 and xi_2 and then stating xi_1 WITH xi_2. Finally, the means of xi_1 and xi_2 are specified in square brackets. The mean of xi_1 is fixed at 0 for identification, and the mean of xi_2 is given a starting value of 2.

OpenMx

The OpenMx script for the second-order latent basis growth model is contained in Script 14.4. The beginning of the script closely follows the specification of the strict invariance model. Here we note the changes and additions. The first change is in the specification of the latent variable variance and covariance matrix. Instead of specifying a full covariance matrix for the first-order factors and placing an identification constraint on the variance of eta_1, we specify only the latent variable variances, give them a starting value of 0.20, and constrain them to be equal using the common label psi. Next, the factor loadings are specified. In the strict invariance script, these parameters were freely estimated but constrained to be equal across time. Now, we place an identification constraint here as we fix the factor loading from each latent variable to the respective science variable to 15.1749088, which was the estimated factor loading for this variable in the strict invariance model. As in the strict invariance model, the factor loadings for reading and mathematics are constrained to be equal across time and labeled lambda_r and lambda_m.

The additions to the script appear after ## Second-Order Growth Specification ##. First, we define xi_1 and xi_2. The factor loadings for xi_1, the second-order intercept, go to the first-order factors and are fixed at 1. The factor loadings for xi_2, the second-order shape factor, also go to the first-order factors. The factor loading to eta_1 is fixed at 0, the factor loading to eta_2 is freely estimated and labeled gamma_22, and the factor loading to eta_3 is fixed at 1 following our typical specification for an unstructured or latent basis growth model. Next, second-order latent variable variances and covariances are specified for xi_1 and xi_2 using connect='unique.pairs'. These parameters are given starting values and labels beginning with phi. Lastly, we specify the mean of the second-order shape factor. This path originates from the constant and goes to xi_2, given a starting value of 2, and labeled kappa_2. We note that the mean of xi_1 is fixed at 0 for identification purposes and was not specified.

Output

Before reporting on the parameter estimates and their interpretation, we discuss model fit. The second-order latent basis growth model showed good fit ($\chi^2(31) = 606.99$, CFI = 0.950, TLI = 0.943, RMSEA = 0.112) and the fit of this model can be compared against the strict invariance model. Comparing these two models, we find that the change in fit was significant ($\chi^2(2) = 6.38$, $p < .05$); however, the change in fit was minimal given the sample size and lack of change in the global and absolute fit indices. This suggests that the growth model was able to adequately capture the mean changes in the first-order factors as well as their variances and covariances.

Script 14.4. OpenMx Script for the Second-Order Latent Basis Growth Model

```
lgm.acad.omx <- mxModel ('Second Order Latent Basis Growth Model, Path Specification',
    type='RAM', mxData (observed=eclsk, type='raw'),
    manifestVars=c('s_g3','r_g3','m_g3','s_g5','r_g5','m_g5','s_g8','r_g8','m_g8'),
    latentVars=c('eta_1','eta_2','eta_3','xi_1','xi_2'),

# Unique Variances
mxPath(from=c('s_g3','r_g3','m_g3','s_g5','r_g5','m_g5','s_g8','r_g8','m_g8'),
    arrows=2, free=TRUE, values=100,
    labels=c('th_s','th_r','th_m','th_s','th_r','th_m','th_s','th_r','th_m')),

# Unique Covariances
mxPath(from=c('s_g3','s_g3','s_g5','r_g3','r_g5','m_g3','m_g3','m_g5'),
    to=c('s_g5','s_g8','s_g8','r_g5','r_g8','r_g8','m_g5','m_g3','m_g8'),
    arrows=2, free=TRUE, values=50,
    labels=c('th_s53','th_s83','th_s85','th_r53','th_r83','th_r85','th_m53','th_m83','th_m85')),

# Latent Variable Disturbance Variances
mxPath(from=c('eta_1','eta_2','eta_3'),
    arrows=2, free=TRUE, values=.2, labels='psi'),

# Factor Loadings
mxPath(from='eta_1', to=c('s_g3','r_g3','m_g3'),
    arrows=1, free=c(FALSE, TRUE, TRUE), values=15.1749088,
    labels=c(NA, 'lambda_r', 'lambda_m')),

mxPath(from='eta_2', to=c('s_g5','r_g5','m_g5'),
    arrows=1, free=c(FALSE, TRUE, TRUE), values=15.1749088,
    labels=c(NA, 'lambda_r', 'lambda_m')),
```

```r
mxPath(from='eta_3', to=c('s_g8','r_g8','m_g8'),
    arrows=1, free=c(FALSE, TRUE, TRUE), values=15.1749088,
    labels=c(NA, 'lambda_r', 'lambda_m')),

# Observed Variable Intercepts
mxPath(from='one', to=c('s_g3','r_g3','m_g3','s_g5','r_g5','m_g5','s_g8','r_g8','m_g8'),
    arrows=1, free=TRUE, values=70,
    labels=c('tau_s','tau_r','tau_m','tau_s','tau_r','tau_m','tau_s','tau_r','tau_m')),

## Second - Order Growth Specification ##
# Factor Loadings
mxPath(from='xi_1', to=c('eta_1','eta_2','eta_3'),
    arrows=1, free=FALSE, values=1),

mxPath(from='xi_2', to=c('eta_1','eta_2','eta_3'),
    arrows=1, free=c(FALSE, TRUE, FALSE), values=c(0,.5,1),
    labels=c(NA, 'gamma_22', NA)),

# Latent Variable Variances & Covariances
mxPath(from=c('xi_1','xi_2'), connect='unique.pairs',
    arrows=2, free=TRUE, values=c(.8,0,.5),
    labels=c('phi_11','phi_21','phi_22')),

# Latent Variable Means
mxPath(from='one', to=c('xi_2'),
    arrows=1, free=TRUE, values=2, labels='kappa_2')

) # Close Model
```

Parameter estimates from Mplus and OpenMx are contained in Output 14.3 and 14.4, respectively. For Mplus, we only list the parameter estimates associated with the second-order growth model because there should not be much change in the parameter estimates associated with the first-order factors. Beginning with the second-order growth factors, the mean of the shape factor (Means of xi_2; kappa_2) was 1.95 and represents the expected mean change in the academic achievement factor from third through eighth grade. Since the scale of the first-order factors is arbitrary, it can be difficult to interpret the magnitude of this parameter. The identification constraints imposed in the model have specified the total variance of the first-order factor in third grade to be approximately one. Thus, the mean change from third through eighth grade represents almost a two standard deviation increase when compared to the amount of between-person differences in academic achievement at third grade. The variance of the second-order intercept and shape factors (Variances of xi_1 and xi_2; psi_11 and psi_22) were both significant, indicating that children significantly varied in their level of academic achievement in third grade and their rate of growth. The covariance between the second-order intercept and shape factors was negative (xi_1 WITH xi_2; psi_21) and transformed into a correlation equaled –0.19. Thus, academic achievement in third grade was slightly negatively associated with the rate of growth from third through eighth grade.

To determine the within-person rate of change at different points in time, we need to consider the factor loadings of xi_2 (xi_2 BY eta_2; gamma_2). The factor loadings

Output 14.3. Mplus Output for the Second-Order Latent Basis Growth Model

MODEL RESULTS

		Estimate	S.E.	Est./S.E.	Two-Tailed P-Value
XI_1	BY				
ETA_1		1.000	0.000	999.000	999.000
ETA_2		1.000	0.000	999.000	999.000
ETA_3		1.000	0.000	999.000	999.000
XI_2	BY				
ETA_1		0.000	0.000	999.000	999.000
ETA_2		0.524	0.006	85.607	0.000
ETA_3		1.000	0.000	999.000	999.000
XI_1	WITH				
XI_2		-0.061	0.019	-3.114	0.002
Means					
XI_1		0.000	0.000	999.000	999.000
XI_2		1.947	0.024	82.219	0.000
Variances					
XI_1		0.982	0.042	23.184	0.000
XI_2		0.110	0.018	6.277	0.000
Residual Variances					
ETA_1		0.024	0.004	6.026	0.000
ETA_2		0.024	0.004	6.026	0.000
ETA_3		0.024	0.004	6.026	0.000

Output 14.4. OpenMx Output for the Second-Order Latent Basis Growth Model

free parameters:

	name	matrix	row	col	Estimate	Std.Error
1	lambda_r	A	r_g3	eta_1	22.98897356	0.296771614
2	lambda_m	A	m_g3	eta_1	21.23548090	0.250448952
3	gamma_22	A	eta_2	xi_2	0.52391537	0.006237537
4	th_s	S	s_g3	s_g3	60.27110458	4.423763569
5	th_r	S	r_g3	r_g3	208.60749540	10.791908950
6	th_m	S	m_g3	m_g3	173.82419834	9.925948880
7	th_s53	S	s_g3	s_g5	28.70353095	4.524295110
8	th_r53	S	r_g3	r_g5	113.25278838	11.188649411
9	th_m53	S	m_g3	m_g5	113.49470209	10.015172838
10	th_s83	S	s_g3	s_g8	6.80230565	6.341068127
11	th_s85	S	s_g5	s_g8	5.73944175	6.344437494
12	th_r83	S	r_g3	r_g8	67.86753635	12.757414077
13	th_r85	S	r_g5	r_g8	78.02129251	12.907379093
14	th_m83	S	m_g3	m_g8	92.86851524	10.894410307
15	th_m85	S	m_g5	m_g8	100.70326575	10.861819735
16	psi	S	eta_1	eta_1	0.02426940	0.004031375
17	phi_11	S	xi_1	xi_1	0.98255711	0.042414332
18	phi_21	S	xi_1	xi_2	-0.06073336	0.019537961
19	phi_22	S	xi_2	xi_2	0.11001589	0.017562896
20	tau_s	M	1	s_g3	51.42363666	0.451225126
21	tau_r	M	1	r_g3	126.33967208	0.708471750
22	tau_m	M	1	m_g3	100.18119852	0.653793246
23	kappa_2	M	1	xi_2	1.94712088	0.023734060

begin at 0.00 in third grade, go to 0.52 in fifth grade, and to 1.00 in eighth grade. Thus, 52% of the total predicted changes from third through eighth grade took place between third and fifth grades. Using these factor loadings and the mean of xi_2, we find that the mean rate of change from third to fifth grade was 0.51 units ((0.52 · 1.95)/2) per year (unit is approximately the third grade standard deviation), whereas the mean rate of change from fifth to eighth grade was 0.31 units (((1 − 0.52) · 1.95)/3) per year. Knowing these mean rates of change, it is easy to visualize how the expected rate of change decreased from third through eighth grade.

The final parameter estimate that we discuss here is the disturbance variance (Residual Variance of eta_1; psi), which was estimated to be 0.02 and represents true variability in academic achievement that was not accounted for by the second-order growth model. To reiterate, our scaling of the first-order latent variables, we can see that adding this disturbance variance to the variance of xi_1 yields 1.01, which is the total expected variance of eta_1.

IMPORTANT CONSIDERATIONS

We cannot stress enough the importance of measurement invariance when studying change over time. Measurement invariance is often assumed because single-indicator models (all models discussed up to this chapter) are typically fit and testing measurement invariance is impossible with such data. Even with multivariate data, this assumption is often untested with longitudinal data because of select and small samples, lack of power, and unestimable models, but when possible, it is necessary to evaluate the degree of measurement invariance present in the observed variables over time. Researchers often make a yes or no decision regarding measurement invariance—either the parameters are invariant or they are not—and we note that this approach may not be appropriate without putting the *degree* of noninvariance in context. That is, it is important for the field to consider effect sizes for measurement noninvariance. One way to think about this is that measurement parameters are never invariant (never exactly identical) and we should consider what degree of noninvariance should prevent further analysis (e.g., change modeling) and what degree of noninvariance we can live with and continue to move forward with our analysis. There has been some research in item response modeling on effect sizes for measurement noninvariance (i.e., differential item functioning), and similar work should be done with continuous indicator factor models.

Beyond tests for measurement invariance, second-order growth models, compared to first-order growth models, have multiple benefits. First, we note that the power to detect variance in change and covariances among changes is greater with second-order models (Hertzog, Lindenberger, Ghisletta, & von Oertzen, 2006; Hertzog, von Oertzen, Ghisletta, & Lindenberger, 2008). That is, it should be easier to detect significant associations involving second-order intercepts and slopes compared with first-order intercepts and slopes. Second, second-order growth models can be fit when there are changes in the measurement of the construct over time. McArdle and Hamagami (2004) fit a second-order growth model to longitudinal intelligence data where the Stanford–Binet was administered when the participants were children, the Stanford–Binet and Wechsler Adult Intelligence Scale were administered when the participants were young adults, and then the Wechsler Adult Intelligence Scale was administered when the participants were adults. Using first-order models would only enable change modeling for specific spans of age (childhood to young adulthood and then young adulthood to adulthood). The second-order growth model enabled the study of changes from childhood through adulthood.

MOVING FORWARD

In the next chapter, we conclude our discussion of modeling change in latent entities with a discussion on using item response models when studying change. This chapter follows the current chapter closely but specifically deals with dichotomous and polytomous observed variables. As in this chapter, we first discuss the importance of establishing measurement invariance with item response models before modeling change.

## 15

Modeling Change with Latent Variables Measured by Ordinal Indicators

In this chapter we combine concepts from the previous two chapters and discuss *item response models*, sometimes referred to as *nonlinear* or *item factor models*, and how they can be combined with longitudinal data analysis and growth models (Curran et al., 2008; McArdle, Grimm, Hamagami, Bowles, & Meredith, 2009; Ram et al., 2005). As with the incorporation of the common factor model in longitudinal data analysis, we discuss how measurement invariance is tested with longitudinal item-level models. Testing measurement invariance with item response models has a separate history from testing measurement invariance with the common factor model (see Reise, Widaman, & Pugh, 1993). In item response modeling, the term *differential item functioning* (DIF; Thissen, Steinberg, & Gerrard, 1986) is used to refer to a lack of measurement equivalence at the item level (similarly, *differential test functioning* is used to refer to a lack of measurement equivalence at the test level) and is often described as testing for *item* (or *test*) *bias*. Regardless of the terms used, the idea of measurement equivalence or invariance is the same. That is, when measurement equivalence holds, differences (cross-sectionally) or changes (longitudinally) can be examined at the latent (factor or ability) level. We proceed with an examination of measurement invariance in much the same way as discussed in the prior chapter; however, we note that there are several approaches to test for measurement invariance in item response models and that testing for measurement invariance is often done on an item-by-item basis as opposed to studying whether a collection of items, as a whole, demonstrate measurement invariance (see Meredith, 1993; Meredith & Horn, 2001; Reise et al., 1993).

As discussed previously, modeling changes in common factors is a logical extension in the structural equation modeling framework, but not in the multilevel modeling framework and note that the multilevel modeling programs discussed here have difficulty fitting such models. We describe `Mplus` and `OpenMx` code for fitting these models to our illustrative data. As with longitudinal common factor models, `WinBUGS`, a freely available program that utilizes Bayesian estimation, is able to fit growth models that are combined with item response measurement models (see Grimm, Kuhl, & Zhang, 2013; McArdle et al., 2009).

ITEM RESPONSE MODELING

Item response modeling is concerned with understanding and modeling the item response process—that is, modeling the probability of a given response. Item response models, as they were originally developed, can be considered a restricted form of the common factor model for dichotomously and/or polytomously scored outcomes. In the history of common factor models, these same models were described as nonlinear factor models (McDonald, 1967) because the link between the common factor and the dichotomous/polytomous items was a nonlinear function (often the normal ogive or probit link). Item response models were originally developed with several assumptions. First, models assumed *unidimensionality*, such that there was a single latent trait (common factor) underlying all item responses; however, multidimensional models (see Wirth & Edwards, 2007) are now common. Second, item responses were assumed to be *conditionally independent*, such that item responses were uncorrelated after accounting for the latent trait. Third, the item response function was assumed to follow the *normal ogive* or *logistic* functions, which, as seen in Chapter 13, are elongated *s*-shaped curves. Currently, logistic curves are the most commonly used item response function because of estimation complexity with the normal ogive function. Commonly used item response models include the two-parameter logistic model (2PL; Birnbaum, 1968) for dichotomously scored responses and the graded response model (Samejima, 1969) for polytomously scored responses. These models, along with their normal ogive counterparts are subsequently described. Comprehensive overviews of item response models, theory, and approaches are found in Embretson and Reise (2000) and de Ayala (2009).

Dichotomous Response Models

The two-parameter logistic model can be written as

$$\Pr(y_{pi} = 1 | \theta_i, \alpha_p, \omega_p) = \frac{\exp(\alpha_p(\theta_i - \omega_p))}{1 + \exp(\alpha_p(\theta_i - \omega_p))} \tag{15.1}$$

where $\Pr(y_{pi} = 1 | \theta_i, \alpha_p, \omega_p)$ is the probability of a correct response (i.e., scoring in the higher of two categories) to item p by individual i conditional upon person and item parameters, α_p is the discrimination parameter for item p, ω_p is the location (difficulty) parameter for item p, and θ_i is the latent trait (ability/aptitude/common factor score) for individual i. Figure 15.1 is a plot of three example item characteristic curves with different discrimination and location parameters. The discrimination parameters were set to 1.03, 0.80, and 2.20 (from the leftmost to the rightmost curve), and the location

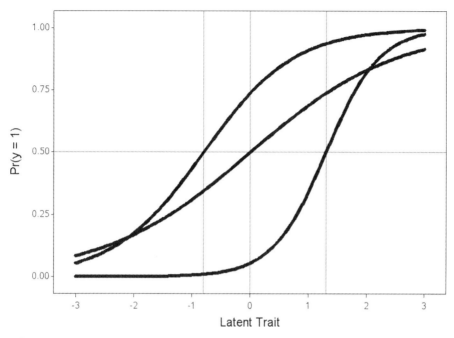

FIGURE 15.1. Item characteristic curves based on the two-parameter logistic model.

parameters were set to –0.80, 0.00, and 1.30, respectively. As seen in these plots, the location parameter refers to the point on the latent trait where an individual is predicted to have a 50% chance of correctly responding to the item. The discrimination parameter references the slope (divided by 4) of the tangent line when the latent trait and the location parameters are equal (i.e., $\theta_i = \omega_p$). Thus, the rate of change in the probability of a correct response when $\theta_i = \omega_p$ is $\alpha_p/4$. Items with greater discrimination parameters have greater changes in the probability for differences in the latent trait when θ_i is near ω_p, indicating that the item can discriminate between individuals with slightly different levels of the underlying ability.

The two-parameter normal ogive model (Lord, 1952) can be written as

$$\Pr(y_{pi} = 1 | \eta_i, \lambda_p, \tau_p) = \Phi(\lambda_p \cdot \eta_i - \tau_p) \tag{15.2}$$

where Φ is the standard normal cumulative distribution function, λ_p is the slope parameter for item p, τ_p is the threshold parameter for item p, and η_i is the underlying latent trait for individual i. Alternatively, the two-parameter normal ogive model can be described using factor analytic terminology (Forero & Maydeu-Olivares, 2009), where the standard normal distribution is first divided by a single threshold, such that

$$y_{pi} = \begin{cases} 0 & if \ y^*_{pi} \leq \tau_p \\ 1 & if \ y^*_{pi} > \tau_p \end{cases} \tag{15.3}$$

where y_{pi} is the observed dichotomous response for individual i on item p, y_{pi}^* is the underlying response propensity for individual i for item p, and τ_p is the threshold for item p. The p underlying response propensities are then linearly related to the common factor, such that

$$y_{pi}^* = \lambda_p \cdot \eta_i + \epsilon_{pi} \qquad (15.4)$$

where λ_p is the factor loading for item p, η_i is the common factor score for individual i, and ϵ_{pi} is the unique factor score of individual i for item p. Typically, the variances of the unique factors are fixed at 1.

Figure 15.2 is a plot of three example item characteristic curves with different slope (factor loading) and threshold parameters based on the two-parameter normal ogive model. The slope (factor loading) parameters were set to 0.76, 0.47, and 1.29 (discrimination parameters from the two-parameter logistic model divided by 1.702) and the threshold parameters were set to –0.81, 0.00, and 1.68 (location parameters from two-parameter logistic model multiplied by λ_p; see Kamata & Bauer, 2008), respectively. The item characteristic curves presented in Figure 15.2 are highly similar to the item characteristic curves from the two-parameter logistic model in Figure 15.1 showing the similarity between the models. Multiplying the slope parameters from the normal ogive model by 1.702 yields the discrimination parameters from the logistic model that are most similar. Based on this specification of the normal ogive model, the threshold parameter refers to the point on the

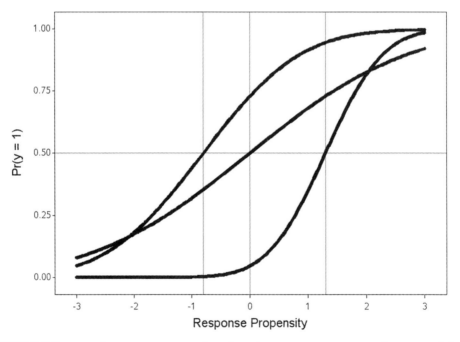

FIGURE 15.2. Item characteristic curves based on the two-parameter normal ogive model.

latent response propensity where an individual has a 50% chance of correctly responding to the item. The slope parameter references the rate of change when the latent response propensity equals the threshold. As before, items with greater slope parameters show greater changes in the probability for differences in the latent response propensity when η_i is near τ_p, indicating that the item can more easily discriminate between individuals with slightly different levels of the underlying ability.

Polytomous Item Response Models

There are several item response models appropriate for polytomously scored items (e.g., partial credit model [Masters, 1982]; generalized partial credit model [Muraki, 1992]; rating scale model; graded response model [Samejima, 1969]; modified graded response model). Here, we describe extensions of the two-parameter logistic and normal ogive models because these models can be fit with structural equation modeling programs (i.e., `Mplus` and `OpenMx`).

The graded response model (GRM; Samejima, 1969) is a straightforward extension of the two-parameter logistic model. The GRM can be written as

$$\Pr(y_{pi} \geq c \mid \theta_i,\, \alpha_p,\, \omega_{cp}) = \frac{\exp(\alpha_p(\theta_i - \omega_{cp}))}{1 + \exp(\alpha_p(\theta_i - \omega_{cp}))} \tag{15.5}$$

where $\Pr(y_{pi} \geq c \mid \theta_i,\, \alpha_p,\, \omega_{cp})$ is the probability of individual i responding in or above category c on item p conditional upon person and item parameters. As with the two-parameter logistic model, item parameters include α_p, a discrimination parameter for item p, and ω_{cp}, a location parameter separating category $c - 1$ from c on item p, and the only person parameter is θ_i, the latent trait for individual i.

Figure 15.3 contains operating characteristic curves (OCCs) for two five-category items with parameters $\alpha_1 = 2.4$, $\omega_{11} = -2.0$, $\omega_{21} = -1.0$, $\omega_{31} = 0.3$, and $\omega_{41} = 2.2$ for the first item and $\alpha_2 = 1.6$, $\omega_{12} = -2.3$, $\omega_{22} = -1.1$, $\omega_{32} = 0.0$, and $\omega_{42} = 1.1$ for the second item. The first curve in each plot represents the probability of responding in the second category or higher, the second curve represents the probability of responding in the third category or higher, and so on. First, we note that for each item the slopes of the curves are the same; however, the slopes of the curves can be different across items (items can be differentially related to the latent trait). Second, the spacing of the OCCs does not have to be the same within or between items, which brings up the idea that the spacing between response categories does not have to be equal. For example, the OCC in Figure 15.3a indicates that it takes a larger difference in the underlying latent trait to go from the fourth to the fifth response categories compared to the difference in the underlying latent trait to go from the second to third or the third to fourth response categories. Thus, the categories for this item are not equally spaced, whereas the categories are approximately equally spaced for the item described by the OCC in Figure 15.3b.

(a) High discrimination and unequal spacing

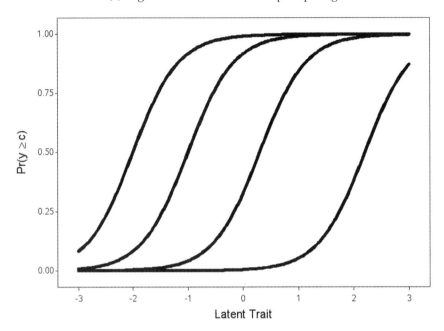

(b) Low discrimination and approximately equal spacing

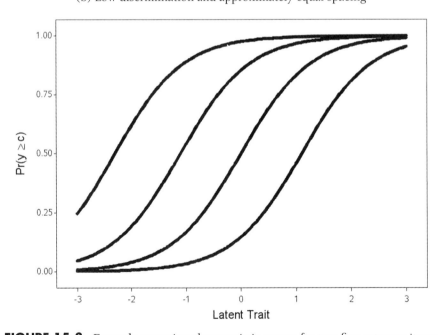

FIGURE 15.3. Example operating characteristic curves for two five-category items.

The probability of responding in each specific category ($\Pr(y_{pi} = c)$) is found through subtraction, such that

$$\Pr(y_{pi} = c|\theta_i, \alpha_p, \omega_{cp}) = \Pr(y_{pi} \geq c|\theta_i, \alpha_p, \omega_{cp}) - \Pr(y_{pi} \geq c + 1|\theta_i, \alpha_p, \omega_{c+1p}) \qquad (15.6)$$

where $\Pr(y_{pi} \geq c|\theta_i, \alpha_p, \omega_{cp})$ is the probability of responding in category c or higher and $\Pr(y_{pi} \geq c + 1|\theta_i, \alpha_p, \omega_{c+1p})$ is the probability of responding in category $c + 1$ or higher. Additionally, the probability of responding in the first category (category 0) is $1 - \Pr(y_{pi} \geq 1|\theta_i, \alpha_p, \omega_{1p})$. Plotting the probability of responding in each category yields category response curves (CRCs), and these are plotted for the two example items in Figure 15.4. From these figures it is easy to see which category is the most likely response for each level of the latent trait. Ideally, and as seen in these figures, each category is most likely at some point along the latent trait. We note that a higher discrimination parameter leads to more peaked curves. Thus, the curves in Figure 15.4a are more peaked than the curves in Figure 15.4b.

The GRM can also utilize the probit link following the two-parameter normal ogive model, which is common in the structural equation modeling framework. In much the same way, the graded response normal ogive model is a cumulative probit model tracking the probability of responding in or above specific categories. This model can be written as

$$\Pr(y_{pi} \geq c|\eta_i, \lambda_p, \tau_{cp}) = \Phi(\lambda_p \cdot \eta_i - \tau_{cp}) \qquad (15.7)$$

where Φ is the standard normal cumulative distribution function, τ_{cp} is the threshold parameter for category c of item p, λ_p is the slope parameter for item p, and η_i is the underlying latent variable measured for individual i. Equation 15.7 leads to OCCs describing the relation between the response propensity and the probability of responding in or above each category (similar to the GRM with the logit link).

As above, the graded response normal ogive model can be described using a factor analytic model where the standard normal distribution is first divided by multiple thresholds. For example, the thresholds for a five-category item would be written as

$$y_{pi} = \begin{cases} 0 & if \quad y_{pi}^* \leq \tau_{1p} \\ 1 & if \quad \tau_{1p} < y_{pi}^* \leq \tau_{2p} \\ 2 & if \quad \tau_{2p} < y_{pi}^* \leq \tau_{3p} \\ 3 & if \quad \tau_{3p} < y_{pi}^* \leq \tau_{4p} \\ 4 & if \quad y_{pi}^* > \tau_{4p} \end{cases} \qquad (15.8)$$

where y_{pi} is the observed dichotomous response for individual i on item p, y_{pi}^* is the underlying response propensity for individual i on item p, and τ_{1p} through τ_{4p} are the

(a) High discrimination and unequal spacing

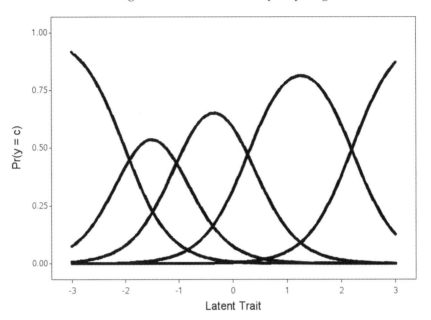

(b) Low discrimination and approximately equal spacing

FIGURE 15.4. Example category response curves for two five-category items.

four thresholds for item p, such that $\tau_{1p} < \tau_{2p} < \tau_{3p} < \tau_{4p}$. More generally, this can be specified as

$$y_{pi} = c \quad \text{if} \quad \tau_{cp} < y^*_{pi} < \tau_{c+1p} \tag{15.9}$$

where $\tau_{0p} = -\infty$ and $\tau_{mp} = +\infty$, where m is the number of response categories, which bounds the observed response to the available response categories (Forero & Maydeu-Olivares, 2009). As in the two-parameter normal ogive model, the p underlying response propensities are linearly related to the common factor such that

$$y^*_{pi} = \lambda_p \cdot \eta_i + \epsilon_{pi} \tag{15.10}$$

where λ_p is the factor loading for item p, η_i is the common factor score for individual i, and ϵ_{pi} is the unique factor score of individual i for item p. As with the two-parameter normal ogive model, the variances of the unique factors are typically fixed at 1.

Measurement Invariance in Item Response Models

The item response models described above can and have been extended to longitudinal data (McArdle et al., 2009; Ram et al., 2005). With longitudinal data, the latent trait or underlying response propensity is time dependent (i.e., θ_{ti}, y^*_{pti}, and η_{ti}) as are the item parameters (i.e., α_{pt} and ω_{cpt} from the logistic model and λ_{pt} and τ_{cpt} from the normal ogive model). A first question in longitudinal item response modeling, much like longitudinal factor analysis, is whether the response process is identical at each measurement occasion—specifically, whether or not the item parameters are invariant over measurement occasions. If item parameters are invariant, then changes in the latent trait or common factor can be modeled. If item parameters are not invariant, then the response process has changed and changes in the latent trait or common factor cannot be modeled without some accommodation (e.g., partial measurement invariance).

Differential item functioning, the study of measurement invariance with item response models, is most often conducted with a grouping variable (e.g., gender) to examine whether the groups have different probabilities of responding in each response category (e.g., probability of correctly answering the question), controlling for differences in the underlying latent trait or latent response propensity. The same idea is carried with longitudinal data. That is, controlling for differences in the underlying latent trait or common factor over time, the same probability of each response category should be observed. This is not to say that the probability of a given response must stay the same over time. It is that the probability should remain the same for individuals measured at different measurement occasions who have the same underlying latent trait or common factor score. These ideas relate directly to the invariance of the item characteristic curves over measurement occasion, which maps onto the invariance of the discrimination (factor loading) and location (threshold) parameters over time.

For simplicity, let's consider that the item is from a math test and that the latent trait represents math ability. In order to examine changes in true math ability, the item characteristic curves must be identical across measurement occasions. Thus, the item parameters must be invariant. If item parameters are different at each measurement occasion, then a person (or two different people) with the same math ability (e.g., 0) at the two measurement occasions would have a different probability of correctly answering the question. In this case, the way in which the item is related to the latent trait has changed, and if the properties of the item have changed, it is impossible to determine how the people changed. For example, Figures 15.5a and 15.5b contain item characteristic curves (based on a logistic response function) for the same item at two measurement occasions (e.g., time 1 and time 2). From these figures, it is easy to see that the probability of a correct response differs at the two measurement occasions for individuals who have the same underlying ability. That is, an individual with a low latent trait (< -0.60) has a higher probability of correctly answering the question at the second measurement occasion, whereas a person with a higher latent trait (> 0.60) has a higher probability of correctly answering the question at the first measurement occasion. Thus, the scales of the two latent traits cannot be directly compared because they relate to different response probabilities at each occasion and therefore, the changes in the latent trait cannot be examined.

Testing for measurement invariance in item response models can be carried out in several different ways (see Muthén, 1985; Muthén & Lehman, 1985; Woods, 2011). However, we take an approach that is similar to how measurement invariance was examined with the common factor model in Chapter 14. That is, in a first step, a configural invariance model is fit with no constraints on the item response parameters at each measurement occasion, and the latent traits or factor scores measured at each measurement occasion are allowed to covary. In the second step, the weak invariance model is fit where equality constraints are imposed on the discrimination ($\alpha_{pt} = \alpha_p$) or factor loading ($\lambda_{pt} = \lambda_p$) parameters, and the change in model fit is evaluated. In the third step, the strong invariance model is fit where the location ($\omega_{cpt} = \omega_{cp}$) or threshold ($\tau_{cpt} = \tau_{cp}$) parameters are constrained to be equal and the means of the latent traits or factor scores are estimated at all measurement occasions, except for the first measurement occasion where the mean is fixed, often at 0, for identification.

Item response models are often fit with more indicators than common factor models with continuous indicators simply because there are more items that are indicative of a latent construct than scores from surveys or tests (that are themselves often composed of multiple items). Given the number of items, it is unlikely that full measurement invariance will hold for all items. In these situations, partial measurement invariance, where item parameters are invariant for a collection of items and noninvariant for another collection of items, is a reasonable solution and should be examined. However, when full measurement invariance does not hold, but partial measurement invariance holds, it is important to note that the *changes* in the underlying latent trait are only based on the items for which measurement invariance holds even though items with noninvariant parameters aid the identification of the latent trait or factor score at each measurement occasion. Following this idea, it is also possible to have different (nonoverlapping) items measuring the latent construct at each measurement occasion as long as measurement invariance holds for the

(a) Time 1

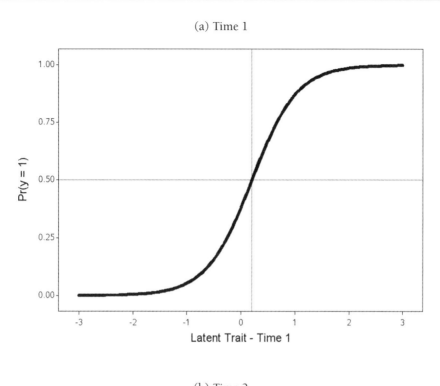

(b) Time 2

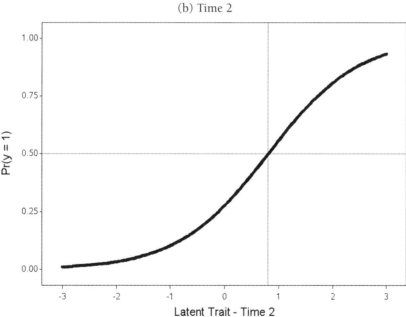

FIGURE 15.5. Example item characteristic curves for a single item at two occasions with different parameters.

overlapping items, which can also vary over measurement occasions (Edwards & Wirth, 2009; McArdle et al., 2009).

SECOND-ORDER GROWTH MODEL

Growth models can be built on item response models (when measurement invariance holds) by replacing the usual observed outcome with the latent trait or factor score measured at each occasion. For example and building on the logistic item response models, a linear growth model for the latent trait can be written as

$$\theta_{ti} = b_{1i} + b_{2i} \cdot t + d_{ti} \tag{15.11}$$

where θ_{ti} is the latent trait for individual i measured at time t, b_{1i} is the intercept or predicted value of θ_{ti} at $t = 0$ for individual i, b_{2i} is the linear slope for individual i relating individual changes in θ_{ti} with changes in t, the chosen time metric, and d_{ti} is the time-dependent disturbance term for individual i at time t. The intercept and linear slope are assumed to be normally distributed with means, variances, and a covariance. The mean of the intercept is fixed at 0 for identification (as in the second-order growth model based on the common factor model and growth models with ordinal indicators), but the mean of the linear slope is freely estimated as well as the intercept and slope variances and their covariance.

Working from the structural equation modeling framework and the probit model, the second-order growth model can be specified as

$$\eta_i = \Gamma\xi_i + \upsilon_i \tag{15.12}$$

where η_i is a $T \times 1$ vector of common factors for individual i, Γ is a $T \times R$ factor loading matrix defining the latent growth factors (e.g., intercept and linear slope in a linear growth model), ξ_i is an $R \times 1$ vector of second-order latent growth factors, and υ_i is a $T \times 1$ vector of latent variable disturbance terms. The second-order factors are assumed to follow a multivariate normal distribution, such that $\xi_i \sim MVN(\kappa, \Phi)$, where κ is an $R \times 1$ vector of latent variable means and Φ is an $R \times R$ covariance matrix. The first-order factor disturbances (υ_i) are assumed to follow a normal distribution, such that $\upsilon_i \sim N(0, \Psi)$, where Ψ is a $T \times T$ diagonal disturbance covariance matrix.

ILLUSTRATION

To illustrate the use of the longitudinal item response model and second-order growth model, we use a random sample of observations from the ECLS-K. In the fall and spring of kindergarten as well as the spring of first grade, teachers completed surveys regarding the children's behavior. Specifically, teachers were asked about the children's level of *interpersonal skills*, *self-control*, and *externalizing* behaviors using a four-point (1–4) scale where higher values indicated more of the behavior. The ECLS-K reports average ratings for each behavior, which we have rounded to the nearest whole number to show how item response models can be incorporated into the study of change. The variables include t1_sc, t1_intp, and t1_ext for the self-control, interpersonal skills, and externalizing behaviors, respectively, measured in the fall of kindergarten. Variables collected in the spring of kindergarten and first-grade begin with t2 and t4, respectively.

STRUCTURAL EQUATION MODELING IMPLEMENTATION

Longitudinal Item Factor Model

Mplus

The Mplus script for a *longitudinal item factor* model with strong factorial invariance fit to the behavior data is contained in Script 15.1. The script begins with the typical components of a title, datafile, and variable names. In the VARIABLE command, the CATEGORICAL option is included, and all variables in the analysis are listed here to treat the variables as being ordinal. The ANALYSIS command lists TYPE=MEANSTRUCTURE with ESTIMATOR=ML and LINK=PROBIT to use maximum likelihood estimation and the probit link.

The MODEL statement begins by defining three latent variables, eta_1, eta_2, and eta_3, which are the latent traits or factors (η_{ti}) measured in the fall of kindergarten, spring of kindergarten, and spring of first grade, respectively. The factor loadings to the self-control items (t1_sc, t2_sc, and t4_sc) are fixed at 1 for identification, and the remaining factor loadings are estimated but constrained to be equal over time by using common labels. For example, the three externalizing items (t1_ext, t2_ext, and t3_ext) have factor loadings that are labeled lambda_e. Next, variances and covariances are specified for the latent variables (eta_1 eta_2 eta_3; and eta_1 WITH eta_2 eta_3; and eta_2 WITH eta_3;), which are all freely estimated. The means of the latent variables are then specified. The mean of eta_1, the latent variable at the first occasion, is fixed at 0 for identification, but the means of eta_2 and eta_3 are estimated. Thresholds are then specified for all items and common labels are supplied for the same threshold for the same item across time. Thus, the first threshold for the self-control items (t1_sc$1, t2_sc$1, and t4_sc$1) are labeled tau_s1.

The configural and the weak invariance models can be specified by modifying this script. The weak invariance model is fit by removing the labels on the thresholds (tau_s1 through tau_e3) to allow them to be freely estimated and fixing the means of the latent variables to be 0 (e.g., [eta_1@0 eta_2@0 eta_3@0];). The configural invariance model is fit by additionally removing the labels associated with the factor loadings (lambda_i and lambda_e).

OpenMx

The OpenMx script for the longitudinal item factor model with strong factorial invariance is contained in Script 15.2. The script begins by defining the observed variables as ordinal using mxFactor and stating the response categories for each item. The model

Script 15.1. `Mplus` Script for the Longitudinal Item Factor Model with Strong Factorial Invariance

```
TITLE: Longitudinal Categorical Factor Model - Strong Invariance;
DATA: FILE= ECLS_Behavior.dat;
VARIABLE:
  NAMES = id t1_sc t1_intp t1_ext t2_sc t2_intp t2_ext
            t4_sc t4_intp t4_ext;
  MISSING = .;
  USEVAR = t1_sc t1_intp t1_ext t2_sc t2_intp t2_ext
            t4_sc t4_intp t4_ext;
  CATEGORICAL = t1_sc t1_intp t1_ext t2_sc t2_intp t2_ext
                t4_sc t4_intp t4_ext;

ANALYSIS: TYPE=MEANSTRUCTURE; ESTIMATOR=ML; LINK=PROBIT;

MODEL:
! Defining Latent Variables
  eta_1 BY t1_sc@1
          t1_intp (lambda_i)
          t1_ext  (lambda_e);
  eta_2 BY t2_sc@1
          t2_intp (lambda_i)
          t2_ext  (lambda_e);
  eta_3 BY t4_sc@1
          t4_intp (lambda_i)
          t4_ext  (lambda_e);

! Latent Variable Variances & Covariances
  eta_1 eta_2 eta_3;
  eta_1 WITH eta_2 eta_3;
  eta_2 WITH eta_3;

! Latent Variable Means
  [eta_1@0 eta_2*0 eta_3*0];

! Observed Variable Thresholds
  [t1_sc$1 t2_sc$1 t4_sc$1] (tau_s1);
  [t1_sc$2 t2_sc$2 t4_sc$2] (tau_s2);
  [t1_sc$3 t2_sc$3 t4_sc$3] (tau_s3);

  [t1_intp$1 t2_intp$1 t4_intp$1] (tau_i1);
  [t1_intp$2 t2_intp$2 t4_intp$2] (tau_i2);
  [t1_intp$3 t2_intp$3 t4_intp$3] (tau_i3);

  [t1_ext$1 t2_ext$1 t4_ext$1] (tau_e1);
  [t1_ext$2 t2_ext$2 t4_ext$2] (tau_e2);
  [t1_ext$3 t2_ext$3 t4_ext$3] (tau_e3);

OUTPUT: RESIDUAL STANDARDIZED;
```

Script 15.2. OpenMx Script for the Longitudinal Item Factor Model with Strong Factorial Invariance

```
(Converting Items of Interest to Categorical Variables
ecls$t1_sc    <- mxFactor(ecls$t1_sc,    levels=c(1,2,3,4))
ecls$t1_intp  <- mxFactor(ecls$t1_intp,  levels=c(1,2,3,4))
ecls$t1_ext   <- mxFactor(ecls$t1_ext,   levels=c(1,2,3,4))
ecls$t2_sc    <- mxFactor(ecls$t2_sc,    levels=c(1,2,3,4))
ecls$t2_intp  <- mxFactor(ecls$t2_intp,  levels=c(1,2,3,4))
ecls$t2_ext   <- mxFactor(ecls$t2_ext,   levels=c(1,2,3,4))
ecls$t4_sc    <- mxFactor(ecls$t4_sc,    levels=c(1,2,3,4))
ecls$t4_intp  <- mxFactor(ecls$t4_intp,  levels=c(1,2,3,4))
ecls$t4_ext   <- mxFactor(ecls$t4_ext,   levels=c(1,2,3,4))

# Strong Factorial Invariance Model
lirt.strong.omx <- mxModel('Strong Invariance Model, Path Specification',
type='RAM', mxData(observed=ecls, type='raw'),
manifestVars=c('t1_sc','t1_intp','t1_ext','t2_sc','t2_intp','t2_ext','t4_sc','t4_intp','t4_ext'),
latentVars=c('eta_1','eta_2','eta_3'),

# Residual Variances
mxPath(from=c('t1_sc','t1_intp','t1_ext','t2_sc','t2_intp','t2_ext','t4_sc','t4_intp','t4_ext'),
arrows=2, free=FALSE, values=1),

# Latent Variable Covariances
mxPath(from=c('eta_1','eta_2','eta_3'),
connect='unique.pairs', arrows=2,
free=TRUE, values=c(5,3,3,5,3,5),
labels=c('psi_11','psi_21','psi_31','psi_22','psi_32','psi_33')),
```

(continued)

383

Script 15.2. (Continued)

```
# Factor Loadings
mxPath(from='eta_1', to=c('t1_sc','t1_intp','t1_ext'),
  arrows=1, free=c(FALSE,TRUE,TRUE),
  values=c(1,1,-1), labels=c(NA,'lambda_i','lambda_e')),

mxPath(from='eta_2', to=c('t2_sc','t2_intp','t2_ext'),
  arrows=1, free=c(FALSE,TRUE,TRUE),
  values=c(1,1,-1), labels=c(NA,'lambda_i','lambda_e')),

mxPath(from='eta_3', to=c('t4_sc','t4_intp','t4_ext'),
  arrows=1, free=c(FALSE,TRUE,TRUE),
  values=c(1,1,-1), labels=c(NA,'lambda_i','lambda_e')),

# Latent Variable Means
mxPath(from='one', to=c('eta_2','eta_3'),
  arrows=1, free=TRUE,
  values=.5, labels=c('alpha_2','alpha_3')),

# Thresholds
mxThreshold(vars=c('t1_sc','t2_sc','t4_sc'), nThresh=3, free=TRUE, values=c(-7,-3,1),
  labels=c('tau_s1','tau_s2','tau_s3')),

mxThreshold(vars=c('t1_intp','t2_intp','t4_intp'), nThresh=3, free=TRUE, values=c(-5,-1,1),
  labels=c('tau_i1','tau_i2','tau_i3')),

mxThreshold(vars=c('t1_ext','t2_ext','t4_ext'), nThresh=3, free=TRUE, values=c(0,2,4),
  labels=c('tau_e1','tau_e2','tau_e3'))

) # Close Model
```

is then specified using `mxModel`. The `mxModel` command begins by stating the datafile along with the manifest and latent variables included in the model. A series of `mxPath` statements follow to specify the model components. The first `mxPath` statement is for the residual variances of the ordinal items. These two-headed arrows (`arrows=2`) begin `from` each observed variable and are fixed (`free=FALSE`) at 1 (`values=1`) following the specification of the normal ogive model. The next `mxPath` statement is for the latent variable variances and covariances. In the strong factorial invariance model, the latent variables (`eta_1`, `eta_2`, and `eta_3`) have estimated variances and estimated covariances. To do this, we use `connect='unique.pairs'` to specify all variances and covariances of the latent variables in a single `mxPath` statement.

The factor loadings for the three latent variables are then specified in the next three `mxPath` statements. For each factor, the factor loading to the self-control item (`t1_sc`, `t2_sc`, and `t4_sc`) is fixed at 1 for identification. The remaining factor loadings are freely estimated but constrained to be equal across time. For example, factor loadings for `t1_intp`, `t2_intp`, and `t4_intp` are constrained to be equal to one another, as are the factor loadings for `t1_ext`, `t2_ext`, and `t4_ext`. As with prior specifications, a common label is used for equality constraints (`labels=c(NA, 'lambda_i', 'lambda_e')`). Next, the latent variable means are specified. The means of the `eta_2` and `eta_3` factors are estimated because this is the strong invariance model and the thresholds (specified next) are constrained to be equal. The means are given starting values of 0 and labeled `alpha_2` and `alpha_3`. The thresholds are specified next using three `mxThreshold` statements. To simplify the `mxThreshold` statements, we have grouped them according to their respective variable. The first `mxThreshold` statement is for the three thresholds for the self-control items, which are freely estimated, given starting values, and labeled `tau_s1`, `tau_s2`, and `tau_s3`. Thus, the three thresholds for this item are constrained to be equal following the strong invariance model. Similar `mxThreshold` statements are then specified for the interpersonal skills and externalizing items. The model is then closed.

The above script can be modified to specify the configural and weak invariance models. For the weak invariance model, the means of the latent variables `eta_1`, `eta_2`, and `eta_3` are fixed to 0, and the equality constraints imposed on the threshold parameters are removed. Thus, in the `mxPath` statement for the latent variable means, `free` is set equal to `FALSE` and the labels are removed. In the `mxThreshold` statements, the labels are changed to be specific to the measurement occasion (e.g., `tau_s11` through `tau_s13` for the three thresholds for the self-control item measured at the first occasion). For the configural invariance model, the equality constraints on the factor loadings are also removed. Thus, in the `mxPath` statements for the factor loadings, the labels are made to be occasion-specific (e.g., `lambda_i1` and `lambda_e1` for the `t1_intp` and `t1_ext` items at the first measurement occasion).

Output

Output for the longitudinal item factor model with strong factorial invariance from `Mplus` and `OpenMx` is contained in Output 15.1 and 15.2, respectively. As a first point of

Output 15.1. `Mplus` Output for the Longitudinal Item Factor Model with Strong Factorial Invariance

MODEL RESULTS

		Estimate	S.E.	Est./S.E.	Two-Tailed P-Value
ETA_1	BY				
T1_SC		1.000	0.000	999.000	999.000
T1_INTP		0.614	0.029	20.969	0.000
T1_EXT		-0.462	0.022	-20.980	0.000
ETA_2	BY				
T2_SC		1.000	0.000	999.000	999.000
T2_INTP		0.614	0.029	20.969	0.000
T2_EXT		-0.462	0.022	-20.980	0.000
ETA_3	BY				
T4_SC		1.000	0.000	999.000	999.000
T4_INTP		0.614	0.029	20.969	0.000
T4_EXT		-0.462	0.022	-20.980	0.000
ETA_1	WITH				
ETA_2		5.727	0.465	12.328	0.000
ETA_3		3.827	0.326	11.727	0.000
ETA_2	WITH				
ETA_3		4.567	0.381	11.974	0.000
Means					
ETA_1		0.000	0.000	999.000	999.000
ETA_2		0.423	0.049	8.634	0.000
ETA_3		0.306	0.058	5.299	0.000
Thresholds					
T1_SC$1		-7.813	0.308	-25.400	0.000
T1_SC$2		-2.967	0.116	-25.675	0.000
T1_SC$3		0.926	0.063	14.738	0.000
T1_INTP$1		-4.871	0.112	-43.372	0.000
T1_INTP$2		-1.514	0.042	-36.411	0.000
T1_INTP$3		1.090	0.039	27.749	0.000
T1_EIT$1		-0.167	0.027	-6.169	0.000
T1_EIT$2		2.011	0.040	50.837	0.000
T1_EIT$3		3.374	0.062	54.551	0.000
T2_SC$1		-7.813	0.308	-25.400	0.000
T2_SC$2		-2.967	0.116	-25.675	0.000
T2_SC$3		0.926	0.063	14.738	0.000
T2_INTP$1		-4.871	0.112	-43.372	0.000
T2_INTP$2		-1.514	0.042	-36.411	0.000
T2_INTP$3		1.090	0.039	27.749	0.000
T2_EXT$1		-0.167	0.027	-6.169	0.000
T2_EXT$2		2.011	0.040	50.837	0.000
T2_EXT$3		3.374	0.062	54.551	0.000
T4_SC$1		-7.813	0.308	-25.400	0.000
T4_SC$2		-2.967	0.116	-25.675	0.000
T4_SC$3		0.926	0.063	14.738	0.000
T4_INTP$1		-4.871	0.112	-43.372	0.000
T4_INTP$2		-1.514	0.042	-36.411	0.000

```
        T4_INTP$3      1.090      0.039     27.749         0.000
        T4_EXT$1      -0.167      0.027     -6.169         0.000
        T4_EXT$2       2.011      0.040     50.837         0.000
        T4_EXT$3       3.374      0.062     54.551         0.000
   Variances
        ETA_1          6.890      0.584     11.794         0.000
        ETA_2          7.928      0.669     11.850         0.000
        ETA_3          8.001      0.666     12.016         0.000
```

Output 15.2. OpenMx Output for the Longitudinal Item Factor Model with Strong Factorial Invariance

```
free parameters:
   name         matrix       row        col      Estimate      Std.Error
1  lambda_i       A       t1_intp     eta_1      0.6122294     0.010915174
2  lambda_e       A       t1_ext      eta_1     -0.4600890     0.005170421
3  psi_11         S       eta_1       eta_1      6.9290607     0.015976345
4  psi_21         S       eta_1       eta_2      5.7565299     0.009902889
5  psi_22         S       eta_2       eta_2      7.9742622     0.030190101
6  psi_31         S       eta_1       eta_3      3.8449325     0.005789941
7  psi_32         S       eta_2       eta_3      4.5955841     0.010414252
8  psi_33         S       eta_3       eta_3      8.0496592     0.016391002
9  alpha_2        M       1           eta_2      0.4238295     0.002193305
10 alpha_3        M       1           eta_3      0.3072734     0.002269799
11 tau_s1   Thresholds    1           t1_sc     -7.8299435     0.151922879
12 tau_s2   Thresholds    2           t1_sc     -2.9724856     0.007081997
13 tau_s3   Thresholds    3           t1_sc      0.9292774     0.010708992
14 tau_i1   Thresholds    1           t1_intp   -4.8688107     0.094284898
15 tau_i2   Thresholds    2           t1_intp   -1.5128191     0.003817751
16 tau_i3   Thresholds    3           t1_intp    1.0899793     0.004588982
17 tau_e1   Thresholds    1           t1_ext    -0.1674869     0.006046656
18 tau_e2   Thresholds    2           t1_ext     2.0100857     0.003166900
19 tau_e3   Thresholds    3           t1_ext     3.3727726     0.044078803
```

discussion, we focus on the fit of this model along with the fits of the configural and weak invariance models. The −2 log likelihood (−2LL) for the strong invariance model was 49,114 (reported in OpenMx or 49,113 [−2 · −24556.340] reported in Mplus). The −2LLs for the configural and weak invariance models were 48,921 and 48,926, respectively. Thus, the move from configural to weak invariance did not lead to a significant increase in model misfit (Δ −2LL = 5 and Δparameters = 4; $\chi^2(4) = 5$, $p = .29$). However, the move from weak to strong invariance resulted in a significant degradation of model fit (Δ −2LL = 188 and Δparameters = 16; $\chi^2(16) = 188$, $p < .01$). The significant decrease in model fit was partly due to the large sample size and partly due to the degree of noninvariance. With maximum likelihood estimation, the global and absolute fit indices are unavailable, which makes it difficult to determine how well or poorly the strong invariance model fit the data (or for that matter, how any of these models fit). As an alternative, we estimated the strong invariance model with weighted least squares in Mplus, which allows for the estimation of global fit indices. When fitting this model, the TLI equaled 0.977, the CFI was 0.971, and the RMSEA was 0.091, which supports that notion that the strong invariance model fit the data adequately. Therefore, we move onto parameter interpretation.

Parameter estimates include the factor loadings for interpersonal skills (t1_intp, t2_intp, and t4_intp) and externalizing behavior (t1_ext, t2_ext, and t4_ext), category thresholds for each item, latent variable variances and covariances, and latent variable means for eta_2 and eta_3. The factor loadings for interpersonal skills (ETA_1 BY T1_INTP; lambda_i) were constrained to be equal and estimated to be 0.61. Similarly, the factor loadings for externalizing behavior (ETA_1 BY T1_EXT; lambda_e) were constrained to be equal and estimated to be –0.46. Given the factor loading pattern, higher factor scores indicate more positive behaviors (self-control and interpersonal skills) and less negative behaviors (externalizing behavior). The standardized factor loadings (reported by Mplus) were all greater than |0.77|, indicating the items were strongly associated with their respective latent variable. We note that the equality constraint is imposed on the *unstandardized* factor loadings. Thus, the standardized factor loadings do, in fact, vary over time.

Next, we focus on the threshold parameters. As with the factor loadings, threshold parameters were constrained to be equal over time. For example, estimates of the three thresholds for the self-control (Thresholds for T1_SC$1 through T1_SC$3; tau_s1 through tau_s3) items were –7.81, –2.97, and 0.93 at each measurement occasion. Similarly, the thresholds for interpersonal skills were –4.87, –1.51, and 1.09, and the thresholds for externalizing behavior were –0.17, 2.01, and 3.37. As discussed above, the threshold parameters divide the underlying response propensity, but in this model the underlying response propensity is not in a standard metric (not standard normal). Thus, interpreting these coefficients in isolation is difficult. We discuss using these parameters in conjunction with the factor loading to derive the predicted proportion of the sample responding in each category after discussing parameter estimates. Since the factor loadings and thresholds were invariant with respect to time, the measurement scale remained constant over time, which allows for changes in response patterns to be purely related to changes in the common factor. The mean of the common factor at the first measurement occasion was fixed at 0 for identification, but the means of the common factor at the subsequent measurement occasions were estimated. The estimated means of eta_2 and eta_3 were 0.42 (Means of ETA_2; alpha_2) and 0.31 (Means of ETA_3; alpha_3) and significantly different from 0, indicating that the mean of the latent variable significantly changed from the first to the second and from the first to the third measurement occasion. The variances of the latent variables were freely estimated and allowed to vary over time. The variances of the three latent variables were 6.89 (Variances of ETA_1; psi_11), 7.93 (Variances of ETA_2; psi_22), and 8.00 (Variances of ETA_3; psi_33) for the first, second, and third measurement occasions, respectively. Therefore, it appeared that the amount of between–person differences in behavior increased over time. The final estimates include the latent variable covariances. The covariance between the common factors at the first and second occasions was 5.73 ($r = .78$; ETA_1 WITH ETA_2; psi_21); the covariance between the first and third occasions was 3.83 ($r = .52$; ETA_1 WITH ETA_3; psi_31); and the covariance between the second and third occasions was 4.57 ($r = .57$; ETA_2 WITH ETA_3; psi_32). The covariances were all positive, significantly different from zero, and strong (correlations were all greater than .50) indicating that individual differences in behavior measured by teachers over time were relatively stable.

The parameters of the model can be utilized to highlight the predicted proportion of the sample responding in each category at each measurement occasion. In Chapter 13 we discussed how estimated proportions can be calculated based on the thresholds and the mean and variance of the underlying latent trait or response propensity at each measurement occasion. The same calculations can be made here with a slight variation. Specifically, the factor loading needs to be taken into account when calculating the variance (or standard deviation) and mean of the response propensity. The variance of the response propensity is equal to the variance of the common factor multiplied by the square of the respective factor loading plus 1 (the residual variance of the probit model) and the mean of the response propensity is equal to the mean of the common factor multiplied by the factor loading. For example, the variance of the response propensity for the externalizing behavior item at the first measurement occasion is the variance of eta_1 (6.89) multiplied by the square of the factor loading (-0.46^2) plus 1, which equals 2.47. The mean of the response propensity for t1_ext is the mean of eta_1 (0) multiplied by the factor loading (-0.46), which equals 0.00. This mean and variance can then be used in conjunction with the thresholds to estimate the expected proportion of the sample responding in each category for each item.

To present this information in a visual format, we embed the distribution of the common factor at each measurement occasion over the CRC for the externalizing behavior item in Figure 15.6. The distribution of the common factors are dashed lines, and the CRC is represented by the solid lines. First, we note that the factor loading for externalizing behavior was negative, which translates into the CRC for the first category appearing on the right-hand side of the figure (higher latent trait corresponds with higher probabilities of lower scores). From this figure, we can determine that the majority of the sample at the first occasion was expected to be rated in the first two categories (dashed distribution on the left) because most of the distribution corresponds with high probabilities for category 1 and 2. This plot also highlights the similarity of distributions for the common factor at the second and third occasions (two dashed distributions to the right), which are nearly coincident.

Second-Order Growth Model

M*plus*

The MODEL statement from the M*plus* script for the second-order linear growth model with a first-order item factor model with strong measurement invariance is contained in Script 15.3. The MODEL statement begins with defining the first-order latent variables. The first-order factors (eta_1, eta_2, and eta_3) are indicated by the behavior rating items collected at each measurement occasion. Common labels are applied to the factor loadings to constrain them to be equal across time. Each latent variable is identified by fixing the factor loading to the self-control item at each measurement occasion (t1_sc, t2_sc, and t4_sc) to 1. First-order factor variances and covariances are then specified. The covariances among the first-order factors are fixed at 0 because these associations are

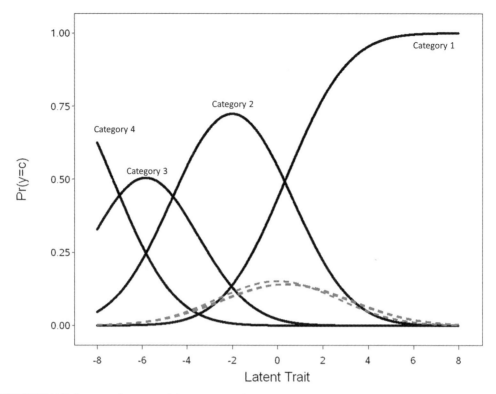

FIGURE 15.6. Distributions of the common factor and response characteristic curves for externalizing behavior.

expected to come from the second-order growth factors. The variances of the first-order factors are constrained to be equal because constraining the residual variances to be equal across time is typical in (first-order) growth models. Next, the first-order factor means and thresholds are specified. The first-order factor means are set equal to 0 because changes in the first-order latent variable means are modeled by the second-order growth factors. The three thresholds per item are specified with equality constraints across time as in the strong invariance model presented above.

In the final part of the script, a linear growth model is specified for the first-order factors. Specifically, the latent variable intercept, `xi_1`, is indicated BY the three first-order factors with factor loadings equal to 1, and the linear slope, `xi_2`, is indicated BY the three first-order factors with factor loadings that change linearly with time. The factor loading to `eta_1` is fixed at 0 to center the intercept at the first measurement occasion (fall of kindergarten), the factor loading to `eta_2` is fixed at 1, and the factor loading to `eta_3` is fixed at 3. The linear slope represents the constant rate of change over a 6-month period. Next, the variances of the intercept and slope are specified by listing the variable names, and their covariance is specified using the WITH statement. Finally, the means of the intercept and slope are specified. The mean of the latent variable intercept is fixed at 0 for identification, and the mean of the slope is freely estimated.

Script 15.3. *Mplus* Script for the Second–Order Growth Model

```
MODEL:
! First-Order Latent Factors
    eta_1 BY t1_sc@1
            t1_intp (lambda_i)
            t1_ext  (lambda_e);
    eta_2 BY t2_sc@1
            t2_intp (lambda_i)
            t2_ext  (lambda_e);
    eta_3 BY t4_sc@1
            t4_intp (lambda_i)
            t4_ext  (lambda_e);

! First-Order Latent Variable Variances & Covariances
    eta_1 eta_2 eta_3 (psi);
    eta_1 WITH eta_2@0 eta_3@0;
    eta_2 WITH eta_3@0;

! First-Order Latent Variable Means
    [eta_1@0 eta_2@0 eta_3@0];

! Observed Variable Thresholds
    [t1_sc$1 t2_sc$1 t4_sc$1] (tau_s1);
    [t1_sc$2 t2_sc$2 t4_sc$2] (tau_s2);
    [t1_sc$3 t2_sc$3 t4_sc$3] (tau_s3);

    [t1_intp$1 t2_intp$1 t4_intp$1] (tau_i1);
    [t1_intp$2 t2_intp$2 t4_intp$2] (tau_i2);
    [t1_intp$3 t2_intp$3 t4_intp$3] (tau_i3);

    [t1_ext$1 t2_ext$1 t4_ext$1] (tau_e1);
    [t1_ext$2 t2_ext$2 t4_ext$2] (tau_e2);
    [t1_ext$3 t2_ext$3 t4_ext$3] (tau_e3);

! Linear Growth Model
    xi_1 BY eta_1@1 eta_2@1 eta_3@1;
    xi_2 BY eta_1@0 eta_2@1 eta_3@3;
    xi_1 xi_2;
    xi_1 WITH xi_2;
    [xi_1@0 xi_2];
```

OpenMx

The OpenMx script to fit the second-order linear growth model built on the longitudinal item factor model is contained in Script 15.4. The script begins by calling the ecls data, listing the manifest variables in manifestVars (which are the categorical versions of the variables; see Script 15.2), and the latent variables in latentVars. The latent variables include both the first-order factors (eta_1 through eta_3) and the second-order factors (xi_1 and xi_2). The model is then specified with a series of mxPath statements along with mxThreshold statements for the item thresholds.

Script 15.4. OpenMx Script for the Second-Order Growth Model

```
lirt.growth.omx <- mxModel('Second Order Growth Model, Path Specification', type='RAM',
    mxData(observed=ecls, type='raw'),
    manifestVars=c('t1_sc','t1_intp','t1_ext','t2_sc','t2_intp','t2_ext','t4_sc','t4_intp','t4_ext'),
    latentVars=c('eta_1','eta_2','eta_3','xi_1','xi_2'),

# Residual Variances
    mxPath(from=c('t1_sc','t1_intp','t1_ext','t2_sc','t2_intp','t2_ext','t4_sc','t4_intp','t4_ext'),
        arrows=2, free=FALSE, values=1),

# First-Order Latent Variable Variances
    mxPath(from=c('eta_1','eta_2','eta_3'), arrows=2, free=TRUE, values=1, labels='psi'),

# Factor Loadings
    mxPath(from='eta_1', to=c('t1_sc','t1_intp','t1_ext'), arrows=1, free=c(FALSE,TRUE,TRUE),
        values=c(1,1,-1), labels=c(NA,'lambda_i','lambda_e')),

    mxPath(from='eta_2', to=c('t2_sc','t2_intp','t2_ext'), arrows=1, free=c(FALSE,TRUE,TRUE),
        values=c(1,1,-1), labels=c(NA,'lambda_i','lambda_e')),

    mxPath(from='eta_3', to=c('t4_sc','t4_intp','t4_ext'), arrows=1, free=c(FALSE,TRUE,TRUE),
        values=c(1,1,-1), labels=c(NA,'lambda_i','lambda_e')),
```

392

```
# Thresholds
mxThreshold(vars=c('t1_sc','t2_sc','t4_sc'), nThresh=3, free=TRUE, values=c(-7,-2,0),
    labels=c('tau_s1','tau_s2','tau_s3')),

mxThreshold(vars=c('t1_intp','t2_intp','t4_intp'), nThresh=3, free=TRUE, values=c(-5,-2,0),
    labels=c('tau_i1','tau_i2','tau_i3')),

mxThreshold(vars=c('t1_ext','t2_ext','t4_ext'), nThresh=3, free=TRUE, values=c(0,2,4),
    labels=c('tau_e1','tau_e2','tau_e3')),

# Growth Model Factor Loadings
mxPath(from='xi_1', to=c('eta_1','eta_2','eta_3'), arrows=1, free=FALSE, values=1),

mxPath(from='xi_2', to=c('eta_1','eta_2','eta_3'), arrows=1, free=FALSE, values=c(0,1,3)),

# Latent Variable Covariances
mxPath(from=c('xi_1','xi_2'), connect='unique.pairs', arrows=2, free=TRUE, values=c(1,0,1),
    labels=c('phi_11','phi_21','phi_22')),

# Latent Variable Means
mxPath(from='one', to='xi_2', arrows=1, free=TRUE, values=.5, labels='kappa_2')

) # Close Model
```

The first mxPath statement specifies the residual variances of the polytomous variables measured at each time point. These paths are two-headed arrows and fixed at 1 following the typical specification of the probit model. Next, the latent variable variances for the first-order latent variables are specified (first-order covariances are accounted for by the second-order growth model). In this mxPath statement, the first-order latent variables are listed as the originating variables; the paths are two-headed arrows, given starting values of 1, and labeled psi to constrain them to be equal over time. The factor loadings are then specified in the next three mxPath statements. These one-headed paths originate from each first-order latent variable and go to the items measured at the same occasion. The factor loadings to the self-control items (t1_sc, t2_sc, and t4_sc) are fixed at 1, whereas the factor loadings to the interpersonal skills and externalizing behavior are estimated, but constrained to be equal over time using common labels (lambda_i for interpersonal skills and lambda_e for externalizing behaviors). The thresholds for the items are then specified with three mxThreshold statements. As with the strong invariance script, the mxThreshold statements are used to define the thresholds for self-control, interpersonal skills, and externalizing behaviors, and the thresholds are held invariant across time. This completes the specification of the first-order (measurement) model.

The second-order growth model is specified with four mxPath statements. First, the factor loadings for the latent variable intercept and slope are specified. The factor loadings for the latent variable intercept orginate at xi_1, go to the first-order factors (eta_1 through eta_3), and are fixed at 1. The factor loadings for the linear slope originate at xi_2, go to the first-order factors, and are fixed values that change linearly with time beginning with 0 to center the intercept at the first measurement occasion (fall of kindergarten). Next, the paths for the second-order latent variable covariance matrix are specified by listing xi_1 and xi_2 as the originating variables and using connect= 'unique.pairs'. These paths are freely estimated and given starting values and labels. The final mxPath statement is for the mean of the slope. This one-headed path goes from the constant (one) to xi_2, is freely estimated, given a starting value of .5, and labeled kappa_2. The model is then closed.

Output

Mplus and OpenMx output from fitting the second-order growth model with a first-order item factor model with strong measurement invariance is contained in Output 15.3 and 15.4, respectively. As in Chapter 14, a first question is whether the second-order growth model fit significantly worse than the strong invariance model. The difference in the $-2LL$ was 132 and the difference in the number of estimated parameters was 3, which indicates that the second-order growth model fit significantly worse than the strong invariance model. However, given our sample size, we have the power to detect minor changes in model misfit. Thus, we fit the second-order growth model using ESTIMATOR=WLSMV in Mplus and found that the model adequately accounted for the observed data, with a TLI of 0.974, a CFI of 0.966, and an RMSEA of 0.095. We therefore discuss the model parameters.

Output 15.3. `Mplus` Output for the Second–Order Growth Model

	Estimate	S.E.	Est./S.E.	Two-Tailed P-Value
ETA_1 BY				
T1_SC	1.000	0.000	999.000	999.000
T1_INTP	0.600	0.029	20.661	0.000
T1_EXT	-0.456	0.022	-20.475	0.000
ETA_2 BY				
T2_SC	1.000	0.000	999.000	999.000
T2_INTP	0.600	0.029	20.661	0.000
T2_EXT	-0.456	0.022	-20.475	0.000
ETA_3 BY				
T4_SC	1.000	0.000	999.000	999.000
T4_INTP	0.600	0.029	20.661	0.000
T4_EXT	-0.456	0.022	-20.475	0.000
XI_1 BY				
ETA_1	1.000	0.000	999.000	999.000
ETA_2	1.000	0.000	999.000	999.000
ETA_3	1.000	0.000	999.000	999.000
XI_2 BY				
ETA_1	0.000	0.000	999.000	999.000
ETA_2	1.000	0.000	999.000	999.000
ETA_3	3.000	0.000	999.000	999.000
XI_1 WITH				
XI_2	-0.742	0.096	-7.767	0.000
Means				
XI_1	0.000	0.000	999.000	999.000
XI_2	0.066	0.020	3.359	0.001
Thresholds				
T1_SC$1	-8.094	0.325	-24.925	0.000
T1_SC$2	-3.163	0.125	-25.297	0.000
T1_SC$3	0.781	0.061	12.765	0.000
T1_INTP$1	-4.942	0.113	-43.728	0.000
T1_INTP$2	-1.599	0.043	-37.598	0.000
T1_INTP$3	0.986	0.038	26.151	0.000
T1_EXT$1	-0.095	0.027	-3.501	0.000
T1_EXT$2	2.087	0.040	51.901	0.000
T1_EXT$3	3.453	0.063	55.150	0.000
T2_SC$1	-8.094	0.325	-24.925	0.000
T2_SC$2	-3.163	0.125	-25.297	0.000
T2_SC$3	0.781	0.061	12.765	0.000
T2_INTP$1	-4.942	0.113	-43.728	0.000
T2_INTP$2	-1.599	0.043	-37.598	0.000
T2_INTP$3	0.986	0.038	26.151	0.000
T2_EXT$1	-0.095	0.027	-3.501	0.000
T2_EXT$2	2.087	0.040	51.901	0.000
T2_EXT$3	3.453	0.063	55.150	0.000
T4_SC$1	-8.094	0.325	-24.925	0.000
T4_SC$2	-3.163	0.125	-25.297	0.000
T4_SC$3	0.781	0.061	12.765	0.000
T4_INTP$1	-4.942	0.113	-43.728	0.000

(continued)

Output 15.3. (*Continued*)

T4_INTP$2	-1.599	0.043	-37.598	0.000
T4_INTP$3	0.986	0.038	26.151	0.000
T4_EXT$1	-0.095	0.027	-3.501	0.000
T4_EXT$2	2.087	0.040	51.901	0.000
T4_EXT$3	3.453	0.063	55.150	0.000
Variances				
XI_1	6.312	0.537	11.756	0.000
XI_2	0.491	0.054	9.171	0.000
Residual Variances				
ETA_1	1.889	0.196	9.640	0.000
ETA_2	1.889	0.196	9.640	0.000
ETA_3	1.889	0.196	9.640	0.000

Output 15.4. OpenMx Output for the Second–Order Growth Model

```
free parameters:
        name       matrix        row        col      Estimate      Std.Error
1    lambda_i           A    t1_intp      eta_1    0.59883090   0.0002106842
2    lambda_e           A     t1_ext      eta_1   -0.45578587   0.0001918320
3         psi           S      eta_1      eta_1    1.89694401   0.0086517445
4      phi_11           S       xi_1       xi_1    6.32224295   0.0008333518
5      phi_21           S       xi_1       xi_2   -0.74209761   0.0002285194
6      phi_22           S       xi_2       xi_2    0.49229792   0.0001967007
7     kappa_2           M          1       xi_2    0.06652350   0.0001405757
8      tau_s1  Thresholds          1      t1_sc   -8.10276182   0.1473712963
9      tau_s2  Thresholds          2      t1_sc   -3.16654612   0.0367364219
10     tau_s3  Thresholds          3      t1_sc    0.78273372   0.0278449740
11     tau_i1  Thresholds          1    t1_intp   -4.94119753   0.0006513041
12     tau_i2  Thresholds          2    t1_intp   -1.59804869   0.0002106411
13     tau_i3  Thresholds          3    t1_intp    0.98559336   0.0002604351
14     tau_e1  Thresholds          1     t1_ext   -0.09524348   0.0001443622
15     tau_e2  Thresholds          2     t1_ext    2.08714471   0.0002751055
16     tau_e3  Thresholds          3     t1_ext    3.45291148   0.0426773544
```

We briefly discuss aspects of the measurement model first before discussing model parameters associated with change. Factor loadings, which were constrained to be equal over time, were estimated to be 0.60 for interpersonal skills (ETA_1 BY T1_INTP; lambda_i) and –0.46 for externalizing behavior (ETA_1 BY T1_EXT; lambda_e). The magnitude of these estimates was nearly identical to the estimates from the strong invariance model. Similarly, estimates of the threshold parameters, which were also constrained to be equal over time, were close in magnitude to the estimates from the strong invariance model. Their magnitudes highlight how few participants were rated using the low categories for the interpersonal skills and self–control items and in the high categories for the externalizing behavior item.

Turning to the estimates of change in behavior, we find that the mean of the linear slope was 0.07 (Mean of XI_2; kappa_2), which was positive and significantly different from zero highlighting how children's positive behaviors were expected to grow from the beginning of kindergarten to the spring of first grade, on average. The variance of the latent variable intercept was 6.31 (`Variance of XI_1; phi_11`) and represents the magnitude of between-child differences in behavior skills in the fall of kindergarten. The variance of the slope was 0.49 and significantly different from zero, indicating that children differed in how their behavior skills changed from kindergarten through first grade. The intercept-slope covariance was −0.74 (`XI_1 WITH XI_2; phi_21`), indicating that children who had poorer behavior in the fall of kindergarten tended to show greater increases in their positive behaviors from kindergarten through first grade. Finally, the disturbance variance of the latent factor was 1.89 (`Residual Variance of ETA_1; psi`) and represents true variability in the first-order factors that was unique from the growth process.

When fitting second-order models, such as these, the estimates of growth can be difficult to interpret, especially because the mean of the intercept was fixed at 0 (for identification, see also Koran & Hancock, 2010). To understand the estimates from such models, we begin by examining the threshold parameters, which provide information regarding the frequency of responses in the fall of kindergarten because the mean of the intercept was fixed at 0. Given the magnitudes of the threshold parameters, it is clear that, in the fall of kindergarten, self-control and interpersonal skills were highly rated, with the majority of responses falling in the highest two categories, and externalizing behaviors had low ratings, with most responses in the first two categories. Based on the growth model, the mean of η_i was predicted to increase slightly (0.07 per 1/2 year) and the standard deviation of η_i was predicted to first decrease slightly (2.51 at the fall of kindergarten to 2.31 at the spring of kindergarten) and then increase slightly (2.51 at the spring of first grade). The magnitude of mean change can be difficult to quantify because we are modeling change in an unobserved entity. One way to contextualize change is by comparing the mean change to the standard deviation of the latent variable intercept. Compared to the standard deviation of the latent variable intercept, the mean change was quite small, and this can be seen in Figure 15.7 where approximate distributions of η_i based on the growth model are overlaid on the thresholds for the interpersonal skills items (as an example). From this figure, it can be seen that the relative frequencies of each response category did not change much from the fall of kindergarten (0 on the x-axis) to the spring of first grade (3 on the x-axis).

IMPORTANT CONSIDERATIONS

Jointly estimating the second-order growth model with a first-order item factor model presented here is often seen as optimal (Grimm et al., 2013) because the scores on the construct of interest do not have to be estimated. However, there are times when this approach is untenable. That is, the item factor model fit here had relatively few items at each measurement occasion, and there were few measurement occasions. Having few items at each measurement occasion and few measurement occasions makes it possible to estimate such models in the structural equation modeling framework, but adding more

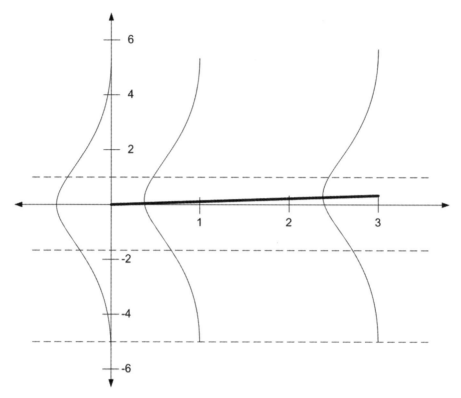

FIGURE 15.7. Approximate distributions of η_i based on the linear growth model plotted against the thresholds for interpersonal skills.

measurement occasions and/or items per measurement occasion will likely lead to non-convergence. In these situations, a sequential modeling strategy (e.g., Curran et al., 2008; McArdle et al., 2009) where factor (ability) scores are estimated first and then treated as observed data in subsequent analyses is a viable alternative.

There are multiple approaches to using item response models to estimate latent variable scores prior to fitting longitudinal (growth) models. The different approaches arise from the question of how to deal with the clustered nature of the longitudinal item response data. The most common approach is to randomly select a measurement occasion for each individual to create a *calibration* sample. An item response model is fit to the calibration sample, item parameters are saved, and then data from all measurement occasions are scored utilizing the previously saved item parameters (see Curran et al., 2008, and Grimm et al., 2013, for examples). This approach is common because each person appears in the calibration sample once (nesting of individuals over time is avoided), data from all measurement occasions are sampled (if items change over time, item parameters from all items can be estimated), and scoring item data using previously estimated item parameters is common.

A second approach is to fit an item response model to all of the longitudinal item-level data without accounting for the clustered nature of the data and estimate factor scores for all persons at each measurement occasion in this single model run (e.g., McArdle et al., 2009). Technically, this model is misspecified because the data are not independently and identically distributed because the same participants appear in the dataset multiple times. However, this approach is able to generate scores for all participants at all occasions and is a viable approach when data are largely incomplete due to the length of the longitudinal study and/or differences in the measurement instruments used to measure the construct (e.g., McArdle et al., 2009).

A third approach is to fit a multilevel item response model to the longitudinal item-level data and estimate factor scores for all persons at all measurement occasions in a single run. The benefit of this approach is that the model accounts for the clustered nature of the observations. Additionally, aspects of measurement invariance can be studied (comparing the within-cluster factor structure to the between-cluster factor structure). However, this approach is not without limitations. The biggest limitation is that the estimated scores, in addition to being based on an individual's item response pattern (as expected), are partially based on the person's individual distribution of factor scores over time. Lastly, we note that we focused on fitting item factor models to binary and ordinal items, but this general approach to modeling is possible with a combination of continuous, count, ordinal, nominal, and binary items (see Bauer & Hussong, 2009; Muthén, 1984, 2001).

MOVING FORWARD

This chapter brings our discussion of modeling change in latent entities to a close. The next collection of chapters focuses on modeling change with latent change (difference) scores and modeling nonlinear change with a focus on the individual rate of change and how the individual rate of change varies over time within and between individuals. We note that the latent variable models discussed in this section can be combined with the modeling frameworks discussed subsequently (see Ferrer, Balluerka, & Widaman, 2008; Grimm, 2006).

# Part V

Latent Change Scores as a Framework for Studying Change

16

Introduction to Latent Change Score Modeling

Latent change score models, originally referred to as latent difference score models (McArdle, 2001, 2009; McArdle & Hamagami, 2001), were developed to study change and time-sequential associations within and between constructs or to study change and time-sequential associations across individuals (e.g., depression for husbands and wives; see McArdle, Hamagami, Kadlec, & Fisher, 2007). Latent change score models led to a revolution in the way multivariate longitudinal data were jointly analyzed by combining aspects of growth models (Meredith & Tisak, 1990) and autoregressive cross-lag models (Jöreskog, 1970) for longitudinal panel data. Here, we consider latent change score modeling as a *framework* (as opposed to a model) for studying change—both a statistical and a theoretical framework.

From a theory standpoint, latent change score models make *time-dependent change* the outcome of interest as opposed to the observed scores, which represent status (or location) at a given point in time. This simple shift to studying time-dependent change as opposed to time-dependent states leads to ideas of dynamical systems, difference equations, and differential equations. Furthermore, developmental researchers are most interested in understanding within-person change, and the latent change score models emphasize within-person change, so there is an appropriate match between this major goal of developmental researchers and the statistical modeling framework. Statistically, the growth models discussed throughout this book can be specified in the latent change score framework (see Grimm, Zhang, et al., 2013). Additionally, the autoregressive cross-lag model, commonly fit to study time-sequential associations in multivariate panel data, can be specified in the latent change score framework. Lastly, several new models emerge from within this framework (see McArdle, 2001; McArdle & Hamagami, 2001; McArdle & Grimm, 2010).

GENERAL MODEL SPECIFICATION

The specification of latent change score models begins with ideas from classical test theory. Following classical test theory, an individual's observed score at a specific point in time can be thought of as a linear combination of the individual's true score at that time point and the individual's unique score at that time point. This can be expressed as

$$y_{ti} = ly_{ti} + u_{ti} \tag{16.1}$$

where y_{ti} is the observed score at time t for individual i, ly_{ti} is the latent true score at time t for individual i, and u_{ti} is the unique score at time t for individual i.[1] Equation 16.1 is essentially a regression equation with y_{ti} as the outcome, ly_{ti} (a latent variable) as a predictor with a regression coefficient equal to 1, and u_{ti} as the residual score.

Next, the true score at time t is a linear combination of the true score at the prior time point $(t-1)$ and the true change *score* from time $t-1$ to time t. This can be written as

$$ly_{ti} = ly_{t-1i} + dy_{ti} \tag{16.2}$$

where ly_{ti} is the true score at time t for individual i, ly_{t-1i} is the true score at time $t-1$ for individual i, and dy_{ti} is the true change score from time $t-1$ to time t for individual i. As in Equation 16.1, Equation 16.2 is a regression equation with a fixed regression coefficient. Specifically, ly_{ti} is the outcome and ly_{t-1i} is the predictor, with a regression coefficient equal to 1. Since ly_{t-1i} and ly_{ti} are consecutive true scores and the regression coefficient for ly_{t-1i} is set to 1, dy_{ti} is the true amount of change that has occurred between the two time points for individual i. The regression models in Equations 16.1 and 16.2 can be specified in the structural equation modeling framework, where the latent true scores and latent change scores are latent variables identified by imposing the constraints inherent in Equations 16.1 and 16.2. These constraints are imposed in the path diagram shown in Figure 16.1, where unlabeled paths are fixed to 1. As seen in Figure 16.1, each observed score (y_1 to y_5) is composed of a latent true score (ly_1 to ly_5) and a unique latent score (u_1 to u_5), and the true scores, with the exception of the first, are composed of the previous true score plus the latent change score (dy_2 to dy_5). The latent change scores have means and variances, the initial true score has a mean and variance, and there are unique variances (variances of u_1 to u_5). Additionally, and not shown in Figure 16.1, covariances are typically estimated among the initial true score (ly_1) and the latent change scores.

If the unique variances (σ_u^2) were set to 0, the latent change model in Figure 16.1 is essentially a respecification of the observed variables into an initial observed variable and a series of change scores (see Rao, 1958). In longitudinal research, we are interested in *change*, so this framework aligns well with the majority of our research questions. Thus,

---

[1]We use the term *unique score* as opposed to *error score* to be consistent with factor analytic terminology.

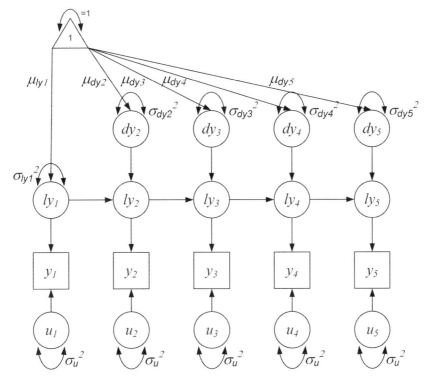

FIGURE 16.1. Path diagram of the basic setup for the latent change framework.

with the latent change framework, change at each time point can be the outcome of inter-est instead of the level or status at each time point.[2]

This latent change score framework leads to the following model for the observed scores

$$y_{ti} = ly_{1i} + \sum_{r=2}^{r=t}(dy_{ri}) + u_{ti} \qquad (16.3)$$

where ly_{1i} is the true score at the first time point ($t = 1$) for individual i, $\sum_{r=2}^{r=t}(dy_{ri})$ is the sum of the latent change scores from the second to the tth time point for individual i, and u_{ti} is the unique score at time t for individual i. Thus, an individual's score at a specific time point is composed of the individual's true score at the initial point in time,

---

[2]We note that the model described in Figure 16.1 (with or without covariances among initial true score and latent change scores) is unidentified. The model can be identified by fixing the unique variance (σ_u^2) to 0 at each time point as previously discussed, which is equivalent to having the first observed score and calculating changes between scores from consecutive measurement occasions. An alternative approach to identification is to constrain the change variances (σ_{dy2}^2 to σ_{dy5}^2) to be equal across time and constrain the unique variances to be equal across time. This specification allows for the separation of latent true scores from observed scores but involves a set of assumptions that can be rejected because the fit of the model can be evaluated.

the accumulation of changes that have occurred up to that point in time, and the unique score at time t for individual i.

As we move forward, we note that the time lag or the distance in time between successive latent *true* scores must be constant. That is, the amount of time elapsed from time $t - 1$ to time t should be equivalent to the amount of time between time t and time $t + 1$ for all t. We note that the constraint of an equal time lag is on the *latent true* scores and not the *observed* scores. For example, McArdle (2001) fit latent change score models to longitudinal intelligence data collected in grades 1, 2, 4, and 6. Thus, the time lag of the observed data varied from 1 to 2 years; however, latent variables, sometimes referred to as *phantom* variables, were utilized as place holders and included in the model to represent latent true scores in grades 3 and 5 to keep a constant time lag for the *latent true* scores. The thought process is that the individuals had a true score in these grades, even though an observed score was not recorded in these grades.

MODELS OF CHANGE

The latent change scores, created by fixed paths between the repeatedly measured observed variables, are now the outcome of interest. Longitudinal models can be specified for the latent change scores, and the model for the latent change scores controls the individual trajectory. McArdle (2001) showed how certain commonly fit growth models (e.g., linear growth) can be specified in the latent change score framework and highlighted how interesting new models can be specified that include time-dependent effects. Grimm, Zhang, et al. (2013) showed how the latent change score framework could be used to specify a wide variety of growth models by writing change equations based on the first derivative of the trajectory equation with respect to time. Models that can be specified in the latent change score framework include any growth model with a first derivative that is defined for all values of time, including fully nonlinear growth models (models discussed in Chapter 12), certain spline models, and the latent basis model. Thus, the flexibility of the latent change score framework enables researchers to fit the majority of models previously discussed and allows for the development of new models that cannot be fit in the traditional growth modeling framework.

In this section, we begin with commonly specified models before moving onto the new models that emerge from this framework. In all cases, we present the change equation and then develop the trajectory equation to compare with the trajectory equation from the traditional growth modeling framework.

Commonly Specified Growth Models

Beginning with the simplest models and moving onto more complex models, the first model for the latent change scores is the *no change* model. In the *no change* model

$$d_{ti} = 0 \qquad\qquad (16.4)$$

indicating that no changes are taking place. The trajectory equation for the *no change* model simplifies to

$$y_{ti} = ly_{1i} + u_{ti} \tag{16.5}$$

which is equivalent to the trajectory equation for the *no-growth* or *intercept-only* model (with slightly different notation) initially discussed in Chapter 3. The parameters in the no change model are the mean of the initial true score (γ_1), the variance of the initial true score (σ_1^2), and the variance of the uniqueness (σ_u^2). Estimates from the no change model are identical to those obtained from the no-growth model. The mapping of the two models is such that the latent intercept (b_{1i}) from the no-growth model is the initial true score (ly_{1i}) from the no change model.

The next model is the *constant change* model, where

$$d_{ti} = g_{2i} \tag{16.6}$$

with g_{2i} termed the *constant change* component, a between-person latent variable. The constant change component, g_{2i}, has a mean (γ_2), variance (σ_2^2), and a covariance with the initial true score (σ_{21}). The constant change model indicates that the amount of change taking place between successive latent true scores is constant within an individual (but allowed to vary between individuals). Expanding the trajectory equation (Equation 16.3) for the first four time points based on the constant change model yields

$$\begin{aligned}
y_{1i} &= ly_{1i} + u_{1i} \\
y_{2i} &= ly_{1i} + g_{2i} + u_{2i} \\
y_{3i} &= ly_{1i} + g_{2i} + g_{2i} + u_{3i} \\
y_{4i} &= ly_{1i} + g_{2i} + g_{2i} + g_{2i} + u_{4i}
\end{aligned} \tag{16.7}$$

which simplifies to $y_{ti} = ly_{1i} + g_{2i} \cdot (t-1) + u_{ti}$. Thus, this model is equivalent to the linear growth model, with the intercept (ly_{1i}) centered at the first time point and the slope (g_{2i}) scaled in terms of the time lag (amount of time) between consecutive latent true scores. Parameters of the constant change model are identical to those obtained from the linear growth model if the intercept is centered at the first measurement occasion and the scale of the linear slope and constant change component are equivalent.

The next model is the linear change model, where the change equation can be written as

$$d_{ti} = g_{2i} + 2 \cdot g_{3i} \cdot (t-1) \tag{16.8}$$

where g_{2i} is the constant change component and g_{3i} is the linear change component. Both g_{2i} and g_{3i} are latent variables with means (γ_2 and γ_3), variances (σ_2^2 and σ_3^2), a covariance with one another (σ_{32}), and covariances with the initial true score (σ_{21} and σ_{31}). Expanding the linear change model for the first four time points yields

$$
\begin{aligned}
y_{1i} &= ly_{1i} + u_{1i} \\
y_{2i} &= ly_{1i} + (g_{2i}) + (2 \cdot g_{3i}) + u_{2i} \\
y_{3i} &= ly_{1i} + (g_{2i} + g_{2i}) + (2 \cdot g_{3i} + 4 \cdot g_{3i}) + u_{3i} \\
y_{4i} &= ly_{1i} + (g_{2i} + g_{2i} + g_{2i}) + (2 \cdot g_{3i} + 4 \cdot g_{3i} + 6 \cdot g_{3i}) + u_{4i}
\end{aligned}
\tag{16.9}
$$

which simplifies to $y_{ti} = ly_{1i} + g_{2i} \cdot (t-1) + g_{3i} \cdot ((t-1)^2 + (t-1)) + u_{ti}$, which is equivalent to the quadratic growth model, but this version of the quadratic is not a direct match to the traditional quadratic growth model (i.e., parameter estimates are not identical). The equivalence can be seen by further simplifying this model to $y_{ti} = ly_{1i} + (g_{2i} + g_{3i}) \cdot (t-1) + g_{3i} \cdot (t-1)^2 + u_{ti}$ and recalling that the traditional quadratic growth model can be written as $y_{ti} = b_{1i} + b_{2i} \cdot (t-1) + b_{3i} \cdot (t-1)^2 + u_{ti}$, where b_{1i} is the intercept, b_{2i} is the linear component, and b_{3i} is the quadratic component. Thus, b_{1i} is equivalent to ly_{1i}, b_{3i} is equivalent to g_{3i}, and b_{2i} is equivalent to $g_{2i} + g_{3i}$. Thus, the constant change component (g_{2i}) in this linear change model is a rotated version of the linear component in the traditional quadratic growth model (b_{2i}). We note that this type of rotation of model parameters is common when specifying traditional growth models in the latent change score framework (see Grimm, Zhang, et al., 2013).

The last commonly specified growth model we present in the latent change score framework is the exponential model. The exponential model, in the traditional growth modeling framework, can be written as

$$
y_{ti} = b_{1i} + b_{2i} \cdot (1 - \exp(-\delta \cdot (t-1)))
\tag{16.10}
$$

where b_{1i} is the intercept, b_{2i} is the change from the intercept to the asymptotic level, and δ is the rate of approach to the asymptote. Within the latent change score framework, the change equation for this exponential model is

$$
d_{ti} = \delta \cdot g_{2i} \cdot (\exp(-\delta \cdot (t-1)))
\tag{16.11}
$$

Combining the change score equation with the trajectory equation for the latent change score model yields

$$
\begin{aligned}
y_{1i} &= ly_{1i} + u_{1i} \\
y_{2i} &= ly_{1i} + (\delta \cdot g_{2i} \cdot (\exp(-\delta))) + u_{2i} \\
y_{3i} &= ly_{1i} + (\delta \cdot g_{2i} \cdot (\exp(-\delta))) + (\delta \cdot g_{2i} \cdot (\exp(-\delta \cdot 2))) + u_{3i} \\
y_{4i} &= ly_{1i} + (\delta \cdot g_{2i} \cdot (\exp(-\delta))) + (\delta \cdot g_{2i} \cdot (\exp(-\delta \cdot 2))) + (\delta \cdot g_{2i} \cdot (\exp(-\delta \cdot 3))) + u_{4i}
\end{aligned}
\tag{16.12}
$$

for the first four time points. This expansion can be simplified to $y_{ti} = ly_{1i} + \delta \cdot g_{2i} \cdot \left(\sum_{r=2}^{r=t} (\exp(-\delta \cdot (r-1))) \right) + u_{ti}$. This equation does not clearly map onto the trajectory equation for the exponential (Equation 16.10); however, we note that changes in $(1 - \exp(-\delta \cdot (t-1)))$ (multiplier of b_{2i} in Equation 16.10) are proportional to changes in $\sum_{r=2}^{r=t} (\exp(-(r-1) \cdot \delta))$.

Expansion 1: Dynamic Noise

McArdle (2001) highlighted how dynamic noise can be incorporated into latent change score models in a straightforward manner by adding a residual term to the latent change equation. For example, the change equation for the constant change model with dynamic noise is

$$d_{ti} = g_{2i} + z_{ti} \tag{16.13}$$

where z_{ti} is a random variable with $z_{ti} \sim N(0, \sigma_z^2)$.

In essence, the latent change score at each time point is not perfectly predicted (in this case by g_{2i}). The inclusion of z_{ti} leads to a stochastic difference or change equation, which is not present in traditional growth models. That is, traditional growth models are deterministic—knowledge of the individual parameters (e.g., intercept and slope) yields value of the latent true score at each point in time, and the inclusion of z_{ti} in Equation 16.13 prevents this from being true. There has not been much research on the incorporation of dynamic noise in latent change score models; however, accurately estimating this type of variability can be difficult and may require many measurement occasions.

Expansion 2: Dynamic Effects

McArdle (2001) and McArdle and Hamagami (2001) showed how dynamic or time-dependent effects could be incorporated into latent change score models. To begin, we expand upon the no change model and include a time-dependent effect. The change score equation for this model can be written as

$$d_{ti} = \pi \cdot ly_{t-1i} \tag{16.14}$$

where π is an estimated parameter and ly_{t-1i} is the true (or latent) score at the prior time point. This model is referred to as the *proportional change* model because the predicted changes are proportional to the state (or status) of the prior true score. In a similar vein, the constant change model can be expanded to

$$d_{ti} = g_{2i} + \pi \cdot ly_{t-1i} \tag{16.15}$$

where g_{2i} is the constant change component and π is the proportional change parameter. This model is referred to as the *dual change* model and is the most commonly fit latent

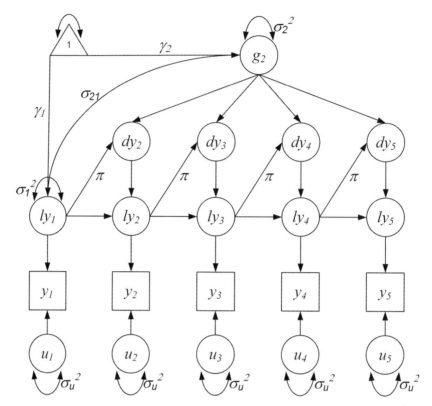

FIGURE 16.2. Path diagram of the dual change model with five time points.

change score model. In this model there is, what is often referred to as, a maturational effect (g_{2i}), as well as the proportional change effect (π). The dual change model yields an exponential growth trajectory (see Grimm, An, McArdle, Zonderman, & Resnick, 2012), and the type of exponential growth trajectory depends on the sign and magnitude of g_{2i}, π, and ly_{1i}. A path diagram of this model is contained in Figure 16.2 with five occasions of measurement with parameters γ_1 and γ_2, which are the means of the initial true score and the constant change component; σ_1^2 and σ_2^2, which are the variances of the initial true score and the constant change component; σ_{21}, which is the covariance between the initial true score and constant change component; σ_u^2, which is the residual or unique variance; and π, which is the proportional change parameter.

ILLUSTRATION

To illustrate the fitting and interpretation of latent change score models, we analyze the longitudinal mathematics data initially subjected to linear growth models in Chapter 3. As a quick reminder, the longitudinal mathematics data were collected from the NLSY-CYA (Center for Human Resource Research, 2009) and the mathematics scores are from the PIAT (Dunn & Markwardt, 1970). As in Chapter 3, *grade at testing* is utilized as the time metric and ranges from second through eighth grade. These data are subjected to a variety of the latent change score models discussed above using the structural equation modeling framework. Latent change score models have almost solely been fit in the structural equation modeling framework. The only exception is presented in Hamagami, Zhang, and McArdle (2009), where WinBUGS (Lunn, Thomas, Best, & Spiegelhalter, 2000) was utilized. Thus, we focus on the structural equation modeling programs to specify latent change score models.

STRUCTURAL EQUATION MODELING IMPLEMENTATION

Dual Change Model

We describe Mplus and OpenMx code for fitting the *dual change score* model since this model combines the constant change and proportional change effects, which makes most of the remaining models simple restrictions. After describing the code and output, we present a table of fit statistics and parameter estimates for the majority of the models discussed above.

Mplus

The Mplus script for the dual change model fit to the longitudinal mathematics data is contained in Script 16.1. The script begins with the typical components of TITLE, DATA, and VARIABLE. The mathematics scores from grade 2 through 8 (math2-math8) are selected for analysis using the USEVARIABLE command. In the ANALYSIS command, we specify MODEL=NOCOVARIANCES; to change the default setting that latent variables are automatically correlated unless they are associated through directional paths. Given the large number of latent variables in latent change score models, this command significantly reduces the length of the programming script.

    The MODEL statement begins with creating latent true scores at each grade. The latent true scores are ly1 through ly7 and defined using the BY command and fixing each factor loading to 1 (e.g., ly1 BY math2@1). These statements follow Equation 16.1 where observed scores are composed of the true score plus the unique score. We note that the true scores (ly1 through ly7) are explicitly defined, but the unique scores are not because the variability of the unique scores is the *residual* variance of the observed variables, which will be specified subsequently. The means and variances of the latent true scores are then specified. The mean and variance of the first latent true score (ly1) are freely estimated, but the means and variances of the subsequent latent true scores (ly2 through ly7) are fixed at 0. The last part of this first section of the script contains statements for the intercepts and residual variances of the observed scores. The intercepts of the observed scores are fixed to 0, and their variances are estimated but constrained to be equal over time following the typical specification of residual variances in growth models (with label sigma2_u).

Script 16.1. Mplus Script for the Dual Change Model

```
TITLE: Dual Change Model - PIAT Mathematics Data;

DATA: FILE = nlsy_math_wide_R.dat;

VARIABLE:
  NAMES = id female lb_wght anti_k1
          math2-math8 age2-age8 men2-men8
          spring2-spring8 anti2-anti8;
  MISSING = .;
  USEVAR = math2-math8;

ANALYSIS:
  TYPE = MEANSTRUCTURE;
  COVERAGE = 0;
  MODEL = NOCOVARIANCES;

MODEL:
!Latent True Scores
     ly1 BY math2@1;        ly2 BY math3@1;
     ly3 BY math4@1;        ly4 BY math5@1;
     ly5 BY math6@1;        ly6 BY math7@1;
     ly7 BY math8@1;

     [ly1*];                ly1;
     [ly2-ly7@0];           ly2-ly7@0;

     [math2-math8@0];       math2-math8 (sigma2_u);

!Autoregressions
     ly2 ON ly1@1;          ly3 ON ly2@1;
     ly4 ON ly3@1;          ly5 ON ly4@1;
     ly6 ON ly5@1;          ly7 ON ly6@1;

!Latent Change Scores
     dy2 BY ly2@1;          dy3 BY ly3@1;
     dy4 BY ly4@1;          dy5 BY ly5@1;
     dy6 BY ly6@1;          dy7 BY ly7@1;

     [dy2-dy7@0];           dy2-dy7@0;

!Constant Change Component
     g2 BY dy2-dy7@1;       g2;
     [g2];                  ly1 WITH g2;

!Proportional Effects
     dy2 ON ly1 (pi);       dy3 ON ly2 (pi);
     dy4 ON ly3 (pi);       dy5 ON ly4 (pi);
     dy6 ON ly5 (pi);       dy7 ON ly6 (pi);
```

Next, and following Equation 16.2, autoregressive paths are specified for the latent true scores, such that the latent true score at each time point is predicted by the latent true score at the prior time point with a regression weight set equal to 1 (e.g., ly2 ON ly1@1). The latent change scores are subsequently defined using the keyword BY. These variables, dy2 through dy7, are specified as one-headed arrows to the latent true scores at each time point (e.g., dy2 BY ly2@1) with weights equal to 1. The means and variances of the latent changes are then specified, and both are set equal to 0 because their expected means and variances are attributable to external sources (i.e., no intercept or dynamic noise).

Now that the latent true scores and latent change scores are defined, we can specify the model for the latent change scores. The dual change model has a constant change component and proportional change effects. First, we specify the constant change component. This latent variable, g2, is defined using the keyword BY with one-headed arrows going to the six latent change scores with weights equal to one (i.e., g2 BY dy2-dy7@1). The constant change component has a mean ([g2*]), a variance (g2), and a covariance with the initial true score (ly1 WITH g2). Finally, the proportional effects are specified using the keyword ON with the latent change score at each time point being regressed on the latent true score at the prior time point (e.g., dy2 ON ly1). These proportional change effects are constrained to be equal across time using the label pi.

The Mplus script can be modified to specify the other latent change models discussed. The constant change model can be specified by removing the proportional effects, and the proportional change model can be specified by removing the constant change component and its associated parameters. Dynamic noise is added by allowing the variances of the latent change scores to be freely estimated instead of being fixed at 0. Often, this dynamic variance, when estimated, is set to be equal over time (e.g., dy2-dy7 (sigma2_dy)). Finally, additional latent variables can be specified to allow for different types of growth trajectories. For example, in the linear change model, the latent variable g3 is specified using the BY keyword with one-headed arrows to the latent change scores with weights that change linearly with time (e.g., 2, 4, 6, 8, 10, 12). This latent variable would have an estimated mean and variance along with estimated covariances with the constant change component and the initial latent true score. The exponential model can be specified by constraining the loadings from g2 to the latent change scores (dy2-dy7) to change according to the nonlinear function of time using the MODEL CONSTRAINT command as in Chapter 11.

OpenMx

The OpenMx script for fitting the dual change model to the mathematics data is contained in Script 16.2. The script begins by calling the dataset and listing all of the manifest and latent variables in the model. The model is then specified with a series of mxPath statements. The first mxPath statement specifies the one-headed arrows from the latent true scores, ly1 through ly7, to the observed variables, math2 through math8. These one-headed arrows are fixed at 1 (free=FALSE, values=1). Next, the autoregressive paths are specified as one-headed arrows between consecutive latent true scores. These parameters are also fixed at 1. The paths to specify the latent change scores come next. These paths are one-headed arrows from the latent change scores, dy2 through dy7, to the latent true scores, ly2 through ly7, and are fixed at 1. The paths to define the constant change component are then specified. These one-headed arrows begin at the constant change

Script 16.2. `OpenMx` Script for the Dual Change Model

```
dcm.math.omx <- mxModel('Dual Change Model, Path Specification',
  type='RAM', mxData(observed=nlsy_math_wide, type='raw'),
  manifestVars=c('math2','math3','math4','math5','math6','math7','math8'),
  latentVars=c('ly1','ly2','ly3','ly4','ly5','ly6','ly7',
                      'dy2','dy3','dy4','dy5','dy6','dy7',
                      'g2'),

# Defining true scores
mxPath(from=c('ly1','ly2','ly3','ly4','ly5','ly6','ly7'),
  to=c('math2','math3','math4','math5','math6','math7','math8'),
  arrows=1, free=FALSE, values=1),

# Autoregressive Effects
mxPath(from=c('ly1','ly2','ly3','ly4','ly5','ly6'),
  to=c('ly2','ly3','ly4','ly5','ly6','ly7'),
  arrows=1, free=FALSE, values=1),

# Defining change scores
mxPath(from=c('dy2','dy3','dy4','dy5','dy6','dy7'),
  to=c('ly2','ly3','ly4','ly5','ly6','ly7'),
  arrows=1, free=FALSE, values=1),

# Constant change component
mxPath(from='g2', to=c('dy2','dy3','dy4','dy5','dy6','dy7'),
  arrows=1, free=FALSE, values=1),

# Variance paths
mxPath(from=c('math2','math3','math4','math5','math6','math7','math8'),
  arrows=2, free=TRUE, values=60, labels='sigma2_u'),

# Latent variable covariance matrix path
mxPath(from=c('ly1','g2'),
  arrows=2, connect='unique.pairs', free=TRUE, values=c(60, 0, 5),
  labels=c('sigma2_1','sigma_21','sigma2_2')),

# Proportional Effects
mxPath(from=c('ly1','ly2','ly3','ly4','ly5','ly6'),
  to=c('dy2','dy3','dy4','dy5','dy6','dy7'),
  arrows=1, free=TRUE, values=0,
  labels='pi'),

# means
mxPath(from='one', to=c('ly1','g2'),
  arrows=1, free=TRUE, values=c(40, 4), labels=c('gamma_1','gamma_2'))

) # close model

dcm.math.fit <- mxRun(dcm.math.omx)

summary(dcm.math.fit)
```

component, g2, and go to the latent change scores, dy2 through dy7, and are also fixed at 1. Now, all of the fixed paths are specified for the dual change model.

The first estimated parameter specified is the residual variance. These two-headed arrows begin and end at the observed variables, math2 through math8, are freely estimated, given a starting value of 60, and labeled sigma2_u. As in the previous growth models specified throughout the book, the residual variances are constrained to be equal across time. Next, the latent variable variances and covariances are specified. In this mxPath statement, connect='unique.pairs' is utilized to specify a full covariance matrix for ly1 and g2. Starting values are provided along with the labels sigma2_1, sigma_21, and sigma2_2 for the variance of the initial true score, the covariance between the initial true score and the constant change component, and the variance of the constant change component.

The proportional change effects are specified in the next mxPath statement. These one-headed arrows begin from the latent true scores, ly1 through ly6, and go to the latent change scores, dy2 through dy7, are freely estimated (free=TRUE), given starting values of 0, and a common label, pi, to constrain them to be equal across time. The final mxPath statement is for the latent variable means. The initial latent true score and the constant change component have estimated means. These one-headed arrows go from the constant, one, to ly1 and g2. These paths are given starting values (i.e., 40 and 4) and labels (gamma_1 and gamma_2). The model is then closed, estimated with mxRun, and the output is printed using summary.

As we noted for Mplus, the constant change and proportional change models can be specified by removing elements of the OpenMx script. The constant change model can be specified by removing the mxPath statement for the proportional change parameter. The proportional change model can be specified by removing the mxPath statement for the factor loadings for g2 and changing the mxPath statements that involve the variance of g2, the covariance between ly1 and g2, and the mean of g2. The linear change model can be specified by adding an mxPath statement to define the linear change component. The mxPath statements for the latent variable covariances and the latent variable means would be expanded to include the additional latent variable. Dynamic noise can be specified through the addition of an mxPath statement for the variances of dy2 through dy7. As noted above, these variances are typically constrained to be equal over time, which can be implemented by using a common label.

Output

The Mplus and OpenMx output for the dual change model fit to the mathematics data is contained in Output 16.1 and 16.2, respectively (for Mplus we only report *estimated* parameter estimates to reduce output length). First, we note that the model fit information provided by Mplus indicates that the dual change model fit the data well with strong global fit indices (e.g., RMSEA less than 0.05, CFI and TLI > 0.95). We now turn to parameter estimates, but return to the model fit information to compare the dual change model against the other fitted models.

Output 16.1. *Mplus* Output for the Dual Change Model

```
MODEL FIT INFORMATION

Number of Free Parameters                          7

Loglikelihood
          H0 Value                        -7895.605
          H1 Value                        -7866.567
Information Criteria
          Akaike (AIC)                    15805.209
          Bayesian (BIC)                  15839.071
          Sample-Size Adjusted BIC        15816.839
          (n* = (n + 2) / 24)
Chi-Square Test of Model Fit
          Value                              58.075
          Degrees of Freedom                     28
          P-Value                            0.0007
RMSEA (Root Mean Square Error Of Approximation)
          Estimate                            0.034
          90 Percent C.I.                     0.021      0.046
          Probability RMSEA <= .05            0.985
CFI/TLI
          CFI                                 0.964
          TLI                                 0.973


MODEL RESULTS

                                             Two-Tailed
              Estimate    S.E.   Est./S.E.     P-Value
DY2     ON
   LY1        -0.241     0.018     -13.387       0.000
DY3     ON
   LY2        -0.241     0.018     -13.387       0.000
DY4     ON
   LY3        -0.241     0.018     -13.387       0.000
DY5 ON
   LY4        -0.241     0.018     -13.387       0.000
DY6     ON
   LY5        -0.241     0.018     -13.387       0.000
DY7     ON
   LY6        -0.241     0.018     -13.387       0.000
LY1     WITH
   G2         13.746     1.699       8.092       0.000
Means
   LY1        32.533     0.434      74.955       0.000
   G2         15.222     0.815      18.687       0.000
Variances
   LY1        71.900     6.548      10.980       0.000
   G2          5.602     0.837       6.695       0.000
Residual Variances
   MATH2      30.818     1.700      18.126       0.000
   MATH3      30.818     1.700      18.126       0.000
   MATH4      30.818     1.700      18.126       0.000
   MATH5      30.818     1.700      18.126       0.000
   MATH6      30.818     1.700      18.126       0.000
   MATH7      30.818     1.700      18.126       0.000
   MATH8      30.818     1.700      18.126       0.000
```

Output 16.2. `OpenMx` **Output for the Dual Change Model**

```
free parameters:
        name    matrix      row       col      Estimate     Std.Error
1         pi        A       dy2       ly1     -0.2410135    0.01798447
2   sigma2_u        S     math2     math2     30.8184687    1.69889645
3   sigma2_1        S       ly1       ly1     71.9004194    6.54300591
4   sigma_21        S       ly1        g2     13.7461381    1.69771623
5   sigma2_2        S        g2        g2      5.6019870    0.83539419
6    gamma_1        M         1       ly1     32.5327261    0.43382728
7    gamma_2        M         1        g2     15.2221890    0.81376519

observed statistics: 2221
estimated parameters: 7
degrees of freedom: 2214
-2 log likelihood: 15791.21
number of observations: 933
Information Criteria:
        | df Penalty | Parameters Penalty | Sample-Size Adjusted
AIC:      11363.2093             15805.21                      NA
BIC:        650.9801             15839.08                15816.85
```

Parameters for the dual change model include the mean and variance of the initial true score (Mean of LY1; `gamma_1` and Variance of LY1; `sigma2_1`), the mean and variance of the constant change component (Mean of G2; `gamma_2` and Variance of G2; `sigma2_2`), the covariance between the initial true score and the constant change component (LY1 WITH G2; `sigma_21`), the proportional change parameter (DY2 ON LY1; `pi`), and the residual variance (Residual Variance of MATH2; `sigma2_u`). The mean of the initial true score was 32.53 and represents the predicted average mathematics score in second grade. The mean of the constant change component was 15.22 and is one of the components of the expected changes over time, with the second coming from the proportional change effect. Because there are two aspects of change in the dual change model, the mean of the constant change component can be difficult to interpret. Additionally, the constant change component functions as an intercept in the change equation, which makes its value dependent on the scale of the observed variable (i.e., adding or subtracting a constant to all the scores alters the mean of the constant change component). And because the constant change component is an intercept in the change equation, it is only interpretable when all other predictors (prior true scores) are zero. In our data, the mathematics scores are never zero in this dataset, which makes the mean of the constant change component an extrapolation from the data and subsequently difficult to interpret in isolation.

Because of these limitations, we describe the overall shape of development by examining the mean of the constant change component and the proportional change parameter together along with the mean of the initial true score. The mean trajectory begins at 32.53 and increases based on two aspects—a maturational effect of 15.22 (mean of the constant change component), which is added at each grade, and the proportional change effect, which serves as a limiting factor because the proportional change parameter was negative (–0.24). Thus, as the scores increase over time, they increase at a slower rate because the proportional change effect strengthens over time (because scores are increasing over time). To illustrate, we calculated the expected mean changes for successive grades. The mean change from second to third grade equaled 7.41 (15.22–0.24·32.52), the mean change from third to fourth grade was 5.63 (15.22–0.24·39.94), and this pattern continues over time. Thus, the mean trajectory is an increasing exponential curve with a decreasing rate of change. The individual predicted trajectories for a random subsample of n = 50 are contained in Figure 16.3. As seen in this figure, all predicted trajectories show this general developmental shape.

The variance of the initial true score was 71.90 and indicates true between-child variability in mathematics scores in second grade. The variance of the constant change component was 5.60 and represents between-child variability in this aspect of change (again parameters associated with the constant change component are difficult to interpret in isolation). The covariance between the initial true score and the constant change component was 13.75, indicating that children with higher true mathematics scores in second grade tended to have greater constant change component scores, indicating greater overall changes from second through eighth grades. Lastly, the variance of the unique scores was 30.82 and indicates the magnitude of within-person fluctuations around the individual smooth trajectories.

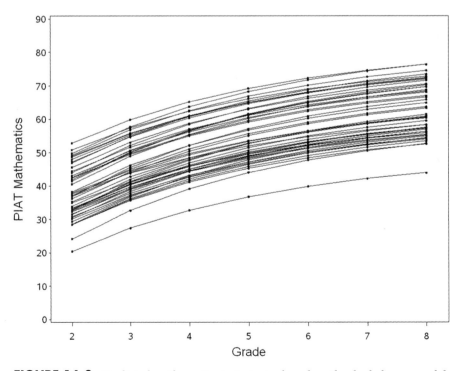

FIGURE 16.3. Predicted mathematics trajectories based on the dual change model.

TABLE 16.1. Fit Statistics for the Latent Change Score Models Fit to Mathematics Data

Model	χ^2	Parameters	BIC	RMSEA	CFI	TLI
No change	1759	3	17,512	0.241	0.000	–0.347
Proportional change	339	4	16,100	0.103	0.634	0.752
Constant change	204	6	15,978	0.081	0.792	0.849
Dual change	58	7	15,839	0.034	0.964	0.973
Linear change[a]	60	10	15,862	0.039	0.958	0.965
Dual change + dynamic noise[a]	53	8	15,840	0.032	0.970	0.976

[a]At least one estimated variance was negative.

Model Fit

Model fit information for the various latent change score models fit to the longitudinal mathematics data is presented in Table 16.1. First, we note that both the linear change model and the dual change model with dynamic noise encountered estimation issues. Of the remaining models, the dual change model was the best-fitting model. The dual change model fit better than the no change model ($\Delta\chi^2 = 1,701$, $\Delta parameters = 4$), the proportional change model ($\Delta\chi^2 = 281$, $\Delta parameters = 3$), and the constant change model ($\Delta\chi^2 = 146$, $\Delta parameters = 1$).

IMPORTANT CONSIDERATIONS

The latent change score framework has had a large impact on longitudinal research and on how researchers conceptualize and study time-dependent change. Most of this impact has been in multivariate models, which are discussed in the next chapter; however, this framework provides benefits for univariate models as well. First, latent change score models have latent variables that represent within-person change between successive time points. Typically, growth models either have a single latent variable that represents within-person change over all time points, as in a linear growth model, or multiple latent variables that contribute to within-person change without a single variable that represents within-person change (e.g., quadratic growth model) because the rate of change varies both within individuals over time and between individuals at different points in time. By incorporating latent change scores at each time point, it is possible to directly examine the mean and variance of the rate of change by calculating expectations for the latent change scores. Furthermore, understanding the effects of time-invariant covariates on the rate of change can also be directly studied when modeling change that is not linear with respect to time (see Grimm, Castro-Schilo, et al., 2013; Grimm, Zhang, et al., 2013). More on this topic is discussed in Chapter 18.

Second, Hamagami and McArdle (2007) extended the latent change score framework to second-order difference scores or latent acceleration models. The acceleration model allows for a variety of nonlinear change trajectories with simple equations for the second-order changes or acceleration scores. For example, the acceleration model can produce sine-type wave trajectories by including effects of prior latent change scores and prior latent true scores (e.g., $a_{ti} = g_{2i} + \pi_1 \cdot d_{t-1i} + \pi_2 \cdot h_{t-1i}$, where a_{ti} is the acceleration, second-order difference, score at time t). We note that latent acceleration models are a discrete analog to the latent differential models developed by Boker and Nesselroade (2002).

Third, by placing an emphasis on within-person time-dependent change, latent change score models allow researchers to fit models that best represent their theory of change. For example, Grimm et al. (2012) fit latent change score models where prior changes were included as predictors of subsequent changes to test a theory regarding how changes in the size of brain structures predicted subsequent changes in memory performance. In essence, the latent change score framework enables researchers to specify their model of change, which may include time-dependent effects, between-person factors, and effects from external forces.

Alternative Specification

Several times we noted that parameters associated with the constant change component were difficult to interpret in isolation when there is a time-dependent (i.e., proportional change) effect, as in the dual change model. An alternative way to specify the dual change model, is to set the mean of the first latent true score to zero (instead of estimating this parameter) and estimate the intercepts of the observed repeated measures with an equality constraint on those intercepts. Thus, in the `Mplus` script the following statements would be adjusted to read

```
[ly1@0];
[math2-math8]    (tau_1);
```

In the `OpenMx` script, the mean vector would be adjusted to

```
mxPath(from='one',
  to=c('math2','math3','math4','math5','math6','math7','math8','g2'),
  arrows=1, free=TRUE, values=c(40,40,40,40,40,40,40,4),
  labels=c('tau_1','tau_1','tau_1','tau_1','tau_1','tau_1','tau_1',
           'gamma_2'))
```

With this specification, the mean of the constant change component is the average change from the first to the second time points; however, variability in the constant change component remains difficult to interpret because variability in change is due to the constant change component and variability in the prior true score.

MOVING FORWARD

In the next two chapters we expand on the latent change score framework by first focusing on multivariate models, where the question of directional time-dependent effects are studied. We then focus on nonlinear models of change and present a modified growth modeling approach with similar goals of identifying between-person differences in within-person change. At this point, it is important to note that latent change score models can be fit as second-order models (Ferrer, Balluerka, & Widaman, 2008) and can be combined with the multiple-group and finite mixture modeling frameworks to study between-person differences in change associated with observed and unobserved groups (see Ferrer, Shaywitz, Holahan, Marchione, & Shaywitz, 2010; Grimm, 2006).

17

Multivariate Latent Change Score Models

Latent change score models were developed primarily to study time-sequential associations between two or more processes that were changing over time. That is, the latent change equations can be extended to include lagged effects from additional variables to jointly model multiple ongoing developmental processes (McArdle, 2001; McArdle & Hamagami, 2001) or lagged effects from other individuals (McArdle, Hamagami, Kadlec, & Fisher, 2007). Prior to the development of latent change score models, models that were typically used to study multiple processes were limited in various respects, and latent change score models were able to address some of these limitations. We begin by reviewing two models that were typically fit to study multiple development processes and then discuss the benefits of moving to the latent change score framework. A bivariate latent change score model is then fit to illustrative data. Finally, we discuss the benefits and limitations of this approach.

AUTOREGRESSIVE CROSS-LAG MODEL

The *autogressive cross-lag* model (see Jöreskog, 1970, 1974, 1979) is often used to examine time-dependent associations between multiple constructs in the structural equation modeling framework. The *bivariate autoregressive cross-lag* model begins with the separation of true score from unique scores. This can be written as

$$y_{ti} = \alpha_t + ly_{ti} + u_{ti}$$
$$x_{ti} = \tau_t + lx_{ti} + s_{ti}$$

(17.1)

where y_{ti} and x_{ti} are the observed scores for the two processes measured at time t for individual i, α_t and τ_t are time-dependent intercepts, ly_{ti} and lx_{ti} are true scores at time t for individual i, and u_{ti} and s_{ti} are the unique scores at time t for individual i. The unique scores are assumed to follow a multivariate normal distribution with zero means, time-invariant variances, and a time-invariant unique covariance; that is,

$$u_{ti}, s_{ti} \sim MVN\left(\begin{bmatrix} 0 \\ 0 \end{bmatrix}, \begin{bmatrix} \sigma_u^2 \\ \sigma_{s,u} & \sigma_s^2 \end{bmatrix}\right)$$

True scores are related over time by autoregressive and cross-lag (cross-variable) effects, such that

$$ly_{ti} = \pi_y \cdot ly_{t-1i} + \delta_y \cdot lx_{t-1i} + z_{ti}$$
$$lx_{ti} = \pi_x \cdot lx_{t-1i} + \delta_x \cdot ly_{t-1i} + v_{ti}$$

(17.2)

where π_y and π_x are autoregressive parameters that indicate the degree to which between-person differences in each true score are stable over time, δ_y and δ_x are cross-lag parameters that indicate the degree to which the prior true state of x (lx_{t-1i}) relates to the current true state of y (ly_{ti}) and vice versa, respectively, and z_{ti} and v_{ti} are time-dependent disturbance or residual terms. In the autoregressive cross-lag model, the covariance matrix for the initial true scores is fully estimated; that is,

$$ly_{1i}, lx_{1i} \sim MVN\left(\begin{bmatrix} 0 \\ 0 \end{bmatrix}, \begin{bmatrix} \sigma_{ly1}^2 \\ \sigma_{lx1,ly1} & \sigma_{lx1}^2 \end{bmatrix}\right)$$

and indicates the amount of between-person variance in true scores at the initial time point and the degree to which between-person differences in true scores are associated at the initial time point. The disturbance terms are also assumed to follow a multivariate normal distribution with time-invariant variances and covariances; that is,

$$z_{ti}, v_{ti} \sim MvN\left(\begin{bmatrix} 0 \\ 0 \end{bmatrix}, \begin{bmatrix} \sigma_z^2 \\ \sigma_{v,z} & \sigma_v^2 \end{bmatrix}\right)$$

To determine the nature of time-sequential associations, a series of four autoregressive cross-lag models is fit with different constraints imposed on the cross-lag parameters. First, a *no cross-lag* model is fit by fixing both cross-lag parameters to 0 (i.e., $\delta_y = \delta_x = 0$). This model serves as a baseline and an initial starting point because there are no cross-variable time-sequential associations. Next, unidirectional models are fit where either δ_y or δ_x is estimated. These models are referred to as $x \to y$ and $y \to x$, respectively. Finally, the *full cross-lag* model, where δ_y and δ_x are jointly estimated, is fit. All models are nested under the full cross-lag model and can be compared with likelihood ratio tests where the differences in χ^2 (or -2 log likelihood) are compared against the difference in degrees of freedom (or the number of estimated parameters).

The autoregressive cross-lag model is an appropriate model to understand time-sequential associations between two or more constructs. The model combines within- and between-person effects, which has been seen as a limitation of this model (Hamaker, Kuiper, & Grasman, 2015). For example, if there are strong autoregressive effects, the model predicts that individuals with higher scores on x (compared to the sample) at time t, will have higher scores on x at time $t + 1$, which is a between-person effect. Additionally, the model predicts that when an individual has a higher score (compared to his or her average) at time t, he or she will have a higher score (compared to his or her average) at time $t + 1$, which is a within-person effect. Thus, the autoregressive and cross-lag parameters represent a combination of between- and within-person effects. With panel data, the between-person effects dominate because sample size tends to be much larger than the number of repeated measurements. Hamaker et al. (2015) proposed an alternative specification of the autoregressive cross-lag model attempting to focus on within-person effects. In this specification, a random intercept is included in the model to account for between-person differences. A second limitation of the autoregressive cross-lag model is that the mean structure of the data is not studied. That is, the autoregressive cross-lag model has a fully specified or saturated mean structure because the intercepts of the oberved variables are perfectly estimated in α_t and τ_t. Thus, the model does not examine within-person change. The autoregressive cross-lag model comes from time-series analysis, where many assessments for a single person are common, and the model was only appropriate when the time-series data were stationary (constant mean and variance over time) and stationarity is not a common attribute of longitudinal panel data. In essence, the autoregressive cross-lag model is only appropriate when the constructs have stopped changing (John J. McArdle, personal communication, May 28, 2010). Therefore, the model can be inappropriate for multivariate panel data where change is observed.

MULTIVARIATE GROWTH MODEL

The *multivariate growth curve* model (MGM) was discussed in Chapter 8. We briefly review the model here because it is often fit to understand the joint development of two processes. A *bivariate linear growth* model can be written as

$$
\begin{aligned}
y_{ti} &= b_{1i} + b_{2i} \cdot \frac{(t - k_1)}{k_2} + u_{ti} \\
x_{ti} &= h_{1i} + h_{2i} \cdot \frac{(t - k_1)}{k_2} + s_{ti}
\end{aligned}
\tag{17.3}
$$

where y_{ti} and x_{ti} are the repeated scores for the two repeatedly measured variables, b_{1i} and h_{1i} are the random intercepts—predicted scores of y_{ti} and x_{ti} for individual i when $t = k_1$, b_{2i} and h_{2i} are the random slopes—predicted linear rate of change for individual i for a one-unit change in t/k_2, t represents the original time metric, and u_{ti} and s_{ti} are time-specific residuals. As in the autoregressive cross-lag model, the residual scores at time t are assumed to follow multivariate normal distributions with zero means and a fully specified covariance matrix; that is,

$$u_{ti}, s_{ti} \sim MVN\left(\begin{bmatrix} 0 \\ 0 \end{bmatrix}, \begin{bmatrix} \sigma_u^2 & \\ \sigma_{s,u} & \sigma_s^2 \end{bmatrix}\right)$$

The growth coefficients (b_{1i}, h_{1i}, b_{2i}, and h_{2i}) are assumed to follow a multivariate normal distribution with estimated means and a fully specified covariance matrix; that is,

$$b_{1i}, b_{2i}, h_{1i}, h_{2i} \sim MVN\left(\begin{bmatrix} \beta_1 \\ \beta_2 \\ \alpha_1 \\ \alpha_2 \end{bmatrix}, \begin{bmatrix} \sigma_{b1}^2 & & & \\ \sigma_{b2,b1} & \sigma_{b2}^2 & & \\ \sigma_{h1,b1} & \sigma_{h1,b2} & \sigma_{h1}^2 & \\ \sigma_{h2,b1} & \sigma_{h2,b2} & \sigma_{h2,h1} & \sigma_{h2}^2 \end{bmatrix}\right)$$

As discussed in Chapter 8, the MGM provides bivariate information about the degree to which the intercepts and slopes across variables are associated as well as how the residuals at a given time point are associated. The benefits of the MGM are that each developmental process is studied with growth models, which allow for the study of within-person change, and that the MGM provides information regarding how changes in the two processes are associated with one another. The main limitation of the MGM is the lack of time-sequential effects or *dynamics*. That is, the MGM provides no information regarding whether the state of one variable predicts the state or changes in the second variable over time, or how changes in one variable may precede changes in the second variable. However, we note that time-dependency can be built into the MGM. First, residual scores can have autoregressive and cross-lag effects (see Grimm, 2007). For example,

$$u_{ti} = \pi_y \cdot u_{t-1i} + \delta_y \cdot s_{t-1i} + z_{ti}$$
$$s_{ti} = \pi_x \cdot s_{t-1i} + \delta_x \cdot u_{t-1i} + v_{ti}$$

(17.4)

where π_y and π_x are autoregressive parameters and δ_y and δ_x are cross-lag parameters. These parameters describe how individual deviations from the growth model are related over time. For example, a positive cross-lag effect for δ_y would indicate that when x_i is higher than predicted by the growth model at time $t-1$ (e.g., positive deviation for s_{t-1i}), then y_i will be higher than predicted at time t (e.g., positive deviation for u_{ti}). This type of model is similar to how some time-varying covariates are handled (see Curran & Bauer, 2011; Wang & Maxwell, 2015).

MULTIVARIATE LATENT CHANGE SCORE MODEL

The *multivariate latent change score* model follows directly from the univariate models discussed in the previous chapter. For a bivariate model, we begin with the separation of true and residual scores for the two observed variables measured at time t. We can write

$$
\begin{aligned}
y_{ti} &= ly_{ti} + u_{ti} \\
x_{ti} &= lx_{ti} + s_{ti}
\end{aligned}
\tag{17.5}
$$

where y_{ti} and x_{ti} are observed scores at time t for individual i, ly_{ti} and lx_{ti} are true scores at time t for individual i, and u_{ti} and s_{ti} are unique scores at time t for individual i. The true scores at time t are then composed of the true score at the prior time point $(t-1)$ and the true change score from time $t-1$ to time t, which can be written as

$$
\begin{aligned}
ly_{ti} &= ly_{t-1i} + dy_{ti} \\
lx_{ti} &= lx_{t-1i} + dx_{ti}
\end{aligned}
\tag{17.6}
$$

where ly_{t-1i} and lx_{t-1i} are the true scores for individual i at time $t-1$, and dy_{ti} and dx_{ti} are true change scores for individual i from time $t-1$ to time t.

Moving to the equations for the latent change scores and building on the dual change score model discussed in the previous chapter, we can write equations for dy_{ti} and dx_{ti} that have constant change components, proportional change (within variable) effects, and *coupling* (across variable) effects. These equations can be written as

$$
\begin{aligned}
dy_{ti} &= g_{2i} + \pi_y \cdot ly_{t-1i} + \delta_y \cdot lx_{t-1i} \\
dx_{ti} &= j_{2i} + \pi_x \cdot lx_{t-1i} + \delta_x \cdot ly_{t-1i}
\end{aligned}
\tag{17.7}
$$

where g_{2i} and j_{2i} are constant change components, π_y and π_x are the proportional change parameters, and δ_y and δ_x are the coupling parameters. This model is referred to as the *bivariate dual change* model and is the most commonly fit bivariate latent change score model. Additionally, the multivariate associations modeled in the MGM (covariances among latent growth factors; covariance among residuals) are included in this model:

$$
ly_{1i},\, g_{2i},\, lx_{1i},\, j_{2i} \sim \mathrm{MVN}\left(
\begin{bmatrix} \gamma_{ly1} \\ \gamma_{g2} \\ \gamma_{lx1} \\ \gamma_{j2} \end{bmatrix},
\begin{bmatrix}
\sigma^2_{ly1} & & & \\
\sigma_{g2,ly1} & \sigma^2_{g2} & & \\
\sigma_{lx1,ly1} & \sigma_{lx1,g2} & \sigma^2_{lx1} & \\
\sigma_{j2,ly1} & \sigma_{j2,g2} & \sigma_{j2,lx1} & \sigma^2_{j2}
\end{bmatrix}
\right)
$$

$$
u_{ti},\, s_{ti} \sim \mathrm{MVN}\left(
\begin{bmatrix} 0 \\ 0 \end{bmatrix},
\begin{bmatrix} \sigma^2_u & \\ \sigma_{s,u} & \sigma^2_s \end{bmatrix}
\right)
$$

The bivariate dual change model combines aspects of growth models and autoregressive cross-lag models. This model is similar to the latent growth model as it is able to capture within-person change and between-person differences in change, and the model is similar to the autoregressive cross-lag model because it captures occasion-to-occasion associations between the variables. A path diagram of the bivariate dual change model is contained in Figure 17.1, where unlabeled paths are fixed at 1. In this figure, unique factors are not specifically drawn, but the variability in the unique factors is equal to the residuals of the observed scores (σ_u^2 and σ_s^2). The latent true scores, ly_2 through ly_5 and lx_2 through lx_5, are composed of the previous true score and the associated latent change score, dy_2 through dy_5 and dx_2 through dx_5, following Equation 17.6. The latent change scores (e.g., dx_2) have three inputs, including the constant change component (e.g., j_2), the previous true score of the same variable (e.g., lx_1), and the previous true score of the other variable (e.g., ly_1). The initial true scores (ly_1 and lx_1) and the constant change components (g_2 and j_2) have means, variances, and covariances with one another. The only model parameter from the bivariate dual change model that is not specified in the path diagram is the unique covariance ($\sigma_{s,u}$).

As in the autoregressive cross-lag model, four bivariate dual change models are often fit to the data to determine the nature of the time-sequential associations. First,

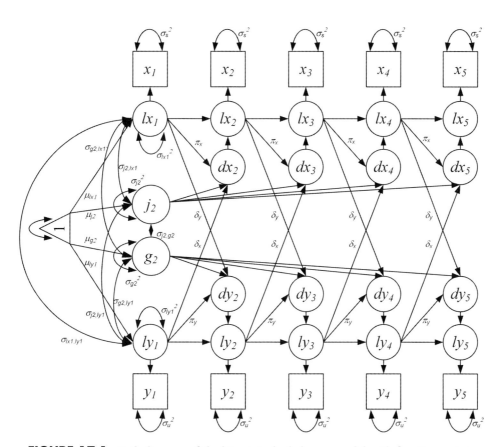

FIGURE 17.1. Path diagram of the bivariate dual change model with five time points.

the *no coupling* model is fit by fixing both coupling parameters to 0 (i.e., $\delta_y = \delta_x = 0$). This model serves as a baseline and posits no cross-variable time-sequential associations. Next, unidirectional coupling models are fit where either δ_y or δ_x is estimated. These models are referred to as $x \to \Delta y$ and $y \to \Delta x$, respectively. Finally, the *full coupling* model, where δ_y and δ_x are jointly estimated, is fit. All models are nested under the full coupling model and can be compared with likelihood ratio tests.

The bivariate dual change model accounts for within-person change and time-sequential associations, but the approach is not without its limitations. First and as noted in Chapter 17, the types of change trajectories are limited with the bivariate dual change score model. In the bivariate case, the change trajectories remain exponential with positive or negative deflections due to the coupling effects (see Grimm, An, McArdle, Zonderman, & Resnick, 2012). The change equations can be expanded in a variety of ways to accommodate different trajectories, although this is rarely done. Second and shared with the autoregressive cross-lag model, the proportional change and coupling effects are a combination of within- and between-person effects, and the between-person effects tend to dominate because sample size is often larger than the number of repeated assessments. Third, in the study of within-person dynamics, changes in the within-person mean are usually discarded before the study of time-sequential associations. In the latent change score approach, the means are not discarded and therefore influence the magnitude and direction of the proportional change and coupling parameters (π and δ).

ILLUSTRATION

To illustrate the fitting and interpretation of the bivariate dual change model, we analyze longitudinal mathematics and reading recognition data, expanding on the mathematics analyses presented in the previous chapter. The mathematics and reading recognition data were collected from the NLSY-CYA (Center for Human Resource Research, 2009), and both the mathematics and reading scores are from the PIAT (Dunn & Markwardt, 1970). The no coupling, two unidirectional coupling and full coupling models were fit to the mathematics and reading data with `Mplus` and `OpenMx`.

STRUCTURAL EQUATION MODELING IMPLEMENTATION

Full Coupling Dual Change Model

We describe `Mplus` and `OpenMx` code for fitting the full coupling model because the no coupling and unidirectional coupling models are simple restrictions of this model. After describing the code and output, we discuss parameter estimates for the full coupling model and then discuss model fit. In the datafile, the mathematics variables are `math2` through `math8`, and the reading variables are `rec2` through `rec8`. In the scripts, we utilize `lm` and `lr` for the latent true scores and `dm` and `dr` for the latent change scores for mathematics and reading, respectively.

Mplus

The `Mplus` script for the full coupling model fit to the mathematics and reading data is contained in Script 17.1. The script begins with the typical components of a title, datafile, and names of observed variables. Here, we focus on the `MODEL` statement. The `MODEL` statement begins with the dual change model for mathematics. This part of the script is nearly identical to the script from the previous chapter. The only change is the label for the proportional change parameter, which is now `pi_m` to indicate the proportional change parameter is for mathematics. The second part of the script is the dual change model for reading recognition. The elements in this part of the script follow the specification for mathematics with naming and labeling differences. The true scores for reading are `lr1` through `lr7`, the change scores are `dr2` through `dr7`, and the constant change factor is `j2`. The label for the residual variance for reading recognition is `sigma2_s`, and the label for the proportional change parameter is `pi_r`. In this script, we provided starting values for a few parameters to aid estimation. As the models have increased in complexity, the need for good starting values has also increased and this is the case with the full coupling dual change model. We provided starting values for the means of the initial true scores, the means of the constant change components, and the proportional change effects. These starting values were obtained from first fitting the dual change model to the mathematics and reading data separately.

The final part of the script, under `!! Bivariate Information`, contains all of the across variable path specifications. First, the covariances between the latent growth factors are specified. These covariances are for the initial true scores, `lm1` and `lr1`, and the two constant change components, `g2` and `j2`. Next, the residual covariances are specified. These seven covariances are between the oberved scores for mathematics and reading recognition at each time point (e.g., `math2 WITH rec2`) and are constrained to be equal across time by the common label, `sigma_su`. The final two collections of paths are for the coupling parameters. First, the coupling parameters from mathematics to changes in reading recognition (e.g., `dr2 ON lm1`) are specified and labeled `delta_r`. Second, the coupling parameters from reading recognition to changes in mathematics (e.g., `dm2 ON lr1`) are specified and labeled `delta_m`. Elements from this script can be removed to specify the no coupling and the two unidirectional coupling models. For example, the no coupling model can be specified by removing the final two collections of statements for the coupling effects. Similarly, the two unidirectional coupling models can be specified by removing one of these two collections of paths.

OpenMx

The `OpenMx` script for fitting the full coupling model to the mathematics and reading recognition data is contained in Script 17.2. The script begins by calling the dataset and

Script 17.1. Mplus Script for the Full Coupling Model

```
TITLE: Bivariate Dual Change Model-Full Coupling;

DATA: FILE = nlsy_math_wide_R.dat;

VARIABLE:
NAMES = id female lb_wght anti_k1
        math2-math8 comp2-comp8 rec2-rec8
        bpi2-bpi8 asl2-asl8 ax2-ax8 hds2-hds8 hyp2-hyp8 dpn2-dpn8 wdn2-wdn8
        age2-age8 men2-men8 spring2-spring8 anti2-anti8;

MISSING = .;
USEVAR = math2-math8 rec2-rec8;

ANALYSIS: TYPE = MEANSTRUCTURE;
          COVERAGE = 0;
          MODEL = NOCOVARIANCES;

MODEL:
!! Mathematics;
! Latent True Scores
    lm1 BY math2@1;           lm2 BY math3@1;           lm3 BY math4@1;
    lm4 BY math5@1;           lm5 BY math6@1;           lm6 BY math7@1;
    lm7 BY math8@1;

    math2-math8 (sigma2_u);   [math2-math8@0];
    lm1;                      [lm1*15];
    lm2-lm7@0;                [lm2-lm7@0];

! Autoregressions
    lm2 ON lm1@1;             lm3 ON lm2@1;             lm4 ON lm3@1;
    lm5 ON lm4@1;             lm6 ON lm5@1;             lm7 ON lm6@1;

! Latent Change Scores
    dm2 BY lm2@1;             dm3 BY lm3@1;             dm4 BY lm4@1;
    dm5 BY lm5@1;             dm6 BY lm6@1;             dm7 BY lm7@1;
    dm2-dm7@0;                [dm2-dm7@0];
```

```
! Constant Change Factor
    g2 BY dm2-dm7@1;        g2;                     [g2*15];
    lm1 WITH g2;

! Proportional Effects
    dm2 ON lm1*-.2 (pi_m);  dm3 ON lm2*-.2 (pi_m);  dm4 ON lm3*-.2 (pi_m);
    dm5 ON lm4*-.2 (pi_m);  dm6 ON lm5*-.2 (pi_m);  dm7 ON lm6*-.2 (pi_m);

!! Reading Recognition
! Latent True Scores
    lr1 BY rec2@1;          lr2 BY rec3@1;          lr3 BY rec4@1;
    lr4 BY rec5@1;          lr5 BY rec6@1;          lr6 BY rec7@1;
    lr7 BY rec8@1;

    rec2-rec8 (sigma2_s);   [rec2-rec8@0];
    lr1;                    [lr1*15];
    lr2-lr7@0;              [lr2-lr7@0];

! Autoregressions
    lr2 ON lr1@1;           lr3 ON lr2@1;           lr4 ON lr3@1;
    lr5 ON lr4@1;           lr6 ON lr5@1;           lr7 ON lr6@1;

! Latent Change Scores
    dr2 BY lr2@1;           dr3 BY lr3@1;           dr4 BY lr4@1;
    dr5 BY lr5@1;           dr6 BY lr6@1;           dr7 BY lr7@1;
    dr2-dr7@0;              [dr2-dr7@0];

! Constant Change Factor
    j2 BY dr2-dr7@1;        j2;                     [j2*10];
    lr1 WITH j2;
```

(continued)

Script 17.1. (Continued)

```
! Proportional Effects
    dr2 ON lr1*-.8 (pi_r);       dr3 ON lr2*-.8 (pi_r);       dr4 ON lr3*-.8 (pi_r);
    dr5 ON lr4*-.8 (pi_r);       dr6 ON lr5*-.8 (pi_r);       dr7 ON lr6*-.8 (pi_r);

!! Bivariate Information
    lm1 WITH lr1;                lm1 WITH j2;
    lr1 WITH g2;                 j2 WITH g2;

    math2 WITH rec2 (sigma_su);  math3 WITH rec3 (sigma_su);
    math4 WITH rec4 (sigma_su);  math5 WITH rec5 (sigma_su);
    math6 WITH rec6 (sigma_su);  math7 WITH rec7 (sigma_su);
    math8 WITH rec8 (sigma_su);

! Math -> Changes in Reading
    dr2 ON lm1 (delta_r);        dr3 ON lm2 (delta_r);
    dr4 ON lm3 (delta_r);        dr5 ON lm4 (delta_r);
    dr6 ON lm5 (delta_r);        dr7 ON lm6 (delta_r);

! Reading -> Changes in Math
    dm2 ON lr1 (delta_m);        dm3 ON lr2 (delta_m);
    dm4 ON lr3 (delta_m);        dm5 ON lr4 (delta_m);
    dm6 ON lr5 (delta_m);        dm7 ON lr6 (delta_m);

OUTPUT: SAMPSTAT;
```

Script 17.2. `OpenMx` **Script for the Full Coupling Model**

```
dcm.fc.omx <- mxModel('Full Coupling Model,Path Specification',
 type='RAM', mxData(observed=nlsy_math_wide, type='raw'),
 manifestVars=c('math2','math3','math4','math5','math6','math7','math8',
                'rec2','rec3','rec4','rec5','rec6','rec7','rec8'),
 latentVars=c('lm1','lm2','lm3','lm4','lm5','lm6','lm7',
              'dm2','dm3','dm4','dm5','dm6','dm7',
              'g2',
          'lr1','lr2','lr3','lr4','lr5','lr6','lr7',
              'dr2','dr3','dr4','dr5','dr6','dr7',
              'j2'),

# defining true scores
mxPath(from=c('lm1','lm2','lm3','lm4','lm5','lm6','lm7',
              'lr1','lr2','lr3','lr4','lr5','lr6','lr7'),
 to=c('math2','math3','math4','math5','math6','math7','math8',
      'rec2','rec3','rec4','rec5','rec6','rec7','rec8'),
 arrows=1, free=FALSE, values=1),

# Autoregressive Effects
mxPath(from=c('lm1','lm2','lm3','lm4','lm5','lm6',
              'lr1','lr2','lr3','lr4','lr5','lr6'),
 to=c('lm2','lm3','lm4','lm5','lm6','lm7',
      'lr2','lr3','lr4','lr5','lr6','lr7'),
arrows=1, free=FALSE, values=1),

# defining change scores
mxPath(from=c('dm2','dm3','dm4','dm5','dm6','dm7',
              'dr2','dr3','dr4','dr5','dr6','dr7'),
 to=c('lm2','lm3','lm4','lm5','lm6','lm7',
      'lr2','lr3','lr4','lr5','lr6','lr7'),
 arrows=1, free=FALSE, values=1),

# defining constant change factor for mathematics
mxPath(from='g2', to=c('dm2','dm3','dm4','dm5','dm6','dm7'),
 arrows=1, free=FALSE, values=1),

# defining constant change factor for reading
mxPath(from='j2', to=c('dr2','dr3','dr4','dr5','dr6','dr7'),
 arrows=1, free=FALSE, values=1),

# unique variance paths
mxPath(from=c('math2','math3','math4','math5','math6','math7','math8'),
 arrows=2, free=TRUE, values=35, labels='sigma2_u'),

mxPath(from=c('rec2','rec3','rec4','rec5','rec6','rec7','rec8'),
 arrows=2, free=TRUE, values=35, labels='sigma2_s'),

# unique covariance paths
mxPath(from=c('math2','math3','math4','math5','math6','math7','math8'),
 to=c('rec2','rec3','rec4','rec5','rec6','rec7','rec8'),
 arrows=2, free=TRUE, values=0, labels='sigma_su'),
```

(continued)

Script 17.2. (Continued)

```
# latent variable variances and covariances
mxPath(from=c('lm1','g2','lr1','j2'),
 arrows=2, connect='unique.pairs', free=TRUE,
 values=c(75, 0, 0, 0, 7, 0, 0, 75, 0, 10),
 labels=c('sigma2_lm1','sigma_g2lm1','sigma_lr1lm1','sigma_j2lm1',
                        'sigma2_g2',  'sigma_lr1g2', 'sigma_j2g2',
                                     'sigma2_lr1',  'sigma_j2lr1',
                                                    'sigma2_j2')),

# proportional parameters
mxPath(from=c('lm1','lm2','lm3','lm4','lm5','lm6'),
 to=c('dm2','dm3','dm4','dm5','dm6','dm7'),
 arrows=1, free=TRUE, values=-.2, labels='pi_m'),

mxPath(from=c('lr1','lr2','lr3','lr4','lr5','lr6'),
 to=c('dr2','dr3','dr4','dr5','dr6','dr7'),
 arrows=1, free=TRUE, values=-.2, labels='pi_r'),

# coupling parameters
mxPath(from=c('lr1','lr2','lr3','lr4','lr5','lr6'),
 to=c('dm2','dm3','dm4','dm5','dm6','dm7'),
 arrows=1, free=TRUE, values=0, labels='delta_m'),

mxPath(from=c('lm1','lm2','lm3','lm4','lm5','lm6'),
 to=c('dr2','dr3','dr4','dr5','dr6','dr7'),
 arrows=1, free=TRUE, values=0, labels='delta_r'),

# means and intercepts
mxPath(from='one', to=c('lm1','g2','lr1','j2'),
 arrows=1, free=TRUE, values=c(30, 15, 30, 15),
 labels=c('gamma_lm1','gamma_g2','gamma_lr1','gamma_j2'))

) # close model

dcm.fc.fit <- mxRun(dcm.fc.omx)

summary(dcm.fc.fit)
```

listing all of the manifest and latent variables in the model. The model is then specified with a series of mxPath statements.

In this specification, we have combined statements for both mathematics and reading recognition, as opposed to presenting them sequentially, to reduce script length. The first mxPath statement specifies the one-headed arrows, which are fixed at one, from the latent true scores for mathematics, lm1 through lm7, and reading recognition, lr1 through lr7, to their respective observed variables. Next, the autoregressive paths, which are also fixed at one, are specified as one-headed arrows between consecutive latent true scores for mathematics and reading recognition. The paths to specify the latent change scores follow. These paths are one-headed arrows from the latent change scores for mathematics, dm2 through dm7, and reading recognition, dr2 through dr7, to the latent true scores, lm2 through lm7 and lr2 through lr7, and fixed at one.

The paths to define the constant change components are then specified. These one-headed arrows begin at the constant change components, g2 for mathematics and j2 for reading recognition, and go to the latent change scores, dm2 through dm7 and dr2 through dr7, and are fixed at one. The residual variances for mathematics and reading recognition are specified in the next two mxPath statments. These two-headed arrows that begin and end at the observed variables, math2 through math8 and rec2 through rec8, are given starting values of 35 and labeled sigma2_u for mathematics and sigma2_s for reading recognition. The residual covariances are then specified as two-headed arrows going from the mathematics variables to the reading recognition variables. These paths are given a starting value of 0 and labeled sigma_su. Next, the covariance matrix for the growth factors, which includes the initial true scores for mathematics, lm1, and reading recognition, lr1, as well as the constant change components for mathematics, g2, and reading, j2, is specified. In this statement, connect='unique. pairs' is specified for a full covariance matrix for these latent variables. Starting values and labels are provided.

The proportional change effects are specified in the next two mxPath statements. These one-headed arrows begin from the the latent true scores, lm1 through lm6 for mathematics, and lr1 through lr6 for reading recognition, and go to the latent change scores, dm2 through dm7 and dr2 through dr7. These paths are given starting values of –0.20 and labeled pi_m and pi_r for mathematics and reading recognition, respectively. Next, the coupling parameters are specified in similar ways. For changes in mathematics, these paths originate at the latent true scores for reading recognition, lr1 through lr6, and go to the latent change scores for mathematics, dm2 through dm7. Similarly, for reading recognition the one-headed arrows go from the true scores for mathematics, lm1 through lm6, and go to the latent change scores for reading recognition, dr2 through dr7. These paths are labeled delta_m and delta_r, respectively, and given starting values of zero. The final mxPath statement is for the latent variable means. The initial latent true scores and the constant change components have estimated means. These one-headed arrows go from the constant, one, to lm1, g2, lr1, and j2 and are given starting values (i.e., 30, 15, 30, 15) and labels (gamma_lm1, gamma_g2, gamma_lr1, and gamma_j2). The model is closed, estimated with mxRun, and output is printed using summary.

The OpenMx script can be modified to specify the no coupling model as well as the two unidirectional coupling models. The no coupling model is specified by removing the mxPath statements for the coupling effects. The unidirectional coupling models are specified, removing one of the two mxPath statements for the coupling parameters.

Output

The Mplus and OpenMx results for the full coupling model fit to mathematics and reading recognition data are contained in Outputs 17.1 and 17.2, respectively. Parameter estimates from this model describe the mean and individual trajectories for mathematics and reading recognition as well as their associations over time. The mean trajectories for mathematics and reading comprehension begin at 32.53 and 34.36 (Mean of LM1 and

Output 17.1. Mplus Output for the Full Coupling Model

MODEL RESULTS

		Estimate	S.E.	Est./S.E.	Two-Tailed P-Value
DM2	ON				
	LM1	-0.295	0.116	-2.550	0.011
	LR1	0.052	0.099	0.528	0.597
DM3	ON				
	LM2	-0.295	0.116	-2.550	0.011
	LR2	0.052	0.099	0.528	0.597
DM4	ON				
	LM3	-0.295	0.116	-2.550	0.011
	LR3	0.052	0.099	0.528	0.597
DM5	ON				
	LM4	-0.295	0.116	-2.550	0.011
	LR4	0.052	0.099	0.528	0.597
DM6	ON				
	LM5	-0.295	0.116	-2.550	0.011
	LR5	0.052	0.099	0.528	0.597
DM7	ON				
	LM6	-0.295	0.116	-2.550	0.011
	LR6	0.052	0.099	0.528	0.597
DR2	ON				
	LR1	-0.487	0.116	-4.205	0.000
	LM1	0.381	0.131	2.915	0.004
DR3	ON				
	LR2	-0.487	0.116	-4.205	0.000
	LM2	0.381	0.131	2.915	0.004
DR4	ON				
	LR3	-0.487	0.116	-4.205	0.000
	LM3	0.381	0.131	2.915	0.004
DR5	ON				
	LR4	-0.487	0.116	-4.205	0.000
	LM4	0.381	0.131	2.915	0.004
DR6	ON				
	LR5	-0.487	0.116	-4.205	0.000
	LM5	0.381	0.131	2.915	0.004
DR7	ON				
	LR6	-0.487	0.116	-4.205	0.000
	LM6	0.381	0.131	2.915	0.004
LM1	WITH				
	G2	14.458	2.186	6.614	0.000
	LR1	57.332	5.464	10.492	0.000
	J2	6.299	3.089	2.039	0.041
LR1	WITH				
	J2	25.979	3.422	7.592	0.000
	G2	10.040	3.054	3.288	0.001
J2	WITH				
	G2	0.791	2.529	0.313	0.755
MATH2	WITH				
	REC2	6.464	1.242	5.204	0.000

MATH3	WITH			
REC3	6.464	1.242	5.204	0.000
MATH4	WITH			
REC4	6.464	1.242	5.204	0.000
MATH5	WITH			
REC5	6.464	1.242	5.204	0.000
MATH6	WITH			
REC6	6.464	1.242	5.204	0.000
MATH7	WITH			
REC7	6.464	1.242	5.204	0.000
MATH8	WITH			
REC8	6.464	1.242	5.204	0.000
Means				
LM1	32.526	0.446	72.895	0.000
G2	15.201	0.932	16.310	0.000
LR1	34.361	0.433	79.267	0.000
J2	10.987	0.939	11.706	0.000
Variances				
LM1	72.734	6.612	11.001	0.000
G2	5.791	1.718	3.37	0.001
LR1	72.256	7.331	9.856	0.000
J2	17.846	6.694	2.666	0.008
Residual Variances				
MATH2	31.439	1.637	19.202	0.000
MATH3	31.439	1.637	19.202	0.000
MATH4	31.439	1.637	19.202	0.000
MATH5	31.439	1.637	19.202	0.000
MATH6	31.439	1.637	19.202	0.000
MATH7	31.439	1.637	19.202	0.000
MATH8	31.439	1.637	19.202	0.000
REC2	33.336	1.784	18.691	0.000
REC3	33.336	1.784	18.691	0.000
REC4	33.336	1.784	18.691	0.000
REC5	33.336	1.784	18.691	0.000
REC6	33.336	1.784	18.691	0.000
REC7	33.336	1.784	18.691	0.000
REC8	33.336	1.784	18.691	0.000

LR1; gamma_lm1 and gamma_lr1), respectively. From there, the mean trajectories are described by their respective change equations, which are

$$dm_{ti} = 15.20 - 0.30 \cdot lm_{t-1i} + 0.05 \cdot lr_{t-1i}$$
$$dr_{ti} = 10.99 - 0.49 \cdot lr_{t-1i} + 0.38 \cdot lm_{t-1i}$$

(17.8)

Beginning with the change equation for mathematics, the mean of the constant change component was 15.20 (Mean of G2; gamma_g2) indicating a constant amount of growth each year, the proportional change effect was −0.30 (DM2 ON LM1; pi_m), indicating a limiting effect on the changes in mathematics based on prior mathematics scores, and

Output 17.2. OpenMx Output for the Full Coupling Model

```
free parameters:
           name   matrix   row     col      Estimate    Std.Error
1          pi_m     A      dm2     lm1    -0.29543517    0.1230187
2       delta_r     A      dr2     lm1     0.38055457    0.1342219
3       delta_m     A      dm2     lr1     0.05227485    0.1050620
4          pi_r     A      dr2     lr1    -0.48665444    0.1191467
5       sigma2_u     S     math2   math2   31.43856473   1.6371060
6       sigma_su     S     math2   rec2     6.46314035   1.2405521
7       sigma2_s     S     rec2    rec2    33.33472560   1.7852697
8     sigma2_lm1     S     lm1     lm1     72.74088290   6.6190641
9     sigma_g2lm1    S     lm1     g2      14.45852853   2.2332946
10     sigma2_g2     S     g2      g2       5.79127306   1.8144241
11   sigma_lr1lm1    S     lm1     lr1     57.33893409   5.4944486
12   sigma_lr1g2     S     g2      lr1     10.03994085   3.1857454
13    sigma2_lr1     S     lr1     lr1     72.25983403   7.3402842
14    sigma_j21m1    S     lm1     j2       6.29880756   3.1894127
15    sigma_j2g2     S     g2      j2       0.78975805   2.6251406
16    sigma_j21r1    S     lr1     j2      25.97918917   3.4731049
17     sigma2_j2     S     j2      j2      17.84760947   6.8938650
18     gamma_lm1     M     1       lm1     32.52558939   0.4483195
19      gamma_g2     M     1       g2      15.20156973   0.9519057
20     gamma_lr1     M     1       lr1     34.36146206   0.4336121
21      gamma_j2     M     1       j2      10.98690301   0.9413406

observed statistics: 4435
estimated parameters: 21
degrees of freedom: 4414
-2 log likelihood: 31364.6
number of observations: 933
Information Criteria:
         | df Penalty | Parameters Penalty | Sample - Size Adjusted
AIC:       22536.602           31406.60                          NA
BIC:        1179.881           31508.21                    31441.51
```

the coupling effect from reading recognition was 0.05 (DM2 ON LR1; delta_m), which was not significantly different from zero, indicating that reading scores were not a *leading indicator* of subsequent changes in mathematics. The change equation for reading recognition begins with the mean of the constant change component, which was 10.99 (Mean of J2; gamma_j2), indicating an annual positive effect on the changes in reading. The proportional change effect was –0.49 (DR2 ON LR1; pi_r), which indicates a limiting factor on changes in reading recognition based on prior reading scores, and the coupling effect was 0.38 (DR2 ON LM1; delta_r), which was significantly different from zero, indicating that mathematics was a positive leading indicator of the subsequent changes in reading recognition.

The variance and covariance parameters of the full coupling model highlight between-person differences in the change trajectories. There was significant variability in mathematics and reading true scores in second grade (Variance of LM1 and

LR1; `sigma2_lm1` and `sigma2_lr1`) as well as significant variability in the constant change components (Variance of G2 and J2; `sigma2_g2` and `sigma2_j2`). We note that the variability in the constant change components does not represent variability in within-person change because the constant change component is only one aspect of the change equation; however, it is the case that individuals with greater scores on the constant change components had greater amounts of change when holding all else constant. The covariance between initial true scores was 57.33 (LM1 WITH LR1; `sigma_lr1lm1`), indicating that the predicted reading and mathematics scores were strongly related in second grade. The covariance between the initial true score for mathematics and the constant change component for mathematics was 14.46 (LM1 WITH G2; `sigma_g2lm1`) and significantly different from zero, suggesting a Matthew effect, such that children with higher true scores in mathematics in second grade tended to show more overall growth. The covariance between the initial true score for mathematics and the constant change component for reading recognition was 6.30 (LM1 WITH J2; `sigma_j2lm1`), suggesting that children with stronger mathematics ability in second grade tended to show more positive growth in reading. The covariance between the initial true score for reading recognition and the constant change component for reading recognition was 25.98 (LR1 WITH J2; `sigma_j2lr1`), indicating a Matthew effect for reading abilities, where children with stronger reading skills in second grade tended to show greater change in reading skills. The covariance between the initial true score for reading recognition and the constant change component for mathematics was 10.04 (LR1 WITH G2; `sigma_lr1g2`), suggesting that students with strong reading skills in second grade tended to show greater changes in mathematics. Finally, the covariance between the constant change components was 0.79 (J2 WITH G2; `sigma_j2g2`) and not statistically significant, indicating that these aspects of change in reading and mathematics were not strongly tied together. We note that this does not mean that changes in mathematics were unrelated to changes in reading because the constant change components are only one aspect of the changes in each construct.

The final estimated parameters are the residual variances and the residual covariance. The residual variances for mathematics and reading recognition were 31.44 (Residual Variance of MATH2; `sigma2_u`) and 33.34 (Residual Variance of REC2; `sigma2_s`), respectively. Lastly, the residual covariance was 6.46 (MATH2 WITH REC2; `sigma_su`), indicating that time-specific unique scores for mathematics were positively associated with the time-specific unique scores for reading recognition.

Individual predicted trajectories for mathematics and reading recognition for a random subsample of $n = 50$ are contained in Figure 17.2. As seen in this figure, the predicted trajectories for both mathematics and reading recognition show the general pattern of rapid initial changes followed slower positive changes. These plots are useful to understand the overall model-based trajectories for mathematics and reading recognition, but only hint at their time-dependent dynamics. For example, on the one hand, trajectories for mathematics are very close to exponential in nature, which indicate a lack of influence from reading recognition to changes in mathematics. On the other hand, the trajectories for reading recognition appear to deviate from the exponential trajectory

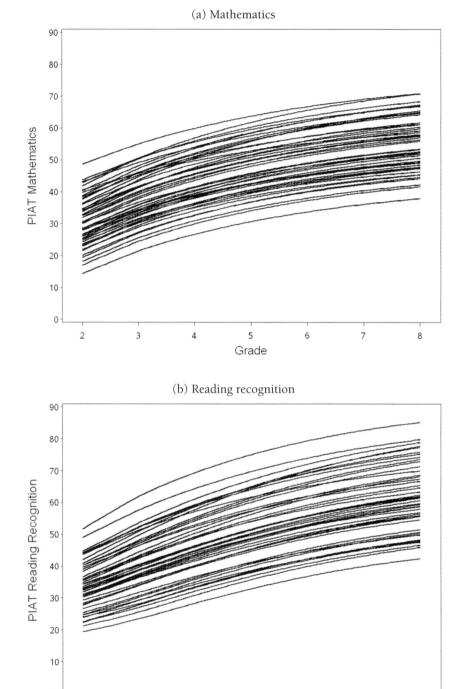

FIGURE 17.2. Predicted trajectories for (a) mathematics and (b) reading recognition based on the full coupling model.

(most clearly seen in the trajectories with lower initial scores), indicating an influence from mathematics.

One way to visualize the dynamic association found between reading recognition and mathematics is to plot a vector field (Boker & McArdle, 1995), which displays the direction and relative magnitude of changes in both reading recognition and mathematics for a given pair of scores. A vector field based on the full coupling model is contained in Figure 17.3. The direction combined with the length of each arrow represents the relative magnitude of the expected changes in both mathematics (vertical axis) and reading recognition (horizontal axis). Additionally, we plotted a 95% confidence ellipse for the true scores in mathematics and reading recognition. Thus, attention should focus on the arrows contained within the ellipse. One way to visualize the dynamics between mathematics on reading recognition with this plot is to imagine a vertical line at a given value of reading recognition (e.g., Reading Recognition = 50) and a horizontal line at a given value of mathematics (e.g., Mathematics = 50) and examine the direction and length of the arrows along these imagined lines. If we focus on the imagined vertical line where reading recognition equaled 50, we see that as mathematics scores increased (moving up the vertical line), the arrows point further to the right, indicating greater increases in reading recognition (i.e., positive coupling from mathematics). The arrows also point less upward, indicating less positive changes in mathematics (i.e., negative proportional change parameter for mathematics). Now, if we focus on the imagined horizontal line where mathematics equaled 50, we see that higher reading recognition scores lead to less positive changes in reading recognition (i.e., negative proportional change parameter

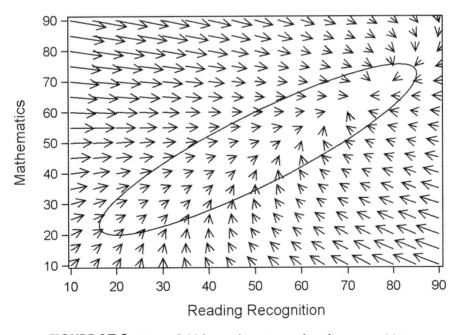

FIGURE 17.3. Vector field for mathematics and reading recognition.

for reading recognition) and very little change in the length of the arrows in the vertical direction, suggesting no effect on changes in mathematics (i.e., nonsignificant coupling from reading recognition to changes in mathematics).

Model Fit

Model fit information for the four bivariate dual change score models fit to the mathematics and reading recognition data is presented in Table 17.1. First, we note that all models adequately represented the data with good global fit information (RMSEA < 0.05, CFI and TLI > 0.95). To decide on the most appropriate model, we conduct likelihood ratio tests by examining the change in the χ^2 compared with the change in the number of estimated parameters. Beginning with the no coupling model and examining the improvement in fit for the two unidirectional coupling models, we can say that the addition of the path from mathematics to changes in reading recognition led to a significant improvement in model fit ($\Delta\chi^2 = 11.6$, $\Delta parameters = 1$, $p < .01$), but the addition of the path from reading to changes in mathematics did not significantly improve model fit ($\Delta\chi^2 = 3.5$, $\Delta parameters = 1$, $p = .06$). Now, starting from the $Math \rightarrow \Delta Read$ model, we can test the improvement in model fit for the full coupling model. The full coupling model did not significantly improve model fit ($\Delta\chi^2 = 0.3$ $\Delta parameters = 1$, $p = .58$). The comparison of the four models suggests that the $Math \rightarrow \Delta Read$ was the best representation of the data of the models fit. This conclusion is consistent with the examination of the significance of the coupling parameters above, which highlight the potential for mathematics to be a leading indicator of changes in reading recognition scores from second through eighth grade.

IMPORTANT CONSIDERATIONS

Bivariate latent change score models are one way to simultaneously examine within-person change and time-sequential associations between multiple constructs. As discussed in Chapter 16, the types of trajectories generated from the latent change score models are limited, given the way the models are typically fit (with a dual change model for each variable). Therefore, if individual trajectories do not follow this type of trajectory, the model can yield biased results. For this reason, it is important to examine global model fit and to interpret effects cautiously if the model does not adequately represent the data.

TABLE 17.1. Fit Statistics for the Four Bivariate Dual Change Models

Model	χ^2	Parameters	BIC	RMSEA	CFI	TLI
No coupling	181.7	19	31,506	0.030	0.969	0.972
Math → ΔRead	170.1	20	31,502	0.028	0.973	0.975
Read → ΔMath	178.2	20	31,510	0.029	0.970	0.972
Full coupling	169.8	21	31,508	0.028	0.973	0.975

We also note that the change equations can be modified in various ways to represent the researcher's theory of change. For example, in Grimm et al. (2012) univariate and bivariate models were extended to include effects from prior change scores to test whether recent changes as opposed to recent levels were the key predictor of subsequent changes. In this work, changes in memory performance were studied in conjunction with changes in the size of the lateral ventricle, and the authors found that prior changes in the size of the lateral ventricle were predictive of subsequent changes in memory performance. Thus, it was not the current size of the lateral ventricle that predicted subsequent declines in memory performance, but how the size of the lateral ventricle had recently changed.

Drawing conclusions from multivariate latent change score models should always be done with caution because such models are almost always fit with two and only two repeatedly measured variables and additional confounding or interacting constructs are excluded from the analysis. Thus, the conclusions are limited to the variables studied as well as the studied timespan (e.g., second through eighth grade). This is why our conclusion highlighted how mathematics is a *potential* leading indicator of changes in reading recognition during the observation period.

In the specification of the bivariate latent change score models, equality constraints were placed on the dynamic parameters (i.e., proportional change and coupling parameters). This is a common approach but is not necessary in most analyses. This constraint is often imposed because of the idea of *constant dynamics*. With constant dynamics, the dynamical system does not depend on the timespan of the observation, and therefore, the change equations do not depend on time. There are, of course, occasions when this constraint is unreasonable for statistical and theoretical reasons. For example, Dogan, Stockdale, Widaman, and Conger (2010) allowed the dynamic parameters to vary over time when studying the joint development of alcohol use and the number of sexual partners. It was found that the coupling parameter from alcohol use to changes in the number of sexual partners shrank over time as participants entered adulthood and began to maintain monogomous relationships. We also note that nonequality constraints can be imposed on the dynamic parameters to statistically test for trends in these parameters (see Grimm, 2006).

The multivariate latent change score framework can be extended in a variety of ways. For example, the multiple-group framework can be combined with the multivariate latent change score framework to examine group differences in the change equations and therefore, group differences in the dynamics (see Ferrer et al., 2010; Grimm, 2006; McArdle & Grimm, 2010). In a similar vein, the finite mixture model can be combined with the multivariate latent change score framework to search for groups of participants with different dynamics (Grimm, 2006; McArdle & Grimm, 2010). Furthermore, Chow, Grimm, Filteau, Dolan, and McArdle (2013) expanded the multivariate latent change score model to allow for *regime switching*, which is an extension of the finite mixture model where class membership is allowed to change over time. In such models, it is thought that there are unobserved groups of individuals with specific sets of dynamics and individuals are allowed to switch between unobserved groups over time, which allows *individual* dynamics to vary over time. Finally, we note that multivariate latent change score models can also be extended to second-order changes to study *acceleration* and their dynamics (see Hamagami & McArdle, 2007).

MOVING FORWARD

In the next chapter, we utilize the latent change score framework to place an emphasis on the within-person rate of change when studying nonlinear change processes (Grimm, Zhang, et al., 2013). That is, in models that are nonlinear with time there is seldom a parameter that represents within-person change because the rate of change varies over time within an individual. Through the use of latent change scores, the within-person rate of change can be studied and examined. Additionally, we discuss work by Zhang, McArdle, and Nesselroade (2012) on growth rate models, where traditional growth models are respecified to allow for the rate of change at a specific point in time to be represented as a parameter.

18

Rate-of-Change Estimates in Nonlinear Growth Models

The benefits of nonlinear growth models are evident from the work reviewed in this book. However, nonlinear growth models do have a key limitation that has not yet been discussed and is related to having a latent variable or random coefficient that represents the within-person rate of change. For example, in the linear growth model, where

$$y_{ti} = b_{1i} + b_{2i} \cdot t + u_{ti} \tag{18.1}$$

b_{2i} represents the instantaneous rate of change for individual i, which is constant within an individual over time, but allowed to vary over individuals. Growth models with non-linear trajectories do not often have a single random coefficient that represents the instantaneous rate of change because the rate of change varies within a person over time as well as varying across individuals at any specific time point. Recent work with latent change score models and transformations of growth models have allowed for a more detailed study of the instantaneous rate of change (Grimm, Castro-Schilo, et al., 2013; Grimm, Zhang, et al., 2013; Zhang et al., 2012). We review these approaches here and return to our example dataset on changes in height with the Jenss–Bayley growth model.

GROWTH RATE MODELS

Zhang, McArdle, et al. (2012) showed how growth models with nonlinear trajectories could be rotated to allow for the rate of change at a specific point in time to be parameterized as a random coefficient. To illustrate this approach, we begin with the Jenss–Bayley growth model initially discussed in Chapter 11. The Jenss–Bayley growth model can be written as

$$y_{ti} = b_{1i} + b_{2i} \cdot t + b_{3i} \cdot (\exp(\gamma \cdot t) - 1) + u_{ti} \tag{18.2}$$

where b_{1i} is the individual intercept (predicted height when $t = 0$), b_{2i} is the individual slope of the linear asymptote, b_{3i} is the vertical distance between the actual intercept and the intercept of the linear asymptote for individual i, $\exp(\gamma)$ is the universal ratio of acceleration of growth at time t to that at time $t - 1$, and u_{ti} is the time-specific residual score, which is assumed to be normally distributed, $u_{ti} \sim N(0, \sigma_u^2)$.

The first derivative of Equation 18.2 with respect to t is

$$\frac{dy_{ti}}{dt} = b_{2i} + b_{3i} \cdot \gamma \cdot \exp(\gamma \cdot t) \tag{18.3}$$

and represents the individual's instantaneous rate of change at time t. This derivative is dependent on time (t), which highlights how the rate of change is expected to vary within an individual over time. Next, a specific time point is selected where the instantaneous rate of change is of interest. For example, if 3 months is chosen (0.25 years), the instantaneous rate of change at 3 months is $dy_{t=0.25i}/dt = b_{2i} + b_{3i} \cdot \gamma \cdot \exp(\gamma \cdot 0.25)$. This equation can be solved for b_{2i} or b_{3i}, and the resultant can be substituted back in Equation 18.2 for the appropriate random coefficient, which allows the rate of change at 3 months to become a random coefficient. For example, solving for b_{2i} yields

$$b_{2i} = \frac{dy_{t=0.25i}}{dt} - b_{3i} \cdot \gamma \cdot \exp(\gamma \cdot 0.25) \tag{18.4}$$

and substituting Equation 18.4 into Equation 18.2 yields

$$y_{ti} = b_{1i} + \left(\frac{dy_{t=0.25i}}{dt} - b_{3i} \cdot \gamma \cdot \exp(\gamma \cdot 0.25) \right) \cdot t + b_{3i} \cdot (\exp(\gamma \cdot t) - 1) + u_{ti} \tag{18.5}$$

which can then be simplified to

$$y_{ti} = b_{1i} + \frac{dy_{t=0.25i}}{dt} \cdot t + b_{3i} \cdot [(-\gamma \cdot \exp(\gamma \cdot 0.25) \cdot t) + (\exp(\gamma \cdot t) - 1)] + u_{ti} \tag{18.6}$$

Equation 18.6 can be specified and fit in the nonlinear multilevel modeling framework or in the structural equation modeling framework (see Grimm & Ram, 2009) as long as appropriate nonlinear constraints are available. The importance of this framework is greatly expanded when studying *determinants of change* because predictors of the instantaneous rate of change at a specific point in time can be evaluated because the rate of change is a random coefficient. More specifically, a time-invariant covariate can be included as a predictor of b_{1i}, $dy_{t=.25i}/dt$, and b_{3i} and the prediction to $dy_{t=.25i}/dt$ is the effect of the predictor on the rate of change at 3 months. Furthermore, the rate of change (i.e., dy/dt) can be located at various ages (e.g., substitute 0.50 for 0.25 in Equation 18.6 to center the rate of change at 6 months) to study how the rate of change varies over time and how the effects of predictors on the rate of change vary over time.

LATENT CHANGE SCORE MODELS

A second approach to examining within-person change in nonlinear growth models is through *latent change score* models (Grimm, Zhang, Hamagami, & Mazzocco, 2013) because the latent change scores represent the within-person rate of change between measurement occasions. To begin, we define true scores (ly_{ti}) and unique scores (u_{ti}), such that

$$y_{ti} = ly_{ti} + u_{ti} \tag{18.7}$$

and then define the latent change scores (dy_{ti}) as

$$dy_{ti} = ly_{ti} - ly_{t-1i} \tag{18.8}$$

As in the previous chapters, we can now write a model for the latent change scores. Specifying growth models based on latent change scores requires the first derivative of model with respect to t. For example, the first derivative of the Jenss–Bayley growth model in Equation 18.2 is written in Equation 18.3. Based on this equation, we can write the following model for the latent change scores

$$dy_{ti} = b_{2i} + b_{3i} \cdot \gamma \cdot \exp(\gamma \cdot t) \tag{18.9}$$

where dy_{ti} is the latent change score at time t for individual i and b_{2i}, b_{3i}, and γ are as defined above. The model in Equation 18.9 is nonlinear with respect to parameters and can be estimated directly within the structural equation modeling framework. In this type of model, b_{2i} is a latent variable with factor loadings to the latent change scores that are set equal to 1, and b_{3i} is a latent variable with factor loadings to the latent change scores set to $\gamma \cdot \exp(\gamma \cdot t)$. We note that in specifying nonlinear growth models in the latent change score framework, it is necessary for the model to have an intercept defined as the true score at the initial time point as we have done in Equation 18.2 (e.g., b_{1i}).

Figure 18.1 is a path diagram of this model with five occasions of measurement, where all unlabeled paths are set equal to 1. The true scores and latent change scores are defined as in Equations 18.7 and 18.8. The intercept, b_1, is indicated by the first true score with a weight equal to one. The latent variables b_2 and b_3 are defined by the latent change scores with weights equal to 1 and $\gamma \cdot \exp(\gamma \cdot t)$, respectively. The latent growth factors, b_1, b_2, and b_3 have estimated means, variances, and covariances. To determine the mean rate of change over time, the mean expectations of the latent change scores can be calculated. Similarly, between-person variability in the rate of change over time can be calculated from the variance expectations of the latent change scores.

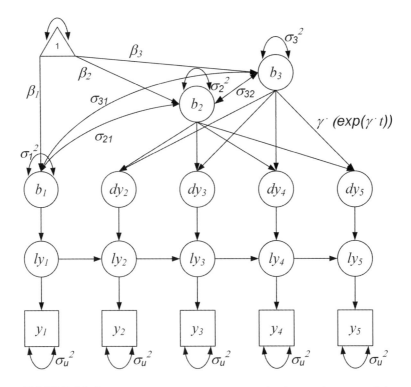

FIGURE 18.1. Path diagram of the Jenss–Bayley latent change model.

Time-invariant covariates can be added as predictors of the growth factors b_1, b_2, and b_3 to understand determinants of between-person differences in these aspects of change (see Chapter 5). A path diagram of such a model is presented in Figure 18.2 with X_1 as the time-invariant covariate. Using this approach, we can calculate the effect of X_1 on the rates of change as the *indirect* effects from X_1 through b_2 and b_3 to the latent change scores dy_2 through dy_5 (i.e., $\beta_{12} + \beta_{13} \cdot (\gamma \cdot (\exp (\gamma \cdot t)))$). For example, the effect of X_1 on the predicted rate of change between *times* 1 and 2 (i.e., dy_2) is $\beta_{12} + \beta_{13} \cdot \gamma \cdot \exp(\gamma \cdot 1)$, which is the indirect effect through b_2 (i.e., $\beta_{12} \cdot 1$) plus the indirect effect through b_3 (i.e., $\beta_{13} \cdot \gamma \cdot \exp (\gamma \cdot 1)$).[1] Additionally, several structural equation modeling programs allow for the calculation of these indirect effects with appropriate standard errors. Thus, the calculation of these indirect effects and their standard errors can be automated.

ILLUSTRATION

To illustrate the fitting of growth rate models and nonlinear growth models based on latent change scores, we utilize the longitudinal height data collected as part of the Berkeley

---

[1] In the latent change models, *time* always begins at 0. Thus, the t of the loading to the first latent change score is 1.

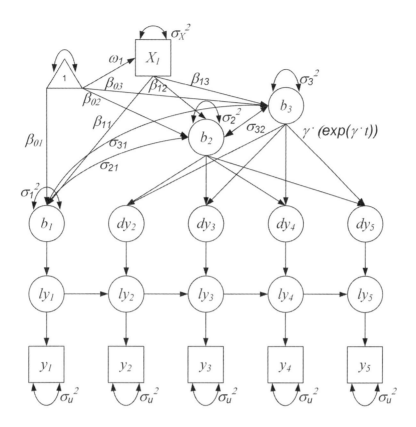

FIGURE 18.2. Path diagram of the Jenss–Bayley latent change model with a time-invariant covariate.

Growth Study and analyzed in Chapters 11, 12, and 13. The Jenss–Bayley growth model was fit as a growth rate model in the multilevel and structural equation modeling frameworks and as a latent change score model in the structural equation modeling framework. In the illustration of the growth rate model, we center the growth rate at 3 months; however, we specified models where the rate of growth was parameterized at each measurement occasion (ages = 1, 3, 6, 9, 12, 15, 18, 24, and 36 months) to describe the instantaneous rate of change over the observation period. Additionally, we included *labor duration* as a time-invariant covariate to illustrate the benefits of these models when including covariates.

MULTILEVEL MODELING IMPLEMENTATION

Jenss–Bayley Growth Rate Model

SAS

The NLMIXED script for the Jenss–Bayley growth rate model of Equation 18.6 with the growth rate centered at 3 months is contained in Script 18.1. The trajectory equation

Script 18.1. NLMIXED Script for the Jenss–Bayley Growth Rate Model

```
PROC NLMIXED DATA = height_long QPOINTS = 5;
    traject = b_1i + dy_i * age/12 + b_3i * (-gamma*exp(gamma*0.25)*(age/12)+(exp(gamma*(age/12))-1));

MODEL hght ~ NORMAL(traject, v_u);
RANDOM b_1i dy_i b_3i ~ NORMAL ([beta_1, beta_dy, beta_3], [v_1,
                                                            c_dy1,  v_dy,
                                                            c_31,   c_3dy,  v_3])

SUBJECT = id;
PARMS
    beta_1 = 50         beta_dy = 31        beta_3 = -18        gamma = -2
    v_1 = 8             v_dy = 12           v_3 = 9
    c_dy1 = 0           c_31 = 0            c_3dy = 0           v_u = 1;

RUN;
```

is specified for the growth rate model with age in months (age) divided by 12 as the timing metric to scale age in terms of years and dy_i representing the rate of change at 3 months (0.25 years in -gamma*exp(gamma*0.25)*(age/12)+(exp(gamma* (age/12))-1)). Next, the outcome, hght, is assumed to follow a normal distibution with a mean equal to the trajectory equation and residual variance labeled v_u. The random coefficients are then defined, which are b_1i, the predicted height for an individual at birth, dy_i, the individual rate of change at 3 months, and b_3i, the vertical distance between the intercept and the intercept of the linear asymptote. These random coefficients are assumed to have a multivariate normal distribution with estimated means ([beta_1, beta_dy, beta_3]) and a fully specified variance–covariance matrix. The random coefficients are random over children (SUBJECT = id) and then starting values are provided for all estimated parameters.

R

The code to specify the Jenss–Bayley growth rate model with the growth rate centered at 3 months using nlme is contained in Script 18.2. The nlme function is called, and the trajectory equation is specified for the growth rate model following Equation 18.6 with age scaled in years (age/12) as the timing metric. The dataset is then specified along with the fixed-effects parameters. The random coefficients (b_1i, dy_i, and b_3i) have fixed-effects parameters, and the gamma parameter is also a fixed-effects parameter. Thus, each of the random coefficients and gamma are listed on the fixed statement. The random line follows, and all the random coefficients are listed to estimate their variances and covariances. The groups line is used to indicate that the random effects are random with respect to subjects. Starting values are then provided for the fixed-effects parameters. Finally, na.action is specified to indicate that observations with incomplete data can be dropped from the analysis.

Output

Select output from the Jenss–Bayley growth rate model fit in NLMIXED and nlme is contained in Output 18.1 and 18.2, respectively. First, we note that the fit of the model was identical to that obtained in Chapter 11, supporting the notion that the models are equivalent. The mean of the intercept was 51.09 cm (beta_1; Fixed effect of b_1i) and represents the average height at birth (*age* = 0). The mean rate of change at 3 months was 31.30 cm/year (beta_dy; Fixed effect of dy_i), and the mean distance between the intercept and the intercept of the linear asymptote was −17.88 cm (beta_3; Fixed effect of b_3i). The gamma parameter was −2.06, and exponentiating this term yields 0.13 (exp (−2.06)), the ratio of acceleration at time *t* to that at time *t* − 1.

The random-effects parameters include the variances of the intercept, the rate of change at 3 months, and the distance between the intercepts and their covariances. The intercept variance was 7.39 (v_1; Random effect of b_1i) and represents

Script 18.2. `nlme` Script for the Jenss–Bayley Growth Rate Model

```
hght.jb.nlme <- nlme(hght~b_1i+dy_i*age/12 + b_3i*(-gamma*exp(gamma*0.25)*(age/12)+(exp(gamma*(age/12))-1)),
      data=hght_long,
      fixed=b_1i+dy_i+b_3i+gamma~1,
      random=b_1i+dy_i+b_3i~1,
      groups=~id,
      start=c(50, 10, -18, -2),
      na.action=na.omit)

summary(hght.jb.nlme)
```

452

Output 18.1. NLMIXED Output for the Jenss–Bayley Growth Rate Model

Parameter Estimates

Parameter	Estimate	Standard Error	DF	t Value	Pr > |t|	Alpha	Lower	Upper	Gradient
beta_1	51.0915	0.3524	80	144.98	<.0001	0.05	50.3902	51.7928	-0.00016
beta_dy	31.3015	0.5519	80	56.72	<.0001	0.05	30.2033	32.3998	0.000103
beta_3	-17.8812	0.4635	80	-38.58	<.0001	0.05	-18.8035	-16.9588	0.000219
gamma	-2.0634	0.07804	80	-26.44	<.0001	0.05	-2.2187	-1.9081	0.000627
v_1	7.3894	1.3519	80	5.47	<.0001	0.05	4.6991	10.0797	0.00004
v_dy	13.3853	2.7796	80	4.82	<.0001	0.05	7.8537	18.9169	0.000017
v_3	9.4219	2.1461	80	4.39	<.0001	0.05	5.1510	13.6929	0.000305
c_dy1	-5.3705	1.6073	80	-3.34	0.0013	0.05	-8.5692	-2.1718	-0.00036
c_31	4.8591	1.4200	80	3.42	0.0010	0.05	2.0332	7.6849	-0.00054
c_3dy	-10.9360	2.3952	80	-4.57	<.0001	0.05	-15.7026	-6.1694	0.000273
v_u	0.6710	0.05003	80	13.41	<.0001	0.05	0.5714	0.7705	-0.00003

Output 18.2. nlme Output for Jenss–Bayley Growth Rate Model

```
Random effects:
 Formula: list(b_1i ~ 1, dy_i ~ 1, b_3i ~ 1)
 Level: id
 Structure: General positive-definite, Log-Cholesky parametrization
          StdDev      Corr
 b_1i     2.7159331   b_1i     dy_i
 dy_i     3.6392135   -0.538
 b_3i     3.0897861    0.581   -0.974
 Residual 0.8192691

 Fixed effects: b_1i + dy_i + b_3i + gamma ~ 1
             Value    Std.Error    DF    t-value     p-value
 b_1i       51.15805  0.3431139    495   149.09931         0
 dy_i       31.16082  0.5243527    495    59.42721         0
 b_3i      -17.98512  0.4540739    495   -39.60836         0
 gamma      -2.02404  0.0619331    495   -32.68117         0
```

between-child variability in height at birth. The variance of the rate of change at 3 months was 13.39 (v_dy; Random effect of dy_i) and represents between-child variability in the instantaneous rate of growth at 3 months. Lastly, the variance of the distance between the intercepts was 9.42 (v_3; Random effect of b_3i) and represents the magnitude of between-child differences in this aspect of development, which is associated with differences in the amount of growth prior to the linear asymptote.

The covariance parameters indicated that birth height was negatively associated with the instantaneous rate of growth at 3 months (c_dy1; Corr between b_1i and dy_i), highlighting how infants who were born taller tended to have slower rates of growth at three months. Birth height was positively associated with the distance between intercepts (c_31; Corr between b_1i and b_3i), indicating that infants who were taller at birth tended to have a shorter distance between their intercepts, which indicated less growth before transitioning to their linear asymptote. Lastly, the covariance between the instantaneous rate of change at 3 months and the distance between the intercepts was negative (c_3dy; Corr between dy_i and b_3i), indicating that infants who were growing more rapidly at 3 months tended to show more growth prior to transitioning to their linear asymptote (i.e., greater distance between the intercepts).

Scripts 18.1 and 18.2 were then modified to center the dy_i random coefficient at different points in time. For example, changing 0.25 in Equation 18.6 to 0.50 would center dy_i at 6 months, and this process was repeated to center dy_i at all measurement occasions. After fitting these models, the fixed- and random-effects parameters for dy_i were entered into a datafile to create a plot of the mean rate of change (i.e., beta_dy or Fixed effect of dy_i) against age along with a 95% confidence interval on the between-person differences in the rate of change (i.e., beta_dy±1.96*SQRT(v_dy)). This plot is contained in Figure 18.3. From this figure we see how the mean rate of change decreased with age and began to stabilize around 24 months to a more or less constant rate of change of less than 10 cm/year. Additionally, we see the large amounts

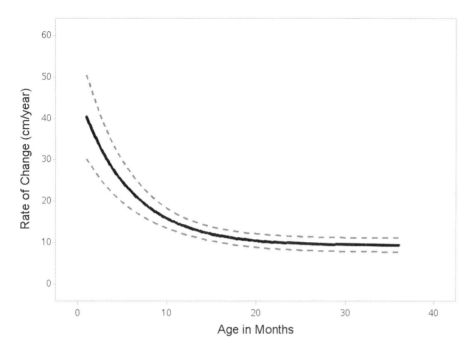

FIGURE 18.3. Plot of the mean rate of change and the 95% confidence interval on between-person differences in the rate of change.

of between-child differences in the rate of change in infancy and how the magnitude of these differences decreased with increasing age.

Next, Scripts 18.1 and 18.2 were modified to include labor duration[2] as a predictor of the three random coefficients of the Jenss–Bayley growth rate model. That is, labor duration was included as a predictor of the intercept (b_1i), the rate of change at 3 months (dy_i), and the difference between the intercepts (b_3i). Additionally, we varied the centering of the rate of change from 1 month through 36 months to examine how the effect of labor duration on the rate of change varied with age. After fitting these models, we output the estimated effect of labor duration on the rate of change along with its standard error and plotted this effect along with its confidence interval against age in Figure 18.4. As seen in this figure, labor duration was negatively related to the instantaneous rate of change in height during early infancy and positively related to the instantaneous rate of change in height from 18 through 36 months of age. Thus, the association between the rate of growth and labor duration was complex because the magnitude and direction of the effect varied as a function of age. Shorter labor durations (potentially easier labors) were associated with a faster growth rate in early infancy, but longer labor durations were associated with faster rates of growth from 18 through 36 months.

---

[2]Labor duration was standardized prior to including it as a predictor.

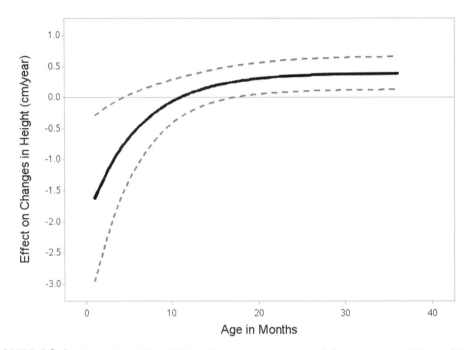

FIGURE 18.4. Plot of the effect of labor duration on the rate of change and its 95% confidence interval.

STRUCTURAL EQUATION MODELING IMPLEMENTATION

Jenss–Bayley Growth Rate Model

We describe Mplus and OpenMx code for fitting the Jenss–Bayley growth rate model using the longitudinal height data from the Berkeley Growth Study. These data are structured in the wide format with a separate variable for each assessment (hght1 through hght36). As above, when fitting the model the timing metric is *age*, scaled in years since birth, and the rate of change is centered at 3 months.

Mplus

The MODEL statement from Mplus is contained in Script 18.3. First, the latent variables are defined using the BY keyword. The intercept, b1, is identified by the repeated height measurements, with factor loadings set equal to 1. The latent variable for the rate of change at 3 months, dy, is defined by the height variables with linearly changing factor loadings. These factor loadings are centered at birth (0 months) and scaled in terms of years. Thus, the factor loading for height measured at 1 month is 0.083, and the factor loading for height at 36 months is 3. The next latent variable, b3, is the difference between the intercepts. The factor loadings for this latent variable are dependent on an

Script 18.3. `Mplus` Script for the Jenss–Bayley Growth Rate Model

```
MODEL:
    b1 BY hght01-hght36@1;
    dy BY hght01@.083 hght03@.25 hght06@.5 hght09@.75 hght12@1
          hght15@1.25 hght18@1.5 hght24@2  hght36@3;
    b3 BY hght01* (L31)
          hght03  (L32)
          hght06  (L33)
          hght09  (L34)
          hght12  (L35)
          hght15  (L36)
          hght18  (L37)
          hght24  (L38)
          hght36  (L39);

    b1*8 dy*1 b3*8;
    b1 WITH dy b3;
    dy WITH b3;
    [b1*50 dy*6 b3*-18];

    hght01-hght36*2 (sigma2_u);
    [hght01-hght36@0];
MODEL CONSTRAINT:
    new(gamma*-2);

    L31 = -gamma*exp(gamma*0.25)*0.0833+(exp(gamma*0.0833)-1);
    L32 = -gamma*exp(gamma*0.25)*0.25  +(exp(gamma*0.25  )-1);
    L33 = -gamma*exp(gamma*0.25)*0.5   +(exp(gamma*0.5   )-1);
    L34 = -gamma*exp(gamma*0.25)*0.75  +(exp(gamma*0.75  )-1);
    L35 = -gamma*exp(gamma*0.25)*1     +(exp(gamma*1     )-1);
    L36 = -gamma*exp(gamma*0.25)*1.25  +(exp(gamma*1.25  )-1);
    L37 = -gamma*exp(gamma*0.25)*1.50  +(exp(gamma*1.50  )-1);
    L38 = -gamma*exp(gamma*0.25)*2     +(exp(gamma*2     )-1);
    L39 = -gamma*exp(gamma*0.25)*3     +(exp(gamma*3     )-1);
```

estimated parameter (`gamma`) and are therefore specified with labels, which will be used in the `MODEL CONSTRAINT` command.

The variances of the latent variables are then specified by listing their names along with appropriate starting values. Next, the covariances between latent variables are specified using the keyword `WITH`. The means of the latent variables are then specified in square brackets along with starting values. Next, the residual variances of the observed variables are specified with a starting value of 2 and labeled `sigma2_u` to force their estimates to be equal across time. The last part of the `MODEL` statement is for the intercepts of the observed scores, which are fixed at 0.

The `MODEL CONSTRAINT` statement is then utilized to impose the nonlinear constraints on the factor loadings for `b3`. The `new()` command is used to create a new parameter, `gamma`, which is given a starting value of –2. The constraints on the factor loadings are then specified. The labels of the factor loadings for `b3` appear on the left-hand side of the equations and the constraint appears on the right-hand side of the equation with the associated age in years varying across the nine constraints. For the Jenss–Bayley growth rate model, the constraint is `-gamma*exp(gamma*0.25)*age+(exp(gamma*age)-1)`, where `age` is set equal to the age in years for each observed variable. To change the centering of the rate of change latent variable, `dy`, the `0.25` in the constraint is changed to the age in years of the chosen centering point (e.g., 0.50 for the rate of change to be centered at 6 months). And as described in Chapter 5, time-invariant covariates can be included as predictors of `b1`, `dy`, and `b3` to examine how the time-invariant covariates predict the rate of change at specific time points.

OpenMx

The `OpenMx` script for fitting the Jenss–Bayley growth rate model to the longitudinal height data is contained in Script 18.4. The script begins by calling the dataset and listing all of the manifest and latent variables in the model. Note that the latent variables include `dy`, the rate of change at 3 months. The model is then specified with a series of `mxPath`, `mxMatrix`, and `mxAlgebra` statements.

The first `mxPath` statement is used to specify the residual variances of the height variables. These paths are two-headed arrows that originate from each height variable (`hght01` through `hght36`), given a starting value of 2, and labeled `sigma2_u` to constrain them to be equal across time. Next, latent variable variances and covariances are specified. In this statement, the latent variables are specified as the originating variables (`from=c(b1,dy,b3)`), and `connect='unique.pairs'` is used to specify all variances and covariances among these variables in one statement. These paths are two-headed arrows, given starting values according to an upper triangular matrix, and appropriate labels.

The next three `mxPath` statements are for the factor loadings to define the latent variables `b1`, `dy`, and `b3`. All factor loadings originate at the latent variable and go to the repeated measures of height. Factor loadings for `b1` are fixed (`free=FALSE`) and set equal to 1. Factor loadings for `dy` are fixed and change linearly with age in terms of years. Thus, the factor loading for the 1-month assessment is 0.0833, and the factor loading for the 36-month assessment is 3. Lastly, the factor loadings for `b3` are specified. These factor loadings are not freely estimated but constrained to follow a nonlinear function of age with an estimated parameter. Thus, we set `free=FALSE` and specify their labels as elements of a matrix, `Load[1,1]` through `Load[9,1]`, which will be subsequently defined. The last `mxPath` statement is for the means of the latent variables. These one-headed arrows originate from the constant (`one`) and go to the three latent variables, are freely estimated (`free=TRUE`), and given starting values and appropriate labels.

The final part of the `OpenMx` script is a series of `mxMatrix` statements and an `mxAlgebra` statement. These statements are required to specify the additional parameter (`gamma`) and to constrain the factor loadings of `b3` to change according to a nonlinear function of age. The first `mxMatrix` specifies the additional parameter. This 9 × 1 matrix has elements that are freely estimated but constrained to be equal due to the common

Script 18.4. OpenMx Script for the Jenss–Bayley Growth Rate Model

```
jb.hght.omx <- mxModel('Jenss Bayley Growth Rate Model', type='RAM',
  mxData(observed=hght_wide, type='raw'),
  manifestVars=c('hght01','hght03','hght06','hght09','hght12','hght15','hght18','hght24','hght36'),
  latentVars=c('b1','dy','b3'),

# residual variances
  mxPath(from=c('hght01','hght03','hght06','hght09','hght12','hght15','hght18','hght24','hght36'),
    arrows=2, free=TRUE, values=2, labels='sigma2_u'),

# latent variable covariances
  mxPath(from=c('b1','dy','b3'), connect='unique.pairs',
    arrows=2, free=TRUE, values=c(10, 0, 0,
                                       1, 0,
                                          10),
    labels=c('sigma2_1','sigma_dy1','sigma_31','sigma2_dy','sigma_3dy','sigma2_3')),

# factor loadings
  mxPath(from='b1', to=c('hght01','hght03','hght06','hght09','hght12','hght15','hght18','hght24','hght36'),
    arrows=1, free=FALSE, values=1),

  mxPath(from='dy', to=c('hght01','hght03','hght06','hght09','hght12','hght15','hght18','hght24','hght36'),
    arrows=1, free=FALSE, values=c(.0833, .25, .5, .75, 1, 1.25, 1.5, 2, 3)),

  mxPath(from='b3', to=c('hght01','hght03','hght06','hght09','hght12','hght15','hght18','hght24','hght36'),
    arrows=1, free=FALSE,
    labels=c('Load[1,1]','Load[2,1]','Load[3,1]','Load[4,1]','Load[5,1]',
             'Load[6,1]','Load[7,1]','Load[8,1]','Load[9,1]')),

# latent variable means
  mxPath(from='one', to=c('b1','dy','b3'),
    arrows=1, free=TRUE, values=c(50, 30, -18),
    labels=c('beta_1','beta_dy','beta_3')),

  mxMatrix('Full', 9, 1, free = TRUE, values = -2, labels = 'g', name = 'gamma'),
  mxMatrix('Full', 9, 1, free = FALSE, values = c(.0833,.25,.5,.75,1,1.25,1.5,2,3), name = 'time'),
  mxMatrix('Full', 9, 1, free = FALSE, values = 0.25, name = 'age_c'),
  mxMatrix('Full', 9, 1, free = FALSE, values = 1, name = 'one'),
  mxAlgebra(-gamma*exp(gamma*age_c)*time+(exp(gamma*time)-one), name='Load')
) # Close Model

jb.hght.fit <- mxRun (jb.hght.omx)

summary(jb.hght.fit)
```

459

label (g), and the matrix is named gamma. The second mxMatrix is also 9 × 1, contains elements that are fixed to values corresponding to the timing of the assessments (age in years), and named time. The last two mxMatrix statements are needed to specify the constants for the nonlinear function of time. The first 9 × 1 matrix is named age_c and is set to 0.25, the time at which dy, the latent variable representing the rate of change, is centered. The second 9 × 1 matrix is named one and set equal to 1, which is also a constant in the nonlinear function of age. Finally, the mxAlgebra statement is specified to constrain the factor loadings of b3 to change according to a specific nonlinear function with an estimated parameter. The constraint is -gamma*exp(gamma*age_c)*time+ (exp(gamma*time)-one). We note that the matrix names are used when specifying the constraint, and the name of the mxAlgebra is Load, which corresponds to the factor loading labels for b3. To change the centering of dy, the value in the age_c matrix is changed. And as described in Chapter 5, time-invariant covariates can be included as predictors of b1, dy, and b3 to examine how the time-invariant covariates predict the rate of change at specific time points.

Output

The Mplus and OpenMx output for the Jenss–Bayley growth rate model fit to the height data is contained in Output 18.3 and 18.4, respectively. Beginning with the means of the latent variables, we find that the mean intercept was 51.11 cm (Means of B1; beta_1), reflecting the predicted mean height of children at birth. The mean rate of growth at 3 months was 31.28 cm/year (Means of DY; beta_dy), and the mean difference between the intercepts was –17.88 cm (Means of B3; beta_3). The estimate of the gamma parameter was –2.06, and exponentiating this value yields the ratio of acceleration, which was 0.13 (exp (–2.06)). There was significant variability in each of the three latent variables. The variance of the intercept was 7.38 (Variances of B1; sigma2_1), the variance of the rate of growth at three months was 13.36 (Variances of DY; sigma2_dy), and the variance of the difference between the intercepts was 9.42 (Variances of B3; sigma2_3).

The covariances among the three latent variables from the Jenss–Bayley growth rate model were all significant. The height at birth was negatively associated with the rate of growth at 3 months (B1 WITH DY; sigma_dy1) and positively associated with the difference between the intercepts (B1 WITH B3; sigma_31). Thus, children who were born taller tended to show a slower rate of growth at 3 months and to transition to their linear rate of growth sooner. The rate of growth at three months was positively associated with the differences between the intercepts (DY WITH B3; sigma_3dy), indicating that children who were growing more rapidly at 3 months tended to take longer to transition to their linear asymptote. Finally, the residual variance was 0.67 (Residual Variance of HGHT01; sigma2_u) and represents individual variability in growth that was not accounted for by the Jenss–Bayley growth rate model.

As in the specifications when using the multilevel modeling software, the rate of change, dy, was centered at each measurement occasion and the beta_dy and sigma2_dy parameters were organized into a datafile along with the centering age.

Output 18.3. Mplus Output for the Jenss–Bayley Growth Rate Model

MODEL RESULTS

		Estimate	S.E.	Est./S.E.	Two-Tailed P-Value
B1	BY				
HGHT01		1.000	0.000	999.000	999.000
HGHT03		1.000	0.000	999.000	999.000
HGHT06		1.000	0.000	999.000	999.000
HGHT09		1.000	0.000	999.000	999.000
HGHT12		1.000	0.000	999.000	999.000
HGHT15		1.000	0.000	999.000	999.000
HGHT18		1.000	0.000	999.000	999.000
HGHT24		1.000	0.000	999.000	999.000
HGHT36		1.000	0.000	999.000	999.000
DY	BY				
HGHT01		0.083	0.000	999.000	999.000
HGHT03		0.250	0.000	999.000	999.000
HGHT06		0.500	0.000	999.000	999.000
HGHT09		0.750	0.000	999.000	999.000
HGHT12		1.000	0.000	999.000	999.000
HGHT15		1.250	0.000	999.000	999.000
HGHT18		1.500	0.000	999.000	999.000
HGHT24		2.000	0.000	999.000	999.000
HGHT36		3.000	0.000	999.000	999.000
B3	BY				
HGHT01		-0.055	0.004	-15.375	0.000
HGHT03		-0.095	0.006	-15.809	0.000
HGHT06		-0.028	0.003	-10.524	0.000
HGHT09		0.136	0.004	30.523	0.000
HGHT12		0.358	0.013	28.320	0.000
HGHT15		0.615	0.021	29.535	0.000
HGHT18		0.892	0.029	31.226	0.000
HGHT24		1.478	0.043	34.661	0.000
HGHT36		2.695	0.067	40.055	0.000
B1	WITH				
DY		-5.359	1.604	-3.340	0.001
B3		4.854	1.419	3.421	0.001
DY	WITH				
B3		-10.926	2.393	-4.567	0.000
Means					
B1		51.106	0.352	145.147	0.000
DY		31.275	0.551	56.743	0.000
B3		-17.877	0.464	-38.531	0.000
Variances					
B1		7.384	1.351	5.467	0.000
DY		13.360	2.774	4.817	0.000
B3		9.424	2.146	4.391	0.000
Residual Variances					
HGHT01		0.670	0.050	13.411	0.000
HGHT03		0.670	0.050	13.411	0.000

(*continued*)

Output 18.3. (Continued)

HGHT06	0.670	0.050	13.411	0.000
HGHT09	0.670	0.050	13.411	0.000
HGHT12	0.670	0.050	13.411	0.000
HGHT15	0.670	0.050	13.411	0.000
HGHT18	0.670	0.050	13.411	0.000
HGHT24	0.670	0.050	13.411	0.000
HGHT36	0.670	0.050	13.411	0.000
New/Additional Parameters				
GAMMA	-2.060	0.078	-26.432	0.000

Output 18.4. `OpenMx` Output for the Jenss–Bayley Growth Rate Model

	name	matrix	row	col	Estimate	Std.Error
free parameters:						
1	sigma2_u	S	hght01	hght01	0.6709178	0.05002753
2	sigma2_1	S	b1	b1	7.3891622	1.35169231
3	sigma_dy1	S	b1	dy	-5.3705598	1.60722221
4	sigma2_dy	S	dy	dy	13.3859797	2.77918533
5	sigma_31	S	b1	b3	4.8598350	1.42009656
6	sigma_3dy	S	dy	b3	-10.9381660	2.39513845
7	sigma2_3	S	b3	b3	9.4251581	2.14645975
8	beta_1	M	1	b1	51.0933316	0.35236203
9	beta_dy	M	1	dy	31.2982305	0.55181261
10	beta_3	M	1	b3	-17.8806570	0.46359367
11	g	gamma	1	1	-2.0629726	0.07802445

These parameters were used to make a plot of the mean rate of change against age along with the 95% confidence interval on the between-person differences in the rate of change (i.e., plot in Figure 18.3). Additionally, the labor duration variable was included as a predictor of the three latent variables (b1, dy, and b3) of the Jenss–Bayley growth rate model. This estimate and its confidence interval were then organized into a datafile to make Figure 18.4. We note that the magnitude of the association between labor duration and the rate of change varied slightly from the estimates obtained from the multilevel modeling framework because of the incomplete data on labor duration and the different approaches to handling incomplete data in the two frameworks.

Jenss–Bayley Latent Change Model

Mplus

The MODEL statement from Mplus for the Jenss–Bayley latent change model is contained in Script 18.5. The script begins by defining the latent true scores following Equation 18.7. We define latent true scores from 0 (ly00) through 36 months (ly36) in 1-year increments. Latent true scores for ages with an associated observed variable are defined using the keyword BY with a fixed weight of 1 (e.g., ly01 BY hght01@1), whereas latent true scores for ages without an associated observed variable are defined using the keyword BY using an observed variable with a fixed weight of 0 (e.g., ly00 BY

Script 18.5. *Mplus* Script for the Jenss–Bayley Latent Change Model

```
MODEL:
!Latent True Scores
ly00 BY hght01@0;
ly01 BY hght01@1;  ly02 BY hght02@1;  ly03 BY hght03@1;  ly04 BY hght04@1;  ly05 BY hght05@1;  ly06 BY hght06@1;
ly07 BY hght07@1;  ly08 BY hght08@1;  ly09 BY hght09@1;  ly10 BY hght10@1;  ly11 BY hght11@1;  ly12 BY hght12@1;
ly13 BY hght13@1;  ly14 BY hght14@1;  ly15 BY hght15@1;  ly16 BY hght16@1;  ly17 BY hght17@1;  ly18 BY hght18@1;
ly19 BY hght19@1;  ly20 BY hght20@1;  ly21 BY hght21@1;  ly22 BY hght22@1;  ly23 BY hght23@1;  ly24 BY hght24@1;
ly25 BY hght25@1;  ly26 BY hght26@1;  ly27 BY hght27@1;  ly28 BY hght28@1;  ly29 BY hght29@1;  ly30 BY hght30@1;
ly31 BY hght31@1;  ly32 BY hght32@1;  ly33 BY hght33@1;  ly34 BY hght34@1;  ly35 BY hght35@1;  ly36 BY hght36@1;

!Autoregressions
ly01 ON ly00@1;  ly02 ON ly01@1;  ly03 ON ly02@1;  ly04 ON ly03@1;  ly05 ON ly04@1;  ly06 ON ly05@1;
ly07 ON ly06@1;  ly08 ON ly07@1;  ly09 ON ly08@1;  ly10 ON ly09@1;  ly11 ON ly10@1;  ly12 ON ly11@1;
ly13 ON ly12@1;  ly14 ON ly13@1;  ly15 ON ly14@1;  ly16 ON ly15@1;  ly17 ON ly16@1;  ly18 ON ly17@1;
ly19 ON ly18@1;  ly20 ON ly19@1;  ly21 ON ly20@1;  ly22 ON ly21@1;  ly23 ON ly22@1;  ly24 ON ly23@1;
ly25 ON ly24@1;  ly26 ON ly25@1;  ly27 ON ly26@1;  ly28 ON ly27@1;  ly29 ON ly28@1;  ly30 ON ly29@1;
ly31 ON ly30@1;  ly32 ON ly31@1;  ly33 ON ly32@1;  ly34 ON ly33@1;  ly35 ON ly34@1;  ly36 ON ly35@1;

!Latent Change Scores
dy01 BY ly01@1;  dy02 BY ly02@1;  dy03 BY ly03@1;  dy04 BY ly04@1;  dy05 BY ly05@1;  dy06 BY ly06@1;
dy07 BY ly07@1;  dy08 BY ly08@1;  dy09 BY ly09@1;  dy10 BY ly10@1;  dy11 BY ly11@1;  dy12 BY ly12@1;
dy13 BY ly13@1;  dy14 BY ly14@1;  dy15 BY ly15@1;  dy16 BY ly16@1;  dy17 BY ly17@1;  dy18 BY ly18@1;
dy19 BY ly19@1;  dy20 BY ly20@1;  dy21 BY ly21@1;  dy22 BY ly22@1;  dy23 BY ly23@1;  dy24 BY ly24@1;
dy25 BY ly25@1;  dy26 BY ly26@1;  dy27 BY ly27@1;  dy28 BY ly28@1;  dy29 BY ly29@1;  dy30 BY ly30@1;
dy31 BY ly31@1;  dy32 BY ly32@1;  dy33 BY ly33@1;  dy34 BY ly34@1;  dy35 BY ly35@1;  dy36 BY ly36@1;

!Means & Variances
hght01-hght36*2 (sigma2_u);      [hght01-hght36@0];
ly00-ly36@0;                     [ly00-ly36@0];
dy01-dy36@0;                     [dy01-dy36@0];
```

(continued)

Script 18.5. (Continued)

```
!Latent Variables
b1 BY ly00@1;
b2 BY dy01-dy36@1;
b3 BY dy01* (L01)
   dy02 (L02)
   dy03 (L03)
   dy04 (L04)
   dy05 (L05)
   dy06 (L06)
   dy07 (L07)
   dy08 (L08)
   dy09 (L09)
   dy10 (L10)
   dy11 (L11)
   dy12 (L12)
   dy13 (L13)
   dy14 (L14)
   dy15 (L15)
   dy16 (L16)
   dy17 (L17)
   dy18 (L18)
   dy19 (L19)
   dy20 (L20)
   dy21 (L21)
   dy22 (L22)
   dy23 (L23)
   dy24 (L24)
   dy25 (L25)
```

```
dy26    (L26)
dy27    (L27)
dy28    (L28)
dy29    (L29)
dy30    (L30)
dy31    (L31)
dy32    (L32)
dy33    (L33)
dy34    (L34)
dy35    (L35)
dy36    (L36);
b1*10 b2*.1 b3*10;
b1 WITH b2 b3;
b2 WITH b3;
[b1*50 b2*1 b3*-18];

MODEL CONSTRAINT:
new(gamma*-2);

L01 = gamma*exp(gamma*1);    L02 = gamma*exp(gamma*2);    L03 = gamma*exp(gamma*3);    L04 = gamma*exp(gamma*4);
L05 = gamma*exp(gamma*5);    L06 = gamma*exp(gamma*6);    L07 = gamma*exp(gamma*7);    L08 = gamma*exp(gamma*8);
L09 = gamma*exp(gamma*9);    L10 = gamma*exp(gamma*10);   L11 = gamma*exp(gamma*11);   L12 = gamma*exp(gamma*12);
L13 = gamma*exp(gamma*13);   L14 = gamma*exp(gamma*14);   L15 = gamma*exp(gamma*15);   L16 = gamma*exp(gamma*16);
L17 = gamma*exp(gamma*17);   L18 = gamma*exp(gamma*18);   L19 = gamma*exp(gamma*19);   L20 = gamma*exp(gamma*20);
L21 = gamma*exp(gamma*21);   L22 = gamma*exp(gamma*22);   L23 = gamma*exp(gamma*23);   L24 = gamma*exp(gamma*24);
L25 = gamma*exp(gamma*25);   L26 = gamma*exp(gamma*26);   L27 = gamma*exp(gamma*27);   L28 = gamma*exp(gamma*28);
L29 = gamma*exp(gamma*29);   L30 = gamma*exp(gamma*30);   L31 = gamma*exp(gamma*31);   L32 = gamma*exp(gamma*32);
L33 = gamma*exp(gamma*33);   L34 = gamma*exp(gamma*34);   L35 = gamma*exp(gamma*35);   L36 = gamma*exp(gamma*36);

OUTPUT: TECH4;
```

`hght01@0`). These place holder or *phantom* variables allow the spacing of latent true scores to be constant, even though the spacing of observed scores is not. Thus, the time lag between consecutive true scores is 1 month, and this is constant from 0 through 36 months. The latent true score at 0 months was created to estimate the mean and variance of height at birth.

In the next section, autoregressive paths are specified between consecutive true scores. These paths are fixed at 1 following Equation 18.8, where the true score at time t equals the true score at time $t - 1$ plus the true change. Completing the second half of this equation, the latent change scores are specified. The latent change scores, `dy01` through `dy36`, are indicated BY the latent true scores, `ly01` through `ly36`, with weights equal to 1. The intercepts and residual variances of the observed, latent true, and latent change scores are then specified. The residual variances of the observed variables are given a starting value of 2 and labeled `sigma2_u` to constrain them to be equal across time. The intercepts of the observed variables, latent true, and latent change scores are all fixed at 0 because their expected means come from the higher-order latent variables that are subsequently specified. Similarly, the residual variances of the latent true and latent change scores are also fixed at 0.

In the next section of the script, the higher-order latent variables are specified. First, the intercept, `b1`, is indicated BY the first latent true score with a weight of 1 (`b1 BY ly00@1`). Next, and following Equation 18.9, the latent variables `b2` and `b3` are specified. These latent variables are indicated by the latent change scores (`dy01` through `dy36`) because the outcome in Equation 18.9 is the derivative of the nonlinear function. The latent variable `b2` is defined BY the latent change scores with weights equal to 1. The factor loadings for `b3` change according to a nonlinear function with an estimated parameter. Thus, the factor loadings are specified and given labels (`L01` through `L36`), which are subsequently used in the MODEL CONSTRAINT command. Next, the variances, covariances, and means of `b1`, `b2`, and `b3` are specified in typical fashion.

The final aspect of the MODEL command is the MODEL CONSTRAINT command where the nonlinear constraints for the factor loadings of `b3` are specified. First, the parameter, gamma, is created using the `new()` statement. Next, the nonlinear constraints are specified, and the nonlinear constraint is $\gamma \cdot \exp(\gamma \cdot t)$. Thus, the factor loadings `L01` through `L36` are set equal to `gamma*exp(gamma*age)`, where `age` is the number of months since birth. The OUTPUT statement requests the TECH4 output, which prints the model implied (expected) means and covariance matrices for the latent variables. In this output, information regarding the mean and variance of the rate of change at each measurement occasion can be obtained.

OpenMx

The OpenMx script for the Jenss–Bayley latent change model is contained in Script 18.6. The script begins with the typical components to specify the datafile and data type along with manifest and latent variables contained in the model. Of note, the latent variables include the growth factors (`b1`, `b2`, and `b3`), latent true scores for each month from 0

Script 18.6. OpenMx Script for Jenns–Bayley Latent Change Model

```
jb.hght.omx <- mxModel('Jenss Bayley Latent Change Model, Path Specification', type='RAM',
mxData(observed=hght_wide, type='raw'),
manifestVars=c('hght01','hght03','hght06','hght09','hght12','hght15','hght18','hght24','hght36'),
latentVars=c('b1','b2','b3',
             'ly00','ly01','ly02','ly03','ly04','ly05','ly06','ly07','ly08','ly09',
             'ly10','ly11','ly12','ly13','ly14','ly15','ly16','ly17','ly18','ly19',
             'ly20','ly21','ly22','ly23','ly24','ly25','ly26','ly27','ly28','ly29',
             'ly30','ly31','ly32','ly33','ly34','ly35','ly36',
             'dy01','dy02','dy03','dy04','dy05','dy06','dy07','dy08','dy09',
             'dy10','dy11','dy12','dy13','dy14','dy15','dy16','dy17','dy18','dy19',
             'dy20','dy21','dy22','dy23','dy24','dy25','dy26','dy27','dy28','dy29',
             'dy30','dy31','dy32','dy33','dy34','dy35','dy36'),

# Residual Variances
mxPath(from=c('hght01','hght03','hght06','hght09','hght12','hght15','hght18','hght24','hght36'),
arrows=2, free=TRUE, values=2, labels='sigma2_u'),

# Latent True Scores
mxPath(from=c('ly01','ly03','ly06','ly09','ly12','ly15','ly18','ly24','ly36'),
to=c('hght01','hght03','hght06','hght09','hght12','hght15','hght18','hght24','hght36'),
arrows=1, free=FALSE, values=1),

# Autoregressive Paths
mxPath(from=c('ly00','ly01','ly02','ly03','ly04','ly05','ly06','ly07','ly08','ly09',
              'ly10','ly11','ly12','ly13','ly14','ly15','ly16','ly17','ly18','ly19',
              'ly20','ly21','ly22','ly23','ly24','ly25','ly26','ly27','ly28','ly29',
              'ly30','ly31','ly32','ly33','ly34','ly35'),
       to=c('ly01','ly02','ly03','ly04','ly05','ly06','ly07','ly08','ly09','ly10',
            'ly11','ly12','ly13','ly14','ly15','ly16','ly17','ly18','ly19','ly20',
            'ly21','ly22','ly23','ly24','ly25','ly26','ly27','ly28','ly29','ly30',
            'ly31','ly32','ly33','ly34','ly35','ly36'),
arrows=1, free=FALSE, values=1),
```

(continued)

467

Script 18.6. (*Continued*)

```
# Latent Change Scores
mxPath(from=c('dy01','dy02','dy03','dy04','dy05','dy06','dy07','dy08','dy09','dy10',
    'dy11','dy12','dy13','dy14','dy15','dy16','dy17','dy18','dy19','dy20',
    'dy21','dy22','dy23','dy24','dy25','dy26','dy27','dy28','dy29','dy30',
    'dy31','dy32','dy33','dy34','dy35','dy36'),
    to=c('ly01','ly02','ly03','ly04','ly05','ly06','ly07','ly08','ly09','ly10',
    'ly11','ly12','ly13','ly14','ly15','ly16','ly17','ly18','ly19','ly20',
    'ly21','ly22','ly23','ly24','ly25','ly26','ly27','ly28','ly29','ly30',
    'ly31','ly32','ly33','ly34','ly35','ly36'),
    arrows=1, free=FALSE, values=1),

# Factor Loadings
mxPath(from='b1', to='ly00', arrows=1, free=FALSE, values=1),

mxPath(from='b2',
    to=c('dy01','dy02','dy03','dy04','dy05','dy06','dy07','dy08','dy09','dy10'
    'dy11','dy12','dy13','dy14','dy15','dy16','dy17','dy18','dy19','dy20',
    'dy21','dy22','dy23','dy24','dy25','dy26','dy27','dy28','dy29','dy30',
    'dy31','dy32','dy33','dy34','dy35','dy36'),
    arrows=1, free=FALSE, values=1),

mxPath(from='b3',
    to=c('dy01','dy02','dy03','dy04','dy05','dy06','dy07','dy08','dy09','dy10',
    'dy11','dy12','dy13','dy14','dy15','dy16','dy17','dy18','dy19','dy20',
    'dy21','dy22','dy23','dy24','dy25','dy26','dy27','dy28','dy29','dy30',
    'dy31','dy32','dy33','dy34','dy35','dy36'),
    arrows=1, free=FALSE,
```

```
labels=c('Load[1,1]',   'Load[2,1]',   'Load[3,1]',   'Load[4,1]',   'Load[5,1]',
         'Load[6,1]',   'Load[7,1]',   'Load[8,1]',   'Load[9,1]',   'Load[10,1]',
         'Load[11,1]',  'Load[12,1]',  'Load[13,1]',  'Load[14,1]',  'Load[15,1]',
         'Load[16,1]',  'Load[17,1]',  'Load[18,1]',  'Load[19,1]',  'Load[20,1]',
         'Load[21,1]',  'Load[22,1]',  'Load[23,1]',  'Load[24,1]',  'Load[25,1]',
         'Load[26,1]',  'Load[27,1]',  'Load[28,1]',  'Load[29,1]',  'Load[30,1]',
         'Load[31,1]',  'Load[32,1]',  'Load[33,1]',  'Load[34,1]',  'Load[35,1]',
         'Load[36,1]')),

# Latent Variable Covariances
mxPath(from=c('b1','b2','b3'), connect='unique.pairs', arrows=2,
free=TRUE, values=c(8,0,0,.1,0,12),
labels=c('sigma2_1','sigma_21','sigma_31','sigma2_2','sigma_32','sigma2_3')),

# Latent Variable Means
mxPath(from='one', to=c('b1','b2','b3'),
arrows=1, free=TRUE, values=c(50, 1, -20), labels=c('beta_1','beta_2','beta_3')),

mxMatrix('Full', 36, 1, free = TRUE, values = -1, labels = 'g', name = 'gamma'),
mxMatrix('Full', 36, 1, free = FALSE, values = c(1, 2, 3, 4, 5, 6, 7, 8, 9,10,
                                                 11,12,13,14,15,16,17,18,19,20,
                                                 21,22,23,24,25,26,27,28,29,30,
                                                 31,32,33,34,35,36), name = 'time'),

mxAlgebra(gamma*exp(gamma*time), name='Load')
) # Close Model
```

(ly00) through 36 months (ly36), and latent change scores from 1 (dy01) through 36 months (dy36). The model is then specified with mxPath, mxMatrix, and mxAlgebra statements.

The first mxPath statement is for the residual variances of the observed variables. These two-headed paths begin from the repeatedly observed measures of height, are freely estimated, given starting values, and labeled sigma2_u to constrain them to be equal over time. Next, the latent true scores are specified. In OpenMx, we only need to specify the latent true scores that have corresponding observed variables. Thus, we specify latent true scores for height at 1, 3, 6, 9, 12, 15, 18, 24, and 36 months. These latent variables are defined by one-headed arrows to their respective observed variables that are fixed (free=FALSE) to 1 (values=1). Next, the autoregressive paths between consecutive true scores are specified. These one-headed arrows connect consecutive true scores with one-headed arrows that are fixed at 1. Thus, they originate from each of the first 36 true scores (ly00 through ly35) and go to the second 36 true scores (ly01 through ly36). The latent change scores are then specified in a similar fashion. These one-headed paths orginate from each latent change score (dy01 through dy36), go to the corresponding latent true score (ly01 through ly36), and are fixed at 1. Now, the latent change and latent true scores are all defined and the growth factors are specified next.

First, the intercept is specified with a one-headed path from b1 to the first true score, ly00, that is fixed at 1. Next, b2, the linear asymptote, is defined with one-headed arrows to the latent change scores that are fixed at 1. The last growth factor, the difference in the intercepts, is defined with one-headed arrows from b3 to the latent change scores. The values of these factor loadings vary according to a nonlinear function with an estimated parameter. Therefore, these factor loadings are not free to vary (free=FALSE) and are labeled Load[1,1] through Load[36,1], which are elements of a subsequently defined mxAlgebra statement. The final two mxPath statements are for the covariances and means of the growth factors. The covariance paths originate from b1, b2, and b3, and connect='unique.pairs' is used to specify covariances among each pair of latent variables. The covariances are then given starting values and labels. The one-headed paths for the means originate from the constant, one, and go to each of the growth factors, are freely estimated, given appropriate starting values, and labels.

The final parts of the OpenMx script include two mxMatrix statements and one mxAlgebra statement to constrain the factor loadings of b3 to change according to a nonlinear function with an estimated parameter. The first mxMatrix statement defines the new estimated parameter. The dimension of this matrix is 36 × 1 because there are 36 factor loadings for b3. The elements of the matrix are freely estimated, given starting values of −1, and labeled g to impose an equality constraint on the elements of the matrix. Finally, the matrix is named gamma, which will be used in the mxAlgebra statement. The second mxMatrix is specified for the timing of the latent change scores. The matrix contains fixed values ranging from 1 to 36 and is named time. Lastly, the mxAlgebra statement specifies the nonlinear function for the factor loadings of b3 following Equation 18.9. The mxAlgebra is named Load, which mirrors the labels of the factor loadings for b3.

Output

Select Mplus and OpenMx output for the Jenss–Bayley latent change model fit to the height data is contained in Output 18.5 and 18.6, respectively. We first note that the fit of the Jenss–Bayley latent change model was identical to the fit of the Jenss–Bayley growth model in Chapter 11, supporting the notion of their equivalence. Turning to the parameter estimates, we begin with the means of the growth factors. The mean of the intercept was 51.09 cm (Means of B1; beta_1), which was the predicted mean height of children at birth. The mean of the linear asymptote was 0.77 (Means of B2; beta_2) and is the predicted mean *monthly* rate of growth during the toddler years. The mean of the difference between the intercepts was –19.51 (Means of B3; beta_3). We note that the estimated mean of b3 is different from the estimate from previous runs of this model (see above and Chapter 11), where the mean difference between the intercepts was –17.88 cm. When utilizing the latent change score framework for fitting nonlinear models, there is a rescaling of certain growth parameters; however, the interpretation of the individual differences in this parameter is retained. The estimate of the gamma parameter was –0.17, and exponentiating this value yields the ratio of acceleration, which is 0.84 (exp (–0.17)).

Output 18.5. Mplus Output for the Jenss–Bayley Latent Change Model

MODEL RESULTS

		Estimate	S.E.	Est./S.E.	Two-Tailed P-Value
B1	WITH				
B2		0.051	0.031	1.641	0.101
B3		5.302	1.549	3.422	0.001
B2	WITH				
B3		0.061	0.044	1.370	0.171
Means					
B1		51.092	0.352	144.983	0.000
B2		0.773	0.014	53.839	0.000
B3		-19.511	0.481	-40.534	0.000
Variances					
B1		7.389	1.352	5.466	0.000
B2		0.005	0.001	4.082	0.000
B3		11.217	2.548	4.402	0.000
Residual Variances					
HGHT01		0.671	0.050	13.411	0.000
HGHT03		0.671	0.050	13.411	0.000
HGHT06		0.671	0.050	13.411	0.000
HGHT09		0.671	0.050	13.411	0.000
HGHT12		0.671	0.050	13.411	0.000
HGHT15		0.671	0.050	13.411	0.000
HGHT18		0.671	0.050	13.411	0.000
HGHT24		0.671	0.050	13.411	0.000
HGHT36		0.671	0.050	13.411	0.000
New/Additional Parameters					
GAMMA		-0.172	0.007	-26.441	0.000

Output 18.6. `OpenMx` Output for the Jenss–Bayley Latent Change Model

```
free parameters:
        name     matrix     row       col      Estimate      Std.Error
1    sigma2_u       S    hght01    hght01     0.670980400    0.050032497
2    sigma2_1       S        b1        b1     7.389475093    1.351926441
3    sigma_21       S        b1        b2     0.051259168    0.031235912
4    sigma2_2       S        b2        b2     0.005135751    0.001258138
5    sigma_31       S        b1        b3     5.302019879    1.549272128
6    sigma_32       S        b2        b3     0.060944216    0.044478289
7    sigma2_3       S        b3        b3    11.217447404    2.548071659
8      beta_1       M         1        b1    51.091521148    0.352396075
9      beta_2       M         1        b2     0.772904804    0.014355921
10     beta_3       M         1        b3   -19.510558876    0.481331366
11          g    gamma        1         1    -0.171949628    0.006503177
```

We note that the ratio of acceleration is scaled in terms of *months*, the timing metric in the fitted model as opposed to *years*, which was the timing metric in previous runs.

As in the previous run of the Jenss–Bayley growth model, there was significant variability in each of the three latent growth factors. The variance of the intercept was 7.39 (`Variances of B1; sigma2_1`), the variance of the linear asymptote was 0.01 (`Variances of B2; sigma2_2`), and the variance of the difference between the intercepts was 11.22 (`Variances of B3; sigma2_3`). In terms of the covariances among the three growth factors, the only significant association was found between height at birth and the difference between the intercepts (`B1 WITH B3; sigma_31`). Thus, children who were born taller tended to transition to their linear rate of growth earlier. Finally, the residual variance was 0.67 (`Residual Variance of HGHT01; sigma2_u`), representing individual variability in growth not accounted for by the Jenss–Bayley latent change model.

In the `Mplus` script, we requested the TECH4 output, which prints the model-based mean and covariance expectations of the latent variables. In `OpenMx`, covariance expectations can be output using `jb.hght.fit$output$expectations`, and mean and covariance expectations can be obtained through a series of `mxMatrix` and `mxAlgebra` statements or through a series of calculations involving the RAM matrices automatically generated by `OpenMx` (see McArdle & McDonald, 1984). The TECH4 output from `Mplus` for the first five latent change scores is contained in Output 18.7. From this information, we can see how the mean monthly rate of growth is expected to decline from 3.60 cm/month to 2.19 cm/month from the first to the fifth month of development. Turning to the estimated covariance matrix for the latent variables, we focus on the diagonal elements to obtain estimates of the magnitude of between-child differences in the rate of change. The variance of the latent change score at 1 month (`DY01`) was 0.22, and therefore the standard deviation was 0.47. An approximate 95% confidence interval of between-child differences in changes at 1 month can be found by multiplying this value by 1.96 and adding and subtracting this product to the mean value. Thus, the majority of children were expected to grow at a rate of 2.67 to 4.52 cm/month at

Output 18.7. Selection of Technical Output 4 from `Mplus`

ESTIMATED MEANS FOR THE LATENT VARIABLES

	DY01	DY02	DY03	DY04	DY05
1	3.598	3.151	2.776	2.459	2.193

ESTIMATED COVARIANCE MATRIX FOR THE LATENT VARIABLES

	DY01	DY02	DY03	DY04	DY05
DY01	0.223				
DY02	0.187	0.157			
DY03	0.157	0.132	0.111		
DY04	0.131	0.111	0.093	0.078	
DY05	0.110	0.093	0.078	0.066	0.056

1 month old. This procedure can be extended to all latent change scores to evaluate the magnitude of the mean change as well as the magnitude of between-child differences in change at each point in time.

A plot of the mean monthly rate of growth along with the 95% confidence interval on the between-child differences is contained in Figure 18.5. As seen in this plot, the monthly rate of growth sharply declined through infancy along with the magnitude of between-child differences. The monthly rate of growth was expected to stabilize around 28 months at a rate of 0.80 cm/month. The magnitude of between-child differences also

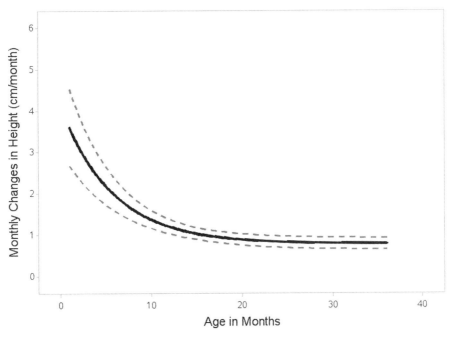

FIGURE 18.5. Longitudinal plot of the monthly mean rate of growth from the Jenss–Bayley latent change model.

stabilized around this age, and the 95% confidence interval on the rate of growth was 0.66 to 0.94 cm/month. This plot mirrors Figure 18.3; however, we note that the scale is different (cm/month vs. cm/year), and the estimates from the latent change approach actually represent the rate of change between the two latent true scores as opposed to the instantaneous rate of change at each measurement occasion. This type of plot can also be made for the latent true scores to obtain the group-based mean predicted trajectory and 95% confidence interval. However, we note that this information can be easily obtained by traditional growth modeling approaches.

As with the multilevel and structural equation modeling specifications of the Jenss–Bayley growth rate model, labor duration was included as a predictor of b1, b2, and b3 in the Jenss–Bayley latent change model to examine the association between the rate of growth and labor duration. Here, we estimated the indirect effects from labor duration to the latent change scores. In *Mplus*, the MODEL INDIRECT: statement can be used to calculate the estimates of the indirect effects and their standard errors. In the MODEL INDIRECT: statement, we list each indirect effect of interest. For example, DY01 IND dur_lbr; through DY36 IND dur_lbr; where dur_lbr is the labor duration variable and DY01 and DY36 are the latent change scores at 1 and 36 months. In OpenMx, estimates of the indirect effects can be calculated using a series of mxMatrix and mxAlgebra statements, and confidence intervals can be obtained using mxCI.

Figure 18.6 is a plot of the association between labor duration and individual changes in height from 1 through 36 months. The association is plotted along with the 95% confidence interval and a horizontal reference line at 0. From this plot, we can see that labor

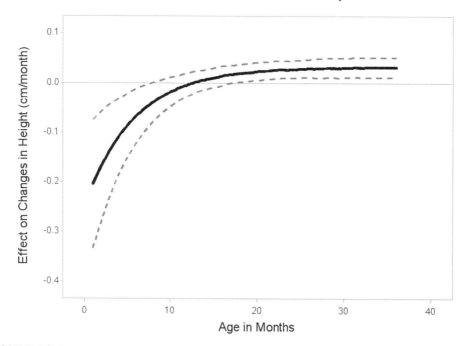

FIGURE 18.6. Longitudinal plot of the effect of labor duration on individual changes in height.

duration was negatively associated with the individual rate of growth from 1 through 7 months; unrelated to growth rate from 8 to 17 months; and positively associated with the individual growth rate from 18 to 36 months. Thus, mothers who were in labor longer tended to have children who grew at a slower rate from 1 to 7 months but grew at a faster rate from 18 to 36 months. This complex association between labor duration and individual changes in height is best studied with the latent change or growth rate frameworks, where this association can be directly estimated along with an appropriate standard error and confidence interval. We note that studying this association with typically specified growth models led to a positive association between labor duration and the slope of the linear asymptote (b2) and a positive association with the difference between the intercepts (b3); however, this information is difficult to translate to a clear picture of the association between labor duration and the individual rate of growth.

IMPORTANT CONSIDERATIONS

The growth rate and latent change approaches to studying the individual rate of change in nonlinear growth models provide information regarding the mean and variance of the individual rate of change at each point in time. This information is not directly or easily obtained from traditional growth modeling procedures. Looking back to the work of Baltes and Nesselroade (1979), we see that the first two rationales of longitudinal research are the direct identification of intraindividual change and the direct identification of interindividual differences in intraindividual change. The growth rate and latent change approaches allow for the direct estimation of parameters related to both rationales when using nonlinear growth models (Grimm, Castro-Schilo, & Davoudzadeh, 2013). The traditional growth modeling approach highlights aspects or characteristics of change in nonlinear growth models. At times, such aspects of change are of great interest (e.g., timing of puberty; see Grimm et al., 2011); however, certain nonlinear growth models have parameters that are not easily interpreted and difficult to map onto theoretical notions of change (e.g., the Jenss–Bayley growth model). For example, the quadratic model has parameters that are difficult to understand in isolation, and it is difficult to understand how the growth parameters are related to the individual rate of change at each point in time. Cudeck and du Toit (2002) discussed a reparameterization to highlight the time at which the function reaches its maximum (or minimum) and the maximum (or minimum) value, as these parameters are more interpretable and understanding variability in such parameters can provide meaningful information. Furthermore, Biesanz, Deeb-Sossa, Papadakis, Bollen, and Curran (2004) discussed how recentering can be used to study individual rates of change in the quadratic model as well as how covariate effects on the rate of change can be examined. The approaches discussed here extend this work to all types of nonlinear growth models. Therefore, this approach is generally recommended, but it is highly recommended when the functional form of change has parameters that are difficult to interpret.

The growth rate and latent change approaches to studying individual change can be extended in a variety of ways. Grimm, Zhang et al. (2013) discussed how individual acceleration can also be studied by extending the latent change framework to second-order changes or latent acceleration scores (Hamagami & McArdle, 2007). Similarly, in the growth rate approach, the second derivative can be estimated and then inserted into the nonlinear model to directly model individual acceleration. Combining these approaches with the multiple-group and growth mixture modeling frameworks allows for the direct study of group differences in the within-person rate of change in nonlinear growth models.

Appendix A

A Brief Introduction to Multilevel Modeling

This appendix briefly introduces the multilevel (or mixed-effects) modeling framework. Excellent complete treatments of multilevel modeling can be found in Raudenbush and Bryk (2002), Bickel (2007), Gelman and Hill (2007), Hox (2010), Snijders and Bosker (2012), Scott, Simonoff, and Marx (2013), and Finch, Bolin, and Kelley (2014). We recommend these sources if you are new to multilevel data and multilevel modeling techniques. If a refresher on multilevel modeling is needed, then we recommend one of several comprehensive papers and chapters on the topic, which include Singer (1998), Hayes (2006), Peugh (2010), and West, Ryu, Kwok, and Cham (2011).

Multilevel or mixed-effects models are a class of models used to analyze data that are collected at multiple levels. The classic example, and one we utilize here, is when data are collected from students who are organized in schools. In this example, data collected from the student are considered lower-level or level-1 data, and data collected from the school are considered higher-level or level-2 data. Another way to discuss these types of data is to say that the students are *clustered* or *nested* within schools or that school is the *cluster* variable. Data from students belonging to the same school are likely to be more related than data from students belonging to different schools, which causes dependency in the data; this dependency must be accounted for to obtain appropriate parameter estimates and standard errors.

A simple multilevel model is the *random intercept* model. The level-1 (student-level) equation for the random intercept model can be written as

$$y_{ij} = b_{0j} + e_{ij} \tag{A.1}$$

where y_{ij} is the observed variable for student i in school j, b_{0j} is the random intercept or the intercept for school j, and e_{ij} is the level-1 residual term for student i in school j. The random intercept, b_{0j}, represents the mean of the outcome for school j, and the residual term, e_{ij}, is student i's deviation from his or her school-level mean. The level-1 residual term is often assumed to be normally distributed with a mean of 0 and an estimated variance, $e_{ij} \sim N(0, \sigma_e^2)$. The level-2 (school-level) equation for the random intercept is

$$b_{0j} = \beta_{00} + u_{0j} \tag{A.2}$$

where β_{00} is the mean intercept and u_{0j} is the level-2 residual term for school j. The level-2 residual term, u_{0j}, is school j's deviation from β_{00}. The level-2 residual is assumed to be normally distributed with a mean of 0 and an estimated variance, $u_{0j} \sim N(0, \sigma_{u0}^2)$. In the multilevel model, β_{00} is a *fixed-effects* parameter because it applies to all scores, and σ_{u0}^2 and σ_e^2 are random-effects parameters because they describe variability (or randomness) in the equation. A first question when fitting multilevel models is whether the ratio of the between-cluster variance to the total variance in the outcome is sizeable. This ratio is termed the *intraclass correlation* (ICC) and is calculated as $\sigma_{u0}^2 / (\sigma_{u0}^2 + \sigma_e^2)$. If the ICC is small ($< 0.05$), then the amount of dependency in the data is small and standard regression models may be appropriate. If the ICC is large (> 0.10), then multilevel models must be specified to account for the dependency in the data.

The multilevel model of Equations A.1 and A.2 can be extended to include predictors at each level of the model. For example, a random intercept model with a level-2 predictor can be written as

Level-1

$$y_{ij} = b_{0j} + e_{ij} \tag{A.3}$$

Level-2

$$b_{0j} = \beta_{00} + \beta_{01} \cdot z_j + u_{0j} \tag{A.4}$$

The level-1 equation remains a random intercept model with no level-1 (student-level) predictors, but the level-2 equation now includes z_j as a predictor of b_{0j}, the random intercept, with coefficient β_{01}. This changes the interpretation of β_{00}, which is now the predicted score for a school with a value of 0 on z_j. The interpretation of β_{01} is similar to the interpretation of any regression coefficient—the expected amount of change in the random intercept for a one-unit change in z_j. Lastly, u_{0j} is the level-2 residual, and its variance represents the amount of unexplained variance in the random intercept.

A multilevel model with a level-1 (student-level) predictor, x_{ij}, can be written as

Level-1

$$y_{ij} = b_{0j} + b_{1j} \cdot x_{ij} + e_{ij} \tag{A.5}$$

Level-2

$$b_{0j} = \beta_{00} + u_{0j}$$
$$b_{1j} = \beta_{10} + u_{1j} \tag{A.6}$$

In this model there is a random intercept, b_{0j}, as well as a random slope, b_{1j}. The random slope allows the effect of x_{ij} to vary over higher-level units. Thus, b_{0j} is the intercept for school j, b_{1j} is the regression coefficient for school j, and e_{ij} is the level-1 residual. In the level-2 equations, β_{00} is the mean intercept over schools, u_{0j} is the deviation from the mean intercept for school j, β_{10} is the mean regression coefficient over schools, and u_{1j} is the deviation from the mean regression coefficient for school j. As above, the individual (level-1) deviations, e_{ij}, are assumed to be normally distributed with a mean of 0 and an estimated variance, $e_{ij} \sim N(0, \sigma_e^2)$. The school-level deviations, u_{0j} and u_{1j}, are assumed to have a multivariate normal distribution with means equal to 0, estimated variances, σ_{u0}^2 and σ_{u1}^2, and an estimated covariance, $\sigma_{u1,u0}$. Of particular interest is whether the effect of x_{ij} varies over schools. That is, whether the effect of x_{ij}, b_{1j}, is random or fixed. This is often tested by examining the significance of σ_{u1}^2, which can be done with a likelihood ratio test (e.g., specifying Equations A.5 and A.6, specifying Equations A.5 and A.6 without u_{1j}, and examining the change in model fit [−2 log likelihood]).

Finally, we can extend Equations A.5 and A.6 to include a level-2 predictor of the random intercept and slope to examine whether the level-2 predictor can account for the variance in the random intercept and slope. This model can be written as

Level-1
$$y_{ij} = b_{0j} + b_{1j} \cdot x_{ij} + e_{ij} \tag{A.7}$$

Level-2
$$b_{0j} = \beta_{00} + \beta_{01} \cdot z_j + u_{0j}$$
$$b_{1j} = \beta_{10} + \beta_{11} \cdot z_j + u_{1j} \tag{A.8}$$

The addition from Equations A.5 and A.6 is the inclusion of z_j as a predictor of b_{0j} and b_{1j}. In the level-2 equation, β_{00} is the expected intercept for school j when z_j equals 0, and β_{01} is the expected change in the level-2 intercept for a one-unit change in z_j. Similarly, β_{10} is the expected regression coefficient for school j (the effect from x_{ij} to y_{ij}) when z_j equals 0, and β_{11} is the expected change in the regression coefficient for a one-unit change in z_j.

ILLUSTRATIVE EXAMPLE

To illustrate the fitting of multilevel models to empirical data, we have organized data from children and schools collected as part of the ECLS-K. The outcomes of interest are student-level reading scores collected in the spring of kindergarten, and the predictors include a student-level predictor, the student's attention as rated by the teacher, and a school-level predictor, the number of school hours per day. The observed student attention was broken down into two separate variables because student-level attention is likely to vary over schools. Thus, the school-level mean of attention was calculated (the average attention score for children in the same school), as well as each student's deviation from their school-level mean. The outcome variable is read_ks, the student-level attention variable is attent_d, the school-level attention variable is attent_m, and the number of hours of school per day is hrs_day. Additionally, the school-level attention variable, attent_m, was mean centered.

Random Intercept Model

To begin, we specified the random intercept model with no predictors (Equations A.1 and A.2). This is often referred to as the *empty* model because there are no predictors, and as discussed above, this model is often fit to calculate the ICC. This model is specified using SAS's PROC NLMIXED in Script A.1. The script begins by calling the NLMIXED procedure and indicating the datafile ecls_school. Next, the level-2 equation is specified for the random intercept. Following Equation A.2, the random intercept, b_0j, is set equal to the sum of its fixed, beta_00, and random, u_0j, components. Next, the level-1 equation is specified without the level-1 residual. On the left-hand side of the equation is pred, which we use as the *predicted* value of the outcome, and on the right-hand side of the equation is the random intercept following Equation A.1. Next comes the MODEL statement where the outcome, read_ks, is assumed to be normally distributed with a mean equal to pred, which was previously defined, and a level-1 residual variance sigma2_e. The RANDOM statement follows, which contains the level-2 random coefficient and its distribution. The random coefficient is u_0j, which is assumed to follow a NORMAL distribution with a mean of 0 and a variance equal to sigma2_u0. At the end of the RANDOM statement, we indicate that the random effects are random with respect to the school_id variable, which is the school identification variable. Next, the PARMS statement is used to provide starting values for the model's estimated parameters. In this empty model, the parameters include beta_00, sigma2_e, and sigma2_u0. The procedure ends with RUN;.

The random intercept model is now specified using the nlme procedure available through R. This programming script is contained in Script A.2. The script begins by naming an object to hold the output from the nlme procedure. This object is called read.empty. In the nlme call, the output read_ks is set equal to (using ~), the fixed effect from

Script A.1. NLMIXED Script for the Random Intercept Model

```
PROC NLMIXED DATA = ecls_school;
*level-2;
    b_0j = beta_00 + u_0j;
*level-1 - without residual term;
    pred = b_0j;

    MODEL read_ks ~ NORMAL(pred,sigma2_e);
    RANDOM u_0j ~ NORMAL([0], [sigma2_u0])
        SUBJECT = school_id;
    PARMS beta_00 = 35 sigma2_e = 80 sigma2_u0 = 20;
RUN;
```

Script A.2. `nlme` Script for the Random Intercept Model

```
read.empty <- nlme (read_ks ~ beta_00 + u_0j,
                        data=ecls_school,
                        fixed=beta_00~1,
                        random=u_0j~1,
                        group=~ school_id,
                        start=c(beta_00=35),
                        na.action="na.omit")

summary(read.empty)
```

the random intercept, `beta_00`, plus the random coefficient, `u_0j`. In this specification, Equations A.1 and A.2 are combined, and this first equation of `nlme` is the predicted value for school *j* as the level-1 residual term is not part of this equation. Next the datafile, `ecls_school`, is specified as the input datafile. This is followed by the `fixed` and `random` statements. In the `fixed` statement, we list `beta_00` as the only fixed-effect parameter, and in the `random` statement, we list the random coefficient, `u_0j`, because we want to estimate the variance of this random coefficient. The `group` statement is then used to indicate the *cluster* variable. In our example, the cluster variable is `school_id`. The `start` statement is used to specify starting values for the fixed-effects parameters, and `na.action` is set to `na.omit` to remove cases with missing values. Lastly, `summary(read.empty)` is specified to print the parameter estimates and model fit indices.

Output from `NLMIXED` and `nlme` is contained in Outputs A.1 and A.2. The mean intercept was 46.44 and indicates the school-level average reading score in the spring of kindergarten. The school-level (level-2) variance was 38.57, and the student-level (level-1) variance was 160.10. These variances can be used to calculate the ICC. The ICC was 0.19 (38.57/(38.57 + 160.10)) indicating that 19% of the variance in spring reading scores was at the school-level and signals that multilevel models should be fit to examine student-level and school-level predictors of reading performance.

Inclusion of Level-1 Predictor

The random intercept model is expanded to include the student's level of attention as rated by the student's teacher in the fall of kindergarten. This is a *student-level* question: Is the student's attention in the fall of kindergarten associated with (predictive of) his or her reading skills in the spring of kindergarten? To control for school differences, we took a preliminary step and decomposed the student's attention score into the school-level mean and the student-level deviation from the school-level mean. The school-level mean is entered as a predictor of the random intercept at level-2, and the student-level deviation is entered as a predictor at level-1. Because the attention measure is centered at the school-mean (*school-mean centered*), this effect is truly a *within-school* effect. We allowed this student-level effect to be random, permitting this effect to vary over schools to highlight how the association between attention and reading achievement may be different in different schools.

Output A.1. NLMIXED Output for the Random Intercept Model

Fit Statistics

-2 Log Likelihood		128828
AIC (smaller is better)		128834
AICC (smaller is better)		128834
BIC (smaller is better)		128848

Parameter Estimates

Parameter	Estimate	Standard Error	DF	t Value	Pr > |t|	Alpha	Lower	Upper	Gradient
beta_00	46.4405	0.2351	878	197.54	<.0001	0.05	45.9791	46.9019	0.270905
sigma2_e	160.10	1.8355	878	87.23	<.0001	0.05	156.50	163.70	-0.0252
sigma2_u0	38.5728	2.3694	878	16.28	<.0001	0.05	33.9223	43.2232	0.084595

Output A.2. nlme Output for the Random Intercept Model

```
Nonlinear mixed - effects model fit by maximum likelihood
 Model: read_ks ~ beta_00 + u_0j
 Data: ecls_school
       AIC       BIC      logLik
   128833.6 128856.7 -64413.82

Random effects:
 Formula: u_0j ~ 1 | school_id
           u_0j Residual
StdDev: 6.17256 12.65722

Fixed effects: beta_00 ~ 1
           Value   Std. Error     DF   t-value   p-value
beta_00  46.42543   0.2339431   15217  198.4475         0

Number of Observations: 16096
Number of Groups: 879
```

The NLMIXED script for this random intercept and slope model is contained in Script A.3. The level-2 equation for the random intercept, b_0j, has been adjusted from the previous script to include attent_m, the school-level attention score, as a predictor with beta_01 as the level-2 regression coefficient. In the level-2 part of the specification, there is now a random slope, b_1j, which is a sum of its fixed effect, beta_10, and its random component, u_1j. The level-1 equation is specified next. The predicted value of the outcome, pred, is now the sum of the random intercept, b_0j, and the random slope, b_1j, multiplied by the student-level attention variable, attent_d. The MODEL and RANDOM statements come next. The MODEL statement has not changed, but the RANDOM statement now includes u_0j and u_1j. These two random coefficients have means set to 0 and a covariance matrix as specified with sigma2_u0 and sigma2_u1

Script A.3. NLMIXED Script for the Random Intercept and Slope Model

```
PROC NLMIXED DATA = ecls_school;
*level-2;
    b_0j = beta_00 + beta_01 * attent_m + u_0j;
    b_1j = beta_10 + u_1j;
*level-1 - without residual term;
    pred = b_0j + b_1j * attent_d;

    MODEL read_ks ~ NORMAL(pred, sigma2_e);
    RANDOM u_0j u_1j ~ NORMAL([0,0], [sigma2_u0,
                                      sigma_u1u0, sigma2_u1])
            SUBJECT = school_id;

    PARMS beta_00 = 11    beta_01 = 0
          beta_10 = 0
          sigma2_u0 = 10 sigma2_u1 = 5 sigma_u1u0 = 0
          sigma2_e = 55;
RUN;
```

as the variance of the random intercept and slope and `sigma_u1u0` as the covariance. As before, SUBJECT = `school_id` is written to indicate that the random effects are random with respect to the school identification variable. The NLMIXED script continues with the PARMS statement where starting values are listed and the procedure is closed with RUN;.

The nlme script for the random intercept and slope model is contained in Script A.4. In this model, `read_ks` is set equal to the level-2 equation for the random intercept with `attent_m` as a predictor, `beta_00` and `beta_01` as fixed-effects parameters, and `u_0j` as the residual random coefficient, plus the level-2 equation for the random slope with `beta_10` as the fixed effect and `u_1j` as the random coefficient multiplied by `attent_d`, the level-1 predictor. The datafile is then specified in the data statement, the fixed-effects parameters are listed in the fixed statement, and the random coefficients are listed in the random statement. The *cluster* variable, `school_id`, is listed in the group statement, starting values for the fixed-effects parameters are listed in the start statement, and `na.action` is set to `na.omit`. The model is then closed with a parenthesis, and the output is printed using the summary command.

Select output from NLMIXED and nlme is contained in Outputs A.3 and A.4. Working through the fixed-effects estimates, `beta_00` was 46.32 and is the predicted spring reading score for a school with a student body that has an average level of attention. `beta_01` was 7.13 and is the predicted increase in the spring reading score for a one-unit increase in the mean school-level attention score. Thus, schools with students who were rated as having higher attention scores were predicted to have higher spring reading scores. `beta_10` was 7.37 and is the predicted mean increase in spring reading score for a one-unit increase in the student's level of attention. This effect is the within-school effect and essentially controls for the school the student attended.

There are four random-effects parameters. The first is the residual variance of the random intercept, `sigma2_u0`, which was 35.49. This is the amount of variance at the school level in spring reading scores that was unrelated to the average level of teacher-rated attention. `sigma2_u1` was 6.00 and is the variance of the random slope, which is the degree to which the effect of attention at the student level varies across schools. Taking the square root yields 2.45, and with this, we can create a 95% confidence interval on the magnitude of the effect of attention within schools. Taking the mean effect, 7.37,

Script A.4. `nlme` Script for the Random Intercept and Slope Model

```
read.attent <- nlme(read_ks ~ (beta_00 + beta_01 * attent_m + u_0j) +
                               (beta_10 + u_1j) * attent_d,
                    data=ecls_school,
                    fixed=beta_00+beta_01+beta_10~1,
                    random=u_0j+u_1j~1,
                    group=~school_id,
                    start=c(beta_00=35, beta_01=0, beta_10=0),
                    na.action="na.omit")
summary(read.attent)
```

Output A.3. NLMIXED Output for the Random Intercept and Slope Model

Fit Statistics

-2 Log Likelihood	126409
AIC (smaller is better)	126423
AICC (smaller is better)	126423
BIC (smaller is better)	126456

Parameter Estimates

Parameter	Estimate	Standard Error	DF	t Value	Pr > |t|	Alpha	Lower	Upper	Gradient
beta_00	46.3177	0.2238	877	206.95	<.0001	0.05	45.8785	46.7570	0.000309
beta_01	7.1314	0.7486	877	9.53	<.0001	0.05	5.6621	8.6007	-0.00006
beta_10	7.3697	0.1731	877	42.57	<.0001	0.05	7.0300	7.7095	-0.00025
sigma2_u0	35.4858	2.1328	877	16.64	<.0001	0.05	31.2998	39.6718	-0.00002
sigma2_u1	6.0036	1.2798	877	4.69	<.0001	0.05	3.4918	8.5155	2.978E-6
sigma_u1u0	13.8426	1.2713	877	10.89	<.0001	0.05	11.3474	16.3379	-0.00004
sigma2_e	136.69	1.6110	877	84.85	<.0001	0.05	133.53	139.85	-3.72E-7

Output A.4. nlme Output for the Random Intercept and Slope Model

```
Nonlinear mixed - effects model fit by maximum likelihood
 Model: read_ks ~ (beta_00 + beta_01 * attent_m + u_0j) + (beta_10 +
 u_1j) * attent_d
 Data: ecls_school
      AIC       BIC     logLik
  126422.7 126476.5 -63204.37

Random effects:
 Formula: list (u_0j ~ 1, u_1j ~ 1)
 Level: school_id
 Structure: General positive-definite, Log-Cholesky parametrization
          StdDev     Corr
u_0j      5.957006   u_0j
u_1j      2.450260   0.948
Residual  11.691486

Fixed effects: beta_00 + beta_01 + beta_10 ~ 1
           Value   Std.Error     DF    t-value    p-value
beta_00   46.31774  0.2238324   15215  206.93043        0
beta_01    7.13143  0.7482553   15215    9.53075        0
beta_10    7.36974  0.1723452   15215   42.76153        0
```

and adding and subtracting 4.80 (1.96 · 2.45) from this mean yields a confidence interval of 3.29 to 11.45. These calculations give an approximate 95% confidence interval on the size of the association between attention and reading scores within schools. Thus, we can see that in certain schools, the effect is quite strong, whereas in other schools the effect is considerably smaller. The covariance between the random intercept and slope, sigma_u1u0, was 13.84, which as a correlation is equal to 0.95. Thus, in schools with higher reading scores, the effect of attention tended to be stronger. The final parameter estimate was the level-1 residual variance, sigma2_e, which was 136.69. This parameter represents variance in spring reading scores within schools that was unaccounted for by student-level attention.

Inclusion of Level-2 Predictor

In the final model presented here, we add a true school-level (level-2) predictor of the random intercept and slope. This variable is the number of school hours per day in kindergarten. As you probably are aware, schools vary in the number of hours per day, with some schools offering half-day programs, some offering full-day programs, and some falling somewhere in between. This variable does not vary within schools and is therefore a true school-level predictor. We include this variable as a predictor of the random intercept and random slope to evaluate whether schools with longer school days tend to have students with higher spring reading scores (effect on the random intercept) and whether the association between attention and reading is stronger (or weaker) in schools with longer school days. The NLMIXED script for this model is contained in Script A.5.

Script A.5. NLMIXED Script for the Full Model

```
PROC NLMIXED DATA = ecls_school;
*level -2;
    b_0j = beta_00 + beta_01 * attent_m + beta_02 * (hrs_day - 5) + u_0j;
    b_1j = beta_10 + beta_11 * (hrs_day - 5) + u_1j;

*level -1 - without residual term;
    pred = b_0j + b_1j * attent_d;

    MODEL read_ks ~ NORMAL (pred, sigma2_e);
    RANDOM u_0j u_1j ~ NORMAL ([0 , 0], [sigma2_u0,
                                         sigma_u1u0, sigma2_u1])
        SUBJECT = school_id;
    PARMS beta_00 = 11    beta_01 = 0
          beta_10 = 0     beta_02 = 0    beta_11 = 0
          sigma2_u0 = 10 sigma2_u1 = 5 sigma_u1u0 = 0
          sigma2_e = 55;
RUN;
```

The NLMIXED script begins with the specification of the level-2 equations for the random intercept and random slope. In the equation for the random intercept, b_0j, is the level-2 intercept, beta_00, and two regression coefficients, beta_01 and beta_02. The level-2 intercept, beta_00, represents the predicted school-level reading score for a school that had 5 hours of school per day and had students with an average level of teacher-rated attention. The two regression coefficients, beta_01 and beta_02, represent the effect of attention at the school level and the effect of hours of instruction, respectively, on the school-level reading score. In the equation for the random slope, b_1j, there is a level-2 intercept, beta_10, and a regression coefficient, beta_11, for the effect of hours per day. This level-2 intercept represents the predicted within-school effect of student attention on spring reading for a school with 5 hours of school per day. The regression coefficient, beta_11, is the effect of the number of school hours per day on the size of the within-school effect of student attention on spring reading. The level-1 equation follows, and in this equation, we have the predicted student-level reading score on the left-hand side of the equation, pred, and the sum of the random intercept and random slope multiplied by the student-level attention variable, attent_d, on the right-hand side of the equation.

In the MODEL statement we list the outcome variable, read_ks, and its distribution. read_ks is assumed to follow a normal distribution with mean pred, which was previously defined, and level-1 variance sigma2_e. The RANDOM line follows where the two random coefficients, u_0j and u_1j, and their joint distribution are defined. u_0j and u_1j are assumed to be normally distributed with 0 means and a variance–covariance matrix as specified. Here, the variances of u_0j and u_1j are sigma2_u0 and sigma2_u1, respectively, and their covariance is sigma_u1u0. The school identification variable, school_id, is listed as the cluster variable using the SUBJECT command. Lastly, starting values are provided for the estimated parameters, and the procedure concludes with RUN;.

The `nlme` script for the random intercept and slope model with a level-2 predictor is contained in Script A.6. The `nlme` procedure is used, and the full model is specified on the right-hand side of the ~. As before, the level-1 and level-2 equations are combined. On the first line, the level-2 equation for the random intercept is specified with the level-2 intercept, `beta_00`, the fixed-effects regression coefficients for school-level attention (`beta_01 * attent_m`) and hours of school per day (`beta_02 * (hrs_day - 5)`), and the residual term (`u_0j`). On the second line, we have the level-2 equation for the random slope with the level-2 intercept (`beta_10`), the effect of hours of school per day (`beta_11 * (hrs_day - 5)`), and the level-2 residual (`u_1j`). This equation for the random slope is multiplied by the level-1 predictor, `attent_d`. Subsequent parts of the `nlme` script are typically specified with the datafile, the name of the fixed-effects parameters (all the `beta` parameters), the name of the random coefficients (`u_0j` and `u_1j`), and listing `school_id` as the cluster variable in the group statement. The model is concluded with starting values for all fixed-effects parameters and the `na.action`.

Output from `NLMIXED` and `nlme` are contained in Outputs A.5 and A.6. Beginning with the fixed-effects parameters describing the random intercept, `beta_00` was estimated to be 46.36, which is the predicted spring mean reading score for a school with 5 hours of daily instruction and a student population with average attention skills. `beta_01`, which was 7.70, is the effect of attention at the school level. Thus, schools with students who were rated as having higher levels of attention were predicted to have higher mean reading scores by 7.70 points for a one-unit change in school-level attention. `beta_02` was 0.63 and is the effect of the number of hours of school on school-level spring reading scores. Thus, schools with longer school days were predicted to have higher reading scores by 0.63 points for each additional hour. Moving to the fixed effects for the random slope, `beta_10` was 7.39 and is the predicted effect of student-level attention on spring reading scores for students in school with 5-hour school days. Thus, within schools, students with higher levels of teacher-rated attention were predicted to have higher spring reading scores by 7.39 points for every one-unit increase in attention. `beta_11` was the effect of school hours per day on this within-school regression coefficient. `beta_11` was not significantly different from 0, suggesting that the within-school association between attention and reading was not dependent on the number of hours in the school day.

Turning to the random-effects parameters, `sigma2_e`, the level-1 residual variance was 136.66 and represents unexplained variance in the level-1 model. Thus, there was sizable variability in student-level reading scores that was not accounted for by student-level attention. The residual variance of the random intercept, `sigma2_u0`, was 34.42 and represents variability in the school-level mean reading scores that was not accounted for by the number of hours in the school day, nor the level of teacher-rated attention in the school. The residual variance of the random slope, `sigma2_u1`, was 6.00 and represents variability in the association between student-level attention and reading scores that was not accounted for by the number of hours in the school day. Lastly, the residual covariance between the random intercept and slope was 13.68 and suggests that there is additional covariation between school-level reading scores and the association between

Script A.6. `nlme` Script for the Full Model

```
read.full <- nlme(read_ks ~ (beta_00 + beta_01 * attent_m + beta_02 * (hrs_day - 5) + u_0j)+
                            (beta_10 + beta_11 * (hrs_day - 5) + u_1j) * attent_d,
                  data=ecls_school,
                  fixed=beta_00+beta_01+beta_02+beta_10+beta_11~1,
                  random=u_0j+u_1j~1,
                  group=~school_id,
                  start=c(beta_00=35, beta_01=0, beta_02=0, beta_10=0, beta_11=0),
                  na.action="na.omit")

summary(read.full)
```

Output A.5. NLMIXED Output for the Full Model

Fit Statistics

-2 Log Likelihood	126383
AIC (smaller is better)	126401
AICC (smaller is better)	126401
BIC (smaller is better)	126444

Parameter Estimates

Parameter	Estimate	Standard Error	DF	t Value	Pr > |t|	Alpha	Lower	Upper	Gradient
beta_00	46.3630	0.2213	877	209.54	<.0001	0.05	45.9287	46.7973	-0.00075
beta_01	7.7015	0.7480	877	10.30	<.0001	0.05	6.2334	9.1696	-0.00001
beta_02	0.6266	0.1299	877	4.82	<.0001	0.05	0.3717	0.8816	0.001942
beta_10	7.3916	0.1731	877	42.70	<.0001	0.05	7.0519	7.7314	0.000217
beta_11	0.05809	0.1003	877	0.58	0.5627	0.05	-0.1388	0.2550	0.000253
sigma2_u0	34.4212	2.0775	877	16.57	<.0001	0.05	30.3438	38.4986	-1.52E-6
sigma2_u1	5.9957	1.2787	877	4.69	<.0001	0.05	3.4861	8.5054	-0.00009
sigma_u1u0	13.6750	1.2504	877	10.94	<.0001	0.05	11.2208	16.1292	-0.00002
sigma2_e	136.66	1.6103	877	84.87	<.0001	0.05	133.50	139.82	-0.00002

Output A.6. nlme Output for the Full Model

```
Nonlinear mixed - effects model fit by maximum likelihood
Model: read_ks ~ (beta_00 + beta_01 * attent_m + beta_02 * (hrs_day - 5) + u_0j ) +
                 (beta_10 + beta_11 * (hrs_day - 5) + u_1j) * attent_d

Data: ecls_school
       AIC      BIC     logLik
    126401.4 126470.5 -63191.69

Random effects:
 Formula: list (u_0j ~ 1, u_1j ~ 1)
 Level: school_id
 Structure: General positive -definite, Log-Cholesky parametrization
            StdDev    Corr
 u_0j       5.866963  u_0j
 u_1j       2.448671  0.952
 Residual  11.690164

Fixed effects: beta_00 + beta_01 + beta_02 + beta_10 + beta_11 ~ 1
          Value      Std.Error    DF      t-value     p-value
beta_00   46.36303   0.2212894    15213   209.51309   0.0000
beta_01    7.70149   0.7476662    15213    10.30071   0.0000
beta_02    0.62662   0.1299268    15213     4.82284   0.0000
beta_10    7.39165   0.1723735    15213    42.88157   0.0000
beta_11    0.05808   0.1002049    15213     0.57960   0.5622

Number of Observations: 16096
Number of Groups: 879
```

491

attention and reading scores within schools, such that schools with higher mean reading scores tended to have a stronger association between attention and reading scores.

MULTILEVEL MODELING AND LONGITUDINAL DATA

Multilevel models are typically applied to longitudinal data because of the dependency that is present in longitudinal data. That is, the repeatedly measured variables are *nested* within participants. Thus, scores from a given individual over time tend to be more highly correlated than scores coming from different individuals at a specific point in time or over time. Multilevel models are able to account for this dependency commonly seen in longitudinal data. With two-level longitudinal data (i.e., repeatedly measured variables nested within participants), a function of time is typically specified at level-1 and is often the only level-1 (time-varying) predictor. Assuming a linear function of time, the random intercept and random slope are individual (level-2) characteristics that can be described by their means, variances, and covariance, and the random slope represents that individual rate of change with respect to time. This random slope is extremely important with longitudinal data because researchers are interested in individual change over time. The mean of the random slope indicates the mean rate of within-person change, and the variance of the random slope indicates the magnitude of between-person differences in the within-person rate of change.

Appendix B

A Brief Introduction to Structural Equation Modeling

We use this appendix to briefly introduce the structural equation modeling (SEM) framework. Excellent treatments of structural equation modeling can be found in Kline (2016), Schumacker and Lomax (2010), Raykov and Marcoulides (2006), Kaplan (2009), and Bollen (1989). We recommend these sources if you are new to structural data analysis techniques. SEM is a *framework* for conducting univariate and multivariate analyses. SEM subsumes most univariate analyses, including the *t*-test, analysis of variance, regression, and multiple regression, and several types of multivariate analysis, including path analysis and confirmatory factor analysis. Over time, the SEM framework has extended into generalized linear models, item response models, multilevel models, and finite mixture models, and most SEM programs now refer to themselves as *general latent variable modeling* programs because of their extensive capabilities.

As a multivariate data analysis framework, SEM is typically used to test a theoretical model against empirical data. The theoretical model can be complex and include observed (manifest) variables as well as unobserved (latent) variables, which are indicated by one or more observed variables. The theoretical model often imposes restrictions on the data, which leads to degrees of freedom, but also causes the model to misfit the empirical data. The level of misfit is judged in relation to the model's degrees of freedom (and potentially alternative models) to evaluate its plausibility. If the model fits the empirical data poorly, then the theoretical model (and the theory that led to its development) is rejected. If the model fits the empirical data well, then the theoretical model (and the theory that led to its development) remains plausible.

SEMs are often presented in matrix notation, and several different notations have been used in the literature (e.g., LiSRel notation, RAM notation). One commonly used notation is the *all-y* notation from LiSRel. In the *all-y* notation, the measurement model, which relates observed variables to latent variables can be written as

$$\mathbf{y}_i = \tau + \Lambda\eta_i + \mathbf{u}_i \tag{B.1}$$

where $\mathbf{y}_i$ is a $P \times 1$ vector of observed variables for individual i, τ is a $P \times 1$ vector of measurement intercepts, Λ is a $P \times Q$ matrix of factor loadings mapping the observed variables on to their respective latent variables, η_i is a $Q \times 1$ vector of latent variable scores for individual i, and $\mathbf{u}_i$ is a $P \times 1$ vector unique factor scores for individual i. The structural model, which relates latent variables to one another, is written as

$$\eta_i = \alpha + \mathbf{B}\eta_i + \mathbf{d}_i \tag{B.2}$$

where α is a $Q \times 1$ matrix of latent variable intercepts, $\mathbf{B}$ is a $Q \times Q$ matrix of latent variable regression coefficients, and $\mathbf{d}_i$ is a $Q \times 1$ vector of latent variable disturbances for individual i. The covariances among the unique factor scores, $\mathbf{u}_i$, are contained in Θ, which is a $P \times P$ matrix, and the covariances among the disturbance factors, $\mathbf{d}_i$, are contained in Ψ. This general model leads to a series of expectations for the covariances among the observed variables as well as a series of expectations for the means of the observed variables. The covariance expectations, Σ, are

$$\Sigma = \Lambda\mathbf{B}\Psi\mathbf{B}'\Lambda' + \Theta \tag{B.3}$$

where Σ is a $P \times P$ matrix of expected covariances. The mean expectations, μ, are

$$\mu = \tau + \Lambda\alpha \tag{B.4}$$

where μ is a $P \times 1$ vector of expected means.

SEMs can also be represented through path diagrams (see Boker, McArdle, & Neale, 2002; Wright, 1921). Path diagrams are visual representations of the SEM and are often used to communicate the complex mathematical underpinnings of such models in manuscripts. Additionally, certain programs allow for model specification with path diagrams (e.g., AMOS). When complete path diagrams are drawn, these diagrams contain all the needed information to calculate model expectations. In a path diagram, squares represent observed variables, circles represent unobserved or latent variables, a triangle is used to represent a constant, which allows the inclusion of mean structures into the diagram, one-headed arrows represent directive (unidirectional) relationships, such as regressions and factor loadings, and two-headed arrows represent symmetric relationships, such as covariances. A path diagram of a latent variable model is contained in Figure B.1. In this diagram, there are two latent variables, η_1 and η_2, that are each indicated by three observed variables (y_1 through y_3 and y_4 through y_6, respectively) and there is a directive path from η_1 to η_2. The parameters in this diagram map onto the specification of the SEM in Equations B.1 through B.4.

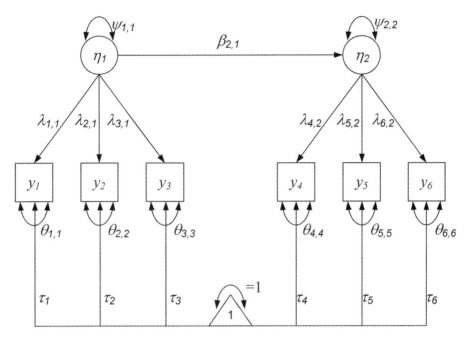

FIGURE B.1. Example path diagram.

An alternative notation for SEMs is with the reticular action model (RAM) notation (McArdle, 2005; McArdle & McDonald, 1984; McArdle & Nesselroade, 2014). In RAM notation, all variables, observed, unobserved, and the constant, are placed in a vector, $\mathbf{v}_i$. Thus, $\mathbf{v}_i$ is a $(P + Q + 1) \times 1$ vector for individual i (P observed variables, Q unobserved variables, and 1 constant). A linear model can then be written for all variables, such that

$$\mathbf{v}_i = \mathbf{A}\mathbf{v}_i + \mathbf{u}_i \qquad (B.5)$$

where $\mathbf{A}$ is a $(P + Q + 1) \times (P + Q + 1)$ square matrix of asymmetric paths (one-headed arrows in the path diagram including factor loadings, regression paths, and intercepts), and $\mathbf{u}_i$ is a $(P + Q + 1) \times 1$ vector of unknown residuals. The expectations of the unknown residuals, $\mathbf{u}_i$, are contained in $\mathbf{S}$, which is a $(P + Q + 1) \times (P + Q + 1)$ square matrix of symmetric paths (two-headed arrows in the path diagram including all variances, covariances, and the two-headed arrow on the constant that is its mean square). Equation B.5 can be solved for $\mathbf{v}_i$, which yields

$$\mathbf{v}_i = (\mathbf{I} - \mathbf{A})^{-1} \mathbf{u}_i \qquad (B.6)$$

where $\mathbf{I}$ is a square identity matrix. The matrix $(\mathbf{I} - \mathbf{A})^{-1}$ is referred to as the *effects* matrix because its calculation yields the total effects (sum of direct and indirect effects) contained in the model. The expectations of Equation B.6 can then be determined, which are

$$M_t = (I - A)^{-1} S(I - A)^{-1\prime}$$ (B.7)

where M_t is the total variable expectations—the sum of the expected covariance matrix and expected mean squares for *observed* and *unobserved* variables (i.e., average sums of squares and cross-products), $(I - A)^{-1}$ is the effects matrix, and S is the model expectations of u_i, which was previously defined. To isolate the expectations for the observed variables, we introduce a filter matrix, F, which is a $(P + 1) \times (P + Q + 1)$ matrix in which its elements equal 1 if the variable is observed (constant counts) and 0 elsewhere. Pre- and postmultiplying the total moment expectations by F (i.e., FM_tF') yields the observed variable expectations, which is the sum of Σ and $\mu\mu'$ defined for the *all-y* notation above.

One benefit of RAM notation is that there is a one-to-one mapping from the matrix algebra to the path diagram. That is, the path diagram in Figure B.1 contains three distinct elements, which map onto the three specified matrices of RAM notation (i.e., A, S, and F). These elements are (1) one-headed arrows (A), (2) two-headed arrows (S), and the distinction between observed and latent variables (F). Furthermore, and as noted earlier, the complete path diagram can be used to calculate model expectations, which follow RAM specification and the work of Wright (1921) (see also McArdle, 2005).

ILLUSTRATIVE EXAMPLE

To illustrate the specification of SEMs using Mplus and OpenMx, the two programs we use throughout the book, we present code to specify a latent variable path model that mimics the model in Figure B.1. The illustrative data were collected as part of the ECLS-K and are academic outcomes measured in the fall and spring of kindergarten. The academic measures include reading, mathematics, and general knowledge, which are used to identify a latent *academic achievement* variable at each time point. As in Figure B.1, the academic latent variable indicated by the observed variables in the spring of kindergarten is predicted by the academic latent variable indicated by the observed variables measured in the fall of kindergarten. A path diagram of this model is contained in Figure B.2. The additional paths in Figure B.2 are the two-headed arrows from read1 to read2, math1 to math2, and gk1 to gk2. These unique covariance paths were added because each indicator is expected to covary more with itself over time than what is expected to be carried by the association between η_1 and η_2.

The Mplus code to fit this model is contained in Script B.1. The script begins with a TITLE, and then the datafile is specified. The datafile, ecls_acad.dat, is an ASCII text file and is located in the same folder (directory) as the input file, which allows us to only specify the file name. Next comes the VARIABLE statement where the names of the variables contained in the dataset are listed under NAMES, the missing value code is specified using MISSING, and the names of the variables that we want to include in the model are listed in the USEVAR statement. We are now ready to specify the structural model, which is contained in the MODEL statement.

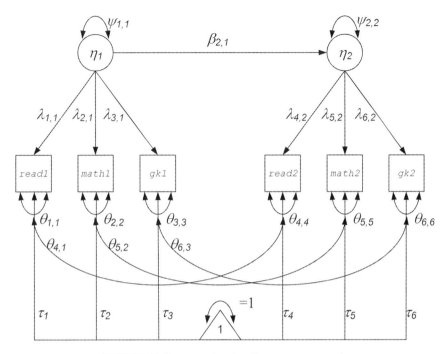

FIGURE B.2. SEM for the illustrative example.

In Mplus several keywords and types of statements are used to specify the SEM. The first keyword we use is BY, which is used to define latent variables by their respective indicators. Thus, in the first model statement, the latent variable eta_1 is indicated BY math1 with a factor loading that is fixed at 1 (@1), read1 with an estimated factor loading, and gk1 with an estimated factor loading. The definition of eta_1 closes with a semicolon. The latent variable eta_2 is then defined in a similar manner as it is indicated by math2 with a factor loading fixed at 1, read2, and gk2 with estimated factor loadings. The fixed factor loadings are identification constraints, which are used to set the scale of eta_1 and eta_2 and ensure that a unique set of parameter estimates exists for this model. In the next statement, the latent variable variances are specified. In Mplus, all variances (residual as well as unique) are specified by listing the variable name. Thus, the statement eta_1 eta_2; indicates that we want to estimate the variances of these latent variables. Similarly, we specify the unique variances of the observed variables by listing these variables in the next statement. This is followed by a series of unique covariances. In Mplus, covariances between two variables (observed or unobserved) are specified using the keyword WITH, which stands for *covaries with*. Thus, in the first of these statements, the variable math1 covaries with math2. Similar statements are written for the reading and general knowledge variables.

Next, we specify the regression coefficient where eta_1 predicts eta_2. In Mplus, regression coefficients are specified using the keyword ON. The statement for the regression coefficient reads eta_2 ON eta_1*.8; and this statement defines eta_2 as the outcome variable and eta_1 as the predictor variable. The *.8 is the starting value for

Script B.1. *Mplus* Script for the Example Model

```
TITLE: Example  Model;

DATA: FILE = ecls_acad.dat;

VARIABLE: NAMES = read1 math1 gk1 lrn_p1
                  read2 math2 gk2 lrn_p2;
    MISSING = .;
    USEVAR = read1 math1 gk1
             read2 math2 gk2;

MODEL:
! Factor  Loadings   (Lambda)
    eta_1 BY math1@1
            read1
            gk1;
    eta_2 BY math2@1
            read2
            gk2;

! Factor Variances (Psi)
    eta_1 eta_2;

! Unique Variances & Covariances (Theta)
    math1  read1  gk1  math2  read2  gk2;
    math1 WITH math2;
    read1 WITH read2;
    gk1  WITH  gk2;

! Latent Variable Regressions (Beta)
    eta_2  ON  eta_1*.8;

! Factor Means (alpha)
    [eta_1@0  eta_2@0];

! Measurement Intercepts (tau)
    [math1 read1 gk1 math2 read2 gk2];

OUTPUT: SAMPSTAT STANDARDIZED TECH1;
```

this parameter. All SEMs require starting values to begin the iterative estimation routines, and most, if not all, SEM programs have default starting values. Using the asterisk, we can override the default starting values to aid model estimation and convergence. The final parts of the MODEL statement are the latent variable means and the measurement intercepts. These parameters are both part of the mean structure, and, in *Mplus*, these parameters are specified by listing the variable name in square brackets. The factor means are set to 0 using the @ function, which is another identification constraint to scale the latent variables. The measurement intercepts are freely estimated.

In the OUTPUT line, we have requested specific types of output. SAMPSTAT stands for sample statistics, and requesting this output is a good way to check that the data were correctly read into *Mplus*. STANDARDIZED requests standardized parameter estimates, and *Mplus* will report different types of standardized parameter estimates, including the fully standardized output (STDXY). Lastly, the TECH1 output prints the full model specification as well as the starting values for each model parameter. This is a good way to ensure that the model was specified correctly. The TECH1 output follows the *all-y* notation, with one notation change: v is used instead of τ.

OpenMx syntax for fitting the example model is contained in Script B.2. The script begins by installing the OpenMx package (you can also do this through the CRAN using install.packages('OpenMx')) using the source statement. Installing OpenMx only has to be done every so often to make sure you are working with the latest version. The OpenMx package is then loaded for this R session using library(OpenMx). The example

Script B.2. OpenMx Script for the Example Model

```
source('http://openmx.psyc.virginia.edu/getOpenMx.R')

library(OpenMx)

acad.omx  <-  mxModel('Example Model',
    type='RAM', mxData(observed=ecls_acad, type='raw'),
    manifestVars=c('read1','math1','gk1','read2','math2','gk2'),
    latentVars=c('eta_1','eta_2'),

# Factor loadings
mxPath(from='eta_1', to=c('math1','read1','gk1'),
    arrows=1, free=c(FALSE,TRUE,TRUE), values=1,
    labels=c(NA,'lambda_21','lambda_31')),

mxPath(from='eta_2', to=c('math2','read2','gk2'),
    arrows=1, free=c(FALSE,TRUE,TRUE), values=1,
    labels=c(NA,'lambda_22','lambda_32')),

# Latent variable variances
mxPath(from=c('eta_1','eta_2'),
    arrows=2, free=TRUE, values=c(60,10),
    labels=c('psi_11','psi_22'))

# Unique variances
mxPath(from=c('read1','math1','gk1','read2','math2','gk2'),
    arrows=2, free=TRUE, values=30,
    labels=c('theta_11','theta_22','theta_33',
             'theta_44','theta_55','theta_66')),

# Unique covariances
mxPath(from=c('read1','math1','gk1'), to=c('read2','math2','gk2'),
    arrows=2, free=TRUE, values=0,
    labels=c('theta_41','theta_52','theta_63')),

# Latent variable regression
mxPath(from='eta_1', to='eta_2',
    arrows=1, free=TRUE, values=.8, labels='beta_21'),

# means and intercepts
mxPath(from='one', to=c('read1','math1','gk1','read2','math2','gk2'),
    arrows=1, free=TRUE, values=30,
    labels=c('tau_1','tau_2','tau_3','tau_4','tau_5','tau_6'))

) # close model

acad.fit = mxRun(acad.omx)

ref = mxRefModels(acad.fit, run=TRUE)

summary(acad.fit, refModels=ref)
```

model is then specified using mxModel. The mxModel procedure begins by providing a title (Example Model), the notation type (RAM), the name of the datafile (ecls_acad), the type of data (raw), and the names of the manifest and latent variables contained in the structural model. The notation type is set to RAM, which is a straightforward way of programming OpenMx that is very much based on the complete path diagram. Alternatively, OpenMx can be programmed using matrices and a series of mxMatrix statements.

After the general model setup is complete, the SEM is specified with a series of mxPath statements. The mxPath statements describe each path (one- and two-headed arrow) in the model. Following the order of specification in Mplus, the first mxPath statements are for the factor loadings of eta_1 and eta_2. The first mxPath statement says that the arrows go from eta_1 to math1, read1, and gk1. These paths are one-headed arrows (arrows=1), are a combination of fixed (free=FALSE) and freely (free=TRUE) estimated values, and are given fixed or starting values of 1 and labels. Since the first factor loading is fixed and the value is 1, the first factor loading is fixed at 1. The remaining factor loadings of eta_1 are freely estimated, and therefore the values statement provides the starting values for these estimated parameters. In the labels statement, the first label is set to NA because the first factor loading is fixed. The remaining factor loadings are given appropriate labels. The second mxPath statement follows the first mxPath statement very closely, with eta_2 as the latent variable and math2, read2, and gk2 as the indicator variables. Additionally, the labels are appropriately changed.

The next two statements are for the variances of the latent and observed variables. In these statements, we list the variables in the from statement, but there is no complementary to statement, which means that these paths begin and end at the same variable. The arrows statement is set to 2 because these are two-headed arrows. These parameters are freely estimated and given appropriate starting values and labels. The labels for the latent variable variances begin with psi to map onto the *all-y* LiSRel notation described above. Similarly, the labels of the unique variances begin with theta. The next mxPath statement is for the unique covariances. These two-headed arrows go from each time-1 variable (math1, read1, gk1) to the respective time-2 variable (math2, read2, gk2). These paths are freely estimated, given starting values of 0, and appropriate labels.

The next mxPath statement is for the regression path between the two latent variables. This one-headed arrow originates from eta_1 and goes to eta_2, is freely estimated, given a starting value of .8, and labeled beta_21. The final mxPath statement is for the intercepts of the observed variables. Following Figure B.2, these are one-headed paths that originate from one, which is used to reference the constant, to each of the observed variables. These paths are freely estimated, given starting values of 30, and appropriate labels. The model is then closed with a parenthesis and run using mxRun. To obtain absolute and incremental fit indices for the fitted model, we use the mxRefModels to automatically fit the saturated and independence (null) models. The output is then printed using the summary command.

Select Mplus and OpenMx output is contained in Outputs B.1 and B.2, respectively. The Mplus output begins with fit information, which is followed by unstandardized (raw) estimates, whereas the OpenMx output begins with the parameter estimates and is followed by the model fit information. Focusing on the fit information, the example model appears to fit the data fairly well. The root mean square error of approximation

Output B.1. *Mplus* Output for the Example Model

```
MODEL FIT INFORMATION

Number of Free Parameters                        22
Loglikelihood
            H0 Value                   -367709.517
            H1 Value                   -367574.510
Information Criteria
            Akaike (AIC)                735463.035
            Bayesian (BIC)              735637.563
            Sample-Size Adjusted BIC    735567.648
            (n* = (n + 2) / 24)
Chi-Square Test of Model Fit
            Value                          270.014
            Degrees of Freedom                   5
            P-Value                         0.0000
RMSEA (Root Mean Square Error Of Approximation)
            Estimate                         0.051
            90 Percent C.I.                  0.046        0.056
            Probability RMSEA <= .05         0.397
CFI/TLI
            CFI                              0.997
            TLI                              0.991
SRMR (Standardized Root Mean Square Residual)
            Value                            0.010

MODEL RESULTS

                                            Two-Tailed
            Estimate      S.E.    Est./S.E.   P-Value
ETA_1    BY
   MATH1       1.000     0.000     999.000    999.000
   READ1       0.892     0.009     102.554      0.000
   GK1         0.575     0.006      89.703      0.000
ETA_2    BY
   MATH2       1.000     0.000     999.000    999.000
   READ2       0.951     0.009     101.979      0.000
   GK2         0.470     0.005      90.199      0.000
ETA_2    ON
   ETA_1       1.224     0.007     175.086      0.000
MATH1    WITH
   MATH2      -0.570     0.645      -0.884      0.377
READ1    WITH
   READ2      43.113     0.782      55.166      0.000
GK1      WITH
   GK2        26.202     0.356      73.594      0.000
Means
   ETA_1       0.000     0.000     999.000    999.000
Intercepts
   READ1      34.791     0.073     475.674      0.000
   MATH1      25.821     0.064     402.153      0.000
   GK1        21.761     0.054     401.270      0.000
   READ2      45.954     0.100     458.478      0.000
```

(continued)

Output B.1. (Continued)

MATH2	36.131	0.084	428.596	0.000
GK2	26.811	0.056	480.977	0.000
ETA_2	0.000	0.000	999.000	999.000
Variances				
ETA_1	74.575	0.994	75.048	0.000
Residual Variances				
READ1	44.894	0.647	69.433	0.000
MATH1	7.887	0.558	14.122	0.000
GK1	32.447	0.389	83.515	0.000
READ2	88.564	1.198	73.928	0.000
MATH2	20.957	0.982	21.337	0.000
GK2	34.343	0.406	84.684	0.000
ETA_2	11.649	0.359	32.447	0.000

(RMSEA), a measure of absolute fit, was 0.051, and models with RMSEAs less than 0.08 are generally considered acceptable. The comparative fit index (CFI) and the Tucker–Lewis index (TLI), two measures of incremental fit, were 0.997 and 0.991, respectively, and models with CFI/TLI values greater than 0.95 indicate good model fit. The chi-square test of model fit was 270.01 on 5 degrees of freedom, suggesting that the model did not fit perfectly, but the goal of perfect fit is often unrealistic.

Moving onto the parameter estimates, we find that the two factors were well defined by their respective indicators. This can be difficult to determine with the unstandardized output and can be more easily seen in the standardized output (STDXY in Mplus and standardized parameters can be requested specifying mxStandardizeRAMpaths(acad. fit, SE=FALSE) in OpenMx). The standardized factor loadings were all greater than 0.60, indicating strong associations between the latent variables and their indicators. The latent variable eta_1 strongly predicted eta_2, with a regression weight of 1.22. The standardized estimate was 0.95. The variances of the factors were 74.58 and 11.65 for eta_1 and eta_2, respectively. The estimate for eta_2 is the disturbance variance—the amount of true variance in eta_2 that was not accounted for by eta_1.

The unique variances indicate the amount of variance that was unexplained by the common factor. We don't go into a detailed discussion about these estimates. The unique factors for reading and general knowledge were strongly related over time. The unique correlation for reading was 0.68, and the unique correlation for general knowledge was 0.79. The final set of estimates are the intercepts for the observed variables, and these parameters should map onto their observed means, so we don't go into a detailed discussion about these estimates.

STRUCTURAL EQUATION MODELING AND LONGITUDINAL DATA

SEM is a commonly used statistical modeling framework for the analysis of longitudinal data beginning with the work of Jöreskog (1979) with the cross-lag model and the work of

Output B.2. OpenMx Output for the Example Model

```
free parameters:
        name    matrix    row     col      Estimate    Std.Error  A
1   lambda_21      A     read1   eta_1    0.8922588    0.008513840
2   lambda_31      A      gk1    eta_1    0.5748677    0.006343646
3     beta_21      A     eta_2   eta_1    1.2237576    0.006964077
4   lambda_22      A     read2   eta_2    0.9505533    0.009391106
5   lambda_32      A      gk2    eta_2    0.4702656    0.005253708
6    theta_11      S     read1   read1   44.8938868    0.638176946
7    theta_22      S     math1   math1    7.8867219    0.506527060  *
8    theta_33      S      gk1     gk1    32.4470291    0.383090959
9    theta_41      S     read1   read2   43.1133738    0.748750590
10   theta_44      S     read2   read2   88.5639343    1.115438278
11   theta_52      S     math1   math2   -0.5698243    0.512431264  *
12   theta_55      S     math2   math2   20.9572064    0.931649836
13   theta_63      S      gk1     gk2    26.2021097    0.346362736
14   theta_66      S      gk2     gk2    34.3432551    0.391361917
15     psi_11      S     eta_1   eta_1   74.5752400    0.954203915
16     psi_22      S     eta_2   eta_2   11.6487048    0.376776831
17      tau_1      M       1     read1   34.7910987    0.073164374
18      tau_2      M       1     math1   25.8211151    0.064235315
19      tau_3      M       1      gk1    21.7612556    0.054261725
20      tau_4      M       1     read2   45.9535899    0.100278272
21      tau_5      M       1     math2   36.1308944    0.084338896
22      tau_6      M       1      gk2    26.8106199    0.055769635

observed statistics: 111311
estimated parameters: 22
degrees of freedom: 111289
fit value (-2lnL units): 735419
saturated fit value (-2lnL units): 735149
number of observations: 20601
chi-square: X2 (df=5) = 270.0144, p = 2.778631e-56
Information Criteria:
      | df Penalty | Parameters Penalty  | Sample-Size Adjusted
AIC:      512841.0              735463.0                     NA
BIC:     -370025.2              735637.6               735567.6
CFI:     0.9971029
TLI:     0.9913086 (also known as NNFI)
RMSEA: 0.05072308 [95% CI (0.04468658, 0.05694658)]
Prob(RMSEA <= 0.05): 0.3967836
```

Meredith and Tisak (1984, 1990) with the latent curve model. The flexibility of the SEM framework and the ability to structure the data in a multivariate form enable researchers to account for the dependency in the data. This framework also enabled researchers to study measurement invariance and measurement bias over time (Meredith, 1993), study how latent entities changed over time (McArdle, 1988), and opened the door to new analyses as the capabilities of SEM programs expanded (e.g., mixture models).

References

Ahmavaara, Y. (1954). The mathematical theory of factorial invariance under selection. *Psychometrika, 19*, 27–38.

Allison, P. D. (2012). Handling missing data by maximum likelihood (SAS Global Forum 2012, Paper 312-2012). Retrieved from *www.statisticalhorizons.com/wp-content/uploads/MissingData ByML.pdf.*

Asparouhov, T., & Muthén, B. (2013). *Auxiliary variables in mixture modeling: 3-step approaches using Mplus* (Mplus Web Notes, No. 15).

Baltes, P. B., & Nesselroade, J. R. (1979). History and rationale of longitudinal research. In J. R. Nesselroade & P. B. Baltes (Eds.), *Longitudinal research in the study of behavior and development* (pp. 1–39). New York: Academic Press.

Bates, D., Mächler, M., & Bolker, B. (2015). Fitting linear mixed-effects models using lme4. *Journal of Statistical Software, 67*(1), 1–48.

Bates, D., Mächler, M., Bolker, B., & Walker, S. (2011). *lme4: Linear mixed-effects models using S4 classes.* R package version 0.999375-38, *http://CRAN.R-project.org/package=lme4.*

Bauer, D. J. (2005). A semiparametric approach to modeling nonlinear relations among latent variables. *Structural Equation Modeling: A Multidisciplinary Journal, 4*, 513–535.

Bauer, D. J., & Curran, P. J. (2003). Distributional assumptions of growth mixture models: Implications for over-extraction of latent trajectory classes. *Psychological Methods, 8*, 338–363.

Bauer, D. J., & Hussong, A. M. (2009). Psychometric approaches for developing commensurate measures across independent studies: Traditional and new models. *Psychological Methods, 14*, 101–125.

Beal, S. L., & Sheiner, L. B. (1982). Estimating population kinetics. *CRC Critical Reviews in Biomedical Engineering, 8*, 195–222.

Beal, S. L., & Sheiner, L. B. (1992). *NONMEM user's guide.* San Francisco: University of California, San Francisco, NONMEM Project Group.

Bell, R. Q. (1953). Convergence: An accelerated longitudinal approach. *Child Development, 24*, 145–152.

Bell, R. Q. (1954). An experimental test of the accelerated longitudinal approach. *Child Development, 25*, 281–286.

Berkey, C. S. (1982). Bayesian approach for a nonlinear growth model. *Biometrics, 38*, 953–961.

Beunckens, C., Molenberghs, G., Verbeke, G., & Mallinckrodt, C. (2008). A latent-class mixture model for incomplete longitudinal Gaussian data. *Biometrics, 64*, 96–105.

Bickel, R. (2007). *Multilevel analysis for applied research: It's just regression!* New York: Guilford Press.

Biesanz, J. C., Deeb-Sossa, N., Papadakis, A. A., Bollen, K. A., & Curran, P. J. (2004). The role of coding time in estimating and interpreting growth curve models. *Psychological Methods, 9,* 30–52.

Birnbaum, A. (1968). Some latent trait models and their use in inferring an examinee's ability. In F. M. Lord & M. R. Novick (Eds.), *Statistical theories of mental test scores* (pp. 397–472). Reading, MA: Addison-Wesley.

Blozis, S. A. (2004). Structured latent curve models for the study of change in multivariate repeated measures. *Psychological Methods, 9,* 334–353.

Blozis, S. A., & Cudeck, R. (1999). Conditionally linear mixed-effects models with latent variable covariates. *Journal of Educational and Behavioral Statistics, 24,* 245–270.

Boker, S. M., & McArdle, J. J. (1995). A vector field analysis of longitudinal aging data. *Experimental Aging Research, 21,* 77–93.

Boker, S. M., McArdle, J. J., & Neale, M. (2002). An algorithm for the hierarchical organization of path diagrams and calculation of components of expected covariance. *Structural Equation Modeling: A Multidisciplinary Journal, 9,* 174–194.

Boker, S., Neale, M., Maes, H., Wilde, M., Spiegel, M., Brick, T., et al. (2011). OpenMx: An open source extended structural equation modeling framework. *Psychometrika, 76,* 306–317.

Boker, S., Neale, M., & Rausch, J. (2004). Latent differential equation modeling with multivariate multi-occasion indicators. In K. van Montfort, J. Oud, & A. Satorra (Eds.), *Recent developments on structural equation models: Theory and applications* (pp. 151–174). Dordrecht, The Netherlands: Kluwer.

Boker, S. M., & Nesselroade, J. R. (2002). A method for modeling the intrinsic dynamics of intra-individual variability: Recovering the parameters of simulated oscillators in multiwave panel data. *Multivariate Behavioral Research, 37,* 127–160.

Bollen, K. A. (1989). *Structural equation modeling with latent variables.* Hoboken, NJ: Wiley.

Box, G. E. (1950). Problems in the analysis of growth and wear curves. *Biometrics, 6,* 362–389.

Browne, M. W. (1993). Structured latent curve models. In C. M. Cuadras & C. R. Rao (Eds.), *Multivariate analysis: Future directions 2* (pp. 171–198). Amsterdam: North-Holland.

Browne, M. W., & du Toit, S. H. C. (1991). Models for learning data. In L. Collins & J. L. Horn (Eds.), *Best methods for the analysis of change* (pp. 47–68). Washington, DC: American Psychological Association.

Bryk, A. S., & Raudenbush, S. W. (1987). Application of hierarchical linear models to assessing change. *Psychological Bulletin, 101,* 147–158.

Burchinal, M., & Appelbaum, M. I. (1991). Estimating individual developmental function: Methods and their assumptions. *Child Development, 62,* 23–43.

Cattell, R. B. (1944). "Parallel proportional profiles" and other principles for determining the choice of factors by rotation. *Psychometrika, 9,* 267–283.

Center for Human Resource Research. (2004). *A guide to the 1979–2002 National Longitudinal Survey of Youth.* Washington, DC: U.S. Department of Labor, Bureau of Labor Statistics.

Center for Human Resource Research. (2009). NLSY79 child and young adult data users guide. Retrieved from *www.nlsinfo.org/pub/usersvc/Child-Young-Adult/2006ChildYA-DataUsersGuide.pdf.*

Chang, W. (2013). *R graphics cookbook.* Sebastopol, CA: O'Reilly Media.

Chow, S. M., Grimm, K. J., Filteau, G., Dolan, C. V., & McArdle, J. J. (2013). Regime-switching bivariate latent change score model. *Multivariate Behavioral Research, 48,* 463–502.

Codd, C. L., & Cudeck, R. (2014). Nonlinear random-effects mixture models for repeated measures. *Psychometrika, 79,* 60–83.

Cudeck, R., & du Toit, S. H. C. (2002). A nonlinear form of quadratic regression with interpretable parameters. *Multivariate Behavioral Research, 37,* 501–519.

Cudeck, R. A., & Klebe, K. J. (2002). Multiphase mixed-effects models for repeated measures data. *Psychological Methods, 7,* 41–63.

Curran, P. J. (2003). Have multilevel models been structural equation models all along? *Multivariate Behavioral Research, 38,* 529–569.

Curran, P. J., & Bauer, D. J. (2011). The disaggregation of within-person and between-person effects in longitudinal models of change. *Annual Review of Psychology, 62,* 583–619.

Curran, P. J., & Bollen, K. A. (2001). The best of both worlds: Combining autoregressive and latent curve models. In L. M. Collins & A. G. Sayer (Eds.), *New methods for the analysis of change* (pp. 105–136). Washington, DC: American Psychological Association.

Curran, P. J., Hussong, A. M., Cai, L., Huang, W., Chassin, L., Sher, K. J., et al. (2008). Pooling data from multiple longitudinal studies: The role of item response theory in integrative data analysis. *Developmental Psychology, 44,* 365–380.

Curran, P. J., & Peterman, M. (2005). *A curious discrepancy between multilevel and structural equation growth curve models with time-varying covariates.* Paper presented at the annual meeting of the Society of Multivariate Experimental Psychology, Lake Tahoe, NV.

Davidian, M., & Gallant, R. A. (1993). The nonlinear mixed effects model with a smooth random effects density. *Biometrika, 80,* 475–488.

Davidian, M., & Giltinan, D. M. (1995). *Nonlinear models for repeated measures data.* London: Chapman & Hall.

Davidian, M., & Giltinan, D. M. (2003). Nonlinear models for repeated measurement data: An overview and update. *Journal of Agricultural, Biological, and Environmental Statistics, 8,* 387–419.

de Ayala, R. J. (2009). *The theory and practice of item response theory.* New York: Guilford Press.

Der, G., & Everitt, B. S. (2014). *A handbook of statistical graphics using SAS ODS.* Boca Raton, FL: CRC Press.

Diggle, P. D., & Kenward, M. G. (1994). Informative dropout in longitudinal data analysis. *Applied Statistics, 43,* 49–93.

Dogan, S. J., Stockdale, G. D., Widaman, K. F., & Conger, R. D. (2010). Developmental relations and patterns of change between alcohol use and number of sexual partners from adolescence through adulthood. *Developmental Psychology, 46,* 1747–1759.

Dunn, L. M., & Markwardt, F. L. (1970). *Peabody Individual Achievement Test Manual.* Circle Pines, MN: American Guidance Service.

Edwards, M. C., & Wirth, R. J. (2009). Measurement and the study of change. *Research in Human Development, 6,* 74–96.

Embretson, S. E., & Reise, S. (2000). *Item response theory for psychologists.* Mahwah, NJ: Erlbaum.

Enders, C. K. (2010). *Applied missing data analysis.* New York: Guilford Press.

Enders, C. K., & Tofighi, D. (2008). The impact of misspecifying class-specific residual variances in growth mixture models. *Structural Equation Modeling: A Multidisciplinary Journal, 15,* 75–95.

Estabrook, R., & Neale, M. C. (2013). A comparison of factor score estimation methods in the presence of missing data. *Multivariate Behavioral Research, 48,* 1–27.

Ferrer, E., Balluerka, N., & Widaman, K. F. (2008). Factorial invariance and the specification of second-order latent growth models. *Methodology, 4,* 22–36.

Ferrer, E., McArdle, J. J., Shaywitz, B. A., Holahan, J. N., Marchione, K., & Shaywitz, S. E. (2007). Longitudinal models of developmental dynamics between reading and cognition from childhood to adolescence. *Developmental Psychology, 43,* 1460–1473.

Ferrer, E., Shaywitz, B. A., Holahan, J. N., Marchione, K., & Shaywitz, S. E. (2010). Uncoupling of reading and IQ over time: Empirical evidence for a definition of dyslexia. *Psychological Science, 21,* 93–101.

Finch, W. H., Bolin, J. E., & Kelley, K. (2014). *Multilevel modeling using R.* Boca Raton, FL: CRC Press.

Flora, D. B., Curran, P. J., Hussong, A. M., & Edwards, M. C. (2008). Incorporating measurement nonequivalence in a cross-study latent growth curve analysis. *Structural Equation Modeling: A Multidisciplinary Journal, 15,* 676–704.

Forero, C. G., & Maydeu-Olivares, A. (2009). Estimation of IRT graded response models: Limited versus full information methods. *Psychological Methods, 14,* 275–299.

Gelman, A., & Hill, J. (2007). *Data analysis using regression and multilevel/hierarchical models*. New York: Cambridge University Press.

Ghisletta, P., & Lindenberger, U. (2003). Static and dynamic longitudinal structural analyses of cognitive changes in old age. *Gerontology, 50*, 12–16.

Grimm, K. J. (2006). *A longitudinal dynamic analysis of the impacts of reading on mathematical ability in children and adolescents*. Unpublished doctoral dissertation, University of Virginia, Charlottesville, VA.

Grimm, K. J. (2007). Multivariate longitudinal methods for studying developmental relationships between depression and academic achievement. *International Journal of Behavioral Development, 31*, 328–339.

Grimm, K. J., An, Y., McArdle, J. J., Zonderman, A. B., & Resnick, S. M. (2012). Recent changes leading to subsequent changes: Extensions of multivariate latent difference score models. *Structural Equation Modeling: A Multidisciplinary Journal, 19*, 268–292.

Grimm, K. J., Castro-Schilo, L., & Davoudzadeh, P. (2013). Modeling intraindividual change in nonlinear growth models with latent change scores. *GeroPsych, 26*, 153–162.

Grimm, K. J., Davoudzadeh, P., & Ram, N. (2015). *Developments in the analysis of longitudinal data*. Manuscript submitted for publication.

Grimm, K. J., Kuhl, A. P., & Zhang, Z. (2013). Measurement models, estimation, and the study of change. *Structural Equation Modeling: A Multidisciplinary Journal, 20*, 504–517.

Grimm, K. J., & Liu, Y. (2016). Residual structures in growth models with ordinal outcomes. *Structural Equation Modeling: A Multidisciplinary Journal, 23*, 466–475.

Grimm, K. J., & Marcoulides, K. M. (2016). Individual change and the timing and onset of important life events: Methods, models, and assumptions. *International Journal of Behavioral Development, 40*, 87–96.

Grimm, K. J., & Ram, N. (2009). Nonlinear growth models in Mplus and SAS. *Structural Equation Modeling: A Multidisciplinary Journal, 16*, 676–701.

Grimm, K. J., & Ram, N. (2011). Growth curve modeling from an SEM perspective. In B. Laursen, T. Little, & N. Card (Eds.), *Handbook of developmental research methods* (pp. 411–431). New York: Guilford Press.

Grimm, K. J., Ram, N., & Estabrook, R. (2010). Nonlinear structured growth mixture models in Mplus and OpenMx. *Multivariate Behavioral Research, 45*, 887–909.

Grimm, K. J., Ram, N., & Hamagami, F. (2011). Nonlinear growth curves in developmental research. *Child Development, 82*, 1357–1371.

Grimm, K. J., Ram, N., Shiyko, M. P., & Lo, L. L. (2013). A simulation study of the ability of growth mixture models to uncover growth heterogeneity. In J. J. McArdle & G. Ritschard (Eds.), *Contemporary issues in exploratory data mining* (pp. 172–189). New York: Routledge.

Grimm, K. J., Steele, J. S., Mashburn, A. J., Burchinal, M., & Pianta, R. C. (2010). Early behavioral associations of achievement trajectories. *Developmental Psychology, 46*, 976–983.

Grimm, K. J., Steele, J. S., Ram, N., & Nesselroade, J. R. (2013). Exploratory latent growth models in the structural equation modeling framework. *Structural Equation Modeling: A Multidisciplinary Journal, 20*, 568–591.

Grimm, K. J., & Widaman, K. F. (2010). Residual structures in latent growth curve modeling. *Structural Equation Modeling: A Multidisciplinary Journal, 17*, 424–442.

Grimm, K. J., Zhang, Z., Hamagami, F., & Mazzocco, M. (2013). Modeling nonlinear change via latent change and latent acceleration frameworks: Examining velocity and acceleration of growth trajectories. *Multivariate Behavioral Research, 48*, 117–143.

Hamagami, F., & McArdle, J. J. (2007). Dynamic extensions of latent difference score models. In S. M. Boker and M. J. Wenger (Eds.), *Data analytic techniques for dynamical systems* (pp. 47–85). Mahwah, NJ: Erlbaum.

Hamagami, F., Zhang, Z., & McArdle, J. J. (2009). Modeling latent difference score models using Bayesian algorithms. In S.-M. Chow, E. Ferrer, & F. Hsieh (Eds.), *Statistical methods for modeling human dynamics: An interdisciplinary dialogue* (pp. 319–348). Mahwah, NJ: Erlbaum.

Hamaker, E. L., Kuiper, R. M., & Grasman, R. P. (2015). A critique of the cross-lagged panel model. *Psychological Methods, 20,* 102–116.

Hancock, G. R., Kuo, W. L., & Lawrence, F. R. (2001). An illustration of second-order latent growth models. *Structural Equation Modeling: A Multidisciplinary Journal, 8,* 470–489.

Harring, J. R., & Blozis, S. A. (2014). Fitting correlated residual error structures in nonlinear mixed-effects models using SAS PROC NLMIXED. *Behavior Research Methods, 46,* 372–384.

Harring, J. R., Cudeck, R., & du Toit, S. H. (2006). Fitting partially nonlinear random coefficient models as SEMs. *Multivariate Behavioral Research, 41,* 579–596.

Harville, D. A. (1977). Maximum likelihood approaches to variance component estimation and to related problems. *Journal of the American Statistical Association, 72,* 320–338.

Hayes, A. F. (2006). A primer on multilevel modeling. *Human Communication Research, 32,* 385–410.

Henson, J. M., Reise, S. P., & Kim, K. H. (2007). Detecting mixtures from structural model differences using latent variable mixture modeling: A comparison of relative model fit statistics. *Structural Equation Modeling: A Multidisciplinary Journal, 14,* 202–226.

Hertzog, C., Lindenberger, U., Ghisletta, P., & von Oertzen, T. (2006). On the power of multivariate growth curve models to detect correlated change. *Psychological Methods, 11,* 244–252.

Hertzog, C., von Oertzen, T., Ghisletta, P., & Lindenberger, U. (2008). Evaluating the power of latent growth curve models to detect individual differences in change. *Structural Equation Modeling: A Multidisciplinary Journal, 15,* 541–563.

Hoffman, L. (2015). *Longitudinal analysis: Modeling within-person fluctuation and change.* New York: Routledge.

Horn, J. L., McArdle, J. J., & Mason, R. (1983). When is invariance not invarient: A practical scientist's look at the ethereal concept of factor invariance. *Southern Psychologist, 1,* 179–188.

Hox, J. (2010). *Multilevel analysis: Techniques and applications* (2nd ed.). New York: Routledge.

Jenss, R. M., & Bayley, N. (1937). A mathematical method for studying the growth of a child. *Human Biology, 9,* 556–563.

Jones, B. L., Nagin, D. S., & Roeder, K. (2001). A SAS procedure based on mixture models for estimating developmental trajectories. *Sociological Methods & Research, 29,* 374–393.

Jones, H. E., & Bayley, N. (1941). The Berkeley growth study. *Child Development, 12,* 167–173.

Jöreskog, K. G. (1970). Estimation and testing of simplex models. *British Journal of Mathematical and Statistical Psychology, 23,* 121–145.

Jöreskog, K. G. (1971). Simultaneous factor analysis in several populations. *Psychometrika, 36,* 409–426.

Jöreskog, K. G. (1974). Analyzing psychological data by structural analysis of covariance matrices. In R. C. Atkinson, D. H. Krantz, R. D. Luce, & P. Suppas (Eds.), *Contemporary developments in mathematical psychology* (pp. 1–56). San Francisco: Freeman.

Jöreskog, K. G. (1979). Statistical estimation of structural models in longitudinal–developmental investigations. In J. R. Nesselroade & P. B. Baltes (Eds.), *Longitudinal research in the study of behavior and development* (pp. 303–352). New York: Academic Press.

Jöreskog, K. G., & Goldberger, A. S. (1975). Estimation of a model with multiple indicators and multiple causes of a single latent variable. *Journal of the American Statistical Association, 70,* 631–639.

Jöreskog, K. G., & Sörbom, D. (1979). *Advances in factor analysis and structural equation models.* Cambridge, MA: Abt Books.

Jung, T., & Wickrama, K. A. S. (2008). An introduction to latent class growth analysis and growth mixture modeling. *Social and Personality Compass, 2,* 302–317.

Kamata, A., & Bauer, D. J. (2008). A note on the relation between factor analytic and item response theory models. *Structural Equation Modeling: A Multidisciplinary Journal, 15,* 136–153.

Kaplan, D. (2009). *Structural equation modeling: Foundations and extensions.* Thousand Oaks, CA: Sage.

Kaplan, D., & Sweetman, H. M. (2006). Finite mixture modeling approaches to the study of growth in academic achievement. In. R. Lissitz (Ed.), *Longitudinal and value added models of student performance* (pp. 130–169). Maple Grove, MN: JAM Press.

Karkach, A. S. (2006). Trajectories and models of individual growth. *Demographic Research, 15,* 347–400.

Kim-Spoon, J., & Grimm, K. J. (2016). Latent growth modeling and developmental psychopathology. In D. Cicchetti (Ed.), *Developmental psychopathology: Vol. 1. Theory and method* (3rd ed., pp. 986–1041). Hoboken, NJ: Wiley.

Kline, R. B. (2016). *Principles and practice of structural equation modeling* (4th ed.). New York: Guilford Press.

Koran, J., & Hancock, G. R. (2010). Using fixed thresholds with grouped data in structural equation modeling. *Structural Equation Modeling: A Multidisciplinary Journal, 17,* 590–604.

Kwok, O., West, S. G., & Green, S. B. (2007). The impact of misspecifying the within-subject covariance structure in multiwave longitudinal multilevel models: A Monte Carlo study. *Multivariate Behavioral Research, 42,* 557–592.

Laird, N. M., & Ware, J. H. (1982). Random-effects models for longitudinal data. *Biometrics, 38,* 963–974.

Lazarsfeld, P. F., & Henry, N. W. (1968). *Latent structure analysis.* Boston: Houghton Mifflin.

Li, F., Duncan, T., Duncan, S., & Hops, H. (2001). Piecewise growth mixture modeling of adolescent alcohol use data. *Structural Equation Modeling: A Multidisciplinary Journal, 8,* 175–204.

Li, L., & Hser, Y. (2011). On inclusion of covariates for class enumeration of growth mixture models. *Multivariate Behavioral Research, 46,* 266–302.

Lindstrom, M. J., & Bates, D. M. (1990). Nonlinear mixed effects models for repeated measures data. *Biometrics, 46,* 673–687.

Littell, R. C., Milliken, G. A., Stroup, W. W., Wolfinger, R. D., & Schabenberger, O. (2006). *SAS for mixed models* (2nd ed.). Cary, NC: SAS Institute.

Little, R. J., & Rubin, D. B. (2002). *Statistical analysis with missing data* (2nd ed.) New York: Wiley.

Little, T. D. (1997). Mean and covariance structures (MACS) analyses of cross-cultural data: Practical and theoretical issues. *Multivariate Behavioral Research, 32,* 53–76.

Little, T. D. (2013). *Longitudinal structural equation modeling.* New York: Guilford Press.

Long, J. D. (2012). *Longitudinal data analysis for the behavioral sciences using R.* Thousand Oaks, CA: Sage.

Lord, F. M. (1952). *A theory of test scores* (Psychometric Monograph Number 7). Richmond, VA: Psychometric Society.

Lubke, G., & Muthén, B. (2007). Performance of factor mixture models as a function of model size, covariate effects, and class-specific parameters. *Structural Equation Modeling: A Multidisciplinary Journal, 14,* 26–47.

Lunn, D. J., Thomas, A., Best, N., & Spiegelhalter, D. (2000). WinBUGS—A Bayesian modeling framework: Concepts, structure, and extensibility. *Statistics and Computing, 10,* 325–337.

Macfarlane, J. W. (1919). The Guidance Study. *Sociometry, 3,* 1–23.

Magnusson, D. (2003). The person approach: Concepts, measurement models, and research strategy. *New Directions for Child and Adolescent Development, 101,* 3–23.

Marceau, K., Ram, N., Houts, R. M., Grimm, K. J., & Susman, E. J. (2011). Individual differences in boys' and girls' timing and tempo of puberty: Modeling development with nonlinear growth models. *Developmental Psychology, 47,* 1389–1409.

Masters, G. (1982). A Rasch model for partial credit scoring. *Psychometrika, 42,* 149–174.

Matange, S., & Heath, D. (2011). *Statistical graphics procedures by example: Effective graphs using SAS.* Cary, NC: SAS Institute.

McArdle, J. J. (1986). Latent variable growth within behavior genetic models. *Behavior Genetics, 16,* 163–200.

McArdle, J. J. (1988). Dynamic but structural equation modeling of repeated measures data. In J. R. Nesselroade & R. B. Cattell (Eds.), *Handbook of multivariate experimental psychology* (2nd ed., pp. 561–614). New York: Plenum.

McArdle, J. J. (1989). Structural modeling experiments using multiple growth functions. In P. Ackerman, R. Kanfer, & R. Cudeck (Eds.), *Learning and individual differences: Abilities, motivation, and methodology* (pp. 71–117). Hillsdale, NJ: Erlbaum.

McArdle, J. J. (1994). Structural factor analysis experiments with incomplete data. *Multivariate Behavioral Research, 29,* 409–454.

McArdle, J. J. (2001). A latent difference score approach to longitudinal dynamic structural analysis. In R. Cudeck, S. du Toit, & D. Sorbom (Eds.), *Structural equation modeling: Present and future* (pp. 342–380). Lincolnwood, IL: Scientific Software International.

McArdle, J. J. (2005). The development of the RAM rules for latent variable structural equation modeling. In A. Maydeu-Olivares & J. J. McArdle (Eds.), *Contemporary psychometrics* (pp. 224–275). Mahwah, NJ: Erlbaum.

McArdle, J. J. (2009). Latent variable modeling of differences and changes with longitudinal data. *Annual Review of Psychology, 60,* 577–605.

McArdle, J. J., & Epstein, D. (1987). Latent growth curves within developmental structural equation models. *Child Development, 58,* 110–133.

McArdle, J. J., Ferrer-Caja, E., Hamagami, F., & Woodcock, R. W. (2002). Comparative longitudinal multilevel structural analyses of the growth and decline of multiple intellectual abilities over the life-span. *Developmental Psychology, 38,* 115–142.

McArdle, J. J., & Grimm, K. J. (2010). Five steps in latent curve and latent change score modeling with longitudinal data. In K. van Montfort, J. Oud, & A. Satorra (Eds.), *Longitudinal research with latent variables* (pp. 245–274). Heidelberg, Germany: Springer-Verlag.

McArdle, J. J., Grimm, K. J., Hamagami, F., Bowles, R. P., & Meredith, W. (2009). Modeling life-span growth curves of cognition using longitudinal data with multiple samples and changing scales of measurement. *Psychological Methods, 14,* 126–149.

McArdle, J. J., & Hamagami, F. (1996). Multilevel models from a multiple group structural equation perspective. In G. Marcoulides & R. Schumaker (Eds.), *Advanced structural equation modeling techniques* (pp. 89–124). Hillsdale, NJ: Erlbaum.

McArdle, J. J., & Hamagami, F. (2001). Linear dynamic analyses of incomplete longitudinal data. In L. M. Collins & A. G. Sayer (Eds.), *New methods for the analysis of change* (pp. 137–176). Washington, DC: American Psychological Association.

McArdle, J. J., & Hamagami, F. (2004). Methods for dynamic change hypotheses. In K. van Montfort, J. Oud, & A. Satorra (Eds.), *Recent developments in structural equation models* (pp. 295–336). London: Kluwer.

McArdle, J. J., Hamagami, F., Kadlec, K., & Fisher, G. (2007). *A dynamic structural analysis of dyadic cycles of depression in the Health and Retirement Study data.* Unpublished manuscript, Department of Psychology, University of Southern California.

McArdle, J. J., & McDonald, R. P. (1984). Some algebraic properties of the Reticular Action Model for moment structures. *British Journal of Mathematical and Statistical Psychology, 87,* 234–251.

McArdle, J. J., & Nesselroade, J. R. (2003). Growth curve analyses in contemporary psychological research. In J. Schinka & W. Velicer (Eds.), *Comprehensive handbook of psychology: Vol. 2: Research methods in psychology* (pp. 447–480). New York: Pergamon Press.

McArdle, J. J., & Nesselroade, J. R. (2014). *Longitudinal data analysis using structural equation models.* Washington, DC: American Psychological Association.

McArdle, J. J., & Wang, L. (2008). Modeling age-based turning points in longitudinal life-span growth curves of cognition. In P. Cohen (Ed.), *Applied data analytic techniques for turning point research* (pp. 105–128). New York: Taylor & Francis.

McArdle, J. J., & Woodcock, R. W. (1997). Expanding test–rest designs to include developmental time-lag components. *Psychological Methods, 2,* 403–435.

McDonald, R. P. (1967). *Nonlinear factor analysis* (Psychometric Monograph Number 15). Richmond, VA: William Byrd Press.

Mehta, P. D., & Neale, M. C. (2005). People are variables too: Multilevel structural equations modeling. *Psychological Methods, 10*, 259–284.

Meredith, W. (1964a). Notes on factorial invariance. *Psychometrika, 29*, 177–185.

Meredith, W. (1964b). Rotation to achieve factorial invariance. *Psychometrika, 29*, 187–206.

Meredith, W. (1993). Measurement invariance, factor analysis and factorial invariance. *Psychometrika, 58*, 525–543.

Meredith, W., & Horn, J. (2001). The role of factorial invariance in modeling growth and change. In A. Saver & L. Collins (Eds.), *New methods for the analysis of change* (pp. 203–240). Washington, DC: American Psychological Association.

Meredith, W., & Tisak, J. (1984). *"Tuckerizing" curves.* Paper presented at the annual meeting of the Psychometric Society, Santa Barbara, CA.

Meredith, W., & Tisak, J. (1990). Latent curve analysis. *Psychometrika, 55*, 107–122.

Millsap, R. E. (1995). Measurement invariance, predictive invariance, and the duality paradox. *Multivariate Behavioral Research, 30*, 577–605.

Millsap, R. E. (2011). *Statistical approaches to measurement invariance.* New York: Routledge.

Molenberghs, G., Fitzmaurice, G., Kenward, M. G., Tsiatis, A., & Verbeke, G. (2015). *Handbook of missing data methodology.* Boca Raton, FL: CRC Press.

Morrison, F. J., Smith, L., & Dow-Ehrensberger, M. (1995). Education and cognitive development: A natural experiment. *Developmental Psychology, 31*, 789–799.

Muraki, E. (1992). A generalized partial credit model: Application of an EM algorithm. *Applied Psychological Measurement, 16*, 159–176.

Muthén, B. (1979). A structural probit model with latent variables. *Journal of the American Statistical Association, 74*, 807–811.

Muthén, B. (1983). Latent variable structural equation modeling with categorical data. *Journal of Econometrics, 22*, 43–65.

Muthén, B. (1984). A general structural equation model with dichotomous, ordered categorical, and continuous latent variable indicators. *Psychometrika, 49*, 115–132.

Muthén, B. (1985). A method for studying the homogeneity of test items with respect to other relevant variables. *Journal of Educational Statistics, 10*, 121–132.

Muthén, B. (2001). Second-generation structural equation modeling with a combination of categorical and continuous latent variables: New opportunities for latent class–latent growth modeling. In L. M. Collins & A. G. Sayer (Eds.), *New methods for the analysis of change* (pp. 291–322). Washington, DC: American Psychological Association.

Muthén, B. (2003). Statistical and substantive checking in growth mixture modeling: Comment on Bauer and Curran (2003). *Psychological Methods, 8*, 369–377.

Muthén, B. (2004). Latent variable analysis: Growth mixture modeling and related techniques for longitudinal data. In D. Kaplan (Ed.), *Handbook of quantitative methodology for the social sciences* (pp. 345–368). Newbury Park, CA: Sage.

Muthén, B., & Asparouhov, T. (2009). Growth mixture modeling: Analysis with non-Gaussian random effects. In G. Fitzmaurice, M. Davidian, G. Verbeke, & G. Molenberghs (Eds.), *Longitudinal data analysis* (pp. 143–165). Boca Raton, FL: Chapman & Hall/CRC Press.

Muthén, B., Asparouhov, T., Hunter, A., & Leuchter, A. (2011). Growth modeling with nonignorable dropout: Alternative analyses of the STAR*D antidepressant trial. *Psychological Methods, 16*, 17–33.

Muthén, B., & Lehman. J. (1985). Multiple-group IRT modeling: Applications to item bias analysis. *Journal of Educational Statistics, 10*, 133–142.

Muthén, B., & Shedden, K. (1999). Finite mixture modeling with mixture outcomes using the EM algorithm. *Biometrics, 55*, 463–469.

Muthén, L. K., & Muthén, B. O. (1998–2012). *Mplus user's guide* (7th ed.). Los Angeles: Muthén & Muthén.

Nagin, D. S. (1999). Analyzing developmental trajectories: A semi-parametric, group-based approach. *Psychological Methods, 4,* 139–177.

National Center for Education Statistics. (2001). *User's manual for the ECLS-K public-use, data files and electronic, codebook.* Washington, DC: U.S. Department of Education.

Neale, M. C., Boker, S. M., Xie, G., & Maes, H. H. (2003). *Mx: Statistical modeling.* Richmond, VA: Department of Psychiatry, Virginia Commonwealth University.

Nylund, K. L., Asparouhov, T., & Muthén, B. (2007). Deciding on the number of classes in latent class analysis and growth mixture modeling: A Monte Carlo simulation study. *Structural Equation Modeling: A Multidisciplinary Journal, 14,* 535–569.

Peugh, J. L. (2010). A practical guide to multilevel modeling. *Journal of School Psychology, 48,* 85–112.

Piaget, J. (1952). *The origins of intelligence in children.* New York: International Universities Press.

Pinheiro, J. C., & Bates, D. M. (1995). Approximations to the log-likelihood function in the nonlinear mixed-effects model. *Journal of Computational and Graphical Statistics, 4,* 12–35.

Pinheiro, J., Bates, D., DebRoy, S., Sarkar, D., & R Development Core Team. (2013). *nlme: Linear and nonlinear mixed effects models.* R package version 3.1–113.

Potthoff, R. F., & Roy, S. N. (1964). A generalized multivariate analysis of variance model useful especially for growth curve problems. *Biometrika, 51,* 313–326.

Preacher, K. J., & Hancock, G. R. (2015). Parameterizing aspects of change as random coefficients. *Psychological Methods, 20,* 84–101.

Preece, M. A., & Baines, M. J. (1978). A new family of mathematical models describing the human growth curve. *Annals of Human Biology, 5,* 1–24.

Ram, N., Chow, S. M., Bowles, R. P., Wang, L., Grimm, K. J., Fujita, F., et al. (2005). Examining interindividual differences in cyclicity of pleasant and unpleasant affect using spectral analysis and item response modeling. *Psychometrika, 70,* 773–790.

Ram, N., & Gerstorf, D. (2009). Methods for the study of development: Developing methods. *Research in Human Development, 6,* 61–73.

Ram, N., Gerstorf, D., Fauth, E., Zarit, S., & Malberg, B. (2010). Aging, disablement, and dying: Using time-as-process and time-as-resources metrics to chart late-life change. *Research in Human Development, 7,* 27–44.

Ram, N., & Grimm, K. J. (2007). Using simple and complex growth models to articulate developmental change: Matching method to theory. *International Journal of Behavioral Development, 31,* 303–316.

Ram, N., & Grimm, K. J. (2009). Methods and measures: Growth mixture modeling, a method for identifying differences in longitudinal change among unobserved groups. *International Journal of Behavioral Development, 33,* 565–576.

Ram, N., & Grimm, K. J. (2015). Growth curve modeling and longitudinal factor analysis. In W. F. Overton & P. C. M. Molenaar (Eds.), *Handbook of child psychology and developmental science: Theory and method* (pp. 758–788). Hoboken, NJ: Wiley.

Ram, N., Grimm, K. J., Gatzke-Kopp, L. M., & Molenaar, P. C. M. (2011). Longitudinal mixture models and the identification of archetypes. In B. Laursen, T. Little, & N. Card (Eds.), *Handbook of developmental research methods* (pp. 481–500). New York: Guilford Press.

Rao, C. R. (1958). Some statistical methods for comparison of growth curves. *Biometrics, 14,* 1–17.

Rao, C. R. (1965). *Linear statistical inference and its applications.* New York: Wiley.

Raudenbush, S. W., & Bryk, A. S. (2002). *Hierarchical linear models: Applications and data analysis methods* (2nd ed.). Thousand Oaks, CA: Sage.

Raykov, T., & Marcoulides, G. A. (2006). *A first course in structural equation modeling* (2nd ed.). Mahwah, NJ: Erlbaum.

Reise, S. P., Widaman, K. F., & Pugh, R. H. (1993). Confirmatory factor analysis and item response theory: Two approaches for exploring measurement invariance. *Psychological Bulletin, 114,* 552–566.

Rogosa, D., Brandt, D., & Zimowski, M. (1982). A growth curve approach to the measurement of change. *Psychological Bulletin, 92,* 726–748.

Rogosa, D. R., & Willett, J. B. (1985). Understanding correlates of change by modeling individual differences in growth. *Psychometrika, 50,* 203–228.

Rubin, D. B. (1976). Inference and missing data. *Biometrika, 63,* 581–592.

Samejima, F. (1969). *Estimation of latent ability using a response pattern of graded scores* (Psychometric Monograph Number 17). Richmond, VA: Psychometric Society.

Schaie, K. W. (1965). A general model for the study of developmental problems. *Psychological Bulletin, 64,* 92–107.

Schumacker, R. E., & Lomax, R. C. (2010). *A beginner's guide to structural equation modeling* (3rd ed.). New York: Routledge.

Scott, M. A., Simonoff, J. S., & Marx, B. D. (2013). *The Sage handbook of multilevel modeling.* Thousand Oaks, CA: Sage.

Seeman, T. E., Berkman, L. F., Gulanski, B., Robbins, R., Greenspan, S., Charpentier, P., et al. (1995). Self-esteem and neuroendocrine response to challenge: MacArthur Successful Aging Studies. *Psychosomatic Research, 39,* 69–84.

Seeman, T. E., Singer, B., & Charpentier, P. (1995). Gender differences in pattern of HPA axis response to challenge: MacArthur Studies of Successful Aging. *Psychoneuroendicrinology, 20,* 711–725.

Sheu, C. F. (2002). Fitting mixed-effects models for repeated ordinal outcomes with the NLMIXED procedure. *Behavior Research Methods, Instruments, and Computers, 34,* 151–157.

Sheu, C. F., Chen, C. T., Su, Y. H., & Wang, W. C. (2005). Using SAS PROC NLMIXED to fit item response theory models. *Behavior Research Methods, 37,* 202–218.

Singer, J. D. (1998). Using SAS PROC MIXED to fit multilevel models, hierarchical models, and individual growth models. *Journal of Educational and Behavioral Statistics, 23,* 323–355.

Singer, J. D., & Willett, J. B. (2003). *Applied longitudinal data analysis: Methods for studying change and event occurrence.* New York: Oxford University Press.

Skibbe, L. E., Grimm, K. J., Bowles, R. P., & Morrison, F. J. (2012). Literacy growth in the academic year versus summer from preschool through second grade: Differential effects of schooling across four skills. *Scientific Study of Reading, 16,* 141–165.

Smith, N., & Blozis, S. A. (2014). Options in estimating nonlinear mixed models: Quadrature points and approximation methods. Western Users of SAS Software 2014 Conference Proceedings. Retrieved from *http://wuss.org/proceedings14/78_Final_Paper_PDF.pdf.*

Snijders, T. A. B., & Bosker, R. J. (2012). *Multilevel analysis: An introduction to basic and advanced multilevel modeling* (2nd ed.). Thousand Oaks, CA: Sage.

Sterba, S. K. (2014). Fitting nonlinear latent growth curve models with individually-varying time points. *Structural Equation Modeling: A Multidisciplinary Journal, 21,* 630–647.

Thissen, D., Steinberg, L., & Gerrard, M. (1986). Beyond group-mean differences: The concept of item bias. *Psychological Bulletin, 99,* 118–128.

Thurstone, L. L. (1947). *Multiple factor analysis.* Chicago: University of Chicago Press.

Tofighi, D., & Enders, C. K. (2007). Identifying the correct number of classes in growth mixture models. In G. R. Hancock, & K. M. Samuelsen (Eds.), *Advances in latent variable mixture models* (pp. 317–341). Greenwich, CT: Information Age.

Tucker, L. R. (1958). Determination of parameters of a functional relation by factor analysis. *Psychometrika, 23,* 19–23.

Tucker, L. R. (1966). Learning theory and multivariate experiment: Illustration by determination of generalized learning curves. In R. B. Cattell (Ed.), *Handbook of multivariate experimental psychology* (pp. 476–501). Chicago: Rand McNally.

Vermunt, J. K. (2010). Latent class modeling with covariates: Two improved three-step approaches. *Political Analysis, 18,* 450–469.

Vonesh, E. F. (1992a). Nonlinear models for the analysis of longitudinal data. *Statistics in Medicine, 11,* 1929–1954.

Vonesh, E. F. (1992b). Mixed-effects nonlinear regression for unbalanced repeated measures. *Biometrics, 48*, 1–17.

Vonesh, E. F., & Chinchilli, V. M. (1996). *Linear and nonlinear models for the analysis of repeated measurements.* New York: Marcel Dekker.

Wang, L., & Maxwell, S. E. (2015). On disaggregating between-person and within-person effects with longitudinal data using multilevel models. *Psychological Methods, 20*, 63–83.

Wang, L., Zhang, Z., McArdle, J. J., & Salthouse, T. A. (2008). Investigating ceiling effects in longitudinal data analysis. *Multivariate Behavioral Research, 43*, 476–496.

West, S. G., Ryu, E., Kwok, O. M., & Cham, H. (2011). Multilevel modeling: Current and future applications in personality research. *Journal of Personality, 79*, 2–50.

Wickham, H. (2009). *ggplot,2: Elegant graphics for data analysis.* New York: Springer.

Widaman, K. F., Ferrer, E., & Conger, R. D. (2010). Factorial invariance within longitudinal structural equation models: Measuring the same construct across time. *Child Development Perspectives, 4*, 10–18.

Widaman, K. F., & Reise, S. P. (1997). Exploring the measurement invariance of psychological instruments: Applications in the substance use domain. In K. Bryant, M. Windle, & S. West (Eds.), *The science of prevention: Methodological advances from alcohol and substance abuse research* (pp. 281–324). Washington, DC: American Psychological Association.

Widaman, K. F., & Thompson, J. S. (2003). On specifying the null model for incremental fit indices in structural equation modeling. *Psychological Methods, 8*, 16–37.

Willett, J. B. (1997). Measuring change: What individual growth modeling buys you. In E. Amsel & K. A. Renninger (Eds.), *Change and development: Issues of theory, method, and application: The Jean Piaget symposium series* (pp. 213–243). Mahwah, NJ: Erlbaum.

Willett, J. B., & Sayer, A. G. (1994). Using covariance structure analysis to detect correlates and predictors of individual change over time. *Psychological Bulletin, 116*, 363–381.

Wirth, R. J., & Edwards, M. C. (2007). Item factor analysis: Current approaches and future directions. *Psychological Methods, 12*, 58–79.

Wishart, J. (1938). Growth-rate determinations in nutrition studies with the bacon pig, and their analysis. *Biometrika, 30*, 16–28.

Wohlwill, J. F. (1973). *The study of behavioral development.* New York: Academic Press.

Wolfinger, R. (1993). Laplace's approximation for nonlinear mixed models. *Biometrika, 80*, 791–795.

Wolfinger, R. D., & Lin, X. (1997). Two Taylor-series approximation methods for nonlinear mixed models. *Computational Statistics and Data Analysis, 25*, 465–490.

Woodman, H. E., Evans, R. E., Callow, E. H., & Wishart, J. (1936). The nutrition of the bacon pig. I: The influence of high levels of protein intake on growth, confirmation and quality in the bacon pig. *The Journal of Agricultural Science, 26*, 546–619.

Woods, C. M. (2011). DIF testing for ordinal items with poly-SIBTEST, the Mantel and GMH tests, and IRT-LR-DIF when the latent distribution is non-normal for both groups. *Applied Psychological Measurement, 35*, 145–164.

Wright, S. (1921). Correlation and causation. *Journal of Agricultural Research, 20*, 557–585.

Zhang, Z., McArdle, J. J., & Nesselroade, J. R. (2012). Growth rate models: Emphasizing growth rate analysis through growth curve modeling. *Journal of Applied Statistics, 39*, 1241–1262.

Zill, N., & Peterson, J. L. (1986). *Behavior Problems Index.* Washington, DC: Child Trends.

Author Index

Subject Index

Note. *f* or *t* following a page number indicates a figure or a table.

About the Authors

Kevin J. Grimm, PhD, is Professor in the Department of Psychology at Arizona State University, where he teaches graduate courses on quantitative methods. His research interests include longitudinal methodology, exploratory data analysis, and data integration, especially the integration of longitudinal studies. His recent research has focused on nonlinearity in growth models, growth mixture models, extensions of latent change score models, and approaches for analyzing change with limited dependent variables. Dr. Grimm organizes the American Psychological Association's Advanced Training Institute on Structural Equation Modeling in Longitudinal Research and has lectured at the workshop since 2003.

Nilam Ram, PhD, is Associate Professor in the Department of Human Development and Family Studies and the Department of Psychology at The Pennsylvania State University. He specializes in longitudinal research methodology and lifespan development, with a focus on how multivariate time-series and growth curve modeling approaches can contribute to our understanding of behavioral change. He uses a wide variety of longitudinal models to examine changes in human behavior at multiple levels and across multiple time scales. Coupling the theory and method with data collected using mobile technologies, Dr. Ram is integrating process-oriented analytical paradigms with data visualization, gaming, experience sampling, and the delivery of individualized interventions/treatment.

Ryne Estabrook, PhD, is Assistant Professor in the Department of Medical Social Sciences at Northwestern University. His research combines multivariate longitudinal methodology, open-source statistical software, and lifespan development. His methodological work pertains to developing new methods for the study of change, and incorporating longitudinal and dynamic information into measurement. Dr. Estabrook is a developer of OpenMx, an open-source statistical software package for structural equation modeling and general linear algebra. He applies his methodological and statistical research to the study of lifespan development, including work on early childhood behavior and personality in late life.